ANCIENT NUBIA

ANCIENT NUBIA

AFRICAN KINGDOMS ON THE NILE

Edited by
Marjorie M. Fisher
Peter Lacovara
Salima Ikram
Sue D'Auria

with photographs by Chester Higgins Jr

The American University in Cairo Press
Cairo   New York

For Marjorie S. and Max,
Andrew and Alissandra,
and to those who strive to uncover
the mysteries of forgotten civilizations
—MF

Endpaper image: Sandstone relief of lion and elephant, from the Lion Temple at Musawwarat al-Sufra. Photo © Chester Higgins Jr 2012.

Copyright © 2012 by
The American University in Cairo Press
113 Sharia Kasr el Aini, Cairo, Egypt
420 Fifth Avenue, New York, NY 10018
www.aucpress.com

Chester Higgins Jr photographs on cover, endpapers, and pp. ii, 4, 6–7, 8–9, 32–33, 37, 68–69, 80–81, 94–95, 96, 97, 100–101, 104–105, 106, 112, 113, 114, 129, 130, 135, 139, 150, 161, 175, 176, 179, 181, 213, 215, 219, 220, 232–233, 260–261, 271, 280–281, 294, 306, 322–323, 355, 359, 377, 380–381, 392–393, 404, 425, 438–439. © 2012 by Chester Higgins Jr
www.chesterhiggins.com

Dar el Kutub No. 24399/11
ISBN 978 977 416 478 1

Dar el Kutub Cataloging-in-Publication Data

Fisher, Marjorie
        Ancient Nubia: African Kingdoms on the Nile/ Marjorie Fisher.—Cairo: The American
    University in Cairo Press, 2012
            p.   cm.
        ISBN 978 977 416 478 1
        1. Egypt—Antiquities   I. Title
        932

1 2 3 4   16 15 14 13 12

Designed by Andrea El-Akshar
Printed in China

CONTENTS

PART II: GAZETTEER OF SITES (FROM SOUTH TO NORTH)

ACKNOWLEDGMENTS

We wish to thank Zahi Hawass, the former minister of state for antiquities, for his support of this project, his article on recent and current Nubia, and his permission to publish material and photographs from Egypt and Nubia in this book. We are very grateful to the other contributing authors—Charles Bonnet, Elizabeth Cummins, Susan K. Doll, Geoff Emberling, Joyce Haynes, W. Raymond Johnson, Christian Knoblauch, Yvonne J. Markowitz, Robert Morkot, Claudia Näser, David O'Connor, Pamela Rose, Mimi Santini-Ritt, Bruce Williams, Janice W. Yellin—for their knowledge, time, and photographs of Nubia. We also wish to thank Chester Higgins for his awe-inspiring photographs of Nubia. His eye for its beauty will inspire others to see into this hidden culture. Moreover, we are indebted to many other scholars for their assistance in creating this book, particularly Julie Anderson, Dorothea Arnold, John Baines, Benjamin Beatty, Christina Blaze, Nancy Reinstein Bettencourt, Bob Brier and Pat Remler, Betsy Bryan, Martin Davies, Margarete Dawson, Rian Dawson, Rania Galal, Jocelyn Gohary, Brigitte Gratien, Melinda Hartwig, Janice Kamrin, Barry Kemp, Margarete Lourie, Colleen Manassa, James Phillips, Tom Phillips, Maarten Raven, Janet Richards, Patrick Vargo, and Terry Wilfong. We are grateful to Thomas R. James, Gustavo Camps, Lorene Sterner, and Laura Brubaker for creating many of the line drawings. For the use of images of their collections, we would like to thank the Ägyptisches Museum und Papyrussammlung der Staatlichen Museen Preussischer Kulturbesitz, Berlin; Ägyptisches Museum Georg Steindorff—der Universität Leipzig; The American Geographical Society Library, University of Wisconsin–Milwaukee Libraries; The British Museum; Collezioni Egittologiche, Università di Pisa; The Egyptian Museum, Cairo; The Garstang Museum of Archaeology, School of Archaeology, Classics, and Egyptology, University of Liverpool; The Griffith Institute, Oxford; Humboldt University; Institut de Papyrologie et d'Egyptologie de Lille; The F.W. Hinkel Archive at the German Archaeological Institute, Berlin; The Metropolitan Museum of Art; The Michael C. Carlos Museum; Museum of Fine Arts, Boston; The Nubian Museum, Aswan; The Peabody Museum of Archaeology and Ethnology, Harvard University; Rijksmuseum van Oudheden, Leiden; Staatliche Sammlung Ägyptische Kunst, Munich; the Sudan National Museum, Khartoum; the Supreme Council of Antiquities, Cairo (now the Ministry of State for Antiquities); the Oriental Institute, University of Chicago; Nicholas Thayer; the Trustees of the Lowell Institute; Jean Walker, Joseph Wegner, and David Silverman and the University of Pennsylvania Museum of Archaeology and Anthropology. We also wish to thank Neil Hewison, Randi Danforth, and Miriam Fahmy of the American University in Cairo Press, and Johanna Baboukis as well as designer Andrea El-Akshar for their patience and perseverance.

xi

FOREWORD

Zahi Hawass

The cultures and civilizations of Nubia have played important roles in the history of the world. The ancient Egyptians were drawn to the area by the mineral wealth of its deserts, and by the luxury materials that came from the far south. Beginning at least in the Old Kingdom, they sent expeditions to bring back products with which they could maintain the cults of their gods and kings. From their tomb biographies, we even know the names of some of the expedition leaders, such as Sabni, Weni, and Harkhuf, who journeyed to Nubia and returned with exotic animals and woods, and of course gold. Of these, perhaps Harkhuf was the most famous, for the wonderful letter from Pepy II that he included on the façade of his tomb at Qubbet al-Hawa in Aswan. In this, the young king specifically mentions the pygmy that Harkhuf is bringing back with him, and urges the official to take great care to bring this unusual person, sacred to the sun god, safely to him in his royal palace.

During the Twelfth Dynasty, the Egyptians established a presence in Lower Nubia, which they controlled through a series of fortresses. This incipient empire was lost at the end of the Middle Kingdom. During the Second Intermediate Period, Egypt was threatened by the kings of

Kush, who conspired with the Hyksos rulers in northern Egypt to defeat the native Egyptians based at Thebes. The ultimate result was that the first kings of the Eighteenth Dynasty took care to secure their southern border, and for much of the New Kingdom, Nubia to the area of the Fourth Cataract was a province of Egypt. The quantities of gold found in Nubia's deserts gained Egypt the reputation of having access to "gold like dust," as the king of the Mitanni writes, for example, to the Egyptian king Amenhotep III in one of the Amarna letters. This empire was lost during the Third Intermediate Period, and by the end of the eighth century BC, it was the Nubian kings of Kush who conquered Egypt, ruling as the Twenty-fifth Dynasty for half a century.

Some scholars have suggested that the Nubian cultures were more advanced than the civilization of Egypt. There is no question that the peoples of Nubia had much to offer, but we must be careful in coming to judgment until more excavation and analysis has been carried out.

I served in Lower Nubia for three months in 1973–74 as an inspector of antiquities for Abu Simbel. I will never forget my first trip, when I traveled on one of the open barges that brought food to this remote site. It took two days, and it was a wonderful way to see the great temples that had been saved by the United Nations Educational, Scientific, and Cultural Organization (UNESCO) before they were prepared for tourism. During this time, I read as much as I could on Nubia, and studied its monuments. The Temple of Ramesses II, in which the king worships himself as a god, is one of the most imposing monuments to survive from pharaonic Egypt. I believe that one of the reasons that this king built this particular temple was not only to inspire awe and fear in the local Nubian population, but also to guarantee his divinity. The most impressive moment I spent here was on February 22, 1974. I arrived, along with many tourists, before sunrise, and watched as the rays of the sun entered the temple and fell on the rock-cut face of Ramesses II carved in the inner shrine, making him equal to the other gods represented here. This extraordinary astronomical feature has no connection with the king's birth or coronation.

It is my great honor to count among my friends Dr. Tharwat Okasha, who spearheaded the campaign to save both monuments, including the temple of Abu Simbel, and to retrieve information from the floodwaters of Lake Nasser created by the building of the Aswan High Dam. This salvage campaign remains as one of the greatest examples of international cooperation the world has ever seen, and the survey and excavation work carried out during the two decades of this venture has helped enormously to build our understanding of the cultures of Lower Nubia. History will write the name of this man in gold because of his dedication to this project. More recently, the Supreme Council of Antiquities has completed the site management of the Island of New Kalabsha, where several Nubian temples were moved during the UNESCO Salvage Campaign. As part of this project, we cleaned and restored the temples of Kalabsha, Beit al-Wali, and the Kiosk of Qertassi, and reconstructed the Temple of Gerf Hussein, whose blocks had been left to gather dust and sand for over twenty years.

Ancient Nubia: African Kingdoms on the Nile is an important addition to the literature on this fascinating region. Today's best scholars in the field have contributed to this volume, and it presents overviews of various key topics, such as art and architecture, religion, animals, burial practices, kingship, women, and jewelry. In addition, it includes the first comprehensive description of all the important archaeological sites excavated so far. This will be of great value to students, the public, and other scholars to help them understand the cultures of Nubia. It also underlines for us the need for more fieldwork in both Lower and Upper Nubia, including surveys and excavations as well as site-management plans for important archaeological areas. I believe that it is time for more cooperation among scholars in this field and the antiquities service in Sudan.

I am so happy to be able to present this book to a wide audience, and hope that it will be published in a number of languages. It will certainly be translated into Arabic, so that it can be made accessible to Arab readers. I would like to offer special thanks here to my friend and colleague Marjorie Fisher. Without her vision and her scholarship, this book would not have been written or published.

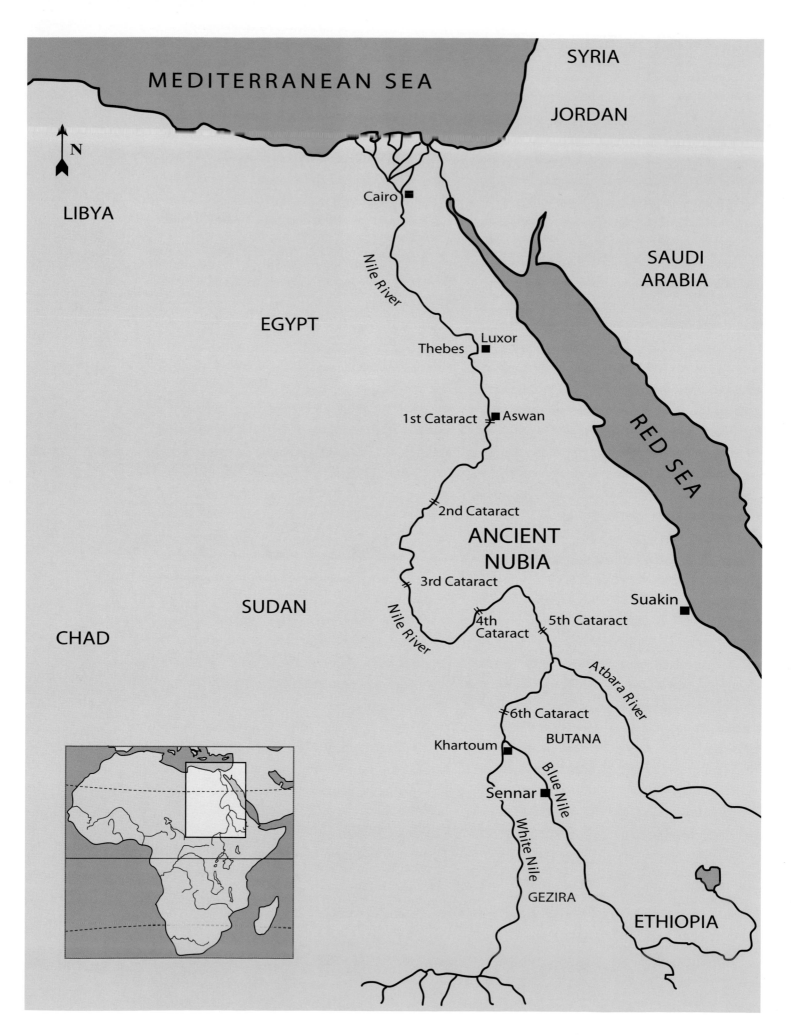

Figure 2. Map of Egypt and Nubia.

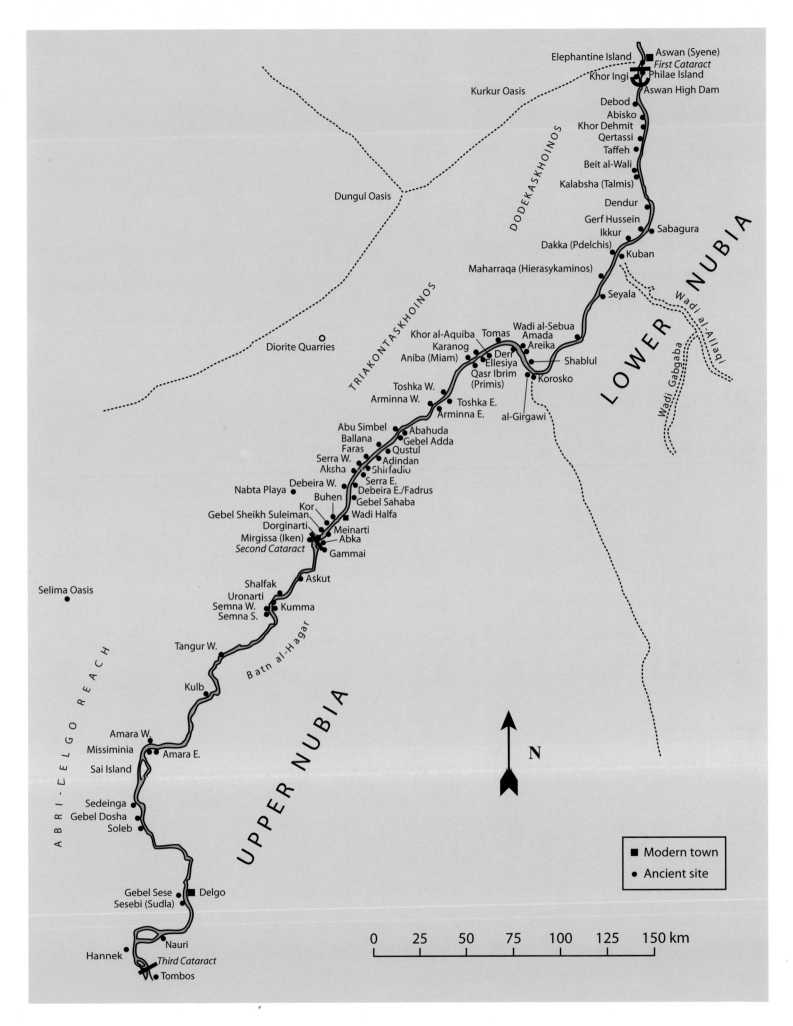

Figure 3. Map of Lower and Upper Nubia from Aswan to the Third Cataract

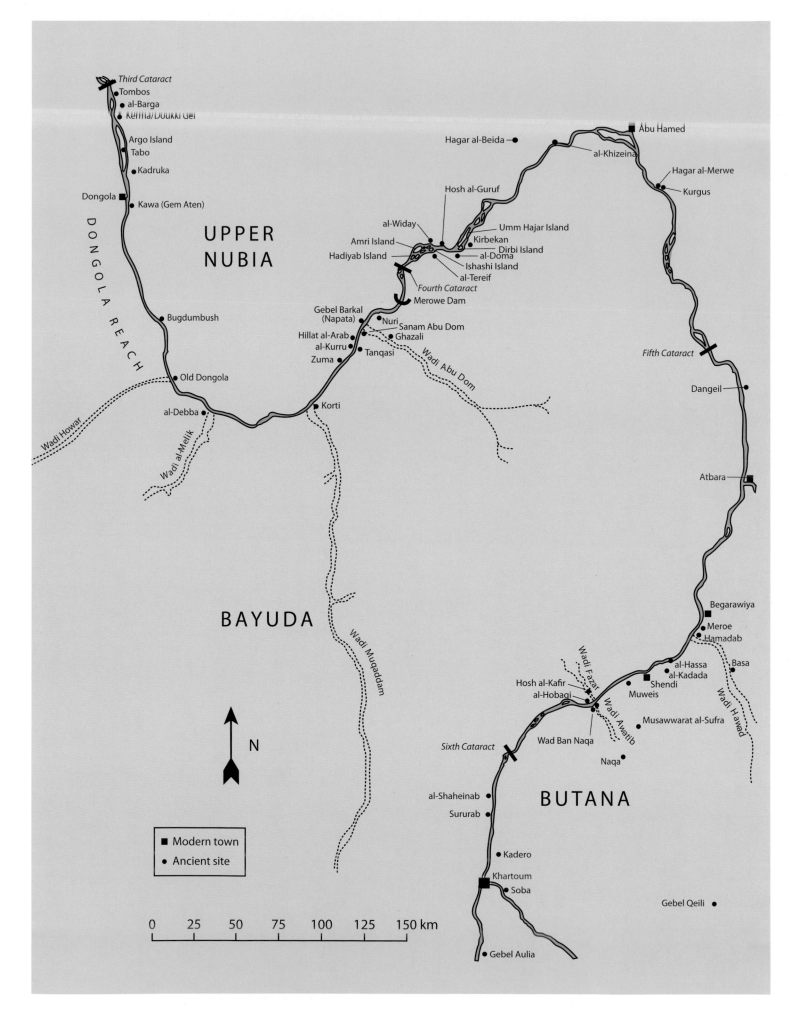

Figure 4. Map of Upper Nubia from the Third Cataract south.

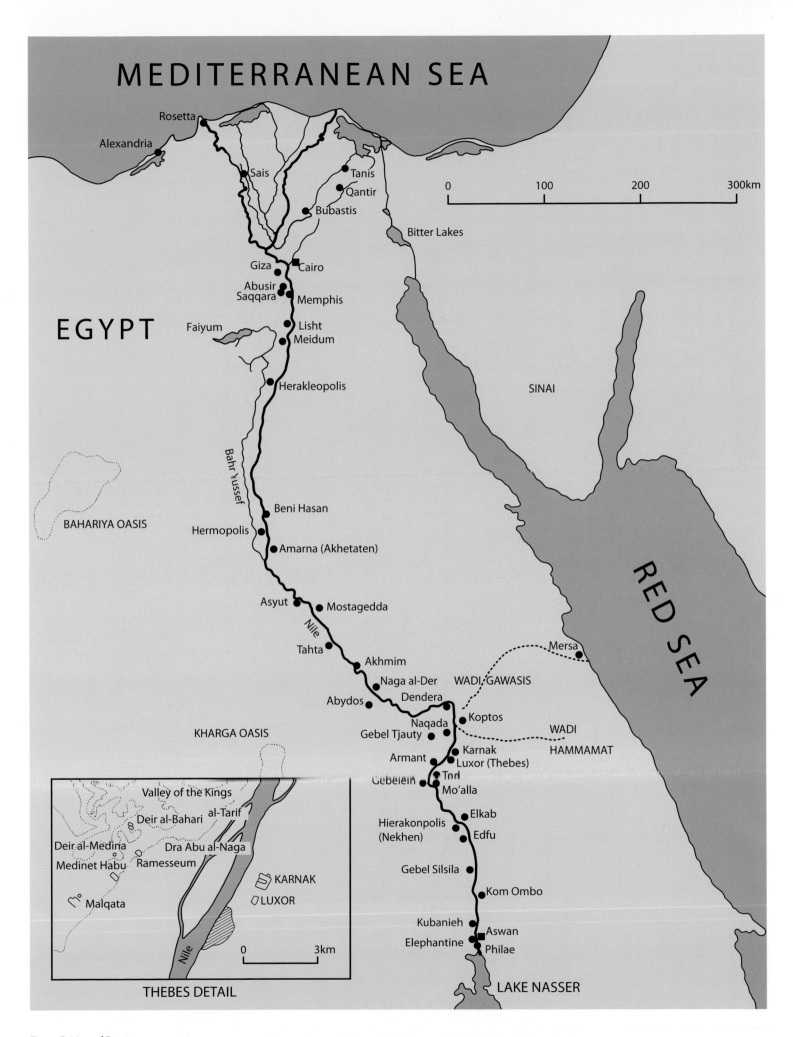

Figure 5. Map of Egypt.

Chronological Table of Egypt, Lower Nubia, and Upper Nubia

	Egypt	Lower Nubia	Upper Nubia
Before 3050 BC	Predynastic Period (to Dynasty 0)	Classic A-Group	Pre-Kerma
ca. 3050–2685 BC	Archaic Period (Dynasties 1–2)	Terminal A-Group	
ca. 2685–2150 BC	Old Kingdom (Dynasties 3–6)	C-Group Ia, Ib	Early Kerma
ca. 2150–2008 BC	First Intermediate Period (Dynasties 7–first half 11)		
ca. 2008–1685 BC	Middle Kingdom (Second half of Dynasty 11–13)	C-Group IIa, IIb	Middle Kerma
ca. 1685–1550 BC	Second Intermediate Period (Dynasties 14–17)	C-Group III	Classic Kerma
ca. 1550–1077 BC	New Kingdom (Dynasties 18–20)	Egyptian occupation	Egyptian occupation
ca. 1076–723 BC	Third Intermediate Period (Dynasties 21–24)	Independent Nubian cultures	Independent Nubian cultures
ca. 722–332 BC	Late Period (Dynasties 25–30) Second Persian Period	Napatan	Napatan
332–30 BC	Ptolemaic Period	Meroitic	Meroitic
30 BC–AD 641	Roman Period	Meroitic Post-Meroitic	Meroitic Post-Meroitic
AD 641–1400	Islamic Period	Christian	Christian
AD 1400–		Islamic	Islamic

Adapted from D. O'Connor, *Egypt's Rival in Africa* (Philadelphia: University Museum, 1993), 7, and *Sudan: Ancient Treasures*, ed. D.A. Welsby and J.R. Anderson (London: British Museum Press, 2004), 315. Table by Thomas R. James.

Chronology of Kushite Rulers

Name of Ruler	Burial	Date
Pre-Dynasty 25		
Ruler A	Ku. Tum. 1	ca. 885–835 BC
Ruler B	Ku. Tum. 2	ca. 865–825 BC
Ruler C	Ku. Tum. 6	ca. 845–815 BC
Ruler D	Ku. 14	ca. 825–805 BC
Ruler E	Ku. 11	ca. 805–795 BC
Alara	(Ku. 9)[1]	ca. 785–765 BC
Early Napatan Kings/Kings of Dynasty 25		
Kashta	(Ku. 8)	ca. 765–753 BC
Piankhi (Piye)	Ku. 17	ca. 753–722 BC
Shabaqo	Ku. 15	ca. 722–707 BC
Shebitqo	Ku. 18	ca. 707–690 BC
Taharqo	Nu. 1	690–664 BC
Tanwetamani	Ku. 16	664–655/53 BC (in Egypt)
Napatan Kings		
Atlanersa	(Nu. 20)	2nd half of 7th century BC
Senkamanisken	Nu. 3	2nd half of 7th century BC
Anlamani	Nu. 6	late 7th century BC
Aspelta	Nu. 8	early 6th century BC
Aramatelqo	Nu. 9	2nd quarter of 6th century BC
Malonaqen	Nu. 5	1st half of 6th century BC
Analmakheye	Nu. 18	middle of 6th century BC
Amani-nataki-lebte	Nu. 10	2nd half of 6th century BC
Karkamani	Nu. 7	2nd half of 6th century BC
Amaniastabarqo	Nu. 2	late 6th century BC
Sikhespiqo	Nu. 4	early 5th century BC
Nasakhma	Nu. 19	1st half of 5th century BC
Malowi-Amani	Nu. 11	middle of 5th century BC
Talakhamani	Nu. 16	2nd half of 5th century BC
Irike-Amanote	Nu. 12	2nd half of 5th century BC
Baskakeren	Nu. 17	late 5th century BC
Harsiyotef	Nu. 13	early 4th century BC
King, name unknown	Ku. 1	middle of 4th century BC
Akhratan	Nu. 14	2nd half of 4th century BC
Amanibakhi	?	2nd half of 4th century BC
Nastasen	Nu. 15	last 3rd of 4th century BC

[1] Questionable rulers and ascribed burials in parentheses.
Key to abbreviations: Ku. Tum. = al-Kurru Tumulus; Ku. = al-Kurru; Nu.= Nuri; Bar. = Gebel Barkal; Beg. = Begarawiya

Name of Ruler	Burial	Date
Late Napatan Rulers		late 4th century to 2nd third of 3rd century BC
Aktisanes	(Bar. 11)	
Ary	(Bar. 14)	
Kash…amani	(Bar. 15)	
Arike-Pi(ankhi)-qo	?	
Sabrakamani	?	

Meroitic Kings and Ruling Queens		
Arkamani I	Beg. S. 6	2nd quarter of 3rd century BC
Amanisaraw [Amanislo]	Beg. S. 5	
Amani-tekha	Beg. N. 4	
Arnekhamani	(Beg. N. 53)	last 3rd of 3rd century BC
Arkamani II	Beg. N. 7	end of 3rd century BC
Adikhalamani (Tabriqo)	Beg. N. 9	1st third of 2nd century BC
King, name unknown	Beg. N. 10	
King, name unknown	Beg. N. 8	
Queen Shanakdakheto	(Beg. N. 11)	2nd half of 2nd century BC
King, name unknown	Beg. N. 12	
Naqyrinsan	(Beg. N. 13)	
Tanyidamani	(Beg. N. 20)	early 1st century BC
King, name unknown	Bar. 2	
Queen, name unknown	Bar. 4	
Queen Nawidemak	Bar. 6	
Amanikhabale	(Beg. N. 2)	
Teriteqas	(Beg. N. 14)	last 3rd of 1st century BC
Queen Amanirenas	(Beg. N. 21)	late 1st century BC
Queen Amanishakheto	Beg. N. 6	
King Natakamani and	Beg. N. 22	2nd half of 1st century AD
Queen Amanitore	Beg. N 1	
(Sotakarora)	?	end of 1st century AD
(Amanitaraqide)	(Beg. N.16)	
Amanakhereqerem	?	end of 1st century AD
Amanitenamomide	Beg. N. 17	2nd half/end of 1st century AD
Queen Amanikhatashan	Beg. N. 18	to middle of 2nd century AD
Tarekeniwala	Beg. N. 19	
Ariteneyesebokhe	Beg. N. 34	
Takideamani	(Beg. N. 29)	
(Arayesebokhe)	(Beg. N. 36)	
Teqorideamani	Beg. N. 28	accession 248/249 AD
(Tamelordeamani)	?	
Yesebokheamani	?	end of 3rd century AD
Queen, name unknown	Beg. N. 26	
Queen, name unknown	Beg. N. 25	End of kingdom, about AD 330–70

Adapted from *Ancient Egyptian Chronology*, ed. E. Hornung, R. Krauss, and D.A. Warburton (Boston: Brill, 2006), 496–98.

INTRODUCTION

Marjorie M. Fisher

For most of the modern world, ancient Nubia seems an unknown and enigmatic land. Only a handful of archaeologists study its history or unearth the Nubian cities, temples, and cemeteries that once dotted the landscape of southern Egypt and Sudan. Its remote setting in the midst of an inhospitable desert and access by river blocked by impassible rapids has lent an air of mystery to Nubia but also a sense of isolation.

Over the past one hundred years, and increasingly during the past twenty years, scholars have begun to focus more attention on the fascinating cultures of ancient Nubia. They have asked and begun to answer such questions as these: Who were the Nubians? What types of buildings did they construct? Where were their cities? What were their religious beliefs? How were they governed? How did they perceive women? How did they interrelate with their neighbors, especially their northern neighbors, the Egyptians? The present book attempts to document some of what has recently been discovered about this unfamiliar realm, with its remarkable history, architecture, and culture, and thereby to fill the gap between the African corridor and Egypt.

This project began eight years ago when a nine-year-old girl, Helena Charles, asked me

for a book explaining the history of Nubia and illustrating what this area looked like. After a thorough search, I was astounded to discover that no such book existed. I decided to undertake a project that might help redress this deficiency, and Dr. Janet Richards suggested I collaborate with Peter Lacovara, Salima Ikram, and Sue D'Auria. We were fortunate as editors to have the contributions of such distinguished scholars on Nubia to greatly enhance this volume's range and insight. It was our sense that a book showing Nubia's vast beauty, as well as the current state of research into its culture, might be of interest to others.

The book is divided into two sections. The first consists of essays that address geography, history, archaeology, art, and architecture in Nubia and various other topics relating to Nubian life: daily life, animals, texts and writing, religion, burial customs, kings and kingship, royal and non-royal women, jewelry, and ceramics. Each essay in this section is written by a specialist on that particular subject. Bibliographies are provided at the end of each section, in case the reader wishes to learn more. Due to the building of the Aswan Dam in Egypt and the Merowe Dam in Sudan, many traces of Nubian civilization have disappeared under water. Yet it is possible to infer that the Nubians chose where to settle based upon trade routes, defensive positions, and the flow patterns of the Nile. It is also clear that Nubian culture was greatly influenced by contact with its northern neighbor, Egypt, as well as its southern neighbors in Sudan and farther south. This contact produced similarities in religious affiliation and architecture, as well as the conflicts that laid waste to numerous sites.

Organized geographically from south to north (the direction in which the Nile flows), the second section (Gazetteer) describes the sites of ancient Nubia that have been excavated. These locations preserve the remnants of a once rich but unfamiliar African civilization.

Part I

HISTORY AND CULTURE

THE LAND OF NUBIA

Peter Lacovara

The term 'Nubia' defines a geographic region that is located in the northeast corner of Africa, encompassing the southern end of Egypt and the northern half of the modern country of Sudan. Straddling the Nile River, it is sometimes referred to in two parts, according to the direction the river flows, Lower Nubia in the north and Upper Nubia in the south. Stretching along the winding course of the Nile River for nearly a thousand kilometers, the area is also sometimes called 'the Middle Nile.' The area is further divided by a series of rapids, called cataracts, which served as boundaries for different regions within Nubia. The First Cataract is at

Figure 7. The Second Cataract as it appeared in the middle of the nineteenth century.

Aswan, where Nubia begins, and the last one, the Sixth, is north of the modern city of Khartoum.

The cataracts were formed when the river ran into outcrops of granite, the hard rock that underlies the lands of Egypt and Sudan. Above this rock, the geology of Egypt and Sudan are very different, and that was to have a profound effect on their respective histories. In the distant past, during the Eocene Period, fifty-five to thirty-nine million years ago, most of Egypt lay under the sea, and deposits of shell, coral, and the remains of other marine life eventually formed a thick bed of limestone. This rock was easily cut into by the river Nile, which formed a wide bed and vast, fertile flood plain that could support a large population and provide great agricultural wealth. At the border of Nubia, however, this floodplain all but disappears, and the soft, orange sandstone that stretches southward confines the river as it runs through vast barren desert. To the east of the Nubian Nile, the terrain is marked by granite and other igneous rocks, including diorite, that form an even more forbidding and desolate landscape, but hold the key to Nubia's importance: gold.

Scholars still debate where the name Nubia came from, but it is tempting to see its origin in the ancient Egyptian word for gold, *nub*, which would be fitting, since Nubia had the ancient world's richest supply of gold. Other names the Egyptians had for Nubia included 'Ta-Sety'—'The Land of the Bow'—undoubtedly because the Nubians, rather than farming, relied on hunting for food and became very skilled with the bow and arrow. Indeed, depictions of Nubian archers are found not only in Egyptian art, but show their fame reached even into the Mediterranean world.

The Classical historians often called the area south of Egypt 'Ethiopia,' incorporating not only the modern country of Ethiopia, but Nubia and the lands beyond. The ancient Egyptian terms for

Figure 8. Kitchener's Island with a view of sand dunes on the west bank of the Nile. Photo © Chester Higgins Jr 2012.

their southern neighbors were similarly vague, and even now scholars debate to which regions their designations refer. Parts of what is known as Lower Nubia were called Wawat by the ancient Egyptians, with outlying areas called Irtjet, Setju, and Yam, although their exact location is much debated. For Upper Nubia, the most common term was Kush, which is often accompanied by the words "vile" or "wretched" to denote the pharaohs' scorn for their principal rival in Africa. 'The Kingdom of Kush' was used twice by the ancient Egyptians to refer to two powerful kingdoms that rose up in Nubia to challenge their control of the Nile. It is yet unclear how, if at all,

these two great Kushite civilizations separated by a millennium were related, but both illustrate the tremendous capacity the Nubians had in overcoming the difficulties of their remote and inhospitable land to become accomplished and powerful societies.

Figure 9. Sand dunes in the Nubian desert. Photo © Chester Higgins Jr 2012.

Bibliography
Butzer, K., and C. Hansen. 1968. *Desert and River in Nubia: Geomorphology and Prehistoric Environments at the* *Aswan Reservoir*. Madison, WI: University of Wisconsin Press.

THE HISTORY OF NUBIA

Marjorie M. Fisher

The Historical Sources

Our knowledge of Nubian political history comes largely from Egyptian textual sources, supplemented by the architectural, archaeological, and other material remains still extant in present-day Sudan. Much material in Lower Nubia now lies under Lake Nasser, permanently flooded after the construction of the Aswan High Dam, while some Upper Nubian sites have been destroyed by the completion of the Merowe Dam at the Fourth Cataract. Nubia's indigenous language, which might offer further insights, was not written down until the Meroitic Period (mid-third century BC to mid-fourth century AD), but the language, although deciphered, can be understood only to a very limited extent today. Therefore, in order to piece together Nubian history, one must explore the region's relations with Egypt, as well as the indigenous sources of data. Nubian history took somewhat different turns in Lower, Middle, and Upper Nubia, but in general it falls into these main periods: Paleolithic, Mesolithic, and Neolithic; Bronze Age Nubia; the Kerma Kingdom; the New Kingdom domination; the Napatan and Meroitic Periods; the post-Meroitic/X-Group Period; the medieval Christian kingdoms; and the Islamic Period.

The Paleolithic Period

The Paleolithic Period can be divided into the Early (Lower) (1,000,000–100,000 BP), Middle (100,000–34,000 BP), and Late (Upper) Paleolithic (34,000–10,000 BP). Paleolithic sites have been found in Lower and Upper Nubia up to the Fourth Cataract, in addition to two sites south of Khartoum. During the Early Paleolithic Period, our hominid ancestors pursued large game using their tools for butchering and food processing. A significant development during the Middle Paleolithic Period was more sophisticated tool assemblages, and use of new stones such as ferrocrete sandstone.

By the Late Paleolithic Period (around 20,000 BP), the people of Lower Nubia were still largely nomadic, living in temporary seasonal dwellings. They sustained themselves by occasionally fishing and fowling in the Nile and hunting wild animals, such as gazelles, hippopotami, wild cattle, and antelope. They left evidence of such activities in the form of petroglyphs and faunal remains in the archeological sites throughout the Nile Valley.

The period from ca. 13,000 to 9000 BC in Lower Nubia and Upper Egypt saw evolving tool assemblages, including groundstone tools, arrows, and microliths. One of the most significant finds from this time is a cemetery at Gebel Sahaba near the

Figure 10. Map of Nubia, ca. 1,000,000 BP–3000 BC, with archaeological sites of the Paleolithic, Mesolithic, and Neolithic Periods.

10

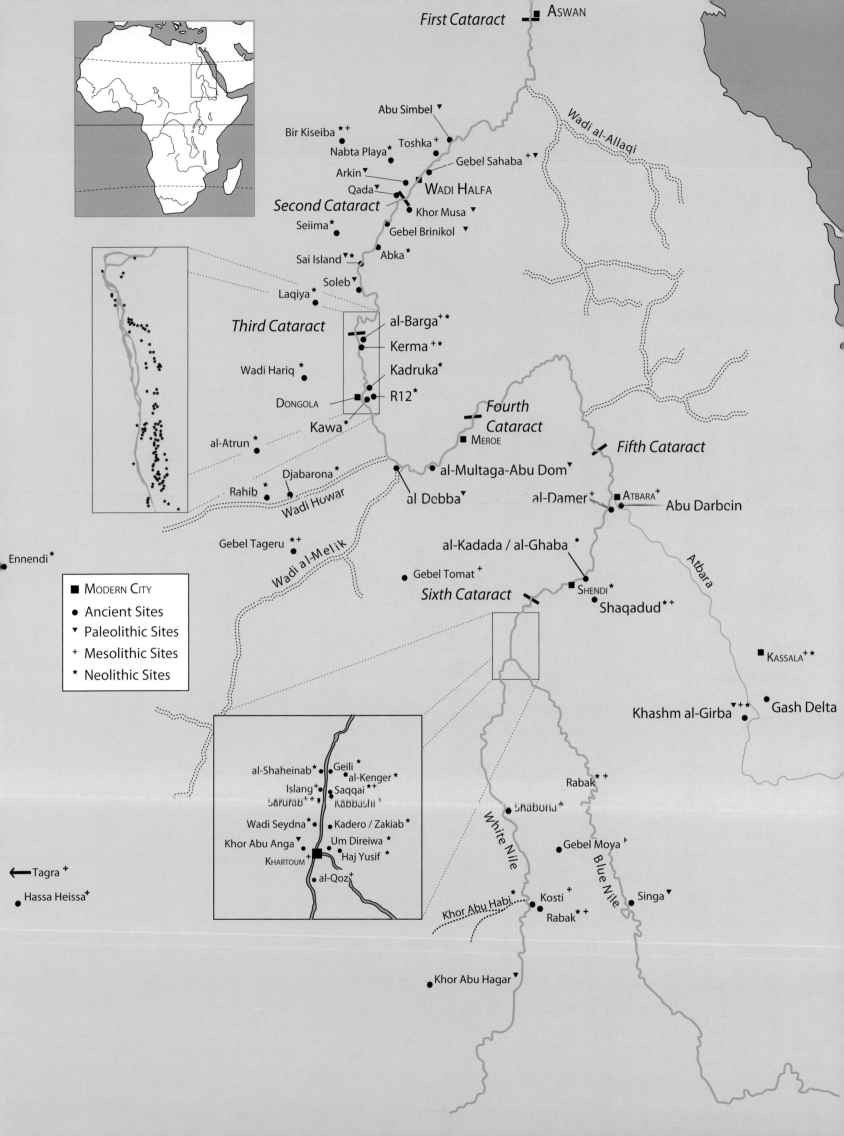

First Cataract
ASWAN

Wadi al-Allaqi

Abu Simbel ▼

Bir Kiseiba ★ +

Toshka +

Nabta Playa ★

Gebel Sahaba + ▼

Arkin ▼

WADI HALFA

Qada ▼

Second Cataract

Khor Musa ▼

Seiima ★

Gebel Brinikol ▼

Sai Island ▼ ★

Abka ★

Soleb ▼

Laqiya ★

Third Cataract

al-Barga + ★

Kerma + ★

Wadi Hariq ★

Kadruka ★

DONGOLA

R12 ★

Kawa ★

Fourth Cataract

al-Atrun ★

MEROE

Fifth Cataract

Djabarona ★

al-Multaga-Abu Dom ▼

Rahib ★

al-Debba ▼

al-Damer +

ATBARA +

Abu Darbein

Wadi Howar

Ennendi ★

Gebel Tageru ★ +

al-Kadada / al-Ghaba ★

Wadi al-Melik

Gebel Tomat +

SHENDI ★

Sixth Cataract

Shaqadud ★ +

KASSALA + ★

Khashm al-Girba ▼ + ★

Gash Delta

al-Shaheinab ★   Geili ★

al-Kenger ★

Rabak ★ +

Islang +

Saqqai ★ +

Sarurab ★ +

Kabbashi +

Shabona +

Wadi Seydna ★

Kadero / Zakiab ★

Gebel Moya +

Khor Abu Anga ▼

Um Direiwa ★

KHARTOUM +

Haj Yusif ★

Kosti +

Singa ▼

al-Qoz +

Khor Abu Habi ★

Rabak ★ +

Tagra +

Hassa Heissa +

Khor Abu Hagar ▼

White Nile

Blue Nile

Atbara

■ MODERN CITY
● Ancient Sites
▼ Paleolithic Sites
+ Mesolithic Sites
★ Neolithic Sites

Second Cataract, which has burials consisting of oval pits covered with stone slabs; multiple bodies were interred in each pit, adults and children alike. Some appear to have died violently, with lithic weapons embedded in such bones as clavicles and eye sockets, but these deaths seem to have occurred at different times, refuting claims that they were caused by single acts of violence or war. The level of violence among the group is nonetheless very striking and is the first evidence of violent death anywhere in the Paleolithic record.

The Mesolithic Period (Epipaleolithic)
In Upper Nubia, the Mesolithic Period (8000–5000 BC) is termed the Khartoum Mesolithic, and in Lower Nubia the Khartoum Variant. The Khartoum Mesolithic sites thus far documented extend southward of the Third Cataract (see map). Khartoum Mesolithic populations seem to have lived close to either a continuous water source—the Nile—or a seasonal water supply—the wadis (valleys or water courses that remained dry except during rains) nearby. The Nile sites and the wadi sites display different assemblages, with grindstones and pottery near the Nile (permanent sites) and various tool assemblages in the wadis (seasonal sites). Many of these sites may have been chosen because after 10,000 BC they became less arid and thus more suitable for nomadic populations.

The Khartoum Variant sites in Lower Nubia were clustered around the Second Cataract and near the Batn al-Hagar. These locations consisted of small camps, indicating their temporary status. Although these sites were near the Nile, fishing implements are curiously missing from finds there, perhaps because the dry conditions rendered this area undesirable for settlement or fishing. Egyptian lithics have also been found at these sites, suggesting some type of contact between Egypt and Nubia.

From this evidence it appears that, during the Mesolithic, hunter/gatherer societies shared the region with semi-sedentary groups. It has been theorized, despite an absence of appropriate tools among the evidence, that the population eventually began to rely increasingly on fishing, as the sites south of the Fifth Cataract suggest; they also began to cultivate cereal crops, as indicated by the appearance of grindstones used to grind grain. Such grinding stones were also used for other forms of food preparation (i.e., beer and porridge), to sharpen tools and bones, and to make colored powder, no doubt for paint or cosmetics.

Around 7000 BC, Mesolithic groups began to decorate their pottery with incised wavy lines and impressed zigzag lines. During the Late Mesolithic Period, pottery in the Khartoum and Shendi regions was ornamented with undulating and zigzag lines and dots impressed with a fish bone or rocker stamp. Burial practices at this time consisted of placing the deceased on the right side in a fetal position, generally without burial goods. Much farther north in Upper Egypt, there were permanent settlements along the Nile, with temporary camps farther away from the river, while in Lower Nubia occupation consisted of basic campsites.

The Neolithic Period
By the time of the Neolithic Period (ca. 5000–3000 BC), there was a distinct transition into settled life, with an increased reliance on domesticated livestock and eventually the cultivation of domesticated crops in certain areas. It has been suggested that a shift in the river's location, as well as increasing aridity near the beginning of the period, led to the movement of the population into the wadis of the eastern Sahara. The regions to which migrants moved were more ecologically favorable for growing crops and herding animals, resulting in significant changes to patterns of living and food production. Seasonal sites located

along the Nile were occupied only in the dry season, in order to be adjacent to a source of water; other sites were near the edge of the seasonally inundated floodplain.

Most Neolithic sites show evidence of domesticated animals, personal adornments made out of bone and ivory, a lithic tradition (bone and stone), grinding stones, and ceramic manufacture, as well as burials and mortuary practices. The huts making up these communities were most likely constructed of reed or reed mats. Some settlements included hearths set into areas of paved sandstone, as found at al-Shaheinab, near Khartoum in Upper Nubia. Another site, near Kerma, dating to 4500 BC, much later in the Neolithic, has rectangular structures, possibly for fences and palisades, as well as circular structures with post holes and hearths. Most archaeologists agree that the Neolithic in Nubia is characterized by large base camps and seasonal smaller camps used for herding animals, in addition to areas in Lower Nubia and northern Upper Nubia that were more permanently settled by farmers.

A majority of Neolithic settlements include burial sites. Early in the Neolithic, burial plots were grouped together into small cemeteries; by the later Neolithic there existed large, complex cemeteries. The deceased were buried mostly in circular pits, in a contracted position surrounded by numerous grave goods. The complexity and variation of goods indicated their social rank, wealth, and possibly their occupation during life, as well as the rituals associated with mortuary practices.

The site of Kadero, north of Khartoum, consists of two settlements and a cemetery. The settlement has yielded Neolithic grinding stones, domestic animals, pottery, and lithics. The cemetery contains at least two hundred burials of male and female adults and children interred over a long period of time. The burials reveal social differentiation, ranging in complexity from graves including little or no funerary goods or pottery to wealthier graves containing varied and elaborate funerary items such as hippopotamus ivory, stone palettes, and adornments like carnelian-bead necklaces. Differences also appear between female and male burials, with some male burials including stone mace heads. Jacques Reinold, who examined the burial goods of one affluent female at Kadero,

Figure 11. Rock inscription at Gebel Sheikh Suleiman.

concluded that women may have had considerable power during this time.

Current research at Kadruka, south of the Third Cataract, yielded even more unusual finds. Some of the largest cemeteries had more than one thousand burials. As at Kadero, these cemeteries spanned a considerable period of time and showed significant social differentiation, but at Kadruka, many cemeteries also suggested complex burial practices. Stelae for the deceased were mounted near some of the graves. Elaborate grave goods consisted of leather, human figurines, bracelets, beads, and pendants; some burials even have hippopotamus-tusk containers and ostrich eggs. These burial goods, as well as the distance of burials from the center of the cemetery, suggested to Reinold a "class-conscious society." Many of the burials had human sacrifices placed next to the deceased, indicating some form of ritual, as well as hearths near the graves for some unknown purpose. Human sacrifices were also apparent at al-Ghaba and al-Kadada, as were animal sacrifices. At Kadruka, dog burials lie at the four cardinal points on the edge of the cemetery, signifying perhaps a protective ritual. Reinold proposes that the animal and human sacrifices may mean that intricate funerary rituals had become an integral social practice.

The site of Kadero yields evidence of domesticated animals such as cattle, sheep, and goats, as well as the cultivation of barley. The population farther north, near the Wadi Howar, also apparently relied strongly on cattle herding, perhaps because Wadi Howar had little permanent water. In Lower Nubia, by contrast, there is less evidence of cattle and goats. All Lower Nubian sites, however, have yielded bones, lithics, potsherds, and grinding stones, while others also have spears, harpoons, and cosmetic boxes, suggesting that domestication of animals may have been less prevalent than fishing, hunting, and growing crops in this area.

Neolithic pottery varies according to region, and is a useful indicator for the identification of regional groups. In the north, the pottery of the Second Cataract area is comparable to that of Upper Egypt, suggesting that the eastern Sahara as well as Egypt may have influenced development in these regions. Until after the Badarian Period (ca. 4400–4000 BC) of Predynastic Egypt, there was an essential continuity throughout the upper Egyptian and lower Nubian Nile region, which did not disappear until the third millennium, that is, around the time of state formation in Egypt.

Bronze Age Nubia

George Reisner divided this period of Lower Nubian history into three successive cultural phases—the A-Group, B-Group, and C-Group—reflecting changes in their material culture. The existence of a B-Group culture, however, which Reisner proposed as an impoverished successor to the A-Group, has been refuted by more recent scholarship. Concurrent with these Lower Nubian phases was the Upper Nubian Pre-Kerma culture, followed by the Early Kerma, Middle Kerma, and Classic Kerma (see chronology chart).

The A-Group (ca. 3700–2800 BC), which is found throughout Lower Nubia from the Wadi Kubanieh north of Aswan to the area just south of the Second Cataract, is characterized by three phases, Early, Classic, and Terminal, ending during the Egyptian First Dynasty, around 2800 BC.

Based upon the archaeological evidence, it appears that A-Group populations cultivated barley, lentils, peas, and forms of wheat, and also maintained domesticated sheep, goats, and cattle; in addition, they supplemented their diet with hunting, gathering, and fishing. Some pottery styles of the A-Group are quite similar to black-topped ware and rippled ware found in Upper Nubia and to black-topped, red-polished ware of the Predynastic Naqada I–II Period in Egypt (ca.

4000–3200 BC). This similarity of style may demonstrate that A-Group cultures had contact, possibly through trade, with their northern and southern neighbors. Nubians of the Classic and Terminal A-Group also produced a distinct style of fine 'eggshell ware' that was burnished and painted in various patterns, as found at the site of Qustul.

Early excavations of A-Group sites concentrated on cemeteries, and so far very few settlement sites have been documented. The main type of burial associated with the A-Group was a rectangular or oval pit with the body in flexed position; the deceased were sometimes clothed in leather loincloths, linen caps, belts, and jewelry. No human sacrifices have been found in these graves.

Grave goods included pottery, amulets, necklaces, and pendants fashioned from shell, ivory, bone, ostrich eggshells, faience, and stone; less frequently occurring objects included ostrich-feather fans, figurines, and copper objects. Some objects were Egyptian in origin (notably at Qustul and Seyala—see below), supporting the theory that the Nubians were engaged in trade with later Predynastic Egypt (ca. 3500–3050 BC). Aswan became a significant trade center between the two cultures. The importance of one Nubian commodity—ivory—to the Egyptians is indicated by the name of the island on which this trade êntrepot was located—Abu, or 'elephant' in ancient Egyptian, later known in Greek as Elephantine.

Burials from the Classic and Terminal periods of the A-Group in Nubia reflect an increasingly differentiated, politically centralized society. The Classic phase in Cemetery 277, just north of the Second Cataract on the east bank of the Nile, provides evidence of this development. Here David O'Connor identified two adjacent sub-cemeteries that may contain separate lineages, each related to a highly powerful and wealthy individual. The importance of these individuals could be seen in the size and quality of the burial

pits and grave goods, including gold beads and imported copper objects, Egyptian pottery, and other imports from Egypt.

The Terminal A-Group Cemetery L at Qustul, excavated by the University of Chicago's Oriental Institute from 1962 to 1964, raised questions about the degree of power held by a leader in their society, whether chief or king. This cemetery included twenty-three graves of considerable size originally surmounted by mounded superstructures, beneath each of which was a subterranean pit with a side chamber. Burial goods were rich and plentiful—for example, large amounts of Egyptian pottery as well as vessels from Palestine/Syria, copper, some gold, and cosmetic palettes made of amethyst and quartz. These tombs were identified as possibly royal, comparable to Egyptian royal tombs of that period; no other site thus far found in Lower Nubia has yielded such magnificent burial goods. Bruce Williams has shown that the occupants of these tombs were contemporary with the Naqada III Period in Egypt and adopted symbols associated with the Egyptian kings, such as those found on a stone incense burner carved with scenes depicting an individual with the White Crown of Upper Egypt, a *serekh* façade, the Horus falcon, and a bull, all motifs associated with Egyptian kingship. These symbols were found earlier in Tomb U-j at the Egyptian site of Abydos, which may be a bit earlier than Cemetery L and also shows evidence of a sophisticated indigenous culture.

The Disappearance of the A-Group and the Egyptian Archaic Period

Around the time of the unification of Egypt (ca. 3050 BC), the A-Group culture in Lower Nubia disappears from the archaeological record. There were no more elite burials at Qustul, indicating the decline of the most powerful people of that area. It is unclear exactly what caused the demise of the A-Group; it may have been the increasing

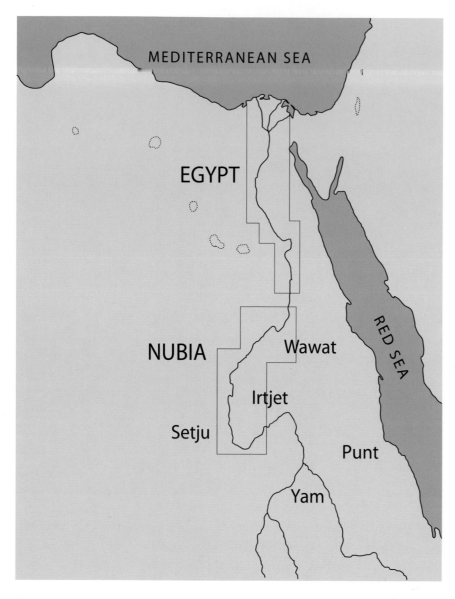

Figure 12. Map of Egypt and Nubia, ca. 3000–2000 BC. The outlines show the approximate extent of Egyptian and Nubian influence during this period.

as Egypt gained dominance in that area. Nubia became important to Egypt because of its location as a corridor to sub-Saharan Africa—the source of such exotic goods as ostrich eggs and feathers, ivory, stones, ebony, vegetable oils, and giraffe tails. Egyptian elites desired these goods for cultural and artistic reasons and hence wanted to trade with or control Nubia in order to acquire them. Finally, during the Egyptian Archaic Period (Dynasties One to Two, ca. 3050–2685 BC), Nubia became of greater concern to Egypt from the standpoint of border security.

The Egyptians thus undertook active campaigns aimed at securing goods from Nubia. An ebony plaque found in the tomb of King Aha at Abydos in Egypt bears the earliest reference to a Nubian battle and victory over Ta-Sety (a name that incorporated both Nubia and the southernmost district of Egypt). Other evidence for campaigns appears on Egyptian rock inscriptions in Nubia referring to raids into this area. A rock inscription dating to Dynasty Zero and located at the Second Cataract at Gebel Sheikh Suleiman near Wadi Halfa (currently housed in the National Museum, Khartoum) may indicate the nascence of Egyptian military operations deeper and deeper into Nubia, though it is unclear how organized these incursions were. A rock inscription near Buhen, also at the Second Cataract, is likewise attributed to an Archaic Period Egyptian king. The lack of indigenous Nubian archaeological evidence and the consequent reliance on exclusively Egyptian materials make our knowledge of this period very sketchy.

The Pre-Kerma Culture

Charles Bonnet identified a 'Pre-Kerma culture' on the eastern periphery of the site of Kerma that is ancestral to the Nubian Kerma culture. Its earliest beginnings in the fourth millennium BC show an affinity to the Abkan and other Lower Nubian Neolithic cultures. Evidence of the Pre-Kerma

political and military power of Egypt, a break in trade networks, population loss through regional warfare, or even climate change. It is possible that some A-Group Nubians moved south to Upper Nubia and were assimilated into the ascendant Kerma culture, while other groups remained in the Second Cataract area, their material culture evolving over many centuries into the assemblages designated by Reisner as the C-Group (ca. 2300–1600 BC). But it is clear that the decline of the A-Group of northern Lower Nubia occurred

culture has subsequently been found throughout middle and northern Upper Nubia and into the Second Cataract region. These Pre-Kerma sites can be distinguished from A-Group cemeteries by their ceramics. Little evidence of contact with Egypt has been found in the Pre-Kerma sites, in contrast with the Lower Nubian A-Group.

Pre-Kerma settlements consisted of groups of round huts supported by posts and defended by palisades. Hearths, food-storage pits, and possible cattle pens were also found within the inhabited areas. Burial pits with small mounds serving as superstructures were often located near the settlements, with burials in a flexed position. These Pre-Kerma burials show evidence of a ritualized and hierarchical social structure, as indicated by the large tumuli at Kerma with hundreds of bucrania (cattle skulls) used to decorate the exterior of the graves.

Unlike the A-Group, the Pre-Kerma culture did not end abruptly with the Egyptian incursions of the first dynasties. Rather it developed into the Early (Ancient) Kerma culture, beginning around 2500 BC.

The C-Group in Lower Nubia

By about 2300 BC, a few centuries after the end of the A-Group, the C-Group appears as a distinct culture in Lower Nubia. C-Group populations seem to have reoccupied many A-Group sites, building more permanent structures—round tents or huts supported by poles, with large slabs for foundations. Three main phases of development have been proposed for this culture. In Phase I, simple dwellings evolved into more complex groups of buildings, some with round or irregular shapes, constructed of materials such as stone, unbaked brick, and/or mud. Frames around the houses were made of poles. The dead were buried in circular graves, with the deceased in a flexed position surrounded by grave goods that were

less ornate than those at Qustul. Phase II is characterized by pottery with more complex designs covering more of the surface than in Phase I. Houses were more complex, constructed of unfired brick, stone, and mud. Some groups of houses were surrounded by a fortified enclosure wall with gates. Burials occupied rectangular graves, sometimes with stones or bricks lining the walls. In the final phase, more Egyptian stamp seals, amulets, jewelry, mirrors, and stone vessels were included in tombs, and animal offerings began to appear in the shafts of these tombs. The end of this phase saw the rapid Egyptianization of the C-Group in the New Kingdom.

C-Group peoples placed great emphasis on cattle as a source of wealth, value, and prestige, judging from the long-horned cows carved on stelae, pottery, and rocks; the ox skulls buried in cemeteries; and the use of cow dung as temper in pottery. They also herded sheep and goats. The cultural importance of such animals is attested in the presence of animal as well as human figurines in graves, along with jewelry, ivory, faience, and colored stones.

Three of the most important C-Group sites are Aniba, Faras, and Dakka. Burial facilities, more elaborate than in earlier periods, were marked by round or oval pits, capped by superstructures consisting of rings of stones filled with gravel. At Aniba, grave markers were made of stone slabs (or stelae), implanted vertically in the ground and sometimes carved with figures of cattle. As previously noted, C-Group people were buried with clothing and sandals mainly of leather, with necklaces and bangles serving as the major types of jewelry. Furthermore, C-Group cultures implemented new styles of burials with mud-brick burial chambers. Above the shaft were monuments made of stone circles filled with rubble and sand. The orientation of the flexed body of the deceased changed over time from east-west to north-south.

The black-topped red pottery of the C-Group shows similarities to that of the A-Group and Korma cultures, but there are also distinct differences in their material culture, such as the so-called polished incised ceramic ware. These vessels were decorated with zigzag lines, hatches, and mosaics; after firing, a white pigment was rubbed over the incised lines, giving it a distinctive appearance.

The Nubian Early C-Group and the Egyptian
Old Kingdom

At the dawn of the Egyptian Old Kingdom (Dynasties Three to Six, ca. 2685–2150 BC), which corresponds to the Nubian Early C-Group, a now strongly centralized and prosperous Egypt desired the commodities of Nubia, including gold, exotic animals, ivory, ebony, and incense. The allure of Nubian goods led Egyptian kings to begin a long series of incursions into Nubia to secure them. Initial efforts to establish trade relations, as well as military campaigns during the Early Dynastic Period, had set the stage for a more complex arrangement during the Old Kingdom. The Egyptian expansion into Nubia during the Fourth and Fifth Dynasties (ca. 2543–2300 BC) had the primary aim of securing access to mines and procuring exotic goods, as is apparent from Egyptian written records. The first king of the Fourth Dynasty, Sneferu, dispatched an expedition into Nubia that brought back prisoners and booty: the Palermo Stone (a fragment of a Fifth Dynasty king list that included a particular event of each king's reign) records the capture of seven thousand prisoners, together with two hundred thousand head of cattle. Securing the Second Cataract by building a fort and settlement there against Nubian incursion became a priority of later Fourth Dynasty rulers. Inscriptions indicating these kings' presence were also found north of the Third Cataract at Kulb.

Khafre of the Fourth Dynasty was evidently interested in Nubian quarrying operations, as the gneiss quarries northwest of Abu Simbel near Toshka yielded stone for his magnificent statue, now in the Cairo Museum. This quarry continued to be exploited during the Fifth Dynasty, as were possibly the gold mines at Wadi al-Allaqi. There also appear to have been minerals originating at Kulb and Tomas in central Lower Nubia, as indicated by inscriptions there. Other expeditions, such as the one to Punt sent by Sahure and Djedkare of the Fifth Dynasty, sought to acquire additional exotic goods. Punt is thought to be located adjacent to the Red Sea, though some scholars have suggested locations as far afield as Somalia and Yemen.

By the Sixth Dynasty (ca. 2300–2150 BC), Egyptian military control over Lower Nubia was beginning to fail; instead, trade and alliances with the Nubians became increasingly important in order to secure goods. Mercenaries from throughout Nubia (Wawat, Irtjet, Setju, Yam, Medja, and Kaau) now began to serve in Egyptian armies. The second ruler of the Sixth Dynasty, Pepy I, used these warriors to help fight the Asiatics who were threatening security in the northeast of Egypt.

Egyptian tomb biographies from this era report numerous expeditions to Nubia on behalf of the rulers. Pepy I's trusted official (and later governor), Weni, inscribed his exploits with the permission of the king on the façade of his tomb chapel: he had ventured to Nubia to procure for Pepy I's successor Merenre the stone for a sarcophagus, its lid, and a pyramidion. Weni's tomb biography makes it clear that Egypt enjoyed peaceful relations with some areas of Nubia, as he oversaw the construction of barges from acacia wood imported from Wawat. Furthermore, he states that foreign chiefs of Wawat, Irtjet, Yam, and Medja (homelands of the Egyptian mercenaries) cut the wood for these ships, indicating either that the Egyptians controlled these areas or, more likely, that they had diplomatic relations with these people and the wood was offered as a tribute or obligation.

An Egyptian tomb biography of the governor Harkhuf at Aswan tells of four expeditions he made to Nubia under Kings Merenre and Pepy II. During Merenre's reign, he set out to "open the way," as the biography puts it, to the Nubian district of Yam. From there, he brought back many beautiful and exotic gifts for the king. He then undertook a second expedition, this time through Irtjet to Yam, claiming that this was the first time an Egyptian representative had visited there. Again he brought back gifts for the king, implying that peace prevailed with this area of Nubia. On a third expedition, Harkhuf returned to Yam, where he reports that the Nubians were fighting among themselves. Harkhuf then followed the chief of Yam to Tjemeh in the west; again they had a peaceful interchange, implying some form of alliance. The conventional view among scholars is that Yam may be associated with Kerma and, if so, that Egypt had begun shifting its interest farther south throughout this period. (O'Connor, however, places Yam in the Butana region.) Harkhuf's final expedition also occurred during the reign of Pepy II. He states that three Nubian areas—Wawat, Irtjet, and Setju—were united under one chief. This chief, accompanied by the troops of Yam, greeted Harkhuf with cattle and goats. Harkhuf also brought back to court a pygmy to perform the "dances of the god." These biographies underscore the complexity of these interactions, the peaceful trade relations that Egypt had with Nubia, and the activities of, and power struggles among, Nubian groups.

Besides using Nubian mercenaries, King Merenre seems to have established a new program to convert Nubian allies to Egyptian customs. Nubian princes were brought back to Memphis, the capital of Egypt at that time, and

Figure 13. Relief of King Amenemhat I from Lisht North, Pyramid Temple of Amenemhat I, ca. 1939–1875 BC. Photograph courtesy of The Egyptian Department, Metropolitan Museum of Art, New York.

educated there in the hope that once they returned to their homes in Nubia, they would maintain their Egyptian affiliation. This policy continued under Pepy II.

Despite these frequent excursions and trade relations, Nubia remained an exotic place to the Egyptians, who had no desire to live—or die—in this alien environment. One Sixth Dynasty noble, Sabni, reports in his tomb biography that he led an expedition into the Nubian desert to recover the body of his father, who had died in battle there. Presumably, Sabni wished not to abandon his father in a foreign land but to give him a proper burial in Egypt, to ensure that he reached the afterworld.

With the collapse of centralized control at the end of the Sixth Dynasty, Nubia was once again free to expand northward. Whatever the cause— famine due to low floods, climatic change in the

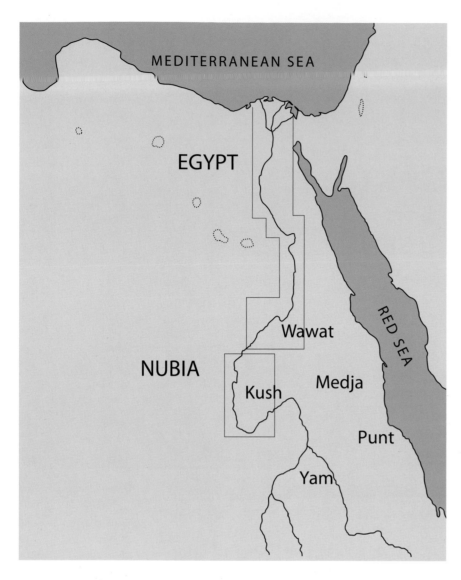

Figure 14. Map of Egypt and Nubia, ca. 2000–1650 BC. The outlines show the approximate extent of Egyptian and Nubian influence during this period.

control of these trade bases in Nubia might have proved too taxing for the available resources.

At the beginning of the First Intermediate Period in Egypt (Seventh to first half of Eleventh Dynasties, ca. 2150–2008 BC), indigenous Nubian populations once again regained control over their land. We do have archaeological evidence from Upper Nubia at this time, most notably from the site of Kerma; as to textual references, in Egypt one inscription from a tomb at Mo'alla mentions grain sent to Wawat in order to prevent a famine, hinting at problems they were experiencing. Egyptians did not control any part of Nubia, and Nubians seem to have remained at peace with their northern neighbor, most likely to maintain trade relations. By the end of this period, however, Egyptian texts refer to armies being sent into Nubia—but do not reveal the outcome of any hostilities.

During the Egyptian First Intermediate Period and early Middle Kingdom (second half of Eleventh to Twelfth Dynasties, ca. 2009–1760 BC), society in Upper Nubia was clearly changing. Many Nubians still lived and worked in Egypt, and a series of stelae from Gebelein seem to indicate that Nubians and Egyptians intermarried. One possible product of such a union is an Egyptian relief that portrays the Eleventh Dynasty Egyptian queen Kemsit, whose face is painted black in some depictions and dark pink in others, possibly indicating a Nubian origin. It has been suggested by many scholars that the other wives or consorts of King Mentuhotep II (ca. 2008–1957 BC) may also have been fully or partially Nubian and that even Mentuhotep II himself may have been of Nubian descent.

Whatever his Nubian connection, Mentuhotep II had a comprehensive plan to regain control of Nubia. Aware of the military skill of Nubian warriors, he incorporated Nubians from some regions into his armies to fight Nubians from other regions, thus protecting Egypt's interests in Nubia

surrounding deserts, the disappearance of certain animals (elephants, giraffes, and rhinoceros), or the breakdown of the centralized government in Egypt—trade between Egypt and Nubia was clearly affected. Morkot has suggested two possible reasons why the Egyptians deserted previously settled areas in Nubia near the end of the Old Kingdom: 1) the increased migration of non-Egyptian people settling in the Nubian Nile Valley, as well as the rise of Kerma as an urban center, and 2) pressures on Egyptian authority and resources elsewhere. Whatever the reason, maintaining traffic

and the rest of Africa. This practice of employing Nubian soldiers in Egypt is illustrated by wooden models, found in a tomb in Asyut belonging to a regional leader, depicting a troop of Nubian archers along with Egyptian soldiers.

To ensure that the Nubians kept their distance from Egypt, Mentuhotep II may have built some fortifications in Lower Nubia. Not content with military force, he also used ritual means in his attempt to destroy his Nubian enemies. Execration Texts, characteristic of the First Intermediate Period and Middle Kingdom, list places and people who were perceived by the Egyptians as hostile, and they mention the names of many of these Nubian enemies. When such texts, written upon pots and statuettes of prisoners, were ritually broken, the intention was that the enemy would magically be destroyed.

Although Nubians were thus mentioned and portrayed on a variety of Egyptian cultural artifacts, little else is known about Egyptian policy in Nubia during this period. There is evidence of three Nubian kings on rock drawings and rock-cut inscriptions in Lower Nubia, although some scholars date this to the Second Intermediate Period, but very little can be discerned about these individuals or the nature of their kingdoms.

Nubian Fortresses in the Egyptian
Middle Kingdom
The Egyptian Middle Kingdom began with another Egyptian effort to expand into Nubian territory. Part or all of Wawat (Lower Nubia) was annexed to Egypt, according to a graffito near Abisko, south of the First Cataract. Mentuhotep II had been able to expand Egyptian interests in Nubia, and the Egyptians regained full control under Amenemhat I at the beginning of the Twelfth Dynasty (ca. 1938–1759 BC). They pushed south in an attempt to secure trade routes and to consolidate control of the area. They now built fortresses along the Nile at the Second Cataract, to protect Egypt's southern border, safeguard Egyptian gold-mining interests (such as the routes through the Wadi al-Allaqi), and tax goods coming overland and downriver into Egypt, as well as to defend against the Kerma polity to the south.

Like his predecessor Mentuhotep II, Amenemhat I may have had some Nubian ancestry. An Egyptian literary text called the *Prophecies of Neferti*, of which we have only New Kingdom copies, refers to a time in the Old Kingdom when a prophet of King Sneferu, Neferti, predicts that an Ameny, or King Amenemhat I, who is the son of a "woman of *t3-sty*" (the name of Nubia or possibly the Aswan nome), will unify Egypt. During the reign of this king, Nubians seem to have been accepted without prejudice as part of the Egyptian population, as indicated by the marriage of these kings to Nubian women and the appointed positions Nubians held in Egyptian society. Yet Nubia was still considered a land for Egyptians to acquire: an inscription at al-Girgawi dating to regnal year 29, possibly associated with Amenemhat I, boasts that his army retook Wawat and built fortresses to protect Egypt's southern borders.

Senwosret I established a power center at the Second Cataract site of Buhen, expanding and fortifying an earlier settlement. A victory decree from Buhen depicts Senwosret facing Montu, the god of war, who stands before him with Nubian enemies. Both Amenemhat I and Senwosret I campaigned to conquer Wawat. The extent of the Nubian threat they perceived is clear from the series of Egyptian fortresses with massive walls that Senwosret I began and Senwosret III completed in Lower Nubia.

During regnal year 8, Senwosret III added fortresses at Semna and Kumma, located on opposite sides of the river, so that no one could pass through this narrow section of the river without being seen. A stela dating to regnal year 16, located at Semna, was duplicated on the island of Uronarti. It reveals that Senwosret III drew his southern boundary at Semna, which he claimed was farther south than his father's boundary. Using the political rhetoric of the time, Senwosret III's inscription stated that the Nubians were cowards, who retreated when they were attacked. He claimed to have captured Nubian women, carried off their children, and killed their cattle while destroying their fields of grain. The inscription ends with Senwosret III's assertion that it was his descendants' duty to maintain this southern border at Semna, to prevent Nubia from attacking Egypt from the south.

Also during Senwosret III's reign, the Nubians of Kush south of the Third Cataract seem to have become more powerful and hostile, and nine more fortresses were built along the Second Cataract to ensure its safety. Once the

Figure 15. Model of Nubian archers, from the Eleventh Dynasty tomb of Mesehty, governor of Asyut.

Nile was secure at the southern boundary, Senwosret III had a channel cut through the First Cataract rocks to allow river traffic to pass through easily to Egypt. Senwosret III was eventually deified and worshiped in Nubia, particularly at Toshka, Buhen, Uronarti, Semna, and Kumma. His cult in Nubia seems to have continued for well over a thousand years.

The effectiveness of Senwosret III's efforts may be seen in the fact that the eighteen inscriptions attributed to his successor, Amenemhat III, at Semna and Kumma lack any reference to hostilities with the Nubians, and this decrease in aggression seems to characterize the later Middle Kingdom interaction with Nubia. The Semna Papyri, a group of documents that were exchanged among the Semna, Mirgissa, and Serra East fortresses, tracked Nubian movements during the late Twelfth Dynasty, speaking not of hostilities but of trade relations between Egypt and Nubia and control of traffic throughout the frontier. The chief point of interaction was at Mirgissa, in the northern sector of the Second Cataract.

As for evidence of the beginning of the Second Intermediate Period, a statue found on the island of Argo is inscribed with the cartouche of the Thirteenth Dynasty king Sobekhotep IV, and the fortresses at Semna and Mirgissa yielded statues whose inscriptions seem to refer to the Thirteenth Dynasty king Wagef and his command over Nubia. This information indicates either that throughout the Middle Kingdom and the beginning of the Second Intermediate Period, Egypt retained some control over Nubia's trade routes and maintained its interest in the fortresses, or that these statues were simply imports to that area. However, by the end of the Thirteenth Dynasty, the area of Kush, which was once a trading partner of the Egyptians, had become a threat. As indicated by evidence at the site of Askut and other Second Cataract forts, Egyptian administrative "expatriates," as Stuart

Tyson Smith describes them, switched their allegiance to Kerma at this time and later back again to the Egyptian pharaoh at the beginning of the Egyptian New Kingdom. Eventually, the expatriates and the native population intermingled and became neighbors, not fighting or competing but living together.

The Kerma Culture and the Kingdom of Kush
The site of Kerma is probably to be identified as the capital of the first Nubian Kingdom of Kush, which first appeared in Egyptian records during the Twelfth Dynasty and then became an increasingly powerful political entity during the Thirteenth Dynasty. There are still many questions regarding, first, whether the state of Kush was the dominant power in Upper Nubia; second, whether there were a number of independent polities in Nubia at that time; and third, whether this area became a centralized state at that time or earlier. But it is clear that this Nubian kingdom was the first to rival Egypt for control of the Nubian Nile Valley.

Two sites that were inhabited about 2050 BC reflect the two different polities found in Nubia at the time: the C-Group site of Areika in Lower Nubia, excavated in the early twentieth century by David Randall-MacIver and C. Leonard Woolley; and Kerma in Upper Nubia, originally excavated by George Reisner and later by Charles Bonnet and the Sudanese Antiquities Service (discussed below).

There are two areas of Areika: the eastern half and the western half were together surrounded by a fortified wall. The eastern half consists of rectangular buildings and seems to have been the center of food production, as indicated by the presence of hearths and bread ovens, a granary, and a courtyard (possibly to hold animals). The western half had irregular and sometimes curved buildings in which people lived, perhaps in a fort. Josef Wegner proposes that the large amounts of Egyptian pottery uncovered in the western half belonged to

Egyptian officers, probably sent to supervise the Nubian troops and the building of the fortress. O'Connor believes that the Nubian populace maintained congenial contact with Egyptians during this period as indicated by their cohabitation at that site.

The cemeteries associated with Areika contain grave goods that offer evidence for C-Group populations in the area: pottery, figurines of animals and people, sandals, jewelry, stone tools, and implements used for making linen. The figurines have been associated not only with burial practices but possibly also with non-funerary religious activity. They were embellished with impressions and marks to imitate tattoos. (Actual tattoos were also found on some of the women buried at Areika.)

During the Egyptian Second Intermediate Period (Fourteenth–Seventeenth Dynasties, ca. 1685–1550 BC), Egypt was politically decentralized, with competing rulers in Lower and Upper Egypt. Because the Egyptians were thus coping with domestic struggles, Nubian groups were once again able to lay claim to Lower Nubia. At some point, the Egyptian soldiers still stationed in Second Cataract forts appear to have switched their allegiance to the increasingly powerful kings at Kerma.

This era is considered the apogee of Nubian power in Kush, as indicated by the royal city at Kerma, which was the earliest and largest city in Upper Nubia. Kerma-culture political groups, apparently dominant in all of Upper Nubia, expanded their territorial control throughout Lower Nubia as far north as Aswan. There are four phases of the Kerma culture: Pre-Kerma (mid-fourth millennium to ca. 2600 BC), Early (Ancient) Kerma (ca. 2500–2050 BC), Middle Kerma (ca. 2050–1750 BC), and Classic Kerma (ca. 1750–1450 BC); a final phase, the Late or Post-Classic Kerma phase, postdates the Egyptian New Kingdom conquest of Nubia.

The city of Kerma was strategically located just south of the Third Cataract, beside a wide fertile plain. Very few settlements of the Kerma culture have been excavated, but at the city of Kerma, during the Pre-Kerma and Early Kerma phases, houses appear to be made of mud and reeds, while later, in the Classic Kerma phase, they are made of stone or mud brick. By the seventeenth century BC, the city had reached its zenith in terms of size and impressive architecture. In the center of the fortified city was a massive mud-brick temple, the Lower or Western Deffufa, which had a pylon-like façade, although unlike Egyptian temples, it was entered from the sides rather than the front. Palace and audience halls were also within the city walls. Residences within the city housed not only the ruler of Kush, but also his family and courtiers, priests, court officials, officers, and soldiers, as well as artisans and servants, all sharing the same urban landscape.

The sophistication of life in this city center is reflected in the furniture, personal equipment, and other goods found in the extensive cemeteries east of Kerma city. Burial practices changed over time, with tombs becoming larger and more elaborate from Early Kerma to Classic Kerma. The deceased, clothed in loincloths or leather kilts and sometimes wrapped in sheepskin, were buried on their right sides in a flexed position with their faces looking north, heads pointed east, and feet west. Accompanying them were pottery and stone vessels as well as jewelry, clothing, tools and weapons, cosmetic vessels, mirrors, and other personal belongings. The bodies were not mummified and were placed on cowhides or on beds. Some of the deceased, most likely the rulers, were accompanied into death by animal and human sacrifices, buried alive. The largest and latest royal tombs are at the southern end of the cemetery, within which hundreds of women, children, and officials were buried.

Egyptian alabaster vases, copper daggers, statues, and statuettes found at Kerma indicate some contact between Kush and Egypt, whether through trade or spoils of war. For instance, a statue found at Kerma of Hepdjefa, a noble from Asyut in Middle Egypt, and also one of his wife Sennuwy, date to the reign of Senwosret III. Rather than being a sign that these individuals visited the city, these statues were probably pillaged from their owner's tomb in Middle Egypt and sent to Kerma. In fact, Egypt was attacked by Kerma, as documented in an inscription recently found at Elkab in Upper Egypt, during which the town was looted. Sobeknakht, governor and hereditary prince of Elkab, mentions how the Egyptians sent a punitive expedition into Nubia. On a vessel found in a tomb at Kerma (Tumulus KIII), dating to the Seventeenth Dynasty, the name Sobeknakht appears with these same titles, establishing that some Egyptian tomb goods were buried with Nubians in Kerma. The implication is that Kerma's reach extended farther north beyond Aswan, possibly as far as Elkab.

In addition to the Kerma culture and the C-Group, another distinct Nubian population was also found on Egypt's southern border at this time. References to the Medjayu appear in Egyptian texts from the late third millennium onward, but less is known of them than of the other groups. The Medjayu, believed to be nomads who acquired food and weapons by trade, first appeared as soldiers or policemen in Egyptian service in the Old Kingdom, but during the Middle Kingdom they apparently became hostile forces fighting the Egyptians in Nubia. They were buried in shallow, round graves reminiscent of frying pans that archaeologists called 'pan graves,' which became a general name for this distinctive culture. The graves contained bows, arrows, and other weapons and were sometimes decorated with painted cattle skulls (bucrania) and goat skulls. They were also provisioned with distinctive forms of pottery (fine black-topped ware cups and bowls with flattened bases) and jewelry, including earrings, as well as Egyptian goods. Pan-Grave remains are found in Lower Nubia and Egypt, as well as in the Eastern Desert as far south as central Sudan, the Red Sea Hills, and the Western Desert. Medjay Nubians are possibly referred to in Papyrus Bulaq, along with the Aushek tribe, in a list of the tribute these groups paid to Egypt.

During the Egyptian Thirteenth Dynasty, some Medjayu were guests at the Theban court. Perhaps as a result of these positive interactions, during the Second Intermediate Period the Medjayu joined forces with the Egyptian king Kamose, the last king of the Seventeenth Dynasty (ca. 1550–1540 BC), to attack the Asiatic Hyksos rulers in Lower Egypt, who were attempting to create an alliance with the Kerma ruler. Kamose then led a campaign into the Second Cataract to recapture Buhen. In doing so, he created a buffer zone between Egypt and the Kerma culture in the south, as well as between Egyptian-ruled territory and the Hyksos in the north. Kamose's brother or son, Ahmose I, eventually succeeded in driving out the Hyksos, and Ahmose I became the first king of a newly unified Egypt, initiating the Eighteenth Dynasty and the New Kingdom. Evidence of Kamose's and Ahmose I's presence in Nubia is seen on rock inscriptions at Arminna, among other places.

Nubia during the Egyptian New Kingdom

The New Kingdom (Dynasties Eighteen–Twenty, ca. 1550–1077 BC) yields a significant amount of Egyptian textual and pictorial evidence about ancient Nubia. Such evidence comes from Egyptian reliefs in tombs and temples, as well as from written documents, which of course reflected Egyptian attitudes toward Nubians, as opposed to the viewpoint of the Nubians themselves.

During the Eighteenth Dynasty, cemeteries, such as that at Soleb, show hardly any trace of traditional Nubian culture. Over a period of eighty-eight years, Egyptians campaigned for control in Nubia during the reign of each successive king. Despite the resistance they met, Egyptian expeditions and campaigns continued until ca. 1460 BC, by which time Egypt had conquered all of Lower and Upper Nubia, including the Kingdom of Kush.

Under the administration of Egypt, Nubia was now divided into two provinces: Lower Nubia, or Wawat, and Upper Nubia, or Kush. Each was placed under a resident official, that is, a viceregal/deputy governor, who reported to the 'King's Son of Kush,' generally termed 'viceroy' by scholars. The deputies were responsible for the collection of tribute for the pharaoh, channeling it through the viceroy of Nubia, who reported directly to the king of Egypt. Although the viceroy was based in Thebes, he would travel to Nubia with the 'Troop Commander of Kush' to collect taxes, acquire tribute and minerals from mining, and oversee the domain. Scenes of tribute from Nubia during this time abound in Egyptian temples.

During the Eighteenth Dynasty, the capital of the region of Wawat was centered at Aniba, while Soleb was the main center of the province of Kush. During the Nineteenth Dynasty, Doukki Gel, Napata, and Amara West gained prominence.

Three main princedoms were created in Lower Nubia at Kuban, Toshka, and Debeira, and possibly six (Sai, Kerma, Bugdumbush, and their subdivisions) in Upper Nubia. Each was headed by a Nubian prince who was raised in the Egyptian court (see below). Within each princedom was a series of towns, each overseen by a governor or mayor. Towns were surrounded by arable land for agriculture, their main source of revenue. Each mayor/governor was responsible for maintaining prosperity in his area.

Even given the limitations of our evidence, Nubia appears not to have been exploited unduly by the Egyptians, in terms of exacting exorbitant revenue or enslaving its people. Clearly, gold and other tribute items were important to the Egyptian economy and were regularly supplied to the pharaoh; however, based on the documentary evidence, it does not appear that excessive amounts were demanded. As in the late Old Kingdom, many Lower Nubian princes and princesses were raised in the Egyptian court. Intermingling with the children of Egyptian courtiers had the effect of integrating these elite Nubians into Egyptian society; the intention was that upon their return home, they would promote Egyptian culture in Nubia and alliances to Egypt. During the New Kingdom, it was also not unusual for a Nubian child to become an official in the Egyptian regime. The rulers of the princedoms of Tekhet and Miam had relatives who may have served in the administration in Egypt itself.

When Ahmose came to the throne at the beginning of the Eighteenth Dynasty, Nubian control of Lower Nubia had been weakened. But the Egyptians needed to secure Nubian gold—for instance, from the gold mines at Wadi al-Allaqi—to demonstrate their wealth and power to the Near East (Levant, Mesopotamia, and Anatolia), and gold was used in political alliances. Moreover, there was a new desire on the part of Egypt to push into Upper Nubia, the reason for which is not as clear, although the trade goods from sub-Saharan Africa along with gold were used to cement Egypt's power in the world.

The biographical inscription of Ahmose, son of Ebana (or Abana), a high-ranking soldier and courtier, in his tomb at Elkab states that the Nubians were pushed back through Lower Nubia, where Ahmose I built a temple at Buhen, site of the Middle Kingdom fort, and strengthened its fortifications. Farther south, above the Second Cataract, there is evidence for Ahmose I's presence: a statue inscribed with the name of Ahmose I, a relief with his wife Ahmose-Nefertari's name upon it, and a statue of his successor, Amenhotep I, found on Sai Island. Since Sai was the capital of the Kushite kingdom of Shaât, its capture was especially significant for the Egyptians. Yet in his campaigns into Nubia, Amenhotep I was apparently never able to push farther south beyond the Third Cataract.

Amenhotep I's successor, Thutmose I, sponsored more campaigns into Nubia than any of his predecessors. He prevailed where Amenhotep I had failed in passing the Third Cataract and taking Kerma. There he decimated the Kerma Nubians, an event described in his rock-cut stela at Tombos in the Third Cataract. Thutmose I resumed control of the Second Cataract Nubian fortresses and enlarged many of them, including those at Kuban, Ikkur, and Buhen. In doing so, he secured the routes to the gold mines. At the same time, he abandoned or downsized many other fortresses that had become redundant once the area leading into the Third Cataract had been conquered. This reduction in military presence did not mean that the Nubians were content under Egyptian sovereignty, however; on the contrary, one inscription at Aswan mentions Nubians being killed in retaliation for a rebellion, and the son of the local chief being captured and presented to the pharaoh.

Not satisfied with securing the Third Cataract, Thutmose I evidently pressed on as far as Kurgus, downstream of the Fifth Cataract. As a display of his control over his Nubian subjects, during his return to Egypt, the pharaoh placed the Kushite leader's corpse at the bow of his boat, head downward, as an admonition to all other Nubians. Along the way north, he established garrisons at Tombos and on Sai Island.

The Nubians were not content under Egyptian rule, and when they learned of the death of

Thutmose I, they mounted another rebellion, which Thutmose II put down. This revolt was curtailed when the son of the ruler of Kush was brought back to Egypt. After this, Nubia seemed to remain peaceful for some time. Goods from Nubia were highly prized by Egyptian pharaohs, and reliefs record their attempts to acquire them, as discussed below. To satisfy this taste for exotic imports, the Egyptians made southern Nubia the point of access to products from sub-Saharan Africa. Campaigns continued under successive pharaohs, as maintaining control of southern Nubia became essential.

No textual material survives to indicate the specific Nubian policies of the next ruler, Hatshepsut. But she built a Hathor sanctuary at Faras and a temple inside Buhen, which Thutmose III later usurped. Her name has also been found on Sai Island. During her co-regency with Thutmose III, there were three or four incursions into Kush in their twelfth regnal year, documented by an inscription at Tangur West. Campaigns in the co-regency regnal years 20 and 21/22 followed. Furthermore, Hatshepsut dispatched an expedition to the land of Punt, thought to be an East African nation, also ruled by a queen, whence she brought back to Egypt a variety of exotic items, recorded on her temple walls at Deir al-Bahari on the west bank at Thebes. Information on the land of Punt and its inhabitants derives from reliefs and references found in Egypt, and from the archaeological site at Mersa/Wadi Gawasis along the Red Sea.

When Thutmose III finally came to the Egyptian throne as sole ruler, he claimed, on a royal stela dating to regnal year 47, to control the area from Asia to Africa. This stela was erected in the temple of Amun-Re at the foot of a rock outcropping at Gebel Barkal in Napata, located between the Third and Fourth Cataracts at the upstream end of the area known as the Dongola

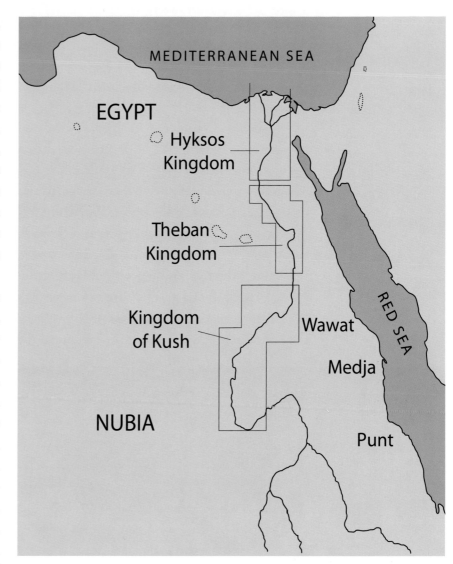

Figure 16. Map of Egypt and Nubia, ca. 1650–1550 BC. The outlines show the approximate extent of the Hyksos, Theban, and Kushite kingdoms during this period.

Reach. Napata was the most important Nubian cult center during Thutmose III's reign, and the god Amun was thought to dwell within the rock (called the 'pure mountain') of Gebel Barkal. The Nubians considered this Nubian Amun a doublet of the Theban Amun, who also dwelled in Gebel Barkal and was believed to be responsible for endowing the pharaoh with the power to rule over Egypt and Kush. Nubians portrayed the god with a ram's head and horns crowned with a sun disc, a form that appears to syncretize the indigenous ram god at Kerma with the Egyptian god

Amun. This way of portraying Amun with a ram's head can also be seen on Egyptian temples in Nubia and Egypt during the New Kingdom. (Further discussion of these gods can be found in "Nubian Religion.")

Besides being a cult center at this time, Napata also served as a stopover between sub-Saharan African routes and Egypt. Consequently, Thutmose III built a garrison town there to secure this area as a major trading post. His interest in Nubia is clear from his inscriptions at Karnak and from those in the Theban tomb of his vizier, Rekhmire, who lists raw materials obtained from Nubia. Thutmose III also followed Hatshepsut's lead in constructing religious edifices, one purpose of which may have been to encourage the Nubians to embrace Egyptian culture. His name is found from Kalabsha in northern Nubia as far south as Argo (Tabo). He began the temple of Amun of Pnubs at Doukki Gel near Kerma, as well as the temple at Amada, which was finished by his son, Amenhotep II. Apparently in an effort to appease the Nubians, he was shown worshiping not only Horus (at Ellesiya in Lower Nubia) and the deified Senwosret III, but also the ancient Nubian god Dedwen. He seems, however, to have been more preoccupied with his victories in Asia than with those in Nubia, as is demonstrated by the predominance of Asia in his annals, a record of some of his accomplishments inscribed on the walls of his buildings at Karnak Temple in Egypt.

Figure 17. Painting in the Eighteenth Dynasty Egyptian tomb of Huy (TT 40) depicting Nubians in procession, carrying offerings to the Egyptian king.

The site of Kurgus, between the Fourth and Fifth Cataracts, was the ultimate Egyptian frontier, with boundary inscriptions there belonging to Thutmose I and Thutmose III. Its proximity to Hagar al-Merwe, which has routes leading to the gold mines, has been suggested as a reason for the Egyptian push that far, as well as the fact that this area might have been part of the northern extent of Kerma.

Thutmose III's successor, Amenhotep II, put forward a definite policy for Asia and Nubia at the beginning of his reign, articulating it on a stela set up in the temple of Amada after he had completed Thutmose III's temple at Napata. By claiming to have executed, with his own hands, six Syrian chiefs/princes, and hanging the seventh upon the temple walls at Napata, he was warning any Nubian individual or town who might resist him: disobey me and die.

During the short reign of Thutmose IV, the title of the viceroy of Nubia became the 'King's Son of Kush,' clearly implying that the Egyptians controlled all of Kush, but there is no evidence that he campaigned there. Thutmose IV's name occurred throughout Nubia: at Buhen, Doukki Gel, and Gebel Barkal, in an addition to the temple at Amada, and in the temple of Amun of Pnubs at Kerma. Many Nubian princes came to the Egyptian court at this time. A few viceroys were themselves Nubian, though the majority were Egyptian. Some scholars maintain that Kushite princesses may have married Egyptian pharaohs, but this cannot be proven, as Morkot points out, since the princesses took Egyptian names once they were married.

The construction of the temple of Amun of Pnubs at Kerma continued during the reign of Amenhotep III, testifying to the ongoing Egyptian presence there. Amenhotep III dispatched two expeditions into Nubia, the first in regnal year 5 and the second near the end of his reign. His in-scriptions do not mention any losses among his troops or large number of prisoners. Nubia was perhaps peaceful or adequately subjugated, or else the pharaoh had other concerns. Egypt had expanded its sovereignty over foreign lands as far as northern Syria and upstream to Kurgus. The creation, decoration, and furnishing of Egyptian works of architecture required the expansion of gold mining and quarrying activities in Nubia. More mines in the Eastern Desert were opened at ancient Ibhet and Ikayta. Princes continued to be schooled in Egypt and envoys carried messages between Egypt and Nubia.

Likewise, during this period, Egyptian building projects proliferated in Nubia. Amenhotep III built temples at Wadi al-Sebua, Kuban, Aniba, Sai Island, and Argo (Tabo), but he is best known for the construction of his temple at Soleb. In addition, Amenhotep III developed in Nubia the idea of paired temples, one masculine and the other feminine. He thus had a companion temple built at Sedeinga, so that there was one for himself and another for his queen, Tiye.

Such activities continued under Amenhotep III's son, Akhenaten. Archaeological and textual evidence places Akhenaten's viceroy in Nubia, campaigning at Wadi al-Allaqi to regain control of the gold mines by putting down a revolt that resulted in grain being stolen. This, however, appears to be a minor pretext. Akhenaten's name was also found on stamped bricks at Buhen. *Talatat* (small sandstone blocks characteristically used in his constructions) have been found at Kerma; at three temples built to Amun, Mut, and Khonsu, and a fourth temple, all at Sesebi; and at Gebel Barkal. Kawa was called Gem Aten, so the town and temple were perhaps founded or renamed in his reign. Another temple at Kawa bears the ancient name Per Gem Aten (House of 'Aten is Found'), dedicated to the sun god whose worship Akhenaten espoused. At the temple of Soleb, William

Murnane showed that Amenhotep III's name was recarved over the name of Akhenaten during the restoration of the old religion, and suppression of Akhenaten, that followed the Amarna Period.

Akhenaten's successor, Tutankhamun, built an Amun temple at Kawa, to which Ramesses II later added his name. Little else is known concerning Nubian policy during the short reign of Tutankhamun, except for paintings in the Theban tomb of his viceroy Huy, which portray Nubians bringing tribute, along with African animals and gold. Also portrayed are two Kushite princesses, confirming the induction of foreigners into the Egyptian court. In addition, Tutankhamun may have built an Amun temple at Gebel Barkal, a sacred site for Nubians. Information is also scarce concerning Horemheb's activities in Nubia at the end of the Eighteenth Dynasty. Possibly, his brief rule left little time for Nubian activities.

During the Eighteenth Dynasty, Nubians and Egyptians were living, possibly marrying, and working alongside each other. The administrative site of Tombos housed a cemetery of Nubians and Egyptian officials. Whereas Egyptians in the Old Kingdom had not considered it desirable to be buried in Nubia (e.g., Sabni had to recover the body of his father from Nubia to be buried in Egypt), during the New Kingdom, Nubians and Egyptians were buried side by side. With the spread of Egyptian interests into Nubia and the Kerma region, previously Nubian settlements apparently came to be shared with Egyptians, as well as new settlements being built along the Nile. Although Egyptians occupied much of Nubia, Nubian chiefs may still have ruled their towns; inscriptive material documents raids they conducted in the early Nineteenth Dynasty.

The beginning of the Ramesside Period (Dynasties Nineteen–Twenty, 1292–1077 BC) was marked by more interest in Lower Nubia than in Upper Nubia on the part of Egyptian

kings. During his short-lived reign, Ramesses I, the first ruler of the Nineteenth Dynasty, built a temple dedicated to Amun-Min at Buhen near the Second Cataract. More is known about the interests of his successor, Sety I, in Nubia. This king undertook one expedition, possibly during his eighth regnal year, to Amara West and Sai Island, where he speaks of a campaign against Irem, upstream of the Fifth Cataract. It also appears from the decoration and style of reliefs that Sety I began a temple at Beit al-Wali in northern Lower Nubia. Moreover, a Nubian rock stela at Nauri details endowments for his famous temple at Abydos in Egypt, and another inscription at the temple of Aksha suggests that he had begun work at Abu Simbel. The gold in Nubian mines still interested Egyptian pharaohs, as evidenced by Sety I, who according to Ramesses II tried unsuccessfully to dig a well at Wadi al-Allaqi.

The temples of Ramesses II in Nubia are the ones most familiar today. This pharaoh constructed or completed eight such temples: at Beit al-Wali, Gerf Hussein, Wadi al-Sebua, Amada, Derr, Abu Simbel, Aksha, and Amara West. The building of these temples was a form of propaganda, possibly to intimidate the Nubians and proclaim Egyptian prowess, according to William Kelly Simpson. In his temple at Abu Simbel, Ramesses II followed Amenhotep III's lead in representing himself as the deified king with the ram's horns of Amun wrapped around his face and a disc upon his head. Again, like Amenhotep III at Sedeinga and Soleb, he had two temples built at Abu Simbel, one for himself and the other for his queen, Nefertari. Ramesses II's expansionistic building policy also appears in the decoration of other temples, but not all reliefs are to be taken as accurate portrayals of royal expeditions and campaigns. On the temples of Beit al-Wali and Abu Simbel, for instance, reliefs document a Nubian campaign that is most likely fictitious (i.e., the Beit al-Wali relief was probably undertaken during the reign of Sety I, when the temple was originally constructed). Ramesses II's name also appears on six further temples, from Aniba in the north to Gebel Barkal in the south.

After Ramesses II's reign, Egypt was forced to turn its attention away from Nubia to focus on disturbances in the Near East. As Merenptah, Ramesses II's heir, defeated the Libyan and Sea Peoples' incursions to protect Egypt's northern borders, the Nubians tried to take this opportunity to regain control of their lands. As a consequence of this process, Merenptah quelled a Nubian rebellion and reasserted Egyptian control, an event described on his stela at Amada.

The final defeat of the Sea Peoples came under Ramesses III of the Twentieth Dynasty. This pharaoh also records Nubian campaigns and victories, although it is clear that Nubian expeditions were less important to him than maintaining order in the Near East.

Ramesses VI is the next pharaoh whose name appears in the record with respect to Nubian activity; his official, Pennout, was the governor of Aniba in Lower Nubia (the capital of Wawat) and was buried there. During the reign of Ramesses XI, the last pharaoh of the Twentieth Dynasty, the position of viceroy of Nubia became critically important when an uprising in Upper Egypt against the king, who resided in the Delta, was put down by the viceroy of Nubia, Panehesy (whose name means 'the Nubian'), and his Nubian troops, perhaps in an attempt to calm the upheaval in Thebes and restore the king's appointee as high priest to power. However, at this time of economic hardship in Egypt, tombs and temples were being looted for their riches; while Panehesy was in the north, his Nubian troops began looting sites in Thebes. From that time on, it is therefore unclear whether Panehesy was a loyalist or an enemy of Ramesses XI.

Herihor, the High Priest of Amun at the time, eventually assumed the official position of viceroy as well as becoming vizier and commander of the army. He virtually controlled Thebes and the area farther south. One reconstruction of history is that Piankh, the son-in-law of Herihor, ultimately succeeded in pushing Panehesy into Nubia. With the deaths of Herihor, Piankh, and Ramesses XI, the New Kingdom came to an end.

Morkot offers an adept summary, from the Nubian point of view, of this long period of relations between Egypt and Nubia, for which most of our information about Nubians derives from

Figure 18. Rock-cut inscription at Tombos, Egyptian late Eighteenth Dynasty, reign of Amenhotep III.

THE HISTORY OF NUBIA

Egyptian sources. In his view, during the Old Kingdom, kings went to Lower Nubia to eradicate the people; during the Middle Kingdom, they tried to conquer them; and during the New Kingdom, they attempted to absorb them into the Egyptian population while benefiting from their resources.

Kushite Kings and the Napatan Period

For the period between the end of the New Kingdom in Egypt and the rise of the Kushite kings of the Twenty-fifth Egyptian Dynasty, we know of very little indigenous archaeological information for Upper Nubia, and nothing for Lower Nubia. Scholars offer numerous theories to explain this apparent depopulation of Lower Nubia from the late New Kingdom onward. Some propose that the Nile may have been low, forcing the population to become nomadic, while others maintain that the inhabitants moved to Egypt, Upper Nubia, or the Eastern Desert. There are problems with each of these theories. A recent theory, propounded by Morkot, is that the gold-mining industry of Wawat collapsed, either because no more ore could be extracted using available technologies, or because the desert dwellers in that area were creating problems, or because it was difficult to mount expeditions at that time. Whatever the case, if mining was no longer possible, then the mining region would have become depopulated, since it was not agriculturally rich enough to sustain large communities. However, even though the population disappeared from archaeological visibility, this does not mean that the Nubians no longer existed there. Downstream from the Fourth Cataract, the site of Hillat al-Arab near Gebel Barkal has tombs containing burials of an indigenous Nubian elite. They date from the end of the New Kingdom or early Third Intermediate Period to the Twenty-fifth Dynasty, indicating a continued presence in that area.

Figure 19. The Great Temple of Abu Simbel at sunrise. Photo © Chester Higgins Jr 2012.

With the decentralization of Egypt during the Third Intermediate Period (Dynasties Twenty-one through Twenty-four, ca. 1076–723 BC), local rulers once again gained control of Nubia. The centers of power were Kerma and Napata, and there seems to have been a resurgence of the Amun cult at Gebel Barkal, near Napata. Egypt could not continue to dominate Nubia, since it had its own difficulties at home. It was not until the Twenty-second Dynasty (ca. 943–746 BC) that Nubian mercenaries are once again documented in Egyptian armies. Then, recognizing the skill and courage of Nubian warriors, the Libyan-descended ruler in Egypt, Sheshonq I, and his successor, Osorkon I, employed Kushites in their armies to fight campaigns in southwest Asia. And Nubian goods were still considered desirable as far away as Mesopotamia; some Assyrian texts mention the giving of gifts crafted from Nubian materials.

During this time, Napata, already prominent during the New Kingdom in Egypt, continued to be an important trade hub. Located near the southern bend of the Nile, Napata is right across the Nile from the site of Nuri with its cemeteries, and from there a road across the Bayuda Desert leads to the city of Meroe. Just south and downstream on the opposite bank from Gebel Barkal is Sanam, a major Kushite center in the eighth and seventh centuries and a stage center route to the southern trade. A little farther downstream were the cemeteries of al-Kurru, on the right bank of the Nile, that is, across from Sanam. Thus the Napata region on both sides of the Nile was a strategic location for access to other areas.

At this point in Nubian history, a powerful local clan arose in the area of Napata that would give rise to the Twenty-fifth Dynasty, which ruled a great nation stretching from the confluence of the Niles to the Mediterranean. Scholars divide what has been termed the "Second Kingdom of Kush" into two successive phases: the Napatan

Period (mid-eighth century BC to mid-third century BC) and the Meroitic Period (mid-third century BC to mid-fourth century AD), so named after the eponymous cities that continued to develop as centers of Nubian culture. The Twenty-fifth Egyptian Dynasty (ca. 722–655/53 BC) is also called the Kushite, Ethiopian, or Nubian Dynasty, because during this time Kush dominated Egypt. Napata is believed to have served as the religious center and Meroe the political center for the Kushite kings. Whether the Kushite realm was unified under one ruler and how it came to control a vast region of Nubia and beyond are uncertain, though numerous suggestions have been made. Explanations based on trade posit that, although gold mining had diminished in importance, the trade in ivory continued to assure the power and prestige of Africa, even in such far-flung places as Assyria and later in Greece.

The Early Napatan Period is characterized by the presence of powerful rulers who by 750 BC controlled all of Nubia. These kings added to the already imposing structure of Amun at Gebel Barkal. They built tombs at al-Kurru in a massive cemetery spanning two wadis and two terraces, as well as tombs at Nuri. The cemeteries at al-Kurru featured pyramids, in front of which were small chapels. Beneath the pyramids were as many as three painted burial chambers, reached by a stairway. Horse burials can also be found in this cemetery, along with their adornments. The cemetery of Nuri, which was first used by King Taharqo, was similar in style to al-Kurru with pyramids, chapels, and chambers beneath them; only three of its chapels remain.

The first Nubian king for whom we have any historical record, Alara (ca. 785–765 BC), is known only from later sources, such as inscriptions of Tarharqo and Nastasen. He seems to have consolidated power over Upper Nubia to the Third Cataract. His probable successor, Kashta (ca. 765–753 BC), extended his rule to encompass Lower

Nubia and seems to have moved north to become accepted as overlord in the Theban area. Kashta was followed by Piankhi (Piye) (ca. 753–722 BC), who, according to his victory stela at Gebel Barkal, captured Thebes, then moved farther north through cities in Upper Egypt, and then to the Memphite region and Western Delta in Lower Egypt, until all of Egypt submitted to him. Morkot has suggested the possibility that Egyptian styles, costumes, and titles were assumed in Nubia during the reigns of Kashta and Piankhi before the conquest of Egypt by Nubians.

After this accomplishment, Piankhi returned to Nubia, leaving Egypt to be reconquered by his brother and successor, Shabaqo. Shabaqo's successors, Shebitqo, Taharqo, and Tanwetamani, incorporated Egypt into the realm of Kush, residing primarily in Memphis but continuing to be buried near Napata and Gebel Barkal.

Powerful as they had become, the Twenty-fifth Dynasty Kushite kings did not destroy Egyptian culture, but rather promoted the revival of earlier styles in the arts, language, architecture, and religion. Egyptian artisans and scribes were taken to Kush to be employed by the Nubian kings. The Kushite kings, having established their royal residence at Memphis, reasserted the importance of the temples at Thebes by siting their local

Figure 20. A fallen statue of Ramesses II at Wadi al-Sebua.

civil and religious administrations there. Further, they adapted the religion of Amun to enhance the renewed emphasis on the position of 'God's Wife of Amun' that had emerged in the previous generations. The holder of this title participated in a theological marriage with a political agenda; that is, the daughter of the king ruling Thebes was designated as the wife of the god, so that the king could control southern Egypt through her. The God's Wife of Amun ruled the south, and this fed into the Nubian tradition of queenship.

The Nubian kings also maintained the commercial relationships that Egyptian kings had developed with the Levant and Assyria. The latter, however, was trying to conquer the Levant and Egypt, so Taharqo spent much of the last decade of his reign fending off Assyrian attacks. Following the attack upon Egypt by the Assyrian king Ashurbanipal in 667 BC and the subsequent sacking of Thebes, during the reign of Taharqo's successor, Tanwetamani, the last Kushite king was expelled from Egypt around 656 BC. After this defeat, the Kushite population continued to develop in the Middle Nile area between the Third and Sixth Cataracts, in an area later dominated by the city of Meroe. The earliest archaeological evidence for the royal cemeteries at Meroe is from around the eighth and seventh centuries BC. King Taharqo is credited with the founding of the cemeteries at Nuri on the left bank of the Nile opposite Gebel Barkal, in which nineteen kings and fifty-four queens were buried.

Nubia during the Napatan Period

Egyptian records from Dynasties Twenty-six through Thirty (664–332 BC), during the Late Period, refer more often to northern rather than southern neighbors, and evidence for Nubian affairs becomes sparser. According to the Nitocris Adoption Stela of Psamtik I of the Twenty-sixth Dynasty, the king consolidated his power in southern Egypt by arranging for his daughter to be adopted as heir to the Nubian God's Wife of Amun Amenirdis II, thus ending Nubian control of that office. His successor Nekau led a campaign in Nubia, as did Psamtik II, who sent a raiding party through the Napatan state as far as the Fourth Cataract and possibly farther upstream in 593 BC. Nothing else is mentioned in the sources until the reign of Ahmose II (Amasis) (570–526 BC), who claimed to have sent an expedition into Lower Nubia, although there is no archaeological evidence of such at the military outpost of Dorginarti, a Late Period fortress situated on an island in the Second Cataract. The temple site of Kawa near Dongola is particularly important for its Napatan inscriptions. Caches of ritually broken royal statuary, some of it at colossal scale, at Doukki Gel, Gebel Barkal, and Dangeil (downstream of the Fifth Cataract), show violent change, perhaps as a consequence of the raid of Psamtik II. The Napatan rulers continued to develop their culture throughout the period from ca. 650 to ca. 300 BC, and they built pyramids at Nuri, as well as temples elsewhere.

Egypt was invaded by Persian forces under Cambyses in 525 BC, ushering in an era of Persian domination (Twenty-seventh Dynasty, 525–404 BC). Egyptian records are silent regarding Nubia during this period, when Egypt was embroiled in internal discord and fighting the might of Persia. There is evidence, however, that one Kushite king, Irike-Amanote (second half of fifth century BC), attempted to regain control over Egypt, to no avail.

The Meroitic Period

From the third century BC onward, Meroe eclipsed Napata as the capital of the Nubian kingdom, and a vast field of pyramids established Meroe as the center for the royal mortuary cult. Thus began the Meroitic Period of Nubian history, which lasted until the mid-fourth century AD.

Figure 21. View of Gebel Barkal with a ram statue of Amun in the foreground and the sacred mountain in the background. Photo © Chester Higgins Jr 2012.

The Kingdom of Meroe included all of Upper Nubia and probably extended as far south as the confluence of the Blue and White Nile or beyond. Lower Nubia became the intermediary between Upper Nubia and Egypt. Meroe had long been an important city, and at its center a large stone enclosure protected many stone palaces, temples, gardens of fruit trees, and later in its development a Roman-style bath and an astronomical observatory. The strategic importance of its location made it the nodal point for travels east to the Red Sea, south to Ethiopia, and farther to sub-Saharan Africa.

After Alexander the Great conquered Egypt in 332 BC, the Kushites took the opportunity once again to reenter Egyptian territory. Ptolemy I, the first ruler of the Ptolemaic Dynasty (305–30 BC), who gradually took power after the death of Alexander, sent an army against the Kushites in 319 BC. His successor, Ptolemy II, dispatched another expedition that recaptured Lower Nubia for Egypt, annexing the northern part of the area between the First and Second Cataracts. Interaction continued between the Kushites and the Egyptians. Trade was renewed as elephants and other prestige goods became important acquisitions for the Ptolemies. This contact in turn stimulated the Kushite economy. The Meroitic populations that lived in Upper Nubia and the Butana, a savannah region east of the Nile, became prominent and powerful in the state. The sites of Musawwarat al-Sufra and Naqa, among others located south of Meroe in the Butana region toward the Sixth Cataract, show evidence of urban planning. Wad ban Naqa, where a type of Meroitic palace was constructed, as well as building activities at sites farther downstream (Amara West, Karanog, and Qasr Ibrim, to mention a few), illustrate the prosperity of the area along with its increased trade.

Meroitic people eventually settled in Lower Nubia. The geographic zones inhabited by Nubians then changed, so that the Meroitic peoples occupied the Nile region, with the Nubai in the area west of the Nile and the Bejai living east of the Nile and south of Egypt. Other tribes included the Troglodytes by the Red Sea, the Blemmyes and Megabaroi (perhaps formerly those known as the Medjayu) near the Red Sea, and the Sembrites near Meroe.

In approximately the third century BC, the immensely important cultural and political center of Meroe acquired walls around its core city. The old Amun temple was replaced with a vast new temple outside the walls. In about the second century BC, the Meroitic writing system was devised, on the model of Egyptian hieroglyphic and demotic. Although the script is alphabetic and has been deciphered, the language itself can be understood only to a very limited extent due to a lack of useful bilingual texts. The Meroitic language probably belongs to the Eastern Sudanic group, but living languages of the same family are far removed from it in date and context.

Improvements in irrigation systems, agriculture, and storage facilities indicate that Meroe housed a sophisticated society. The pottery was beautifully decorated and technically very fine. Major crops at this time included sesame, date palms, and grain (sorghum in particular), and animal husbandry included oxen, sheep, goats, and horses.

In 207–186 BC, Nubians attempted to regain control of Lower Nubia at a time when Upper Egypt was rebelling against Ptolemaic rule. As a result, that area had two cultures living together side by side: the Egyptians participating in the cults at the temple of Philae at the frontier south of Aswan, and the Nubian indigenous culture there and farther south. The Ptolemies began building many temples in Lower Nubia. Eventually the Kushites gained the upper hand in the region, even though they were eventually defeated during the

Meroitic-Roman War in 29–21/20 BC. Despite their defeat, they still controlled most of southern Nubia, with the Roman border at Hierasykaminos (Maharraqa). Lower Nubia, for a time ruled by Rome in the north and Meroe in the south, became very prosperous in the first to fourth centuries AD. Once the Romans had withdrawn from Lower Nubia around AD 298, the Nobadians encroached, possibly from the Western Desert, and the Blemmyes from the Eastern Desert. The Blemmyes established themselves in the area of Dodekaskhoinos. During this time, relations between the Nobadians and Blemmyes and the Egyptians in the north were unsettled.

Post-Meroitic Period/X-Group (ca. AD 350–641)
Meroe remained the capital of the Meroitic state until the early fourth century AD, after the Axumite (Aksumite) Empire conquered the Meroitic kingdom. It was succeeded by three regional cultures represented by finds at Ballana and Qustul in Lower Nubia, Tanqasi in the region of Napata, and al-Hobagi in the region of Meroe. As a result, the burials in impressive pyramids characteristic of the Meroitic Period disappeared, and tumuli reappeared during the post-Meroitic Period. The deceased were buried in a flexed position, and in general single burials were most common. Royal burials, however, continued to use some objects in the tradition of the Meroitic Period, as at Qustul and Ballana (see below), with rich burial goods such as silver crowns. These burials also included human and animal sacrifices, which mostly appear in the sloping passages that led to the doorways to the burials. Important burials were not limited to Qustul and Ballana; in Sudan, cemeteries at Gammai, al-Khizeina, Hagar al-Beida, Tanqasi, Zuma, and al-Hobagi also had massive tombs. Meroe remained a powerful center, though not of the same prestige as in the Meroitic Period, as other dominant realms appeared.

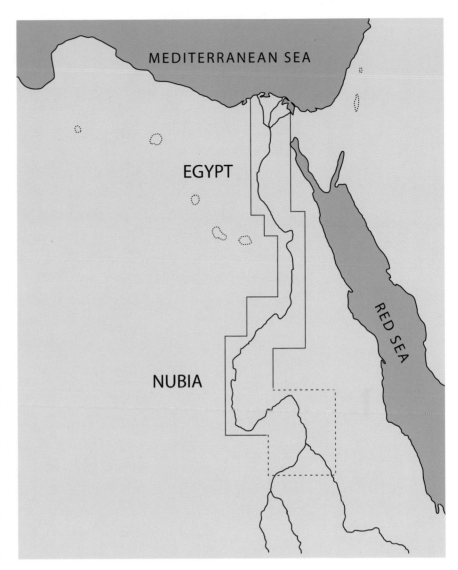

Figure 22. Map of Egypt and Nubia during Dynasty Twenty-five, ca. 765–655 BC. The outlines show the approximate extent of Egyptian and Nubian influence during this period.

Eventually, a Nobadian king, Silko, conquered the Blemmyes in the mid-fifth century, as indicated by his inscription on the walls of Kalabsha temple. The main cemeteries for the Nobadians were at Qustul and Ballana, identified by Reisner as the X-Group. The various pottery styles they introduced are useful in identifying the chronology of this region as Early, Classic, and Late. Early and Classic pottery styles are found at the royal/elite cemeteries at Qustul (beginning around AD 370–80) and then at Ballana (beginning around AD 420). A very early transitional style of pottery is found in the Second Cataract region, and a late post-Meroitic phase occurs from the Batn al-Hagar region to the Third Cataract. Also appearing in this region are possible wine presses, suggesting wine production, as well as a developed form of basketry, while iron tools and weapons become common in burials.

One of the most significant developments during the post-Meroitic period was the appearance of the animal-powered *saqya* waterwheel for irrigation. This invention permitted agricultural expansion into new regions, new types of crops, and year-round cultivation. This expansion, in turn, affected the location of settlements. Since Nile inundation was no longer the determining factor for agriculture, settlements took root in previously unsettled areas of Lower Nubia.

Christian Period/Medieval Period
(ca. AD 641–1400)

By the Christian Period, Nubia was divided into three regional kingdoms: Nobadia in Lower Nubia, whose capital was at Faras; Makuria in Upper Nubia, with a capital at Old Dongola; and Alwa (Alodia), with its northern boundary above the Fifth Cataract and a capital at Soba on the Blue Nile. Each region was converted to Christianity around AD 580 by means of envoys sent from rival missions (as mentioned by John of Ephesus and John of Biclar of the sixth century AD). The two northern regions of Nobadia and Makuria engaged in frequent hostilities with each other, which may explain the presence of a fortified wall surrounding Old Dongola. By the early 600s AD when Persia occupied Egypt, Nobadia and Makuria were united under the Makurian king, whose deputy resided first at the old Nobadian capital of Faras and later in various other formerly Nobadian locations. At this time, both regions acknowledged the authority of the Patriarch of Alexandria in Egypt.

Arab armies unsuccessfully attempted to conquer the Makurian capital of Old Dongola in AD 651; in fact, much of what we know for the period after 641 comes from the sometimes unreliable accounts of Arab historians and travelers who recounted what they saw. As Meroitic writing had earlier disappeared (in the fourth century), other forms of writing now arose: Greek, Coptic, and written Nubian (Old Nubian), alongside texts in Arabic. Since Nubians were now often literate, we can illuminate this time based on written documents, including inscriptions left on shrines by pilgrims, as well as the descriptions of Arab travelers who wrote about them.

Throughout the Christian Period, numerous churches were built in Nubia, as well as settlements with dwellings of mud brick and burnt brick. Churches were built in and around pagan buildings. Some pagan edifices were converted to churches, and Christian sanctuaries were even built next to pyramid cemeteries, as at Nuri. However, the majority of the churches were original constructions built within and near the settlements, towns, and monasteries they served, and they could be owned and built by private individuals as well as by kings. Church buildings decreased in size over the course of the Christian Period, paralleling a development in Byzantine architecture, so that they could almost be called chapels.

Burial practices also changed, from the pagan post-Meroitic tumuli style with numerous burial goods to Christian burials with few or no funerary goods. Often the deceased was placed in a rectangular grave surmounted by a small structure, which in more elaborate burials was plastered and painted and sometimes took the shape of a cross with a rounded or vaulted ceiling. Remains were wrapped in a shroud with a brick above the head, and a lamp was often deposited within the tomb. In addition, multiple burials occurred during this period.

Monasteries were also built—ranging in size from small to sprawling establishments—and some were possibly associated with pottery manufacturing. Settlements expanded, and new forms of architecture arose over time, such as the late 'castle-houses,' composed of two levels: a lower level made of stone and an upper level of mud brick. These houses occur in Lower Nubia, sometimes along with watchtowers. Domestic building techniques and materials used during the Christian Period include stone, barrel vaulting, and high-quality red brick and mud brick. Religious themes began to be expressed through artistic forms such as painting, crafts, architecture, and literature. Design elements appear that also characterize the Christian Period elsewhere: fish, crosses, doves, and the like.

High-quality pottery in the Christian Period was decorated with Christian and traditional African motifs in complex banded patterns that were also often related to the ceramics of the Byzantine and Muslim worlds. While the amount and type of ceramics certainly provide information on relative wealth, progressive changes provide important chronological information. Trade is documented by the appearance of foreign wares from Egypt, China, and possibly Iran, mostly found at the Alwa capital of Soba, but also at richer sites as far north as Lower Nubia. At this time, the Christian populations of Nubia apparently enjoyed good relations with their Muslim neighbors, to judge from a treaty in which, after several Arab military attempts to conquer Nubia, the Nubians traded slaves to the Muslims in return for commodities.

Records show that at this time Alwa, once a lowly power, became a formidable kingdom whose king rivaled and possibly overshadowed that of Makuria, although the exact territorial extent of this kingdom is unknown. Excavations at Soba reveal an impressive site with numerous churches, some with cemeteries attached. Build-

ings made of mud brick, and some of wood, were mostly rectangular, although some post holes for circular buildings have been discovered. Monumental buildings, such as large churches (two of which may have been cathedrals) and royal residences, have also been found. Hand-made black-topped burnished ware continued to be manufactured, while wheel-made 'Soba ware' (brown or black slip coated over polychrome painted bowls and basins) was devised. Other vessels from Egypt and Makuria, as well as Islamic glass, found in limited quantity at this site, represent trade or imports.

During the post-Meroitic Period, Makurians lived mainly on the west side of the Nile, possibly to take advantage of irrigation opportunities through the use of the *saqya*, as David Edwards postulates, but conclusions remain tentative because of the lack of excavations in this area for this period of time. During the Christian Period, the fortified capital at Old Dongola was large and sprawling like its counterpart at Soba, and may have contained multi-level houses and palaces, as well as many churches. Surrounding this area were workshops, monasteries, churches, and houses.

Figure 23. A palimpsest painting at Wadi al-Sebua of Ramesses II, holding flowers and facing the back niche, where the figure of St. Peter was later painted during the Christian occupation of the temple.

Although important new towns came into being during the Christian Period, many of Nobadia's post-Meroitic cities were also reoccupied at this time. Settlements were fortified—possibly to stave off conflicts with their northern and southern neighbors, as well as those in the Eastern and Western Deserts. Agriculture was important in this region, although as in the post-Meroitic Period, the Dodekaskhoinos was sparsely populated in the Early Christian Period. By the end of the Christian Period, very few churches and settlements survived in Lower Nubia compared to the area of Makuria in the south.

By the 1300s, Alwa had broken up and essentially dissolved under pressure from Arab invaders, while Makuria's capital at Old Dongola succumbed to occupation by the Muslim ruler, Kanz ed-Dawla, in 1323. That dynasty disintegrated in the face of repeated attacks by Arab armies and the Mamluk rulers of Egypt around 1365. A Christian capital was set up at Dotawo, probably Gebel Adda in Lower Nubia, for a time; some political structures remained in place. At the end of the Christian Period, about 1400, despite an influx of Arab and Islamic peoples, some areas still retained their independence and Christian beliefs.

Islamic Period (1400–)

By 1400, Nubian populations had mostly converted to Islam. A new Arab power arose in eastern Sudan, around Suakin, under Abdullah the Gatherer. In the south, near the White Nile, a group known as the Funj arose and successfully challenged Abdullah, founding the great Funj Dynasty at Sennar, which expanded to incorporate most of Nilotic and Eastern Sudan. In the later sixteenth century, the Ottoman Empire, which had conquered Egypt in 1517, made a number of attempts to penetrate Sudan; these were finally stopped in a defeat at Hannek at the Third Cataract. This cataract became the frontier between the two empires until 1821.

Over the millennia, Nubia flourished because of its resources and its location as a trade corridor between Egypt and sub-Saharan Africa. Its inhabitants maintained their own culture in terms of language, burials, religion, art, and architecture, even during colonial episodes. Influences from Egypt are clear in burial styles, and to a lesser extent pottery, and some merging of the Egyptian and Nubian cultures was inevitable, given that the two areas formed part of the same region along the Nile. Yet throughout the ebb and flow of its history, Nubia's rich culture persisted and developed in its own unique ways.

Bibliography

Arkell, A.J. 1950. "Varia Sudanica." *JEA* 36:24–40.

Baines, J. 2009. "On the Background of *Wenamun* in Inscriptional Genres and in Topoi of Obligations among Rulers." *Text-Thebe-Tonfragmente: Festschrift für Günter Burkard*. ÄAT 76:27–36.

Bard, K.A. 2008. *An Introduction to the Archaeology of Ancient Egypt*. Oxford: Blackwell Publishing.

Bard, K.A., and S.B. Shubert. 1999. "Gebel Barkal." In *Encyclopedia of the Archaeology of Ancient Egypt*, 325–27. London and New York: Routledge.

Bicke, S. 2002. "Aspects et fonctions de la déification d'Amenhotep III." *BIFAO* 102:63–90.

Bonnet, C. 1991. "Upper Nubia from 3000 to 1000 BC." In W.V. Davies, ed., *Egypt and Africa: Nubia from Prehistory to Islam*, 112–17. London: British Museum Press.

———. 1997a. "A-Group and Pre-Kerma." In D. Wildung, ed., *Sudan: Ancient Kingdoms of the Nile*, 36–49. Paris and New York: Flammarion.

———. 1997b. "C-Group." In D. Wildung, ed., *Sudan: Ancient Kingdoms of the Nile*, 50–71. Paris and New York: Flammarion.

———. 1997c. "The Kingdom of Kerma." In D. Wildung, ed., *Sudan: Ancient Kingdoms of the Nile*, 88–116. Paris and New York: Flammarion.

———. 2004. "The Kerma Culture." In D.A. Welsby and J.R. Anderson, eds., *Sudan: Ancient Treasures: An Exhibition of Recent Discoveries from the Sudan National Museum*, 70–91. London: British Museum Press.

Bonnet, C., et al. 1984. "Les fouilles archéologiques de Kerma (Soudan): Rapport préliminaire des campagnes de 1982–1983 et de 1983–1984." *Genava*, n.s., 34: 5–45, i–xxii.

Bonnet, C., and D. Valbelle. 2005. *The Nubian Pharaohs: Black Kings on the Nile*. Cairo: American University in Cairo Press.

Bourriau, J. 1991. "Relations between Egypt and Kerma during the Middle and New Kingdoms." In W.V. Davies, ed., *Egypt and Africa: Nubia from Prehistory to Islam*, 129–44. London: British Museum Press.

Callender, G. 2000. "The Middle Kingdom Renaissance." In I. Shaw, ed., *The Oxford History of Ancient Egypt*, 148–83. Oxford: Oxford University Press.

Darnell, J.C., and C. Manassa. 2007. *Tutankhamun's Armies: Battle and Conquest during Ancient Egypt's Late Eighteenth Dynasty*. Hoboken, N.J.: John Wiley and Sons.

Davies, N. de G., and A.H. Gardiner. 1926. *The Tomb of Huy, Viceroy of Nubia in the Reign of Tut'ankhamun (No. 40)*. London: Egypt Exploration Society.

Davies, V. 2001. "Kurgus 2000: The Egyptian Inscriptions." *Sudan & Nubia* 5:46–58.

———. 2003. "Kush in Egypt: A New Historical Inscription." *Sudan & Nubia* 7:52–54.

Dunham, D. 1970. *The Barkal Temples*. Boston: Museum of Fine Arts.

Edwards, D.N. 1998. "The Nubian A-Group: Perceiving a Social Landscape." Paper delivered at the Ninth International Conference for Nubian Studies, Boston.

———. 2004. *The Nubian Past: An Archaeology of the Sudan*. New York: Routledge.

Eide, T., T. Hägg, and R.H. Pierce. 1994–2000. *Fontes Historiae Nubiorum: Textual Sources for the History of the Middle Nile Region between the Eighth Century BC and the Sixth Century AD*. 4 vols. Bergen: University of Bergen, Department of Classics.

Emery, W.B., H.S. Smith, and A. Millard. 1979. *Excavations at Buhen I. The Fortress of Buhen: The Archaeological Report*. Egypt Exploration Society Memoirs 49. London: Egypt Exploration Society.

Fischer, H.G. 1961. "Nubian Mercenaries of Gebelein during the First Intermediate Period." *Kush* 9:44–80.

Garcea, E.A.A. 2004. "The Palaeolithic and Mesolithic." In D.A. Welsby and J.R. Anderson, eds., *Sudan: Ancient Treasures: An Exhibition of Recent Discoveries from the Sudan National Museum*, 20–24. London: British Museum Press.

Geus, F. 2004. "Funerary Culture." In D.A. Welsby and J.R. Anderson, eds., *Sudan: Ancient Treasures: An Exhibition of Recent Discoveries from the Sudan National Museum*, 274–307. London: British Museum Press.

Guichard, J., and G. Guichard. 1968. "Contributions to the Study of Early and Middle Paleolithic of Nubia." In F. Wendorf, ed., *The Prehistory of Nubia*. Dallas: Southern Methodist University Press.

Habachi, L. 1969. "Divinities Adored in the Area of Kalabsha, with a Special Reference to the Goddess Miket." *MDAIK* 24:169–83.

Helck, W. 1980. "Ein 'Feldzug' unter Amenophis IV. gegen Nubien. *SAK* 8:117–26.

Honegger, M. 2004a. "El-Barga." In D.A. Welsby and J.R. Anderson, eds., *Sudan: Ancient Treasures: An Exhibition of Recent Discoveries from the Sudan National Museum*, 31–34. London: British Museum Press.

———. 2004b. "The Pre-Kerma Period." In D.A. Welsby and J.R. Anderson, eds., *Sudan: Ancient Treasures: An Exhibition of Recent Discoveries from the Sudan National Museum*, 61–69. London: British Museum Press.

Jacquet-Gordon, H., C. Bonnet, and J. Jacquet. 1969. "Pnubs and the Temple of Tabo on Argo Island." *JEA* 55:103–11.

Jesse, F. 2004. "The Neolithic." In D.A. Welsby and J.R. Anderson, eds., *Sudan: Ancient Treasures: An Exhibition of Recent Discoveries from the Sudan National Museum*, 35–60. London: British Museum Press.

Kemp, B.J. 1991. *Ancient Egypt: Anatomy of a Civilization*. New York and London: Routledge.

Kendall, T. 1997a. *Kerma and the Kingdom of Kush 2500–1500 B.C.: The Archaeological Discovery of an Ancient Nubian Empire*. Washington, D.C.: National Museum of African Art, Smithsonian Institution.

———. 1997b. "Kings of the Sacred Mountain: Napata and the Kushite Twenty-fifth Dynasty of Egypt." In D. Wildung, ed., *Sudan: Ancient Kingdoms of the Nile*, 161–203. Paris and New York: Flammarion.

———. 2002. "Napatan Temples: A Case Study from Gebel Barkal." Tenth International Conference for Nubian Studies. Rome: La Sapienza University.

———. "Recent Field Work at Jebel Barkal, 2007–08: National Corporation for Antiquities and Museums of Sudan [NCAM] Mission, 2008." http://www.univie.ac.at/afrikanistik/meroe2008/abstracts/Abstract%20Kendall.pdf

———. 2010. "Jebel Barkal: History and Archaeology of Ancient Napata." National Corporation of Antiquities and Museums of Sudan [NCAM]. http://www.jebelbarkal.org

Krzyżaniak, L. 1992. "Some Aspects of the Later Prehistoric Development in the Sudan as Seen from the Point of View of the Current Research on the Neolithic." In F. Klees and R. Kuper, eds., *New Light on the Northeast African Past: Current Prehistoric Research*, 267–73. Africa Praehistorica 5. Cologne: Heinrich-Barth-Institut.

———. 2004. "Kadero." In D.A. Welsby and J.R. Anderson, eds., *Sudan: Ancient Treasures: An Exhibition of Recent Discoveries from the Sudan National Museum*, 49–52. London: British Museum Press.

Leclant, J. 1997a. "Egypt in Sudan: The New Kingdom." In D. Wildung, ed., *Sudan: Ancient Kingdoms of the Nile*, 119–42. Paris and New York: Flammarion.

———. 1997b. "Egypt in Sudan: The Old and Middle Kingdoms." In D. Wildung, ed., *Sudan: Ancient Kingdoms of the Nile*, 72–86. Paris and New York: Flammarion.

Liverani, I. 2004. "Hillat el-Arab." In D.A. Welsby and J.R. Anderson, eds., *Sudan: Ancient Treasures: An Exhibition of Recent Discoveries from the Sudan National Museum*, 138–47. London: British Museum Press.

Mariette, A. 1869–80. *Abydos: Description des fouilles exécutées sur l'emplacement de cette ville*. 2 vols. Paris: A. Franck.

Marks, A.E. 1991. "Relationships between the Central Nile Valley and the Eastern Sudan in Later Prehistory." In W.V. Davies, ed., *Egypt and Africa: Nubia from Prehistory to Islam*, 30–39. London: British Museum Press.

Morkot, R. 2000. *The Black Pharaohs: Egypt's Nubian Rulers*. London: Rubicon Press.

———. 2007. "Tradition, Innovation, and Researching the Past in Libyan, Kushite, and Saïte Egypt." In H. Crawford, ed., *Regime Change in the Ancient Near East and Egypt: From Sargon of Agade to Saddam Hussein*, 141–64. Proceedings of the British Academy 136. Oxford: Oxford University Press.

Murnane, W. 2000. "Soleb Renaissance: Reconsidering the Nebmaatre Temple in Nubia." *Amarna Letters* 4 (Fall): 6–19, 160.

Nordström, H. 1972. *Neolithic and A-Group Sites*. Scandinavian Joint Expedition to Sudanese Nubia 3:1. Uppsala: Scandinavian University Press.

O'Connor, D. 1991. "Early States along the Nubian Nile." In W.V. Davies, ed., *Egypt and Africa: Nubia from Prehistory to Islam*, 145–65. London: British Museum Press.

———. 1993a. *Ancient Nubia: Egypt's Rival in Africa*. Philadelphia: University Museum, University of Pennsylvania.

———. 1993b. "Chiefs or Kings? Rethinking Early Nubian Politics." *Expedition* 35, no. 2: 4–14.

Priese, K.-H. 1997a. "The Kingdom of Napata and Meroe." In D. Wildung, ed., *Sudan: Ancient Kingdoms of the Nile*, 207–42. Paris and New York: Flammarion.

———. 1997b. "Meroitic Writing and Language." In D. Wildung, ed., *Sudan: Ancient Kingdoms of the Nile*, 253–64. Paris and New York: Flammarion.

Randall-MacIver, D., et al. 1909. *Areika*. Oxford: Oxford University Press.

Reinold, J. 2000. *Archéologie au Soudan: Les civilisations de Nubie*. Paris: Editions Errance.

———. 2004. "Kadruka." In D.A. Welsby and J.R. Anderson, eds., *Sudan: Ancient Treasures: An Exhibition of Recent Discoveries from the Sudan National Museum*, 42–48. London: British Museum Press.

Reinold, J., and L. Krzyżaniak. 1997. "6,000 Years Ago: Remarks on the Prehistory of the Sudan." In D. Wildung, ed., *Sudan: Ancient Kingdoms of the Nile*, 9–36. Paris and New York: Flammarion.

Reisner, G.A. 1910. *The Archaeological Survey of Nubia, Reports for 1907–1908*. 2 vols. Cairo: National Printing Department.

Rilly, C. 2008. "Les textes méroïtiques de l'île de Saï." *Kush* 19:139–77.

Shinnie, P.L. 1996. *Ancient Nubia*. London: Kegan Paul International.

Simpson, W.K. 1982. "Egyptian Sculpture and Two-dimensional Representation as Propaganda." *JEA* 68:266–71.

Smith, H.S. 1972. "The Rock Inscriptions of Buhen." *JEA* 58:43–82.

———. 1991. "The Development of the 'A-Group' Culture in Northern Lower Nubia." In W.V. Davies, ed., *Egypt and Africa: Nubia from Prehistory to Islam*, 92–111. London: British Museum Press.

Smith, S.T. 1995. *Askut in Nubia: The Economics and Ideology of Egyptian Imperialism in the Second Millennium BC*. London: Kegan Paul International.

Spence, K., and P. Rose. 2009. "New Field Work at Sesebi." *EA* 35:21–24.

Strudwick, N. 2005. *Texts from the Pyramid Age*. Writings from the Ancient World 16. Atlanta: Society of Biblical Literature.

Taylor, J.H. 1991. *Egypt and Nubia*. London: British Museum Press.

Török, L. 1997. "The Kingdom of Kush: Napatan and Meroitic Periods." In D.A. Welsby and J.R. Anderson, eds., *Sudan: Ancient Treasures: An Exhibition of Recent Discoveries from the Sudan National Museum*, 132–37. London: British Museum Press.

Valbelle, D. 2004. "Egyptians on the Middle Nile." In D.A. Welsby and J.R. Anderson, eds., *Sudan: Ancient Treasures: An Exhibition of Recent Discoveries from the Sudan National Museum*, 92–108. London: British Museum Press.

Wildung, D. 1997. "The Kingdom of Meroe." In D. Wildung, eds., *Sudan: Ancient Kingdoms of the Nile*, 243–50. Paris and New York: Flammarion.

Williams, B.B. 1986. *The A-Group Royal Cemetery at Qustul: Cemetery L*. Excavations between Abu Simbel and the Sudan Frontier, Part 1. *OINE* 3. Chicago: Oriental Institute.

Žába, Z. 1974. *The Rock Inscriptions of Lower Nubia (Czechoslovak Concession)*. Prague: Universita Karlova.

THE EARLY EXPLORATION AND ARCHAEOLOGY OF NUBIA

Peter Lacovara

While the major monuments of Egypt were familiar to people even before Napoleon's great expedition at the close of the eighteenth century, Nubia remained inaccessible to all but the most adventurous of travelers. Accounts and sketches of the antiquities of Nubia were not seen until the explorations of Frédéric Cailliaud (1820s), John Lowell (1830s), and most importantly, Karl Richard Lepsius (1840s).

The most spectacular discovery of this early period was the treasure found by Giuseppe Ferlini (see sidebar, "The Treasure of a Nubian Queen"), but it was not fully appreciated or understood at the time.

It was not until the beginning of the twentieth century that Nubian archaeology would come into its own, ironically, as much of Nubia was about to be lost. The long-forgotten land was to be changed forever with the enlargement of the first dam at Aswan beginning in 1908. Realizing the destruction to archaeological sites that would take place, the Egyptian Antiquities Service engaged a young American Egyptologist, George Andrew Reisner, to study the area of Egyptian Lower Nubia, which would soon be covered forever by the floodwaters of the new reservoir. Reisner had trained at Harvard and in Berlin, had excavated for the University of

California, and then went on to become curator at the Museum of Fine Arts in Boston. A painstakingly systematic scholar, he devised the prototypical archaeological survey that became the ancestor of modern salvage archaeology. The Archaeological Survey of Nubia began its work in September 1907, with Reisner as director, assisted by Cecil M. Firth and A.M. Blackman. The goals of the Survey were "the recovery of all the archaeological and [anthropological] material and the reconstruction of the history of the district." The chronological framework that Reisner devised in which to order his finds remains the basis for Nubian archaeology today. Without historical records to name the cultures he discovered, he began with the earliest identifiable culture and named it the "A-Group" (=Archaic Egypt) and ended with the X-Group (=Byzantine Period). The rest of the alphabet was left in between should other cultures be added. Reisner left the Survey after the first season, in 1908, but Firth continued until 1911 with a rapid publication of 150 sites they had excavated. Soon after this pioneering work in Lower Nubia, a number of expeditions were sent out by the University of Pennsylvania, Oxford University, and the Austrian government; also at this time, John Garstang began work at the fabled city of Meroe in Upper Nubia.

Figure 24. Harvard University–Museum of Fine Arts, Boston excavations at the Second Cataract: The north end of Dabenarti and the cataract west of Mirgissa, with notes by excavator, January 1915. Photograph © 2012 Museum of Fine Arts, Boston.

The Harvard University–Museum of Fine Arts, Boston Excavations in Sudan: Kerma

Reisner's interest in the history of Nubia remained after his preliminary excavations in Egyptian Nubia, and wishing to continue his studies of Nubian history, he applied to the Sudanese government to survey and excavate the area around Halfa, particularly the New Kingdom site of Sesebi. However, once in Sudan, he was urged by the local authorities to work farther to the south at the site of Kerma, which was threatened by an agricultural irrigation project.

At Kerma, to the east of the Nile above the Third Cataract is a wide lush plain with two massive mud-brick ruins. These structures were called *deffufa* in the local Nubian dialect. Around the larger one, the Lower Deffufa, were the remains of the ancient town. The other, the Upper Deffufa, was situated in an enormous necropolis among great earthen tumuli, some hundreds of feet in diameter.

Previous to Reisner's work here, sporadic examples of a particularly fine black-topped pottery cup had appeared in excavations in Egypt, where they were mistakenly attributed to another Nubian culture, the so-called Pan-Grave culture. Examples had also appeared in some of the sites discovered in the First Survey, but at Kerma, Reisner's expedition found thousands of examples of the finest workmanship and in a myriad of forms.

The Kerma artisans were remarkably adept at working with a variety of materials. They produced large faience-tile inlays, glazed-quartz jewelry and sculpture, as well as deadly bronze daggers. Through trade and warfare, the Kingdom of Kerma eventually became powerful enough to invade and control the southernmost portion of Egypt and enter an alliance with the Hyksos against the Theban kings of the Second Intermediate Period.

By this date, Kerma had grown to be the center of a large and powerful state. Its kings were buried in huge earth mound graves nearly three hundred feet across. The bodies in the main burials were placed on elaborately carved and inlaid beds; they were not mummified or placed in coffins, as was the Egyptian custom. Pottery, weapons, food, and clothing for the afterlife were placed in the graves, along with sacrificial offerings of animals and humans. As many as four hundred people were buried alive in some of the great royal burial mounds. Large funerary chapels, such as the Upper Deffufa, were also built in connection with these latest graves and were decorated with wall paintings and inlaid with faience tiles.

The Lower Deffufa, also a religious structure, was located at the center of the settlement surrounded by workshops and storehouses where raw materials and imported Egyptian goods were kept, and objects for cultic and royal use were manufactured. The Kerma kings imported vast quantities of Egyptian material to decorate the chapels and outfit their tombs, including jewelry, stone vessels, and sculpture.

Reisner was misled by the Egyptian imports and interpreted the site as an Egyptian outpost that gradually became 'Nubianized' and impoverished. In fact, Reisner had the order of the material he discovered reversed, and one can see the indigenous growth of a great kingdom from smaller, native beginnings.

The Harvard/Boston Excavations
at the Second Cataract Forts
Kerma material was also found in the remains of a series of Egyptian frontier fortresses built in the area of the Second Cataract in the Middle King-dom. Reisner and his team excavated a number of these between 1923 and 1932.

This stretch of the Nile is one of the most inhospitable of all. Here, trackless desert wastes bound the river. Although largely barren agriculturally, the area was rich in gold and valuable as a conduit to the interior of Africa, enabling the trading of ivory, ebony, gold, and animal skins.

The Second Cataract is known as the Batn al-Hagar, or 'the belly of rocks,' for the numerous rounded granite boulders that appear here. It was a dangerous passage filled with eddies and hidden rocks that even sank one of the Boston expedition's own boats! To take advantage of the opportunity provided by this topography, Senwosret I (ca. 1900 BC) began the construction of a series of forts in the area of the Second Cataract, which acted not only as garrisons, but also as trading posts.

These forts were massive structures built of mud brick with moats, parapets, crenelated battlements, and drawbridges, bearing a striking resemblance to medieval castles, which had their roots in the architecture brought to Europe in the Islamic conquest.

The Boston Museum excavated five of the forts: the twin fortresses of Semna and Kumma, Uronarti, Shalfak, and Mirgissa. The largest of the forts in the region, Buhen, was excavated by the University of Pennsylvania. Of particular interest were the objects of daily life that had belonged to the soldiers and their families who were stationed here. They possessed not only weapons, but also mirrors and jewelry of great beauty, as well as charming toys and examples of 'folk art' produced to make their harsh life more pleasurable. Indeed, the hardships of life in the area got to one of Reisner's crew so badly that he became obsessed with what he thought was a sort of 'Loch Ness Monster' that he thought he saw swimming among the rocks of the cataract!

Continued on p. 52.

THE TREASURE
OF A NUBIAN QUEEN

Peter Lacovara and Yvonne J. Markowitz

As entertaining—and perhaps as true—as one of the tales of the Arabian Nights, the story of finding a treasure of gold and jewels in the top of a pyramid at Meroe in Sudan, recounted by Giuseppe Ferlini (ca. 1800–76), remains one of the most controversial discoveries in Nubian archaeology. Ferlini was an Italian physician who was appointed surgeon-major to the Egyptian army. In 1830 he was posted with a detachment to Sudan, and became intrigued by rumors of great riches hidden in the ancient ruins. He requested permission from the local authorities to conduct 'excavations' at a number of sites near Khartoum, and proceeded to explore the area despite warnings against desert bandits, who were ready to encroach on any discoveries.

Ferlini could not be dissuaded, and so he engaged Antonio Stefani, an Albanian merchant living in Khartoum, to act as his partner. Together they hired thirty men, purchased camels and food, and set out for the site of Naqa in August 1834. Sailing north, they reached Wad ban Naqa and marched eight hours across the scorching desert to Naqa. Here, they were forced to build shelters to protect the team from prowling lions. After a few days of digging with meager results, along with the deaths of five camels from heat and a lack of water, Ferlini abandoned the site in the hope of finding a more profitable and hospitable location. He returned to the banks of the Nile, to the temple at Wad ban Naqa, where he attempted to remove a great stone altar from the ruins. The altar proved too heavy to dislodge, and so they journeyed northward and eventually wound up at the villages of Begarawiya, the site of the fabled ancient city of Meroe.

Stefani suggested excavating in the town ruins, but Ferlini, fresh from his unsuccessful experiences with temple sites at Naqa and Wad ban Naqa, set his sights on the pyramid tombs located on the desert scarp to the east. The first few tombs Ferlini opened contained little more than stripped bones left by ancient robbers. He decided to give it a final try, tackling one of the largest pyramids in the Northern Cemetery.

The pyramid, Begarawiya North 6 (Beg. N. 6), measured eighty-eight feet high and sixty-one feet square at the base. It had so impressed the French traveler Frédéric Cailliaud that he made a careful sketch of it during his visit to the site in 1821. Lacking an appreciation for ancient architecture, Ferlini had his men climb to the top of the pyramid and tear it apart, hurling the stones, one by one, down the sides. In an 1838 publication, as related by E.A.W. Budge in 1907, Ferlini recounted:

> We made the men remove the largest of the stones which covered the upper part, and then we were able to see that the chamber was rectangular in shape, and that its walls were formed of flat stones laid one upon the other, and that . . . the chamber was from six to seven feet long, and about five feet high. The first object that met our gaze was a large mass covered over with a white piece of linen or cotton cloth, which however, so soon as it was touched, fell into dust. Under this was a rectangular funerary couch, or bier of wood. . . . Under this bier I found the vessel, which contained objects wrapped up in a piece of linen similar to that which I have just mentioned. Close to the vessel, on the floor of the chamber, there were arranged symmetrically by means of thread, necklaces formed

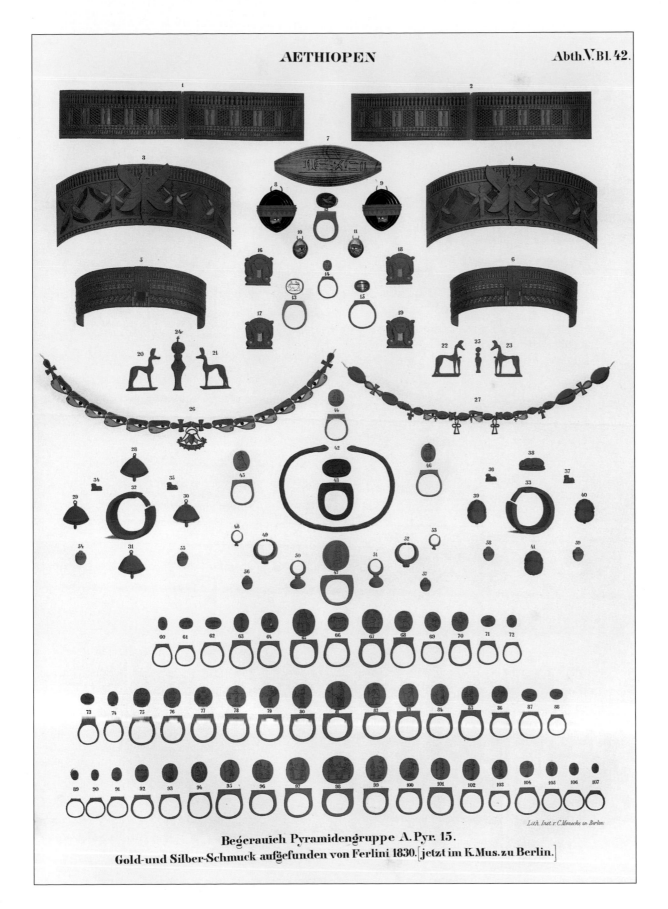

Begerauieh Pyramidengruppe A.Pyr. 15.
Gold-und Silber-Schmuck aufgefunden von Ferlini 1830. [jetzt im K.Mus.zu Berlin.]

Lith. Inst. v. C.Monecke in Berlin.

Figure 25. Silver and gold objects found by Ferlini at Meroe.

Figure 26. Gold lotus-flower pendant from the Ferlini treasure. Bildarchiv Preussischer Kulturbesitz/ Art Resource, New York.

Figure 27. Gold, glass paste, and carnelian "shield ring" with ram head of Amun before a chapel. Bildarchiv Preussischer Kulturbesitz/ Art Resource, New York.

of beads made of glass paste, coloured stones, a number of amulets, small figures of gods, a metal eye-paint case, little round boxes, a saw, a chisel and several other objects.

Ferlini recorded that farther down in the pyramid he found a chamber with two imported bronze vessels elaborately decorated with heads of Dionysus. After the pyramid was dismantled to the level of the chapel, he cleared the area around the base and found a path leading under the eastern wall of the chapel. Digging

down about eight feet, he discovered the remains of a masonry wall. At this point, Ferlini dismissed his workmen so he could continue the excavation in secret.

Ferlini was rewarded beyond his wildest dreams. He had discovered what must have been the largely intact burial of Queen Amanishakheto (late first century BC). He later recorded that he removed the gold and jewels, hiding them in leather bags for fear that a glimpse of the treasure might tip off the local bandits. For further security, he hid the loot in the sand by his tent.

The workmen, sensing that an important find had been made, returned with weapons, determined to receive just payment or a share of the treasure. Stefani persuaded Ferlini that it would be foolish for the two of them to engage in battle with the armed band. Instead, they managed to slip away in the middle of the night, sailing upstream on the Nile. By prior arrangement with a loyal workman, their supplies were transported overland by camel. Two weeks later, Stefani and Ferlini caught up with the convoy that had made the hazardous journey across the desert from Abu Hamed to Korosko. From there, they continued on to Cairo with the treasure, and shortly thereafter Ferlini departed for Italy.

After returning to his home in Bologna in 1837, Ferlini put his finds on display, and they became the subject of great controversy. The treasure was so unlike anything discovered in Egypt or elsewhere that it was roundly denounced as a forgery. Some considered the jewels a collection of stray Roman pieces that Ferlini had picked up on the market in Egypt. Eventually, part of the treasure was purchased by King Ludwig I of Bavaria, father of the infamous "mad" Ludwig. Soon afterward, the great German Egyptologist Richard Lepsius became intrigued with the treasure, particularly after his expedition to Sudan, and persuaded the Berlin Museum to add the remainder of the hoard to its collections.

Much of the doubt surrounding the authenticity of the treasure was caused by Ferlini's tale of its discovery. Many found the idea of a secret chamber at the top of the pyramid absurd. The story was dismissed by the father of Meroitic studies, Dows Dunham, as a clever ruse concocted by Ferlini to throw others off the trail, so that he could later return and find more treasure. Dunham concluded that the treasure undoubtedly came from the burial chamber, based on his personal experience excavating other Meroitic pyramids.

The most logical explanation of the treasure tale is that Ferlini, after demolishing the pyramid and finding nothing, shifted his attention to the area around the chapel. The wall he recorded as being beneath the chapel must have been none other than the wall of the burial chamber. It was at this point that Ferlini dismissed his workmen and continued on alone. If one examines the account and compares it to the actual circumstances of the burial, it becomes clear that Ferlini was extrapolating the situation he found in the actual burial chamber to fictitious caches in the body of the pyramid. The two caches mirror the two rooms of the burial chamber as found in other Meroitic pyramids. The cloth-covered wooden couch was actually the bier placed over the burial, such as those found during the same period in Roman Egypt and depicted in some of the burial chambers at Meroe. Even the location of the bronze pot he records as situated on the floor below the 'couch' is typical of the placement of such vessels in other Meroitic tombs.

When the burial chamber of Beg. N. 6 was opened by George Reisner and Dows Dunham in 1921, they

discovered that although the blocking material was intact, the tomb had been extensively plundered. Unlike most of the robbed tombs at Meroe, which were entered via the stairway, the tomb had been breached by a tunnel dug down from the side of the chapel, the exact spot in which Ferlini had been digging. Ferlini's ruse worked. Although he never returned, later explorers knocked the tops off most of the Nubian pyramids looking for gold. It was not until the work of Reisner and Dunham that the true design of the Nubian pyramids was revealed.

Figure 28. Gold signet ring with a pair of rulers and a child. Bildarchiv Preussischer Kulturbesitz/ Art Resource, New York.

Figure 29. Gold and glass bracelet of Queen Amanishakheto. Bildarchiv Preussischer Kulturbesitz/ Art Resource, New York.

Continued from page 47.

The Middle Kingdom forts were restored and enlarged in the Eighteenth Dynasty when they were reoccupied by Egyptian forces. In addition, a series of temples were built not only in the forts but elsewhere throughout Nubia. Living more or less at peace beside the forts was another local Nubian culture known as the C-Group. Reisner had already encountered this culture during the First Archaeological Survey, and at the time of the Second Survey in 1929–34, Georg Steindorff had discovered a large C-Group cemetery beside the fort at Aniba.

After the excavations at Kerma had finished in 1916, one of Reisner's Harvard students, Oric Bates, worked at the Meroitic site of Gammai and obtained important late Meroitic material for the Boston Museum and for Harvard. The other members of the crew, including Dows Dunham, Reisner's most accomplished student, headed south to the Fourth Cataract region and the 'Holy Mountain,' Gebel Barkal.

Excavations at Gebel Barkal

Reisner's richest finds came from his excavations in the area around the Fourth Cataract, the great heartland of later Nubian civilization. This included the most important of all religious centers of the later Kingdom of Kush, Gebel Barkal —the Karnak of Nubia. Reisner also dug all the great royal cemeteries that surrounded it: al-Kurru, Nuri, and tombs at Barkal itself.

With the defeat of the Kerma Kingdom at the beginning of the Eighteenth Dynasty, the Egyptians began a policy of constructing a series of temples as the main administrative centers in Nubia. These were first set up in the reoccupied Egyptian forts. By the mid-New Kingdom, the forts were largely abandoned, and great temples were constructed on their own. Ramesses II built a series of temples south of Egypt's border, the most impressive of which was the great temple at Abu Simbel.

What was to become the most important temple complex in Nubia, however, was that dedicated to Amun at Gebel Barkal. The first temple here seems to have been established by Thutmose III, and the complex continued to be expanded by nearly every pharaoh of Dynasties Eighteen and Nineteen through Ramesses II. It continued to function long after Nubia had again asserted its independence at the end of the New Kingdom.

Following the decline of Egyptian royal authority over Nubia, a powerful local dynasty emerged centered at Gebel Barkal. These rulers allied themselves with the Thebans, and in 725 BC, the Nubian king Piankhi (Piye) had assumed control over all of Egypt and Nubia. Piankhi founded the Twenty-fifth or Kushite Dynasty in Egypt and established Egypt's last great cultural renaissance.

Because Napata, the city at Gebel Barkal, remained both the chief cult center of the kingdom and the burial place of its kings, the age is known as the 'Napatan Period.' Reisner and his assistants worked at Gebel Barkal in 1916 and 1919–20, and at the surrounding royal cemeteries at Gebel Barkal itself, at Nuri in 1916–1918, and the earliest cemetery of Piankhi and his ancestors at al-Kurru in 1919.

Because of their importance in determining the history of Nubia, Reisner excavated all four major royal cemeteries of the later Nubian state, dating from the ninth century BC to the mid-fourth century AD. Of the hundreds of tombs discovered—at the sites of al-Kurru, Nuri, Gebel Barkal, and Meroe—more than 350 were built as pyramids and were assignable to at least seventy-six successive generations of rulers. By determining a building sequence for these tombs, Reisner was able to develop a chronology for all these rulers, largely in the absence of any historical records.

Figure 30. Nuri excavation camp looking northwest, with *shawabti*s of Taharqo being sorted, March 19, 1917. Harvard University–Boston Museum of Fine Arts Expedition. Photograph © 2012 Museum of Fine Arts, Boston.

Figure 31. Golfing in the desert at Meroe Camp. Photograph courtesy of Philippa Dunham Shaplin.

Excavations at Meroe

To record the final chapters in Nubian history, Reisner and the Harvard-Boston Expedition moved south to Meroe and between 1921 and 1923 excavated some fifty royal pyramids that were built along the tops of two desert ridges east of the ancient city. They had also been looted, but he did recover a wealth of imported bronze lamps and metal vases, stone vessels, jewelry, and items of exquisite local craftsmanship.

Perhaps as the result of raids on Gebel Barkal by Egyptian armies, or more likely due to economic developments, the center of Nubian civilization shifted southward to Meroe, below the Sixth Cataract. This move marks the later stage of Nubian history and is known as the Meroitic Period.

Culturally as well as geographically, it was very different from the Napatan Period. While the Meroitic Nubians were still influenced by Egyptian traditions, the Meroitic Nubians were also in contact with new cultures from the Greco-Roman world and central Africa. Their art and architecture combined these influences in highly original ways, and they began to express their own language in an alphabetic script of their own devising. The language is known as Meroitic and still remains largely undeciphered.

Figure 32. Begarawiya North cemetery from the top of Pyramid 7, March 1922. Harvard University–Museum of Fine Arts excavations. Photograph © 2012 Museum of Fine Arts, Boston.

Meroe, which had become the chief royal residence probably as early as the sixth century BC, became at this time the center of an empire that included not only much of Lower and Upper Nubia, but probably extended its influence far south of modern Khartoum. Important as an iron-working center, the capital itself was a huge city with a great stone-walled enclosure at its center, including palaces, temples, gardens, even Roman-style baths and an astronomical observatory.

In 24 BC, a brief war with Rome over control of Lower Nubia resulted in a peace treaty that endured until the collapse of Meroe in the fourth century AD, probably in part due to wars with the kingdom of Axum in eastern Ethiopia. Nubia fragmented politically in this period into a number of provincial kingdoms that Reisner termed the X-Group. The pottery and objects from this period combine a lively local variation of painted ceramics and adaptations of Byzantine jewelry and styles, as found in the Museum's excavations at Gammai and in later burials at Kerma.

Later Work in Nubia

Due to an additional raising of the dam at Aswan, W.B. Emery and Lawrence Kirwan conducted excavations at Ballana, discovering large royal tombs of the X-Group culture filled with a

PETER LACOVARA   55

wealth of treasures exhibiting the confluence of Byzantine styles with survivals of the last of the ancient Egyptian traditions. Little work was done in Nubia subsequently, until a plan for a massive new dam to be built at Aswan was unveiled in the 1950s.

A substantial international salvage effort was called for in order to rescue the monuments and investigate the sites that would be covered by a vast new reservoir that would cover most of Lower Nubia (see "Saving Nubia's Legacy"). More than two dozen expeditions participated in the salvage campaign, excavating dozens of sites and moving more than thirty monuments, including the massive temples at Abu Simbel.

In Sudanese Nubia, the salvage effort was led by William Y. Adams. Trained in the American Southwest, he brought a new, anthropologically-based perspective to Nubian archaeology, and his synthesis and publication of the information of the salvage campaign revitalized Nubian archaeology.

Recent years have seen continued efforts to excavate and salvage a number of notable sites, in particular the excavations of the University of Geneva under the direction of Charles Bonnet at Kerma. The re-exploration of the city and cemeteries originally excavated by Reisner has added much to our picture of the area in both earlier and later times, and has elucidated what Reisner had uncovered. Likewise, the work of Friedrich Hinkel at Meroe has yielded remarkable new insight into the design and construction of the pyramids.

Prehistoric Nubia has also been a major focus of work in recent years, notably by Fred Wendorf, Anthony Marks, and Jacques Reinold, which has shed new light on the origins of Nubian culture.

Recent construction of a dam in Sudan at the Fourth Cataract has prompted another salvage campaign effort (see "Archaeological Salvage in the Fourth Cataract, Northern Sudan [1991–2008]") and promises to reveal much about this little-understood area.

Bibliography

Adams, W.Y. 1977. *Nubia, Corridor to Africa*. Princeton, NJ: Princeton University Press.

Bonnet, C., ed. 1990. *Kerma, Royaume de Nubie: Catalogue de l'exposition*. Geneva: Musée de Genève.

Budge, E.A.W. 1907. *The Egyptian Sudan*. Vol. 1. London: Kegan Paul, Trench, Trübner and Sons.

Dunham, D., 1967. *Second Cataract Forts*. Vol. 2: *Uronarti Shalfak Mirgissa*. Boston: Museum of Fine Arts.

———. 1972. *Recollections of an Egyptologist*. Boston: Museum of Fine Arts.

Dunham, D., and J. Janssen. 1960. *Second Cataract Forts*. Vol. 1: *Semna Kumma*. Boston: Museum of Fine Arts.

Emery, W.B. 1948. *Nubian Treasure: An Account of the Discoveries at Ballana and Qustul*. London: Methuen and Co.

Emery, W.B., and L. Kirwan. 1935. *The Excavations and Survey between Wadi es-Sebua and Adindan, 1929–1931*. Cairo: Government Press.

Ferlini, J. 1838. *Relation historique de fouilles opérées dans la Nubie*. Rome: Salviucci.

Hinkel, F.W. 1982. "Pyramide oder Pyramidenstumpf? Ein Beitrage zu Fragen der Planung, konstruktiven Baudurchführung und Architektur der Pyramiden von Meroe." *ZÄS* 109, no. 2: 127–48.

Markowitz, Y.J., and P. Lacovara. 1996. "The Ferlini Treasure in Archaeological Perspective." *JARCE* 33:1–9.

Marks, A.E., et al. 1968. "Survey and Excavations in the Dongola Reach." *CA* 9:319–23.

Reinold, Jacques. 2000. *Fouilles françaises et franco-soudanaises: Contribution à l'histoire du Soudan*. Khartoum: Section française de la Direction des antiquités du Soudan.

Reisner, G.A. 1910. *Archaeological Survey of Nubia: Report for 1907–08*. Vol. 1. Cairo: Egyptian Government Printing Office.

Steindorff, G. 1935. *Aniba*. Vol. 1. Service des antiquités de l'Égypte. Mission archéologique de Nubie 1929–1934. Glückstadt and Hamburg: J.J. Augustin.

Wendorf, F., ed. 1968. *The Prehistory of Nubia*. Dallas: Southern Methodist University Press.

SAVING NUBIA'S LEGACY

Zahi Hawass

In ancient times, the southern border of Egypt lay at the First Cataract, where an outcropping of granite interrupts the flow of the Nile River. Beyond lay the land of Nubia, which stretched from the First to the Sixth Cataract and encompassed a distance of about 250 kilometers. This region is traditionally divided by scholars into Lower Nubia, which is within the borders of modern Egypt, and Upper and Southern Nubia, both of which are today located in Sudan. In ancient times, Lower Nubia was known as Wawat, Irtjet, and Setju; Upper Nubia was divided into Sai and Yam, and was also called Kush. Later on, the name Kush was given to all of Nubia. The earliest mention of the name Nubia appears in the early-first-century AD *Geography* by the Classical author Strabo, who cites the work of the third-century BC mathematician Eratosthenes. Many believe that the name Nubia derives from the ancient Egyptian word *nub*, which means 'gold.'

Until recently, archaeology in Nubia was focused on the northern part of the region. From the late nineteenth and early twentieth centuries, much of this was salvage work stimulated by the creation of the Aswan Dam, completed in 1902, then expanded in 1912 and 1936, whose reservoir gradually began to inundate the area and threaten the monuments there. The most important of the early expeditions were led by the British, and then by George Reisner, who was director of the Archaeological Survey of Lower Nubia and later excavated in the south. David Randall-MacIver and Leonard Woolley also carried out significant early excavations in Lower Nubia.

Plans for a new High Dam at Aswan were made first in 1946 and finally implemented beginning in 1960. The dam was completed by 1964, and represents one of the greatest Egyptian national achievements since the pyramids, as it controls the once irregular flood and provides electrical power for the many villages that line the banks of the Nile. However, it was recognized that the effects of the dam would not be entirely positive, as the expanded reservoir would submerge still more of the ancient monuments of Lower Nubia.

The Story of the Nubia Salvage Campaign
The salvage of the monuments of Lower Nubia is one of the great success stories of our time. Since 1955, UNESCO has been cooperating with Egypt's Documentation Center to record the Nubian temples. In 1958, the American ambassador, Raymond A. Hare, and the director of the Metropolitan Museum of Art, James J. Rorimer,

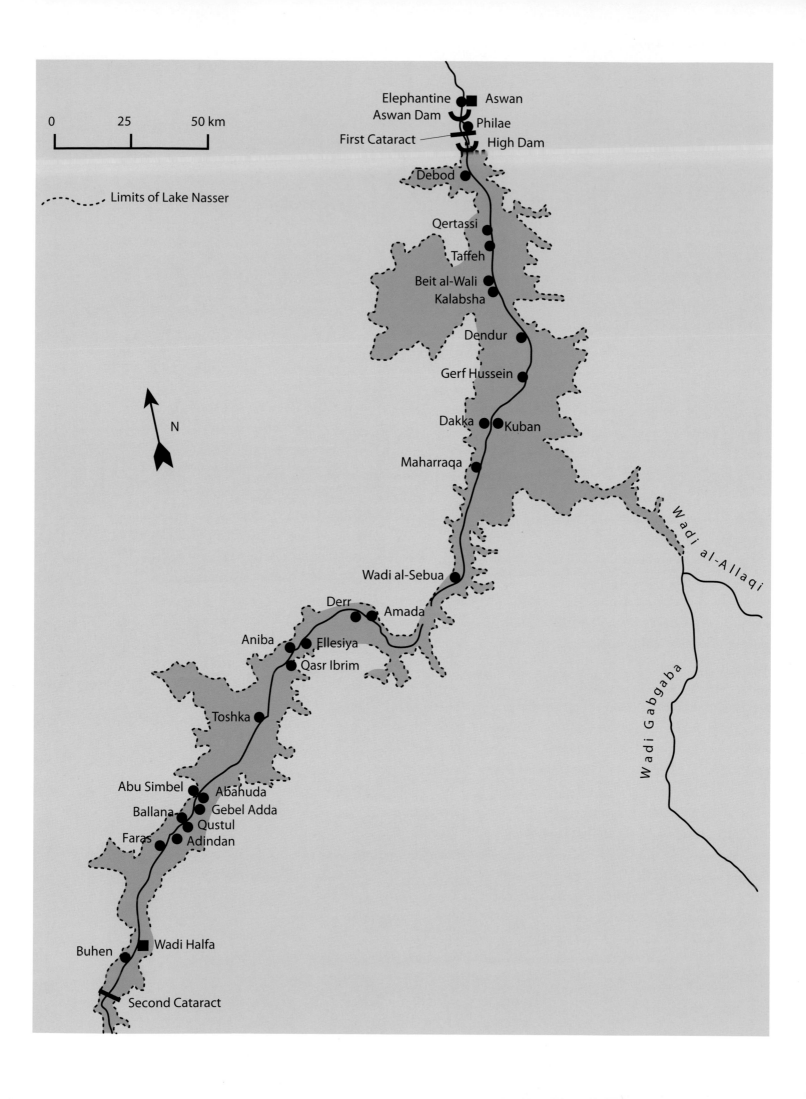

0   25   50 km

- - - - Limits of Lake Nasser

N

Elephantine   Aswan
Aswan Dam
First Cataract   Philae
                      High Dam
        Debod
        Qertassi
        Taffeh
        Beit al-Wali
        Kalabsha
        Dendur
        Gerf Hussein
        Dakka   Kuban
        Maharraqa

        Wadi al-Sebua
        Derr
Aniba   Amada
        Ellesiya
        Qasr Ibrim
Toshka

Abu Simbel   Abahuda
Ballana   Gebel Adda
        Qustul
Faras   Adindan

Wadi al-Allaqi

Wadi Gabgaba

Buhen   Wadi Halfa

Second Cataract

visited Egypt's minister of culture, Dr. Tharwat Okasha, and asked him if they could buy one or two of the temples that would be drowned after the construction of the dam. Already concerned, this brought home to Dr. Okasha the necessity for immediate and decisive action. In January 1959, he had the opportunity to meet René Maheu, acting director of UNESCO, and show him the locations of seventeen threatened temples on a map of the area from Wadi Halfa South to Aswan, along with photographs of these monuments that he had put on the walls of his office at Abdin Palace. At this meeting, Okasha proposed that UNESCO should lead a global campaign to save the monuments of Lower Nubia. He told Maheu that Egypt would provide a sum of money, but would need much assistance. Within twelve hours of Maheu's return to Paris, Maheu called Okasha and handed the phone directly to UNESCO's director-general, Vittorino Veronese. UNESCO was convinced, and ready to commit; all that was needed was an official letter of request from the Egyptian government.

Dr. Okasha met with President Gamal Abd al-Nasser, and explained the project to him; Nasser agreed that Egypt could pay one-third of the cost. In April 1959, Okasha sent a second letter to UNESCO, asking for technical and financial help to save the temples of Nubia, and appointed a committee to be led by Anwar Shokry, director of the Egyptian Antiquities Organization at that time. The goals of the campaign were to be: first, the recording of all accessible monuments in Lower Nubia; second, excavation of all known archaeological sites in the region; and finally, the transfer of all the threatened temples from their current locations to safety. These goals were written in a letter sent by Okasha to UNESCO, and also given to Christiane Desroches Noblecourt, who was a great supporter of the campaign, to deliver by hand. In July 1959, a delegation from UNESCO came to meet the Egyptian experts, and the parties agreed on the points outlined in Okasha's letter.

The next step was for UNESCO to announce the campaign. An office in Cairo, directed by Shehata Adam, was opened to manage the work. A planning conference was held in October 1959 at the Nubian Documentation Center; thirteen experts in the fields of archaeology, geology, engineering, and architecture attended the conference. They stayed in Nubia for ten days, meeting each day on a boat. At the end of the conference, Okasha was able to announce that the first monuments to be addressed would be the temples of Abu Simbel. Cut into the cliffs along the east bank of the Nile near the Second Cataract, these magnificent temples were built to honor Ramesses II and his chief wife Nefertari (ca. 1279–1213 BC). The UNESCO council earmarked US$110,000 for research into this project.

Dr. Okasha used to tell a story about something that happened to René Maheu. In January 1960, he was riding with Gamal Mokhtar, who later became the head of the Egyptian Antiquities Organization, going from Wadi Halfa to Abu Simbel to visit the temples, in a jeep with no windows. They reached the border just as darkness fell, and the border police, thinking they were drug smugglers, greeted them with guns. Fortunately, Dr. Mokhtar was able to explain the mission to the police, who allowed them to go. But their adventures were not over—later, the car got stuck in the sand, and Maheu and the others had to push it out.

On March 8, 1960, with the agreement of Okasha, UNESCO issued an international call for the participation of countries and organizations in the campaign. An honorary committee was appointed under Gustav VI of Sweden, with a twelve-member subcommittee (eight foreigners and four Egyptians) to support him. The press was invited to come and visit Nubia, and tell the world about this important initiative.

Figure 33. Map of sites within Lake Nasser.

Figure 34. Blocks from the dismantled temples of Dendur, Debod, Ellesiya, and Taffeh on Elephantine Island, 1964.

Salvage excavations began in 1960, and Egypt began work to dismantle the temples of Taffeh and Debod, moving them to Elephantine Island at Aswan. A second conference was held, this time with a committee consisting of representatives from twenty-four countries. At the top of the agenda for this conference were the Abu Simbel project, an expedition to study the other temples, and a project to save the temples of Philae. Egypt committed 3.5 million Egyptian pounds to rescue the temples of Abu Simbel, within a time frame of seven years, and UNESCO began the process of building cooperation between Egypt and other countries.

Two major projects were proposed for the salvage of Abu Simbel. One, offered by the French,

suggested surrounding the temples with a high concrete wall; the other, from the Italian engineer Piero Gazzola, proposed the transfer of the temples to higher ground. Gazzola's project was chosen, and on June 20, 1961, the Swedish firm VBB (Vatten-byggnadsbyrån) was given the contract. The cost was estimated at US$78 million, of which Egypt provided 20 million.

In order to raise more funds, Egypt sent an exhibition of artifacts from the tomb of Tutankhamun to twelve cities in the United States. First Lady Jacqueline Kennedy attended the opening in November 1961 at the National Gallery of Art in Washington, DC. At this event, Okasha presented the American people with a small Old Kingdom statue. The only unfortunate mishap associated with this exhibition happened while it was in Texas, accompanied by the great Egyptologist Ahmed Fakhry as its curator. On March 13, 1962, the press announced that the staff held by one of the *shawabti*s (funerary figurines) was missing. A day later, the American ambassador to Egypt, John Badeau, informed Dr. Okasha that the Associated Press had reported that the staff had been found. However, Fakhry sent a report to Okasha stating that he believed the staff had gone missing during the transfer of the artifacts from one city to the other. While the American police were investigating the case, a replica of the staff had been made and put with the *shawabti*; the Associated Press had assumed that the replica was the real thing. The staff was never found, but as a result, the American authorities paid much more attention to the treasures and guarded them diligently for the rest of the exhibition.

President Kennedy asked Congress to agree to donate US$10 million from the sale of wheat to Egypt toward the salvage campaign, of which 6 million would go to the temples of Philae, 2.5 million to the temples of Nubia (other than Philae and Abu Simbel) and to pay for the American expedition to Nubia, and 1.5 million for the other monuments in Sudan. This gesture truly launched the international effort, and many other countries began to participate in the salvage effort. The Abu Simbel project was completed in September 1968, and five hundred people from all over the world came to celebrate the reopening of the temples; the project to save Philae was inaugurated in 1971 and completed in 1980; and the overall campaign was also completed in 1980.

The salvage of the two temples at Abu Simbel will be remembered forever. The engineers worked to build a concrete dam in front of the temples to protect them until the dismantling process was complete. A dome was built in the new location, which was two hundred meters east and sixty-five

meters higher than their original spot, so that the temples would still look as if they were carved into the cliff face. The archaeological and restoration work was, in itself, a miracle of planning and organization. The numbering of the pieces was carried out flawlessly, and the restoration and conservation of the temples was one of the most successful scientific projects ever carried out in the field of archaeology. The salvage of Philae was also very important, and beautifully managed: a

Figure 35. Heads from the Abu Simbel Great Temple during salvage.

dome was built around the partially submerged monuments and the water was drained, then the temples were dismantled and moved to a nearby island, where they were reconstructed.

Egypt thanked the countries that helped by giving them statues and even, in four cases, whole monuments: the Roman Period temples of Debod, Taffeh, Ellesiya, and Dendur were given to Spain, the Netherlands, Italy, and the United States, respectively, and are now displayed in Madrid in the Parque de Rosales, near the Spanish royal palace; at the Rijksmuseum van Oudheden in Leiden; at the Museo Egizie in Turin; and at the Metropolitan Museum of Art in New York.

The government of Sudan, under the leadership of the minister of education, Ziada Arbab, also asked UNESCO to help save the monuments in the part of Nubia that lies within their territory. Unfortunately, many of the most important structures here, such as a series of Middle Kingdom fortresses and many magnificent churches, could not be moved, because they were built of mud brick. Instead, these buildings (some of which had been excavated and recorded earlier) were carefully documented, and a number of frescoes were removed from the churches and transported to museums. Several stone monuments were saved: the temple of Ramesses II at Aksha (with sponsorship from France); the tomb of Djehutyhotep at Debeira; the temple of Buhen (with help from the United Kingdom); and the temples of Semna East (the Netherlands) and West (Belgium). Under the supervision of German architect Friedrich W. Hinkel, these were dismantled and re-erected in the National Museum at Khartoum. The principal expert sent by UNESCO was Dr. William Y. Adams, who was indispensable to the work. Representing Sudan were the commisioner for archaeology, Sayyid Thabit Hassan Thabit, and especially the inspector for the Wadi Halfa area, Sayyid Nigmeddin Mohamed Sharif, who later

became the commissioner for archaeology; both of these men were key to the success of the documentation and salvage efforts. Their achievements are especially extraordinary in light of the fact that life in Sudan was disrupted by war and political upheaval during the course of the campaign.

The Temples of New Kalabsha

Many people know the stories of the Abu Simbel and Philae temples. Far fewer people know about the other temples that were rescued during the Nubia Salvage Campaign. Four of these, the Temple of Kalabsha, the Temple of Beit al-Wali, the Kiosk of Qertassi, and the Temple of Gerf Hussein, were dismantled in the 1960s and moved from their original locations to the modern island of New Kalabsha, which lies only 750 meters south of the High Dam at Aswan. These four temples date from different eras of Egyptian history; the island today, which has been the focus of a recent site-management plan, is becoming an important tourist destination, designed to tell the stories both of Nubia in ancient times and of the modern rescue of the past.

The largest freestanding temple from Nubia, the Temple of Kalabsha was originally located fifty-six kilometers to the south west of Aswan in an area known to the ancients as Talmis. The temple as it is configured today dates primarily to the reign of Augustus Caesar (30 BC), who demolished an earlier temple built by King Arkamani of Meroe (at the end of the third century BC) in order to make room for a larger structure. The principal god worshiped at Kalabsha was Mandulis, an African sun god who was associated with Horus; among the other deities represented in the temple's decoration are Osiris, Isis, and the fertility god Min.

The pylon of the temple leads to an open forecourt with a stone-tiled floor and colonnades to the north, east, and south. Beyond the forecourt

Figure 36. The Great Temple of Abu Simbel during salvage.

is a hypostyle hall, once decorated with scenes of the pharaoh making offerings to the gods. The hypostyle hall led to the most sacred part of the temple, which consists of three chambers that follow one upon another, culminating in the sanctuary proper. The first of these chambers also has a doorway in its south wall, from which a stairway leads to a small gallery on the roof, perhaps dedicated to Osiris. In addition to the original offering scenes, the temple walls bear a variety of Demotic, Coptic, and Greek graffiti, including several crosses, indicating that the temple was later used as a church. Associated with the temple were a sacred well and a birth house *(mammisi)*. In the northeast corner of the enclosure, on a lower level than the rest of the temple and accessed via a stairway, is a small chapel dating to the Ptolemaic Period.

The Temple of Kalabsha was exposed to the danger of partial inundation after the completion of the first Aswan Dam in 1902. After the height of the dam had been increased for the second time, the temple was flooded for nine months every year. When the creation of Lake Nasser in the 1960s threatened to submerge the temple forever, Egypt appealed to UNESCO for help. The

Federal Republic of Germany made a financial contribution of DM 6 million to finance the project, and also provided scientific and practical help.

In 1961, the German engineering company Hochtief was awarded a contract for the dismantling and transfer of the temple, to be carried out under the supervision of the German Archaeological Institute in Cairo. While this company was making their preparations, Khor Ingi, a rocky outcropping near the site of the High Dam, was selected for the new location of the temple. A decision was made to transfer two other monuments to this location as well—the rock-cut temple of Ramesses II at Beit al-Wali and the Greco-Roman kiosk at the village of Qertassi.

The work of dismantling and moving the Kalabsha temple took over a year to complete, beginning in May 1962 and finishing in late 1963. During this time, thirteen thousand blocks of stone weighing a total of twenty thousand tons were moved. The project faced problems such as intense heat and the difficulty of dismantling and cutting the sandstone blocks forming the fabric of the temple, which had been restored earlier by Alexandre Barsanti. Transporting these blocks more than fifty kilometers from their original site also presented significant challenges. Following the successful re-erection of the temple on Khor Ingi, this island was renamed New Kalabsha. In 1971, the Ptolemaic gate of the earlier temple was

Figure 37. Beit al-Wali during dismantling, 1963.

donated to the Federal Republic of Germany, and was reconstructed in the Egyptian Museum, Berlin.

Dating back to the Greco-Roman Period, the Kiosk of Qertassi was constructed on a rocky outcropping about forty kilometers south of Aswan. The single-chambered kiosk, which was dedicated to the goddess Isis, is entered from the north, between two columns with Hathoric capitals; a smaller entrance lies to the west. Inside there are four columns topped with floral capitals; all but those on the south are connected by screen walls. The only remaining decoration here is a relief depicting a Ptolemaic king in front of Osiris and Horus, carved on the northwest column. Like the small temples of Dendur and Debod, this kiosk may have been built as a way station. In 1963 the kiosk was dismantled, moved to a new location just southeast of the newly relocated Temple of Kalabsha, and reassembled.

The Temple of Beit al-Wali, originally situated fifty-five kilometers to the south of Aswan, is the earliest of Ramesses II's Nubian temples. It is simple in plan, consisting of an open forecourt, a hypostyle hall, and a sanctuary. The walls of the forecourt bear particularly interesting scenes showing the pharaoh, accompanied by two of his sons, engaged in battle with the Nubian army, then seated while receiving the tribute of the defeated enemy. Other scenes here show the king's victories over Libyan and Asiatic foes. The west end of the open forecourt contains three entrances to the rock-cut hypostyle hall, which was decorated with additional victory scenes, as well as images of the pharaoh with various gods and goddesses. A door in the hypostyle hall provides access to the sanctuary, in the back of which there is a niche where three now-destroyed seated statues, likely Ramesses II between two gods, were carved. The well-preserved decoration of this hall includes additional images of the king with deities, including scenes showing the king being suckled by the goddesses Anukis and Isis. During the Coptic era, Beit al-Wali was converted into a church.

Egypt and UNESCO enlisted the help of the United States to save the temple of Beit al-Wali. The Egyptian Antiquities Authority contracted an Arab company to carry out the salvage operation, and the temple was successfully dismantled and reconstructed on the modern island of New Kalabsha in 1963.

The Temple of Gerf Hussein was originally located on the west bank of the River Nile, eighty-seven kilometers south of the First Cataract. Built, like Beit al-Wali, during the reign of Ramesses II, it is partly freestanding, and partly cut into a rock formation covered with drawings and inscriptions from prehistory on, and thus most likely considered sacred in some way. The temple, whose construction was supervised by the viceroy of Kush, Setau, was consecrated primarily to Ptah, Ptah-Tatenen, Hathor, and Ramesses II himself, and consists of a porticoed forecourt flanked by ambulatories, a hypostyle hall, an antechamber with side rooms, and a triple sanctuary. The walls of the forecourt were decorated with reliefs of the pharaoh in the company of various gods, as well as images of his sons; these scenes are in general not well preserved. Beyond the court, the rock façade of the temple is carved into the shape of a pylon. On the east and west walls of the rock-cut hypostyle hall are scenes showing the king victorious over his enemies; carved into the north and south walls are niches filled with images of the king accompanied by deities. Against each of the six columns that support the ceiling are colossal figures of Ramesses II.

The pillars of the antechamber are adorned with reliefs of the pharaoh worshiping various gods. In the center of the three innermost shrines is the remnant of a stone plinth that was probably used as a resting place for the god's sacred boat during festival processions. In the west wall is a niche containing rock-cut statues of Ptah, Ramesses II, Ptah-Tatanen, and Hathor.

In 1961, the Egyptian Antiquities Authority cleaned the inside walls of the Temple of Gerf Hussein, making some of the painted scenes visible once more. The forecourt, the architraves, and many stone blocks bearing superb scenes and reliefs were moved to the island of New Kalabsha in 1962, while the finest of the statues of Ramesses II were taken to the Nubia Museum. Stored to the south of the Temple of Kalabsha, the elements of Gerf Hussein were left unreconstructed, and eventually were enveloped in sand.

Site Management

After their removal to New Kalabsha, the temples of Kalabsha, Beit al-Wali, Qertassi, and especially Gerf Hussein continued to face threats to their long-term preservation and survival. Lack of ongoing maintenance allowed dirt to accumulate. In addition, the long-term infestation of the reconstructed temples by thousands of bats had left a deposit of excrement and blood on the interior walls that was thick enough to obscure their reliefs and inscriptions. In light of these problems, it was decided to implement a project to clean and restore the temples of Kalabsha and Beit al-Wali. At the same time, plans were made

Figure 38. The flooded temple at Wadi al-Sebua, in its original location.

to make access to the island easier, in order to take advantage of the tourists visiting the High Dam and taking the Nile cruises operating between Aswan and Abu Simbel.

To make the site more accessible, a landing place equipped with stairways leading to the principal axis of the Temple of Kalabsha was installed. In addition, the monuments on the island were linked by access points and stone-paved footpaths, thus outlining the ideal itinerary for the visitor. A further improvement was the introduction of illumination designed to accentuate the architectural and decorative elements of the temples without damaging the scenes. In order to further enhance the visitors' experience of the island and to protect the monuments, many stone architectural elements, apparently from a pre-Ptolemaic temple at Kalabsha that had been stored haphazardly next to the reconstructed Temple of Kalabsha, were placed in an open-air display.

In November 2000, a major project was inaugurated, as part of the overall site-management plan, to reconstruct the Temple of Gerf Hussein. Thousands of stone elements were uncovered—carved blocks, as well as pieces of statues, column capitals, and bases carrying the name of Ramesses II. After a year and a half, a study of these fragments of the Temple of Gerf Hussein was completed, and the reconstruction began. The all-Egyptian mission entrusted with this task included members of the Archaeological Supervision Department, the Architectural Surveying and Documentation Department, and the Photographic Documentation Department, as well as a number of architects, structural engineers, and a surveying engineer. It took three months for the actual reconstruction to be completed, and a part of the temple can now be visited on New Kalabsha.

A number of additional monuments have also been included in the new visitor path. One of the most important of these is a stela carved by Amenmobi, the viceroy of Kush under Sety I (ca. 1290–1279 BC), at a site 238 kilometers south of Aswan. Reconstructed from four pieces, this was erected on a concrete base several meters from the *mammisi* of the Kalabsha temple. In addition, a number of rock-cut graffiti from the prehistoric period on, depicting subjects such as animals and scenes of hunting and sailing, were moved here, along with a Twenty-sixth Dynasty stela of Ahmose II (570–526 BC). Many of these monuments are now on display. As a consequence of the site-management plan, the island of New Kalabsha has become an open-air museum spanning the history of Lower Nubia from the prehistoric through the Greco-Roman eras. The most beautiful time of day to visit Kalabsha is about one hour before sunset. As the sun sinks below the horizon, the lights on the island come on, allowing the visitor to enjoy the reconstructed temples in an atmosphere of mystery and magic.

Recent and Current Archaeology in Nubia

Nubian archaeology has come to the fore over the past decades. Understanding the Nubian cultural sequence, as well as the relations between Egypt and its neighbors to the south, has come to be considered an essential part of a basic grounding in Egyptology. There has been a resurgence of interest in the principal Nubian sites, and a number of missions are currently working or have recently worked in the region. For instance, Pamela Rose of the Egypt Exploration Fund is working now at the fortress of Qasr Ibrim, once located atop a cliff, and now on an island in the midst of Lake Nasser.

In Egyptian Nubia, we are focusing on site management, which includes expanding carefully planned tourism, with limits to the number of tourists and clearly laid-out visitor paths to the temples that have been salvaged, via cruises on Lake Nasser that go from Philae to Abu Simbel and back. One of the new site-management plans is designed to protect the site of Abu Simbel. A wall, equipped with security cameras, has been built to mark the archaeological zone surrounding the temples, and visitors enter through a gate with x-ray machines. There is also now a visitors' center, where displays highlight the salvage campaign and introduce the site to tourists, and new facilities such as restrooms and cafeterias have been built. A landing stage has been added to accommodate the boats from Philae, and there is also a new parking lot, away from the site: most people walk to the temples, but there are cars for visitors with special needs. We have also constructed new administrative offices for the inspectors, police, and technical staff who monitor and maintain the temples. Inside the temples, wooden paths have been added to protect

the original floors. Similar site-management projects have been completed for the rescued temples of Wadi al-Sebua, Dakka, Maharraqa, and Amada, and the Twentieth Dynasty tomb of Pennout.

The Nubian Salvage Campaign shows the power of international cooperation, and highlights the role that an organization like UNESCO can play in facilitating collaboration among countries.

It was also important because it raised public awareness of our shared cultural heritage, encouraging individuals around the world to participate in saving the ancient monuments. The campaign was initiated and implemented through the passion and initiative, and then the diplomatic and organizational skills, of Dr. Tharwat Okasha, whose great work on behalf of cultural heritage will always be remembered. There were many other great people behind this project, such as the director and vice director of UNESCO, and Gamal Mokhtar, who continued the campaign and was responsible for making Egypt's Antiquities Service an internationally recognized organization.

Exploration and excavation of Sudanese Nubia's sites will continue into the future. This area is now a major focus of interest and scholarship, and the information being gathered from the fascinating sites of this region is adding a great deal to our understanding of human history.

The excavations of the Sudanese World Heritage Site of Gebel Barkal, which were begun in the early 1900s by George Reisner for Harvard University and the Boston Museum of Fine Arts, were continued in the 1970s by Sergio Donadoni for the University of Rome La Sapienza, and in the 1980s by Timothy Kendall of the BMFA. In 2003, while working at the site of Kerma, one-time capital of Kush, a Swiss team from the University of Geneva discovered a marvelous cache of statues representing Twenty-fifth Dynasty Nubian rulers.

Salvage Archaeology in Sudanese Nubia
The area is still threatened by modern development. The first in a series of new dams to harness the power of the Nile and its feeders and tributaries has been constructed. The Merowe Dam, which has stopped the flow of the river in northern Sudan, will produce 1,250 mega-watts of hydro-electric power, and cost more than US$2 billion. It has displaced more than fifty thousand people,

Figure 39. The temple of Philae at night. Photo © Chester Higgins Jr 2012.

moving them from their current homes and farms on the riverbank either into the desert or to the outskirts of Khartoum. In addition, it has destroyed many archaeological treasures, some of which have been submerged through the reservoir created behind the sixty-foot dam, and others of which have been damaged by the changes wrought on the local environment.

Fortunately, salvage work has been carried out in the region. Over the course of several seasons of survey and excavation, which began in 1999, many archaeological sites were identified and recorded over an area of forty kilometers. This was carried out by the British Museum in cooperation with the Sudan Archaeological Research Society (SARS). In the winter of 2006, SARS, as part of the Merowe Dam Archaeological Salvage Project, sent five teams to the field to conduct a survey of the area from Amri to Kirbekan in the Fourth Cataract region. The team, joined by Cornelia Kleinitz's rock-art survey, reported findings from ten different medieval-period sites in the areas of al-Doma, Hadiyab, al-Tereif, and on the islands of Umm Hajar, Dirbi, and Ishashi.

These excavations yielded a number of new discoveries, including small Christian box graves; a settlement where traces of a series of stone hearths and what could possibly have been storage units remain; and a post-medieval village retaining the interiors of several houses, approximately two meters high, as well as a circular hut apparently used as a kitchen. The islands of Umm Hajar, Dirbi, and Ishashi, respectively, yielded three groups of structures including stone hut circles, all believed to be from the medieval Christian period; two well-preserved crevice graves containing intact human remains; and a large stone-walled structure enclosing a three-roomed building, tentatively dated to the post-Meroitic period. In the area near al-Tereif, a cow burial was discovered, with extensive skeletal remains and grave goods. Finally, the rock-art survey identified and marked a number of rock-art panels that hopefully can be moved to modern Merowe, and marked 390 blocks from an early Kushite pyramid, scheduled to be moved to the new Fourth Cataract Museum.

The 2006–2007 season concluded the survey of the Fourth Cataract region. It is hoped that SARS can continue its salvage work in the Northern Dongola Reach, where settlements from the Kerma period, a great number of Neolithic cemeteries, and the city of Kawa are all sites that have yet to be examined.

The results of this salvage work have been extraordinary, and have helped to clarify the history and prehistory of this previously little-known area. It is clear that the region was far more important than it has traditionally been considered. The archaeological potential of the area is enormous, and has only just begun to be explored.

Bibliography

Hawass, Z. 1998. "The Relations between Egypt and the Southern Borders from the New Kingdom until Alexander the Great." In El Sayed Hamid, ed., *Anthropology Egypt. The Second Anthropology Conference: Egypt and Africa.* Cairo University Faculty of Arts. Cairo: Cairo University Press.

———. 2000. *The Mysteries of Abu Simbel: Ramesses II and the Temples of the Rising Sun.* Cairo: American University in Cairo Press.

———. 2004. *The Island of Kalabsha.* Cairo: Supreme Council of Antiquities Press.

Okasha, S. 2010. "Rameses Recrowned: The International Campaign to Preserve the Monuments of Nubia, 1959–68." In S.H. D'Auria, ed., *Offerings to the Discerning Eye: An Egyptological Medley in Honor of Jack A. Josephson,* 223–43. Leiden and Boston: Brill.

Welsby, D. 2007. "The Merowe Dam Archaeological Salvage Project: The Sudan Archaeological Research Society's Amri to Kirbekan Survey, 2006–2007," 12 February 2007. http://www. britishmuseum.org/ research/projects/merowe_dam_project.aspx

Archaeological Salvage in the Fourth Cataract, Northern Sudan (1991-2008)

Geoff Emberling

The Aswan Dam salvage campaign of the 1960s was by far the most intensive archaeological investigation of ancient Nubian society throughout a landscape and in all periods of history up to that date. That salvage project provided a wealth of information about life in Lower Nubia that stimulated new syntheses of Nubian history as well as a series of museum exhibitions. The basic publication of the Aswan Dam salvage campaign is still underway more than thirty years later, and it continues to be a rich source of data for new interpretations.

Salvage archaeology in general produces a level of detailed survey and excavation across historical periods that is otherwise rarely achieved in archaeological research. At the same time, salvage situations do not allow for the usual development of research questions and archaeological methods that accompany projects conducted under less imminent threat, and there is inevitably a significant and irrevocable loss of historical knowledge.

Salvage projects can also intersect with modern politics and modern lives in particularly intense ways. Archaeologists in salvage areas live among the people who are being displaced, and most projects rely on local people for labor as well as housing, hospitality, and other forms of assistance. Although most archaeologists come into the field planning to focus on historical research and avoid modern politics, it can be difficult in salvage situations to separate the two.

The difficulties and potential of salvage projects are both illustrated by the recently completed salvage project at the Fourth Cataract of the Nile in northern Sudan. Plans to build a dam at Merowe (not to be confused with the ancient city of Meroe) led to an increasingly intensive international salvage project from 1991 to 2008, when the dam was completed and the area flooded. Teams from Sudan, Poland, England, Germany, the United States, and Hungary (in rough order of initial work in the region) worked in often difficult conditions in an increasingly rigorous effort to document and recover what evidence they could.

Although the Fourth Cataract salvage project did not have high-profile monumental architecture—like the temples of Ramesses II at Abu Simbel that captured international attention during the Aswan project—archaeological survey, excavation, and ethnographic work in the area have provided significant data on all periods and have already considerably altered our understanding of some periods of the Nubian past.

The Fourth Cataract

Archaeological knowledge of Nubia remains relatively sparse and uneven compared to other major early civilizations. One particularly poorly known area was the Fourth Cataract, a region approximately 170 kilometers long that before 1991 had received almost no sustained archaeological attention.

Nile cataracts are extensive areas in which the river floodplain is narrow, the current is strong, and islands and rocky areas in the riverbed make navigation difficult. The Fourth Cataract is especially difficult to traverse by boat because it is among the longest of the cataracts, but also because of its orientation—traveling upstream on the Nile is possible elsewhere because the prevailing winds blowing south allow use of sails, but since the Nile flows toward the southwest in the Fourth Cataract, sailing upstream is generally not possible in that stretch of the river.

At the downstream end of the Fourth Cataract are Nubian monuments of the Napatan and Meroitic Periods (mid-eighth century BC to mid-fourth century AD), including the temples and palaces of Gebel Barkal, the royal pyramids of al-Kurru and Nuri, and presumably the associated capital cities of the Napatan empire, which have yet to be definitively located. One important land route from Napata itself led northwest across the Nubian Desert to the region of modern Dongola, while another cut southeast across the Bayuda Desert to Meroe.

The upstream end of the Fourth Cataract, near modern Abu Hamed, was the terminus of a route that traveled across the Nubian desert from the Second Cataract some three hundred kilometers to the north. This was the presumed route of two Egyptian armies in the New Kingdom that continued south to Kurgus, where Thutmose I and Thutmose III left inscriptions on the dramatic rock outcrop at Hagar al-Merwe.

It has long been thought that the Fourth Cataract was sparsely occupied because of the difficulties in navigation, because of the scarcity of viable agricultural land in the region, and because the major routes crossing the surrounding desert bypass the region entirely. The Fourth Cataract salvage showed that this was not the case. A survey of the north bank of the river recorded 762 sites in roughly half the affected area; in a very general sense, one could estimate that a full-coverage survey would have identified 1,500 sites on each bank and a comparable number on the islands throughout the cataract, or some 4,500 sites dating from the Paleolithic to Islamic Periods, and that there were undoubtedly more that a survey would not have found.

It will be some time before the archaeological finds are published, but some have already altered our understandings of Nubian history. Among the many notable discoveries were the extensive remains of the Kerma period (ca. 2500–1450 BC), which significantly extend the known distribution of this culture; an absence of clear Egyptian occupation during the New Kingdom; the base of a pyramid of Napatan date; and a significant medieval manuscript found in the remains of a church. A brief survey of other finds shows the ways in which the Fourth Cataract fits into—and alters our understanding of—broader patterns of Nubian history.

The earliest archaeological finds appear to be those of the Paleolithic (Middle Stone Age), as early as perhaps 175,000 BP. Paleolithic sites were mostly scatters of stone tools, but at least one Upper Paleolithic site contained faunal remains from about 30,000 BP.

A significantly greater number of Mesolithic and Neolithic sites have been noted. They are generally located on higher ground, corresponding to substantially higher Nile levels from ca. 7000 to 4000 BC. Interestingly, very few Neolithic burials have been noted. Typology and chronology of these sites remain to be worked out in detail, and it is not yet clear if settlement in the area was continuous from Neolithic into later times. There is, for example, relatively little evidence of Pre-Kerma occupation (ca. mid-fourth millennium to 2500 BC in the Kerma basin), and it may be that the corresponding Fourth Cataract variant has not yet been recognized.

It is clear, however, that beginning in about 2500 BC, an increasing number of people were buried with Kerma-style ceramics in the Fourth Cataract. Relatively few settlement sites of any Kerma periods are known. The nature of the cultural connection is not entirely clear—are these the burials of people migrating into the Fourth Cataract from the Kerma region, or people arriving from elsewhere who established and maintained trade and cultural connections with Kerma? Study of the ceramics shows that some vessels were traded from Kerma and others were made locally in the Kerma style. There are also local components of the ceramic assemblage that are not known in Kerma itself.

The intensity of occupation significantly increased throughout the Fourth Cataract in the Middle and Classic Kerma Periods (ca. 2050–1450 BC), the time when the power of Kush increasingly threatened Egyptian rule in Lower Nubia. Preliminary studies of human remains of these

Figure 40. Middle Kerma period burials at al-Widay I in the Fourth Cataract area. The stone tumuli have been removed from some of the burials, showing the small round burial pits.

Figure 41. Sid Ahmed Mustafa and Abdel Rahim Ibrahim from the Fourth Cataract area excavating remains of Kerma period domestic architecture at Hosh al-Guruf, a site with rich gold deposits having occupation in the Neolithic, Kerma, and Napatan periods.

periods suggest a population with a life expectancy in the mid-twenties. Demographic studies should ultimately be able to suggest whether this population would have required significant immigration or could have developed from the existing Early Kerma population.

The increased occupation and its evident trade connections with the city of Kerma have led many scholars to conclude that the entire Fourth Cataract (and beyond) was a part of the Kingdom of Kush in the early second millennium BC.

Movement of goods from Kerma to the Fourth Cataract is represented by ceramics and scarabs, while the other side of the exchange was likely provided by gold extracted from alluvial gravels in the Fourth Cataract. Scattered rock drawings of boats like those pictured at Kerma support the notion of a connection between the two areas. Interestingly, the cattle that are an important component of wealth in burials at Kerma itself are scarcely present in Fourth Cataract burials of this

time, although they are extensively represented in the corpus of rock art. The picture that emerges of the Kingdom of Kush is of a decentralized polity in which the connections between center and periphery are extractive in nature—tribute in gold reciprocated by gifts of relatively low value. Yet it is also increasingly clear that Kush was a potent military power, able to draw on geographically extensive alliances to threaten Egypt itself.

An interesting issue that will require more research is the presence of Pan-Grave style pottery in Classic Kerma cemeteries in the Fourth Cataract. In Lower Nubia and Upper Egypt, Pan-Grave pottery is known largely in distinct cemeteries or graves, and it is interpreted there as a marker of the Medjayu, a largely nomadic group known in texts mainly of Egypt's Second Intermediate Period (ca. 1685–1550 BC). In the Fourth Cataract context, however, preliminary indications are that the local versions of this distinctive ceramic style are scattered across cemeteries of this date. Pan-Grave pottery may thus acquire different meanings across its area of distribution, and it remains to be understood how and where it was made and distributed before we can begin to understand the range of social differences it might mark.

There had been some question about the extent of Egyptian control of this region during the New Kingdom (ca. 1500–1100 BC in the Fourth Cataract area), but the salvage project has resolved this question—there were no Egyptian settlements in the Fourth Cataract, but a few sites do contain New Kingdom trade goods (ceramics, mainly) in association with a larger quantity of Late Kerma material. The continuing existence of Kushite culture in this area supports the idea of some continuity between Kush in the Kerma periods and its resurgence more than five hundred years

later under the Napatan Dynasty. A local burial phenomenon in the Fourth Cataract, so-called Dome Graves, may reflect changes in group identities and an increased nomadic component of the population in the centuries around 1000 BC.

The Napatan Dynasty arose just downstream of the Fourth Cataract in the ninth century BC (although the exact chronology remains uncertain), and significant remains of Napatan date were found in the area. The most spectacular find, and the most surprising, was the remains of a pyramid found in the middle of the cataract region, some seventy kilometers upstream of the monumental center of Gebel Barkal. The pyramid structure had been largely destroyed, but its presence suggests potential connections between the Napatan elite and the Fourth Cataract. A single

Figure 42. Screening excavated deposits at Hosh al-Guruf.

clay sealing bearing the impression of the seal of the Napatan queen Khensa was also found at a gold-extraction site just across the river from the pyramid. In spite of these significant connections, occupation in the Napatan and subsequent Meroitic Periods was significantly less evident than Kerma occupation had been.

After the collapse of the Meroitic Empire during the fourth century AD, the Fourth Cataract once again became a focus of burials—post-Meroitic burials are ubiquitous throughout the region. Early studies of skeletal remains of this period suggest a significantly increased incidence of traumatic injury, suggesting a new level of violence and political instability. Post-Meroitic settlement sites were recognized under the gravel layer that covers much of the Fourth Cataract by one team, but other teams did not succeed in locating them—it is clear that our knowledge of settlement in this period is highly skewed. This raises basic questions about the representativeness of our sample of settlements and burials in other periods: Have we simply not known where to look for Kerma settlements or Neolithic burials?

Finds of medieval periods, both Christian and later Islamic, included a surprising number of fortresses along the Nile, as well as churches and associated cemeteries and settlements. The Fourth Cataract was part of the Christian kingdom of Makuria, centered at Old Dongola. The abundance of remains of this period in the Fourth Cataract may partially be explained by the introduction of the waterwheel *(saqya)* and the relative political stability of the time.

In addition to these results specific to each historical period, some larger questions emerge from the Merowe Dam salvage project. One concerns the broad use of the landscape beyond settlement and burial sites. Rock art was ubiquitous in the Fourth Cataract, and studies of its chronology, location, and meanings are in their early stages. Similarly, many teams noted the existence of low walls running across the landscape, some undoubtedly related to water retention, others perhaps to hunting or territorial marking.

Another set of issues surrounds the subsistence economy. Because the river valley is particularly narrow in the Fourth Cataract, the variation between high and low water was extreme (as much as eight to ten meters difference). In times before the introduction of the water wheel, this would have made extensive irrigation difficult, and agriculture would presumably have been limited to areas that could be planted as the Nile flood receded. We do not yet know which crops were grown at which periods—whether wheat and barley introduced from Egypt or millet and sorghum introduced from the south—or indeed whether year-round settlement was possible throughout the Fourth Cataract with these agricultural restrictions. This raises further questions about the extent of connection between Fourth Cataract settlement and nomadic groups of the deserts on either side of the Nile. Botanical remains were poorly preserved in the Fourth Cataract in general, although finds of sorghum in late Meroitic contexts provide one datum. It is possible that continuing analyses, including studies of human remains, may provide a clearer picture.

Finally, a range of ethnographic and ethnoarchaeological studies were made, paralleling in part the work done in the Aswan Dam salvage project. Among many other results, this work suggests the longstanding importance of gold as a resource in the Fourth Cataract.

Conclusion
The survey and excavation phase of the Merowe Dam Archaeological Salvage Project has ended, but finds in the Fourth Cataract will continue to provide insight into Nubian history as publication and analytical studies develop in years to come.

Bibliography

Adams, W. 1977. *Nubia: Corridor to Africa*. Princeton, NJ: Princeton University Press.

Ahmed, S.E.M. 2004. "The Merowe Dam Archaeological Salvage Project." In D. Welsby and J. Anderson, eds., *Sudan: Ancient Treasures*, 308–14. London: British Museum Press.

Baker, B. 2008. "Post-Meroitic to Early Christian Period Mortuary Activity at Ginefab: The 2007 Field Season of the UCSB-ASU Fourth Cataract Project." In B. Gratien, ed., *Actes de la 4e Conférence Internationale sur l'Archéologie de la 4e Cataracte du Nil*, 217–24. *CRIPEL*, Supplément 7.

Daszkiewicz, M., et al. 2002. "Composition and Technology of Pottery from Neolithic to Christian Periods from Jebel el-Ghaddar and from the Karima-Abu Hamed Region, Sudan." *Archéologie du Nil Moyen* 9:65–87.

Davies, W.V. 2001. "Kurgus 2000: The Pharaonic Inscriptions." *Sudan & Nubia* 5:46–68.

Edwards, D. 2004. *The Nubian Past: An Archaeology of the Sudan*. London: Routledge.

Emberling, G., and B. Williams. 2010. "The Kingdom of Kush in the 4th Cataract: Archaeological Salvage of the Oriental Institute Nubian Expedition, 2007 Season." *Gdansk Archaeological Museum African Reports* 7:17–38.

Fernea, E.W., and R. Fernea. 1991. *Nubian Ethnographies*. Prospect Heights, IL: Waveland Press.

Fuller, D. 2004. "The Central Amri to Kirbekan Survey: A Preliminary Report on Excavations and Survey 2003–04." *Sudan & Nubia* 9:4–10.

Gabriel, B., and P. Wolf. 2007. "Geoglyphs at the Fourth Nile Cataract (Sudan)." In C. Näser and M. Lange, eds., *Proceedings of the Second International Conference on the Archaeology of the Fourth Nile Cataract*, 28–33. Meroitica 23. Wiesbaden: Harrassowitz.

Gladykowska-Rzeczycka, J., and A. Pudlo. 2005. "Anthro-pological Analysis of Human Skeletal Remains from the GAME Concession Excavations (1996–2004)." *Gdansk Archaeological Museum African Reports* 4:31–37.

Haberlah, D. n.d. "Culture of the Manasir." http:// www2. hu-berlin.de/daralmanasir/

Kleinitz, C. 2007. "Rock Art and Archaeology: The Hadiab Survey." *Sudan & Nubia* 11:34–41.

Näser, C. 2006. "Die Humboldt University Nubian Expedition 2006: Arbeiten auf Us und Mograt." *Der Antike Sudan. MittSAG* 17:89–116.

———. 2007. "Die Humboldt University Nubian Expedition 2007: Arbeiten auf Us und Sur." *Der Antike Sudan. MittSAG* 18:41–50.

Paner, H., and Z. Borcowski. 2005. "Gdansk Archaeological Museum Expedition. A Summary of Eight Seasons' Work at the Fourth Cataract." *Gdansk Archaeological Museum African Reports* 4:89–115.

Trigger, B. 1976. *Nubia under the Pharaohs*. London: Thames and Hudson.

Welsby, D. 2003. *Survey above the Fourth Nile Cataract*. BAR International Series 1110. Oxford: Archaeopress.

———. 2004. "The SARS Amri to Kirbekan Survey: Excavations at the Pyramid, Site 4–F–71." *Sudan & Nubia* 9:2–3.

Welsby, D., and I. Welsby Sjöström. 2006–2007. "The Dongola Reach and the Fourth Cataract: Continuity and Change during the 2nd and 1st Millennia BC." *CRIPEL* 26:379–98.

Wenig, S., S. Hochfield, and E. Riefstahl, eds. 1977. *Africa in Antiquity: The Arts of Ancient Nubia and Sudan*. Brooklyn: Brooklyn Museum.

Wolf, P., and U. Nowotnick. 2005. "The Second Season of the SARS Anglo-German Expedition to the Fourth Cataract." *Sudan & Nubia* 9:23–31.

Zurawski, B. 2007. "Survey and Excavations in Shemkhiya, Dar el-Arab and Saffi Island." *Polish Archaeology in the Mediterranean* 17:323–35.

The Art and Architecture of Early Nubia: The A-Group to the Kerma Culture

Peter Lacovara

The artistic accomplishments of the ancient Nubians have long been overshadowed by those of the pharaonic Egyptian state to the north and have never been fully appreciated as unique and expressive aesthetic accomplishments on their own. Indeed, given limited resources and population in the Middle Nile, much of what they were able to produce was as outstanding as that of Egypt's best artists.

Moreover, the Nubians were fundamentally more experimental and adventurous than their neighbors, and we have begun to realize that even in their borrowings from Egypt, the Nubians were hardly simple copyists, but were quite ingenious in reinventing technologies and motifs to suit their purposes.

Given the lack of good stone for sculpture throughout most of Nubia, much of the local artistic energy went into ceramics rather than into stone sculptures and vessels.

Up until the First Dynasty (ca. 3050–2890 BC), Lower Nubian and Upper Egyptian material culture were remarkably similar, although already much of the Nubian ceramic production was superior. The Nubian A-Group rapidly distinguished itself with the creation of extremely fine ceramic vessels, perhaps influenced by earlier Nubian cultures, such as the Abkan. Some extremely rich A-Group graves of local rulers have been discovered, with some particularly finely crafted objects. A mace from a wealthy tomb at Seyala had a handle covered with gold leaf and decorated with rows of animals. The animal-phyle motif, which had come into Egypt from Mesopotamia in the late Predynastic Period, continued on through much of the early phases of Nubian civilization. The succeeding C-Group, Pan-Grave, and Kerma cultures show a persistence of many of the A-Group traditions and suggest a connection between these cultures that is still not fully understood.

The C-Group people appear to have been, at least in part, nomadic pastoralists, and cattle, sheep, and goats figure prominently in their art. Small figurines of these animals have been found in C-Group graves, along with human figurines that are remarkably sophisticated abstractions of the human form. Animal figures, also abstractly rendered, are found on grave stelae and incised on ceramic vessels.

Some C-Group settlements have been discovered and are composed of small groups of structures built of dry stone masonry that seem to evolve from round structures to more rectilinear units.

The so-called Pan-Grave culture, associated with the Medjayu of Egyptian texts, was widespread throughout Lower Nubia and into Upper Egypt. Their graves are decorated with painted cow, sheep, and goat skulls often decorated with geometric patterns. One skull from Mostagedda combines the typical patterns of red and black dots painted on the skull along with the eyes of the animal, and in the center of the skull a unique portrait of a Nubian warrior, perhaps the tomb owner himself. The figure carries a bow and has a battleaxe strapped to his back. He wears a long, colorful Nubian leather kilt along with an Egyptian-style broad collar. A panel beside the figure is inscribed in Egyptian hieroglyphs for an "owner of the river" or "owner of horns," which seems appropriate, as the deceased was buried with about forty pairs of horns.

Medjayu soldiers and police have been portrayed on stelae from the Middle Kingdom (ca. 2008–1685 BC) and the Second Intermediate Period (ca. 1685–1550 BC), but these are presumably made by Egyptian artists and depict them in a more Egyptianized way. Janine Bourriau has pointed out that the Pan-Grave cemeteries located within Egypt do show a gradual acculturation over time. Similarly, Manfred Bietak defined a 'Mixed Culture' in Lower Nubia that combined traces of a number of Nubian groups.

Some of this cultural admixture may have been created by expansion northward of the Kerma culture in the Second Intermediate Period. It is the Kerma culture that is the largest and most notable of all these groups, and its vast city and cemeteries located at the Third Cataract have been a rich repository of some of Nubia's most distinctive monuments and artistic achievements.

At the center of the city is a large mud-brick structure known as the Lower or Western Deffufa. The structure evokes an Egyptian temple with a massive pylon out front, but it is clearly a local

Figure 43. A-Group gold foil-covered mace handle with animal phyle decoration from Seyala.

design based only on the outward form of an Egyptian temple and indeed may have been comparable, or even larger, than anything that existed in Egypt at the time. Like an Egyptian temple, it formed the center of the city and was surrounded by storerooms and workshops. Many of the workshops contained fragments of Egyptian sculpture and stone vessels that had been brought there to rework into jewelry and other objects.

In the cemetery were a number of similar structures, including one known as the Upper or Eastern Deffufa. These were also religious structures, but served as funerary chapels. They were decorated with remarkable paintings, one of which showed a flotilla of ships, along with a number of scenes of animal phylae, including hippos and giraffes. They were also decorated with faience tiles, some of which were fragments of Egyptian faience that had been reworked to use in the decoration

Figure 44. The Upper or Eastern Deffufa at Kerma. Photo © Chester Higgins Jr 2012.

Figure 45. C-Group black-top pottery bowl with incised bovine figures.

Figure 46. Kerma culture, glazed quartzite lion sculpture.
Photograph © 2012 Museum of Fine Arts, Boston.

of the chapels, as in sandstone ceiling blocks with floral-pattern inlay. However, it also appears that large quantities of faience were produced on site as architectural decorations in the pattern of cavetto cornices, torus moldings, and a version of the Egyptian *kheker* frieze, along with images of striding lions and bound captives.

In addition to this production of faience, the faience glaze itself was used on local carvings of milky quartz that included a large scorpion figure, lions, and even a funerary bed, as well as possibly a sphinx. Massive glazed stones also served as altars and as pyramidia for the large tumuli in the cemetery. Unfortunately, the glaze proved fairly fugitive, and its most successful application was on quartz crystal used for jewelry.

The graves contained large quantities of jewelry, ceramics, imported Egyptian objects, and furniture. The principal burial was placed on a wooden bed with sculpted bull's legs and sometimes with an inlaid footboard. These were decorated with ivory inlays, cut and sometimes colored, in geometric shapes in the form of local flora and fauna, along with such mythical beasts

Figure 47. Kerma, Tumulus K III showing cross walls. Photograph © 2012 Museum of Fine Arts, Boston.

Figure 48. Kerma culture pottery bowl with spiral decoration. Photograph © 2012 Museum of Fine Arts, Boston.

as the Egyptian deity Taweret or a local invention of a flying giraffe. They may have been protective images, functioning in much the same way as the Egyptian magic wands of the Middle Kingdom.

Similar images were also cut out of sheets of mica and used as spangles on leather garments, also found in the tombs. Another ornament was a silver headdress in the form of an abstracted Egyptian vulture wig.

The large tumuli were impressive feats of architecture in and of themselves, and they gradually developed an internal buttress system, which may have influenced the development of casemate architecture in Egypt. Although the Kingdom of Kerma was destroyed by the Egyptian armies of the New Kingdom, the arts of the early Nubian cultures would have significant influence on the art of New Kingdom Egypt, as well as the other Nubian cultures that were to follow.

Bibliography

Adams, W.Y. 1977. *Nubia, Corridor to Africa*. Princeton, NJ: Princeton University Press.

Bietak, M. 1987. "The C-Group and the Pan-Grave Culture in Nubia." In T. Hägg, ed., *Nubian Culture: Past and Present*. Stockholm: Almquist and Wiksell.

Bourriau, J. 1991. "Relations between Egypt and Kerma during the Middle and New Kingdoms." In W.V. Davies, ed., *Egypt and Africa: Nubia from Prehistory to Islam*. London: British Museum Press.

El-Sayed, R. 2004. " r^c n *Mḏȝi.iw*—lingua blemmyica—*tu bedawie*. Ein Sprachenkontinuum im Areal der nubischen Ostwüste und seine (sprach-)historischen Implikationen." *SAK* 32:351–62.

Reisner, G.A. 1923. *Excavations at Kerma I–III and IV–V*. Harvard African Studies 5. Cambridge, MA: Harvard University Press.

THE ART AND ARCHITECTURE OF NUBIA DURING THE NEW KINGDOM: EGYPT IN NUBIA

Marjorie M. Fisher

A study of architecture and art in Nubia during the New Kingdom (Eighteenth–Twentieth Dynasties, ca. 1550–1077 BC) is inevitably hampered by the partial or complete destruction of so much material. Little is known of Nubian remains, because of a dearth of excavation, but also because Egypt had incorporated Lower Nubia into its realm as a province: what is known is based on Egyptian tombs, temples, and written documents, as well as temple reliefs and minimal excavation finds. Although Upper Nubia retained some independence from its northern Egyptian neighbors, which can be surmised from the lack of Egyptian settlements in its territory, Egypt evidently infiltrated Upper Nubia up to Kurgus. Nubia was clearly influenced artistically by Egypt during this period: Nubian potters may have learned how to make wheel-made pots from Egyptian craftsmen, though handmade Nubian pottery continued to be produced throughout this period.

Nubian buildings, settlements, and art were overshadowed in the archaeological record by construction on the part of the Egyptian pharaohs exercising their control over the region. Whereas earlier Nubian religious life is attested mainly by tombs and graves, the Nubian populace was now introduced to Egyptian temple styles, which had previously existed only at Kerma. Newly adopted pyramid-shaped mud-brick structures with enclosed courtyards set in front of them, like that found at Debeira, are reminiscent of Egyptian private tombs of the New Kingdom.

Temple architecture also drew on Egyptian prototypes, particularly at the sacred site of Gebel Barkal. Egyptians associated the high mountain there with their god Amun, and constructed a temple complex there dedicated to Amun of the holy mountain. Later, in the Napatan Period, Gebel Barkal became an important religious center for Nubian kings.

Many of these Nubian buildings, constructed of soft local sandstone, have suffered from weathering or were razed in either ancient or modern times. In addition, numerous monuments in Lower Nubia were moved or flooded when the Aswan Dam was built in the 1960s. Therefore, when examining this period, one is now limited to examining the surviving relocated Egyptian temples and their art styles, which had often been influenced by the local Nubian culture. Despite these challenges, this chapter will attempt to define some trends in architecture and art in Egyptian-influenced Nubia.

Opposite top:
Figure 49. The Temple of Semna.

Opposite bottom:
Figure 50. Relief of king holding offerings from Buhen Temple.

84

Figure 51. Eighteenth Dynasty block statue of Amenemhat from Buhen.

Figure 52. Eighteenth Dynasty round-topped stela from the tomb of Amenemhat at Debeira West.

By the beginning of the New Kingdom, Egypt had regained sovereignty from the Hyksos and began expanding its authority southward to Gebel Barkal, just north of the Fourth Cataract, and even farther upstream to Kurgus, north of the Fifth Cataract. As a result of the Egyptian incursion, Kerma, a once-thriving city south of the Third Cataract, saw a gradual abandonment of its necropolis, settlement, and temple area.

Nubian monuments and settlements became peripheral to an expansive Egyptian building program. There were three phases of Egyptian construction during the New Kingdom in ancient Nubia. In Phase 1, from the early Eighteenth Dynasty into the reign of Thutmose III, Egypt consolidated its presence in Nubia by enlarging the fortresses of the Middle Kingdom and securing settlements in Upper Nubia. In Phase 2, from the reign of Thutmose III to the end of the Eighteenth Dynasty, kings built new temples in Upper Nubia and around existing settlements in Lower Nubia. In Phase 3, associated with the Nineteenth and Twentieth Dynasties, isolated Egyptian temples were constructed in various locations throughout Nubia.

Nubia in the Early Eighteenth Dynasty

During the Eighteenth Dynasty, Egyptian pharaohs enlarged existing Middle Kingdom forts as well as building more fortresses along the Nile to monitor river traffic. Nubians, including the Pan-Grave people in Lower Nubia and the descendants of the Kerma culture in Upper Nubia, were resettled with Egyptian subjects and as a result became assimiliated with Egyptian culture.

As Egyptians pushed farther into Nubia during the New Kingdom, the number of Egyptian fortresses, cities, and structures rose from sixteen in the Middle Kingdom to at least twenty-eight in the New Kingdom. It is likely that more will be found, as is suggested by the early New Kingdom temple found recently at Doukki Gel. During this first construction phase, Egyptian control eventually extended all the way to the Fourth Cataract at Gebel Barkal and possibly beyond. The New Kingdom kings were determined to reinforce and expand their fortresses, as well as establishing larger and/or more numerous temples within fortress complexes. City temples dating to the early Eighteenth Dynasty are known at (from north to south) Amada, Aniba, Faras, Buhen, Sai Island, and Gebel Barkal, while rock-cut temples of this period (see the section "Nubia during the Nineteenth and Twentieth Dynasties," below) can be found at Ellesiya and Gebel Dosha. The building of more intramural temples—that is, temples built within a larger structure—in the Eighteenth Dynasty can be seen at Buhen, which by the New Kingdom had a total of four: the north temple of Isis or Hathor, built by Ahmose and restored by Amenhotep II; the south temple of Horus of Buhen, attributed to Hatshepsut and Thutmose III, which was built on the site of a Middle Kingdom temple; and the so-called Original Temple, built by Hatshepsut, Thutmose II, and Thutmose III over a Middle Kingdom chapel, possibly of Senwosret I. Buhen became increasingly important during the New Kingdom, as is indicated by the amount of archaeological material found there. Buhen temples appear to be oriented toward the southeast, although this is not the case for all temples in Nubia. Some others seem to change orientation based on the flow of the Nile and the orientation of the cliff faces, which dictate the orientation of buildings.

The north temple at Buhen, which was built by Ahmose, the first ruler of the Egyptian Eighteenth Dynasty, is different in structure from the southern temple built by Hatshepsut of the Eighteenth Dynasty. The south temple consists of a massive outer wall leading into an open room with pillars (peristyle court). The temple structure itself is located within this pillared area. Two entrances take one through a vestibule, then into three chambers, the center of which is the sanctuary. The room on the south side forms a corridor leading to another room that runs across the back of the other two rooms. The northern temple, by contrast, is entered through a large, thick gate that is built into the enclosure wall, leading into a pillared forecourt, which leads in turn through two elongated gated vestibules. At the back of the vestibules are three rooms, the middle one of which was most likely the sanctuary. This structure is similar to the freestanding temples discussed below.

Artworks of the Egyptian New Kingdom—painting, sculpture, relief, and small objects—have been found scattered throughout Nubia. Many of these artifacts can now be seen in the Nubia Museum at Aswan or the Sudan National Museum in Khartoum. They display certain attributes that characterized Egyptian art throughout its three-thousand-year history—notably symmetry, balance, and particular patterns of representation, all embodying conceptions of Egyptian religion, politics, and daily life. The craftsmen who created these representations followed a canon of proportion and expressed an ideology that constrained individual creativity. In addition, any given work of art was often executed not by one individual but by many, each performing a single function. In Egypt, for example, to create a large wall relief, one person

Figure 53. Sandstone statue of Amenhotep I from Sai Island.

Figure 54. Red quartzite kneeling statue of Amenhotep II from the Temple of Kumma.

sketched the wall, another corrected the drawing, another painted the relief, another detailed it, and others carved it. Further, the entire composition was divided into sections, so that each artist was responsible for finishing one section. These trends possibly carried over to Nubia. The quality of each piece depended on the intended patron (whether royal or private), the quantity of resources made available to the craftsmen, the period in which it was created, and where the piece was to be located, with pieces farther back in a tomb or room sometimes being of inferior quality. Egyptian art clearly influenced Nubian material culture during the New Kingdom, but Nubian artistic styles also persisted, particularly in the minor arts. Furthermore, much of New Kingdom Nubian art may have been crafted by Egyptians and completed by Nubians or vice versa.

Much of the known New Kingdom sculpture and painting so far discovered in Nubia come from the temples and sites that

were relocated during the flooding caused by the Aswan High Dam. The style of the statuary and carved-relief paintings is similar to that found in Egypt, displaying the Egyptian emphasis on portraying individuals in a stylized and idealized form. The Nubian variant was adapted to the type of stone found in Nubia and by Nubian artisans involved in its production. For example, the block statue, a typical New Kingdom form that portrays a seated person with knees drawn up and wearing an enveloping cloak, was adopted by the Nubians. One example, found at Buhen, is now in the Sudan National Museum. Dating to the reign of Hatshepsut and Thutmose III and belonging to a member of the Nubian elite named Amenemhat, a scribe, this statue represents a Nubian, but its overall style is Egyptian. Its beautiful carving shows a good sense of proportion, as seen in the facial features and ears. Less beautifully executed are the inscriptions on the front, reflecting perhaps a hand less familiar with Egyptian hieroglyphs.

Another piece, also in the Sudan National Museum, was found at the tomb of a different Amenemhat, at Debeira West.

Figure 55. Stela of Amenhotep III from Sedeinga.

This round-topped stela is beautifully carved and inscribed in Egyptian. In the lunette at the top of the stela is a scene similar to those seen on Egyptian stelae: a couple seated, one behind the other.

The materials available to Nubian artisans also left their mark on the Egyptian-influenced art found in Nubia. During the New Kingdom, sandstone—the main stone quarried in Nubia—was used frequently for sculpture, especially for sphinxes and for Akhenaten's colossi (see section "Nubia in the Later Eighteenth Dynasty," below). Sandstone statuary appears heavier in proportion than that carved from harder stones, such as granite or schist, and may reflect or contribute to the local style. Sandstone was easier to shape in three dimensions because of its soft nature, but less durable for finer carving. For example, a sandstone statue of Amenhotep I, found on Sai Island and currently in the Sudan National Museum, shows the king with a wide neck, short legs and body, and large feet—presumably either to deter breakage or as a matter of style. (Even so, the head has broken off over time.) On the other hand, the inscriptions covering the throne upon which he sits are beautifully incised, suggesting an adept craftsman. This statue was most likely painted as well.

A statue of his predecessor, Ahmose I, executed in the same manner and medium, was also found at the same site on Sai Island. Though these kings lived a generation apart, they have similar features; Dominique Valbelle suggests that the heads of both statues were disproportionately small because they were sculpted at a local workshop. The beautifully carved inscriptions point to an artist with a higher level of skill than that of the sculptor.

Egyptian paintings found in Nubia from this time period adhere to the canon of proportion established in Egypt. A relief from the temple of Hatshepsut and Thutmose III at Buhen that por-

Figure 56. Stela of Sety I in the traditional pharaonic pose of smiting an enemy while grasping a hank of hair, from the temple at Amara West.

trays the king before the god might just as easily have been carved on a temple wall in Egypt.

Nubia in the Later Eighteenth Dynasty

Phase 2 is characterized by the appearance of fortified temple towns south of the First Cataract and north of the Fourth Cataract at Amada, Faras, Sai, Soleb, Sesebi, Doukki Gel, Kawa, and possibly at Sedeinga and Gebel Barkal. Two other sites of the Nineteenth Dynasty may have been part of this phase: Amara West and Sedeinga. Fortified temple towns could either simply consist of a wall around the temple or could exhibit a more substantial means of fortification. Although many of these sites were first settled during earlier periods, notably the Middle Kingdom (that is, Faras and Sai), they continued into later times. According to Irmgard Hein, the change from Phase 1 to Phase 2 indicates a shift from military control of the areas to an Egyptian colonization of Nubia.

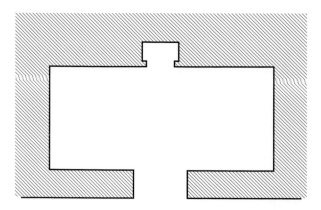

Figure 57. General plan of a private cliff tomb of the Nineteenth and Twentieth Dynasties. Based upon the tomb of Pennout at Aniba.

During this era, Egyptian temples were built on pre-existing sites in Lower Nubia and in areas in Upper Nubia that were less susceptible to Egyptian domination. These freestanding Egyptian temples take several standard forms. They typically consist of a pylon gateway leading to a pillared court (which may be an open court/peristyle court), a pillared hall, and a sanctuary. Variations of this plan occur with fewer or additional rooms within the temple. In contrast to the reliefs on pylons in Egypt where the king is shown overpowering his enemies, the first pylon in Nubian temples portrays the more peaceful scene of the king and the god embracing. From there a pillared hall leads to a vestibule and the sanctuary, as at Dakka, Amada, Aksha, Amara, Soleb, Doukki Gel, Kawa, and Gebel Barkal. The towns at these sites had been built long before the Egyptian temples were constructed.

The chief sites of Akhenaten's activity in Nubia include Sesebi and Doukki Gel, although it now seems that during the Amarna Period, there may have been more construction than previously thought (see sidebar, "Akhenaten in Nubia"). Building resumed under Tutankhamun with the temple of Kawa, then the rock-cut temple of Abahuda under Horemheb. These construction projects related to the resurgence of the Amun cult under Tutankhamun.

At these New Kingdom temple sites in Nubia, deities began to assume new roles and representations. Syncretized Nubian and Egyptian gods and goddesses were painted on temple walls. At Kerma,

the god Amun-Re, the chief god of Thebes in Egypt, was intermingled with a Nubian ram headed deity. Other gods and goddesses also rose to prominence, such as Horus of Aniba, a Nubia-specific version of an Egyptian god who became important in the reign of Thutmose III.

Royal deification appears on temple walls dating to Phase 2. Worship of the deified king is first attested in Egypt in private tombs dating to the reign of Thutmose III. Here the king is shown representing the sun god Re, Osiris, Amun, and others, enshrined in *djet* (eternal) time and worshiped by the deceased. This iconography was adapted by Thutmose IV, Amenhotep III, and later Ramesses II for their own living deification. In Nubia, this royal deification iconography first appears at Soleb Temple during the reign of Amenhotep III. Here the king appears with a lunar crescent and solar disc upon his head and a curled ram's horn around his ear, reflecting the assimilation of the Nubian and Egyptian ram cult of Amun-Re with the cult of the king. The appearance of the lunar crescent and sun disc has been interpreted to relate to solar aspects of the Amun-Re cult and an association with the lunar god Khonsu (see below).

As in the previous phase, the materials available in Nubia influenced the art that was produced. Some royal statuary of this phase is carved from materials different from those usually employed in Egypt; for instance, several statues of Amenhotep III were carved in peridotite, a local greenish igneous rock. Other stone was used for sculpture placed in both Egypt and Nubia: one red quartzite statuette of Amenhotep II discovered at the temple at Kumma, now in the Sudan National Museum, shows the kneeling king holding a pot in each hand. This stone was used in royal statuary found in other places in Nubia as well. The high-quality carving is similar to that found in Egypt. A statue of Amenhotep II, of which only the upper part of the torso exists, also made of red quartzite, was found at the Isis Temple of the Meroitic Period at Wad ban Naqa. It is currently in the Berlin Ägyptisches Museum und Papyrussammlung. However, Jean Leclant has determined that it most likely derived originally from Kumma and was placed with the other statue.

A sandstone relief of Amenhotep III, found in a Great Necropolis tomb at Sedeinga and currently in the Sudan National Museum, is the upper part of the lunette of a round-topped stela. Here the king offers incense to Amun of Soleb, who is positioned in front of the deified image of Amenhotep III himself. This fascinating composition shows the deified king wearing a disc placed into a crescent moon. Ram's horns, associated with Amun of Nubia, are curved around the pharaoh's ears, further showing the integration of the Egyptian Amun and the Nubian Amun. As mentioned above, this style of representation as both sun and moon also appears on the deified Amenhotep III at Soleb and was later adopted by Ramesses II, for instance at the Great Temple of Abu Simbel.

Continued on page 94.

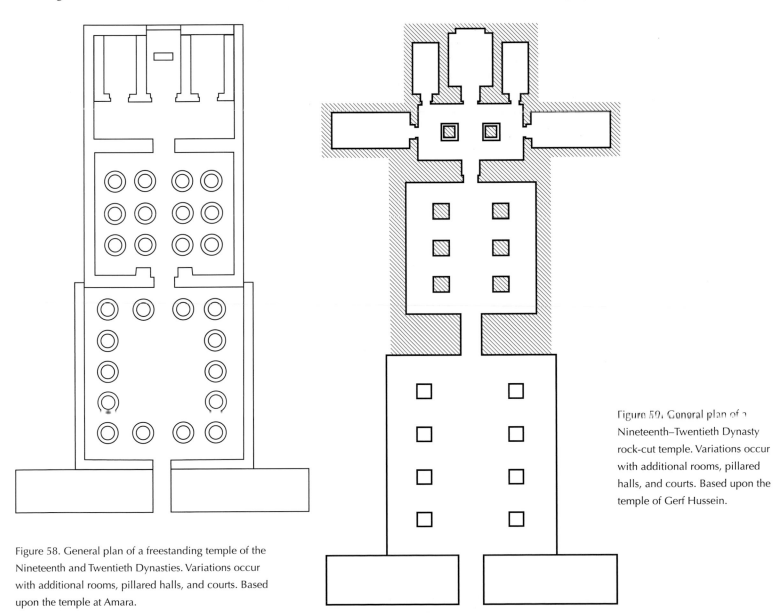

Figure 58. General plan of a freestanding temple of the Nineteenth and Twentieth Dynasties. Variations occur with additional rooms, pillared halls, and courts. Based upon the temple at Amara.

Figure 59. General plan of a Nineteenth–Twentieth Dynasty rock-cut temple. Variations occur with additional rooms, pillared halls, and courts. Based upon the temple of Gerf Hussein.

AKHENATEN IN NUBIA

W. Raymond Johnson

Scholars have assumed that Amenhotep III's son Amenhotep IV, who changed his name to Akhenaten in the fifth year of his reign, had little interest in Nubia outside of the exotic trade goods that passed through it and into Egypt from farther south, and we know that a military campaign occurred in his year 12 when that flow of goods was briefly interrupted. Recent archaeological investigations, however, have revealed the presence of more Akhenaten-period temple complexes in Nubia than was hitherto suspected, even at the better-known sites such as Kerma and Gebel Barkal. It is interesting to note how many temples of Akhenaten are found in close proximity to—or part of—those of his father Nebmaatre Amenhotep III, who built extensively throughout Nubia.

The northernmost site in Nubia where Akhenaten's building activities have been noted is Amada, two hundred kilometers south of Aswan and the First Cataract. This mid-Eighteenth Dynasty temple complex is just south of the Amenhotep III-period sites of Kuban (where a chapel was built dedicated to the jackal-headed Wepwawet at the head of the Wadi al-Allaqi, with its gold mines) and Wadi al-Sebua, with Amenhotep III's small rock-cut sanctuary for the god Horus. Immediately to the west of Wadi al-Sebua at Amada, Akhenaten augmented the earlier Thutmoside temple complex of Amun-Re and Re-Horakhty with an elaborate sandstone kiosk platform, sixteen by sixteen meters, supported by papyrus columns, approached by a stone stairway from the river. Later in his reign, Akhenaten erased the figures of Amun in the main temple, leaving the other gods and goddesses intact. While the kiosk was rebuilt and reinscribed later by Sety I, who also restored the Thutmoside temple, material found in the later walls of the kiosk—blocks and part of a stela—date the original construction to early in Akhenaten's reign (there is a similar structure at Kuban nearby that is probably contemporary). Up until the construction of the Aswan Dam, the platform and stairway were still visible, but the structure is now covered by the waters of Lake Nasser.

The next cluster of Amenhotep III- and Akhenaten-period sites is found just north of the Third Cataract. Here Amenhotep III built two great temple complexes, one at Sedeinga (Adaya) dedicated to Queen Tiye (mother of Akhenaten) as a manifestation of Hathor, and another at Soleb, where Amenhotep III's own cult as the creator god was celebrated in lavish style in the middle of a large, fortified settlement. Akhenaten inscribed the front pylon and gateway of the Amenhotep III Soleb temple with figures of himself worshiping 'Amun Lord of Nubia' but also his deified father 'Nebmaatre Lord of Nubia,' here crowned with the sun's disc and lunar crescent. Even when Akhenaten later eradicated the figures of Amun in the complex, he left his deified father's figures intact (also all gods other than Amun, as elsewhere). After Akhenaten's death, his cartouches were covered with plaster and reinscribed for Amenhotep III (brilliantly noted by William Murnane), the only known instance where figures of Akhenaten were ever posthumously appropriated and not simply destroyed.

Linked to Soleb by a contemporary road—and underscoring the close relationship of the two sites—is Akhenaten's own fortified temple complex and settlement at Sesebi (Sudla). Here Akhenaten built a triple shrine to the Theban triad Amun, Mut, and Khonsu, but then later rededicated the monument to the cult of the Aten. In one of the southern sanctuaries, Akhenaten constructed an enigmatic, subterranean crypt whose inscribed walls depict him in the field of offerings—a scene usually found in tombs—seated before various deities including Atum, 'Amun Lord of Nubia,' and the deified Amenhotep III. After Akhenaten's death, Sety I rededicated the monument to the Theban triad, covering Akhenaten's reliefs with plaster and recarving the walls and columns with his own reliefs. At the north of the site was a separate solar temple, and on the south a royal residence.

South of the Third Cataract and just north of the site of Kerma in the fortified settlement at Doukki Gel (ancient Pnubs), the remains of a temple of Akhenaten were recently discovered; it was constructed with the small *talatat* blocks particular to Akhenaten (54 by 26 by 24 cm), decorated in his distinctive style and featuring offering scenes to the rayed Aten/disc. The temple was left standing after Akhenaten's death but was, again, modified by Sety I, who plastered over the original decoration, and later by Ramesses III, before it was completely dismantled in the Twenty-fifth Dynasty. A bit farther to the south at Argo, also called Tabo, a temple with reliefs of Amenhotep III was dismantled to construct a Twenty-fifth Dynasty temple to the god Amun. Immediately to the south lies the site of Kawa, whose ancient name, Per Gem Aten (House of 'Aten is Found'), suggests that the temple to Amun of Tutankhamun, plastered over, reinscribed, and rebuilt by Taharqo, was originally another Akhenaten temple.

Kerma, Tabo, and Kawa lie at the northern terminus of an overland caravan route to the great religious center of Gebel Barkal, fifteen kilometers upriver from the Fourth Cataract and four hundred kilometers north of Khartoum. Considered to be the Nubian residence of the god Amun from the Eighteenth Dynasty on, the temple complex there is built against a dramatic sandstone butte that features a natural rock spur on its southern side that the ancient Egyptians associated with a rearing uraeus cobra; depictions of Amun of Gebel Barkal often show the god within a shrine fronted by a gigantic cobra. Barkal mountain itself was considered to be a manifestation of the primeval mound of creation and the original home of the sun god's—and king's—cobra uraeus, the Eye of Re, of tremendous significance for Egyptian kingship. Probably not coincidentally, Gebel Barkal also appears to have been the southernmost site of Akhenaten's building activities in Nubia. Very recently (2007), an Aten temple was uncovered in the foundations of a later temple (B 500), constructed of *talatat* blocks that replaced an earlier Thutmoside Amun temple. The Aten temple shows three Amarna phases and, once again, was not destroyed or dismantled after Akhenaten's death, but was modified in the post-Amarna period and rededicated to Amun. In addition to this temple, the emplacements for six additional Akhenaten-period chapels were also discovered, all constructed of *talatat*, which formed a line of sanctuaries in front of the Barkal cliffs. This surprising new material indicates that the site was of tremendous importance to Akhenaten, and appears to have been a major cult center during his reign.

It is becoming increasingly clear that Akhenaten's presence and interest in Nubia were much greater than was previously thought, and a reassessment is definitely in order. Like the kings before and after him, Akhenaten was interested in controlling the flow of exotic goods from Africa: ebony, ivory tusks, animal pelts, ostrich feathers, similar goods, and most important of all, gold. The cluster of Amenhotep III and Akhenaten temples in the vicinity of the Wadi al-Allaqi and the sites south of the Second Cataract can be easily linked to earlier Eighteenth Dynasty gold-mining activities, as was the area around Soleb, just north of the Third Cataract. But the activities of Akhenaten south of the Third Cataract, in Kerma, Argo, and Kawa, as well as Gebel Barkal, much farther upriver—all outside of the main gold-mining areas—seem more linked to the cultic significance of these sites. Akhenaten's newly discovered, large temple complex at Gebel Barkal, in particular, strongly suggests that the earlier association of the site as the residence—and origin—of the 'fiery eye' of the sun god—and the source of divine kingship itself—continued to be celebrated in Akhenaten's Aten cult. Amenhotep III's obsession—and identification—with the sun cult in Nubia seems now matched by his son's own interest. It appears that Nubia played as key a role in Akhenaten's Aten cult as in the Amun cult before it.

Continued from page 91.

Nubia during the Nineteenth
and Twentieth Dynasties

Phase 3 ushered in a significant period of new temple construction by Egyptians in Nubia. But it was not until the reign of the second pharaoh of the Nineteenth Dynasty, Sety I, that two new administrative cities were built: Aksha in Lower Nubia and Amara West in Upper Nubia. Barry Kemp has categorized these cities surrounded by massive defensive walls as temple cities, because temples with their own cultural and economic systems were central to the larger settlements. Aksha was soon abandoned, perhaps because it was too close to Aniba, the administrative center of Lower Nubia. Amara West, on the other hand, prospered, possibly because of its central location between the Second and Third Cataracts with easy access to gold mines and proximity to a caravan route to the Selima Oasis. Sety I also had many Nubian temples restored, notably in order to reestablish the Amun-Re and Re-Horakhty cults in Amada and Sesebi, and he built a chapel to Amun at Gebel Barkal.

Ramesses II, the son of Sety I, added to or built seven temples throughout Nubia (Beit al-Wali, Gerf Hussein, Wadi al-Sebua, Derr, Abu Simbel, Aksha, and Amara West). He also continued restoration of and additions to previously built temples at numerous sites and continued support of other existing buildings. His son, Merenptah, did not continue these building projects in the south, with the possible exception of Kuban, as he was forced to contend with the incursions of Libyans and others in the north. Instead he focused on maintaining many already-existing Nubian temples, as did his successor Amenmesse, including restorations at Abu Simbel and Amara. Similarly, the remaining pharaohs of the Nineteenth Dynasty attempted no new construction other than a chapel of Sety

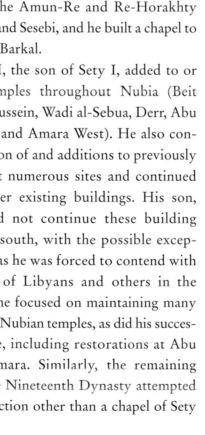

Figure 60. Relief from the tomb of Pennout. Photo © Chester Higgins Jr 2012.

II at Debod and an addition in Buhen. During the Twentieth Dynasty, royal building projects and inscriptions are apparent only at Kuban, Aniba, Buhen, and Dorginarti. By that date, kings no longer had the resources to send expeditions into Nubia, and maintenance of existing temples was all that was possible at many sites.

Like earlier cult buildings, Egyptian Nineteenth and Twentieth Dynasty temples in Nubia followed a standardized plan. They were either rock-cut, partly or fully cut into a rock face or escarpment, or they were freestanding. According to Hein, the rock-cut type may have been inspired in part by the Egyptian creation myth, in which the gods reside in and issue forth from a primeval mound, represented by the rock face; hence the sanctuary of the temple is within the escarpment. The part of these temples that lies outside may

have likewise materialized the notion that the gods created humans to dwell upon the earth. Another theory proposed by Hein is that the rock-cut temple developed naturally from the T-shaped private tombs of the Eighteenth Egyptian Dynasty. But it is equally possible that the rock-cut temple was developed from within Nubia itself.

Within the category of rock-cut temples are two subtypes: mortuary chapels/private cliff sites and gods' temples/royal sites. The private subtype has one rock-cut room with a niche in the back for cult images. The royal subtype has several halls and rooms eventually leading to the sanctuary, which is flanked by additional ritual rooms.

The private cliff site type is best represented by two chapels: that of the viceroy Setau of the reign of Ramesses II at Qasr Ibrim, and also a chapel at Faras. The Qasr Ibrim site is typical of Eighteenth

Figure 61. The temple of Beit al-Wali, interior of the vestibule. Photo © Chester Higgins Jr 2012.

Figure 62. Relief of the king given life and luck by the god Khnum, from the interior of the temple of Beit al-Wali. Photo © Chester Higgins Jr 2012.

Dynasty cliff tombs found in Egypt that consisted of one square or rectangular room with a niche on the back wall for a cultic image. In the case of the viceroy Setau's chapel, the cult images were of Horus of Miam, Hathor of Ibshek (the temple of Hathor and Nefertari at Abu Simbel), and the deified Ramesses II. At Faras, his commemorative chapel consists of a square room with a niche in the back for the cultic images. The deities honored are not certain, but Hein assumes the images may represent Hathor of Ibshek and Ramesses II.

A later cliff tomb of Pennout dating to the reign of Ramesses VI consists of one room running east to west and a sanctuary north of the main room on the center axis that focuses on three statues cut into the rock. The main room is decorated in the painted sunk relief typical of Egyptian late-New Kingdom private tombs. Reliefs on the west side of the tomb are dedicated to the afterlife and the weighing of the heart ritual—predictably,

given that the west is associated with the afterlife. On the east side are represented events of Pennout's life. Although this tomb is associated with an Egyptian official, it is unclear whether Pennout was actually Egyptian. Given the ancient Egyptian preference for burial in Egypt, it is equally possible that Pennout was a Nubian who worked in the Egyptian administration and was thus buried in Nubia. His family members also had Egyptian-style decorated tombs in Nubia, implying that they too were Nubian members of the Egyptian administration.

Differing in format from private cliff chapels, royal rock-cut temples are best represented by those of Ramesses II at Beit al-Wali, Gerf Hussein, Wadi al-Sebua, Derr, and Abu Simbel. Ramesses II seemed to prefer building rock-cut temples rather than freestanding temples in Nubia. Many of these Lower Nubian temples were moved by UNESCO when the construction of the Aswan

High Dam created Lake Nasser in the 1960s. As with the fortresses, their original sites were chosen for their location along the Nile, the availability of arable land adjacent to them, their proximity to trade routes and mining operations, and the vantage point they provided for monitoring Nile traffic. Hein further surmises that cultic worship of the sun dictated where Ramesses II built his temples. His earliest temple at Beit al-Wali was the farthest north, and each subsequent temple to the south could have served as a cultic station visited during the king's symbolic journey in praise of the sun god. This is illustrated later in Ptolemaic Nubia, where another myth of Hathor shows her as an angry goddess, who is the sun god's eye. She travels south from Aswan into Nubia in winter and returns north in spring. Although this myth dates to the Ptolemaic Period, its origin must have been further back in Egyptian history and could draw on the same mythological principles as those materialized in the Ramesside temples.

The rock-cut temples of Ramesses II share similar features: a pylon or gate leads through a first pillared hall or peristyle court, either of which has pillars with attached colossal statues of the king in his ceremonial kilt, leading into a pillared hall, then into a transverse room or vestibule. At the back of the vestibule are three rooms, the center one being the sanctuary, featuring a niche for statues of the gods and king or an elongated offering room. Other adjoining rooms and an adjacent chapel are parallel to the sanctuary. In addition, some temples have storage rooms off the vestibule or first pillared hall. Finally, there may be additional courtyards in front of the first pillared hall/peristyle court, as at Derr and Wadi al-Sebua.

Again, the orientation of these Nubian rock-cut temples varies depending on the orientation of the Nile and of the rock face into which they are built. They face broadly to the east on the west bank and to the west on the east bank.

Reliefs in Rock-cut Temples

Two types of pictorial compositions characterize the rock-cut temples of Ramesses II: military scenes showing the king smiting enemies of Egypt, and cultic scenes that portray him with the gods. The incomplete state of many temples makes it difficult to discern fine-grained trends in temple decoration, but certain standard components of their reliefs can be established. The relief scenes on Egyptian rock-cut temples in Nubia are essentially the same as those in Egypt proper, except that the use of desert gods and motifs, southern enemies, and elements with Nubian religious associations are incorporated in the decoration more prominently. Egypt's enemies are portrayed much as they are in Egypt proper: in military scenes, the king overcomes the human enemies of Egypt in the form of Asians and Nubians, as well as symbolic enemies such as chaos. In cultic reliefs, the king interacts with the gods in order to maintain order for the populations over which he rules.

Military reliefs are normally carved on the exterior walls and the first pillared hall/peristyle court of a temple. If there were additional halls before the first pillared hall, then battle scenes might also be shown there. These military scenes often indicate specifically which enemy the Egyptians are fighting, in the detail of the figures, the accompanying captions, and their location in the temple. For example, as Nubia is south of Egypt, Nubian battle reliefs occupy the southern wall; as Asia is north of Egypt, Asiatic battle reliefs take up the northern wall. Again in standardized images, the sons of Ramesses II are represented in battle scenes and his sons and daughters in processional scenes on the first pillared halls/peristyle courts of many of his temples. On the gate or pylon of the temples, Ramesses II is portrayed in a ritual with the gods or fighting his enemies. Nubians adopted this style of relief on the pylons of their own temples years later during the Napatan and

Meroitic Periods, but in their versions the king is portrayed in relief on one side and the queen on the other, for example at the temple of Naqa from the first century AD.

A sandstone stela associated with Sety I, found in the temple at Amara West and currently in the Sudan National Museum, portrays the king holding the feathered headdress of his Nubian enemies with his left hand, while with his right hand he raises a scimitar to strike them. The relief describes his battle against the region of Irem in Nubia or possibly to the south of Nubia. This smiting motif was common in Egyptian reliefs of all periods. It shows the king destroying and controlling evil as symbolized by foreigners.

Cultic scenes appear in all Egyptian temples in Nubia, both freestanding and rock-cut. Ritual reliefs with the gods appear from the first pillared hall/peristyle court to the back of the temple. Numerous gods are depicted, the primary god being a variation of Amun-Re, the sun god. As Amun-Re became the ultimate focus of the Egyptian pantheon, so too did he become the main god in Nubia. Variations of the sun god appear in the form of Re and Re-Horakhty; a separate chapel on the north side of the pylon of the Great Temple of Abu Simbel is dedicated to Re-Horakhty. Other prominent Egyptian gods who appear in Nubia include Osiris, Isis, Mut, Hathor, Ptah, and Khnum. Most of these gods can in one form or another be associated with the sun god, Amun-Re.

Labib Habachi was the first scholar to isolate trends in temple representations of the gods in Nubia. He established that certain gods appear to be associated with specific cardinal directions more than others. Other scholars, such as Hein, have built on this foundation, hoping to ascertain the preferences of Egyptian artists for where to locate the various gods throughout the decorative scheme of the temples. Extensive damage to the temple walls has, however, made this a daunting task.

Figure 63. Ramesses II being suckled by the goddess Isis, on a wall relief at Beit al-Wali.

Specific deities tend to appear most often in the sanctuaries of the temples dedicated to them. In addition, the sun god Amun-Re appears in all Nubian temples in that most sacred area. As mentioned earlier, in New Kingdom temples, he is depicted with ram's horns curled around his ears, most likely an adaptation of the Nubian ram cult mentioned above. For example, at the temple of Kawa (Gem Aten), Amun is again depicted with ram horns during the reign of Tutankhamun. Similarly, the Small Temple at Abu Simbel is dedicted to Hathor and thus contains representations of that goddess throughout its decorative scheme. Many of the temples also incorporate Nubian representations of Horus, such as Horus of Baki, Miam, and Buhen. These local forms augmented the standard Egyptian pantheon of the state gods. The Nubian God Dedwen, for example, who supplies incense for the gods and burns incense at the royal birth, first appears in the Egyptian Pyramid Texts around 2400 BC. His presence continues throughout New Kingdom Egypt and there are temples dedicated to him by Thutmose III at Uronarti and Semna West. He is further identified on reliefs at the temples at Ellesiya, Semna East, and Gebel Barkal.

Cultic reliefs portray the king acting on behalf of humanity as a whole. The Egyptians considered Egypt to be the center of the world, but in Nubia they included local populations, which they considered more or less annexed to Egypt. The king worshiped either before the gods or before a deified version of himself. This standard portrayal of the king in Egypt proper appears in Nubia, too, with many more examples known from Nubia than Egypt. The self-worship of the deified king began in Nubia with Senwosret III at Buhen, Thutmose III in Ellesiya, and then most importantly Amenhotep III at Soleb and Sedeinga, and was adopted by Ramesses II in all his rock-cut temples except the Small Temple at Abu Simbel associated with his wife, Nefertari.

Just as in Egypt, the color palette of the reliefs found in temples was dictated by the period in which they were painted. For instance, Ramesses II favored black, red, and yellow colors in his Nubian temples more than the softer palette preferred by Eighteenth and Nineteenth Dynasty predecessors such as Amenhotep III and Sety I.

Statuary in Rock-cut Temples

Royal rock-cut temples contain two types of statuary: one type cut out of the rock face on the interior and exterior of the temple, and a second, freestanding type, found within the temple or decorating the façade. In the sanctuaries at the back of these temples, all the gods are cut out of the living rock. In general plastered then painted, these rock-cut statues are stouter and less refined than freestanding ones. The neck and ankles are wider to support the statue, since it is carved into the mountain. According to W. Raymond Johnson, Ramesses II's style and proportions changed over time; while earlier statues (like those at Abu Simbel) are proportionally more slender and appealing to modern eyes, the later figures became stockier and cruder, possibly due to the speed of construction.

The colossal statues of Ramesses II at Abu Simbel incorporate small figures of his children, his wife, and his mother adjacent to his legs. These colossal statues offer visitors their first impression when approaching the temple, which materializes Ramesses II's strength and power. The statuary of Ramesses II and his queen on the Small Temple at Abu Simbel is smaller in size and unfinished. Both sets of rock-cut colossal statues on the large and small Abu Simbel temples were originally plastered and beautifully painted.

Within the temples, standing statues abutting pillars depict the king wearing a ceremonial sporran. These statues, carved from the rock, appear along the main axis in the pillared halls in all the rock-cut temples of Ramesses II except that of Derr,

Figure 65. Relief of Ramesses II worshiping Amun-Re, himself in deified form, and Mut, from the Great Temple at Abu Simbel.

where they are placed facing the entryway, perhaps because of the direction of the flow of the Nile at that location.

Freestanding Temples

The two freestanding temples of Ramesses II, Amara West in Upper Nubia and Aksha in Lower Nubia, were built in colonial settlements previously established by Sety I. Both settlements were important residential and administrative centers and possibly storage centers as well, being located along trade routes where agricultural land was available.

Each of these temples consists of a pylon leading to a peristyle court with pillars around it. The Amara temple is much larger than the Aksha temple, with more rooms. These freestanding temples show a similar layout of the sanctuary and other rooms.

Statuary for freestanding temples was similar to that in rock-cut temples. The carving of the facial features was more finely executed than in the statuary of rock-cut temples. One sandstone statue of Ramesses II (of which only the upper torso and head remain), now in the Munich Staatliche Sammlung Ägyptischer Kunst, shows the figure of the king holding a crook, *was* scepter, and flail in his right hand. He wears the traditional *nemes* headdress but appears to have had a sun disc, now missing, mounted upon his head. This characteristic element of solar deification is here represented in Ramesses II statuary, as identified by Leclant.

In conclusion, the location and character of Egyptian architecture in Nubia throughout the New Kingdom was probably dictated in the first instance by the topography of the region of Nubia, as well as by the relative security of Egyptian control at the time when a particular structure was begun. Egyptians attempted to incorporate natural rock formations into their buildings so that they could coalesce both Egyptian and Nubian cultic beliefs. In so doing, they created new architectural

Following pages:
Figure 66. The Small Temple in the foreground and Great Temple of Ramesses II in the background at Abu Simbel.
Photo © Chester Higgins Jr 2012.

Figure 67. The interior of the Great Temple of Abu Simbel, looking down the central axis. Photo © Chester Higgins Jr 2012.

forms of rock-cut temples that merged Egyptian and Nubian styles as well as pantheons. Such assimilation was a natural outgrowth of Egyptian and Nubian encounters over time. Conventional indigenous forms began to incorporate new artistic trends and developed into a style that later could be seen in Egypt, specifically during the Twenty-fifth Dynasty. The conflation of Egyptian and Nubian gods and goddesses portrayed on New Kingdom temple walls demonstrated Egypt's ability to encompass coexisting beliefs and thereby harmonize relations with the Nubians. Similarly, Nubians incorporated and adapted Egyptian styles in their architecture and art. It is hoped that future excavation in Upper and Lower Nubia will yield a better understanding of Nubian art and architecture during this period. What is clear is that while Egyptian occupation left its imprint on Nubian art and architecture, the pattern also worked in reverse, with Nubian influence on Egyptian iconography, architecture, and religious ideology.

Bibliography

Arkell, A.J. 1950. "Varia Sudanica." *JEA* 36:24–40.

Bard, K.A. 2008. *An Introduction to the Archaeology of Ancient Egypt.* Oxford: Blackwell Publishing.

Bard, K.A., and S.B. Shubert. 1999. "Gebel Barkal." In *Encyclopedia of the Archaeology of Ancient Egypt*, 325–27. London and New York: Routledge.

Bicke, S. 2002. "Aspects et fonctions de la déification d'Amenhotep III." *BIFAO* 102:63–90.

Blackman, A.M. 1937. "Preliminary Report on the Excavations at Sesebi, Northern Province, Anglo-Egyptian Sudan 1936–7." *JEA* 23:145–51.

Bonnet, C. 1991. "Upper Nubia from 3000 to 1000 BC." In W.V. Davies, ed., *Egypt and Africa: Nubia from Prehistory to Islam*, 112–17. London: British Museum Press.

Bonnet, C., et al. 1984. "Les fouilles archéologiques de Kerma (Soudan): Rapport préliminaire des campagnes de 1982–1983 et de 1983–1984." *Genava*, n.s., 32:5–20.

Bonnet, C., and D. Valbelle. 2006. *The Nubian Pharaohs: Black Kings on the Nile.* Cairo: American University in Cairo Press.

Bourriau, J. 1991. "Relations between Egypt and Kerma During the Middle and New Kingdoms." In W.V. Davies, ed., *Egypt and Africa: Nubia from Prehistory to Islam*, 129–44. London: British Museum Press.

Darnell, J.C., and C. Manassa. 2007. *Tutankhamun's Armies: Battle and Conquest during Ancient Egypt's Late Eighteenth Dynasty.* Hoboken, NJ: John Wiley and Sons.

Davies, N. de G., and A.H. Gardiner. 1926. *The Tomb of Huy. Viceroy of Nubia in the Reign of Tut'ankhamun (No. 40).* London: Egypt Exploration Society.

Davies, V. 2001. "Kurgus 2000: The Egyptian Inscriptions." *Sudan & Nubia* 5:46–58.

Dunham, D. 1970. *The Barkal Temples.* Boston: Museum of Fine Arts.

Garcea, E.A.A. 2004. "The Palaeolithic and Mesolithic." In D.A. Welsby and J.R. Anderson, eds., *Sudan: Ancient Treasures: An Exhibition of Recent Discoveries from the Sudan National Museum*, 20–24. London: British Museum Press.

Habachi, L. 1969. "Divinities Adored in the Area of Kalabsha, with a Special Reference to the Goddess Miket." *MDAIK* 24:169–83.

Hein, I. 1991. *Die Ramessideische Bautätigkeit in Nubien.* GOF 4, Vol. 22. Wiesbaden: Otto Harrassowitz.

Helck, W. 1980. "Ein 'Feldzug' unter Amenophis IV. gegen Nubien." *SAK* 8:117–26.

Jacquet-Gordon, H., C. Bonnet, and J. Jacquet. 1969. "Pnubs and the Temple of Tabo on Argo Island." *JEA* 55:103–11.

Junker, H. 1911. *Der Auszug der Hathor-Tefnut aus Nubien.* Berlin: Verlag der Königlichen Akademie der Wissenschaften, in Commission bei G. Reimer.

Kemp, B.J. 1991. *Ancient Egypt: Anatomy of a Civilization.* New York and London: Routledge.

Kendall, T. 2008. "Recent Field Work at Jebel Barkal, 2007–08: National Corporation for Antiquities and Museums of Sudan [NCAM] Mission, 2008." http://www.univie.ac.at/afrikanistik/meroe2008/abstracts/Abstract%20Kendall.pdf

———. 2010. "Jebel Barkal: History and Archaeology of Ancient Napata." National Corporation of Antiquities and Museums of Sudan [NCAM]. http://www.jebel-barkal.org

Leclant, J. 1997. "Egypt in Sudan: The New Kingdom." In D. Wildung, ed., *Sudan: Ancient Kingdoms of the Nile*, 118–42. Paris and New York: Flammarion.

Macadam, M.F.L. 1955. *The Temples of Kawa II: History and Archaeology of the Site.* London: Oxford University Press.

Morkot, R. 1988. "The Excavations at Sesebi (Sudla) 1936–38." *BSF* 3:159–64.

Murnane, W. 2000. "Soleb Renaissance: Reconsidering the Temple of Nebmaatre in Nubia." In *Amarna Letters* 4:6–19. San Francisco: KMT Communications.

O'Connor, D. 1991. "Early States along the Nubian Nile." In W.V. Davies, ed., *Egypt and Africa: Nubia from Prehistory to Islam*, 145–65. London: British Museum Press.

Redford, D.B. 1984. *Akhenaten, the Heretic King.* Princeton, N.J.: Princeton University Press.

Reisner, G.A. 1910. *The Archaeological Survey of Nubia: Reports for 1907–1908.* 2 vols. Cairo: National Printing Department.

Shinnie, P.L. 1996. *Ancient Nubia.* London: Kegan Paul International.

Simpson, W.K. 1982. "Egyptian Sculpture and Two-dimensional Representation as Propaganda." *JEA* 68:266–71.

Smith, H.S. 1991. "The Development of the 'A-Group' Culture in Northern Lower Nubia." In W.V. Davies, ed., *Egypt and Africa: Nubia from Prehistory to Islam*, 92–111. London: British Museum Press.

Spence, K., and P. Rose. 2009. "New Field Work at Sesebi." *EA* 35:21–24.

Strudwick, N. 2005. *Texts from the Pyramid Age.* Writings from the Ancient World 16. Atlanta: Society of Biblical Literature.

Taylor, J.H. 1991. *Egypt and Nubia.* London: British Museum Press.

Valbelle, D. 2004. "Egyptians on the Middle Nile." In D.A. Welsby and J.R. Anderson, eds., *Sudan: Ancient Treasures: An Exhibition of Recent Discoveries from the Sudan National Museum*, 92–121. London: British Museum Press.

Williams, B. 1986. *The University of Chicago Oriental Institute Nubian Expedition.* Vol. 3, Part 1: *The A-Group Royal Cemetery at Qustul: Cemetery L.* Chicago: University of Chicago Press.

THE ART AND ARCHITECTURE OF KUSHITE NUBIA

Peter Lacovara

The Kushite kings of the Twenty-fifth Dynasty and their Napatan successors not only brought about a renaissance in art and architecture in Egypt, but also created a new artistic idiom for Nubia that would survive for nearly a millennium. Although much of the revivalism of the period was dismissed by earlier, Egypto-centric scholars as mere copying, we now see that it is in fact a complex and studied reinvention of past styles, and a reinterpretation of pharaonic motifs and themes.

We know little about the forebears of the Twenty-fifth Dynasty. The ancestral tombs at al-Kurru are tumulus graves of ancient Nubian tradition, and the ceramics associated with them are a combination of local handmade wares and Egyptian imports.

However, with the expansionist designs of Kashta and his successors, we see a rapid transformation in the cemeteries at al-Kurru. The tombs change from the traditional tumulus burial to a pyramid, although ones more closely modeled on private New Kingdom Egyptian examples, and there is a proliferation of imported Egyptian wares. Alongside the imports from Egypt, we have locally manufactured products inspired by pharaonic traditions, including *shawabti*s, coffins, offering tables, stelae, and amulets.

In Egypt, mirroring the texts that recorded the takeover of the country and extolled the piety of the Nubian kings and their devotion to the established norms of society, the new rulers were anxious to show themselves in traditional forms. Large-scale statues of Shabaqo and Taharqo were set up at Karnak Temple depicting the kings in a standard pose, but with the tightly fitting cap-crown favored by the Nubian kings. Taharqo is also depicted as a sphinx, and in numerous votive bronze figures.

The Divine Votaresses ("God's Wives") of Amun built their funerary chapels within the temple precinct of Medinet Habu, following the Third Intermediate Period predilection for locating important burials within temple grounds for safeguarding.

Piankhi (Piye) as well as his successors continued to rule from Napata, but he installed his sister, Amenirdis, in the office of God's Wife to act as his representative in Thebes. Her tomb chapel is a small rectangular sandstone temple fronted by a small pylon gate, with a forecourt with four columns fronting a sanctuary containing a holy of holies with battered sides, torus molding, and cavetto cornice. The walls are decorated in sunk relief with depictions of Amenirdis

Figure 68. Limestone relief from the tomb of Mentuemhat, Mayor of Thebes.

and her adopted successor, Shepenwepet II, and spells drawn from the ancient Pyramid Texts. Adjoining this chapel to the west was a similar one that was later subdivided for three burials: Shepenwepet II; her adopted daughter, Nitocris, who was her ultimate Saite successor; and Nitocris's actual mother, Queen Mehytenweskhet. Taharqo also built a new gateway entrance to the earlier temple to Amun that had been begun at the site by Hatshepsut (and Thutmose III in the Eighteenth Dynasty).

The Twenty-fifth Dynasty pharaohs undertook their most ambitious building projects, not surprisingly, at Karnak. The great First Pylon, begun by Taharqo but never finished, greets visitors at the first glimpse of the temple complex today. He also erected an enormous kiosk in the First Court behind the pylon, and one of its monumental papyrus columns still majestically rises there today. He also erected other colonnades in

the temple and built a number of small shrines around the periphery of the great temple of Amun, including one to Osiris Hekadjet.

Under Nubian rule, a number of imposing private monuments were created as well, particularly in Thebes. The largest and most celebrated of these is the tomb of the Mayor of Thebes, Mentuemhat. The tomb is situated in front of the temples at Deir al-Bahari, in part to make use of the Hatshepsut causeway. The entrance to the tomb runs south off the causeway, parallel to a massive, arched mud-brick pylon. Below this is a warren of open courts, vestibules, and subterranean chambers numbering over fifty rooms, many decorated with exquisite reliefs. Sadly, the tomb has been badly plundered since antiquity, but many examples of the refined, delicate carving can be found in museums throughout Europe and the Americas. The relief carving is inspired by earlier pharaonic styles, particularly from the Old and New Kingdom, with

Figure 69. Bronze statuette of Taharqo.

Figure 70. Colossal granite gneiss statue of Aspelta from Gebel Barkal. Photograph © 2012 Museum of Fine Arts, Boston.

stock scenes being carefully adapted to fit the decorative program of the sepulcher.

There were some outstanding sculptures produced at this time, both of private officials, such as Mentuemhat and Harwa, and of the rulers Taharqo and Shabaqo, in particular, in both bronze and stone, and ranging in size from small votives to colossal sculptures.

What is remarkable about the Twenty-fifth Dynasty copyists is their understanding of the stylistic phases of Egyptian art, distinguishing scenes derived from Old, Middle, and New Kingdom sources. The most amazing of these is a stela, now in the Cleveland Museum of Art, that is done in an Archaic style evoking the slab stelae of the first dynasties.

Within the context of this revivalism, however, the Nubians were able to add distinctive qualities of their own. As is usually the case in Egyptian art, the physiognomy of the reigning king becomes the standard of beauty for that age. The portraits of Nubians and Egyptians alike during this period reflect this, with a broader face and distinctive almond-shaped eyes with prominent lower rims, and the so-called Kushite fold, a swelling on the cheeks on either side of the nose.

Another aspect of sculpture from this period is an interest in more exotic stones, such as petrified wood, peridotite, and serpentine, aside from the more standard materials (black, gray, and red granite, 'Egyptian alabaster' [calcite or travertine], limestone, graywacke, and quartzite). A group of statues in Berlin carved in red quartzite mimics Old Kingdom wooden tomb sculptures.

This archaism can also be seen in relief carving. The most oft-remarked example is at the temple of Kawa, which depicts the king as a sphinx trampling Libyan enemies that is copied, right on down to the names of the crushed victims, from Old Kingdom originals at Saqqara and Abusir. However, such slavish copying is not usually the case. One can see a more original approach to using Egyptian models on the barque altar of Atlanersa from Gebel Barkal. Here the traditional Egyptian motif of the 'baptism of pharaoh' has been reworked into a propagandistic summary of royal power. What is evident here again is the defined physique, more reminiscent of Assyrian than Egyptian art.

In Nubia itself, both during the Twenty-fifth Dynasty and after, one can see a more distinctive Kushite art style. The royal sculptures from Gebel Barkal are different from those at Karnak, being more stylized both in their facial features and their exaggerated musculature. Carved out of

Figure 71. Granite gneiss barque stand of King Atlanersa, from Gebel Barkal. Photograph © 2012 Museum of Fine Arts, Boston.

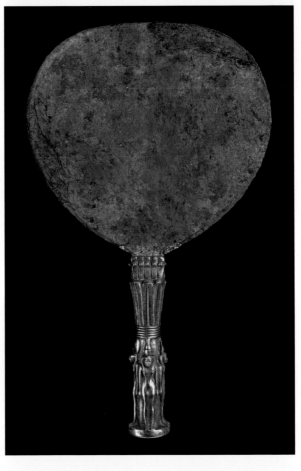

Figure 72. Gilded silver and bronze mirror of Shabaqo. Photograph © 2012 Museum of Fine Arts, Boston.

Figure 73. Quartzite statue of Horemakhet, son of Shabaqo and High Priest of Amun. Photo © Chester Higgins Jr 2012.

local gray granite, these fragmentary sculptures were found ritually buried in a number of pits in the temple precinct; presumably they had been smashed by the invading armies of Psamtik II. The two largest statues found represent Aspelta and Anlamani, standing. They depict the kings wearing the four ostrich plumes of Nubian royalty on their heads as well as the double uraeus, and have roughened areas on the crown, kilt, and where sandals, armbands, and three ram-pendant necklaces would have been covered with gold leaf.

A group of statues remarkably similar to these was found at Doukki Gel recently by Charles Bonnet. They too must have been destroyed by the invading Egyptians and interred in sacred ground. Even more recently, statues of Taharqo and Senkamanisken were uncovered at Dangeil, much farther south than large-scale Napatan remains heretofore had ever been found. These too had been smashed, but whether this was due to an Egyptian incursion this far south or for some other reason is unclear at the moment.

If this was the result of Psamtik's forces, then that would give added weight to the speculation that the political and cultural shift southward toward Meroe at the end of the Napatan Period was a response to the threat of another Egyptian attack. In any regard, the Napatan phase of the Second Kingdom of Kush gave way to the Meroitic, a far more eclectic and inventive era in Nubian art and culture.

Bibliography

Adams, W.Y. 1977. *Nubia, Corridor to Africa*. Princeton, NJ: Princeton University Press.

Bonnet, C., and D. Valbelle. 2006. *The Nubian Pharaohs: Black Kings on the Nile*. Cairo and New York: American University in Cairo Press.

Dunham, D. 1950. *Royal Cemeteries of Kush*. Vol. 1: El Kurru. Boston: Museum of Fine Arts.

———. 1970. *The Barkal Temples*. Boston: Museum of Fine Arts.

Josephson, J. 1997. "Egyptian Sculpture of the Late Period Revisited." *JARCE* 34:1–20.

Russmann, E.R. 1974. *The Representation of the King in the XXVth Dynasty*. Brussels and Brooklyn: Fondation égyptologique reine Elisabeth.

———. 1994. "Relief Decoration in the Tomb of Mentuemhat (TT34)." *JARCE* 31:1–19.

Wenig, S. 1978. *Africa in Antiquity: The Arts of Ancient Nubia and the Sudan*. Brooklyn: Brooklyn Museum.

The Art and Architecture of Meroitic Nubia

David O'Connor

The Kingdom of Kush, founded by the ancestors of the Twenty-fifth Dynasty, is divided into two phases named after the principal centers of power. The earlier Napatan Period was centered in the area of the Fourth Cataract around the city of Napata, the cemeteries of al-Kurru and Nuri, and the great temple complex at Gebel Barkal. Over time and for a number of reasons, the city of Meroe in the south began to eclipse Napata in importance, so much so that

Figure 74. The temple pylon at Naqa. Photo © Chester Higgins Jr 2012.

Figure 75. Meroe at sunset.
Photo © Chester Higgins Jr 2012.

the royal burial ground was shifted to the former. The southern ascendancy is known as the Meroitic Period, and it lasted some six hundred years (ca. 250 BC–AD 350), ruled by the heirs of the Napatan Dynasty. Their annals were written in Meroitic, a local language for which an alphabet had been invented by AD 100. In the preceding Napatan Period, Egyptian hieroglyphs were used for monumental inscriptions.

The territory covered by the Meroitic kingdom was perhaps even larger than that of the Napatan Period. It included Lower and Upper Nubia, and futher to the south, the 'Gezira,' or the Blue and White Niles and the territory between them. Sites partly or largely Meroitic in culture extend along the Blue Nile as far south as Sennar, about three hundred kilometers upstream, and the same may be true for the White Nile, though this area has yet to be fully explored.

In the north, Lower Nubia became increasingly important to the Meroites. Art and archaeology inform us about the lifestyles of Meroitic royalty, and representations of the kings and queens show them wearing distinctive clothing and regalia based on Egyptian costume, but adding a more original ensemble as time went on. Over most of the body was worn a close-fitting white robe topped with a fringed shawl dyed red and decorated with tassels, or, for more vigorous activities, a knee-length kilt. There was a variety of crowns, some modeled after those of an Egyptian pharaoh, but also a distinctive cap-like head covering, decorated with two uraci. Meroitic rulers additionally displayed a rich array of sumptuous jewelry, often bearing rams' heads, the emblem of the state god, Amun. The king was also often depicted with weapons: a bow and arrows, a sword slung in a scabbard across his back, or a spear.

The capital city Meroe, covering about one square mile, has not been fully excavated, but it is clear that there were not only large temples

Figure 76. Bronze hanging lamp with leaf handle and griffin-head hook. Photograph © 2012 Museum of Fine Arts, Boston.

Figure 77. The "Venus of Meroe."

but also clusters of palaces and other public and domestic buildings, including a Roman-style bath. The foundation of the town goes back to as early as 500 BC. It was also a center of iron-working, and large slag heaps and a smelting furnace were discovered within the boundaries of the city.

In the desert to the east of the city, along a series of desert scarps, were the royal tombs. The structures were always pyramidal, built either of

Figure 78. Painted and gilded glass chalice from a tomb in the western necropolis of Sedeinga. The inscription reads "Drink and you shall be alive!"

rough stone or masonry or, after AD 50, of red brick or rubble covered with plaster. Queens, princes, nobles, and even some commoners were also buried under pyramids, with an attached chapel like those found in association with the king's tomb. However, only the royal chapels were fronted by pylon gateways. The burial chambers were situated below ground and accessed by an external rock-cut stairway.

However important the king was, the world view of the Nubians was dominated by a pantheon of gods and goddesses. The king certainly had a unique relationship to these powerful beings, and in temples at least, he is the only one shown as performing the cultic rites for them. Isis, Amun, and Apedemak are the chief deities worshiped in the temple cults. Amun was the state god and had many temples throughout the land, but the one at the capital, Meroe, was the largest, as large as the great temple at Gebel Barkal. Isis's cult center was at Philae, where she was venerated by Nubian pilgrims as well as the Egyptians. Amun and Isis are shown in fully human form, but Apedemak, a local god, is shown with a lion's head and a human body or a serpentine form, perhaps influenced by the art of India. His principal temples lay in the south, at places like Meroe, Naqa, and Musawwarat al-Sufra. Other gods of Egyptian origin included Osiris, Anubis, Horus, and Mut, but some deities were purely Nubian, like Mash, whose cult is found so far only at one place, Karanog. Two other important gods were hunter gods of the desert, Arensnuphis and Sebiumeker, and are usually represented as guardian statues in front of temples.

Temples were constantly being built and rebuilt throughout Nubia, and some were in or near great cities, but temples were probably also associated with smaller settlements like Meinarti. The larger temples are better known and are generally of two basic types. One is Egyptian in style, with a pylon, forecourt, columned offering hall, and a sanctuary at the rear that was surrounded by smaller rooms. The other type is peculiar to Nubia and is composed of a single square chamber with a pylon-shaped entry. This sort of temple was probably constructed for many gods, but is particularly associated with Apedemak.

Although many of the Meroitic gods were Egyptian in origin, and some of the scenes on temple and funerary chapel walls, for example, follow Egyptian patterns, the Meroitic Period saw a much greater diversion from Egyptian canons than the Napatan Period. The dress and regalia worn by gods and kings may have been modeled on Egyptian prototypes, but they are far more elaborate and less formulaic than their pharaonic predecessors. Egyptian artistic conventions were changed, recombined, and joined with influences from the Hellenistic Mediter-ranean, as well as local traditions, to form a new stylistic vocabulary through which the Nubians could express their own world view.

In the north, Meroitic Lower Nubia flourished throughout the second and third centuries AD, but in the fourth century, political, social, and artistic traditions underwent large-scale change with the fall of Meroe and a shift of emphasis once again to the north. These later X-Group or 'post-Meroitic' societies moved even further away from Egyptian antecedents. The pyramid tomb was eventually abandoned, and there was a return to the mound or tumulus burial.

Meroitic painting and artistic traditions continued with the conversion of Nubia to Christianity and survived until the Islamic conquest of Nubia. Incorporated into the wider Islamic world, much of the distinctiveness of Nubian culture gradually faded away.

Bibliography

Adams, W.Y. 1977. *Nubia, Corridor to Africa.* Princeton, NJ: Princeton University Press.

O'Connor, D. 1993. *Ancient Nubia: Egypt's Rival in Africa.* Philadelphia: University Museum.

Shinnie, P. 1967. *Meroe: A Civilization of the Sudan.* New York and Washington: Praeger.

Wenig, S. 1978. *Africa in Antiquity: The Arts of Ancient Nubia and the Sudan,* vols.1–2. Brooklyn: Brooklyn Museum.

Woolley, C.L., and D. Randall-MacIver. 1911a. *Karanog, The Romano-Nubian Cemetery 1–2.* Eckley B. Coxe Jr. Expedition to Nubia, vols. 3–4. Philadelphia: University Museum.

———. 1911b. *Karanog, the Town.* Eckley B. Coxe Jr. Expedition to Nubia, vol. 5. Philadelphia: University Museum, University of Pennsylvania.

KINGS AND KINGSHIP
IN ANCIENT NUBIA

Robert G. Morkot

There are numerous texts from Egypt that illuminate aspects of kingship, but for the cultures of the Nile Valley south of Egypt, there is remarkably little. Much of what has been written about kingship in 'Nubia' has been influenced by Egyptian models, and by the work of Greek writers of the Hellenistic Period (ca. 300–30 BC). There have also been some presumptions by western scholars, based upon anthropological data and ideas of what is considered to be 'typical' of Africa. This has been particularly significant in the development of ideas about matrilineal succession.

Much of the direct evidence is therefore from archaeology and from depictions. Inevitably this is material that is—and has been—frequently analyzed subjectively rather than objectively. What is very clear from the evidence is that the Nile Valley south of Egypt, and the surrounding desert regions (particularly the Eastern Desert), had political units that responded to both Egyptian activities and to those of their other neighbors. These states expanded and absorbed others, and at times rivaled Egypt in power. They differed from Egypt in that they did not use writing in the same way as that highly bureaucratic society did.

From the earliest of Lower Nubia's archaeological periods, the A-Group, there is evidence from the enormous tumulus burials in the cemeteries at Qustul and Seyala. Their scale is generally accepted as indicative of rulers: whether we choose to style them 'chiefs' or 'kings' largely reflects our own attitudes. The burials at Qustul, near Abu Simbel, included artifacts that carried iconography that clearly related to the early Egyptian kingship, leading Bruce Williams, in a highly controversial study, to claim that the Egyptian pharaonic monarchy developed in Lower Nubia, rather than in Egypt itself. Williams's arguments were based on artifacts that were later shown to be Egyptian imports. Nevertheless, it is now agreed that the Qustul cemetery shows the emergence of a powerful state in Lower Nubia that was contemporary with the development of kingship in Egypt. Harry Smith re-examined the material from the cemetery of Seyala, also in Lower Nubia. This too contained imported material with Egyptian royal iconography. Smith argued that the Seyala 'chiefdom' or kingdom developed at the same time as the Qustul kingdom but was subsumed into the expanding Qustul state, which was itself destroyed by the Egyptians during the First Dynasty.

Egyptian texts of the later Old Kingdom refer

to the rulers of parts of Nubia, showing that despite Egyptian military actions in the First Dynasty, new states had developed throughout the Nile Valley and deserts. The Egyptians use the term *wer*, which is applied to foreign rulers in both Africa and Asia, but without any indication of the extent of their territories. The first chiefdoms or kingdoms named are Irtjet, Wawat, Yam, and Medja. The last of these, Medja, is certainly the Eastern Desert. In a long inscription of the Sixth Dynasty, the official Harkhuf gives accounts of his journeys into Nubia: these have been the subject of numerous attempts to identify where the places that he visited, notably Yam, were actually located. In the Nile valley south of Aswan, Harkhuf names Wawat, Irtjet, and Setju. Wawat was later used as the name of the Egyptian province between the First and Second Cataracts, but opinion is divided as to whether Irtjet and Setju were also between the First and Second Cataracts, or in the region farther south between the Second and Fourth Cataracts. By the last of Harkhuf's journeys, they had both been subsumed into Wawat. Yam, the focus of Harkhuf's expeditions, is even more difficult to locate, and places in the Nile Valley, the Butana, and to the west of the Nile have all been suggested. Many scholars have accepted the proposal of Karl-Heinz Priese that Yam should be identified with Kerma, and the later Meroitic toponym Ireme/Areme, but this too presents problems. What these late Old Kingdom Egyptian records do tell us is that the region to the south had a range of states, and that some of those states expanded and absorbed their neighbors.

A collection of documents from the late Old Kingdom and the Middle Kingdom, known as the Execration Texts, records foreign rulers who were considered to be enemies of Egypt. The texts are often written on models of bound captives, and were clearly used in rituals to control hostile forces. They carry the names of rulers and the territories

Figure 79. Bronze figure of King Taharqo, from Gebel Barkal, Great Temple of Amun, B 501. Photograph © 2012 Museum of Fine Arts, Boston.

that they ruled, and show a deep Egyptian knowledge of the political geography of parts of Nubia. Unfortunately, many of the territories named cannot be placed precisely. One state, Yam-nas, is said to have a female ruler, named Satjyt.

None of the Egyptian evidence gives us information on the way that the Nubian rulers displayed

Figure 80. Carnelian necklace with ram's-head pendant.

figures wearing the White Crown of Upper Egypt. The rulers named, however, are certainly not Egyptian kings. It seems likely that the Nubian rulers were following the model of Egypt. Some archaeologists think that the inscriptions belong to the period following the Middle Kingdom.

From southern Nubia, Kush, we have even richer evidence. In the northern part of the Dongola Reach of the Nile, south of the Third Cataract, the city of Kerma emerged as the focus of a powerful trading kingdom. Its origins lie in a much earlier period, whose archaeological levels are only now being examined, but it rose to its most powerful during the Twelfth Dynasty and succeeding Second Intermediate Period. At Kerma, a large royal audience hall was excavated. Rebuilt many times, it took the form of a vast circular hut, with a conical roof. Adjacent was a 'palace' complex built in mud brick, and showing the influence of Egyptian architects and techniques. The Kerma kingdom increased its power as the trading partner of Egypt in the Twelfth Dynasty, and eventually expanded to take control of Lower Nubia, and threatened Egypt itself. At its zenith, Kerma was trading directly with the Hyksos rulers of the Egyptian Delta. The kings were buried in vast tumuli, and numerous of their subjects were killed and buried with them. The kings are referred to in the Kamose Stela, an account of the expansion of the Theban kingdom against Kush and the Hyksos. From this it is clear that the Kushite king maintained diplomatic letter correspondence with the northern ruler and planned to invade southern Egypt. A stela from the fortress of Buhen, which had been taken over by the Kushites, shows us one of the kings, wearing the White Crown of Upper Egypt. The kingship therefore combined traditional elements—the audience hall and retainer burials—with aspects of iconography taken from the pharaonic monarchy. In Lower Nubia, there are more rock drawings that appear to show

their power, or what attributes they adopted; as yet, we have no images of these earliest rulers. With the Egyptian Middle Kingdom, our evidence grows richer. In Lower Nubia, a series of rock inscriptions probably belongs to the period of Egyptian expansion in the Eleventh and early Twelfth Dynasties. Egyptian texts record the conquest of Nubia between the First and Second Cataracts, and the opposition of local rulers. The rock inscriptions have cartouches in the conventional Egyptian style and are accompanied by local rulers, wearing the traditional feather head-dress; these were presumably subordinate to the Kerma kings.

Although the Egyptian pharaohs of the early New Kingdom did, after a long struggle, destroy the Kerma kingdom, they retained local rulers throughout Nubia. These *weru* are quite well documented, and their families were integrated into the Egyptian administration. The sons of rulers were taken to Egypt to be educated at the Egyptian court. In their own tombs, they are shown as Egyptian, in skin coloring (red-brown) and in costume. By contrast, in Egyptian scenes where they appear as foreign vassals of the pharaoh, they are depicted with dark-brown skin, and a mixed traditional (Nubian or Kushite) and Egyptian costume, with feather headdress, earrings, cheetah skins, and bead chokers. The Kushite word for 'king'—*kor* (later *qore*)—also appears in Egyptian texts at this time.

The emergence of kingship in Kush following the end of Egyptian rule around 1100 BC is still debated by archaeologists. The new Kushite kingdom adopted many features of the pharaonic kingship, but also shows indigenous traditions. Passing through the phases generally known as Napatan (ca. mid-eighth century to mid-third century BC) and Meroitic (ca. mid-third century BC–mid-fourth century AD), there are continuities, but numerous changes. Most importantly, a distinctive way of depicting rulers was developed around the time that the Kushite state expanded and conquered Egypt (ca. 710 BC), and this con-tinued in use, with some modifications.

The Napatan-Meroitic idea of the king showed him as muscular—physically powerful with broad chest and shoulders, narrow waist, and strong upper arms. The head is generally rather rounded and the neck quite long and straight. The principal item of regalia is a close-fitting cap, which usually has a diadem encircling

it, sometimes covered with rearing snakes. The other notable feature is the double uraeus: two rearing cobras on the king's forehead, their bodies weaving back over his head. Unlike an Egyptian pharaoh, the king is usually shown wearing large pendant earrings, which take the form of a ram's head (representing the god Amun) crowned with a solar disc. A cord with three rams' heads usually circles the king's neck. Later Meroitic kings are shown wearing a distinctive tasseled sash and a long fringed cloak, knotted on one shoulder.

Figure 81. Objects from the tomb of Aspelta (Nuri Pyramid 8). Photograph © 2012 Museum of Fine Arts, Boston.

The ideology of kingship certainly incorporated Egyptian elements, although whether this was consistent is impossible to know. The two Egyptian kingship traditions are used. In one the king appears as Horus, the son of the goddess Isis, and in the other he is the son of the god Amun and the queen. Inscriptions tell us that the kings (certainly down to around 300 BC) were crowned in the temple of Amun at Gebel Barkal and then visited the other temples of Amun (at Sanam, Kawa, and Pnubs) in the northern part of the kingdom.

Over the long span of the Napatan and Meroitic kingdoms, there may have been different tribal groups and dynasties with different traditions, but it is very difficult to penetrate the list of surviving royal names. There is no ancient king list, and it has to be reconstructed, primarily from the evidence from the royal cemeteries at Nuri, Barkal, and Meroe.

Hellenistic writers have caused problems in our understanding of kingship. One episode, relating to a Nubian king called Ergamenes, tells us that priests of Amun had the power to give the order when kings should die. The Greek writer relates that Ergamenes, who was a contemporary of Ptolemy II and had had a Greek education, went to the temple and slew the priests. As with so much in Greek writing on political systems, Meroe has been used as a location on the fringe of the known world in which to place a discussion of political philosophy: this episode is more about Greek culture than it is about Meroe. Yet, because there are similar Meroitic royal names (for example, Arkamani) of roughly the right period, scholars have argued that there was a historical foundation to this episode. They argue that this 'barbaric' practice was carried out only in the Late Napatan Period (itself seen, subjectively, as a low point based on the archaeological evidence). Anthropological parallels from more recent societies of southern Sudan and Uganda have also been brought into play. The Late Napatan Period can thus be argued to conform to our notions of what an African kingship *should* be like, even though there is no indigenous evidence to support the Greek writer.

Similar ideas have affected the interpretation of the evidence for female rulers and matrilineal succession. It has to be stressed that the existence of female rulers in any society is not necessarily connected with matrilineage. Indeed, matrilineage is usually a succession of *male* rulers who inherit through a female line, rather than from their fathers. In one type of matrilineal succession, a male ruler is succeeded by the son of his sister, practiced, for instance, among the Bemba of Zambia and the Kom Dynasty of Bamenda Grassfields (Cameroon).

The most influential discussion of matrilineage in Kush was appended to the translation of a group of inscriptions mostly of the reign of Taharqo (690–664 BC) excavated at Kawa. In two inscriptions, Taharqo states his relationship to an earlier Kushite king, Alara, which is through his own mother. This was combined with other genealogical material, and evidence relating to a group of royal women who officiated in the priestly capacity of 'God's Wife of Amun,' to argue that the kingship was matrilineal. One key Assyrian text tells us that Taharqo was succeeded by "his sister's son" Tanwetamani: so he may have been, but this may not have been the *reason* for the latter's succession. A key problem is that the terms of relationship employed in the texts (written in Egyptian) are extremely vague: 'sister,' 'son,' and 'brother' can all have far wider implications than the precise terms that we expect. What we can say about the Napatan Period is that royal women do figure quite prominently in texts and temple scenes. There was certainly an emphasis placed on female ancestors, but that does not necessarily indicate that the royal succession passed through the female line. The inscription of King Aspelta records the ancestry of his mother through the female line, but again, we do not know what the purpose of this text was, and even if it does relate to succession, it implies that many of these women were married to kings who would have been their (half-) brothers.

In most cases we do not know the relationship of a king to his predecessor, but we do know that most kings were sons of kings. Again this indicates that even if a matrilineal system was in place, most of the 'heiresses' were married to male relatives. Despite the difficulties presented by the archaeological and textual evidence, many scholars still insist on succession through the female line as a reality. This must, to some extent, be influenced by the idea of what we expect an African society to be like. Yet any examination of kingship throughout Africa shows that patrilineal succession is as frequent, if not more so, than matrilineal. It must also be noted that, irrespective of what underlying ideological base there may be, power struggles within the ruling family are to be expected.

A number of large royal inscriptions from Gebel Barkal and Kawa record the accession of kings, and these generally refer to the role played by the "royal brethren" and the army. They note the "election" of the ruler by his brethren and by the army, again glossing any assertion of power by the new king. The new king then traveled to Gebel Barkal to be acknowledged and accepted by the god Amun. It was there that he was crowned, and in one instance we are told that this was where the crowns of earlier kings were kept.

Royal women clearly played an important role in the early Napatan state, even if that role is rather difficult to interpret. The second historical period in which women figure very prominently is the second century BC to the first century AD. At this time, a number of women carried the title

rendered into Greek (and more recent European languages) as *kandake* (Candace). These women are referred to in Hellenistic and Roman literature as well as on indigenous monuments.

In one instance, Roman writers are dealing with contemporary events, and their accounts can be taken as having some, albeit biased, historical evidence. This episode follows the Roman capture of Egypt, and the defeat of Cleopatra. The Romans needed to consolidate their southern border, but were faced with an invasion of the Meroitic army. The army was led by the *kandake*, who is described as a woman of masculine appearance and blind in one eye. Ultimately peace was achieved by treaty,

Figure 82. Scene of the lion god Apedemak holding a lion and elephant on a leash, and worshiped by the king and queen. From the temple at Musawwarat.

and the Meroites gained what they wanted. There is undoubtedly a clear historical basis to this, but the choice of details and the prejudices of the author are interesting. The *kandake*, both during the events and in the narrative, must have been compared with that other powerful female threat the Romans had already faced in Egypt, Cleopatra. The Egyptian queen was portrayed as beautiful, clever, and politically astute; the Meroitic queen is placed within a different genre. In reality, she and her armies posed a serious threat to the security of Egypt's frontier.

Discussion of the role of the *kandake* has focused on her relationship to the *qore* (king): was the *kandake* (1) the wife of the *qore* and mother of the Crown Prince (or successor); (2) sister of the *qore* and mother of the Crown Prince; or (3) mother of the *qore*? At present, these questions remain unanswerable.

The religious role of the 'queen' was largely Egyptian-derived, or any local traditions were associated with Egyptian models. The queen represented the goddess Isis, as mother and protector of her son Horus. The king was also seen as the product of the union of the god Amun with the queen.

The problem of interpretation is that the Meroitic monuments generally promote the Egyptian elements of religion and ideology, but many other smaller objects (such as seal rings) show that there was a far more complex set of ideas underlying kingship. The Egyptian-style monuments are part of a process by which the earlier kings legitimized their rule in Egypt, which then became part of their own tradition.

One key indigenous aspect of kingship in the Meroitic Period was legitimacy through the god Apedemak. Although depicted in conventional Egyptian style with a lion head and human body, Apedemak was a god of the savannah lands around Meroe who had both solar (war) and lunar (agriculture) aspects. In temples from around 300 BC into the Roman Period, he is shown presenting the king with slaves, a large bow and arrows, and *dhurra* (millet), the staple crop.

The nature of the Nubian states, which do not appear to have had the large bureaucracy of Egypt, required strong rulers, and consequently the succession must have been dominated by power struggles within the ruling family. The king was both a military leader and priest. His power came from the Egyptian Amun and the indigenous lion god Apedemak, and Egyptian and indigenous influences are also reflected in the titles and iconography of the kingship. So many Egyptian features are present in the surviving Nubian monumental building that much of the indigenous element is either lost, or stands out as an 'unusual' element (such as the role of the *kandake*).

Bibliography

Lohwasser, A. 2001. "Queenship in Kush: Status, Role and Ideology of Royal Women." *JARCE* 38:61–76.

Morkot, R.G. 1991. "Nubia in the New Kingdom: The Limits of Egyptian Control." In W.V. Davies, ed., *Egypt and Africa: Nubia from Prehistory to Islam*, 294–301. London: British Museum Press.

———. 1999. "Kingship and Kinship in the Empire of Kush." In S. Wenig, ed., *Studien zum Antiken Sudan. Akten der 7. Internationalen Tagung für meroitistische Forschungen vom 14. bis 19. September 1992 in Gosen bei Berlin*, 179–229. Meroitica 15. Wiesbaden: Harrassowitz.

Smith, H.S. 1991. "The Development of the 'A-Group' Culture in Northern Lower Nubia." In W.V. Davies. ed., *Egypt and Africa: Nubia from Prehistory to Islam*, 92–111. London: British Museum Press.

Williams, B.B. 1980. "The Lost Pharaohs of Nubia." *Archaeology* 33:12–21.

———. 1986. *The A-Group Royal Cemetery at Qustul: Cemetery L*. Excavations between Abu Simbel and the Sudan Frontier, Part 1. *OINE* 3. Chicago: Oriental Institute.

NUBIAN RELIGION

Janice W. Yellin

The ancient Nubians worshiped their gods on hilltops and in caves as well as at the graves of their dead. Until the Egyptian conquest of Nubia in the New Kingdom, the ancient Nubians were non-literate. With the exception of the Kerma culture, they did not construct permanent religious structures until after the Egyptians began building temples in Nubia. So for the most part, until the Egyptian conquest, only their burials record their beliefs. This lack of texts and of physical evidence (other than from burials) means that elite Nubian religion is largely undocumented until the Napatans adopted Egyptian language and religion, and that evidence for non-elite religion is sparse in all periods. We do know that the magical belief in, and use of, objects and prayers to achieve a desired result was a pervasive part of its religious practices, and that images and words were imbued with the power to actualize the concepts or objects they referenced. The burials of all Nubians demonstrate that they believed in some form(s) of an afterlife and developed various burial customs to achieve it.

In those areas that the Egyptians eventually colonized, elite and non-elite religion developed separately, particularly during Egypt's New Kingdom. The religion of the governing elites reflected their extensive and knowledgeable *direct* contact with Egyptian religion. For the most part, non-elites had less contact with Egyptian religion, and so their beliefs did not become nearly as Egyptianized. However, certain Egyptian cults and burial practices were adopted by both groups. In the mid-eighth century BC this situation changed in terms of elite religion when the Napatan and then the ensuing Meroitic Dynasty 'officially' adopted Egyptian religion and language. Napatan elite religion mirrored Egypt's very closely, but during the Meroitic Period, there were local gods and Meroitic interpretations of Egyptian religion that revealed hitherto unknown indigenous beliefs. Reconstructing ancient Nubian religion during these two dynasties challenges us to find the indigenous gods and practices underlying the ones elites adopted from the Egyptians, while also searching the archaeological record for information as to the beliefs of ordinary Nubians. After the Meroitic Period, Egyptian influences disappeared and indigenous features again dominated elite and non-elite burials and everyday cults.

Figure 83. Napatan gilded silver figure of Amun.

The Impact of Egypt upon Nubian Religion during the New Kingdom

Egyptians formally introduced their religion into Nubia when they built temples at their First and Second Cataract trading forts during the Middle Kingdom. Political, economic, and social connections with Egypt were intensified when Nubia became a province during the New Kingdom. A number of large and small temples, which were dedicated to Egyptian gods and rulers, decorated by Egyptians, and staffed by their priests, were built throughout Nubia as far south as Napata. These spread official pharaonic state religion among the population, while non-official Egyptian beliefs entered Nubian popular religion through the intermarriage of local women with the Egyptian soldiers and workers who lived in Nubia.

For the most part, the Egyptian gods adopted by Nubians underwent a 'Nubianization.' Many were associated with pre-existing Nubian deities and developed new qualities and iconography as a result. The cult of Amun is a good example of this process. Of the Egyptian gods worshiped by Nubians, Amun was the most prominent and deeply entrenched. In his Egyptian form, he is pictured as a human-headed male, but by the New Kingdom, he was worshiped by Egyptians and Nubians as a ram or a ram-headed male who was associated with fertility and water (= the Nile inundation). These traits developed from Amun's absorption of indigenous Nubian ram deities, such as the ram god(s) at Kerma, who were associated with fertility and water. (Although numerous images and objects representing rams and ram-headed deities span many centuries, the lack of textual materials makes it difficult to ascertain whether these represent multiple ram gods or different manifestations of a single one.) During the New Kingdom, distinctive Nubian Amun cults were connected to particular temples, the most important of which was at Gebel Barkal

(Napata). There were also Nubian gods 'shared' by both cultures. Dedwen, a god originally from Lower Nubia, was an ancient falcon god linked to Horus in Egypt and later in Nubia. Egyptians and Nubians worshiped Anukis and Satis, who are typically paired with another ram-headed god associated with water, Khnum. This trio, from the First Cataract region, was associated with the source of the Nile's annual inundation that was believed to originate in this area.

The period following Egypt's withdrawal at the end of the New Kingdom is considered a 'dark age' because of the lack of written texts and archaeological remains. Nubia is thought to have reverted to simpler political units and to have lost contact with Egyptian traditions, including religious ones. However, current research is demonstrating that this perception is not accurate. The Semna Temple text of the Nubian Queen Kadimalo has been interpreted by John Darnell to reflect an organized Nubian state in the Second Cataract region that continued to honor Egyptian gods during Egypt's Twenty-first Dynasty, but the dating of this inscription has been questioned by Karola Zibelius-Chen. Tombs at Hillat al-Arab near Napata, published by Irene Vincentelli, which contained Egyptian religious elements, were in use from the Nineteenth Dynasty until the beginning of the Napatan Period, and demonstrate a complex social organization and ongoing Egyptian influence on Nubian religion during this 'dark age.'

Napatan Period Elite Religion

The dating of the first Napatan Dynasty burials at al-Kurru is controversial, but evidence currently supports an early to mid-eighth century BC date for the tomb of Alara, the ancestor of the dynasty. The earliest types of burials were indigenous, but within a few generations, royal tombs evolved into pyramid burials. Concurrently, elite religion

Figure 84. Twenty-fifth Dynasty wooden ram's head. Photograph © 2012 Museum of Fine Arts, Boston.

became Egyptianized, and Egyptian-style temples dedicated to Egyptian gods were constructed at a number of sites. Early Napatan kings might have adopted Egyptian religion because it offered them prestige and a model for the development of a theocratic centralized state. Napatan state religion, particularly the cult of Amun, was focused on establishing and supporting the divine basis for kingship. However, elite Nubians also demonstrated a long-held and genuine devotion to Egyptian gods, many of whom had been worshiped in Nubia for a millennium. How thoroughly these ideas, drawn on Egyptian religion, penetrated into the general population is not clear, and the members of the literate priestly class who shaped and actively supported the state cults constituted a very small percentage of the population.

As in Egypt, Amun, chief of the gods, was the sovereign's 'divine father' who expressly selected and gave him kingship. Amun's main consort was Mut, but occasionally she was replaced by one of the Egyptian/Nubian goddesses, Satis or Anukis. The ruler's power was affirmed during coronation ceremonies at Amun's major temples. Once crowned, rulers built or renovated Amun's temples to underscore their relationship to him. The ancestor of the Twenty-fifth Dynasty kings, Alara, who introduced this Egyptian model for legitimating his descendants, built a temple at Kawa, and succeeding rulers built, expanded, or renovated temples in Kush and Egypt. After the Napatan conquest of Egypt, royal daughters became the God's Wife of Amun (his high priestess) in Thebes, another example of the Napatans' clever exploitation of Amun's theology for dynastic purposes. Amun of Napata was the most important of the Nubian Amuns. As early as the New Kingdom, Gebel Barkal—the large mountain near Napata—was considered his birth and dwelling place by the Egyptians, who paired him with the human-headed Amun of Thebes. The clear distinction made by the Egyptians between Amun of Thebes and the ram-headed Amun(s) indicates their consciousness of the gods' indigenous origins. The Amun Temple at Barkal was supported by a considerable priesthood and was a vibrant religious center whose impact on Nubian state religion was profound.

The custom of associating a god, most notably Amun, with a particular site or shrine was a consistent feature in Nubian religion that continued through the Meroitic Period. The localization (= 'the capture') of deities at specific sites, through the construction of shrines in their honor, still occurs in modern southern Sudan, as recorded by the anthropologist Douglas Johnson. At each modern site, a clan has constructed and maintained one or more shrines, giving that clan a special claim both to the god and to the territory placed under the god's dominion by their shrine(s). For semi-nomadic people, this is a way to establish a claim to territory they may not occupy continuously, or to identify a territory to which they wish to stake a claim. Ceremonial meetings at these

shrines also provide an opportunity for both newly formed and pre-established clan groupings to be integrated into their larger community. Since some members of ancient Nubian society were also clan-based and/or semi-nomadic, their identification of a god with a particular shrine/locale may reflect the same dynamic. If so, then Amun of Kawa was a god localized at Kawa whose shrine 'identified' a territory belonging to a different clan than the territory claimed by the clan who established a shrine to Amun at Pnubs (Doukki Gel, near Kerma). The inclusion of localized aspects of gods in the Napatan pantheon provided a way through which the kings brought established clans under their control.

In addition to Amun, three Egyptian mother goddesses, Mut, Hathor, and Isis, were particularly prominent. All were associated with the queen mother through her important role in the birth and legitimation of the rulers, and as a result their cults eventually merged, with Isis becoming the most visible of the three. As the consort of Amun, the vulture goddess Mut played a significant role in the myth of royal legitimation, which was celebrated in her speos (rock-cut) temple at Gebel Barkal (B 300). Like Amun, she had various aspects linked to different cult places (that is, 'Mut of Thebes,' 'Mut of Napata,' and 'Mut of Nubia'). When shown with Amun, Mut was a human-headed female wearing a vulture headdress, a crown also worn by queens. By the Meroitic Period, Mut was overshadowed by Isis, with whom she shared a number of attributes. Hathor, as 'mistress of gold,' was first introduced by Egyptian gold mining expeditions into Nubia, but it was as the mother of Horus, the divine aspect of the living ruler, that she earned her place in Napata. In kingship theology, she was closely associated with Isis, and their identities blended. Isis was often depicted wearing Hathor's crown of cow horns surmounted by a disc. Napatan queens typically wore this crown with two feathers.

Isis was the most important of the Kushite goddesses. Her cult was so well established by the New Kingdom that the Egyptians gave her the title 'Mistress of Kush.' By Egypt's Third Intermediate Period, she had evolved into a demiurge who was 'mistress of heaven, earth, and the underworld.' The Nubians' devotion was based in part on the broad appeal of these beliefs, which they encountered through their involvement in Nubian temples, particularly at Philae, but also on the universal appeal of Isis as an all-encompassing mother goddess. Her protection of both the living and the dead made her one of the few gods worshiped by all Nubians. Within state religion, her theology had developed to the point that, as the mother of the living Horus (ruler), she was linked to Amun, his divine father, rather than to her husband, Osiris. As the ruler's mythic mother, Isis conveyed divine kingship by nursing him. When the monarch was crowned, the queen mother needed to be present and was specifically identified as Isis, who had nursed and protected her son Horus (the king). The identification of the queen mother with Isis, who bestowed and legitimated kingship, created a divine basis for a king's power.

Figure 85. Relief of Satet, Horus, and Isis from the Lion Temple at Musawwarat al-Sufra. Photo © Chester Higgins Jr 2012.

Figure 86. Unfinished granite stela with the figure of Osiris, from the chapel of the Pyramid of Senkamanisken at Nuri. Photo © Chester Higgins Jr 2012.

As in Egypt, Horus had different personae based on whether he was considered the son of Hathor or of Isis and Osiris. Several were adopted in Nubia, most notably the infant Horus, who was nursed and protected by Isis, and the adult Horus (a falcon or falcon-headed human wearing the double crown of the pharaoh), who avenged Osiris's murder and assumed the throne. Napatan kings were particularly linked to Horus when their legitimacy was being stressed.

Other Napatan-Egyptian gods included Anukis, Satis, Bastet, Bes, Onuris, and Thoth. Satis and Anukis both sometimes appeared as Amun's consorts. Anukis had her own cult at Kawa, where she appeared as his consort and was accompanied by Satis, who completed a divine family triad. The relative prominence of Bastet and Bes in Nubia, as compared to Egypt, sug-

gests that, like Amun and Isis, these deities had characteristics in common with Nubian gods. The cat goddess, Bastet, had a temple at Tare that was visited by the new ruler during his coronation journey, indicating that her cult played an important role in kingship theology. Elite Napatan names included hers, and Bastet amulets were found in elite graves. Bes was a minor deity in official Egyptian religion but was popular in its folk religion, where he was associated with the protection of women in childbirth. This latter role may account for his presence in Mut's (a divine mother) Gebel Barkal temple. Bes amulets were also placed on bodies, so his protective role appears to have been given a fairly broad application. Dietrich Wildung suggested in 2004 that his popularity may be due to his Nubian origins, as is suggested by his Egyptian titles 'Lord of Punt' and 'Ruler of Nubia.' He was depicted frontally as a squatting male with a semi-human face on a lion's head, a type of representation that may reflect an original association with magical practices and/or his foreign (possibly Nubian) origins. Onuris, a hunter god, was a consort of Hathor when she was linked with Tefnut, an aspect of Hathor that was particularly associated with Nubia in the Egyptian myth of the Eye of Re. Thoth, most prominently worshiped in Egypt as the ibis-headed god of writing, appeared infrequently in Nubian temples in this role. Instead, he appears more often as a giver of ritual purification alongside Horus during the king's coronation. This was a secondary role in Egypt, indicating that his role in kingship dogma was more important in Nubia.

Napatan state gods were worshiped either in temples dedicated to them or as guests in temples to which there was a theological connection. Freestanding temples, their organization and ceremonies followed Egyptian models. Amun temples were the most numerous. The idea of creating permanent, interior spaces within which a god was housed and worshiped was not inherently Nubian. Taharqo had to import Egyptians to construct temples and to instruct the Nubian elite on their rituals. As in Egypt, Napatan temples had large gateways (pylons) leading to an open courtyard followed by a hypostyle hall, pronaos, and then sanctuary. Only their gateways and courtyards were accessible to the public, and the placement of large royal statues in public areas suggests that the ruler would have been worshiped by the populace as a divine intermediary, according to László Török. Napatans also built rock-cut (speos) temples, such as the Mut Temple at Gebel Barkal (see "Nubian Popular Religion," below).

Temples and their priesthoods played a role in the political life of the Napatan state. The king was selected from a pool of candidates by the priests of Amun at Gebel Barkal, demonstrating how politically powerful this priesthood was. Many other temples were also powerful and wealthy, since the ruler gave them endowments of land, cattle, and people to support their activities, particularly after a military victory. Priests were organized into classes, each of which had a different status and set duties within the temples. High-ranking royal males, including princes, served as important priests. Queens and kings' sisters served as priestesses for Isis and other goddesses. Females, royal and otherwise, were the musicians of temple rituals and are shown playing sistra (rattles) while pouring libation offerings for the god(s).

Temple activities and festivals followed Egyptian models; however, the daily offering rites to the temple's god(s) appear to have been less important and complex. Cyclical festivals with processions of priests carrying a barque with the god's image from the temple along a preordained route were important. Night processions lit by torches and oil lamps must have been particularly dramatic for those who witnessed them. Almost every Napatan temple had a sanctuary in which its processional barque could be kept, and kiosks stood before temples to house the barques during festivals when they would leave the confines of the temple proper. Most official festivals were to ensure the fertility of the land and its ruler, as well as to (re-)legitimate royal power. The New Year Festival was perhaps the most important of these, because it linked the annual renewal of royal power with the annual inundation of the Nile. Amun and Isis in particular had processions as part of their cultic celebrations. The prominence given to processions suggests they were an indigenous religious practice that was shared with, rather than derived from, Egypt (see "Nubian Popular Religion").

As noted, permanent freestanding temples do not appear to be indigenous and were not built by Nubians before the Early Napatan/Dynasty Twenty-five period in Kush. Instead, natural settings, notably caves and hilltops, were indigenous places of worship. It is also likely that shrines built of perishable materials were erected at sacred locales. The Napatans constructed speos temples that had freestanding or rock-cut façades behind which sanctuaries were cut into the cliff or hillside. Speos temples might have developed from the tradition of worshiping in caves. The speos temples in Gebel Barkal testify to the numinous power of this sacred mountain. There is evidence at Barkal and other locations that a sacred cave predated some speos temples. The numbers of New Kingdom Nubian speos temples, including Abu Simbel, have led Egyptologist Robert Bianchi to propose that this temple type originated there and was adopted by the Egyptians. Whatever its origins, the chronological range and numbers of these cave-like temples demonstrate how meaningful they were to Nubians.

Napatan Period Elite Funerary Religion

Elite beliefs about the afterlife and how to achieve it were based on Egyptian ones. At the beginning of the Early Napatan/Dynasty Twenty-five period in Kush, pyramids (derived from private Egyptian New Kingdom pyramid burials in Nubia) and mastaba-type superstructures replaced tumuli burials; mummies in coffins replaced shroud-wrapped bodies resting on beds, and rituals of food offerings to sustain the dead were changed to follow Egyptian practices. In royal burials, Susan Doll (2008) has demonstrated that Egyptian concepts were expressed by the knowledgeable use of ancient mortuary texts from Egyptian temple archives. Napatan texts, particularly those from Taharqo's lakeside temple at Karnak, indicate that the merging of Amun-Re and Osiris that occurred during the Third Intermediate Period in Thebes was also incorporated into the Napatan cult of Osiris. Osiris had a number of cult places in Nubia, and the deceased was identified with Osiris who, according to Egyptian traditions, was mummified, buried, and cared for by his wife Isis along with Anubis, the god of the necropolis. Isis was invoked as the protector of the dead. Anubis was her companion and fellow offering-giver. The disappearance of all evidence for mummification shortly after the end of the Napatan Period indicates that it did not become a true part of Nubian funerary practices. However, animal offerings/ sacrifices of cattle, and more rarely horses, continued to be a traditional Nubian element in wealthy burials.

Meroitic Period Elite Religion

During the Meroitic Period, the capital moved from Napata to Meroe, a regional center in the southern half of the country. Far from the epicenter of Egyptian religious traditions at Napata, and perhaps belonging to a different ethnic or family group from the Napatans, the Meroitic elite followed a religious path less attuned to these traditions. Nubian gods and cultic practices became a more prominent component of official and popular religion against a backdrop of Egyptian religious influence that waxed and waned over the course of the Meroitic Period. The Egyptian influences were most felt during periods when Meroitic rulers built temples in Lower Nubia, priests served at Philae, and royal ambassadors and pilgrims visited Egyptian Nubian temples, particularly the Isis Temple at Philae. During some of these periods, such as the mid-third century BC and early first century AD, religious monuments and texts demonstrated a 'scholarly' interest in pharaonic Egyptian religion that derived in part from the use of Egyptian temple archives, but at the same time there were indigenous practices shared by all classes of Meroitic society (see "Nubian Popular Religion"). As a result, Meroitic state religion and, to a lesser extent, popular religion, was a dynamic mix of indigenous, pharaonic, and Greco-Roman Egyptian beliefs.

Our understanding of Meroitic religion is imperfect because of the near total absence of translatable texts. Fortunately, ongoing research and excavations are offering new information. A plaque discovered by Dietrich Wildung at Naqa in 2000 and published in 2004 finally revealed the name of the shadowy goddess, Amesemi, who is the lion god Apedemak's consort. A god's name from an inscription found at Qasr Ibrim might, according to Karl-Heinz Priese, belong to a Meroitic version of Bes, indicating a hitherto unknown cult place and priesthood. As more such discoveries are made, Meroitic religion will be better understood.

Of the Napatan-Egyptian gods worshiped by Meroitic elites, Amun remained important, but the status of other gods changed. Mut became less prominent, while Anubis, Thoth, and Nephthys grew in stature. The appearance of indigenous gods, including a lion-headed, bellicose god originating near Meroe called Apedemak, is particularly notable. Amun's worship as an independent deity may have become less robust as the Meroitic Period progressed. His temple at Barkal continued to function, but it had lost its central role in the political/religious life of the Nubian state. Although there were Amun temples in the Meroitic heartland, most notably at Meroe and Naqa, he did not appear to develop particularly vibrant local southern forms (that is, Amun of Meroe). Even in the south, he was worshiped primarily as Amun of Napata or Amun of Thebes. Although the Meroitic state continued for two more centuries, the last Amun temples were constructed in the second half of the first century AD by the rulers Amanitore and Natakamani, who were noted Egyptophiles. Amun's primacy as the royal dynastic god was challenged by Apedemak, who also appears in temple scenes legitimating and empowering the ruler. When Amun appears in temple scenes pertaining to royal power, he sometimes holds objects associated with Apedemak. Furthermore, Amun's associations with water and fertility were given new emphasis in his Naqa Temple, because these were traits he shared with Apedemak.

Isis vied with Amun and Apedemak for prominence in official religion and may well have overshadowed them among the non-elite population. Within royal circles, as a mother goddess and the mother of Horus, her cult continued to shape the role of the King's Mother. Isis had temples in Meroe and Qasr Ibrim, had places as a guest in other temples, and had priests who were called 'King's Son' (a reference to her role as the mother of the ruler). In non-mortuary contexts, as the royal mother, Isis was linked with Apedemak or Amun rather than Osiris. As a companion to Apedemak, she absorbed his bellicose qualities and so was shown offering the sovereign arrows and prisoners. The tendency to

consider Isis as a demiurge, already visible during the Napatan Period, reached its full development. Hailed as 'mistress of heaven, mistress of the underworld,' she was a deity who offered protection in both life and death. Meroitic priests served in her temple at Philae, which was also a major pilgrimage site. The annual boat pilgrimages of her statue from Philae to the temples at Debod and Dakka would have made her cult accessible and vivid to the general population.

Hathor was far less prominent than Isis, and when represented in temples, she seemed to exist primarily as a counterpoint to Isis. There is no evidence of an independent cult site. Based on depictions of Hathor on jewelry belonging to the ruling queens Amanishakheto and Shanakdakheto, Hathor appears to have had a particular relationship to them, perhaps in her role as a divine mother. There are occasional references to Mut as a mother goddess associated with the queen, but her importance diminished after the Napatan Period.

Horus continued to be revered in ways already known from the Napatan Period, most notably as the son of Hathor or Isis and as the protector of the ruler. He also had a number of distinct local cults, but no known temple can be associated with them, perhaps because he was worshiped in indigenous, perishable shrines at these sites. As in contemporary Egypt, Horus was depicted as a divine child who was nursed by Isis or as an adult falcon-headed male with warrior aspects. As royal gods, he and Thoth were shown with the new ruler in temple coronation scenes. While little is known about Thoth, he did have an important and wealthy cult center at Pnubs, so Thoth might have even been more prominent in Nubia than Horus. Thoth was also occasionally depicted in southern Meroitic temples as the scribe of the gods, and also appears as a baboon, but in this form his cult is obscure. Jaroslaw

Lewczuk notes only three examples of Thoth as a baboon, a statuette from Faras and two grafitti from the Great Enclosure at Musawwarat al-Sufra. The small statuette from Faras shows Thoth in the role of a scribe.

Bes appeared in a variety of locales. In temples, he is found most notably on pillars (temple at Wad ban Naqa) and on column bases (Meroe KC 104). The introduction of Dionysus's cult into Meroe, and his resemblance to figures in Dionysus's entourage of satyrs, might explain the depiction of Bes in contexts in which there were references to Dionysus, such as the 'Royal Bath' at Meroe. Given his associations with childbirth, other locales in which Bes appeared may have been female cult places.

Indigenous Cults

Apedemak, the most important indigenous god, was represented as a lion, or more often as a lion-headed Egyptian-style god. He also had a rarer indigenous form as a lion-headed snake that appears in his Lion Temple at Naqa and in a burial from Semna South. His numerous temples are all in the Butana region from which he originated. Apedemak's southern origin is reflected in the near absence of his cult in the northern half of the country and his continued worship in the area around Meroe into the late Meroitic/post-pyramid period (post AD 350). His earliest known temple at Musawwarat al-Sufra is dated to ca. 220 BC, but given his local origins, he was probably worshiped earlier in the Butana region. Of particular interest are two rock shrines that were carved in the hillside above Temple F (Naqa 500) at Naqa that were noted by Inge Hofmann and Herbert Tomandl. Each contained a rock-carved frontal face of a lion (=Apedemak), representing a rare example of an indigenous god in an indigenous setting. A later Lion Temple (15 BC–AD 15) proves that Apedemak had an enduring cult at this locale.

As a warrior/hunter god who defended the ruler, destroyed royal enemies, and conferred divine kingship, Apedemak often carried a bow and arrows and offered prisoners to the ruler. Like Amun, he was a creator god associated with fertility and water, particularly the Nile's annual inundation. As noted, Apedemak sometimes replaced or paralleled Amun in the state religion. In this context, Isis would be paired with him, as well as with Amun. In other contexts, he had a distinctly Meroitic consort, Amesemi, who wore short curly hair or a snug cap surmounted by two falcons on a crescent.

The gods Sebiumeker and Arensnuphis, who (re-)emerged in the Meroitic Period, were often paired. Enigmatic in origin, neither has yet been associated with a particular cult temple in Meroitic territory. Their images flanked, or were placed over, temple entrances so that they could serve as guardians, perhaps because of their shared aspects as warriors and hunters. Of the two, Sebiumeker is not as well documented. His name, which was Egyptian, may have been written as Sabomakal in Meroitic. Worshiped as a life giver (through association with the Egyptian god Atum) and a warrior, he typically appeared in human form wearing a short kilt, the double crown of Egypt, and the divine beard. He may have had an important place as a 'guest,' so to speak, in a Musawwarat al-Sufra temple. His better-known companion, Arensnuphis, was depicted in either human or lion form. When shown in human form, he wore a short kilt, a tall feather crown, and divine beard. He had a temple at Philae and so was sometimes associated with Isis. Egyptian texts also associated him with the Egyptian/Nubian god Dedwen, who was also from this region, and Egyptian and Meroitic references suggest a connection to the hunting god, Onuris. There are conflicting theories as to whether he was originally Egyptian or Kushite, in part because his name is Egyptian and means 'good companion' *(iry hms nefer)*. How-

ever, whether this was his original name, or if this was a later change from a Nubian name, is uncertain. Arensnuphis was worshiped in both Nubian and Ptolemaic temples of the First to Second Cataract region, adding to the uncertainty concerning his origins.

Satis and Anukis were recognized by Meroites as gods of the First Cataract region, and along with an obscure Meroitic goddess, Miket, they continued their association with the ram-headed god Khnum. Satis and Anukis were mentioned in several inscriptions as divine relations/protectors of the ruler.

There are a number of Meroitic gods whose names, but little else, are known. Mandulis and Aqedise (perhaps a form of the moon god Khonsu) were obscure Meroitic deities, and an inscription of an official from Karanog, Haramadeye, refers to other obscure gods (Mash, Ariten, Amanete, and Makedeke), which, as Derek Welsby pointed out, further demonstrates how much remains to be learned about Meroitic religion.

Figure 87. Sandstone corbel with the ram-headed Amun flanked by two manifestations of Apedemak, from Temple 100 at Musawwarat al-Sufra. Photo © Chester Higgins Jr 2012.

Hellenistic Cults

Hellenistic gods, most notably Serapis and Dionysus, joined the Meroitic pantheon as a result of Meroe's contact with the Mediterranean world via Ptolemaic and Roman Egypt. Serapis did not appear as an independent deity, suggesting that he never developed a true cult in Meroe. His occasional images and inscriptions identify him primarily with Amun, but on at least one occasion he was linked with Apedemak, which reflected Serapis's status in Egypt as the Ptolemaic dynastic god. Most of his appearances were in minor contexts, primarily on rings and amulets. Dionysus, however, did have a cult. As in contemporary Egypt, he was identified with Osiris, because he was a god of fertility who offered his followers an opportunity for rebirth. The full extent of his worship is uncertain, but there is evidence that it was long lived, since he figured in decorations from the first phase of the enigmatic 'Royal Baths' at Meroe (ca. second century BC) and in a royal palace at Gebel Barkal (early first century AD).

Temples

A traditional Egyptian ground plan was used in only a handful of Amun Temples. Most other temples contained one sanctuary (naos) or two rooms (pronaos and naos). Many were built on podia with ramps leading to their entrances, a design that might have been meant to evoke the indigenous practice of worshiping on sacred high places. Occasionally a temple had more than one naos to house one or more guest gods. The most complex, dramatic podium temple was the 'Sun Temple' at Meroe. Speos temples, probably also Nubian in origin, continued to be constructed for local forms of Amun, whose cults survived because of their local origins. At Gebel Qeili, a cave shrine with decoration depicting a Meroitic queen and prince before the ram-headed Amun of Napata demonstrates that the indigenous custom of worshiping in natural sacred places continued to play a part in official religion, while daily rites in state temples continued to focus on offerings for the temples' god(s). Central to these rites was a libation ritual that served as an offering while consecrating the other gifts upon which it was poured. Wine and milk libations were often given, but in this desert country, cool water was the most important libation.

Each temple's calendar included weekly and monthly temple feasts, as well as larger annual festivals. In Meroe, the New Year Festival and perhaps the Choiak Festival, both from Egypt, celebrated and linked the rebirth of Osiris to agrarian renewal and royal legitimacy. Processions, during which the gods' boats were carried into and through public spaces, played an important role in all festivals, and there were processional ways at Meroe leading from the royal enclosure to temples. There were also royal processions. A ruler's reign began and ended with processions at his/her coronation and funeral. Processions created experiences in which communal and personal religious expressions were conjoined.

Supporting royal power and control remained the major focus of official religion and its temples. One Meroitic innovation was the construction of large temple complexes for the state gods, including Amun and Apedemak at Musawwarat al-Sufra, Naqa, and Basa. Their location in arid locations in the Butana to the east and southeast of Meroe, away from major population centers, suggests that they were used to bringing the pastoralists who lived on the edges of the Meroitic polity under some degree of state control because, as convincingly argued by David N. Edwards, Meroitic society appeared to have been organized in sedentary and semi-nomadic clan groups. Each of these temple complexes had at least one large *hafir* (water reservoir) that was used by semi-nomadic pastoralists for their herds. Small

Apedemak temples also had *hafirs* in a more modest, but still effective, iteration of state control. The temples and their decoration presented the Meroitic rulers and state gods as the providers of these *hafirs*. Most of the scenes carved on the temples' inner and outer walls depicted rites that legitimated and demonstrated aspects of royal power. Large images and statues of the rulers were placed at the temples' gateways and in their outer courtyard(s). Since commoners only had access to these areas and not to the gods within the temples, these impressive royal images were worshiped as intermediaries to the temple's gods. In addition, larger religious complexes, such as Musawwarat al-Sufra and Naqa, probably also served as pilgrimage centers for the more settled, agrarian population. The large Meroitic temple complexes could have functioned much like some modern shrines in the southern Nile Valley, in that both these modern and ancient religious centers served as gathering places for various social, economic and/or ethnic groups during important religious events. At these times, the differences between these groups would be mediated so that they could be incorporated into a coherent social entity.

Meroitic Period Elite Funerary Religion

Isis, Osiris, and Anubis were the primary mortuary gods. The deceased became Osiris after burial and so was depicted as Osiris on his funerary monuments. In prayers and images, Isis overshadowed Osiris, since Osiris (= the deceased) was only the passive recipient of her offerings and protection. Her popularity was fed by her cult at Philae, where hundreds of Egyptian and Meroitic pilgrims watched as her statue left the temple every ten days to give offerings at the nearby tomb of Osiris. Anubis shared this rite with Isis, and through his associations with her and with cattle he became responsible for providing sustenance

in the afterlife. In elite funerary contexts, other gods, such as Horus and Thoth, appeared in secondary roles. Horus was a protector and offering giver. Thoth, who was always paired with Horus in royal chapel offering scenes, also made separate appearances proclaiming the funerary offerings to be given as part of the burial rituals in those same chapels, a role derived from Egypt. The cult of Dionysus, which also offered its initiates an afterlife, appears to have made some inroads in the funerary religion. Grapevines and grapes decorated at least one royal pyramid chapel in Meroe as well as some offering tables, particularly in Nubia.

Like their predecessors, Meroites believed that their afterlife depended on the provision of food and drink to sustain it. Evidence from their burials, most particularly the disappearance of mummification after the early Meroitic Period, indicates that the crucial transformation to the afterlife was not achieved through rituals associated with mummification, but most likely by rituals that were performed at the time of burial. Even in elite burials, the multiple reuses of tombs, and the careless handling of the bodies already within them, indicate that after a burial was completed, as Claudia Näser has noted, the physical remains of the dead were unimportant. Although the afterlife did not rely on the mummification and continued existence of an earthly body, the deceased was still identified with Osiris and nurtured by Anubis and Isis.

Egyptian influences on mortuary religion were more prevalent in the northern than in the southern half of the country, and a number of elite cemeteries with Egyptian-style pyramid and mastaba burials were found in Upper and Lower Nubia. Extended burials and the use of coffins reflect the contemporaneous influence of Egyptian burial customs. In the south, elite burials influenced by Egyptian religion were found only in and around Meroe; otherwise, various types of indigenous burial customs prevailed.

Thanks to the scenes carved in the royal and elite pyramid chapels and additional evidence from elite graves, we can reconstruct what their burials might have been like. On the day of interment, the deceased was accompanied to his/her tomb by a procession that could include palm-branch-bearing clan members, courtiers, ululating dancers, and drummers, as well as cattle and fowl to be sacrificed as offerings. At the tomb, priests impersonating Isis, Anubis, and other gods made offerings and poured libations. Before or after these offerings, the body was placed in the tomb with food and possessions. Human sacrifices, also known from the Kerma period, were possibly made as part of a small number of elite burials at Meroe's Western Cemetery. The limited temporal and geographic distribution of this rite throughout ancient Nubian history has led Török to suggest that human sacrifice may have been practiced only by certain ethnic/clan groups.

In a final communion with the deceased, members of the community shared a funerary meal that ended with a ritual of 'breaking of the pots,' both of which were ancient and widespread Nubian traditions. The meal's remains and broken ceramics were placed before the sealed tomb entrance prior to filling in its access ramp. A superstructure, which often included a small chapel or niche on its east side, was then constructed over the wealthier graves. To provide for ongoing offerings, an offering table and stela carved with offering scenes and prayers were placed in the offering area. Sometimes a *ba*-bird statue, which was a human-headed bird representing a spiritual aspect of the owner, looked down on the offering area from a niche cut into the superstructure's east face. When the superstructure was completed, rites finalizing the burial process might have been performed in the offering area.

The end of the Meroitic Dynasty marked, for the most part, the end of millennia of Egyptian religious influence in Nubia. Temples were no longer built, existing ones were abandoned, and indigenous burial customs were the rule, including tumuli with contracted non-Egyptian burial types. However, new excavations of post-Meroitic elite burials south of Meroe at al-Hobagi (see "al-Hobagi") that had been directed by the late Patrice Lenoble indicate that Isis libation rites and other elements of Meroitic/Egyptian funerary religion continued to be practiced for several generations, perhaps by descendants of elites from the nearby royal capital.

Nubian Popular Religion

Nubians worshiped numinous forces of the natural world that they believed were immanent in certain animals and places. Rock-cut speos temples, high places, and caves, as well as small rocks that were found in tombs and temples, indicate that mountains and their stones were believed to be important sources of numinous power.

Among their gods were the ram gods who were absorbed by Amun; the female goddesses who were absorbed by Isis and, to a lesser extent, by Mut and Hathor; and the lion god Apedemak. Indigenous beliefs shared by all Nubians can be seen in non-Egyptian features of state religion. For example, the role of royal women in kingship dogma and the widespread popularity of Isis suggest the prior and/or concomitant existence of indigenous mother goddesses. The greater importance of Anubis and Bes in Kush relative to their place in the Egyptian pantheon might reflect the existence of indigenous gods with similar cultic features. Anubis's importance as an offering-giver was connected to his more obscure associations with cattle, which resonated in Nubia, rather than his connection to mummification, which did not.

As noted, Nubian gods were worshiped in caves and on hilltops imbued with divine forces, locales in which the sacred and profane could intersect. These sites remained places of worship for the Nubians even after the construction of the state-built temples. In these locales, Nubians could pray directly to their deities without the mediation of a formal priesthood. It is not always apparent why certain sites were sacred. In the case of hilltops, many, such as Gebel Barkal, were visually distinctive. Some sacred hilltops had small shrines, but others appear to have had no structures. These have been identified by the remains of the offering vessels, graffiti, and inscribed objects left by worshipers. Caves were sacred because Nubians considered living rock an animate matrix in which numen or deity resided. It could be that particular sites were selected because their stone matrix was believed to have possessed particular numinous power. One of the most well-known natural cave shrines at Seyala was in use from A-Group to Roman times and had man-made niches and religious paintings on its walls and ceilings. The cave shrine at Gebel Qeili was decorated with images of a queen and prince, indicating that all levels of Meroitic society may have visited them. Many tombs, including royal ones, held sacred rocks. A piece of green feldspar wrapped with metal wire and tied with wax knots (evidence for magical practices) was found in Taharqo's tomb. Sacred stones were also apparently left for or used as temple offerings. During 2008, excavations led by Timothy Kendall in Gebel Barkal's Temple B 700-sub 2 found 620 stones that were left within this small shrine by Napatan worshipers. Many others were probably not recovered. These stones were very specific and consistent variations of spherical forms, naturally occurring imitations of recognizable forms (women's torsos, phalli, animals, and so on), or particularly attractive, naturally

Figure 88. Apedemak in the form of a snake, from the Lion Temple at Naqa. Photo © Chester Higgins Jr 2012.

polished specimens. Several were wrapped with gold wires like ones found in the Napatan burials of Queen Khensa at al-Kurru and King Taharqo at Nuri.

Beginning with the large-scale introduction into Nubia of Egyptian religion during the New Kingdom, its influence on popular religion continued until the end of the Meroitic Period. Egyptian beliefs and practices became part of the religious life of ordinary Nubians. The intermarriage of Nubian women with Egyptian workers and soldiers (see "Texts and Writing in Ancient Nubia") during the New Kingdom, and to a lesser extent during the Twenty-fifth Dynasty, would have been an avenue for the introduction of non-elite Egyptian beliefs into popular religion. In addition, non-elite Nubians worshiped Egyptian gods by visiting their temples and participating in their ceremonies from the New Kingdom on. Through these channels, Amun, Isis, Anubis, and to a lesser extent other Egyptian gods, came to be worshiped by ordinary Nubians, although the beliefs attached to them might have been different and included more indigenous features than those held by elites. This merger of indigenous and Egyptian elements in popular religion can be seen in the continued use of sacred spaces and the offerings of rocks in certain temples. In some cases, sacred spaces were used to worship Egyptian gods, particularly Amun and Isis. Nicholas Millet found sixteen graffiti carved on a single hilltop in Lower Nubia. Three of these graffiti were dedicated to local forms of Amani, but another addressed Isis of Philae and Isis of the Abaton, indicating that more than one god was worshiped on this hilltop and that at least one of them, Isis, was not from the immediate vicinity. At Qasr Ibrim near the Amun Temple and its oracle, there was an open-air podium that had paving stones carved with human feet with their owner's name inscribed in them.

Practices in Nubian Popular Religion

Graffiti

The practice of drawing graffiti on the sides of rock outcroppings and in sacred places was an extremely ancient form of prayer. Simple depictions of offerings, such as animals, wine jars, offering tables, or even feet, were carved to invoke the god's favor and to remind the god of the supplicant's presence. Images were therefore a type of prayer that could be left by the non-literate, while literate worshipers left hundreds of short prayers, often with the supplicant's name in Meroitic and, in rare cases, Egyptian, that addressed the god(s) of the site. The existence of written prayers alongside crude graffiti of offerings demonstrates that these sites were visited by all classes of Nubian society.

Libation

The pouring of a liquid offering was, either of itself or when poured on other offerings to consecrate them, a ritual practice found in all levels of society. It is one of the oldest known rituals, since libation vessels were found in Neolithic graves by Jacques Reinold, among others. Napatan and Meroitic libation scenes show a priest/priestess or deity performing them, but throughout Nubian history ordinary persons probably also poured libations for their gods or for their dead. The vessels they used ranged from ritual vessels to ordinary ones typically used to store fluids. Water was the most common fluid, but milk and wine were also given. Libations were celebrated throughout Nubian-built temples. Basins, sometimes in the shape of an ankh, were set into the ground in front of temple entrances, and libation altars were placed in outer courtyards where non-elite Nubians would have had access to all of them. In cemeteries, libations were poured upon the graves, perhaps on a regular schedule. At wealthier graves, they were poured upon an offering table with a spout that allowed the fluid to flow into the ground and to the tomb below it.

Magic

Magic was important in popular religion. The presence of small amulets and other objects in ordinary as well as in elite Nubians' graves testifies to their belief in the efficacy of images to create desired outcome(s), typically of protection or well-being. In the state cult, evidence for magic can also be found in the images of bound prisoners, who were impaled beneath the flagpoles in front of temples.

Oracles

The uses of oracles and the divination of dreams to reveal divine intentions were well documented in Napatan royal inscriptions, and in the Meroitic Period, petitions to the oracle at Qasr Ibrim, translated by John Ray, show that they were also available to, and used by, ordinary Kushites. Ray translates a letter written in Demotic (Text 2) requesting that the oracle be "relentlessly questioned" as to the fate of an imprisoned acquaintance and as to whether Amun's displeasure is responsible for the prisoner's misfortune. Questions written as graffiti on temple walls might have been intended for the temple's gods as another form of oracle. Individual pilgrimages to shrines were sometimes motivated by the desire to receive oracular guidance.

Pilgrimage

The evidence for the popularity of pilgrimages among Meroites suggests this may have been an indigenous practice. Pilgrimages by communal groups and individuals might have been made to important sacred places, such as the cave at Seyala, long before there was written evidence for them. Meroitic pilgrims from all levels of society visited the Isis Temple at Philae and the Temple of Amun at Qasr Ibrim, leaving hundreds of graffiti with prayers and offerings on the temples' walls. Pilgrims would have traveled to petition an oracle for protection, information, healing, and to attend religious events, such as Isis of Philae's visit to Osiris's tomb at Abaton. In addition to Egyptian and Nubian temples in the First and Second Cataract regions, the large sanctuaries at Gebel Barkal, Naqa, Basa, and Musawwarat al-Sufra were the focus of individual and organized group pilgrimages.

Processions

Processions, which played an important role in pilgrimage rites and the festivals of state temples, were also part of ordinary communal religious and political expressions. While the manner in which processions were depicted on a temple's walls was essentially Egyptian, the depictions of funerary processions in Meroitic pyramid chapels show processions with community members carrying sheaves of grains and bringing offerings that were indigenous. Funerary processions like these were practiced, albeit on a more modest scale, at every level of society.

Popular Funerary Religion

A belief in an afterlife was always part of Nubian funerary religion. The variety of funerary practices dating from the Neolithic Period onward perhaps reflects the distinctive beliefs of different ethnic groups, as well as the later impact of Egyptian religion. In general, early graves were simple pits that might contain food offerings, amulets, personal items, animal burials, and more rarely, evidence for human and animal sacrifices. By the early to mid-second millennium BC, there were changes that suggest the introduction of Kerma culture funerary beliefs into a wider sphere of Nubian society. Burials became more elaborate and included bed burials and the building of superstructures. Burials that reflected other indigenous practices were stairway or pit graves with the dead placed in a contracted position on his/her side, sometimes wrapped in a shroud and sometimes also resting on a bed.

The influx of Egyptians during the New Kingdom led to the adoption of Egyptian practices by large numbers of Nubians. Egypt's impact on what is typically a very conservative form of religious expression indicates how deeply its religion penetrated Nubian culture. This was perhaps aided by intermarriages, as evidenced by a New Kingdom cemetery containing both Egyptian (male) and indigenous (female) burials found by Stuart Tyson Smith at Tombos. A Nubian-style burial most often had a shaft that led to an axial chamber containing the deceased, who was placed on his/her back with various combinations and quantities of jars, bowls, jewelry, and weapons. These bodies were not mummified and lacked any of the accoutrements that accompanied mummified burials. Instead, bodies were often wrapped in shrouds before being placed in simple wooden coffins.

Napatan and Meroitic burials continued to demonstrate a variety of types that included the contemporaneous use of Egyptian and Nubian-style burial practices, sometimes even within the same cemetery. Four different tomb types were excavated at Sanam Abu Dom in the north, suggesting that different family groups in that area followed separate burial traditions, including some Egyptian ones. The use of distinct burial practices by different clans/groups is perhaps also documented in the south at Meroe, where two quite separate but contemporary early Napatan cemeteries, the Western and Southern Cemeteries, were used by residents of comparable economic and cultural status. With the end of Egyptian religious influences after the Meroitic Period, even elite burials were essentially indigenous in nature.

The lack of any type of mummification after the early Meroitic Period indicates that Nubians did not hold Osirian or other beliefs tied to the preservation of the body to ensure an afterlife. Once a burial had been completed, the physical remains of the dead were unimportant and handled roughly when tombs were reused, sometimes not too long after the original burial. Therefore, the ceremonies performed at the time of burials were crucial for the afterlife of their occupants.

Water libations were the single most important offering of the burial ceremony. In the dry, hot land of Kush, it was the most essential of all gifts, and even the poorest burials had at least a cup in them. In Egyptianized burials, water offerings took on an additional meaning as the life-giving Nile inundation that sprang from the tomb of Osiris near Philae, a pilgrimage site. A funerary meal, the last communion between the living and dead, was also fundamental. Remains of such meals are found in burials from the post-Neolithic to post-Meroitic Periods, and graves of all periods and of all classes often had intact or broken food and drink vessels buried near them. The breaking of vessels used for this repast was another common feature, perhaps symbolizing a breaking of the link between the living and dead. Sometimes intact or broken vessels were deposited outside the sealed burial chamber in a final rite prior to filling the entrance shaft. Broken Meroitic funerary pots and burned animal bones have been found piled around the bottoms of hills in Lower Nubia and around Meroe. Apparently there were funerary meals on their summits that ended with a ceremonial destruction of the remains by throwing them from the hilltop. Patrice Lenoble (1992) found two such hilltops near Meroe that had tumuli (which may have been over burials) around their bases, suggesting that burial places were sometimes selected because of their proximity to a hill suitable for these rites. Napatan and Meroitic royal and non-royal cemeteries were also often located on hilltops.

The local gods to whom ordinary Nubians turned in death are unknown, but images and symbols of Anubis and Isis were placed on or in humble Napatan and Meroitic graves, either in the form of amulets or on offering tables and stelae. In many instances, these burials reused older, elite offering tables with their original images still upon them, or made do with crude offering tables that had Anubis and Isis scratched on their surfaces, demonstrating that Anubis and Isis were venerated even by the humblest members of Nubian society.

Conclusion

Gifts to their gods and to their dead, which Nubians of all socioeconomic classes left on hilltops, in caves, in temples, and in tombs, speak eloquently to their belief that the world they inhabited was charged with divine forces that would hear their prayers and receive their offerings. These natural forces were manifested in animals, such as the ram (Amun) and the lion (Apedemak), in the forms of mother goddesses (Isis, Mut, Hathor), and in other forms still unknown. In Nubian daily life, the gods who controlled the physical environment could be implored, placated, and queried. Among all classes of ancient Nubians,

there was a belief in an afterlife that depended on a proper burial and offerings; unlike ancient Egypt, this afterlife was not linked to an ongoing earthly physical presence, and whatever was needed was magically supplied by ritual performed at the time of the burial.

As Nubia's interactions with pharaonic Egypt strengthened, the adoption of Egyptian religion to express Nubian ideas intensified among elites and, to a lesser extent, non-elites. However, the Egyptianized appearance of Nubian religion during the New Kingdom, Napatan, and Meroitic Periods is misleading. Indigenous traditions were never entirely subsumed by Egyptian ones, even during the peak of Egyptian religious influence during the Napatan Period. The long-lived elements taken from Egyptian religion, such as the worship of Amun, Isis, and Anubis, survived because they resonated with aspects of indigenous religion. The ancient Nubians' adaptations of Egyptian religion consistently reveal that their culture shaped and informed its uses.

Bibliography

Barnard, A., and J. Spencer, eds. 1996. *Encyclopedia of Social and Cultural Anthropology.* London: Routledge.

Bianchi, R.S. 2004. *Daily Life of the Nubians.* Westport: The Greenwood Press.

Darnell, J.C. 2006. *The Inscription of Queen Katimala at Semna: Textual Evidence for the Origins of the Napatan State.* New Haven, Conn.: Yale Egyptological Seminar.

Doll, S.K. 1978. "Texts and Decoration on the Napatan Sarcophagi of Anlamani and Aspelta." PhD diss., Brandeis University.

———. 2008. "The Ritual of the Royal Ancestors at Nuri." Communication. Eleventh International Conference for Meroitic Studies, Vienna, September 1–September 4, 2008. Vienna: University of Vienna, Department of African Studies.

Edwards, D.N. 2003. "Ancient Egypt in the Sudanese Middle Nile: A Case of Mistaken Identity?" In D.N. Edwards, ed., *Ancient Egypt in Africa,* 137–50. London: University College London.

———. 2004. *The Nubian Past: An Archaeology of the Sudan.* London: Routledge.

Frankfurter, D. 1998. *Pilgrimage and Holy Space in Late Antique Egypt.* Leiden: Brill.

Gamer-Wallert, I. 1983. *Der Löwentempel von Naq'a in der Butana (Sudan).* Tübingen: Reichert.

Geus, F. 2003. "Two Seasons at Sai Island (1996–1997)." *Kush* 18:61–79.

———. 2004. "Funerary Culture." In D.A. Welsby and J.R. Anderson, eds., *Sudan: Ancient Treasures: An Exhibition of Recent Discoveries from the Sudan National Museum,* 274–307. London: British Museum Press.

Hofmann, I. 1987. *Die Bedeutung des Tieres in der meroitischen Kultur.* Vienna: Druckerei St. Gabriel.

———. 1995. "Die meroitische Religion. Staatskult und Volksfrömmigkeit." In *Aufstieg und Niedergang der römischen Welt* 18, no. 5: 2801–68. Berlin: Walter de Gruyter.

Hofmann, I., and H. Tomandl. 1986. *Unbekanntes Meroe.* BSF Supplementary vol. 1. Vienna: Mödling.

Johnson, D.H. 1990. "Fixed Shrines and Spiritual Centres in the Upper Nile." *Azania* 25:41–56.

Kendall, T. 2008a. "Recent Field Work at Jebel Barkal, 2007–08: National Corporation for Antiquities and Museums of Sudan [NCAM] Mission, 2008," http://www.univie.ac.at/afrikanistik/meroe2008/abstracts/Abstract%20Kendall.pdf

———. 2008b. "Report of the NCAM Mission to Jebel Barkal Season's Activities: February 29–March 31, 2008 (The New Kingdom Architecture)." Unpublished report submitted to NCAM.

Lambek, M., ed. 2002. *A Reader in the Anthropology of Religion*. Malden, MA: Blackwell Publishing.

Lenoble, P. 1992. "Cônes de déjections archéologiques dans des djebels à cimetières tumulaires proches de Méroé." *BSF* 5:73–92.

———. 1997. "La petite bouteille noire: Un recipient Meroeën de la libation funéraire." *Archéologie du Nil Moyen* 7:143–62.

Lenoble, P., et al. 1994. "Le sacrifice funéraire de bovinés de Meroë à Qustul et Ballana." In C. Berger-El Naggar et al., eds., *Hommages Leclant*. Bibliothèque d'étude 106/1–4, 269–83. Cairo: IFAO.

———. 2002. "El-Hobagi." In D.A. Welsby and W.V. Davies, eds., *Uncovering Ancient Sudan: A Decade of Discovery by the Sudan Archaeological Research Society*, 193–97. London: Sudan Archaeological Research Society.

Lewczuk, J. 1983. "Studies on the Iconography of Thoth in the Art of the Kingdom of Kush: Napatan and Meroitic Periods." *GM* 69:45–61.

Millet, N.B. 1984. "Meroitic Religion." *Meroitica* 7:111–21.

Morris, B. 1987. *Anthropological Studies of Religion: An Introductory Text*. Oxford: Oxford University Press.

Näser, C. 1999. "Cemetery 214 at Abu Simbel North: Non-elite Burial Practices in Meroitic Lower Nubia." In *Recent Research in Kushite History and Archaeology: Proceedings of the Eighth International Conference for Meroitic Studies*, 131:19–29. London: British Museum Press.

Priese, K.-H. 1996. "Die Götterwelt von Meroë." In *Sudan. Antike Königreich am Nil*, 267–300. Tübingen: Ernst Wasmuth Verlag.

Ray, J.D. 2005. *Demotic Papyri and Ostraca from Qasr Ibrim*. London: Egypt Exploration Society.

Reinold, J. 2004. "Kadruka." In D.A. Welsby and J.R. Anderson, eds., *Sudan: Ancient Treasures: An Exhibition of Recent Discoveries from the Sudan National Museum*, 42–48. London: British Museum Press.

Rondot, V. 2010. "Les Dieux de Méroé." In M. Baud, A. Sackho-Autissier, S. Labbé-Toutée, eds., *Méroé: Un empire sur le Nil*, 189–201. Paris: Musée du Louvre Editions.

Séguenny, E. 1984. "Quelques éléments de la religion populaire du Soudan ancien." *Meroitica* 7:149–55.

Smith, S.T. 2003. *Wretched Kush: Ethnic Identities and Boundaries in Egypt's Nubian Empire*. New York: Routledge.

———. 2007. "Death at Tombos: Pyramids, Iron and the Rise of the Napatan Dynasty." *Sudan & Nubia* 11:2–14.

Török, L. 1997. *The Kingdom of Kush: Handbook of the Napatan-Meroitic Civilization*. Leiden: Brill.

———. 2002. *The Image of the Ordered World in Ancient Nubian Art: The Construction of the Kushite Mind, 800 BC–300 AD*. Leiden: Brill.

———. 2009. *Between Two Worlds: The Frontier Region between Ancient Nubia and Egypt, 3700 BC–AD 500*. Leiden: Brill.

Vincentelli, I. 1999. "Some Remarks on Burial Customs at Hillat El Arab." In *Recent Research in Kushite History and Archaeology: Proceedings of the Eighth International Conference for Meroitic Studies*, 131:45–54. London: British Museum Press.

———. 2006. *Hillat el-Arab: The Joint Sudanese-Italian Expedition in the Napatan Region, Sudan*. Sudan Archaeological Research Society Publication 15. London: British Museum Press.

Welsby, D.A. 1996. *The Kingdoms of Kush: The Napatan and Meroitic Empires*. London: British Museum Press.

Wildung, D. 1996. *Sudan. Antike Königreich am Nil*. Tübingen: Ernst Wasmuth Verlag.

———. 2004. "Kushite Religion: Aspects of the Berlin Excavations at Naga." In D.A. Welsby and J.R. Anderson, eds., *Sudan: Ancient Treasures: An Exhibition of Recent Discoveries from the Sudan National Museum*, 174–85. London: British Museum Press.

Yellin, J.W. 1989. "The Impact of Egyptian Religion on Meroitic Society." Paper presented at Fifth International Conference for Meroitic Studies, Khartoum, Sudan.

———. 1995. "Egyptian Religion and Its Ongoing Impact on the Formation of the Napatan State." *CRIPEL* 17:243–66.

Žabkar, Louis V. 1975. *Apedemak, Lion God of Meroe: A Study in Egyptian-Meroitic Syncretism*. Warminster: Aris & Phillips Ltd.

Zibelius-Chen, K. 2007. Review of *The Inscription of Queen Katimala at Semna: Textual Evidence for the Origins of the Napatan State* by J. Darnell. *BiOr* 64:377–87.

Burial Customs
in Ancient Nubia

Peter Lacovara and Christian Knoblauch

While the cultures of ancient Nubia and Egypt were linked in many ways, burial customs often diverged along the Middle Nile from those to the north, particularly during periods when the pharaonic presence in Nubia was limited.

Early Nubia

Late Neolithic burials throughout the Nile Valley show remarkable similarity and demonstrate the necessity for provisioning the dead, which was to become so significant in later times. A cemetery at Kadero near the Sixth Cataract yielded a number of richly furnished graves that included tools, jewelry, cosmetic implements, and fine, decorated pottery, probably made specifically for burial. As in Egypt, bodies were placed in a contracted position in shallow round or oval graves apart from settlement sites. A distinction that appears in these early graves and that continues on is the inclusion of animal bones, usually for decorative purposes, in Nubian burials. This also reflects the importance of pastoralism to the economy. Multiple burials in a single grave also suggest possible human sacrifice, which was also to become important in later Nubian mortuary custom. As in Egypt, burials of infants and very young children are rare, suggesting a different method of disposal for them.

Later burials in the north in the Third and Second Cataract regions display the development of increasing social stratification, with the appearance of singularly larger and more richly provisioned graves for the Pre-Kerma and A-Group cultures. A series of large tombs discovered at Qustul, although badly robbed, still contained not only large amounts of jewelry and fine and imported pottery, but also symbols associated with kingship in Egypt. These burials were marked with a large, mounded superstructure, which was to become the default tomb type throughout later Nubian history.

While different grave architecture developed in Archaic Egypt, along with coffin burials and mummification, within the Nubian groups the Neolithic traditions persisted. In the C-Group, Early Kerma, and Pan-Grave cultures, tumuli were the preferred monuments, although they were constructed in rather different ways. For the C-Group, the superstructures above the burials were constructed of dry stone masonry arranged in a cylindrical shape, sometimes with an appended offering chapel. They could also be marked with standing stone slabs, sometimes decorated with incised designs including cattle.

Pottery was both left in the offering chapel and interred with the deceased, along with jewelry and personal items. The body was dressed and laid out in a semi-contracted position, usually with the head to the east and facing north, as was standard in Egypt and Nubia.

C-Group cemeteries are found throughout Lower Nubia (see "The C-Group in Lower Nubia"), even within the proximity of the Egyptian fortresses in the Second Cataract, but they are at a distinct remove in location and tradition from the burials of the Egyptians garrisoned there.

Middle Kingdom Fort Burials

Although the Egyptians had erected fortresses in Lower Nubia during the early Twelfth Dynasty, it was not until the late Twelfth Dynasty that there is any evidence for associated burial activity. This may be due to the well-known aversion of Egyptians to a burial in foreign lands, but it more likely reflects a new policy whereby rotating garrisons and support staff were replaced by a more permanent presence, including families that lived and died in Nubia. From the late Twelfth Dynasty onward, cemeteries were con-

secrated in the vicinity of nearly all of the Egyptian fortresses, indicating a rapidly burgeoning expatriate population.

The earliest graves at the Mirgissa fortress were simple rectangular pits in which the deceased was laid supine in a rectangular wooden coffin. At this early stage, there were very few grave goods, indicating the relatively low social status of the first wave of émigrés. Where grave goods were present, these consisted almost entirely of ceramics drawn from the sphere of everyday life, in line with the Egyptian practice of offering the deceased a last ritual meal.

During the early Thirteenth Dynasty, grave wealth and size increased. The subterranean component of the tomb now consisted of a vertical access shaft, at the bottom of which was cut a small chamber intended for the interment of a single or double burial. The deceased was still placed supine in a wooden rectangular coffin, but well-preserved examples from Mirgissa show that some of these coffins were now decorated externally with funerary texts and depictions of the goddesses Isis and Nephthys. On the interior there were excerpts from the Egyptian Coffin

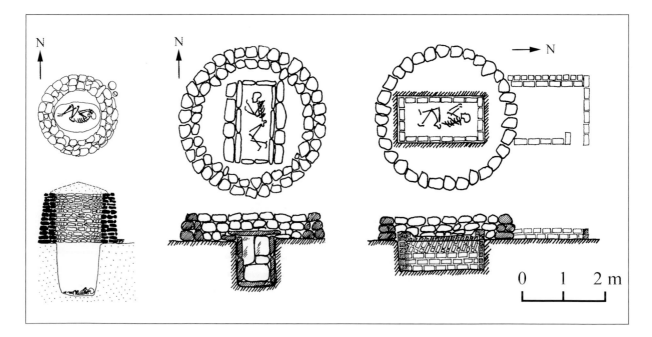

Figure 89. Schematic representation of graves of the early and late C-Group.

Texts. Cartonnage masks, placed over the head and shoulders of the deceased, played an important role in the preparation of the body for burial. Splendid polychrome examples from Mirgissa document the close identification of the deceased with the Egyptian god of the dead, Osiris.

Although Egyptian central control over the fortresses waned some time during the Thirteenth Dynasty, Egyptian populations remained in Nubia, and it was around this time that grave size and wealth increased noticeably. For the first time, rectangular mud-brick offering chapels with decorated offering stones were constructed above the burial chambers. The burials also became more impressive: one very important individual from Buhen was buried with a gold ring, an armband of twisted gold wire, and two long necklaces. One of these was one meter long and featured gold tubular beads interspersed with spherical amethyst beads and two gold leonine finials. Both gold and amethyst were local products and indicate the probable source of wealth for these new elites. In other burials from the same cemetery, there are indications of colonists' connections to the north. These include Egyptian-made stone vessels and small ceramic juglets originating in the tradition of Middle Bronze Age cultures of the Levant. Connections to the south are attested to by an increasing amount of Kerma pottery found in Egyptian cemeteries alongside non-Egyptian burial practices. While the nature of this evidence is ambiguous, it is clear that the fortress populations were excelling in their role as trade intermediaries between Egypt and Kerma. Part of this success must lie in the co-opting of local Nubians into the enterprise, as documented in the Semna dispatches.

Burials of Egyptianized Nubians, both of the local C-Group population as well as the desert Medjay or Pan-Grave people, show a growing proliferation of Egyptian imports and customs, lasting into the New Kingdom.

Pan-Grave and Kerma Cultures

The Pan-Grave culture gets its name from burials found in Egypt where the superstructures had been denuded, and the shallow, round graves reminded archaeologists of frying pans. They are similar to the tombs of both the contemporary C-Group and Kerma cultures and are also found decorated with painted animal skulls, one from Mostagedda in Egypt depicting a Pan-Grave warrior with his weapons. Pan-Grave cemeteries are found throughout southern Upper Egypt and Lower Nubia. In Egypt they were originally isolated within Egyptian cemeteries,

Figure 90. Funerary mask from Mirgissa.

Figure 91. Kerma tumulus decorated with applied stone.

but gradually the cultures seemed to merge, as was also the case in Lower Nubia, where graves with mixed Pan-Grave, C-Group, and Kerma traditions are found.

Some well-preserved graves of the Early Kerma period provide a great deal of information on the mortuary customs of the age. Here the bodies were flexed and lying on beds as if sleeping, and sometimes covered with leather or linen blankets. Again, the individuals wore clothing and jewelry that they would have worn in life, and the tomb was provided with pottery, objects of daily use, and, occasionally, human or animal sacrifices. Around the earthen tumulus above the grave were placed offerings of pottery vessels, and the grave could be decorated with animal skulls, usually cattle or sheep and goats. Some mounds have been found decorated with geometric patterns

of black and white stones, in imitation of the black incised ceramics of the period.

Throughout the second millennium, the elite graves at Kerma grew larger and larger, with a proliferation of grave goods and human sacrifices. The culmination of this trend was in the massive royal tumuli built at the end of the Second Intermediate Period. These were huge earthen mounds seventy meters across. They later developed a complex system of internal crosswalls built in mud brick to stabilize the structure, with large mud-brick chapels built nearby. They were richly provisioned with grave goods, including masses of fine-ware ceramics, notably the famous Kerma beakers; imported Egyptian stone vessels and sculpture; weapons; tools; and jewelry. The principal burial was off a central corridor in a side room, as had been the case in the A-Group tumuli.

The body was placed on a bed that was finely carved of ebony, standing on supports carved in the shape of cows' legs and decorated with ivory inlaid footboards. The corridor was also littered with the bodies of human sacrifices; as many as four hundred individuals were buried alive to accompany the king into the next world. Other individual graves were later added, cut into the sides of the tumulus.

Figure 92. Classic Kerma bed burial.

New Kingdom Nubia

With the destruction of the Kerma state at the beginning of the New Kingdom and the reoccupation of Lower Nubia, Egyptian burial customs began to influence the local Nubian populations. This is particularly observable in key areas previously occupied by the Nubian C-Group. The largest single Nubian cemetery of this period is at Fadrus in the region of Debeira, ancient Tekhet. Unlike in earlier burials in the region, the bodies are uniformly extended and contain almost exclusively Egyptian pottery and stone vessels. Group burials, a trait observable in the Egyptian burials of the Second Intermediate Period, also occur, as do typical types of Egyptian grave architecture. Interestingly, the graves are poor in specialized Egyptian funerary goods. Moreover, there was no evidence of a facility for a mortuary cult. This could imply that the 'Egyptianization' of the C-Group was superficial, but it also may simply be an indication of the relatively low socioeconomic status of those buried at Fadrus.

The social elites of Tekhet were powerful local princes who were responsible for the administration of the Egyptian occupation. Their tombs were located a short distance downstream from Fadrus. In contrast to the lower-status burials, the tombs of the brothers Djehutyhotep and Amenemhat were rich in Egyptian mortuary objects and symbolism. Of particular importance are the paintings from the tomb of Djehutyhotep, which

Figure 93. Reliefs in the tomb of Pennout.

Figure 94. Painted burial chamber of Queen Qalhata, wife of Shebitqo, at al-Kurru, Pyramid 5. Photo © Chester Higgins Jr 2012.

conform to contemporary Egyptian canons, and a magnificent tomb stela from the tomb of Amenemhat, on which the tomb owner is depicted making offerings to his mother and father. The conceptualization and the performance of the graveside mortuary cult were therefore purely Egyptian. The burial goods from the tomb of Hekanefer, Prince of Miam, provide an insight into the afterlife beliefs of the local elite. Stone and faience *shawabti*s, small mummiform figurines inscribed with a ritual text, were included in the burial. Their purpose was to undertake any work required of the deceased in the afterlife. Hekanefer

also possessed a winged heart scarab bearing a text that implored his heart not to betray him during the judgment of the dead. Both object types belong to the standard Egyptian New Kingdom repertoire of burial goods and attest to an orthodox, Egyptian perception of the afterlife.

The burials in the Debeira area and the Lower Nubian hinterland gradually declined in wealth, and there are very few burials that can be dated with assurance to the second half of the Egyptian New Kingdom. This may indicate a depopulation of this area, or a shifting in burial location to important regional centers such as Aniba (ancient

Miam). Here, on the great plain to the west of the fortified town, a large cemetery of tombs developed. The substructure of these tombs invariably consisted of multiple burial chambers in which large groups of people were buried. Some of these tombs had superstructures in the form of small mud-brick pyramids fronted by an enclosed courtyard. Similar tomb structures are found throughout the zone of Egyptian occupation, including the area above the Second Cataract at sites such as Sai, Soleb, and Tombos. The appearance of Egyptian burial customs in the previous heartland of the Kerma kingdom can be attributed to a policy of external colonization by the Egyptians and a large-scale adoption of Egyptian burial customs by the Kerma population. Despite the overwhelming nature of the evidence for Egyptianization, new data from Tombos demonstrates

that some aspects of Kerma burial practice survived the Egyptian occupation and were stressed in burial rituals of local women.

Later Nubian Traditions

With the loss of Egyptian control over Nubia at the end of the New Kingdom, local mortuary tradition, most strikingly among the elites, reasserted itself. At al-Kurru, near the Fourth Cataract, there are a series of large tumuli datable to the late Third Intermediate Period. These burials are thought to belong to the ancestors of the kings of the Twenty-fifth Dynasty. The earliest burials clearly belong to the long-standing Nubian tradition of an earthen or dry-stone mound grave with a shaft and side niche for the burial. These later evolve into more impressive monuments with brick enclosure walls and fronted by small chapels.

Figure 95. *Shawabtis* of King Taharqo. Photograph © 2012 Museum of Fine Arts, Boston.

Figure 96. Reconstruction
of a Meroitic pyramid.

With the beginning of the Nubian conquest of Egypt in the Twenty-fifth Dynasty, we see a radical transformation in the burial customs in the royal cemeteries around the capital at Napata. The traditional tumulus, at least for the kings and queens, was abandoned in favor of the pyramid, although in a very different version from the great monuments of Egypt's Old and Middle Kingdoms. These pyramids are smaller and much steeper than Egyptian pyramids and were built of local sandstone blocks. The chapels and burial chambers followed more closely the pattern developed in the later tumuli, with a chapel out front and a burial chamber entirely built under the ground. Some of the burial chambers were painted with scenes and patterns evocative of Egyptian private tombs of the period.

The inspiration for the pyramid superstructure can be found in the style of private pyramids of the Egyptian New Kingdom, and those found in Nubia most probably provided the inspiration for the new burial type. The largest of all the Nubian pyramids belonged to Taharqo and was built at Nuri rather than the cemetery of his ancestors at al-Kurru. It ultimately was 51.75 meters square at the base and 40 to 50 meters high.

Although these burials had all been extensively plundered, still a large number of objects and fragments of the funerary furniture were found within them by the expedition of Harvard University and the Museum of Fine Arts, Boston. They were provided with *shawabti*s in the fashion of Egyptian tombs, but numbering in the thousands, made of faience or carved in stone. The treatment of the bodies also followed Egyptian tradition, with canopic jars (attesting to mummification), funerary amulets, and coffins inlaid with semiprecious stones and covered with gold leaf. Massive granite sarcophagi to house the royal coffins were found in the tombs of Anlamani and Aspelta.

Private burials of this period are less well attested, but seem to follow Nubian traditions more closely. In the cemetery at Meroe, and even more so at provincial sites such as Sanam, we also see a persistence of Nubian tradition with uncoffined bed burials in a contracted position.

Later royal pyramid burials are found at Gebel Barkal, and in Meroe as that city grew in prominence and eclipsed Napata as the capital of the country. These were also fronted by decorated chapels that survive in a far better state of preservation and record scenes of their royal occupants receiving offerings, and images of Osiris and other deities.

After the fall of Meroe, the pyramid tradition continued in sites like Karanog, but ultimately we see a return to ancient burial customs with the tumuli at Ballana and Qustul, Zuma, and elsewhere.

Figure 97. Reconstruction of a painted stone *ba*-bird statuette from Karanog.

Bibliography

Bietak, M. 1966. *Ausgrabungen in Sayala—Nubien 1961–1965. Denkmäler der C-Gruppe und der Pan-Gräber-Kultur.* Berichte des Österreichischen Nationalkomitees der UNESCO-Aktion für die Rettung der Nubischen Altertümer 3. Österreichische Akademie der Wissenschaften, Philosophisch-Historische Klasse, Denkschriften. Vienna: Hermann Böhlhaus Nachf.

———. 1987. "The C-Group and the Pan-Grave Culture in Nubia." In T. Hägg, ed., *Nubian Culture: Past and Present,* 113–23. Stockholm: Almquist and Wiksell.

Bonnet, C., et al. 2000. *Edifices et rites funéraires à Kerma.* Paris: Errance.

Dunham, D., and J. Janssen. 1960. *The Second Cataract Forts.* Vol. 1: *Semna Kumma.* Boston: Museum of Fine Arts.

———. 1967. *The Second Cataract Forts.* Vol. 2: *Uronarti Shalfak Mirgissa.* Boston: Museum of Fine Arts.

Knoblauch, C. 2008. "The Egyptian Cemeteries in Lower Nubia during the First Half of the Second Millennium B.C." PhD diss., Macquarie University.

Lacovara, P. 1986. "The Funerary Chapels at Kerma." *CRIPEL* 8:49–58.

Randall-MacIver, D., and C.L. Woolley. 1911. *Buhen.* Eckley B. Coxe Junior Expedition to Nubia 7. Philadelphia: University Museum.

Reisner, G.A. 1923. *Excavations at Kerma, Parts I–III and IV–V.* Harvard African Studies 5 and 6. Cambridge, MA: Harvard University Press.

Säve-Söderbergh, T., and L. Troy. 1991. *New Kingdom Pharaonic Sites: The Finds and the Sites. SJE* 5:2.

Simpson, W. K. 1963. *Heka-nefer and the Dynastic Material from Toshka and Arminna.* New Haven: Peabody Museum of Natural History of Yale University.

Smith, S.T. 2003. *Wretched Kush: Ethnic Identities and Boundaries in Egypt's Nubian Empire.* London: Routledge.

TEXTS AND WRITING IN ANCIENT NUBIA

Susan K. Doll

The story of texts and writing in Nubia is intimately bound up with its history as a culture alternately conquered and colonized, conquering and building empires. It is also a story of the interaction of languages of official communication and languages of everyday life, the effects of language imperialism, second-language use as policy and necessity, and the flowering of literacy in a native language. Sadly, while we can see the results of some of the political and military successes and failures of Nubian civilization on archaeology and history, we can only guess at their effects on language and texts. For much of the period in question, Nubia produced no texts or writing of its own.

The earliest examples of texts referring to Nubia are actually found in Egypt and are written in the ancient Egyptian language. These first begin to appear in the Egyptian Old Kingdom (ca. 2685–2150 BC), and they record Egyptian incursions into Nubian territory, mostly to confiscate natural resources and imported goods, to take slaves and cattle, and to keep the Nubians from uniting and creating competitive states. The Egyptian writers only give us information sufficient to persuade the reader that they are clever, courageous, and strong. Nubians are named, they revolt and are punished, they offer to or otherwise provide the Egyptians with gifts or duty of various kinds, and they do obeisance, but we rarely learn anything more about them. No written evidence from the Nubian side of this story has ever been found, and most probably the Nubians did not use written records at this time.

Between the lines, we conclude that there must have been several centers of economic and political activity in Nubia, and they must have been fairly wealthy, since luxury goods and cattle could be obtained from them in large numbers. How the urban and commercial areas such as Kerma were managed, and how communication was conducted, we do not know. The Nubians must have been powerful and threatening, since the Egyptians sent numerous military expeditions to attack them and built many forts at crucial locations to keep them under control. These conditions continued throughout the Egyptian Middle Kingdom (ca. 2008–1685 BC), during which we know of the Nubians again only through Egyptian records. They provide individual names of rulers and districts, but little context in which to put them. Did Nubians resisting Egyptian incursions communicate through message runners? Or did pockets of resisters operate independently, without much communication? We do not know.

Later, during the Second Intermediate Period (ca. 1685–1550 BC), a record of an intercepted letter shows that communications could be sent to Nubian rulers with the expectation that they would be read and acted upon, but if the Nubians were literate in their own language, as well as in Egyptian as a second language, we have no evidence of it. As the intercepted letter shows, handling written communication in the Nubian court(s) was no problem; doubtless many officials were fluent in Egyptian and Nubian languages, and perhaps even in languages from farther afield. However, even from the excavations at the great state of Kerma, we still have no textual evidence to show us how official records were kept or communication conducted within Nubia between Nubians.

From the Egyptian New Kingdom (ca. 1550–1077 BC), many written records were found in Nubia itself, but again, these are written exclusively in Egyptian. Egyptians used their native language to mark out territory under their control, conduct their business and daily affairs, and provide the textual necessities for Egyptian-style burial and religious observance. Some of their

Figure 98. A stela of King Nastasen.

a   b

Figure 99. The sarcophagus of King Aspelta. Photograph © 2012 Museum of Fine Arts, Boston.

bureaucratic communication with Nubians certainly took place on a visual level. The body of an Asiatic chief hung from the fortress walls at Napata, the figure of the pharaoh on a temple pylon triumphant over his Nubian foes—these symbols represent the type of official information the Egyptians thought the Nubians needed about their status as subjects. Although many Nubians living in Egypt have left records in Egyptian, often funerary in nature, Nubia itself is still silent on its own situation. There are good reasons to assume that one of the local languages spoken in Nubia at this time was an early form of Meroitic, the language of the later kings, but Egyptian at this time was the imperial language, the language of power, commerce, and diplomacy in much of the Middle East, not only in northeastern Africa. The effects of language imperialism are known from many areas and eras, and are so strong that

it may not even have occurred to Egypt's neighbors that their own languages could be written down and employed to their own great benefit. We can assume that they used their own languages for private verbal communication, and Egyptian when things needed to be recorded or official business conducted.

It is useful to try to imagine how this might have worked on the level of daily life. There are two questions, the answers to which will help us understand language use in daily life at this time and also subsequent developments. First, what happened in the border areas where significantly large groups of speakers of both languages lived? Did they associate with each other, and to what extent? Second, if Nubians and Egyptians lived for prolonged periods in close association, what sociolinguistic consequences might this have had?

It is, of course, impossible to answer these

questions based on written texts because, as we have seen, written texts at this point in time are in Egyptian only. Based on other similar situations in other parts of the world at different times, however, some developments can be supposed. Happily, we can postulate based on solid, new archaeological evidence. It is increasingly clear that along the borders, Egyptians and Nubians were interacting on many levels, even as families. There are settlements that have yielded artifacts and other evidence of cultural mixing. Stuart Tyson Smith has shown that at Askut (an Egyptian 'colony' in Nubia and occupied during the Middle Kingdom, Second Intermediate Period, and New Kingdom by Egyptians and Nubians), there is good evidence for Nubians and Egyptians living side by side, probably even in the same households. The archaeological evidence for the existence and domestic role of Nubian women in this mixed society is particularly strong. These women left quite clear evidence of their preferences for Nubian cookery and religious beliefs.

Where food and religion go, language is not far behind. We can expect that there were children born of unions between Egyptian men and these Nubian women, and that these children spoke Nubian, learned at their mothers' or nurses' knees, and probably also Egyptian, learned from their fathers and perhaps from teachers or playmates. Children in such a community might then have been bilingual. The languages they learned would naturally have reflected the variants or dialects spoken by their parents and neighbors, and might not always have used the same structures or lexis found in today's standard Egyptian dictionaries and grammar books. Such linguistic 'breeding grounds' are both ideal and typical for the formation of pidgin languages, interlanguages, and later creoles. Indeed, from the sociolinguistic standpoint, it would

Figure 100. The Coronation Stela of King Aspelta.

have been almost impossible for something of the kind not to have happened. Witness only the manifold varieties of communication methods created in previous centuries as European languages and those of the rest of the world came into contact during the ages of discovery and colonization. It is possible that Egyptian first became a 'Nubian' language at this very time—a socially, commercially, and politically useful language to have in one's repertoire, used at some significant level of mastery and frequency by many Nubians living in areas of contact and mixing. While these developments can be supposed, it is still impossible to trace them textually or archaeologically, and we are unable to guess how they may have played out during subsequent periods. As it was the dominant language of the time, however, Egyptian would have been mastered by any Nubian yearning for the good life.

Although we have Meroitic names preserved in earlier Egyptian texts, the inscription of Queen Kadimalo/Karimala at Semna fort near the Second Cataract is possibly the first identifiable text written by, for, and about Nubians. Not surprisingly, it was written in Egyptian. Its date is uncertain, but it would seem to belong to the beginning of the Third Intermediate Period (the Twenty-first and Twenty-second Dynasties, ca. 1076–746 BC). This means it was composed during the so-called Nubian Dark Age (Donald Redford's 'Silent Years') between the end of Egyptian control (although we are not able to pinpoint the exact dates) and the rise of a line of kings buried at al-Kurru who eventually conquered Egypt. The name of the primary female figure in the inscription, Kadimalo, can be read as two known Meroitic words and means 'Good Lady.' Kadimalo is thus one of our proofs of the pre-Napatan existence of Meroitic, appearing many centuries before Meroitic was ever written down and used administratively to manage an empire.

A recent translation and commentary on this text by John Darnell attempts to affirm the dating and readability of the inscription, long described as degraded and untranslatable. It shows significant familiarity with contemporary Egyptian and describes an important though unidentifiable 'issue' or problem (md.t) in Kadimalo's kingdom, caused by the abandonment of the god Amun. An opponent named Makaresh is mentioned and relegated to the sidelines, while the cult of Amun is returned to its position of primacy under Kadimalo, who uses her successful military campaign as an apparent plea for confirmation of her rulership.

The text summons to the imagination a Kushite/Meroitic cultural and historical profile with detail that scholars could hardly have dared to hope for at this early time—a state under Amun, a queen who was militarily and politically active and powerful, a portrait of a political, religious, and military situation in some turmoil, and the use of the Egyptian language in a form typical for the early Third Intermediate Period in Egypt. If Darnell's picture is correct, this last point is particularly important, suggesting, as it does, continuing contact with Egypt proper, and corroborating other such evidence in the form of lists of Nubian products delivered to Egypt at this time. Importantly, the text shows not only that the writer knew the form of Late Egyptian current at the time, but also that the writer, at least, was a full participant in the Late Egyptian language community, using the same referents and contemporary literary allusions. The question of whether Kadimalo herself was an ancestor or an opponent of the royal predecessors buried in the early tombs at al-Kurru cannot now be answered, but she spoke a language that most probably belonged to the same language family, and certainly adhered to the religious and political positions that the al-Kurru family later adopted and that were so successful for it.

Figure 101. The Meroitic alphabet.

Hieroglyph
Cursive Letter
Phonetic Value
or
or
a
e
i
y
w
b
p
m
n
n(i)
r
Hieroglyph
Cursive Letter
Phonetic Value
l
kh
kh
s
sh
k
q
t(i)
te
te
z

Beginning with the Twenty-fifth Dynasty in Egypt (ca. 753–655 BC), there is a relative abundance of textual material from Nubian kings. None of it is written in their first language; in fact, there was clearly a political decision to adopt an earlier form of imperial Egyptian, at least for monumental inscriptions. No longer did the Nubians use Egyptian as a second language, in whatever form it was spoken contemporaneously in its home country, as Kadimalo had done. Nubians now took steps to possess, shape, and determine the course of the official language of Egypt for themselves—that is, they returned the official language of their former colonizer to something approaching the form used some seven to eight hundred years earlier. Interestingly enough, that period was the New Kingdom, when Nubia was so closely integrated into the Egyptian empire. This return to the use of what was already an ancient version of the former colonizer's language could well have had deep emotional significance to the Egyptian or Nubian reader, as it demonstrated that Egyptian was in Nubian hands and was equally now a Nubian language. It is unimportant whether each Nubian in Egypt spoke Egyptian perfectly—the collective impression is what counts here. Kushite courtiers were sophisticated members of the Egyptian speech community; they had mastered the idioms, the genres, literary references, and subtleties of specialized usages, and had even changed the history of the language. No better definition of balanced bilingual skills exists.

Psychologically, there is a significant difference between passively happening to use a second language because it gives you a larger audience, and actively choosing to use it as the administrative language of communication for your own empire. If Karimala used a late form of Egyptian, the imperial lingua franca of her time, to record her successes and hopes, the Kushite pharaohs did something quite different. They made Egyptian their own and changed the language to suit themselves. Only Egyptian was worthy to express and represent Nubian prowess and power on imperial monuments, as only Norman French was appropriate for English kings for centuries after 1066.

The texts produced by the great Nubian kings of the Twenty-fifth Dynasty are quite remarkable. Not only did they successfully recreate what was then an ancient form of the Egyptian language, replete with erudite literary allusions and echoes of earlier writers and themes, but also they often achieved a newness and freshness of expression that belied the potential stodginess of using an older form of the language. Kushite Egyptian is sometimes so direct that the reader wonders if it was not indeed composed, at least in part, by the kings themselves. One wonders how such vital turns of phrase and the expressions of passionate belief, personal quirks, and general exuberance could have been achieved if the composition process had involved significant amounts of translation and counter-translation between a Nubian monolingual king and scribal speakers of Late Egyptian. One suspects that at least some of the kings had considerable control of the Egyptian language themselves, if they were not native speakers of some Nubian version of Egyptian already. And this is certainly possible—some of the variants of Egyptian that must have been used in border communities during the New Kingdom could have survived and still have been spoken by Nubian groups some centuries later. And why not? What language could have been more useful for trade, politics, and commerce in a world dominated by Egypt? Adopting classical Egyptian, the ultimate conferrer of literary status, for official communications may have actually been a natural and comfortable, as well as unavoidable, choice for the Nubian rulers of Egypt.

A rare aspect of retained first-language use among the new Nubian pharaohs is their naming custom. Although Kushite kings adopted Egyptian names for their titularies, in order to tie themselves to the power and success of earlier native Egyptian kings, they all seem to have possessed personal names in their native language. Naming customs are very diverse, and generalizations are very dangerous. However, names seem unique to the individual in Kush, although we can identify certain elements within names that appear relatively often. Completely duplicate names are rare. Contrast to this the case in Egypt, where we can trace the popularity of certain names over centuries in many families. This contrast suggests that Nubian naming customs were not a matter simply of fashion, and that names were not passed along in families or bestowed to honor ancestors or patrons. The Kushite tradition for personal naming seems to be more one of 'custom-made' names for each individual (perhaps derived from an event during the individual's earlier life or some liminal rite). If Nubian names were 'custom-made,' it would be a strong sign that however useful and comfortable an Egyptian 'persona' might have been among Nubians, native naming customs still had power in the home and family. In the cases where we are dealing with Nubians who have Egyptian personal names (see below), even among later rulers such as Harsiyotef, we might have an example of naming customs resulting from the family's originally being Egyptian or of mixed ethnicity, although anyone could simply have adopted Egyptian naming customs for a religious or some other purpose unknown to us now.

As mentioned above, there are many fascinating texts produced during the Twenty-fifth Dynasty. At the beginning, the decision to revert to classical Egyptian might well have been made during the reign of Piankhi (Piye), as texts in the

re-engineered language begin with his great Triumphal Stela describing his army's move northward and the submission of northern Egyptian kinglets, with content ranging from details of the conquest and Piankhi's philosophy of war to his religious beliefs and obsession with horses.

Figure 102. Stela with Meroitic text. Photo © Chester Higgins Jr 2012.

Piankhi's Triumphal Stela is one of the most studied documents written in Egyptian.

The overall success of the policy to use an older form of Egyptian can be demonstrated by the inscription on the Shabaqo Stone, a religious text on an object from the time of Nubian rulership of Egypt. Scholars are still not in complete agreement on the original composition date of this theological text. Is it a copy of something much older, rescued from the depths of an ancient and dusty temple library by Nubian antiquarians and historians of religion, or was it composed in an ancient style by researchers contemporary with the Nubian king whose name it bears? Most modern scholars now think it likely that the text is contemporary with Shabaqo and thus of Nubian composition, but there is still some debate, demonstrating how successfully 'antiquated/archaized' the language really is. It may well be that both Egyptians and Nubians of the time were indeed deceived and thought the text to be much older.

There are many examples of stelae with secular content from the Napatan Period. A series issued by King Taharqo shows his particular interest in inundation and rain in Nubia, the physical conditioning of his soldiers, troubles in his political paradise, temple donations, and probable references to his political interventions in Palestine. Tanwetamani's Dream Stela relates the story of how a dream about two serpents caused him to take the throne and attempt to restore Egypt to the rule of Nubia.

Of kings who ruled after the loss of Egypt, Anlamani and Aspelta have both left us stelae on their enthronements. Additionally, Aspelta's so-called Banishment Stela tells of political problems in the Napatan kingdom and a possible assassination attempt, and another describes the pious and politically effective creation of a pyramid and mortuary cult for Prince Khaliut, a long-dead son of Piankhi.

One of the most interesting of Aspelta's texts describes the investiture of Kheb, a female family member, into a temple position. Of the eleven king's officials who present Kheb as candidate for the position, only two have Egyptian names. Of the fifteen witnesses to the candidature, priests of the Temple of Amun, about half have names that are wholly or partly Egyptian, but those individuals are not among the exclusive group of the most highly placed Prophets of Amun, all of whom have Meroitic names. If names follow ethnicity, it may be important that at this point so soon after Dynasty Twenty-five, Egyptian names are seldom found among the most powerful members of the court or high priesthood at the temple at Gebel Barkal. Interestingly, of the two scribes mentioned in the stelae, men who might have had some responsibility for the multiplicity and literary excellence of the texts from Aspelta's reign, we find the name Marabiwamani (Meroitic), the king's chief scribe, and thus possible creator of monumental inscriptions such as Aspelta's Election and Banishment Stelae; and Nesmut (Egyptian), the chief temple scribe, who may have had, as probable caretaker of the great library of Barkal, a part in the remarkable textual decoration in the pyramid of Aspelta and of his monumental sarcophagus.

Even deeper into the Napatan Period, King Irike-Amanote has left us a text showing significant facility with the Egyptian language, although many scholars have remarked that the forms of the signs and grammar are not 'up to standard.' This typical scholarly attitude toward Napatan use of Egyptian reflects an old idea that some forms of a language are socially and educationally inferior to others—and are therefore to be stigmatized. Modern linguists have discarded the concept of stigmatized dialects and varieties. However, for many scholars in the Nubian field, differences between Napatan Egyptian and Middle Kingdom Egyptian are still a sign of language degradation and scribal incompetence, as if the Egyptian language itself were a sacred museum object that must be preserved by everyone in its 'original state,' whatever that was, and not a living language like any other, a tool to be used, altered, and adapted further in the hands of all speakers, non-native and native alike.

Indeed, Carsten Peust has already addressed the question of how Egyptian, when used by non-native speakers in Nubia, began to develop into a new variety or dialect. His study of late Napatan stelae texts, such as those by Harsiyotef, Nastasen, and Ary, treats differences between Egyptian and Napatan Egyptian as features of a newly developing dialect, albeit one more affected by Late Egyptian rather than by languages spoken in Nubia. This 'dialect' might later have developed into a new language, as happened in Europe when the imperial language, Latin, was used for centuries by non-Romans, and eventually split into the Romance languages. Differences reflect not a degradation of Egyptian, but the beginnings of the change of the ancient Egyptian language into a new form, as developed by second-language speakers.

This process of development in Napatan Egyptian did not continue long enough for Egyptian to develop a descendant in the way that French, for example, developed from Latin. The Meroitic language, still waiting on the sidelines for its official written appearance, was a living language, used daily, and scholars serving libraries like that at Gebel Barkal were not powerful enough to preserve classical Egyptian in the face of a living language. At some point, Meroitic simply took over in importance, and the imperative to use it officially overwhelmed any desire to remain traditionally connected with Egypt linguistically.

In any case, the use of language, texts, and writing in Nubia was changing yet again at this time. More use was made of contemporary varieties of Egyptian in the rapidly expanding world of the centuries before Christ. Ptolemaic Egyptian texts were brought from Philae, and hymns to non-Egyptian gods were newly composed in Nubia using elements of Late Egyptian. Most importantly, we now see, during the reign of the queen Shanakdakheto at Naqa, the first use of written Meroitic, a native language of Kush with a long history. This development signifies a huge change in Nubian thought on the traditional proprieties of language use, and it is clear evidence that language policy in Kush was consciously planned and open to review. Whereas the acknowledged policy had always been to use Egyptian, the new policy was to use the native language for official communication. Whether this had nationalistic, dynastic, economic, or practical causes is unknown at the moment.

Written Meroitic appears rather suddenly in the archaeological record, sometime around the reign of Shanakdakheto, the first Meroitic reigning queen, and this suddenness probably reflects the reality of its invention. Meroitic, which may well have been spoken for a thousand years or more in Nubia and thus probably underwent its own significant but unrecorded internal changes, now appears in written form. Someone simply devised an alphabet for it. It seems a logical step, but it was not. The great old imperial languages of the time were written in complicated scripts with hundreds if not thousands of signs, and this complexity was undoubtedly valued and revered. There were not many stimulants for change in the form of models of efficient alphabets available, although Greek was the most well known in Nubia. In any case, use of an alphabet is not a sine qua non, as the Chinese and Japanese demonstrate daily. A new alphabet, in monumental hieroglyphic form and in a separate script form, was nonetheless created, exclusively for Meroitic.

Figure 103. Stela of Tanyidamani. Photograph © 2012 Museum of Fine Arts, Boston.

Invented alphabets usually do not have a development period. They are traditionally reported to have been put together by one individual, whose name is often revered. Pronunciation clues (letters, syllabic signs) are routinely chosen from scripts familiar to the inventor. These visual 'hints' are married to the articulated sounds (consonants and vowels, or syllables) necessary for the language being scripted, and it then remains only to teach new users how to use the alphabet to sound out their own language. Adopted or borrowed letters need not be matched to the same sound with which they were associated in the original language.

It is not even always necessary for the creator to be literate—a syllabary consisting of eighty-six signs (borrowed from English letters) for the North American Cherokee language was invented by the non-reader and Native American Sequoyah. The syllabary was called 'Talking Leaves' and in a short time the first newspaper written in the new alphabet appeared, attracting large numbers of enthusiastic, newly literate readers. The Koreans use an invented alphabet, Hangul, with signs borrowed from Asian scripts. Hangul is said to have been invented by a king. The Armenian alphabet was created along much the same principles, by one individual borrowing signs from other scripts in the area. Meroitic writing is thus a typical member of the invented alphabet group, with signs borrowed from Egyptian, but used in a very different way to spell out syllables.

The advantages of this new script, for the ruling class, must have been numerous. An alphabet is easy to learn, and facilitates communication immensely. Although there must have been conservative resisters to this very modern literacy technology, and also to the concomitant change of official language, new users certainly wielded expanded power in their ability to pass along information to armies, construction crews, subordinates in other centers of power, and commercial partners. One person who had mastered the alphabet could now read aloud in the native language for the edification of all listeners. The stela of Tanyidamani, the first known long text in Meroitic, was set up in public areas of the temple complex at Gebel Barkal, and as László Török suggests, was probably read aloud to the general public. No translator was necessary, since the stela was composed in the native language. Public readings of announcements, official texts, letters, and so on could have become commonplace. Instead of employing individuals who had mastered Egyptian and its difficult hieroglyphic script as a second language, a Meroitic administration could now teach the new system with its twenty-three signs to officials anywhere in the empire in a matter of days. Use of written Meroitic would have been advantageous politically, financially, dynastically, militarily, economically, and undoubtedly socially. It may well also have been a nationalistic statement and source of pride, as other invented alphabets have been.

We might even go so far as to posit a sort of cultural revolt against the imperial language of ancient Egypt, as we see now in parts of Wales and Scotland against English, and with the Basque language in France and Spain. A language is at the heart of a culture, and there comes a point at which cultural and linguistic pride triumphs over theory and habit. People naturally want to use their own language, rather than the one first imposed on them by colonists and conquerors, then used as a political or organizational convenience. What was once convenient and practical eventually becomes inconvenient and senseless. This process can and does occur naturally, and should not be overlooked during scholarly ruminations over the loss of the Nubians' educated elite and its intellectual inability to continue using an old imperial second language. It would, indeed, have been unnatural for the Kushites to continue using

classical Egyptian, particularly as the Egyptian language and Egypt were changing so dramatically in late antiquity. As to the ruler presiding over this new development, we will probably never be able to answer the question of whether Shanakdakheto initiated the new alphabet herself, commissioned it from others, or resisted it as long as she could.

Naturally, once the use of script passed into the hands of the scribal class and later into the hands of the population as a whole, changes were made in the forms of the signs, some perhaps intentional improvements, but some also occurring as a natural result of general, public use of the alphabet. Alphabetic and syllabic signs can change over time unless they are literally 'set in stone' by the invention of printing, which did not happen. Many texts appear to have been written on papyrus, leather, or perhaps other natural materials such as wood or even leaves. Unfortunately, due to the climate, we have very few examples of Meroitic written on perishable materials, but it is hardly to be believed that the Meroites had no cheap, convenient writing materials available. The increasing similarity of some signs over time points to the existence of very experienced readers and writers, treating words as entire visual groups rather than as individual letters to be sounded out, and for whom sign similarity would not have been a hindrance to comprehension. Surely these experienced readers and writers had convenient writing materials at hand.

The Meroitic decision to use word dividers (two or three dots after a complete word) in writing is an interesting one. In modern times, of course, many languages place spaces between words. This facilitates reading even for native users, especially if they are not fluent readers, and is, as a by-product, of particular help to readers from a different language background. Ancient Egyptian, however, did not use any method of separating words, nor did most languages in the ancient world. Sentences therefore present themselves initially to the learner as strings of signs. Until sufficient vocabulary and grammar skills are developed, a second-language reader has to spend some time deciding where one word ends and another begins. It is conceivable that the Nubians, coerced for centuries into learning and using Egyptian as a second language for communication, simply decided at the time of the creation of their own script to make life easier and just separate the words.

In any case, apparently substantial numbers of businessmen, officials, scribes, and others learned to write. It certainly seems that, at least by the later Meroitic Period, literacy was not only an advantage exclusive to the scribal classes, but a tool that was much more widespread in the 'professional' population. There is now considerable evidence that new generations read and studied texts written by previous generations, a continuation of the scholarly attitude that the Napatans had long taken toward earlier religious and secular literature written in Egyptian.

Ironically, as soon as the Nubians begin to use their native language, we become unable to understand them. Although there is a good deal of material, including a few historical stelae, we basically cannot read it. Like some other ancient languages, for example, Etruscan, Meroitic cannot be translated, although we can pronounce it. Texts on offering tables are the only exception to this, containing, as they do, mostly names and a few of the words we do know. However, great strides in the understanding of the language have recently been made by the French Meroiticist Claude Rilly, who has very much increased the likelihood that we will be able to translate Meroitic soon by identifying lexical and morphological relationships between Meroitic and certain Northeastern Sudanic languages. This is enabling his team to begin increasing its lexical and grammatical base. Rilly has also furthered the study of the use of the script and its changes over time as a way to date inscriptions, objects found with them, and possibly kings' reigns as well. These developments give hope to all scholars and students that we will soon be able to understand much more Meroitic and finally open a window on late antiquity in this fascinating area of ancient northeast Africa.

Bibliography

Darnell, J.C. 2006. *The Inscription of Queen Katimala at Semna: Textual Evidence for the Origins of the Napatan State.* Yale Egyptological Studies 7. New Haven, CT: Yale Egyptological Seminar.

Eide, T., et al., eds. 1994. *Fontes Historiae Nubiorum: Textual Sources for the History of the Middle Nile Region between the Eighth Century BC and the Sixth Century AD.* Vol. 1: *From the Eighth to the Mid-Fifth Century BC.* Bergen: University of Bergen, Department of Classics.

Peust, C. 1999. *Das Napatanische: Ein ägyptischer Dialekt aus dem Nubien des späten ersten vorchristlichen Jahrtausends: Texte, Glossar, Grammatik.* Monographien zur Ägyptischen Sprache 3. Göttingen: Peust & Gutschmidt Verlag.

Priese, K.H. 1976. "Studien zur Topographie des 'äthiopischen' Niltales im Altertum und zur meroitischen Sprache." *EAZ* 16:315–29.

Redford, D.B. 2004. *From Slave to Pharaoh: The Black Experience of Ancient Egypt.* Baltimore: Johns Hopkins Press.

Rilly, C. 2004. "The Importance of Nara for the Study of the East African Past." May 2004. http://www.shaebia.org/cgibin/artman/exec/view.cgi?archive=9&num=2714

Smith, S.T. 2003. *Wretched Kush: Ethnic Identities and Boundaries in Egypt's Nubian Empire.* New York: Routledge.

Török, L. 1997. *The Kingdom of Kush: Handbook of the Napatan-Meroitic Civilization.* Leiden: Brill.

———. 2002. *The Image of the Ordered World in Ancient Nubian Art: The Construction of the Kushite Mind, 800 BC–300 AD.* Leiden: Brill.

Daily Life in Ancient Nubia

Peter Lacovara

Compared to the rich textual and pictorial record of everyday life in ancient Egypt, our information on Nubian society is very limited. We do know that the lack of a broad, fertile floodplain along most of the Nubian Nile made agriculture of far less importance, and thus the ancient Nubians were more reliant on hunting and herding of sheep, goats, and cattle for food and clothing.

Certainly the need to bring down wild game gave the Nubians their much-vaunted ability with the bow and arrow, which would also lead them to be employed as police and soldiers by the Egyptians and to spread their fame as archers throughout the ancient world. Likewise, the importance of cattle, sheep, and goat herding would also have a profound impact on Nubian society, as manifested in their art and even in their religion.

This need for a semi-nomadic existence probably revealed itself in the creation of seasonal encampments, particularly in the earliest periods. Small settlements built of post and wattle and daub or dry stone masonry structures are found throughout Nubia at all periods and must be evidence, at least in part, of this wandering existence.

Larger and long-lived settlements, such as the vast city at Kerma, document another, more urban type of life. Developing over many centuries, the settlement at Kerma grew to be the capital of a large and powerful kingdom by the classical phase of the culture during the Second Intermediate Period in Egypt. The city was roughly circular in shape and surrounded by a large defensive dry moat and wall. It was quartered by two main roads running north to south and east to west, intersecting in the center of the town, the whole corresponding to the shape of an idealized urban plan depicted in the Egyptian hieroglyph, *niwt*.

At the intersection of the two avenues was an immense mud-brick temple known as the Lower or Western Deffufa. Fronted by a massive pylon entrance, this temple was surrounded by workshops and storerooms and had been rebuilt and enlarged many times over the centuries. As was the case with Egyptian temples, it must have played an important economic role in the functioning of the city. The town itself was home to a large royal palace, chapels, and storage magazines, along with a multitude of habitations, both rectangular mud-brick buildings as well as more traditional round post-hole dwellings. In addition to the town, farther afield some farmsteads have been excavated in the countryside that clearly were provisioning this population center.

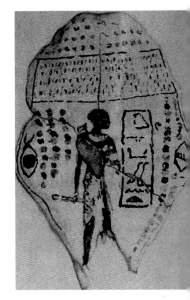

Figure 104. Pan-Grave painted cow skull from Mostagedda.

167

Kerma's wealth came not just from military conquest, but also from its control of trade, both along the Nile and through desert caravan routes. The area was an important conduit for river traffic going farther down the Nile, and the Egyptians had sought to maintain control of it and levy taxes on goods being shipped north when they controlled Lower Nubia in the Middle and New Kingdoms. The forts they built to control commerce also served as centers for gold processing. Gold-washing stations and assay paraphernalia have been found in the forts, which were populated not only by garrisons of Egyptian troops but also by treasury officials.

In the barren stretches of the Second Cataract, food had to be shipped in to feed the residents of the forts who received rations from government storehouses. Fishhooks and net sinkers found at the forts indicate that the inhabitants supplemented their diet by

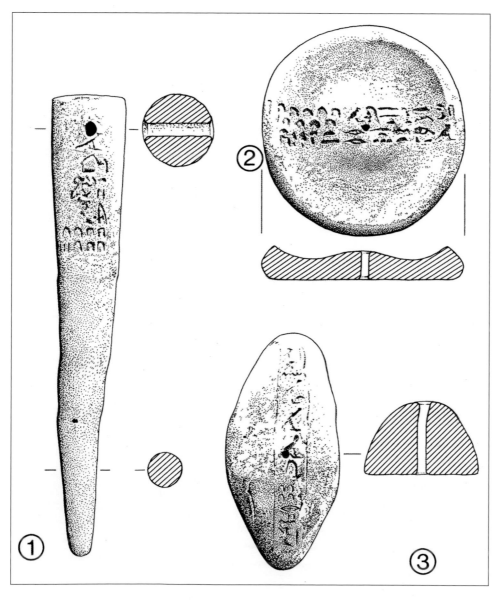

Figure 106. Wood ration token from the Second Cataract Forts.

catching fish in the river. Within the forts, they lived in small communities either in barracks or in houses, some of them quite well appointed, and worshiped in small chapels that were dedicated to Egyptian gods and local deities.

During the later New Kingdom, large Egyptian cities and temples were built throughout Lower Nubia. The Egyptian and Nubian populations seem to have coexisted in this area, and Nubians served as interpreters for trading and military expeditions sent farther south.

The rise of the Kingdom of Napata illustrated the continuing process of Egyptianization of the Nubian population that had begun in the New Kingdom. Although the remains of the capital city have yet to be discovered, the vast temple complex at Gebel Barkal, built originally by the Egyptian pharaohs of the New Kingdom, but greatly expanded upon by the Nubian rulers, indicates its importance as a regional center. Situated at the base of a large, flat-topped mountain visible for many kilometers, the place was an ideal spot to serve as a destination of traders and travelers alike.

Associated with the temples were royal palaces and vast bakeries, much like those found in an Egyptian temple complex. A resident priesthood would have maintained the temple cults and overseen the redistribution of temple gifts and offerings.

When conflict, shifting trade patterns, and possibly climatic conditions forced the kingdom to focus on its southern frontier in the Meroitic Period, advances in irrigation, such as the water-wheel or *saqya*, made agriculture feasible in the areas around Meroe, and another large urban center was constructed, with some features adopted from classical cities, including a Roman bath and an astronomical observatory. The description of Meroe by the classical historians recorded that, much like the earlier town of Kerma, it had houses built of both wickerwork and mud brick.

By far, however, most Nubians probably lived in small villages or seasonal encampments, which have not been well represented in the archaeological record, but regional surveys such as those recently conducted in the Third and Fourth Cataract areas are beginning to round out our picture of ancient Nubian settlement patterns.

Figure 105. Drawing of Nubian village life from an incised bronze bowl found at Karanog.

Bibliography

Trigger, B.G. 1976. *Nubia under the Pharaohs*. London: Thames and Hudson.

Shinnie, P. 1967. *Meroe: A Civilization of the Sudan*. New York and Washington: Praeger.

WOMEN IN ANCIENT NUBIA

Joyce Haynes and Mimi Santini-Ritt

Non-royal Kushite Women

The information about non-royal Nubian women is far from complete. This is primarily because there are so few excavated non-royal burial grounds. There are also very few visual representations of women and even fewer pieces of inscriptional evidence. However, from graves of different periods we do have some knowledge about clothing and jewelry. The A-Group and C-Group burials indicate that loincloths of leather and linen, as well as leather sandals and caps, were worn. From Kerma burials there are similar types of clothing, but at this time they are often far more richly decorated with mica and beads of faience, shell, gold, and silver. In addition to elaborate mica-covered caps, leather net coverings adorned their heads. Tunics and skirts of linen or leather were decorated with beads, red stain, or pierced patterns.

Over fifteen hundred non-royal graves were excavated in Sanam by F.Ll. Griffith in 1923. Among them were numerous graves dating from 800 to 600 BC that contained non-royal female skeletal remains. From these graves it is evident that adornment continued to be as important for the non-royal women as it was for the royal. A great variety of types of jewelry was found in these graves. The clothing too continued to be decorated, here with bronze circular bosses. Tomb 1516 contained an especially large number of jewelry items, which ornamented nearly every part of the body from top to bottom. The hair was covered with a cap made out of blue-glazed Eye of Horus beads. Earrings with pendants and a bronze band at the forehead with pendant tubular flower were present. Cuffs and bangles made of bronze and faience adorned the wrists. There were a number of bronze rings, and strings of beads and scarabs were found on the forearms. Eight faience plaques strung with beads were around the neck and on the chest. Many of these types of jewelry elements were found in the royal repertoire as well.

Inscriptional evidence for non-royal women in Nubia is scant. We know that a non-royal woman could have a stela made for her grave, as one of the few known inscribed pieces is a funerary stela dating to the Napatan Period (fourth century BC) from Begarawiya, now in the Museum of Fine Arts, Boston, made for a woman named Pasalta. While we know little about her, she must have been a woman of high status. There is slightly more inscriptional evidence of non-royal Kushite women in Egypt from Theban tombs. The tomb of Tjesreperet, the nurse of one of Taharqo's daughters, was found at Thebes (TG 924, 690–664 BC). Her elaborate inner and outer coffins were found with floral garlands placed on top. Theban tomb VII in the Asasif contained a coffin belonging to a woman named Kheril, clearly depicted as Kushite. Another Theban tomb belonging to Senneferi contained the burial equipment of a Kushite woman named Nyiw who had the title of 'Follower,' *sedjem-ash (sḏm-ꜥš)*. Her father was Padiamun, Prophet of Amun in Kawa.

There is also further substantiation of non-royal Kushite women living in Egypt, married to Egyptians, and participating in religious cults. Two women, Khikhy and Qeqiry, dating to the Late Period, can be identified as Kushite. They each hold the title 'Follower of Mut,' and both are shown offering mirrors to the goddess Mut. An unnamed woman on a stela in the Louvre, identified as Kushite by her garment, is shown offering a mirror to Re-Horakhty. Another religious title for a woman named Taneferher on a stela in Leiden was 'Songstress of the Interior of Amun.' While her name is Egyptian, she is shown with what appears to be a typical Kushite tail on her garment, indicating a Kushite costume.

In the second century AD there is a rare glimpse of a non-royal woman with her family. It is engraved on a bronze bowl in the Museum of Fine Arts, Boston. Here a woman is kneeling before a dome-shaped hut, accompanied by a standing man and a female figure who is probably her daughter. They are approached by two young men and a procession of cattle. Her short-cropped hairstyle was always the favored Nubian style. While modest, her adornment consists of what appears to be a collar and necklace of pendant beads, as well as bracelets and armlets. The details of an elaborately patterned skirt indicate the continuation of well-known skirt decorations popular at least as far back as the Kerma burials. The

Figure 107. Silver amulet of a goddess suckling Queen Neferukakashta, from al-Kurru, Pyramid 52. Photograph © 2012 Museum of Fine Arts, Boston.

hairstyle and costume of the second-century non-royal woman do not seem dramatically different from what one might have seen more than a millennium earlier.

Napatan Queens

The Napatan queens were a powerful group of women whose titles reflect their prominence and prestige in the royal family: King's Mother, Great King's Wife, King's Wife, King's Daughter, and King's Sister are all frequent designations. A Napatan king could have many different queens, and each queen could have one or more of these titles. Most queens bore the title 'King's Wife,' but usually only one was referred to as the 'Great King's Wife.' The meaning of this latter title is unclear, because there appears to be no correlation between the Great King's Wife and the mother of the succeeding king. In fact, no woman called King's Mother is recorded as also being a Great King's Wife or even a King's Wife.

Kings valued their female relatives highly. It was the duty of the king to honor his female ancestors by making funerary offerings to them (as on Stela Kawa VI, now in the Khartoum Museum). Kings commonly prayed for their mothers' welfare. Anlamani, on his Enthronement Stela, asks the god to "Have regard for my mother, and establish her children on earth." The King's Mother was a highly significant individual, so much so that some scholars argue that the maternal bloodline determined who was an acceptable candidate for kingship. Taharqo, on Stela Kawa IV, quotes his ancestor, King Alara, as praying for the children of the queen, namely future kings: "Look upon the womb of my ⌐mothers⌐ (?) for me and establish their children on earth. Act for them as you acted for me, and let them attain what is good." Although the pattern to the line of succession is unclear, one thing is known: The king had to be born to a woman who had the title Sister of a King.

Taharqo and Aspelta both trace back their female ancestral lines to the start of the Napatan royal family in order to legitimize their kingship. Taharqo's genealogy shows that his mother Abalo was the Sister of a King and niece of King Alara, founder of the reigning family (as named on Stelae Kawa IV and Kawa VI). On his Enthronement Stela (now in the Egyptian Museum, Cairo), Aspelta records the speech of the god Amun legitimizing Aspelta's rule, as presented by László Török in his 2002 publication:

> His father was my son, the Son-of-Re [father's name in a cartouche now missing], justified; and his mother is King's Sister, King's Mother, Mistress of Kush, and Daughter of Re, Nasalsa, may she live for ever, whose mother [again] was the King's Sister, Divine Adoratrice of Amun-Re, king of the gods of Dominion, [name in a cartouche now missing], justified. Her mother was the King's Sister [name in cartouche now missing], justified.

Another four female ancestors are similarly listed, the earliest of whom bears the additional title Mistress of Kush. While a king often cited the name of his mother, this is a rare instance in which the king names his earthly father, by means of the speech of Amun. The king's divine father was Amun; it was his godly father that was of importance. Aspelta's dynastic legitimacy was therefore based both on his divine father and his mother's relationship to a long line of King's Sisters.

At the coronation ceremony, the King's Mother was intimately connected with legitimizing the king—so much so that the ceremony could not occur without her ritual participation at its conclusion. Taharqo, Anlamani, Aspelta, and Irike-Amanote all refer to the journeys that their mothers made to see them crowned. Anlamani relates that he sent a courtier to the "circle of king's sisters" to bring his mother Nasalsa to his coronation. Taharqo's mother Abalo traveled all the way from Napata to Memphis for this purpose. "She was exceedingly joyful after seeing the beauty of His Majesty, as Isis saw her son Horus appearing on the throne of his father after he had been a youth in the swamp of Chemmis" (Tanis Stela). The text continues to say that everyone then bowed their heads to the ground to the King's Mother and rejoiced that mother and son were reunited, as Isis and Horus had been.

The King's Mother played an active role in the coronation, as it was she who made a speech to Amun asking him to grant her son kingship. The coronation speeches made by Abalo and Nasalsa were preserved on stelae by their sons, as published by Robert Ritner.

> Recitation by the king's sister and king's mother, the Mistress of Kush, [Nasalsa]. "I have come before you, O Amon-Re, Lord of the Thrones of the Two Lands, great god. (2) Foremost of his harem, who knows his name and who gives valor to the one who is loyal to him. May you establish your beloved son [Aspelta], living forever in this chief office of Re, so that he might be greater in it (4) than all the gods. May you multiply his years of life on earth like (those of) the sun disk in heaven. May you give to him all life and dominion issuing from you, all health issuing from you, all joy issuing from you and appearance upon the throne of Horus forever."

Nasalsa is actually depicted presenting this speech on Aspelta's Enthronement Stela. The kneeling Aspelta is shown receiving kingship from Amun of Napata and Mut. Nasalsa faces them and makes her direct appeal to Amun.

King's Wives were also important at the coronation. In one known instance, rather than a King's Mother, it is Piankhi's (Piye's) Great Wife Pekereslo who makes the coronation speech. In coronation scenes of Kings Taharqo, Tanwetamani, Harsiyotef, and Nastasen, both the King's Mother and King's Wife are shown. The king with his mother appears on one side of the scene and the king with a wife on the other. Both royal women are represented participating in the coronation, shown holding sistra and making libation offerings.

It is possible that Napatan queens and King's Mothers themselves may have been crowned or enthroned. The Chaliut Stela from Gebel Barkal B500 states that King Aspelta was on the Horus throne with Nasalsa "as Isis was with Horus." Some scholars believe that this may mean that she was a regent or co-regent. King Nastasen's stela says that his mother Pelcha "was given the crown of Napata." The full implication of this is not known. Nastasen's Great(?) Wife Sachmach has a Horus name and is referred to as "king" at both the beginning and end of her stela from Gebel Barkal B551. Unfortunately, the rest of the inscription is barely decipherable. Some suggest she may have been a ruling queen, a precursor for the Meroitic ruling queens that follow.

The names of King's Mothers always appear in cartouches, in two instances preceded by Daughter of Re. Those of King's Wives are often in cartouches as well. Queens and King's Mothers had titles that paralleled many of those of the kings. They were known as Mistress of the Two Lands, Mistress of Upper and Lower Egypt, Mistress of Foreign Lands, Mistress of Egypt/Ta-Sety/Kush, and the like. Other titles relate to their standing at court, High Born, First of His Majesty, King's Acquaintance, Mistress of all Women. Their cultic roles were also reflected: Mistress of the *j3mt* Scepter, Great One of the *hts*-Scepter, Sistrum Player before Amun-Re. The

Figure 108. Relief of the God's Wives of Amun Amenirdis I and Shepenwepet II in the temple of Medinet Habu in Thebes.

variety and incidence of titles is much greater in the Twenty-fifth Dynasty than in later Napatan times. The same can be said for epithets, which include 'the one who satisfies the heart of the king through that which she performs daily'; 'the one who causes the king's heart to rejoice on account of all that she says'; 'the one who is united to the limbs of the god'; 'the sole ornament of the king'; 'sweet of love'; 'great in grace'; and so on.

Queens could also share in rites normally reserved for kings in Egypt. One such rite was being suckled by a goddess. A winged goddess suckles a queen on a silver amulet from the tomb of Neferukakashta, wife of Piankhi. Also referencing this rite is a breast-shaped, double-spouted silver bowl found in the tomb of Khensa, Great Wife of Piankhi. By being breast-fed by a goddess, divinity and the potential for ceremonial rebirth were passed on to the queen. This iconography in

Egypt was reserved only for kings, with a single exception—the God's Wife Shepenwepet I, who is thus represented in a relief from the Osiris-Hekadjet Chapel at Karnak (see below). Other than this example, the concept of a queen being suckled by a goddess appears to be indigenous to Kush.

Queenship was viewed as an essential component of governing, necessary for guaranteeing the kingship. The king and queen together ensured the continued existence of the kingdom by maintaining both worldly and cosmic order. Queens and especially King's Mothers were frequently represented on reliefs and stelae, along with the king, playing an active role as priestesses of the royal cult of the god Amun. There are numerous representations of them rattling the sistrum and pouring libations. A Napatan queen could address the gods directly, and was likened to a goddess. As such, the queen was a mediator between the earthly and divine realms.

Figure 109. Statue of the
God's Wife of Amun,
Ankhnesneferibre from Karnak,
Dynasty Twenty-six. Photo ©
Chester Higgins Jr 2012.

Many royal women held other important cultic positions. Some titles include Chantress of Amun, Chief Priestess of Hathor, and Priestess of Mut. Typically, the king would make the original appointment. Taharqo records that his ancestor Alara, the founder of the ruling family, dedicated one (or more) of his sisters to be priestesses of the god Amun. As one of these priestesses was Taharqo's grandmother (and therefore not celibate), the nature of this office was clearly different from that of the God's Wife of Amun at Thebes (see below). King Anlamani installed four of his sisters (including his sister-wife Madiken) as sistrum players in the temples of Napata, Kawa, Pnubs, and Sanam—one in each of the four administrative regions of Nubia. In one case, a position was passed on for three generations: from King's Mother Nasalsa to her daughter Queen Madiken (wife and sister of both King Aspelta and King Anlamani) and thereafter to Madiken's daughter Henuttakhbit.

The God's Wife

The position of the God's Wife (*ḥmt-nṯr*) of Amun at Thebes, along with her designated successor the Divine Adoratress (*dwȝt-nṯr*), was by far the most important cultic position held by a royal woman. The title God's Wife had existed in Egypt since the Eighteenth Dynasty and was usually held by a King's Wife or King's Daughter. In the Napatan Period, the position was passed on from one female relative of the king to another by means of adoption. According to most scholars, the God's Wife was a celibate priestess consecrated solely to the service of the god Amun. During the Twenty-fifth Dynasty, the powers and responsibilities of the God's Wife of Amun (note that at this time the god's name is never actually specified) were twofold. She held the highest religious office in Thebes, surpassing even that of the High Priest of Amun, and was also the de facto ruler of the

Theban area, given powers and rights usually reserved for the king alone. This office moved beyond its cultic role and became perhaps the most influential political role held by a woman.

When the Kushite King Kashta (ca. 765–753 BC) secured Upper Egypt as part of his kingdom, one of his first acts was to make his daughter, Amenirdis I, the adopted daughter and therefore successor of the reigning God's Wife of Amun of Thebes, Shepenwepet I, daughter of Osorkon III. By doing this, he guaranteed the loyalty of Upper Egypt, as his daughter would be its virtual ruler. He also gained ideological and political justification for his reign. Amenirdis I adopted her niece Shepenwepet II, daughter of King Piankhi, as her daughter-successor, who in turn adopted her niece Amenirdis II, daughter of Taharqo. During the Kushite rule in the Twenty-fifth Dynasty, the position God's Wife of Amun was at its peak of power. The Kushite control over the position ended in the reign of Psamtik I (ca. 655 BC), when he arranged for his own daughter, Nitocris I, to be installed as the next successor.

As the spouse of Amun, the God's Wife was identified with the goddess Mut, and as a living god, she maintained contact between the earthly sphere and the heavenly realm. In fact, the God's Wife and Amun himself could be depicted as the same size in reliefs. Likened to the king, she was shown participating in acts of adoration, coronation, consecration of offerings, giving *maat* (see glossary), performing foundation rites, and even having her own *sed* (jubilee) festival. Importantly, just like the king, she was believed to have been suckled by a goddess. She also had her name written in a cartouche. Shepenwepet II was called 'sovereign of the two lands' and was even represented twice as a sphinx. In Twenty-fifth Dynasty Thebes, it was always the God's Wife rather than the queen who was shown at the

Figure 110. Painting of Queen Qalhata from her burial chamber at al-Kurru. Photo © Chester Higgins Jr 2012.

king's side or in symmetrical scenes. Many of the rights and privileges of the God's Wives were mirrored in the unusually powerful role played by Kushite queens.

The God's Wife presided over a body of priestesses called 'The Inner Abode of Amun' and was head of a large household with her own court and an extensive staff, including her own major-domo, scribes, chamberlains, and doorkeepers. As such, she wielded substantial economic power. The Kushite God's Wives lived in Egypt and adopted Egyptian names. These priestesses were buried in Egypt, and elaborate tomb chapels for Amenirdis I and Shepenwepet II have been found in Egypt at Medinet Habu. Beneath them were vaulted burial chambers similar to the Napatan royal tombs, and although they were found largely empty, a bronze bed fitting was discovered, suggesting that the God's Wives might have been buried there according to Napatan custom.

Napatan Dress

The God's Wives adopted the Egyptian style of the day. They wore tight sheath dresses over their slender bodies and long elaborate wigs. Rarely were they shown with the short curly hairstyle of the Kushite women. They most commonly wore a vulture headdress, often topped with two tall feathers of Amun, supplemented at times with a sun disc.

In contrast to the God's Wives, the other Napatan royal women wore a uniquely Kushite dress style, known primarily from reliefs. There is only one nearly complete sculpture of a Napatan queen, a life-size striding statue of Amanimalol (second half of seventh century BC), now headless, from the cache at Gebel Barkal B500A. The costume usually consisted of an under dress, over which a wide cape, often worn open, was knotted at one or both shoulders. This cape could

have fringed or striped trim and was usually represented as transparent, so that the slender torso and legs were visible. At times, a scarf or cloth was worn over the shoulder, the end of which dangled down the back in a triangle. The outfit was frequently completed by a 'tail' hanging down below the hem of the dress in the back. This distinctly Kushite feature has been interpreted by some as a fox tail.

A rare example of the queen in a panther skin and tassels, attire known more commonly from depictions of Meroitic kings, can be seen in the relief of the north wall of Kawa Temple T, Room D. Sandals in a variety of styles were worn, although sometimes the queens were barefoot. Royal Napatan women were depicted with very modest amounts of adornment. They were traditionally shown with broad collars and occasionally with bracelets, but little else is worn. Anklets and earrings were rarely shown.

Other than the God's Wives of Amun, royal Napatan women did not wear wigs. Their curly hair was traditionally worn very short. At times little pendants or braids tied off with tassels or beads appeared at the back of the head. Headdresses varied; most were the same as those worn by kings. The most common was the basic king's crown, consisting of a skullcap with a diadem fronted by a uraeus (or uraei) and backed by two streamers. There were many variations in the diadem decoration and style of uraei; there was also a variety of elements that could top the crown. The King's Mother often wore just the skullcap crown, with only one uraeus. The queens could wear the skullcap alone or with additions, most frequently the double-feather crown or double-feather crown with sun disc and horns. At times, they wore the Egyptian queens' vulture headdress. Another queens' headdress was a fillet with a lotus blossom or uraeus at the forehead, sometimes shown with streamers at the back. A very unusual headdress or hairstyle consisted of one to four long slender bobbing elements that appear to stand up on the top center of the head. The number of elements may be associated with rank. When depicted together, the King's Wives and the King's Mother always wore different crowns. A relief of Atlanersa's female relatives shows queens of varying ranks wearing different headdresses. The variety of crown types increases, particularly in later Napatan times.

Napatan Burials

Both males and females were buried in the royal cemeteries of al-Kurru and Nuri. Al-Kurru was the earliest royal cemetery, used until the time of Taharqo, who moved the royal burial ground to Nuri. In both cemeteries, the queens' tombs were located in areas close to, but separate from, those of the kings. At al-Kurru, the more important queens were buried in pyramids in a small field to the south of the kings, the less important queens to the north, and a few low-ranking royal women were buried in a group of very small graves crammed together to the far north. At Nuri, queens were buried in three groups to the south, west, and north of Taharqo's tomb, whereas the kings were all buried to the east. The most prestigious of the queens' pyramids belong to the Kings' Mothers and were located near Taharqo's pyramid. The King's Wives' pyramids were mainly in two rows in the northern group. Located the farthest from Taharqo's pyramid is a group of small shaft tombs, no doubt for lesser royal women.

Queens were often buried in elaborate graves very similar to those of the kings. A typical royal Napatan tomb consisted of a pyramidal superstructure, often with a chapel and sometimes also a cult stela on the east. Stairs led down to the burial area, consisting of one or more chambers.

Most of the burials had been badly plundered, but there is evidence for nesting wooden sarcophagi with bronze-rimmed inlaid stone eyes. The sarcophagi could be placed on funerary beds or on coffin benches. Numerous heart scarabs, amulets, and jewelry of precious metal and stones (including gold finger caps) were placed on the body. The tomb goods also included hundreds of *shawabtis*, mirrors, canopic jars, offering tables, and fine vessels of travertine, metal, and pottery. Queen Mernua, one of the few queens from the Napatan Period found buried at Meroe, had a coffin ensemble that was relatively undisturbed. It consisted of three nesting anthropoid coffins, a silver gilt mummy mask, and beadnet covering. Overall, luxury grave goods in the queens' burials were comparable to those found in the kings'.

Napatan Queens in Egypt

Evidence indicates that Napatan queens traveled to and possibly lived in Egypt. A group of five royal women of the Twenty-fifth Dynasty appears to have been buried in one area of the cemetery at Abydos. Most notable of this group were the Great

Figure 111. Fragment of a steatite stela depicting King Amanikhabale presenting broad collars to the ram-headed Amun and human-headed Mut. Photo © Chester Higgins Jr 2012.

King's Wife Isisemchebit, Pekereslo (Kashta's daughter and wife of Piankhi), and Paabtameri (King's Sister, King's Daughter). Many scholars equate Paabtameri with Pabatma, which would make her Kashta's wife and the mother of Pekereslo and Amenirdis I. Also there are sculpture fragments of Kushite queens from Karnak. One from the hypostyle hall was inscribed for Queen Khensa, and another from Temple A of the Mut precinct belonged to a larger-than-life-size statue of an unnamed King's Mother. It is known from texts that Queen Abalo visited Egypt for Taharqo's coronation. Taharqo's queen, members of the harem, and the crown prince were in Memphis when captured and deported by Esarhaddon, according to Assyrian sources.

There is also evidence for 'diplomatic' marriages. A King's Daughter Amenirdis (who may or may not have been Amenirdis II) was a wife of the Egyptian vizier Mentuhotep (according to the stela of Mentuhotep in Cairo). She is shown wearing Egyptian clothing, yet her hairstyle is distinctly Kushite. Also, Wedjarenes, granddaughter of a Kushite king, possibly Piankhi, was the third wife of Mentuemhat, mayor of Thebes. In Mentuemhat's tomb, she is represented as both Nubian and Egyptian, depending on whether the scene had a Nubian or Egyptian religious context. The Nitokris Adoption Stela makes it clear that Wedjarenes owned extensive property in her own right and remained in Egypt after the end of the Twenty-fifth Dynasty.

Meroitic Queens

The queen as an independent ruler is first seen in the Meroitic Period. However, the vital and active role that Napatan queens, and especially the God's Wife of Amun, played in rulership set the stage for this development. Meroitic queens inherited many of the rights and privileges of the Napatan queens, but they further expanded their role to include additional kingly responsibilities. Ruling queens now performed rituals previously reserved for the king, such as smiting the enemy, holding up the sky, and being crowned.

The concept promoted by classical writers that all the Meroitic queens holding the title Candace or *kandake (kn-ti-ky/ktke)* were independently ruling queens is no longer substantiated. Not every *kandake* was a ruling queen. It is more likely that the *kandake* was sister of the king (possibly the king's eldest sister) and the mother to the successor to the throne. Complete understanding of this position still eludes us, as there are many gaps in the inscriptional evidence. The title *kandake* may have been seen as early as the time of Queen Sar...tine (beginning of the third century BC), although this reading is now suspect, and was used until the time of Queen Amanitore (second half of the first century AD), who is the last attested to carry the title *kandake*. Michael Zach has listed seven *kandake*s for this time period. Three of these were also called *qore*, or ruler, namely Amanirenas, Amanishakheto, and likely Amanitore. This title, *qore*, was definitive proof that the queen had taken the throne. However, it is possible that a given queen lacks the title *qore* due to poor preservation or archaeological accident. In these cases, iconography could demonstrate that she was a ruling queen. Such features would include sitting on the lion throne, wearing or carrying the other kingly insignia detailed below, or having kingly titles such the Son of Re *(s3 Rʿ)* preceding her cartouche. However, the queen's name in a cartouche alone does not necessarily mean that she was a ruling queen.

The first woman to take the Meroitic throne was Queen Shanakdakheto (second half of the second century BC). Even though she does not have the title *qore*, her royal accoutrements, and her burial place with other rulers in the Northern Cemetery, rather than in the Western Cemetery

5261.

Figure 112. Sandstone Meroitic funerary stela of Lapakhidaye, from Aksha cemetery (Serra West). Photo © Chester Higgins Jr 2012.

Figure 113. Queen Amanishakheto smiting enemies on the temple pylon at Naqa.

where the non-ruling queens were buried, indicate that she was a ruling queen. There is a basalt life-size pair statue from Begarawiya of her (looking rather slender, as opposed to her more corpulent appearance in reliefs) and a prince who touches her headdress's streamers in a gesture of the act of coronation (now in the Egyptian Museum, Cairo). This sculpture is especially significant, because there are very few such sculptures known of queens. The prince also makes a similar gesture in her funerary chapel and is, in fact, always with her. It was common in Meroitic relief for a ruling queen to be accompanied by a prince (see below).

There is an exceptional time period, from about 50 BC to AD 40, in which there are four independently ruling queens. Three are successive: Nawidemak, Amanirenas, and Amanishakheto,

closely followed by Amanitore. The latter two are perhaps the most famous and well documented of the Meroitic queens, known from their inscriptions, temples, tombs, and tomb goods.

Queen Nawidemak took the throne after three generations of male rulers. Curiously, she did not build her pyramid in Meroe, as was customary, but moved it back to Gebel Barkal, where she built Pyramid 6. Possibly this shift to a new burial area indicated a change of dynasty. Her title, *qore* but not *kandake*, was found with her name on a gold-covered statue base.

Queen Amanirenas, consort of King Teriteqas, was shown accompanied by Prince Akinidad. After the death of King Teriteqas, Queen Amanirenas ascended to the throne, and Prince Akinidad continued to appear in her company on her monuments. Amanirenas is possibly the unnamed *kandake* against whom the Roman prefect in Egypt was said to fight when the Roman troops advanced to Napata, according to Strabo, the Greek geographer.

After the death of Amanirenas, Queen Amanishakheto was represented with Akinidad; his presence likely indicates that Amanishakheto was the successor of Amanirenas. It has been suggested that here, as well as in the case of Queen Shanakdakheto, the accompanying male was in some way involved in legitimizing the queen's rule. Queen Amanishakheto built several temples at Wad ban Naqa, as well as a lavish residence with a second story and possibly an atrium. Her mud-brick palace, 3700 square meters, is one of the largest found to date. Her pyramid at Meroe

Figure 114. Queen Amanitore and King Natakamani doing homage to the god Apedemak on the Naqa temple west wall.

was vandalized in 1834 by an Italian doctor named Guiseppe Ferlini, who was stationed in Egypt and had traveled to Sudan (see "The Treasure of a Nubian Queen"). Near the top of the pyramid in a small chamber, according to Ferlini, he found a hoard of jewelry. This location is much debated by scholars, as there has never been any indication of such a treasure in this part of any other pyramid. The bracelets, rings, amulets, and necklace elements were made of gold, silver, semiprecious stones, and inlaid glass. Several of the rings appear to depict scenes from the birth of a king on their bezels.

Amanitore was the last of the well-known Meroitic ruling queens. She was co-regent with King Natakamani, an unusual form of rulership that may have been influenced by contemporary Ptolemaic co-regencies in Egypt. Amanitore and Natakamani were responsible for the building and restoration of numerous temples in Napata, Meroe, Meroe City, Amara, and Wad ban Naqa. Theirs was a particularly prosperous period in Meroitic history. One of the most spectacular temples they built was the temple of Naqa. Remarkable images of the king and queen flank the entry pylon, the king on the left and the queen on the right, a juxtaposition seen throughout the temple. They each are smiting enemies that they hold by the hair. In this scene, the queen is depicted in an unusual role as fierce protector of the country and upholder of *maat*, a role traditionally reserved for the king.

While there were other ruling queens in Kush, they were minor figures. In general, over the late Meroitic Period there was an overall decline in the role of the monarchy, and rulers, both male and female, were reduced to a cultic function.

Most Meroitic queens were buried at Meroe. The queens' pyramids were not segregated from from the kings' as they had been in Napatan times. Meroitic queens' burials were, in appearance, not very different from Napatan queens' burials. The pyramid superstructure with burial chambers directly below was similar, although gradually the pyramids became smaller and less well built. Also in the first century AD, the outside access to the burial chamber by stairs was eliminated. Stelae and offering tables were still employed in the funerary rituals. Over the course of the Meroitic Period, the custom of using mummies, cartonnage, *shawabti*s, and coffins diminished. Although the contents of the graves were badly plundered, it is clear that they were still using lavish grave goods.

Meroitic Dress

The Meroitic queens' dress contained many of the same elements as the Napatan queens' dress. One new feature was that the long, wide robe of the Meroitic queens was now closed and was not transparent, so her legs were no longer visible. Features that were worn by Napatan kings but were new to the Meroitic queens' costume include the triple-ram-head necklace, ram-head earrings, and ram horns encircling the ears. Ruling Meroitic queens were often depicted wearing the same costume as the king, including insignia such as the 'royal sash' worn diagonally across the chest, one or more long tasseled bands worn over the shoulder, a panther skin, flails, palm and pine-cone scepters, and snake staff. Another less common look of the Meroitic queen shows her bare breasted, wearing only a long, often patterned, skirt.

The Kushite crown at this time takes on multiple new superstructures, reflecting the new powers of the ruling queen. The double crown of Egypt, the *atef* crown, and the *hemhem* crown were shown on ruling queens and kings. Each could be worn either alone or as elements of composite crowns. The Kushite skullcap, now sometimes secured by a chin strap, continued to be worn by both kings and queens.

Adornment reaches new heights of luxury in the Meroitic Period. In addition to broad collars, multiple necklaces become common. Especially noteworthy are the large ball-bead necklaces, often with sizeable amulet pendants suspended. Multiple bangle bracelets, armlets, and anklets gain popularity. A new item seen on queens is 'gauntlets,' wide, ornate bands covering the entire forearm. Another interesting new style that sets apart Meroitic queens is their long pointed fingernails.

A dramatic change also occurs in the way that the Meroitic queens were depicted. They now were shown, especially in relief, with heavy, powerful physiques, appearing nearly double the weight of the representations of Meroitic kings and goddesses. Hints of this corpulence started to be seen in the late Napatan Period. Representations of Meroitic queens in the round are rare; two examples found by John Garstang at Meroe in 1913 are quite stout, as is another example in the Museum of Fine Arts, Boston. Curiously, in two other sculptures, Queen Nawidemak's gold statuette and Queen Shanakdakheto's basalt pair statue, the queens are not shown as corpulent, but are rather more in keeping with the standard of the Napatan Period queens.

Conclusion

Our understanding of Kushite women is still incomplete. Overall, there is not a great deal of source material. What exists is often fragmentary and subject to a great deal of speculation and debate. Meroitic material remains largely undeciphered. What we do know is that in the Napatan and Meroitic Periods, royal women attained a status that had not been seen before. They were revered as ancestors and mothers of kings. As rulers, priestesses, and goddesses they attained unprecedented levels of involvement in royal and cultic roles. A clearer, more detailed picture of these Kushite royal women will emerge only with continued research and excavation.

Bibliography

Gitton, M., and J. Leclant. 1977. "Gottesgemahlin." *LÄ* 2: 792 ff.

Griffith, F.Ll. 1923. "Oxford Excavations in Nubia 18–25: The Cemetery at Sanam." *LAA* 10:73–171.

Kahn, D. 2005. "The Royal Succession in the 25th Dynasty." *MittSAG* 16:143–63.

Lohwasser, A. 2001a. *Die königlichen Frauen im antiken Reich von Kusch.* Meroitica 19. Wiesbaden: Harrassowitz.

———. 2001b. "Queenship in Kush: Status, Role and Ideology of Royal Women." *JARCE* 38:61–76.

Morkot, R.G. 1999. "Kingship and Kinship in the Empire of Kush." In S. Wenig, ed., *Studien zum antiken Sudan: Akten der 7. Internationalen Tagung für meroitistische Forschungen vom 14. bis 19. September 1992 in Gosen bei Berlin*, 179–229. Meroitica 15. Wiesbaden: Harrassowitz.

Ritner, Robert K. 2005. *Inscriptions from Egypt's Third Intermediate Period.* Boston: Brill.

Török, L. 1987. *The Royal Crowns of Kush: A Study in Middle Nile Valley Regalia and Iconography in the 1st Millennia B.C. and A.D.* Cambridge Monographs in African Archaeology 18, BAR International Series 338.

———. 2002. *The Image of the Ordered World in Ancient Nubian Art: The Construction of the Kushite Mind, 800 BC–300 AD.* Boston: Brill.

Zach, M. 1992. "Meroe: Mythos und Realität einer Frauenherrschaft in Antiken Afrika." In E. Specht, ed., *Nachrichten aus der Zeit*, Reihe Frauenforschung, Vol. 18, 73–114. Vienna: Wiener Frauenverlag.

———. 2001. "Gedanken zur *kdke* Amanitore." In C. Arnst, I. Hafemann, and A. Lohwasser, eds., *Begegnungen: Antike Kulturen im Niltal*, 509–20. Leipzig: Wodtke and Stegbauer.

Nubian Adornment

Yvonne J. Markowitz

The urge to adorn the body with jewelry is a uniquely human endeavor of considerable antiquity. Jewelry is, in fact, the oldest and most resilient of the decorative arts, transcending time and place. Although the forms and techniques used to make jewelry have varied over the millennia, its creation and use have remained constant due to its psychological utility and ability to serve as a powerful cultural signifier.

In most cultures, the earliest adornments were made of organic substances such as blossoms, seeds, and plant fiber. These rarely survive. Shell, however, is more durable and was used around 3000 BC in Nubia to make simple bangles and flat, disc-shaped beads. About a hundred of these are strung together in an A-Group assemblage from Lower Nubia. However, it is the hard stone bangle in this group that would have been the most prized. This ornament would have taken more skill and time to fabricate and would have been resistant to deterioration over time. The mica fragment in the assemblage was possibly used as a mirror, an important grooming accessory. Later, at Kerma around 1700 BC, mica would be used as a raw material to create decorative textile appliqués.

A range of jewelry forms and materials dating to around 2000 BC (C-Group culture) was discovered at the site of Aniba in northern Nubia by Georg Steindorff. Most common were cowrie shells (genus *Cypraea*) whose backs have been shaved off so they can be strung together at the ends and then worn flat on the body. We know that in Egypt young women wore them as girdles in the hopes of promoting fecundity, and it is possible that the same was true during this time period in Nubia. However, cowries are versatile shells and are used in countless ways throughout Africa to this day.

Also from Aniba, but somewhat later in date, is a group of faience amulets that appear to be Egyptian in origin. The circular amulets with various designs on the base are typical of First Intermediate Period Egyptian stamp seals, while other elements, such as the sacred eye, the falcon, the ankh, the *heh*, and the bead forms are all known Egyptian types.

While disc beads, bangles, and cowrie shells appear in many cultures throughout the world, some forms of adornment serve as cultural markers. This is the case with the matched sets of arm ornaments worn by the famed bowmen (the Medjayu) of the Nubian Pan-Grave culture. Contemporaries of C-Group peoples, these warriors were in the employ of the pharaoh and lived on Egyptian soil.

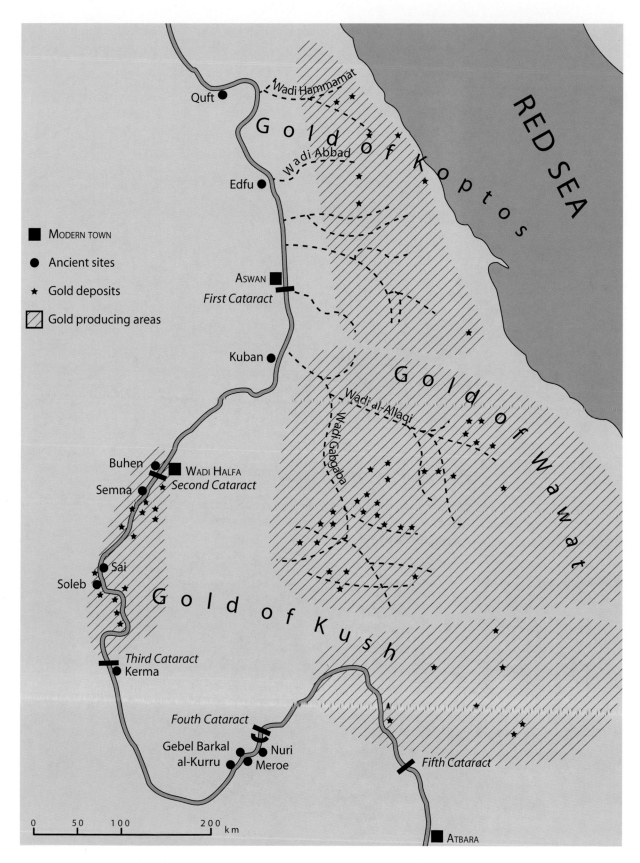

RED SEA

Quft ●

Wadi Hammamat

G o l d   o f   K o p t o s

Wadi Abbad

Edfu ●

■ MODERN TOWN

● Ancient sites

★ Gold deposits

▨ Gold producing areas

ASWAN ■
First Cataract

Kuban ●

Wadi al-Allaqi

Wadi Gabgaba

G o l d   o f   W a w a t

Buhen ●
■ WADI HALFA
Semna ●   *Second Cataract*

Sai ●
Soleb ●

G o l d   o f   K u s h

Third Cataract
Kerma ●

Fouth Cataract

Gebel Barkal ● ● Nuri
al-Kurru ● ● Meroe

Fifth Cataract

0   50   100   200 km

■ ATBARA

Figure 115. Map of Nubian gold deposits.

They are recognizable in Egyptian wall paintings by their distinctive dress and adornments.

In ancient times, Egypt's southern neighbor was called Nubia, perhaps based on the Egyptian word *nbw*, meaning gold. Alluvial gold in the form of nuggets and grain-sized particles was readily available along the banks of the Nile around Kerma—the so-called Gold of Kush. An even greater quantity—the Gold of Wawat—was extracted from quartz deposits in the Eastern Desert. The gold from Koptos, mined by the Egyptians, was largely depleted by 1500 BC, so Nubia became a very important source of gold in the Mediterranean world during the second millennium BC.

Early Kerma

The earliest inhabitants of the area located south of the Third Cataract, who lived around 2000 BC, had an affinity for carved shell and ivory jewelry. When Dows Dunham published his unique finds from Early Kerma burials, he noted several ornaments with no known parallels. He concluded that they were earrings, based on his observation that there were often two per interment and that they were usually located in the region around the head. However, it is difficult to imagine how they would have been worn on the ears. A more reasonable conclusion is that these objects were hair

Figure 116. Ivory stud earring. From Kerma, Tumulus IV, grave 440x. Photograph © 2012 Museum of Fine Arts, Boston.

Figure 117. Pair of ivory cuff bracelets from Kerma, Tomb KN 35. Photograph © 2012 Museum of Fine Arts, Boston.

ornaments. To secure the adornment, you would slide a clump of hair near the scalp through the narrow notch, achieving a ponytail-like effect. This lifts the hair away from skin, making it more comfortable in a warm climate.

As for the ears, ivory hoops were fashionable among Nubians, as illustrated in a later painting from the Theban tomb of the senior Egyptian treasury official, Sobekhotep. Here, Nubians wearing such hoops offer the products of tropical Africa to Sobekhotep, who receives the goods on behalf of Thutmose IV. Among the tribute items are gold ingots, ebony logs, carnelian, giraffe tails, a leopard skin, and a live baboon. Interestingly, the earring, so popular among Early Kerma peoples, did not become stylish among Egyptians until around 1500 BC, perhaps a direct influence from the south.

That earrings were important accessories in Nubia is evidenced by the numbers of ivory studs found in Early and Classic Kerma tombs—a form completely different in conception from the hoop. These too, would become popular in Egypt at a later date.

While ivory bangles continued to be crafted and worn throughout Kerma's history, it was during this period that they were modified into cuffs. This is a timeless design, easier to put on and remove. A pair of cuffs recovered from one burial indicates that such ornaments were sometimes worn stacked on one wrist, suggesting that the Nubians were less inclined to adorn the body with bilateral, symmetrical ornaments than the Egyptians.

Classic Kerma

Like the Egyptians, Kerma's ruling elite valued hard stones such as carnelian—a stone readily available in the Nile Valley and often used to create amulets and beads. Kerma craftsmen also made ornaments out of silver, a material not found in northeastern Africa but obtained through

Figure 118. Ivory cuffs in situ on right wrist, from Kerma, tomb KN 35.

trade with Egypt and Western Asia. Surviving examples of silver jewelry are made of thin metal sheet and wirework, suggesting the material was used sparingly.

Unique to Kerma are the bright-blue beads of glazed quartz. These beads are dazzling when held to the light, especially when the quartz is transparent. George Reisner and his team (published by Dows Dunham) found thousands of these small ornaments—one tunic alone had more than three thousand beads attached. These adornments were very difficult to produce, as the application of heat during the glazing process caused many beads to crack. One wonders why these ancient peoples were willing to expend so

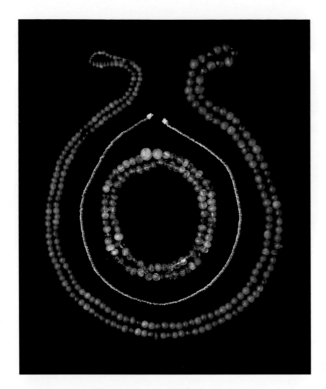

Figure 119. Necklaces of carnelian, silver, and blue-glazed quartz. From Kerma South Cemetery K 332, K 426, and K 423. Photograph © 2012 Museum of Fine Arts, Boston.

Figure 120. Necklace of blue faience ball beads and a blue-glazed quartz pendant from Kerma, K XB-61. Photograph © 2012 Museum of Fine Arts, Boston.

much time and effort fabricating these decorative elements. The desire to have a blue colored bead was not the motivating factor in glazing the quartz, because Kerma residents both imported and produced objects made of blue faience—a man-made, quartz-based ceramic. In all likelihood, the quartz was imbued with magical properties, possibly the result of its association with the mining of gold, a substance with deep religious significance and the lifeblood of the Nubian economy. Nubians also made use of six-sided natural crystals, which they used as pendants on necklaces and girdles. This fascination with quartz would continue throughout the course of Nubian history.

Many of the ornaments found at Kerma during the Classic Period demonstrate a lively trade with Egypt for small luxury goods. It was not uncommon to find Egyptian imports, such as hard stone amulets, incorporated into ornaments of Nubian manufacture. In one necklace, found in an intact male burial, the blue faience stars and a cylindrical silver pendant amulet case were products of Egypt, while the carnelian and blue-glazed quartz beads were made locally. Interestingly, cylindrical amulet cases in Egypt were worn exclusively by women during the Middle Kingdom. An example in the Brooklyn Museum contains garnet pebbles, a red stone associated with the goddess Isis that offered protection to women. It is difficult to know what meaning such amulets had in Nubia—it may be that it was simply an exotic import that elevated the status of its wearer.

Unlike Egypt, where paintings, relief, and sculpture provide a context in which to understand when, how, and why certain ornaments were worn, there is little documentary material of this type from Kerma. As a result, some ornaments are difficult to interpret within the framework of Nubian culture. Such is the case with a large, heart-shaped pendant made of carnelian.

The ornament has a widthwise boring at its apex, indicating that it was meant to be suspended with the split facing downward.

One thought is that the pendant may have been an attempt to create a three-dimensional ornament imitating the Egyptian *demedj* amulet— itself a rather elusive amuletic device worn by Egyptian royalty and high officials. In the Cairo statue of the Middle Kingdom ruler Amenemhat III (1818–1773 BC), the king wears the amulet on a string with several cylinder beads. We do know that the residents of Kerma were familiar with Egyptian Middle Kingdom statuary, but one can only speculate on the source of inspiration for this unusual jewel.

The large fly pendants found in the burials of Nubian warriors are less of a mystery. They are typically made of ivory or bronze and were sometimes found in pairs. Such ornaments were much admired by Queen Ahhotep of Egypt, who was buried with three large gold flies and two silver flies. Ahhotep was the mother of Kings Kamose and Ahmose, rulers credited with bringing an end to foreign domination of Egypt around 1550 BC. It appears that the Egyptians adopted the fly as their own military decoration, paying silent homage to the skills and valor of Nubian fighters.

The inhabitants of Kerma also mined mica to create fanciful appliqués that were sewn onto leather caps and possibly tunics. Mica is a difficult material to work with—it is inflexible, exfoliates at whim, and is easily cracked. It does, however, have a sparkling, reflective surface that shimmers in sunlight. In one excavated grouping, which was probably applied to a head covering, the surface of the appliqués has been lightly incised and patterned. Some surviving micas even have the remains of paint in select areas. As for motifs, there are border, and numerous plant and animal forms— all very similar to the ivory inlays used to decorate Kerma beds.

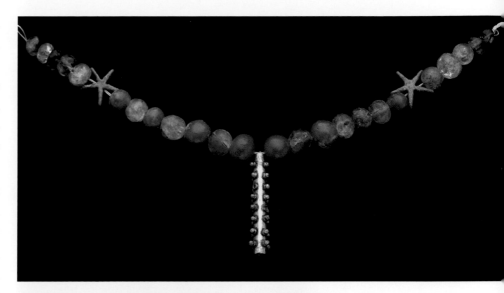

Figure 121. Silver, blue-glazed quartz, carnelian, and faience necklace from Kerma, tomb K 1067. Photograph © 2012 Museum of Fine Arts, Boston.

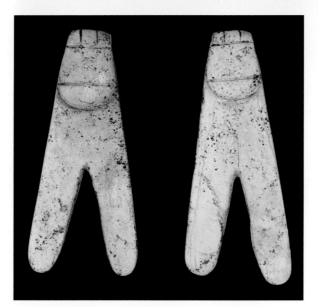

Figure 122. Ivory fly pendants from Semna, tomb S 579. Photograph © 2012 Museum of Fine Arts, Boston.

Second Cataract Forts

With Kerma's decline and the ascendancy of Egypt during the sixteenth century BC, the Egyptian presence at a series of forts in the north, near the Second Cataract, was greatly increased. Several of these forts, which also served as trading posts, were excavated by the Harvard University– Museum of Fine Arts, Boston team, who found evidence of their use in commerce. Excavations at Uronarti Island, Halfa Province, provide insights into daily life at these centers, and it is not surprising that stone weights to measure precious

Figure 123. Mica appliqués, from Kerma KX, tomb 1039x.
Photograph © 2012 Museum of Fine Arts, Boston.

materials were found in various sizes at different locations. Some examples bear the hieroglyphic sign *nbw*, for gold.

It may be that, in the forts, gold extracted from mines was made into circular ingots, as illustrated in several Theban tomb scenes, including a tribute scene from the tomb of Huy, who served as Tutankhamun's viceroy in Nubia; a scene from the tomb of Sobekhotep, where gold ingots hang from the arm of the first tribute bearer; and in a wall painting showcasing Nubian luxury goods from the tomb of Rekhmire. In the latter example, several Nubian baskets are heaped with gold ingots, and there are leopard skins, feathers, ebony, and a charming pet monkey in the top register.

Napata

Strong Egyptian influence in Nubia continued well into the first millennium BC. During that time, many Egyptians migrated to Nubia, establishing permanent settlements. As in the past, around 800 BC, a period of weakness and vulnerability in Egypt coincided with the emergence of a powerful Nubian dynasty. This time, however, the leaders unified the Nile Valley and presided over both lands. The ancestors of that dynasty came from the town of Napata, south of Kerma, near the Fourth Cataract. The kings, known as the

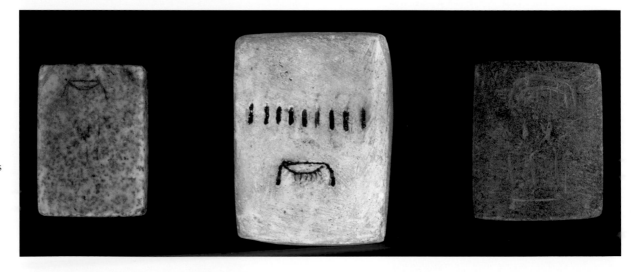

Figure 124. Stone weights for weighing gold, from Uronarti Island, Halfa Province. Photograph © 2012 Museum of Fine Arts, Boston.

Twenty-fifth or Kushite Dynasty, incorporated many Egyptian ideas and customs into Nubian culture. This acculturation, however, occurred within the context of Nubia's unique ethnic, linguistic, and material infrastructure. And in Upper Nubia, during the first millennium BC, gold was king.

Emblematic of the centrality of gold in Napatan culture is the alluvial nugget jewel. The first known example belonged to an ancestor of Piankhi, the first Kushite king of Egypt. This mid-eighth century BC chieftain was buried in a pit grave under a circular gravel mound at al-Kurru, an early Kushite cemetery located southwest of Napata. Although the grave was partially plundered in antiquity, the Harvard-Boston Expedition found several items of jewelry in situ around the head, chest, and left hand of the deceased. They include a gold lunate earring, a plain gold finger ring, and two necklaces. The thirty-millimeter nugget, pierced for suspension and inscribed with a dedication to the god Amun, was part of one of the neck ornaments. The suspension boring, artfully placed by the ancient craftsman within an elongated outgrowth of the gold, simulates a bail

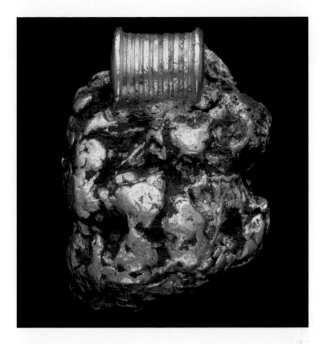

Figure 125. Gold nugget pendant, from Meroe, Beg. W 859. Photograph © 2012 Museum of Fine Arts, Boston.

(suspension hoop), while smoothing of the face provided a flat surface for the inscription. It reads, "The Lord (god) Amun, may he give the perfect life," a dedication illustrating the relationship between an earthly material (gold) and the divine or magical. Its inclusion in a royal burial also marks the nugget as a prestige or status item. In fact, two of the thirteen nugget pendants recov

Figure 126. Reconstructed gold collar, from al-Kurru, Tumulus 1. Photograph © 2012 Museum of Fine Arts, Boston.

Figure 127. Hathor-headed crystal amulet case, from al-Kurru KU 55. Photograph © 2012 Museum of Fine Arts, Boston.

Figure 128. Ram-headed amulet case, from al-Kurru KU 55. Photograph © 2012 Museum of Fine Arts, Boston.

Figure 129. Gold winged-Isis pectoral, from Nuri, pyramid of Amani-nataki-lebte. Photograph © 2012 Museum of Fine Arts, Boston.

ered from Napatan tombs at nearby Nuri and Meroe come from royal burials. These later nuggets—smaller and uninscribed—were found among the plundered remains of two queens buried over a century apart. The first, a gold nugget pierced for stringing found in the Nuri tomb of Queen Malaqaye (around 664 BC) is ten millimeters in length. In the case of Queen Madiken, buried at the same site around 500 BC, the twelve-millimeter-long nugget was found on a gold wire torque. Other items on this wire include two granulated ring beads and a rough, triangular pendant of amazonite (microcline).

Another nugget, the largest so far recovered from ancient Nubia, comes from an intact male burial in the Western Cemetery at Meroe. It was found around the neck of the deceased, the stringing material, either leather or flax, long disintegrated. Soldered to this fifty-gram specimen is a hand-fabricated gold bail whose internal edges show signs of wear, a clear indication that this bold and substantial ornament was worn in life as well as death. Electron microbe analysis determined that the nugget is about 91 percent gold, 8.8 percent silver, and 0.08 percent copper. Very similar findings were obtained for the bail, while the solder was found to contain about 78 percent gold, 12 percent silver, and 10 percent copper. Also around the neck of the deceased was an unworked lump of amazonite with a boring for suspension. This material, durable and no doubt highly valued for its color, also had divine and royal connections. An earlier specimen inscribed for King Taharqo (690–664 BC), which is held in the Brooklyn Museum, uses to advantage the edge of the crystal for a funerary inscription. As with the early nugget jewel, this royal pendant reinforces the connection between an indigenous natural form and position, power, and religion.

Although the burials of these early leaders were plundered, Reisner found that a significant

amount of gold remained—enough from one burial to reconstruct a gold collar. The form, which resembles an Egyptian broad collar, was most likely dictated by its five spacer-beads. It has a small central pendant—an element that probably does not belong on the collar. It is important because it represents an attempt to imitate granulation, a technique where solid gold balls are fused onto a gold sheet—except here, there is no gold

Figure 130. Faience winged goddess amulet, from al-Kurru 51. Photograph © 2012 Museum of Fine Arts, Boston.

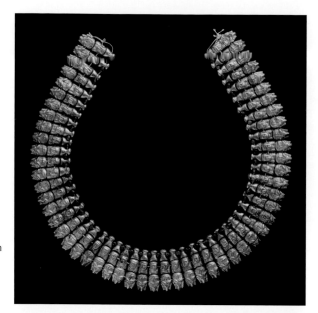

Figure 131. Gold and carnelian necklace, from Meroe, Beg. W. 263. Photograph © 2012 Museum of Fine Arts, Boston.

Figure 132. Bracelet with an image of Hathor, from Gebel Barkal, Pyramid 8. Photograph © 2012 Museum of Fine Arts, Boston.

sheet, just the balls. Perhaps a piece of mica was used in lieu of gold sheet during the heating process, so that the gold balls fused to one another rather than a metal substrate. Afterward, the mica could have been easily removed.

Somewhat later burials at al-Kurru give testimony to the sumptuous adornments owned by Napatan elites. For example, one queen of King Piankhi (ca. 753–722 BC) was interred with several extraordinary jewels worn around her neck. The finest is a Hathor-headed, cylindrical amulet case made of gold and rock crystal. The pendant is similar to sculptural gold and semi-precious ornaments made in the royal workshops of the Egyptian Delta capital, Tanis, around 1000 BC.

Piankhi may, in fact, have acquired Egyptian-made jewels for his queens, and knowing their preference for rock crystal, returned with this extraordinary pendant. The ornament is about two inches high and features the head of the goddess Hathor on a crystal orb that has a lengthwise boring into which a hollow gold tube has been inserted.

The pendant was recently x-rayed in the hope of identifying its contents. Based on similar examples in the Phoenician world, it was expected to contain a folded metallic sheet inscribed with magical imagery and/or texts. However, the results were negative—the cylinder appeared empty.

Another crystal amulet case from the same queen's tomb is surmounted by a gilt silver ram's head, now missing its sun disc. Although the natural crystal is hexagonal, the column has been carved so there are eight fluted sides—a time-consuming process that suggests that the octagonal form was of magical significance. Unfortunately, the base, gold cylinder, and its contents were removed at some point.

While a case can be made for considering many of the precious metal/hardstone pendants from al-Kurru royal burials as being of Egyptian origin, a silver pendant from another queen's tomb represents a cultural blending, a mix commonly found in Napatan iconography. This silver amulet shows Queen Neferukakashta being embraced and suckled by a goddess, probably Mut, the patron goddess of the royal women of the Twenty-fifth Dynasty (see illustration in "Women in Ancient Nubia"). Neferukakashta grasps the wrist of the hand that offers the breast, while the goddess's other arm encircles the queen's shoulder and rests on the queen's breast. The goddess wears the vulture headdress and a crown consisting of a diadem with bovine horns and the solar disc. The claw of the vulture touches the queen's uraeus, and its outstretched wing caresses the goddess. Mut wears a tight sheath that reveals her slenderness,

while the queen's body expresses the more volup-
tuous Kushite feminine ideal.

Less bound to the tricolor scheme (red, blue,
and green) found on Egyptian jewelry, the Kushites
often selected common Egyptian forms made of
stones with unusual colors. One example is a pendant in the form of a miniature ritual vessel made
of a rosy-lilac amethyst, which features the god
Thoth carved out of a luminous blue chalcedony—
the stone most likely from a West Asian source.

As for the regalia worn by Kushite kings, it
was simple and distinctive—a close-fitting cap
encircled by a diadem, two uraei attached to the
diadem, and a cord necklace with three pendant
ram heads. Examples have not survived, but numerous representations, including a bronze sculpture
of King Taharqo, have (see illustration in "Kings
and Kingship in Ancient Nubia"). However, several earrings from Napata have been excavated,
suggesting that the ram manifestation of Amun
took many jeweled forms.

The Kushite kings largely copied Egyptian
burial practices. They erected pyramid superstructures with offering chapels, cut vaulted burial
chambers in the bedrock, and mummified the dead.
A winged Isis pectoral, Egyptian in design, was
fabricated from gold sheet that has been worked in
repoussé and chased. It would have been sewn
onto the linen covering the body of the deceased.

Nearly all of the Napatan queens were buried
with a selection of relatively large faience amulets
that were of Nubian manufacture. A popular form
was that of the winged goddess, shown here with
pendulous breasts and heavy thighs. Made of blue-
green glazed faience, they depict a nude, winged
goddess crowned with a sun disc, uraeus, and
feathers. The wings bend sharply downward, and
on each arm is a uraeus crowned with horns and
a sun disc. The identity of the goddess is uncertain, but like the silver amulet featuring the queen
suckled by the goddess, the body of the deity has

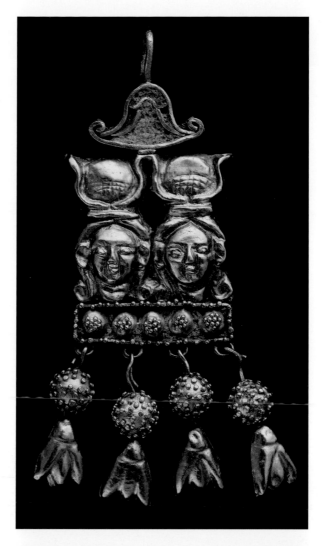

Figure 133. Gold Hathor
earring from Meroe, Pyramid
W.5, no. 6. Photograph © 2012
Museum of Fine Arts, Boston.

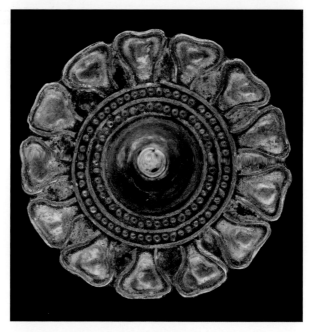

Figure 134. Ear stud from
Meroe. Photograph © 2012
Museum of Fine Arts, Boston.

pronounced curves. Many of these large amulets were once parts of necklaces where the beads were either flat faience discs or simple spheres.

Near the end of the seventh century BC, the Kushites were driven out of Egypt by the Assyrians and moved their residence to Meroe in the south. They continued, however, to be buried at Nuri, just south of the Fourth Cataract. The best-preserved pyramid and burial at Nuri belonged to King Aspelta. The objects recovered from the tomb hint at the wealth, grandeur, and tastes of Napata's ruling elite and demonstrate the sophistication and capabilities of Kushite artisans. A jeweled alabaster vessel from Aspelta's tomb is a good example (see illustration in "Kings and Kingship in Ancient Nubia"). The decorative gold collar on this object has hundreds of cells created by metal strips. These spaces were once filled with Egyptian blue—a faience-like material. The stone pendants are made of carnelian, blue-green amazonite (microcline), and magnetite. Since magnetite deposits in the region are scarce, it is possible that a meteor served as the source for this stone and that it was considered magical.

Meroe

Jeweled marvels would also characterize the next and final flourishing of ancient Nubia. The location of this activity was Meroe (between the Fifth and Sixth Cataracts), and the date is the mid-third century BC to the mid-fourth century AD. It was an age of powerful queens, long-distance trade, and extraordinary jewelry. The surviving ornaments come largely from tombs, many of which were systematically excavated by Reisner and published by Dunham, including the royal burials in the Northern Cemetery.

However, before Reisner began his excavations in the early decades of the twentieth century, the site was explored by treasure hunter Giuseppe Ferlini, an Italian-born military doctor working in Khartoum in the 1830s. His spectacular discovery of a cache of outstanding adornments in the tomb of Queen Amanishakheto gives testimony to the material wealth of Meroitic royals and the artistic skills of Nubian craftsmen (see sidebar, "The Treasure of a Nubian Queen").

Although the tombs at Meroe had been largely plundered by the time of Reisner's arrival, the archaeologist and his team were able to recover numerous jewels in a variety of forms. They include necklaces, diadem ornaments, pendants, earrings, bracelets, and signet rings. Some ornaments have hollow gold or faience beads with images of deities, particularly the deities Isis, Hathor, and Amun. Others have intriguing composite imagery, as demonstrated in a necklace with multiple pendants featuring human and ram heads. Others demonstrate the skills of Meroe's glass artists, who created colorful beads, pendants, inlays, rings, and gilt-glass items. Meroe was known for its advanced glass works, and the gold-in-glass beads produced there were traded throughout the ancient world.

By the third century BC, Nubian craftsmen had perfected the process of enameling on metal, a decorative technique that largely replaced the setting of colored stones in channels (cloisons). A unique ring in the form of a rearing uraeus demonstrates their mastery of champlevé enameling, a technique not in general use in antiquity. This highly sculptural ornament is made of heavy silver sheet that was once gilded. Located on the surface of the snake's hood are three pairs of recesses that have 'carved-out' cells with tool marks that suggest the use of a metal graving tool. Enamel inlays, presumed to have filled the cells, are now missing. Even more experimental is a double-hinged bracelet recovered from a queen's burial at Gebel Barkal. All three sections of this wrist ornament have applied gold appliqués surrounded by colored enamels. The reddish enamels in the upper and lower registers of the two large sections, made by a very specific percentage of copper oxide added to the powdered silica, are unparalleled, as red enamels are very difficult to produce—a fact not lost on the classical Greeks, who used cinnabar to obtain a red effect.

As in earlier times, earrings were very popular during the Meroitic Period. The fact that so many different forms—kidney wires with drops, studs, flares, and plugs—were in use indicates the importance of ear adornment in Meroitic culture. These small ornaments also demonstrate the skills of Nubian metalsmiths, whose works reveal a mastery of filigree wirework, granulation, casting, chasing, repoussé, and inlaying. One gold and enamel ear stud, made of reddish gold, indicates that they were able to achieve color by controlling the alloys—in this case, a higher percentage of copper, not found in naturally occurring gold, was used.

Another common jewelry form in Meroe was the signet ring, a finger ornament typically made of cast gold, although silver, bronze, and iron were also used. There is no evidence that these were functional adornments employed as seals, but rather served as powerful amuletic devices. The motifs used include seated and standing deities, falcons, uraei, rams, vultures, and the Meroitic lion god, Apedemak. In one example, the circular, deeply cut intaglio bezel features four lions' heads symmetrically arranged around a central cobra with a sun disc. Rings were sometimes

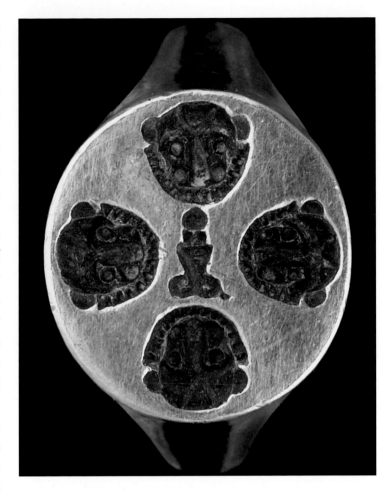

Figure 135. Signet ring from Meroe, Beg. W 333. Photograph © 2012 Museum of Fine Arts, Boston.

worn on several fingers and occasionally stacked, a practice popular among the Romans.

At the close of the Meroitic Period, jewelry production underwent a decline. There was a tendency to use fewer precious materials, and the fine-honed skills of the metalsmith were no longer evident. The variety of forms was also diminished, as was the use of an extensive, rich imagery.

Bibliography

Dunham, D. 1950–63. *The Royal Cemeteries of Kush.* 5 vols. Cambridge, MA: Harvard University Press/Museum of Fine Arts, Boston.

———. 1982. *Excavations at Kerma, Part VI: Subsidiary Nubian Graves, excavated by the late George A. Reisner in 1915–1916, not included in his Excavations at Kerma, I–III and IV–V.* Boston: Museum of Fine Arts.

Markowitz, Y.J. 2002. "The Hathor Crystal Pendant: An Ancient Nubian Amulet Case in the Museum of Fine Arts, Boston." *Adornment* 3, no. 4 (Summer): 1–5.

Steindorff, G. 1935–37. *Aniba.* Vols. 1–2. Service des antiquités de l'Egypte. Mission archéologique de Nubie 1929–1934. Glückstadt and Hamburg: J.J. Augustin.

Welsby, D.A., and J.R. Anderson. 2004. *Sudan: Ancient Treasures: An Exhibition of Recent Discoveries from the Sudan National Museum.* London: British Museum Press.

Nubian Ceramics

Christian Knoblauch and Peter Lacovara

Nubian pottery belongs to one of the oldest ceramic industries on earth and is marked by a degree of conservatism in regard to technology, form, and surface treatment: until the late second millennium BC, when the potter's wheel was introduced into Nubia by the Egyptians, Nubian ceramic was exclusively handmade. Tellingly, despite the new technology, handmade pottery continued to be produced by Nubians then and indeed in all subsequent periods up to the present day. Pottery was an integral utilitarian as well as ceremonial component of Nubian culture, and ceramic sherds are a common feature of all post-Paleolithic archaeological sites. Ceramic is thus one of the most useful tools available to archaeologists. The most basic information it provides may relate to the date, function, and cultural identity of a particular site. Increasingly, however, ceramics are being used as a sensitive indicator of the degrees to which prehistoric Nubian cultural groups of the Nile Valley and surrounding lands were related to each other and communicated with one another, through the observation of shared technological as well as decorative traits. Ceramics have also proven useful in investigating changes to patterns of subsistence and habitation, ascertaining levels of social complexity and craft specialization in a given context, as well as evaluating the varying effects of Egyptian imperialism upon Nubian material culture and ritual.

The faint beginnings of pottery production in Nubia can be traced back to the Qadan culture (ca. 13,000–9000 BC), named after the site Qada in the vicinity of the Second Cataract, where the earliest fired potsherds have been found. In the following Mesolithic Period (ca. 8000–5000 BC) the intensity and quality of ceramic production increased, despite there being little corresponding evidence for either the pursuit of agriculture or the domestication of animals. Thin-walled and hard-fired bowls were made of a fine quartz-tempered paste and decorated from rim to base with complex incised and impressed patterns, including wavy lines and dashes. Around 7000 BC, this essentially Nile Valley pottery tradition was replaced by the adoption of so-called dotted wavy line pottery. The latter is one particularly diagnostic element of a widespread Saharan ceramics tradition whose introduction may be sought in the flow of peoples and ideas from the eastern Sahara into the Nile Valley at this time. Mesolithic ceramic development is well documented for central Sudan but is far less well known for Lower

Nubia and until recently, hardly at all for Upper Nubia, where suitable sites are known but have yet to be systematically excavated.

The state of knowledge concerning Nubian Neolithic pottery in comparison is more satisfactory. During the fifth and fourth millennia BC, Nubian pottery shows affinity with a widespread ceramics tradition that covered the Eastern and Western Deserts, the Egyptian Nile Valley, and Lower and Upper Nubia, as well as central Sudan, pointing to the free flow of information and ideas between these areas. Certain forms, firing technologies, and the mode of application and appearance of decorative motifs are common to all areas, although each area developed its own distinctive style. In Upper Nubia and central Sudan, potters of the fifth through the fourth millennia BC produced distinctive, handmade caliciform beakers—

round-based vessels with everted rims. Related types have been recorded in Lower Nubia, Nabta Playa, and in the Tasian phase of the Badarian culture of Predynastic Upper Egypt. The decoration of examples from Upper Nubian sites such as Kadruka and Kawa consisted of alternating registers of incised linear or impressed geometrical patterns and plain burnished surfaces. Attention was drawn to the decorative elements by highlighting them with white gypsum. Although characteristic of Upper Nubia and central Sudan, caliciform beakers were in fact rare and derived predominantly from wealthy graves. More representative of the bulk of the ceramic assemblage was a wide variety of handmade open shapes—bowls and cups—with smoothed or polished plain surfaces, black or incised rims, and all-over rippled surfaces. The pottery of the Abkan Neolithic culture that

Figure 136. Khartoum Mesolithic potsherds.

Figure 137. A-Group redware bowl with triangle motif, from Dakka. Photograph © 2012 Museum of Fine Arts, Boston.

Figure 138. C-Group incised ware from Aniba N.

pled surfaces, the latter being particularly common in the Classical-A Group assemblage. The succeeding Terminal A-Group (ca. 3200–2800 BC) is in part defined by the introduction of painted eggshell ware, an elegant conical form with extremely thin walls decorated by a wide array of painted motifs, including linked inverted triangles. It attests to the high degree of skill attained by A-Group potters. Other differences between the Classical and Terminal A-Group pottery assemblages included a reduction in the frequency of rippled and black-topped ware and an increase in the importance of vessels with plain red surfaces. Importantly, the last decorative elements common to both Nubian and Upper Egyptian Neolithic cultures had by this time disappeared from the Egyptian Nile Valley, where a preference for undecorated surfaces had taken hold. Egyptian storage jars that were partially manufactured on a turning device have been found in A-Group graves in Lower Nubia but do not appear to have influenced the technology of the A-Group ceramic assemblage. Incised figural additions to some of these pots suggest how their utilitarian Egyptian identity was transformed into something quite different by their A-Group owners.

Farther south in the Kerma Basin, the ceramics of the roughly contemporary Pre-Kerma culture show noticeable points of divergence from the Neolithic pottery of the same region. Presumably this is due to the chronological gap of nearly a thousand years that separates the two. On the other hand, Pre-Kerma pottery does exhibit some similarities with certain A-Group decorative features, such as all-over rippled surfaces and black tops, but other features, such as rippled rims and the common use of fish bones to execute horizontal lines of incised decoration, are distinctively Pre-Kerma. The Pre-Kerma shape corpus consists predominantly of plates and dishes, as well as deep basins with slightly pointed bases and

developed in Lower Nubia during the fifth millennium BC was initially largely undecorated, identifiable rather by the characteristic sandy fabric from which it was made. Ceramic belonging to the latest phase of this culture—the Terminal Abkan, dated to the first half of the fourth millennium BC—includes black-topped vessels and vessels with rippled surfaces.

The terminal Abkan overlaps chronologically with the early Classical phase of the Lower Nubian A-Group culture (ca. 3500–3200 BC), and the two ceramic traditions shared a number of features, including darkened and black rims as well as rip-

restricted rims. Like elsewhere in Nubia, the most common ceramic fabrics exhibit a distinct shift from predominantly quartz-rich fabrics to those containing a higher component of silt and organic matter. This is perhaps to be related to changing patterns of subsistence and habitation that took place in the late Neolithic Period.

The transition from the Pre-Kerma to the Early Kerma (ca. 2500–2050 BC) is marked by an increase in the use of polished black-topped vessels, a feature that would become characteristic of all subsequent phases of the Kerma culture. Both open and closed vessels were decorated using this technique, whereby a vessel was placed rim-down on an oxidizing organic substance during firing, resulting in a blackened interior and blackened rim exterior. Other decorative techniques of the Early Kerma included the incised hatching of rims and all-over incised geometric and banded decoration on a black or gray background, reminiscent of contemporary bowls produced by the early C-Group, a cultural group that had moved into Lower Nubia at this time (see below). This probably indicates a common or overlapping origin for the two groups. At first, the form repertoire demonstrated clear links to the deep basins with slightly pointed bases of the Pre-Kerma Period, but as the Early Kerma progressed, these were replaced by a wide variety of small, roughly hemispherical bowls with rounded bases. Deep spherical and biconical vessels with restricted, direct rims—the closed shapes of the Early Kerma—were eventually augmented by ovoid and spherical jars with thickened and short, vertical rims. During the following Middle Kerma Period (ca. 2050–1750 BC), these jars gained short, flaring necks with thickened, rounded-to-angular rims and were characteristically decorated with incised geometric and linear motifs around the base of the neck and the shoulder. The small black-topped bowls of the Middle Kerma Period also underwent

Figure 139. "Gilded ware" pottery vessel from Mirgissa.

Figure 140. Classic Kerma pottery. Photograph © 2012 Museum of Fine Arts, Boston.

changes. The hemispherical shape type persisted but was joined at first by bowls with distinctive S-shaped profiles, and then in the latest stages of the Middle Kerma Period by very thin-walled bowls with flattish bases and steep, straight sides. The latter type preempted the deeper and distinctive range of open-shaped, black-topped pottery produced during the Classic Kerma Period (ca. 1750–1450 BC), of which the flared 'tulip' beakers are the most famous representatives. These beakers often had a secondary band of silvery polished surface below the blackened rim, an effect achieved by a combination of cleverly controlled firing and careful clay selection. The black-topped ware of the Classic Kerma Period was evidently produced by highly skilled craftsmen whose experimentation with form and technology resulted in an aesthetically pleasing and rich oeuvre of vessels, including delicately spouted jars and vessels with complex, corrugated side walls. Such

Figure 141. New Kingdom pot from Buhen.

vessels were highly prized cultural markers and can be found on sites throughout the area of Kerma domination, hinting at both the large scale of production as well as the highly effective modes of distribution and communication that the Kerma state could draw upon.

For much of the same period (ca. 2300–1600 BC), the C-Group was the dominant Nubian cultural group in Lower Nubia. The most diagnostic ceramic type here was the distinctive assemblage of black, polished hemispherical bowls. With the exception of the rims, which were often decorated independently, the entire exterior surfaces of these vessels were filled with complex and well-organized incised/impressed patterns. The incisions were sometimes highlighted by the application of a white or colored substance. Over time, the decorative programs shifted from multiple fields of linear bands, rectilinear shapes, and occasional curvilinear motifs, to the use of zigzag and checkered patterns. The latest stage of these bowls bore motifs reliant on the patterned repetition of diamond-shaped fields. Similar motifs were reproduced on characteristic footed hemispherical bowls and on small globular to ovoid jars. The latter were sometimes inscribed with figural motifs, which included the depiction of local fauna. For the period between ca. 2000 and 1750 BC, Lower Nubia and the C-Group came to be politically dominated by the Egyptian state, whose physical presence in Lower Nubia was often directed toward C-Group population centers. Despite this, C-Group pottery production shows little or no sign of Egyptian influence, and only very small amounts of Egyptian pottery of this date have been found in C-Group graves and settlements. The Egyptian pottery that has been found in C-Group contexts appears to be earlier and dates to the period directly before or just after the initial Egyptian conquest. It has been suggested that the resilience of C-Group material culture during the Egyptian occupation was a form of cultural resistance in the face of overwhelming Egyptian military and political might. The end of the C-Group ceramics tradition can be traced to the period of Kerma occupation of Lower Nubia (ca. 1750–1450 BC), when a mixture of Egyptian, Kerma, C-Group, and Pan-Grave features predominated.

The ceramics of the Pan-Grave culture, a Nubian people whose territory may be sought in the Eastern Desert and Red Sea Hills (as well as into Egypt itself), was clearly related to both the C-Group and Kerma pottery, all three probably deriving from a common tradition. This is especially discernible in the shape, decoration, and surface finish of the repertoire of simple, utilitarian open shapes that dominated the Pan-Grave assemblage. In the absence of a good context, it is not always straightforward to distinguish Pan-Grave pottery from the pottery of the other contemporary Nubian groups. Recent research suggests that the method of applying the decoration (incision rather than impression), the restriction of the black-topped surface to the area of the offset rim, and the use of burnishing rather than polishing may help define the Pan-Grave tradition.

The vibrancy of the Nubian cultural traditions of the third and the first half of the second millennia BC was dealt a serious blow by the reconquest of Lower Nubia and the conquest of Upper Nubia by the Egyptians during the New Kingdom (ca. 1550–1077 BC). The pottery of the elites and that used in burials overwhelmingly conformed to the standard Egyptian New Kingdom wheel-made ceramic corpus. Egyptian potters evidently resided and worked at the major Egyptian centers in Nubia, producing pottery to meet local demands. Despite this, Nubian handmade pottery continued to be produced, albeit in smaller quantities than previously, and neither the selection of raw material nor the methods

of manufacturing were influenced by Egyptian ceramics technology. The coexistence of wheel-made pottery and handmade Nubian pottery is characteristic of all subsequent periods of Nubian pottery until the present.

Despite the predominance of Egyptian ceramic types in the areas administered under the New Kingdom, the creativity and inventiveness of the

Figure 142. Painted and incised Napatan Period pottery beakers from Gammai.

Figure 143. Barbotine cup. Photograph © 2012 Museum of Fine Arts, Boston.

PLATE 42

8174. G 526

8293. G 162

8202. G 297

8171. G 156

See ch. vii

8177. G 271

PAINTED POTTERY

Figure 144. Meroitic
pottery from Karanog.

Nubian potters still managed to assert itself, as it did earlier, where a micaceous slip was applied to standard Middle Kingdom vessels to give them a shimmering surface called 'gilded ware.' An Eighteenth Dynasty example of such artistic skill is seen in a red-polished pitcher with a charming depiction of a gazelle added to the neck.

Nubian pottery also had an effect on Egyptian ceramics, as seen in the appearance in the late Second Intermediate Period of red and red-polished bowls and cups with painted black bands around the rims that clearly imitate the pottery of the Pan-Grave and Kerma cultures. The post-conquest potters of Kerma still produced pottery that was derivative of, though less finely finished and varied than, that of the Classic Phase of the civilization. The pottery of this so-called Kerma Recent Phase is found throughout Nubia and into early New Kingdom contexts at Thebes.

While handmade pottery of Nubian tradition continued to be manufactured in Egyptian-occupied Nubia, these wares were largely domestic and utilitarian products and have been largely overlooked in archaeological work, publications, and museum collections. This lack of information makes our understanding of the Nubian cultural transitions to the first millennium unclear.

Some Napatan wares still continue many of the forms and decorative motifs found in the pottery of their Nilotic ancestors. Two extraordinary beakers from a Napatan tomb at Gammai show an affinity to the wares of the A- and C-Groups. In the south, one can see examples of a form perhaps descended from the Kerma beaker. Unfortunately, the ceramic repertoire of the royal tombs at al-Kurru and Nuri is dominated by imported Egyptian wares, notably amphorae; therefore, we do not have a well-dated corpus of local wares. Some of the ancestral tombs at al-Kurru have handmade, incised vessels similar to those found in the Meroitic repertoire.

In contrast to the Napatan Period, there is a wealth of indigenous ceramic material published from the succeeding Meroitic Period; however, this still remains imperfectly understood, despite the pioneering studies of William Y. Adams. In part, this is due to a lack of corresponding well-dated settlement corpora and ancillary datable material in tomb groups. A further complication may be differential date ranges between the decorated wares and the far more conservative handmade traditions. The situation is further confused by the differences between the pottery from the capital in Upper Nubia and the succeeding kingdoms in Lower Nubia, and to what degree this difference reflects geographic versus temporal variability.

Figure 145. Late Meroitic black-incised pottery beer jar with stamped pattern. Photograph © 2012 Museum of Fine Arts, Boston.

Figure 146. Painted Meroitic pottery from Karanog.

Different fabrics are used in Upper and Lower/Middle Nubia, and the elaborate stamped decoration found, particularly on cups, in the south are rarer in the north. There does appear to be some overlap between pottery forms that belong to the later Meroitic and those that have been traditionally called 'post-Meroitic.' The handmade black-polished beer jars occasionally decorated with incision are a classic example of this type. Alongside such crude products, however, wheel-made fine wares and painted pottery continue in the north after the fall of Meroe and, if anything, become more elaborate. The more inventive products of the provincial potters at places such as Karanog represent some of the finest artistic achievements of ancient Nubia.

Bibliography

Adams, W.Y. 1964. "An Introductory Classification of Meroitic Pottery." *Kush* 12:126–73.

Bietak, M. 1968. *Studien zur Chronologie der Nubischen C-Gruppe.* Berichte des Österreichischen Nationalkomitees der UNESCO 5. Vienna: Böhlau in Komission.

Bourriau, J. 2004. "Egyptian Pottery Found in Kerma Ancien, Kerma Moyen and Kerma Classique Graves at Kerma." In T. Kendall, ed., *Nubian Studies 1998: Proceedings of the Ninth Conference of the International Society of Nubian Studies, August 21–26, 1998,* Boston, Massachusetts, 3–13. Boston: Northeastern University.

Dunham, D. 1950. *Royal Cemeteries of Kush.* Vol. 1: *El Kurru.* Boston: Museum of Fine Arts.

Dunham, D., and O. Bates. 1927. *Excavations at Gammai,* 1–124. Harvard African Studies 8. Cambridge, MA: Peabody Museum of Harvard University.

Edwards, D.N. 1999. "Meroitic Ceramic Studies I: A Preliminary Study of the Meroe West Cemetery." *Meroitic Newsletter* 26:53–77.

Gatto, M. 2006. "Prehistoric Nubian Ceramic Tradition: Origin, Development and Spreading Trajectories." In I. Caneva and A. Roccati, eds., *Acta Nubica: Proceedings of the Tenth International Conference of Nubian Studies, Rome, 9–14 September 2002,* 103–106. Rome: Istituto Poligrafico e Zecca dello Stato, Libreria dello Stato.

Giuliani, S. 2006. "Defining Pan-Grave Pottery." In K. Kroeper, M. Chlodnicki, and M. Kobusiewicz, eds., *Archaeology of Early Northeastern Africa in Memory of Lech Krzyżaniak,* 647–58. Poznań: Poznań Archaeological Museum.

Heidorn, L.A. 1994. "Historical Implications of the Earliest Pottery from the Tombs at El Kurru." *JARCE* 31:115–20.

Holthoer, R. 1977. *New Kingdom Pharaonic Sites: The Pottery.* Scandinavian Joint Expedition to Sudanese Nubia 5:1. Lund: Scandinavian University Books.

Honegger, M. 2004a. "The Pre-Kerma Period." In D.A. Welsby and J.R. Anderson, eds., *Sudan: Ancient Treasures: An Exhibition of Recent Discoveries from the Sudan National Museum,* 61–69. London: British Museum Press.

———. 2004b. "The Pre-Kerma: A Cultural Group from Upper Nubia prior to the Kerma Civilisation." *Sudan & Nubia* 8:38–46.

Knoblauch. C. 2011. "Not All that Glitters: A Case Study of Regional Pottery Production in Lower Nubia during the Middle Kingdom." *Cahiers de la céramique égyptienne* 9:167–83.

Lacovara, P. 1987. "The Internal Chronology of Kerma." *BSF* 2:51–74.

Nordström, H. 1972. *Neolithic and A-Group Sites.* Scandinavian Joint Expedition to Sudanese Nubia 3:1. Uppsala: Scandinavian University Press.

———. 2004. "Pottery Production." In D.A. Welsby and J.R. Anderson, eds., *Sudan: Ancient Treasures: An Exhibition of Recent Discoveries from the Sudan National Museum,* 248–52. London: British Museum Press.

Nordström, H., and J. Bourriau. 1993. "Ceramic Technology: Clays and Fabrics." Fascicle 2 in D. Arnold and J. Bourriau, eds., *An Introduction to Ancient Egyptian Pottery,* 149–90. SDAIK 17. Mainz am Rhein: von Zabern.

Privati, B. 1990. "Les ateliers de potiers et leur production." In C. Bonnet, ed., *Kerma, royaume de Nubie,* 121–31. Geneva: Mission archéologique de l'Université de Genève au Soudan.

———. 1999. "La céramique de la nécropole orientale de Kerma." *CRIPEL* 20:41–69.

Reinold, J. 2001. "Kadruka and the Neolithic in the Northern Dongola Reach." *Sudan & Nubia* 5:2–10.

Salvatori, S., and D. Usai. 2006. "Report on the R12 Neolithic Cemetery, Northern Dongola Reach (Kawa, Sudan)." In I. Caneva and A. Roccati, eds., *Acta Nubica: Proceedings of the Tenth International Conference of Nubian Studies, Rome, 9–14 September 2002,* 197–201. Rome: Istituto Poligrafico e Zecca dello Stato, Libreria dello Stato.

Säve-Söderbergh, T. 1989. *Middle Nubian Sites.* Scandinavian Joint Expedition to Sudanese Nubia 4:1–2. Partille: Paul Åström.

Török, L. 1986. "Meroe, North and South." *Proceedings of the Sixth International Conference for Nubian Studies, Prepublications of Main Papers, Uppsala, 11–16 August 1986.* Bergen: Klassisk Institutt and Society for Nubian Studies.

Wolf, W. 1937. "Gefäße: I Tongefäße." In G. Steindorff, ed., *Aniba 2,* 125–38. Glückstadt, Hamburg, and New York: J.J. Augustin.

From Food to Furniture: Animals in Ancient Nubia

Salima Ikram

Evidence for the different roles that animals played in Nubian culture throughout history comes from burials, settlements, temples, excavated objects, and rock art. Animals were a crucial component of Nubian culture and economy: they were a measure of wealth; a source of raw materials for a vast variety of products ranging from food to furniture; cherished pets; valued work animals; trade goods; played a crucial role in religious beliefs; and provided iconographic and artistic inspiration. Thus, the variety of animals found in Nubia encompassed both wild and domesticated species, although the emphasis was on the latter.

The Nubians of all periods, like many other ancient peoples, measured their wealth in livestock and grain. The most valued animals were cattle, providing meat, milk, blood, and hides. Representations of these animals in rock art are among the earliest figural art made by the Nubians, and indicate that some of the first denizens of the area were cattle herders. Cattle were followed in importance by sheep, goats, and donkeys. Horses, once they arrived in Nubia post-1550 BC, were highly valued and were also another measure of wealth, albeit, as far as we can tell, one that was not consumed. The exploitation of wild animals such

as hippopotami, elephants, antelope, desert hare, fish, ostrich and other wild birds, lions, and rhinoceri was minor, especially after the Neolithic Period, and most of these featured more prominently in the iconography than the economy, save when it came to trade, particularly with Egypt.

For the Egyptians, Nubia was not only the source of gold, but also of other precious objects, serving as the gateway to the rest of Africa, and whether or not the items originated in Nubia itself, Nubia was seen as the source for all this wealth. Elephant ivory; giraffe tails; the skins of leopards, panthers, and cheetahs; ostrich eggs and feathers; and live animals, such as cattle, or the more exotic ones such as giraffes, elephants, and a vast variety of monkeys all wended their way from Nubia to the north.

Animals in Nubia did not feature in sacred and secular life only in a positive manner; they also were regarded as dangerous, destructive creatures that could poison, maul, or eat people, as well as pests and vermin that threatened food supplies. A gerbil found at Sai dating to the Pre-Kerma Period attests to the problem of protecting grain and other foodstuffs from vermin. Even today, householders in Sudan often suspend foodstuffs from the rafters in order to protect them from rats, mice, gerbils, and jerboas that are endemic to the environment and great gourmands.

Food

Throughout the history of Nubia, cattle *(Bos taurus)* provided the most important source of nourishment, and a manifestation of wealth. These animals were domesticated in the Eastern Sahara about 8000 BC from the wild aurochs, *Bos primigenius*, which was native to the area. There is some discussion as to whether other breeds of cattle, such as zebu *(Bos indicus)*, existed in Nubia. Certainly there is a painting in the funerary chapel K XI at Kerma showing cattle that look as if they have humps. Whether they are zebu or extremely well-fed animals that have developed enormous fatty deposits and are being taken for sacrifice is unclear. However, thus far no osteological evidence has come to light to support the existence of zebu at Kerma, a site that has the largest number of cattle bones excavated anywhere in Nubia.

Prior to domestication, cattle were hunted or trapped. The flesh of one well-fed animal could feed well over two hundred people if they ate in moderation. In addition to meat, cattle supplied milk and its by-products. Although there is no specific evidence for this in ancient Nubia, ethnographic parallels from the Nuer indicate that they might also have been a source of blood that could be cooked (maybe with milk, fat, or cereals), or even taken from a live animal and consumed fresh without harming the creature. Due to the strength of the bulls, and the fact that cattle yielded the most amount of food, these animals obtained a high status in Nubian culture, and thus became the favored animals for temple offerings.

Massive numbers of cattle were slaughtered to mark the passing of a ruler or a member of the elite. This custom was common throughout Nubian history in many areas of the country, and

was most obviously practiced at Kerma. Whether all these animals were kept in the surroundings of the town or brought in specifically for the funerary rites from elsewhere is unknown—certainly grazing land in the immediate area would be insufficient for such large numbers of animals. While the cattle's heads (bucrania) were used to mark the tombs and a few portions of the body were buried with the dead, the remnants were consumed in the town, as is attested by zooarchaeological evidence.

Ovicaprids (sheep and goats) followed bovids (cattle) in importance as a food source. They were probably the mainstay of the diet for the majority of the population, as their bones are found in several settlement sites. These animals, particularly goats, were well adapted to the varied climate and in addition to grazing could scavenge for food among the middens and alleys of villages and towns. Since these animals are small, they are more convenient to raise, because they require less food and less space to graze than cattle. Thus when they are slaughtered, they can be consumed by a smaller group of people, and were the more common food for family groups in daily life, while cattle were probably more often slaughtered for

Figure 147. C-Group ceramic animals.

Figure 148. Cattle skulls in situ around a tumulus at Kerma.

festivals or by rulers and the elite. Ovicaprid remains were also given as offerings to the dead.

There is little evidence for pig consumption in Nubia until the Christian Period, when examples of pig bones are found at Qasr Ibrim. However, this absence of suid remains might be more an accident of archaeology rather than a reflection of reality. Only two bones of a domestic pig have been found at Kerma in the Middle Kerma Period (ca. 2050–1750 BC). Perhaps these animals required too much moisture to survive to be a very successful food source for the ancient Nubians.

Curiously, archaeological evidence suggests that in addition to being used as draft animals, donkeys were also sometimes eaten. Donkeys seem to have been unique among the equids as a food source; there is no evidence for any other equids having been consumed.

Except for the earliest periods of history, zoo-archaeological evidence suggests that hunted animals did not provide a significant amount of food. However, wild creatures did augment the standard diet. Thus, hippopotami, desert hare, gazelle, and other antelope were hunted for sport, as well as to provide fresh delicacies for the table.

The Nile and its tributaries were a constant and dependable source of food for the Nubians. Fish provided an easy and cheap source of protein for everyone: anglers with their poles and hooks could fish for dinner, and commercial fishermen could spread their nets to catch fish to trade in the markets. Fish bones have been recovered from sites dating from the Paleolithic onward throughout Nubia. The most commonly consumed fish seem to have been different types of catfish (*Clarias* sp. and *Synodontis* sp.), Nile perch *(Lates niloticus)*, African barbel *(Barbus bynni)*, and bulti or tilapia (*Tilapia* sp.), to name but a few. At Kerma, archaeologists have discovered jars filled with small fish bones (from *Hydrocynus* sp. as well as a few remains from *Barbus* sp.) dating to the Middle Kerma Period. These are the remains of ancient salted fish, similar to the *fasikh* that has been consumed in Sudan and Egypt up until today. Shell remains found in settlements suggest that freshwater shellfish, as well as river and land snails, augmented the diet. In light of the clear evidence for fish consumption in Nubia throughout history, the remarks made by King Piankhi (Piye) (ca. 753–722 BC) on his Victory Stela (see illustration in this chapter) stating that fish eating was an abomination to the palace are odd—perhaps fish were proscribed to the royal or priestly classes? Certainly fish were enthusiastically consumed by all other ranks!

Birds, particularly water birds, were also a rich source of protein and were consumed, together

Figure 149. Meroitic painted and gilded glass chalice from Sedeinga, with figure holding ducks and an antelope. Photo © Chester Higgins Jr 2012.

with their eggs. Remains of many varieties of geese, ducks, storks, cranes, and other waterfowl indicate that poultry was a common and accessible food source. The variety of birds would have been more diverse in the spring and fall, during the course of migration. As in Egypt, the chicken came late to Nubia and thus far there is little evidence for any great popularity in the region, although this might be an accident of preservation. Clearly the diet of the Nubians was rich in protein from a variety of sources.

Friends and Furnishings
In addition to supplying food, animals provided many other services. Dogs were used for hunting and herding, and many were prized pets, serving as the constant companions of their owners. At Musawwarat a graffito shows a hunter with his hound, with what is probably the animal's name inscribed above it in Meroitic. Images of rulers and their dogs, such as that of Queen Amanitore and her pet dog, held on a leash, even appear in temples, such as the Temple of Apedemak at Naqa. In the Neolithic Period (fourth millennium) dogs were found buried at al-Kadada, while several burials at Kerma feature dogs buried at the feet of their owners (for example, Tombs 25 and 67), as do the much later tombs at Ballana and Qustul (fourth to sixth centuries AD), where many of the dogs were buried complete with collars and leashes.

Perhaps even more valued than the dog was the horse. After their introduction into Nubia, horses became prized possessions and were used to pull chariots as well as for riding. Unlike the Egyptians, who did not seem to have been keen riders, the Nubians quickly became adept horsemen, noted not only for their prowess in riding, but also for breeding and handling horses. Horses were ridden in military contexts, and perhaps also for pleasure as well as for state occasions: King Nastasen (fourth century BC) mounted a 'Great Horse' to take him to his coronation at the temple at Gebel Barkal. Kushite horses and grooms swelled the ranks of the chariotry in Assyria and Egypt, particularly in the seventh century BC. In Assyria one Kushite even bore the title Chariot Driver of the Prefect of the Land. This association of Nubians with expert horsemanship persisted

into the Greek and Roman Periods, when Nubian horsemen were represented on ceramics, in statuary, and referred to in texts. A Ptolemaic or Roman relief from Temple 250 at Meroe depicts a large group of armed horsemen—truly an impressive display of cavalry. In the early medieval periods, and even later on, the Shaiqiya tribe of Dongola was well known for their fighting stallions that could kick and leap at the enemy.

One of the most noted horse lovers was the Kushite king Piankhi (Piye), who erected a stela at Napata that recorded his adventures during his conquest of Egypt. In this he recounts how he became enraged when he entered the stables of Nimlot (in ca. 728 BC), the defeated ruler of Hermopolis, and discovered the pathetic and starved state of his horses. The lunette of the stela depicts these very horses, and their salvation by Piankhi was also depicted on the walls of the temple of Amun at Gebel Barkal. Horses were so important to him that they accompanied the king into the afterlife, and he had a team of his horses buried outside his tomb at al-Kurru. This custom was adopted by three of his successors. Four groups of horse graves were found at al-Kurru, located northwest of pyramids K.1–K.55. Each group consisted of a team for a four-horse chariot. Inscriptions found in each burial indicated that each team belonged to a different king of the Twenty-fifth Dynasty: Piye, Shabaqo, Shebitqo, and Tanwetamani. The horses, which had been sacrificed, were buried as if they were standing up, facing northeast. Their bodies were adorned with bead nets enhanced with cowrie shells, faience and silver amulets, and large bronze ball beads. They had also worn silver collars and plumed headdresses with silver supports. In Meroitic royal burials, horses also wore bells decorated with images of prisoners; one such bell shows bound prisoners lying on the ground with their eyes being pecked out by vultures that stand on or beside them, and are reminiscent of similar scenes found in Egyptian art. This habit of horse burials persisted quite late in Nubia. The tombs at Ballana and Qustul included the burials of the owners' horses, complete with trappings, as well as camels and donkeys. The animals were poleaxed and their heads were present.

Donkeys were also important in Nubia, particularly prior to the advent of the horse. Their primary function was as draft animals, although they were sometimes consumed. Naturally, with both horses and donkeys present, mules and hinnies were bred. The temple of Sanam depicts a series of mules being ridden as well as being used as draft animals. Camels were introduced quite late into Nubia and therefore, as in Egypt, did not figure extensively in their culture until the Late Antique or early medieval periods. They first began to appear on objects, and in use, during the Meroitic Period.

Elephants also featured in the lives of the Nubians from the earliest periods, when they were portrayed in rock art. They were exploited initially as food, then as a source of ivory, and finally, much later (ca. fourth century BC onward) as draft and military animals. In the temple of

Figure 150. Avenue of sandstone ram sculptures at Naqa. Photo © Chester Higgins Jr 2012.

Figure 151. Petroglyphs at Gerf Hussein depicting giraffes.

Figure 152. Petroglyph of elephant near Kalabsha.

Apedemak at Musawwarat al-Sufra, rows of elephants lead bound prisoners as offerings to the god; similar scenes also appear at the temple at Naqa. Several other almost life-size sculpted elephants wearing trappings grace the temple and its surroundings, even guarding a throne. A column at the same site features a Meroitic king wearing a double crown, riding an elephant, with its handler holding the animal's trunk. Some scholars have suggested that the sprawling ruin christened the 'Great Enclosure' at Musawwarat al-Sufra was a massive elephant stable where they were fed, kept, and perhaps trained for use in battle. Alternatively the enclosure has been identified as a place to pen pack animals during massive festivals. During the Ptolemaic era, there is some evidence that suggests that Egypt's king sent emissaries up the Nile, perhaps to purchase war elephants from the Kushite rulers. These war elephants also adorn Meroitic lamps (second century AD), and might also have marched with Hannibal.

Animals were a major source of clothing, furniture, jewelry, and other objects used in daily life. Leather from cattle and possibly goats and gazelles was used to fashion caps and garments favored by the chieftains of the A-Group. A loincloth found at Kerma still had cattle hair adhering to it. Shields, quivers, footwear, and other items were also manufactured out of leather. Elite burials of the Middle Kerma Period feature cow hides covering the deceased (for example, tomb 70), with goatskin serving the same purpose in other

periods throughout Nubia. Many finds of leather bags in tombs indicate their use both in this life and the next.

Bone and horn were used to fashion implements ranging from cosmetic spoons, pins, vessels, beads, and awls to archer's guards. They were also cut into shapes, sometimes in the form of the deities Taweret and Bes, or animals, such as hyenas, and used as inlays to decorate beds. Feathers were utilized as arrow fletches as well as for the elaborate ostrich-feather fans found in the tombs of the A-Group and in Kerma. Turtle shells provided sounding boxes for musical instruments, and might have also been used as shields. Ostrich eggshells were a source for beads,

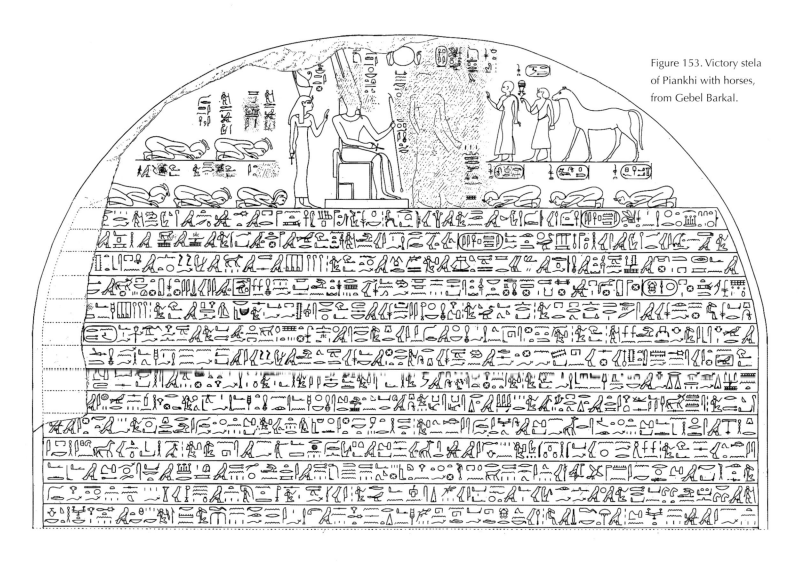

Figure 153. Victory stela of Piankhi with horses, from Gebel Barkal.

as well as containers to hold liquid; some such vessels were enhanced by etchings. One example shows an image of a crocodile. Surprisingly, despite the number of crocodiles that populated the Nile, representations of them are relatively few, save on Meroitic ceramics, where they are more commonly featured. Ivory from elephants and hippopotami was used to make beads, bracelets, armlets, and figurines. Entire hippopotamus tusks served as containers, and depictions at Kawa dating from the reign of Taharqo show that elephant tusks were used as trumpets. Indeed, elephant-tusk trumpets were used recently in the time of the Mahdi in the late nineteenth century. They were covered with a skin membrane, and blown into from the side. Entire shells, particularly cowrie, were used as pendants, beads, or decoration, while other shells were used as containers or broken up to make beads. Coral from the Red Sea was prized as jewelry, and carved into small beads or larger pendants.

Animals not only provided the raw materials so vital to the everyday life, comfort, and survival of the Nubians, but also served as inspirations for adorning the objects that they used in their daily life. Gaming pieces were carved or cast in the form of sitting or ram-headed lions, while stone, ceramic, and faience vessels took the form of ducks, fish, antelope, or other creatures. In addition to the gut and hide used to make furniture, bed and chair legs take the form of bull's feet. Figures of giraffes, hyenas, and the hippopotamus deity, Taweret, carved out of mica, adorned leather caps and were inlaid into beds. Faience tiles featuring animals were used as decorative wall inlays. Faience images also seem to have been used to decorate clothing. In Kerma, plaques showing scorpions have been found on the clothing of ritually sacrificed people who were buried with their rulers. The scorpions' tails point to the heads of the deceased, perhaps intimating that they had been put to death with some form of poison. Scorpion amulets have also been found at other sites, including Qasr Ibrim, as tokens to protect against scorpion stings, no doubt a frequent threat in the desert. On a lighter note, animal-shaped ceramic figurines that might have been toys, decorations, or served some ritual purpose are found in settlements and tombs. Painted images of cattle, birds, giraffes, snakes, fish, frogs, crocodiles and other creatures adorn ceramic vessels, making them pleasing to the eye, while other vessels are enhanced with quirky handles or lids modeled in the form of animals, such as leopards and lions. It is surprising that images of monkeys are rarely found in Nubian art—certainly the Nubians exported these creatures to Egypt, where they are commonly depicted animals, despite being imported rather than native.

Figure 154. Painted decoration of lions attacking a man, from a Kerma pot.

Ritual, Religion, and Representations

Animals featured extensively in Nubian religion of all periods, and after contact with Egypt, many elements of Egyptian iconography were incorporated and adapted to fit into those of the Nubian kingdoms. As in Egyptian sepulchers, many Nubian tombs, such as those at Kerma (particularly Chapel K XI, with its images of hippopotami, wading birds, bulls, and giraffes) and Meroe depict animals in contexts of daily life as well as religious iconography, specifically in association with the ruler who had dominion over all living things. However, the most striking use of animals is in the funerary cult, rather than in tomb decoration. From the Neolithic Period onward, and possibly before, animal burials were common. Cattle, goats, sheep, dogs, horses, and even lions and fish have been found in tombs throughout Nubia, dating from all periods of history. These animals served a multiplicity of purposes: joints of meat from cattle and ovicaprids served as food offerings for the deceased, while entire animals with their trappings, buried with or near someone, were an indication of wealth and a manifestation of an afterlife that would require all that had been used in life on earth. Thus, teams of horses, cattle, sheep, goats, camels, and dogs were interred with their owners, sometimes, particularly in the case

Figure 155. Sandstone relief of lion and elephant, from the Lion Temple at Musawwarat al-Sufra. Photo © Chester Higgins Jr 2012.

of C-Group burials, augmented with pottery figures of some of these creatures. During the Middle Kerma Period, sheep, goats, and dogs were placed in leather bags and buried with the deceased. As no indication of trauma was detected, and the animals showed signs of struggling, perhaps these animals were asphyxiated. In the tomb of Prince Arikankharer at Meroe, the animal interments were augmented by the burial of a man who might have been an animal handler. Unusual animal burials have been found at Sanam (500 BC) in the form of three lions and two fish. Although lion burials are known from Archaic Egypt, thus far no other examples have been found in Nubia.

Cattle were particularly prominent in funerary culture. At Toshka, graves dating to the period between 12,000 and 9,000 BC are crowned with the skulls of wild cattle (Bos primigenius). This custom continues on throughout Nubian history, with the fifth millennium BC graves at al-Ghaba marked by bucrania (cattle skulls), as well as some of the tombs at al-Kadada (fourth millennium BC). Some of the tombs at Kerma dating to the Middle Kerma Period have hundreds of bucrania marking tumuli, all 'looking' in at the deceased; presumably

Figure 156. Figure of elephant at Musawwarat al-Sufra. Photo © Chester Higgins Jr 2012.

Figure 157. Watercolor copy of a Meroitic wall painting, probably from a palace at Meroe (ca. second–third century AD), representing a youth rather improbably carrying two elephants. Possibly this scene was an illustration of a myth that is now lost to us, or, less likely, the youth is bringing tribute.

most of the meat from the bodies of these animals would have been consumed as part of the funerary rites. Some of the horns of these animals are deliberately deformed into curious shapes, a custom that is still found in some parts of East Africa. Tombs of the Pan-Grave culture feature small pits nearby that contain the partial bucrania of cattle, gazelles, and goats painted with red and black dots whose precise function is unknown, although doubtless ritual in nature. One cattle skull fragment shows a hunter (perhaps the deceased) surrounded by a pattern of dots. These animal heads not only indicated the rank and wealth of the deceased, but also presumably encoded a promise of fertility in the form of rebirth for the dead.

Another curious animal interment at Kerma is that of lambs wearing elaborate headdresses made out of ostrich feathers, with pendants hanging down from each horn. Perhaps these animals allude to the god Amun and invoke his protection for the deceased. Indeed, some scholars posit that the manifestation of Amun as a ram originates in Nubia, where the Egyptian Amun fused with one or a series of important local ram gods. This might explain why, particularly in Nubia, Amun is shown with horns from different types of rams: *Ovis longipes palaeoaegyptiacus* and *Ovis aries africana*.

The interment of teams of chariot horses not only displayed the wealth and status of the deceased, but also had an iconographic role in Nubian religion. Horses were associated with the sun god, and in Near Eastern art, solar deities are shown mounted on a horse, an image that was adopted by the Nubians. The idea of the sun god crossing the sky in a chariot was common to several cultures. To further emphasize the identification of horses with solar deities, many of the plume holders crowning the heads of the Kushite steeds were decorated with an image of the Egyptian sun god Re in the form of a falcon. Thus, horse burials served

as an offering to the sun god and identified the deceased ruler with the sun who was reborn daily.

Other funerary rituals also evoke animal iconography. The human burials on beds whose legs are like those of cattle, with the body placed on a cowhide, evoke the Heavenly Cow and the goddess Nut. Indeed, one of Tutankhamun's funerary beds took the form, in wood, of the Heavenly Cow. The Egyptian idea of the *ba* or soul in the form of a bird with a human head was also adopted by the Nubians from the eighth century BC on, if not before, albeit with a slight iconographic twist. Nubian *ba* statues have both human and bird bodies.

Animal imagery that is similar to that of the ancient Egyptians is particularly marked in royal and cult iconography. Serpents, bulls, and lions are all related to kingship. The Nubian rulers of Egypt sport a double uraeus on their brow to indicate that with the blessing of the sun god, they are kings of two countries: Egypt and Nubia. The king appears as a leonine sphinx, the only human portion of his anatomy being his face. Kings also hold leashed lions, showing their dominion over the king of the beasts, as well as identifying the ruler himself with lions and lion deities. Lions also serve as sentinels, identified with the king and the god Apedemak, god of war and fertility. As with sphinxes, they guard gateways to temples and palaces, and, in a more Kushite tradition, man-made reservoirs known as *hafir*s. Vultures with extended wings protect kings and the queen or the ruling queen (Candace), as they do with their Egyptian counterparts. The many cattle burials associated with the tombs of rulers emphasize their strength and power. Nubian pharaohs also allude to their close relationship with the Egyptian god Amun by wearing ram's horns.

All the Egyptian totemic relationships between animals and gods are observed in Nubia. Thus, the goose of Geb, the scarab beetle of Khepri, the cat of Bastet, the cow of Hathor, the crocodile of Sobek, and the raptor of Horus are all found in Nubian temples. The Egyptian pantheon is augmented by local divinities, such as the lion-headed Apedemak; the hunter god Sebiumeker, shown with his companion, Arensnuphis, another god of the hunt; the hawk-headed god, Hemen; and Mandulis and Breith, the divine brothers shown as falcons with human heads. Thus, temples are adorned with images of all of these gods in their semi-animal form. Some purely Nubian touches in temples are the number of representations of elephants, in both two and three dimensions. These creatures do not seem to have been divine themselves, but were more a manifestation of the subjugation of might by the king, as well as by the god Apedemak. Apedemak is often shown holding elephants and lions on leashes, thus expressing his dominion over two of the most impressive wild animals in Africa.

The *hafir* is the Nubian answer to the Sacred Lake found in Egyptian temples. Some of these, such as that at Musawwarat, measure as much as 250 meters across, with a depth of six meters. These seem to have served both a practical and a religious function involving water supply for consumption as well as purification. Unlike their Egyptian counterparts that are sometimes stone edged, but otherwise unmarked, these are often protected by stone lions and frogs. Presumably the frogs also serve as a magical encouragement for the water supply to increase.

A particularly engaging cultic image from Nubia comes from Gebel Barkal and illustrates the significance that the Nubians conferred upon certain animals. The mountain of Gebel Barkal takes the form of a cobra that rears up and faces the rising sun. From different angles it seems to be wearing different royal crowns. This likeness to the cobra is undoubtedly why the Nubians chose this as one of their most sacred sites. Thus, the emblem of Amun of Gebel Barkal is a serpent with a ram's head, a fitting union of Amun and Re.

For the Nubians, animals were a vital part of their physical and spiritual existence. They supplied food for practical and cultic purposes, raw materials for tools, weapons, clothing, and furniture, and were a source of iconographic inspiration and totems or manifestations of the gods. They were also an aspect of the world that evoked curiosity: the tomb of Queen Khensa at al-Kurru contains her natural history collection consisting of rocks, pebbles, sea urchin fossils, and a variety of sea shells. Thus, the intellectual, spiritual, and physical life of the Nubians was closely entwined with that of the animals around them.

Bibliography

Adams, W.Y. 1977. *Nubia, Corridor to Africa*. Princeton, NJ: Princeton University Press.

Bietak, M. 1987. "The C-Group and the Pan-Grave Culture in Nubia." In T. Hägg, ed., *Nubian Culture: Past and Present*, 113–23. Stockholm: Almquist and Wiksell.

Bökönyi, S. 1993. "Two Horse Skeletons from the Cemetery of Kurru, Northern Sudan." *Acta Archaeologica Academiae Scientiarum Hungaricae* 45:301–16.

Bonnet, C., ed. 1990. *Kerma, royaume de Nubie. Catalogue de l'Exposition*. Geneva: Musée de Genève.

Bonnet, C., et al. 1989. "Sépultures à chiens sacrifiés dans la vallée du Nil." *CRIPEL* 11:25–39.

Bonnet, C., and D. Valbelle. 2006. *The Nubian Pharaohs: Black Kings on the Nile*. Cairo: American University in Cairo Press.

Chaix, L. 1980. "A Preliminary Note on the Faunal Remains of Kerma (Soudan)." In C. Bonnet, ed., *Kerma 1979–1980*, xv–xvii. Geneva: Etienne and Christian Braillard.

———. 1988. "Le monde animal à Kerma (Soudan)." *Sahara Preistoria e Storia del Sahara* 1:77–84.

———. 1993. "The Archaeozoology of Kerma (Sudan)." In W.V. Davies and R. Walker, eds., *Biological Anthropology and the Study of Ancient Egypt*, 175–85. London: British Museum.

———. 2000. "Animals and the Dead at Kerma (Sudan) 2500–1500 BC: Archaeological Data and Interpretations." In L. Bodson, ed., *Ces animaux que l'homme* choisit d'inhumer. Contribution à l'étude de la place et du rôle de l'animal dans les rites funéraires. *Journée d'étude, Université de Liège, 20 mars 1999*, 15–39. Liège: University of Liège.

———. 2002. "La faune des peintures murales du temple K XI." In C. Bonnet, ed., *Edifices et rites funéraires à Kerma*, 162–75. Paris: Errance.

Dunham, D. 1950–1963. *The Royal Cemeteries of Kush*. 5 vols. Cambridge, MA: Harvard University Press/Museum of Fine Arts, Boston.

Edwards, D.N. 2004. *The Nubian Past: An Archaeology of the Sudan*. New York: Routledge.

Emery, W.B. 1938. *The Royal Tombs of Ballana and Qustul. Archaeological Mission of Nubia, 1929–34*. Cairo: Government Press.

Evans-Pritchard, E.E. 1969. *The Nuer: A Description of the Modes of Livelihood and Political Institutions of a Nilotic People*. New York: Oxford University Press.

Gautier, A. 1986. "La faune de l'occupation néolithique d'El Kadada (secteurs 12–22–32) au Soudan Central." *Archéologie du Nil Moyen* 1:59–111.

Griffith, F.Ll. 1923. "Oxford Excavations in Nubia: The Cemetery of Sanam." *LAA* 10:73–171.

Heidorn, L.A. 1997. "The Horses of Kush." *JNES* 56, no. 2: 105–14.

Kendall, T. 1982. *Kush: Lost Kingdom of the Nile*. Brockton: Brockton Art Museum.

Lenoble, P. 1994. "Une monture pour mon royaume: Sacrifices triomphaux de chevaux et de méhara d'El Kurru à Ballana." *Archéologie du Nil Moyen* 6:107–30.

Lohwasser, A. 2006. "Tiere und deren Verehrung in Nubien."

In V. Vaelske et al., eds., *Ägypten. Ein Tempel der Tiere*, 114–16. Berlin: Achet.

El Mahi, A.T. 1996. "The Wildlife of the Sudan in a Historical Perspective." *BSF* 6:89–113.

Morkot, R.G. 1997. "There Are No Elephants in Dongola: Notes on Nubian Ivory." *CRIPEL* 17, no. 3: 147–54.

Reisner, G.A. 1920. "Note on the Harvard–Boston Excavations at el-Kurru and Barkal in 1918–1919." *JEA* 61:61–64.

Shinnie, P.L. 1967. *Meroe: A Civilisation of the Sudan*. London: Thames and Hudson.

Török, L. 1991. "Iconography and Mentality: Three Remarks on the Kushite Way of Thinking." In W.V. Davies, ed., *Egypt and Africa: Nubia from Prehistory to Islam*, 195–204. London: British Museum Press.

Vila, A. 1987. *Le cimetière Kermaïque d'Ukma Ouest: La prospection archéologique de la vallée du Nil en Nubie Soudanaise*. Paris: Éditions du Centre national de la recherche scientifique.

Wildung, D., ed. 1997. *Sudan: Ancient Kingdoms of the Nile*. Paris and New York: Flammarion.

Williams, B.B. 1991a. "A Prospectus for Exploring the Historical Essence of Ancient Nubia." In W.V. Davies, ed., *Egypt and Africa: Nubia from Prehistory to Islam*, 74–91. London: British Museum Press.

———. 1991b. *Noubadian X-Group Remains from Royal Complexes in Cemeteries Q and 219 and from Private Cemeteries Q, R, V, and W, B, J, and M at Qustul and Ballana*. Excavations between Abu Simbel and the Sudan Frontier, Part 9. *OINE* 9. Chicago: Oriental Institute.

Part II

GAZETTEER OF SITES
(FROM SOUTH TO NORTH)

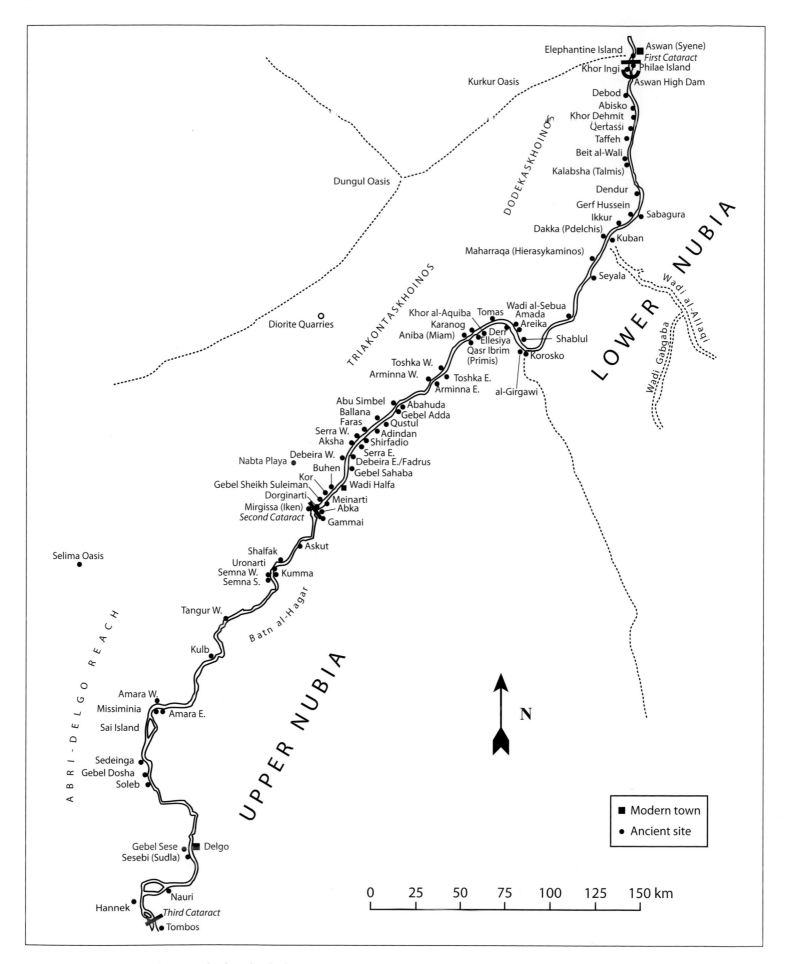

Figure 158. Map of Upper and Lower Nubia from the Third Cataract to Aswan.

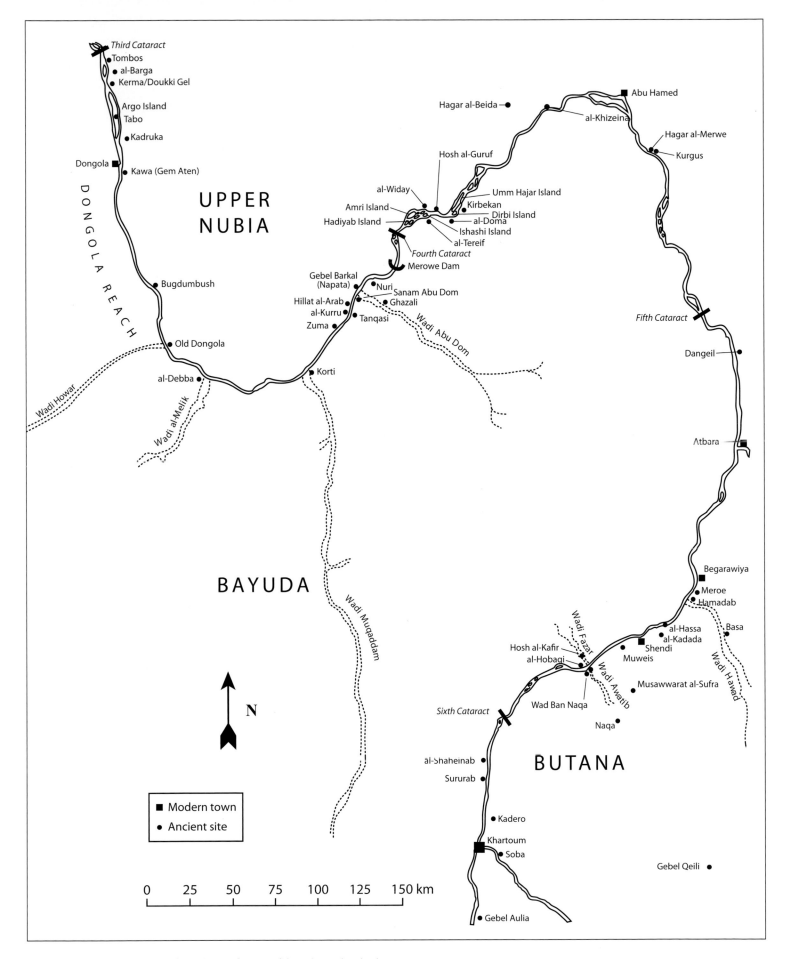

Figure 159. Map of Upper Nubia from the confluence of the Niles to the Third Cataract.

GEBEL QEILI

Peter Lacovara

The victory inscription carved on the rock at Gebel Qeili is the southernmost Meroitic monument known, situated east of the Blue Nile in the Butana steppe. It depicts King Sherkarer standing on bound captives and holding a spear and bow and arrows. Before him the sun god Helios offers a group of tethered captives and a bouquet of sorghum. The combination of a Hellenistic god and Nubian motifs illustrates the cosmopolitan nature of the kingdom, even at its remotest extent.

Figure 160. The Meroitic king Sherkarer, the god Helios, and captives, from a rock inscription at Gebel Qeili.

Bibliography

Adams, W.Y. 1977. *Nubia, Corridor to Africa*. Princeton, NJ: Princeton University Press.

Török, L. 1997. *The Kingdom of Kush: Handbook of Napatan-Meroitic Civilization*. Leiden: Brill.

NAQA

Janice W. Yellin

The ancient Nubian royal city of Naqa is one of the largest archaeological sites in Sudan, measuring approximately 1.5 kilometers north to south and one kilometer east to west. Along with Meroe and Gebel Barkal, it is one of the most important royal centers of the Meroitic Period. Naqa is 170 kilometers northeast of Khartoum on the Butana plateau, a region considered to be the Meroitic heartland. Naqa was well situated for trade to and from the Nile Valley, which may in part explain its existence, size, and importance. A major Meroitic site far from the Nile River, it is strategically located at the junction of a number of wadis, the most important being the Wadi Awatib. This network of wadis, which served as trade routes throughout this region, was linked to the royal distribution center of Meroe. The inhabitants of Naqa would have depended on a rainy season to grow their crops, and on the two large *hafir*s (reservoirs) that were built on the southern edge of the town for drinking water for themselves and their herds. Derek Welsby has speculated that the water from the *hafir*s would not been adequate for farming needed to sustain a large sedentary population year round. The earliest date for Naqa's formal settlement, approximately 135 BC, derives from an inscription in Meroitic hieroglyphs from the sanctuary of Temple F (discussed below), and the latest known dated materials are from the second century AD.

The site's location beside the small mountain of Gebel Naqa reflects the indigenous practice of worshiping upon, in, and beside sacred high places (see "Nubian Religion"). Naqa would have been an impressive town. As described by Karla Kroeper and Lech Krzyżaniak, the large temple of Amun, which was plastered white and partially painted with red and blue designs on a light yellow background, stood on a raised terrace dominating a town area filled with large stone and brick palace and administrative complexes, as well as other painted temples of varying sizes. One can imagine the impact this expression of state authority and Meroitic royal power would have had on the nomads and semi-nomads living on the edge of the Meroitic state who would have come to Naqa to trade, and/or to bring their herds to the large state-built and maintained *hafir*s at the site. Naqa's temples and their rituals, palace and administrative complexes, and *hafir*s would have helped bring the semi-nomadic population of the Butana region under the sway of their distant rulers in Meroe.

Research History

In modern times, the site was first visited in 1822 by Linant de Bellefonds and slightly later by Frédéric Cailliaud (1823), who published drawings of it. The careful plans and drawings of the site and some of its temples by Richard Lepsius in 1844 have been the only documents available for study of Naqa and its temples until the mid-twentieth century, when limited explorations of its temples were undertaken by expeditions from Humboldt University in Berlin under Fritz Hintze, and Tübingen University in 1978 and 1980 under Ingrid Gamer-Wallert and Karola Zibelius-Chen. From 1995 to 2006, more extensive excavations were led by Dietrich Wildung for the Ägyptisches Museum und Papyrussammlung Staatliche Museen zu Berlin in collaboration with the Poznań (Poland) Museum's director, Lech Krzyżaniak, and the National Corporation for Antiquities and Museums, Sudan. The expedition created an accurate plan of the site with a superimposed grid for future work and conducted a surface survey of the site's administrative area. Its primary focus was on the excavation, recording, and conservation of the best preserved temples, particularly the Amun temple, as well as the Lion Temple, the so-called 'Roman' Kiosk, and Temple F (Naqa 500), work that has greatly expanded our understanding of these structures and various aspects of Naqa's history. The expedition also found several new temples, noted a number of large cemeteries, and located at least one area in which non-elite inhabitants probably lived.

The Recorded Temples

There are numerous temples at Naqa. In addition to previously known temples such as the Amun Temple, Lion Temple, 'Roman' Kiosk, Temple F (Naqa 500), and Temple G, several one-room, unexcavated temples have been identified by the Ägyptisches Museum expedition in an area near the Lion Temple.

The Large Amun Temple (Naqa 100)

The impressive remains of this 135-meter-long sandstone temple, the largest at Naqa, were an excavation and conservation priority for the Ägyptisches Museum expedition under Wildung's direction. The avenue of sphinxes and much of the temple have been reconstructed as part of their on-site conservation efforts.

The temple's design reveals a combination of local and Egyptian features. Like the Egyptian-derived Amun temples at Meroe and Gebel Barkal, it has a pylon, hypostyle hall, offering hall, and sanctuary. The temple is approached through an alley of six ram-headed sphinxes with small figures of King Natakamani between their front legs. As in many other Egyptian and Nubian temples dedicated to Amun, the visitor encounters a small ritual chapel (20 meters by 6.8 meters) in front of its first pylon. At Naqa, the chapel was between the third and fourth set of sphinxes. A ram-headed sphinx of Amun of Napata was discovered abutting the rear exterior wall of the temple. This would have been in a one-room chapel serving the same role as an Egyptian contra-temple that was accessible to the public. Kushite features include its construction on a thirty-three-meter-wide podium with three access ramps on its north, west, and south sides.

As on a typical Egyptian and Kushite temple pylon, the ruler is shown smiting traditional enemies of the state. Unlike Egypt, however, not only the king but a ruling queen participated in this ancient duty of kingship, reflecting the Meroitic institution of ruling queens (*kandakes*). Cartouches reveal that these rulers are King Natakamani and Queen Amanitore, thereby dating this temple to their reigns in the second half of the first century AD.

Where preserved, the exterior and interior walls are covered with relief scenes that confirm the rulers' legitimacy and power as leaders of the

Meroitic state. Among the finds made by the Ägyptisches Museum expedition were fragments of finely carved, inscribed stelae and statuary found in the hypostyle hall, a carved altar in the sanctuary, and a plastered and painted altar in a court on the temple's northern side. While all demonstrate a high level of artistry, there are interesting differences in the nature of Egyptian and Kushite influences in each.

Before it was destroyed by an earthquake about 150 years after its completion, this temple on its high podium would have dominated the site, communicating to all who visited Naqa the power and prominence of both Amun and his designated representatives, the Meroitic rulers, Natakamani and Amanitore.

Amun Temple (Naqa 200)

In 2004, the Egyptian Museum team excavated another, smaller Amun temple south of the large Amun temple's entrance ramp that was built by a little-known ruler, Amanakhereqerem. Its plan differs from the ground plan of the larger Amun temple in that its sanctuary is divided into three chambers, perhaps for Amun, Mut, and Khonsu. Before these sanctuaries there are two pronaoi rather than a pronaos and hypostyle hall. The dating and place of King Amanakhereqerem in Meroitic royal chronology is uncertain. Until the discovery of his temple, he was known only from two ram sculptures from Soba with his name on them, an omphalos (small freestanding shrine) from Gebel Barkal, and three rams found at al-Hassa. Based on the form of the letters in a Meroitic cursive inscription with the king's name in it, Claude Rilly has tentatively dated Amanakhereqerem to the first century AD, either before or after Natakamani and Amanitore, rather than to the second century AD, as suggested by László Török in 1997. Based on its decorations and architecture, Wildung believes that it was built

Figure 161. Naqa: Kiosk in the foreground, and Apedemak temple in the background. Photo © Chester Higgins Jr 2012.

either right before or right after the Amun and Lion Temples and that these temples along with the 'Roman' Kiosk are to be understood as being part of a planned sacred landscape.

Apedemak Temple (Naqa 300)

This fairly intact small, one-room temple of indigenous Kushite design stands to the west of the large temple of Amun. Like other Kushite one-room temples, it is on a podium and is dedicated to the lion-headed god, Apedemak, who like Amun is associated with kingship and fertility. According to Friedrich W. Hinkel, the temple had a wooden roof and a small wooden shrine on a masonry base along the back wall of its sanctuary. A layer of red, compacted sand found below the temple's foundation suggests that there was an earlier temple below this one. To the north, south, and west of the temple stand the remains of walls that perhaps belonged to magazines and priests' quarters, as well as the possible remains of temenos walls.

While some of the decorations of this temple are particularly interesting for the originality of their style and iconography, the pylon and exterior side walls follow Egyptian/Napatan traditions in representation. Like the large Amun Temple, Natakamani (south side) and Amanitore (north side) are depicted on the pylon. They are shown in the traditional act of smiting prisoners to demonstrate their ability to protect the kingdom from its traditional enemies, and thus legitimate their roles as rulers. Relief scenes carved on the side exterior walls show the king and queen in the presence of Egyptian and Kushite gods. The king, queen, and crown prince stand before a row of five female gods on the north exterior wall and five male gods on the south one. More distinctively original are depictions of Apedemak on the narrow sides of the pylons and on the rear exterior wall of the temple. On the pylon, a lion-headed snake emerges from an acanthus base, and on the back wall a three-headed, four-armed, lion-headed, human-bodied Apedemak gives offerings and legitimates the queen on his right and the king on his left. These unusual depictions of Apedemak have generated a great deal of discussion as to their meaning and origins, including speculation of Indian influences in Meroe (now discounted after much investigation). It is generally accepted that both images reflect local expressions of Apedemak's cult derived in some degree from Ptolemaic Egyptian models. A similar depiction of the lion-headed snake on the pylons' edges was also found at Semna South in Nubia during the excavation of its Meroitic Period cemetery by Louis V. Žabkar in the 1960s. Žabkar's investigation of this image led him to various Ptolemaic Egyptian examples and to the conclusion that this composite depiction is derived from Egyptian and Ptolemaic traditions—for example, figures drawn in Egyptian royal mortuary texts with an upright snake's body that were surmounted by the head of a different animal that share elements with the lion-headed snake found at Naqa and Semna South. The three-headed, four-armed Apedemak on the rear exterior wall is seen by Wildung and others as the expression of multiple simultaneous actions by the god to the king and queen beside him and the viewer before him. According to Žabkar, this type of representation also has Ptolemaic Egyptian antecedents. Originality in the blending of borrowed images with Meroitic concepts is also seen in reliefs on the interior walls of the temple. There, Hellenistic influences (also found in the use of the acanthus base for the snake-bodied Apedemak on the pylon) are given free play in the depiction of a frontal male god with a full beard who resembles Serapis or Zeus. Throughout the temple, the typical Meroitic stylistic practice of depicting Kushite figures, with much fuller proportions and broader shoulders than Egyptian gods, was followed.

Roman Kiosk (Naqa 361)

The Hellenistic influences that appear in some of the Lion Temple's decorations are more strongly present (in combination with traditional Egyptian features) in the architecture of the so-called 'Roman' Kiosk. Uniquely, the kiosk has an Egyptian-style doorway and lintel, but its sides have columns with Corinthian capitals and arched windows with decorative details in Roman style. There is still not full agreement as to the purpose, date, and relationship of this unique structure to the Lion Temple. Although it was built near the front of the latter, its direct and intentional relationship to the Lion Temple has been questioned because the Kiosk stands off to the side of that temple's central axis, rather than directly along its main axis. However, this same spatial relationship between a temple and a chapel can also be found at Temple F (Naqa 500). It may be that at Naqa, chapels with ritual associations to temples were not always built along the main axis of that temple. Sculptures associated with Hathor, including a small lintel with her head carved on it, were found in or near the so-called 'Roman' Kiosk by Wildung. These objects have led him to suggest that the Kiosk was a chapel to the goddess Hathor. The 'Roman' Kiosk (or Hathor Chapel if Wildung's attribution is correct), which had been dated as early as the first century AD and as late as the third century AD, as noted by Wildung and Kroeper, is now dated to the first century AD by Rilly, based on the letter forms used to write a Meroitic graffiti carved on its wall. Further evidence for a first-century AD date may also be found in similarities in the design and manufacture of the star-filled border under the ceilings of both this structure and the more securely dated first-century AD Lion Temple as noted by Hinkel.

Temple to Amun, Mut, and Khonsu (Naqa 500)

This small temple at the base of Gebel Naqa is the earliest dated structure at the site. The name of a queen, Shanakdakheto, carved into its sanctuary's niche, dates it to her reign, ca. 135 BC. The hieroglyphic texts carved on its interior walls are the oldest known example of the written Meroitic language. Scenes in badly preserved reliefs indicate that the temple was dedicated to the Egyptian triad of Amun, Mut, and Khonsu. It was damaged in 1834 by the Italian treasure hunter Giuseppe Ferlini. Above the temple are two niches carved into the cliff face, which contained frontal lions' heads carved in high relief, suggesting that Apedemak was the original 'owner' of the temple and reflecting his close association with Amun as a dynastic god. There are the unexcavated remains of a small kiosk in front of but somewhat off the temple's main axis, and a large three-room structure before the pylon's left side.

In addition to these temples, there are several others identified by Lepsius, for example, Temple G near the great *hafir*, and by James Knudstad and Rosa Frey in the administrative center near the Lion Temple, that await excavation and further study.

The Townsite

The habitation areas of the site have not been excavated or fully identified. In 1995, a survey of an area near the Lion Temple, which is marked by large mounds (some as high as four meters) of stone, mud brick, and other rubble, was conducted after a rough surface clearing. Right below the surface of this area, Knudstad and Frey were able to find and draw the complete plans of three buildings, one of which had twenty-three rooms laid out around a central court with fluted stone columns that were built of lime-plastered rubble, as well as to draw the partial plans of four others. During the second season, more of this area was surveyed and more enclosures farther to the northwest, which were the farthest limits of the site's formal development, were identified. They were made with foundations of rubble walls with plaster-covered mud-brick walls built on them. Constructed on podia, these structures were accessed by ramps or stairs. Faience tiles and a few sculptures found on the site indicate their interiors were decorated. Knudstad and Frey identified this as an area composed of official structures and temples built in courtyards surrounded by large separate enclosures.

In the past, the lack of evidence for ordinary dwellings led Török to speculate that Naqa was not really an urban settlement, but rather both a trade center for the royal government and a home to a specialized, elite population living around its important sanctuaries. However, an area outside the town center where there might be modest dwellings of a non-elite population has tentatively been identified, based on the surface collection of potsherds. Naqa needs a more systematic search for other settlement areas before it can be ascertained whether it was a royal center or an urban settlement with a substantial population.

Although the area near the Lion Temple that was explored by Knudstad and Frey was divided roughly in half by thick stone walls, there is no evidence of fortifications around the town. The enclosures were agglutinative and grew from south to north. Their common orientation suggests that there was some degree of urban planning at the site. Several gates indicated that the general approach to Naqa was from the north. Two one-room temples were found, one with a peristyle (Naqa 600) and one with a pylon (Naqa 700) like the Lion Temple. A third temple (Naqa 800) had the very large feet of a statue in front of it, indicating that a monumental sculpture stood before it, similar to other Meroitic temples.

The Cemeteries

Hundreds of tumuli graves have been identified in the many cemeteries surrounding the site, but none of these cemeteries have been excavated. One particularly large cemetery lies along the mountain chain that marks the northeast border of the Wadi Awatib, stretching several kilometers from Gebel Naqa to Gebel Matruka. Hundreds of stone tumuli graves, up to four meters high and fifteen meters long, probably date to the Meroitic and post-Meroitic Periods. A few fragmentary *ba*-statues were found in this area. In addition to other similar cemeteries close to the boundaries of the site, there is an unusual one to the south of this area with long narrow rows of stones (in lieu of round or oval tumuli) laid out like the shape of a body, according to Wildung and Kroeper.

Bibliography

Bellefonds, L.M.A. 1822. *Bankes Manuscript*. National Trust, U.K.

Cailliaud, F. 1823. *Voyage à Méroé au fleuve Blanc, au-delà du Fâzoql, à Syouah et dans cinq autres oasis: fait dans les années 1819, 1821, et 1822*. Paris: L'Imprimerie Royale.

Gamer-Wallert, I. 1983. *Der Löwentempel von Naq'a in der Butana (Sudan)*. Vol. 2: *Die Wandreliefs*. Wiesbaden: Reichert.

Gamer-Wallert, I., and K. Zibelius-Chen. 1983. *Der Löwentempel von Naq'a in der Butana (Sudan)*. Vol. 1: *Forschungsgeschichte und Topographie*. Wiesbaden: Reichert.

Hinkel, F.W. 1997. "Meroitic Architecture." In D. Wildung, ed., *Sudan: Ancient Kingdoms of the Nile*, 391–417. Paris and New York: Flammarion.

———. 1998. "Naga Project (Sudan)—Egyptian Museum, Berlin. The Lion Temple at Naga. Results of Investigation in 1996." *Archéologie du Nil Moyen* 8:231–30.

Hintze, F. 1959. "Preliminary Report of the Butana Expedition 1958 Made by the Institute for Egyptology of the Humboldt University, Berlin." *Kush* 7:171–96.

Knudstad, J., and R. Frey. 1998. "Naga Project (Sudan)—Egyptian Museum, Berlin. The City Survey 1995–

1996, Seasons 1 and 2." *Archéologie du Nil Moyen* 8:193–202.

Kroeper, K., and L. Krzyżaniak. 1998. "Naga Project (Sudan)—Egyptian Museum, Berlin. The Amun Temple Complex. Preliminary Report, Seasons 1 and 2." *Archéologie du Nil Moyen* 8:203–16.

Kröper, K., Sylvia Schoske, and Dietrich Wildung, eds. 2011. *Königsstadt Naga/Naga Royal City*. Berlin: Ägyptisches Museum und Papyrussammlung Staatliche Museen zu Berlin.

Lepsius, K.R. 1849–59. *Denkmaeler aus Aegypten und Aethiopien: nach den Zeichnungen der von Seiner Majestät dem Könige von Preussen Friedrich Wilhelm IV. nach diesen Ländern gesendeten und in den Jahren 1842–1845 ausgeführten wissenschaftlichen Expedition auf Befehl Seiner Majestät herausgegeben und erläutert von C.R. Lepsius*. Leipzig: G. Wigand.

Priese, K.H. 1998. "Naga Project (Sudan)—Egyptian Museum, Berlin. Epigraphic Documentation 1996." *Archéologie du Nil Moyen* 8:217–21.

Rilly, C. 2004. "Meroitic Paleography as a Tool for Chronology: Prospects and Limits." Paper presented at Tenth International Conference of Meroitic Studies, Paris.

Rocheleau, C. 2008. *Amun Temples in Nubia: A Typological Study of New Kingdom, Napatan and Meroitic Temples*. Oxford: Archeopress.

Török, L. 1997. *The Kingdom of Kush: Handbook of the Napatan-Meroitic Civilization*. Leiden: Brill.

———. 2002. *The Image of the Ordered World in Ancient Nubian Art: The Construction of the Kushite Mind, 800 BC–300 AD*. Leiden: Brill.

Weferling, U. 1998. "Naga Project (Sudan)—Egyptian Museum, Berlin. Contributions to Geodesy." *Archéologie du Nil Moyen* 8:191–92.

Welsby, D.A. 1996. *The Kingdoms of Kush: The Napatan and Meroitic Empires*. London: British Museum Press.

Wildung, D. 1998. "Naga Project (Sudan)—Egyptian Museum, Berlin. Preliminary Report 1995–1996, Seasons 1 and 2." *Archéologie du Nil Moyen* 8:183–90.

———. 1999. "Naga. Die Stadt in der Steppe. Grabungen des Ägyptischen Museums im Sudan. Vorbericht I." *Jahrbuch der Berliner Museen* 41:251–66.

———. 2001. "Naga. Die Stadt in der Steppe. Grabungen des Ägyptischen Museums im Sudan. Vorbericht II. Statuen aus dem Aumn-Tempel." *Jahrbuch der Berliner Museen* 43:303–30.

———. 2004. "Kushite Religion: Aspects of the Berlin Excavations at Naga." In D.A. Welsby and J.R. Anderson, eds., *Sudan: Ancient Treasures: An Exhibition of Recent Discoveries from the Sudan National Museum*, 174–77. London: British Museum Press.

Wildung, D., and K. Kroeper. 2006. *Naga, Royal City of Ancient Sudan*. Berlin: Ägyptisches Museum und Papyrussammlung Staatliche Museen zu Berlin.

Žabkar, L.V. 1975a. *Apedemak, Lion God of Meroe: A Study in Egyptian-Meroitic Syncretism*. Warminster: Aris & Phillips Ltd.

———. 1975b. "Semna South, the Southern Fortress." *JEA* 61:42–44.

Zibelius-Chen, K. 1983. *Der Löwentempel von Naq'a in der Butana (Sudan)*. Vol. 3: *Die Inschriften*. Wiesbaden: Reichert.

MUSAWWARAT AL-SUFRA

Claudia Näser

Musawwarat al-Sufra, located about 180 kilometers northeast of the modern Sudanese capital Khartoum, is a key site of the Meroitic Period (ca. mid-third century BC–mid-fourth century AD)—and certainly its most enigmatic. The site lies about seventy kilometers southwest of Meroe and thirty kilometers away from the Nile Valley, in what is today the semi-arid landscape of the Keraba, in the Butana. The core zone of the site extends over roughly 3.5 by 1 kilometers.

The central feature of Musawwarat is the so-called Great Enclosure, which covers an area of about 43,000 square meters and consists of several building complexes, partly erected on artificial terraces, connected by ramps, corridors, and passages, and surrounded by huge walled courtyards. The function, as well as the exact dating of this unique assemblage, is widely debated, not least because it almost completely lacks a formal decoration, that is, reliefs and related inscriptions, which could aid its interpretation. Long-term archaeological investigations, which nevertheless have so far only covered parts of the structure, revealed that the Great Enclosure was rebuilt and extended numerous times. While conventionally eight main building phases are differentiated,

recent studies by Pawel Wolf suggest that their number is actually smaller. The core of the Great Enclosure is the so-called Temple 100 on the central terrace, which was rebuilt at least four times. The extant structure dates from building phase 6, to which most other standing remains of the Great Enclosure also belong. This phase has long been related to the reign of the early Meroitic king Arnekhamani (ca. last third of third century BC), thanks to fragments of his throne name, Kheperkare, which are preserved on columns in the so-called Western Chapel. If this attribution were correct, the earlier phases of the Great Enclosure would date back to pre-Meroitic, that is, Napatan times. However, Kheperkare was also the throne name of Natakamani, whose reign (ca. second half of first century AD) is considered to have been the heyday of the Meroitic Empire. Recently, it has been suggested by Tim Karberg that building phase 6 should be attributed to him rather than to Arnekhamani. Several indications support this redating.

As Pawel Wolf summarized in his detailed review of all approaches, the function of the Great Enclosure is still very much debated. Its first excavator, Fritz Hintze, suggested that it was a religious site and pilgrimage center, whose central

Figure 162. Map of the valley of Musawwarat with the known archaeological features.

Following pages:
Figure 163. View of the Central Terrace of the Great Enclosure at Musawwarat al-Sufra. Photograph courtesy of Peter Lacovara.

238

Temple 100 was dedicated to Amun-Re, while its courtyards served as gathering and sheltering places for the large crowds coming from the Nile Valley during religious festivals. Later researchers saw it as a national shrine, the main place of worship of the lion god Apedemak, a palace and place of investiture of the Meroitic kings, or even an elephant training camp.

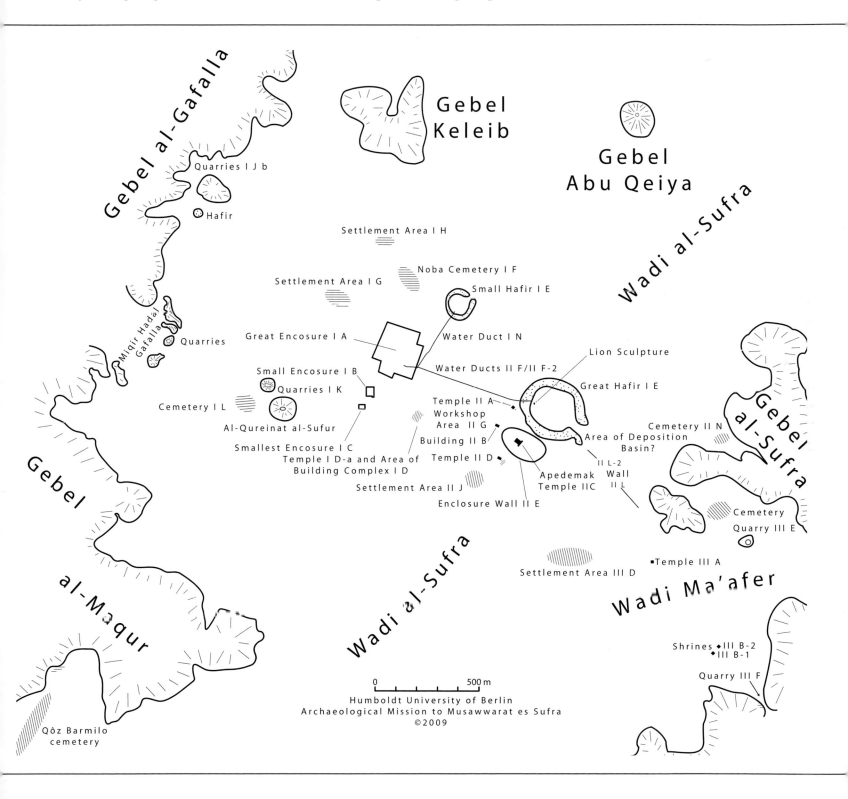

Gebel al-Gafalla

Quarries I J b

Hafir

Gebel Keleib

Gebel Abu Qeiya

Wadi al-Sufra

Settlement Area I H

Noba Cemetery I F

Settlement Area I G

Small Hafir I E

Miqir Hadal Gafalla

Quarries

Great Encosure I A

Water Duct I N

Lion Sculpture

Small Encosure I B

Water Ducts II F/II F-2

Great Hafir I E

Quarries I K

Cemetery I L

Temple II A

Al-Qureinat al-Sufur

Workshop Area II G

Cemetery II N

Gebel al-Sufra

Building II B

Area of Deposition Basin?

Smallest Encosure I C

Temple II D

II L-2

Temple I D-a and Area of Building Complex I D

Apedemak Temple IIC

Wall II L

Settlement Area II J

Gebel al-Maqur

Enclosure Wall II E

Cemetery Quarry III E

Settlement Area III D

Temple III A

Wadi al-Sufra

Wadi Ma'afer

Shrines ◆III B-2
◆ III B-1

Qôz Barmilo cemetery

Quarry III F

0   500 m

Humboldt University of Berlin
Archaeological Mission to Musawwarat es Sufra
©2009

Today, it is widely accepted that the three main structures of the Great Enclosure (complexes 100, 200, and 300) represent temples—however, due to the lack of relief decoration, their dedicatory deities cannot be determined conclusively. A thorough analysis by Dieter Eigner suggests that many ancillary rooms situated around these temples were used during the preparations of the cult activities and during the presence of the kings at the religious ceremonies. Recent investigations revealed a large garden with plantation pits, water basins, and a subterranean water reservoir in the courtyards east of Temple 100, and the dumping place of a pottery workshop in a courtyard north of Temple 200. These findings enrich our picture of the Great Enclosure as a religious assemblage with multiple, frequently remodeled installations supporting the ceremonial activities.

Recently, important progress has been made toward understanding the technological and logistical prerequisites for establishing and maintaining a site like Musawwarat. For Meroitic times, the Keraba can be pictured as a dry savannah. Then, as now, the yearly summer rains were the only available source of water. In order to develop the locale as a main religious center, a continuous availability of substantial amounts of water was needed throughout, or at least during major parts of, the year. This requirement was met by the so-called *hafir*s, monumental water reservoirs, of which four were found at Musawwarat and its immediate environment.

The largest one, the so-called Great Hafir, is situated approximately five hundred meters east of the Great Enclosure. It is the only monument of its type that has so far been archaeologically investigated. Structurally, *hafir*s consist of two main components: a reservoir basin surrounded by an embankment and a sequence of inlet installations, designed to channel, direct, and clear the incoming water. The embankment of the Great Hafir has a diameter of about 250 meters and still stands up to eight meters high. In the east, it has an opening flanked by two straight earthworks, which frame the inner part of the inlet area. The reservoir basin was originally about fifteen meters deep, and its volume can be calculated to about 262,000 cubic meters.

The Great Hafir at Musawwarat is a technological masterpiece of the highest rank. Its construction presupposed an in-depth knowledge of hydrological and geomorphological conditions, and its maintenance required constant attention, a large work force, and a complex logistical organization. This recognition adds new facets to our picture of Musawwarat, showing that it was a site of surprisingly complex resource management and a stimulus of technological innovation. It has been argued by Thomas Scheibner that the construction of at least one *hafir* must have preceded all other large-scale building activities at the site, and recent C-14 dates indeed support an origin of the Great and the Small Hafir in pre-Meroitic, late Napatan times.

Still, many questions remain unanswered, for example, how the smaller structures all over the site—which include two smaller enclosures, the famous Apedemak Temple, several other shrines, workshops, habitation areas, and cemeteries—tie in with its general function. Or why exactly this harsh and remote spot, a two-day trip away from the Nile, was chosen to establish a major religious center. However, the monuments of Musawwarat impressively document the interest of the Meroitic rulers to extend their direct sphere of influence into areas beyond the Nile Valley, their ability to implement massive building schemes in such a faraway location, and the amount of logistical and administrative power they were able to mobilize toward this end.

Bibliography

Edwards, D.N. 1999. *Musawwarat es Sufra III: A Meroitic Pottery Workshop at Musawwarat es Sufra: Preliminary Report on the Excavations 1997 in Courtyard 224 of the Great Enclosure.* Meroitica 17, 2. Wiesbaden: Harrassowitz.

Eigner, D. 2010. "Where Kings Met Gods: The Great Enclosure at Musawwarat es Sufra." *Der Antike Sudan. MittSAG* 21:7–22.

Karberg, T. 2010. "Musawwarat es-Sufra: A Meroitic Terrace Temple in a Nubian Perspective." In W. Godlewski and A. Łajtar, eds., *Between the Cataracts: Proceedings of the Eleventh International Conference for Nubian Studies, Warsaw University, 27 August–2 September 2006. Part 2, fascicule 2: Session Papers.* PAM Supplement Series 2.2/2, 571–76. Warsaw: Warsaw University Press.

Näser, C. 2010. "The Great Hafir at Musawwarat es-Sufra: Fieldwork of the Archaeological Mission of Humboldt University Berlin in 2005 and 2006." In W. Godlewski and A. Łajtar, eds., *Between the Cataracts: Proceedings of the Eleventh International Conference for Nubian Studies, Warsaw University, 27 August–2 September 2006. Part 2, fascicule 1: Session Papers.* PAM Supplement Series 2.2/1, 39–46. Warsaw: Warsaw University Press.

———. 2011. "Early Musawwarat." In V. Rondot, F. Alpi, and F. Villeneuve, eds., *La pioche et la plume: Autour du Soudan, du Liban et de la Jordanie: Hommages archéologiques à Patrice Lenoble*, 317–38. Paris: Sorbonne PUPS.

Scheibner, T. 2004. "Neue Erkenntnisse zur Wasserversorgung von Musawwarat es Sufra (I). Das übergeordnete Wasserversorgungssystem—Teil I: Wassergewinnung und -speicherung." *Der Antike Sudan. MittSAG* 15:39–64.

———. 2005. "Archäologie, Verantwortung und Kulturerhalt: Die Rettungskampagne am Großen Hafir von Musawwarat 2005." *Der Antike Sudan. MittSAG* 16:15–33.

Wolf, P. 2001a. "Die Untersuchungen zur Baugeschichte an der Nordseite der Zentralterrasse." *Der Antike Sudan. MittSAG* 11:16–23.

———. 2001b. "Die Höhle des Löwen. Zur Deutung der Großen Anlage von Musawwarat es Sufra." In C.-B. Arnst, I. Hafemann, and A. Lohwasser, eds., *Begegnungen: Antike Kulturen im Niltal: Festgabe für Erika Endesfelder, Karl-Heinz Priese, Walter Friedrich Reineke, Steffen Wenig*, 473–508. Leipzig: Verlag Helmar Wodtke und Katharina Stegbauer.

———. 2004. "Fieldwork of the Humboldt University of Berlin at Musawwarat es Sufra 1993–2000: A Summary." In S. Wenig, ed., *Neueste Feldforschungen im Sudan und in Eritrea: Akten des Symposiums vom 13. bis 14. Oktober 1999 in Berlin*, 47–62. Meroitica 21. Wiesbaden: Harrassowitz.

WAD BAN NAQA

Janice W. Yellin

Wad ban Naqa (Meroitic name: 'Irbiklb), like the nearby town of Naqa to its southwest, lies inland from the Nile so that it could be situated on a network of wadis that served as an important trade route between the Nile Valley, the royal city of Meroe, and the outer fringes of the Meroitic state. The site, approximately one hundred kilometers north of Khartoum, was built between two converging branches of the Wadi Kirbikan.

Wad ban Naqa is relatively unexplored. The site is currently being excavated by a Czech Republic expedition headed by Pavel Onderka of the National Museum, with the participation of several other Czech institutions and the Kestner-Museum in Hannover, Germany. During the first excavation season (2009) Onderka's team carried out a general survey of the site and its cemeteries. The main focus was on the central area with its palace, circular structure, and temples. One goal will be to conserve the palace of Amanishakheto. They also uncovered a previously unknown site, EAD e-Wakar, nearby.

Previously, this large site was known only from the visits of mid-nineteenth century travelers (for example, Frédéric Cailliaud, Linant de Bellefonds, Georg Gustav Erbkam). The Royal Prussian Expedition of Richard Lepsius mapped and made drawings of the site and its monuments. In addition, Lepsius's expedition brought back four stone monuments from the site, the most important of which is the barque stand of Natakamani and Amanitore from the Southeast Temple. Bilingual inscriptions, including the names of these two rulers, written in both Egyptian hieroglyphs and Meroitic cursive on each of its four sides, were used by F.Ll. Griffith to identify the phonetic values of alphabetic signs used in Meroitic cursive inscriptions.

Said Hassan Thabit, the first Sudanese head of the Sudanese Antiquities Department, with Jean Vercoutter, conducted the first excavations at the site (1958–60) and discovered the remains of a large brick two-story palace belonging to Queen Amanishakheto (end of first century AD). This palace, approximately sixty-one meters square, was accessed by ramps. Its ground floor had several large chambers, as well as approximately sixty smaller rooms that probably served as storage magazines. Evidence suggests that the palace had a second floor with an audience hall and living quarters, as are found in the royal palace at Meroe and in Natakamani's palace at Gebel Barkal. Small elements of painted and gilded relief indicate that some of these chambers were lavishly decorated.

Wad ban Naqa might have been an urban center with a sedentary population that developed near the royal religious center of Naqa. Recent excavations at the site of Muweis by Michel Baud, the Louvre Museum, suggest that there may have been a parallel situation between the religious center of Musawwaret al-Sufra and the nearby site of Muweis, to that of the religious center of Naqa and the nearby site of Wad ban Naqa. Based on early evidence that Muweis was a large urban center, Aminata Sackho-Autissier has proposed that Muweis was the habitation site for the nearby royal religious center of Musawwaret al-Sufra, which, like Naqa, has not offered archaeological evidence for a large sedentary population.

In 2009, the Czech National Museum expedition discovered a rectangular building, labeled the North Temple, to the north of the palace. About fifty meters to the south of the palace, there is a mysterious circular structure known since the time of Lepsius. Constructed of mud brick, it has a diameter of about twenty meters, and walls that are 3.70 meters thick and, in some places, up to five meters high. There are eroded walls belonging to magazines that were once attached to it. The round form suggests a *hafir*, but in a February 2011 interview posted on the website *Archaeology Daily News*, the expedition leader Pavel Onderka indicated that this beehive-shaped structure clearly served a religious purpose in the service of an as-yet-unidentified god. A small temple (Wad ban Naqa 600) lies nearby. Two small buildings to the east of the palace are also temples. The nearest and smaller of the two (Wad ban Naqa 400) has a pylon, but its ground plan is incomplete. In the same February 2011 interview Onderka revealed that his expedition discovered that the so-called small temple was built between

the first century BC and the first century AD and was in continual use until the end of the Meroitic state. It was probably dedicated to Sebiumeker or, less likely, Apedemak, both indigenous lion gods. The larger, farther temple (Wad ban Naqa 500) has a pylon, a first court with eight columns, a tripartite second court, and a three-room sanctuary with side chambers. To the west of the palace, lying under a mound about eighty meters long, are a large temple (Wad ban Naqa 300), called the Typhonium by Lepsius, and the Southeast Temple. The so-called Typhonium was identified as a *mammisi* (a divine birth temple) by Lepsius and others because it had columns carved with the Egyptian/Nubian god Bes (Greek name: Typhon) and columns with Hathor heads, since both of these deities can be associated with childbirth. However, László Török argues that this is the Isis Temple at Wad ban Naqa that is referred to in an inscription from Musawwarat al-Sufra. The nearby Southeast Temple had three shrines with three barque stands found by Lepsius—two for Isis and one for Hathor—indicating that the barques of these goddesses could have been brought to it from the nearby Isis temple during ritual processions. Török argues that the dedication of these barque stands to Isis and to Hathor, who is closely linked with Isis, support the larger temple's identification with Isis rather than as a *mammisi*. Two of these barque stands have disappeared, and the third is the one Lepsius took to the Berlin Museum.

During its 2009 season of surveying the site, the Czech expedition noted cemeteries adjacent to the site, and to the north of the palace are two tumuli burials that date to the post-Meroitic era. These await future exploration.

Bibliography

Bellefonds, L.M.A. de. 1822. *Bankes Manuscript*. National Trust, U.K.

Cailliaud, F. 1823. *Voyage à Méroé et au Fleuve Blanc, au-delà du Fazoql, à Syouah et dans cinq autres oasis fait dans les années 1819, 1821, 1822*. Paris: L'Imprimerie Royale.

Czech Expedition to Wad ban Naqa. Home page. http://www.hedvabnastezka.cz/cestopisy/archeologicka-expedice-do-wad-ben-naga?highlightWords=wad+ben+naqa (in Czech)

"Czech Team Excavates Ancient Sites Dedicated to Nubian Gods." *Archaeology Daily News*. http://www.archaeologydaily.com/ news/201102026035/Czech-team-excavates-ancient-sites-dedicated-to-Nubian-gods.html

Erbkam, G.G. 2008. *Tagebuch meiner egyptischen Reise (in der Transkription von Elke Freier herausgegeben von der Arbeitsgruppe Altägyptisches Wörterbuch der Berlin-Brandenburgischen Akademie der Wissenschaften)*. http://pom.bbaw.de/erbkam

Griffith, F.Ll. 1911. "Meroitic Inscriptions. Part I. Sôba to Dangêl." In J.W. Crowfoot, *The Island of Meroe*. London: Egypt Exploration Fund.

Hinkel, F.W. 1997. "Meroitic Architecture." In D. Wildung, ed., *Sudan: Ancient Kingdoms of the Nile*, 391–417, fig. 48. Paris and New York: Flammarion.

Priese, K.H. 1984. "Wad Ban Naqa 1844." *FuB* 24:11–29.

Sackho-Autissier, A. 2008. "The Material Culture of Muweis Site (Meroe Region): First Data." *Eleventh International Conference for Meroitic Studies, Vienna, September 1–September 4, 2008*. Vienna: University of Vienna, Department of African Studies.

Société des cultures nubienne. Introduction. http://- nubie-international.fr/accueil.php?a= page100000&lang=en

Török, L. 2002. *The Image of the Ordered World in Ancient Nubian Art: The Construction of the Kushite Mind, 800 BC–300 AD*. Leiden: Brill.

Vercoutter, J. 1962. "Un Palais des 'Candaces,' contemporain d'Auguste (fouilles à Wad-ban-Naga 1958–1960)." *Syria* 39:263–99.

AL-HOBAGI

Janice W. Yellin

The site of al-Hobagi, with its modest number of tumuli burials (seven in all), has changed our understanding of the late- and post-Meroitic history of Nubia and demonstrated how much still remains to be learned about Nubian history. Located near the Sixth Cataract on the west bank of the Nile some seventy kilometers south of Meroe, its seven tumuli lie on the gravel terrace beside the Wadi Fazar, and a nearby structure at Hosh al-Kafir lies within the wadi proper. Today the area, between the Nile flood plain and sandstone hills, supports animal husbandry and agriculture that rely on rain and the Nile River. Other than these eight monuments, there are no other visible ruins at the site. Unexcavated graves and tumuli in other regional cemeteries appear to date to the pre-Christian and Christian Periods.

A Franco-Sudanese expedition led by Patrice Lenoble in 1985–90 excavated two of the tumuli and part of the large enclosure at nearby Hosh al-Kafir. The large structure at Hosh al-Kafir may have had a military use. An enclosure wall built of rough stone slabs and dry earth mortar walls approximately one meter thick had two small entrances that controlled access to the large open area and smaller central twelve-room brick or mud structure that lay within the wall. The small area of this enclosure excavated by Lenoble had only a meager amount of animal remains but many military objects such as arrowheads. These finds led him to theorize that this structure was a military camp rather than a ritual structure associated with the tumuli burial, as might first be assumed because of the structure's proximity to the burials. However, further exploration is needed to clarify its use(s).

The seven tumuli built of piled stones are scattered on the nearby gravel plain over an area of approximately five kilometers. Impressive in scale, each was originally surrounded by an elliptical enclosure wall and range between thirty and forty meters in diameter. They still stand approximately four to five meters high. To date, only two of these burials have been excavated. Although both were robbed in antiquity, the thieves took only the most precious materials, and there was still a wealth of objects left relatively undisturbed in their burial chambers. When talking about his entry into each of these burial chambers (both occupied by males, whom he presumed to be kings), Lenoble describes a dramatic scene in which the dead owner was laid out on a funerary bed. Immediately around him were hundreds of weapons such as arrows, bows, and spears. Slightly farther away from the body were vessels for food and drink, as well as special vessels made of bronze that were intended for ritual uses such as libations and incense offerings. The quality of many objects, especially the bronze bowls, is quite high. Evidence for animal sacrifices, including camels, dogs, cattle, and horses, was also found in the burials. Those entering the tomb at the time of burial would have been presented with a dramatic image of their dead leader as a warrior rich in possessions and well cared for within Egyptian-Meroitic funerary traditions.

The compilation of practices and beliefs found in these burials and the implications for our understanding of the post-Meroitic Period are fascinating. The use of a tumulus, bed burial, and horse sacrifice(s) are very ancient Nubian traditions. However, the bed burials and tumuli structures were not part of Meroitic royal/elite burial practices at Meroe and Gebel Barkal. Their use fits well into the idea, discussed below, that the Meroitic Period ended with the fall of the royal dynasty at Meroe, since Meroitic royal burials are most essentially marked by the use of pyramids rather than tumuli, as well as by the use of stone coffin benches to receive the body rather than bed burials. Therefore the external appearance of the tumuli at al-Hobagi indicates that the Meroitic royal tradition has ended. So their excavator was very surprised to discover that despite these differences, the decoration and uses of the objects placed inside them nonetheless follow Meroitic religious traditions and royal practices very closely. The images on the bronze ritual objects clearly indicate that burial beliefs, as at Meroe, are modeled on ancient Egyptian ones, including the worship of Osiris, Isis, and Horus. The various military objects in the tombs construct the same image of the warrior king as seen in the chapels of

the last royal pyramids at Meroe. Finally, the last known inscription in Meroitic signs is carved on one of these bowls. Because recognizable Meroitic words are part of the inscription, it can be assumed that the inscription had a good Meroitic source. The connections between these burials and the last royal burials at Meroe are undeniable. What remains problematic is how to interpret this connection to build a history of the events after the end of Meroe.

Until Lenoble excavated these tumuli, it was assumed that the Meroitic Period and its elite culture ended with the collapse of royal power at Meroe in the fourth century AD and that its territories followed several different paths of development during what is called the post-Meroitic and/or X-Group Period. However the clear use of, and relationship to, Meroitic royal and religious traditions at al-Hobagi has led to the re-evaluation of this assumption. Lenoble believed that the owners of these tumuli were kings who continued the Meroitic state after its supposed end in the fourth century AD, and that these burials and other tumuli burials, such as those at Ballana and Qustul, belong to a culture and period that should be called 'Post-Pyramidal Meroitic.' Others, such as László Török, argue that the Meroitic Period and culture ends with the fall of the royal dynasty at Meroe in the fourth century AD and with the incursions of new populations, such as the Noba in Meroitic territories. If Meroitic culture did end with the fall of Meroe, then the burials at al-Hobagi belong to local dynasts, who were imitating Meroitic forms to enhance their status within a relatively small area. The untimely death of Patrice Lenoble in 2007 ended his work at al-Hobagi. A more complete understanding of Sudanese history after the fall of the royal dynasty at Meroe awaits data from new excavations at al-Hobagi and other later sites.

Bibliography

"El Hobagi." Section française de la Direction des Antiquités du Soudan (SFDAS), http://www.sfdas.com/blog/?page_id=10

Lenoble, P. 1996. "The Division of the Meroitic Empire and the End of Pyramid Building in the 4th Century AD: An Introduction to Further Excavations of Imperial Mounds in the Sudan." In D. Welsby, ed., *Eighth International Conference for Meroitic Studies*, 157–98. London: British Museum Press.

———. 1997. "Les tumulus impériaux des IVe, Ve et VIe siècles de notre ère. Une fausse énigme." *Dossier d'Archéologie*. Hors-série 6 (Soudan): 82–86.

———. 2002. "El-Hobagi." In D.A. Welsby and W.V. Davies, eds., *Uncovering Ancient Sudan: A Decade of Discovery by the Sudan Archaeological Research Society*, 193–97. London: British Museum Press.

Lenoble, P., and Nigm ed Din Mohammed Sharif. 1992. "Barbarians at the Gates? The Royal Mounds of El Hobagi and the End of Meroë." *Antiquity* 66, no. 252: 626–35.

Reinold, J. 2000. *Archéologie au Soudan: Les civilisations de Nubie*. Paris: Editions Errance.

Török, L. 1996. "The End of Meroe." In D. Welsby, ed., *Eighth International Conference of Meroitic Studies*, 133–56. London: British Museum Press.

Muweis

Janice W. Yellin

The site of Muweis, which is located approximately 400 kilometers north of Khartoum, was first identified by Ahmed Sokari and the late Patrice Lenoble during their 2003 survey of the area. Excavations by the Louvre Museum under the direction of Michel Baud, which began in 2007, reveal that Muweis was an urban center dating to the Meroitic Period. The discovery of Meroitic eggshell fine ware in the palace area has led Baud to propose that the earliest settlement at Muweis dates at least to the early first century AD, a date which is also given for the similar palace of Amanishakheto at Wad ban Naqa. Currently many small objects found throughout the excavated areas of Muweis date to the first to fourth centuries AD. Among these objects are small clay human figures, seals, and seal rings.

Investigations of the site have focused on two large mounds, the Eastern and Western Hills, which are approximately 150 meters apart, and on the central area of the town that lies between them. Preliminary survey work on the Western Hill suggests that it was a settlement area, and areas excavated on the Eastern Hill have revealed many levels of mud-brick structures with evidence for human occupation. Evidence for pottery and iron

metal manufacturing was found on the northeastern part of this hill. A large number of potsherds and three kilns were uncovered in that area along with numerous examples of ceramic products, and iron slag suggests there were also iron-smelting furnaces that have yet to be excavated. Among the most interesting finds in this area are small baked-clay figurines, which appear to be female fertility figures and have features reflecting their African origins. Many show scarification and tattooing. South of this area is a habitation zone with what is thought to be eight building phases, some of which were separated by long phases of inactivity, indicating that Muweis was inhabited for a very long time.

The center of the site is now a large, sandy plain. It appears that, as in many other urban sites of the Meroitic Period, the central part of the town contained large official buildings and shrines that were built perpendicular to a major avenue. Although formal excavations have not begun in the central area, a survey using magnetometry revealed a large building or complex close to the southeastern edge of the Western Hill. Test trenches indicate there were several levels of buildings, and the finds from at least one level are clearly Meroitic. The same survey revealed the outlines of several other structures and shrines in the central area. During the 2009 season, the remains of what appears to be the site's major temple dedicated to Amun, as well as two smaller temples (J and M) that were oriented perpendicular to it along a sacred way, were surveyed. In temple J, fragments of painted relief showing a queen, prince, and gods, along with two partial cartouches with the beginning of a name that could belong to one of Natakamani's and Amanitore's (second half of first century AD) sons, indicate that Muweis was among the many preexisting sites these rulers remodeled. Palace A, temple J, and the ceramic kilns FA are currently under excavation.

Still in the early stages of excavation, the large red-brick, two-story palace of Gala'a al-Howara (a mound area on the central plain) is oriented to the processional way on its southern edge. There are indications that its ground floor bears a general similarity to the plan of the palace at Wad ban Naqa, which led to its identification as a palace building. Like other Meroitic palaces, it appears to have had ground-floor casement and storage rooms, with the living and official areas on its second floor. Decorative architecture elements, faience tiles and plaques, as well as fragments of painted plaster, have been found in it. Aminata Sackho-Autissier has indicated that some of its faience decorations were similar to ones found at

Figure 164. Muweis, Palace A, first century AD, view to north.

Tabo and Kawa in sacred buildings, as well as at the palace in Wad ban Naqa.

According to Baud, Muweis was a royal urban center belonging to a fairly dense network of such small, recently identified urban centers built along the right bank of the Nile approximately ten kilometers apart that included Hamadab, al-Hassa, and Dangeil near the royal capital at Meroe. These served as both royal residences and royal administrative centers during the Meroitic Period.

Bibliography

Baud, M. 2008. "The Meroitic Royal City of Muweis: First Steps into an Urban Settlement of Riverine Upper Nubia." *Sudan & Nubia* 12:52–63.

———. 2010a. "Méroé: Un mond urbain." In M. Baud, A. Sackho-Autissier, and S. Labbé-Toutée, eds., *Méroé: Un empire sur le Nil*, 211–14. Paris: Musée du Louvre Editions.

———. 2010b. "Mouvweis. Une ville riveraine de la région de Méroé." *Dossiers d'Archéologie*. Hors-série 18 (March 2010): 14–19.

Evina, M. 2010. "Painted Kraters from the Meroitic City of Muweis." Abstract. *Twelfth International Conference for Nubian Studies, London, August 1–August 6, 2010*. London: British Museum.

Lenoble, P., and A. Sokari. 2005. "A Forgotten Meroitic Agglomeration in the Region of Meroe: el-Muweis." *Sudan & Nubia* 9:59–61.

Lewczuk, J. 1983. "Studies on the Iconography of Thoth in the Art of the Kingdom of Kush: Napatan and Meroitic Periods." *GM* 69:45–61.

Maillot, M. 2010. "The Palace of Muweis in the Shendi Area: A Comparative Approach." Abstract. *Twelfth International Conference for Nubian Studies, London, August 1–August 6, 2010*. London: British Museum.

Sackho-Autissier, A. 2008. "The Material Culture of Muweis Site (Meroe Region): First Data." *Eleventh International Conference for Meroitic Studies, Vienna, September 1–September 4, 2008*. Vienna: University of Vienna, Department of African Studies.

AL-HASSA

Janice W. Yellin

The site of al-Hassa, which is situated approximately 180 kilometers north of Khartoum on the right bank of the Nile, was first noted by John Burckhardt in 1814, and later by Linant de Bellefonds and Frédéric Cailliaud in 1822. Al-Hassa was rediscovered in 1975, when a ram-headed sphinx inscribed with the name of a little-known Meroitic king, Amanakhereqerem, was found while digging an irrigation canal. Excavations first began in 2000 under the direction of the late Patrice Lenoble and now led by Vincent Rondot for the French Section of the Directorate on Antiquities of Sudan, in cooperation with the Sudanese National Corporation for Antiquities and Museums. This extensive site, which is thirty kilometers south of the royal capital of Meroe, is one of several currently under excavation that promise to reshape our understanding of the political and economic organization of the Meroitic state. Like the sites of Muweis and Hamadab, which are also on the Nile's east bank and near the capital in the area known as the Island of Meroe, al-Hassa was a secondary royal site where state business, including the smelting of iron for weaponry, occurred. As Rondot and others have noted, proximity of these sites to the royal capital at Meroe allowed

iron smelting and weapon manufacturing to be under close state control.

Since 2002, excavation efforts have focused on the investigation of an Amun Temple that was built in two phases. The later temple, which was enlarged and changed, is very similar to Amun Temple 200 at Naqa. The later ground plan brings it closer to traditional Egyptian temple plans and demonstrates the importance of Egyptian religious forms in this period. Based on inscriptions found in association with both the Naqa and the earlier al-Hassa temples, they appear to have been constructed by King Amanakhereqerem, whose reign is currently dated to the late first century AD. It is not yet clear if he was also responsible for the second, larger phase of the al-Hassa temple. According to an inscription, this temple was dedicated to Amun of Tabakh, which was also probably the Meroitic name for this town. The Amun temple was made of brick, with stones used primarily for the columns. Evidence indicates that exterior relief decorations were plastered and painted. The temple founded by Amanakhereqerem was later rebuilt with a somewhat different plan that included the addition of three rooms in a new sanctuary area. Behind the temple was a separate contra-temple with a ram-headed statue of Amun and an altar.

253

This is only the second example (the other is in the large Amun Temple at Naqa) of this Egyptian temple feature in Nubia. Again, as at Naqa and other Amun temples, the pylon of the temple was approached through an avenue of ram-headed sphinxes with small figures of the king between their forelegs. In 2008, three ram sphinxes, one with the first complete Meroitic dedication inscription ever found, confirmed Amanakhereqerem's role in building the first temple and provided further evidence for dating him to the late first century AD. Based on the forms of the Meroitic cursive used for the dedication inscription, Claude Rilly dates it to AD 80–90. It is still not known who rebuilt the temple—the same king later in his reign or a successor.

In 2005, excavations in the sanctuary of the temple yielded two interesting groups of objects. A cache of objects built into the naos stand was followed by the discovery of a group of objects in their original locations on the sanctuary's floor, giving insights into cultic activities in the sanctuary. Among the objects found in situ on the floor were Neolithic weapons from much earlier graves, statues imported from Egypt, Meroitic faience, and local pebbles in unusual shapes. The pebbles reflect an ancient Kushite religious practice, perhaps derived from a belief in the numinous power of the sacred mountains from which they may have come, or because their natural shape(s) had religious symbolism (see "Nubian Religion"). The most striking of the finds from the sanctuary was the bronze head of a Meroitic queen, used for the top of a staff or cane, which is notable for the African nature of its aesthetic and features. The magnometrical survey of the site indicated there are a number of additional official buildings. Even after more than ten years of excavation, al-Hassa still promises to add much to our understanding of life in a royal Meroitic urban center.

Bibliography

Burckhardt, J. L. 1822. *Travels in Nubia*. London: John Murray.

Cailliaud, F. 1823–27. *Voyage à Méroé et au Fleuve Blanc, au-delà du Fazoql, à Syouah et dans cinq autres oasis fait dans les années 1819, 1821, 1822*. 4 vols. Paris: L'Imprimerie Royale.

Lenoble, P., and V. Rondot. 2003. "A la redécouverte d'El-Hassa. Temple à Amun, palais royal et ville de l'empire méroïtique." *CRIPEL* 23:101–11, 164–66.

Rilly, C. 2010. "Le royaume de Méroé." *Afriques: Varia*. http://afriques.revues.org/379

Rocheleau, C. 2008. *Amun Temples in Nubia: A Typological Study of New Kingdom, Napatan and Meroitic Temples*. Oxford: Archeopress.

Rondot, V. "Un établissement urbain méroïtique à proximité de la capitale impériale. Fouille engagée en 2000." Section française de la Direction des Antiquités du Soudan. http:// www.sfdas.com/blog/?page_id=9

———. 2010a. "El-Hassa, un nouveau temple à Amon dans la region de Méroé." *Dossiers d'Archéologie*. Hors-série 18 (March 2010): 32–37.

———. 2010b. "Le matériel cultuel du temple à Amon d'el-Hassa." In M. Baud, A. Sackho-Autissier, and S. Labbé-Toutée, eds., *Méroé: Un empire sur le Nil*, 236–39. Paris: Musée du Louvre Editions.

———. Sudan: al-Hassa. "Méroé Island Project." France Diplomatie. http://www.diplomatie.gouv.fr/en/france-priorities_1/archaeology_2200/archaeology-notebooks_2202/africa-arabia_2240/sudan-el-hassa_5988/index.html

———. 2008. "The Temple to Amun at el-Hassa: What We Know after Six Digging Campaigns." Abstract. *Eleventh International Conference for Meroitic Studies, Vienna, September 1–September 4, 2008*. Vienna: University of Vienna, Department of African Studies.

HAMADAB

Janice W. Yellin

Excavations at the site of Hamadab, approximately 205 kilometers north of Khartoum, promise to increase our understanding of Meroitic urban settlements. This site, which is on the right bank of the Nile less than two miles south of Meroe, is at the meeting of the Wadi Hawad and the Nile. The wadi served as a trade route to the Nile, so this location would have been well suited for commerce on behalf of the royal government at Meroe, as well as for its defense against threats from its southern territory. Now a large mound with two distinct areas (the northern upper and southern lower towns), Hamadab is near a branch of the Nile that fills during the winter. The Meroitic cemetery is probably in the large, unexcavated mound south of the residential area. The first excavation at Hamadab was conducted in 1914 by John Garstang at the end of his work at Meroe (1909–14) and was focused solely on the excavation of the temple (H 1000) and the large stelae of Prince Akinidad and Queen Amanirenas that stood before its entrance. In 2001, a team from Humboldt University (Berlin) in cooperation with the National Corporation for Antiquities and Museums, Khartoum, and the University in Shendi (Sudan), under the leadership of Pawel Wolf, began excavations of the town site. Since 2007, the German Archaeological Institute has also sponsored this undertaking.

The first seasons of exploration at Hamadab were conducted primarily through the use of magnetometry and surface clearing. Traditional excavations in selected areas of the site are now underway, and as a result some of the first theories about Hamadab, its structures and purpose have been rethought. Results from work that is currently primarily focused on the fortified upper town suggest that Hamadab, despite its proximity to the capital of Meroe, was an independently functioning urban center with an economically varied population that, based on what appears to be an administrative center (H 3000) in the southern part of the upper town, had its own system of governance rather than serving as a religious complex or satellite of Meroe. The density of its population and absence, to date, of evidence for on-site food production suggest that it relied on nearby areas for its food, making it an urban center in the truest sense.

Because excavations have not reached the earliest settlement levels, the date of Hamadab's founding is not known. There is evidence that Hamadab was occupied from the later first century BC, and Wolf believes that the town was probably abandoned, like so many other sites, at the end of the Meroitic Period (fourth century AD). Its decline might have begun earlier, because a late Meroitic burial found in the upper town along the inner side of the southern fortification wall indicates that this part of the town was not in active use by the late Meroitic Period.

The site is large and its archaeological remains deep (up to four meters in the center of the upper town), so it will be many years before a full understanding of the site can be achieved. Nonetheless, the excavations at Hamadab offer some of the first information indicating an urban Meroitic town in which there is a separation of habitation from industrial areas. The upper town, with its large central avenue leading to the main temple (H 1000) and a large open plaza, shows definite evidence it was designed by a central authority. It was surrounded by a wall with city gates at the termini of the main avenue. Based on his excavations, Wolf has developed a tentative overview of Hamadab's history. The upper town, including the religious area with the Amun Temple (H 1000) plus administrative and domestic areas, was founded during the reigns of Amanirenas and Akinidad (phase C, late first century BC). In phase B, the city wall was rebuilt after its collapse, the main avenue was widened and extended, and the Amun temple may have been rebuilt. During phase A, the latest one, several of these main public structures may have again undergone some rebuilding and the city moved beyond the walled northern upper town into an area to its south that contained zones dedicated to the manufacturing of various goods.

The center of the upper town included a sacral area with Temple H 1000. The later phases (B–A) of the temple have either been eroded or were removed by Garstang when he excavated it. In 2002, Wolf re-examined the temple. The deity for whom the modest, mud-brick shrine with stone doorframes and columns was built is uncertain, but may have been Amun. It was entered through a portal that led to a long, narrow pronaos with two columns at its far end. This room opened to a sanctuary with an altar. On the north side there were two rooms that are larger than the entire shrine. These were entered through the pronaos, and their purpose is unclear. The temple and adjacent rooms were essentially empty of small finds, although Wolf found an uninscribed copper alloy statuette of the Meroitic god Sebiumeker near the sanctuary that dates to the second century BC on stylistic grounds. The erection of two important royal stelae by Prince Akinidad and Queen Amanirenas in front of such a small shrine was unusual and speaks to the importance Hamadab held for them. Based on the forms of the Meroitic cursive letters used to write the stelae's inscriptions, Claude Rilly has confirmed they date to the reigns of Akinidad and Amanirenas in the late first century BC. This dating as well as what Rilly is able to translate of the Meroitic inscription on the smaller of the two stelae suggest that they contain information pertaining to events in Strabo's account of the Meroites' attack on the Roman garrison at Syene and their battles with the Roman prefect, Petronius Gallius. However, there is no definite evidence that these stelae were erected to mark this war, and current thinking is that they contained annals recording and commemorating accomplishments during the reigns of Akinidad and Amanirenas, including their attack on Syene.

The northern half of the upper town was filled with densely packed dwellings, some of which were two stories high. These were framed by narrow streets radiating off the main avenue. Residences were created by the addition or subdivisions of rooms to an original dwelling, changes that eventually filled the entire buildable areas framed by the narrow roads to create irregularly shaped apartment blocks. Some of these combined dwellings consisted of up to sixty rooms. Plaster painted red, yellow, or white often covered these mud-brick buildings. Ovens and other finds indicate the domestic functions of various rooms. So far, larger elite dwellings, such as found at Meroe and other sites, have not been found, suggesting that for the most part Hamadab was populated by non-elite Meroites.

The southern half of the upper town is still largely unexplored, but may have had areas of domestic dwellings as well as areas for manufacturing. A substantial building in the southeastern corner (H 3000) is the only other monumental structure so far identified (the temple is the other). Based on its similarities to Meroitic official structures, it may have served an administrative function.

The extensive area of the unfortified lower town has not yet been excavated and is known through magnetometry and other survey methods. It appears to be largely composed of various zones devoted to the production of specific kinds of products. There is clear evidence for iron smelting, as well as for ceramic, glass, textile, and faience production. Objects such as bronze vessels, Roman glass, and archer's rings that were retrieved from some recently pillaged tombs demonstrate that some of Hamadab's citizens enjoyed relatively high status and wealth, and testify to its success as an urban manufacturing and, based on its location at the terminus of the Wadi Hawad, perhaps also as a trading center.

Bibliography

Eide, T., T. Hagg, R.H. Pierce, and L. Török, eds. 1996. *Fontes Historiae Nubiorum: Textual Sources for the History of the Middle Nile Region between the Eighth Century BC and the Sixth Century AD.* Vol. 2: *From the Mid-Fifth to the First Century BC.* Bergen: University of Bergen.

Garstang, J. 1916. "Fifth Interim Report on the Excavations at Meroë in Ethiopia." *LAA* 7:1–24.

Griffith, F.Ll. 1917. "Meroitic Studies IV: The Great Stele of Prince Akinizaz." *JEA* 4:159–73.

Leclant, J., et al. 2000. *Répertoire d'Épigraphie Méroïtique: Corpus des inscriptions publiées. REM 1001 à 1278.* Paris: Académie des Inscriptions et Belles-Lettres.

Rilly, C. 2008a. "The Linguistic Position of Meroitic: New Perspectives for Understanding the Texts." *Sudan & Nubia* 12:2–12.

———. 2008b. "New Advances in the Understanding of Royal Meroitic Inscriptions." Abstract. *Eleventh International Conference for Meroitic Studies, Vienna, September 1–September 4, 2008.* Vienna: University of Vienna, Department of African Studies.

Rocheleau, C. 2008. *Amun Temples in Nubia: A Typological Study of New Kingdom, Napatan and Meroitic Temples.* Oxford: Archeopress.

Wolf, P. 2002a. "Die Ausgrabung in Hamadab bei Meroe: Erste Kampagne, Frühjahre 2001." *Der Antike Sudan.* MittSAG 13:92–104.

———. 2002b. "Die Ausgrabung in Hamadab bei Meroe: Zweite Kampagne, Frühjahre 2001." *Der Antike Sudan.* MittSAG 13:105–11.

———. 2004. "Hamadab—das Haupquartier des Akinidad?" *Der Antike Sudan.* MittSAG 15:83–98.

———. 2008. "Insights into Development and Lifestyle of a Meroitic Urban Settlement." *Proceedings of the Eleventh International Conference for Meroitic Studies, Vienna, September 1–September 4, 2008.* Vienna: University of Vienna, Department of African Studies.

———. 2010. "Season 2010 at Domat al Hamadab." Unpublished report to the National Corporation of Antiquities and Museums.

Wolf, P., U. Nowotnick, and C. Hof. 2010a. "Investigating the Meroitic City of Hamadab." Abstract. *Twelfth International Conference for Nubian Studies.* London: British Museum.

———. 2010b. "Investigating the Meroitic Town of Hamadab: An Overview after Season 2010." *Twelfth International Conference for Nubian Studies.* London: British Museum.

MEROE

Janice W. Yellin

Meroe lies between the Fourth and Fifth Cataracts of the Nile River, some 209 kilometers north of Khartoum. The town was situated near the Nile's fertile right bank, while the terrain immediately beyond the settlement area is arid and dotted with low, barren, rocky hills. Nearby, an opening to the Wadi Hawad connected Meroe with its outlying territory, the Butana Savannah, and thence to southern trade routes.

Ancient Greek and Roman authors wrote knowledgeably about Meroe, which was once the center of a kingdom whose elites participated in the religious, political, and economic life of Egypt and the greater Mediterranean world. Yet, after it was abandoned, its location was forgotten until a Scottish adventurer, James Bruce, rediscovered it in 1772. Thereafter, Meroe was visited by travelers, treasure hunters, and the occasional scholar. Modern exploration of the site began with John Garstang's expedition in the Royal City and environs during 1909–14. From 1965 to 1984 and 1999 to 2010, excavations in the Royal City and the Northern Mound have been sponsored by various academic institutions, most notably a joint expedition of the Department of Archaeology of the University of Calgary, Canada and the Uni-

versity of Khartoum under the direction of Peter Shinnie and Ali Hakim that was conducted with only a few intermittent interruptions from 1965 to 1984. This expedition worked in the town area only. Our understanding of the site's history is imperfect because less than half has been investigated, and even the most heavily explored area, the Royal City, is problematic due to Garstang's unsatisfactory early-twentieth-century excavation techniques that included rapid excavation of important areas such as the royal palace, coupled with poor record keeping and incomplete publication of his findings. The recent Sudanese–Canadian expedition to Meroe under the direction of Krzysztof Grzymski contributed much to our understanding of the site and kingdom that bears its name. One such example is its work in the Amun Temple that has led to a new, more accurate ground plan that supersedes Garstang's, as well as the discovery of new architectural elements, sculptures, and inscriptions, all of which allow for a clearer understanding of this important temple. Work in Palace 750, imperfectly explored by Garstang, demonstrates that it had undergone at least two significant periods of construction prior to a major rebuilding in the second century AD. Excavations in areas of the city outside the royal enclosure would further expand our understanding of the site's development and early history.

The earliest settlement, which can be dated to approximately 1000 BC, was initially rural. The increasing density of its dwellings reflects a process of urbanization that corresponded to the rise of the Napatan dynasty and the town's development as an early Napatan center. Napatan presence can be seen in the construction of buildings with Napatan-style bricks and Napatan ceramics in the area of Palace 750, as well as in the hundreds of Napatan burials in the Southern and Western Royal Cemeteries. By the late seventh century BC, Meroe was a royal residence for a part of each year. When at Meroe, the royal family resided in a palace (M 292–298) and celebrated religious rites in a nearby Amun temple (M 294) that included the annual New Year Festival reconfirming the king's divine right to rule. The construction of the large 'Sun Temple' (M 250) during the sixth century BC reflects the site's importance; nonetheless kings and their major queens continued to be buried near Napata.

The inception of the Meroitic Period (mid-third century BC) was marked by royal burials at Meroe. Within three generations of these burials, the appearance of new cultural features and the commencement of major building projects in the town, which would ultimately transform it into an impressive royal center, indicate that a Meroitic branch of the royal family had come into power. During the Meroitic Period, Meroe included a walled Royal City, non-royal habitation and industrial areas on the Northern and Southern Mounds, and temples both within and outside of the town, as well as three royal necropolises and a late, post-Meroitic private cemetery. Smelting furnaces with considerable amounts of iron slag and numerous pottery kilns uncovered in the Northern Mound demonstrate that it was a manufacturing center. Some archaeologists have proposed that

Nile channels were dug through parts of the site, but there is as yet no evidence for them according to its current excavator, Krzysztof Grzymski. He estimated that its maximum area was approximately 450,000–500,000 square meters with approximately 8,800–13,800 inhabitants, while in 2004 David Edwards wrote that the total area was smaller and that its population consisted of no more than a few hundred households.

For the first two centuries of the Meroitic Period, the Royal City and its monuments underwent phases of expansion that transformed it into a planned urban center. A major rebuilding of the town at the beginning of this period included a new palace (M 294), a massive stone wall around the Royal City, and the so-called Royal Bath (M194–195). Grzymski believes that older sections of the Amun Temple (M 260), east of the enclosure wall, may also date to this time. Many new temples were built. In addition to temples for Isis (M 600) and Apedemak (M 6), an enigmatic temple, Temple M 292, may have served as a royal victory shrine, because a head of a sculpture of Augustus was buried under its threshold. Throughout the Royal City, the architecture and ornamentation of important buildings demonstrated contemporary influences from Ptolemaic, Hellenistic, and Roman Egypt.

Meroitic town planning demonstrated a creative use of architectural scale and spatial relationships that allowed the population to experience the close connection between the royal, religious, and economic aspects of Meroitic society. The palace had only modest living quarters, but it was provided with large columned audience halls for ceremonial functions. Nearby courtyards that were surrounded by numerous magazines for storing trade goods were also important components. During the late first century AD, the palace, which continued to be linked with nearby storage magazines and granary buildings (M 740), was also

Following pages:
Figure 165. Reconstructed pyramids and chapels at Meroe. Photo © Chester Higgins Jr 2012.

connected via a processional way to the Amun Temple. László Török has argued that together these structures resulted in a monumental complex that reflected the close interplay among royal, divine, and economic powers in the Meroitic state.

Urban planning also expressed the religious basis of royal power. Over time, processional ways that led into large courtyards for public gatherings were constructed, and temples were aligned along them or at their termini. These were used by the populace during religio-political festivals that (re-)confirmed the divine legitimization of the ruler. From approximately the third century BC on, the Palace (M 294) was oriented toward the entrance to the Amun Temple, the largest and most important temple at the site. During religious events, inhabitants would have watched or joined with the ruler along a processional way from within the Royal City to the Amun Temple, a route that Török argued symbolically expressed the divine father/son, i.e., Amun/king relationship that formed the theological basis of Meroitic kingship. A later processional way leading from the Amun Temple's entrance toward the royal cemeteries might have expressed a connection between royal funerary cults and Amun.

Meroitic use of architecture to express theological/political ideas may well explain the design of two unusual structures, the 'Royal Bath' and the 'Sun Temple.' The 'Royal Bath,' west of palace M 295, is a unique, colonnaded, red-brick water sanctuary with a large central water tank surrounded by colorfully painted sculptures and frescoed walls. The structure, which was built well after the city was established, underwent several phases of renovation demonstrating strong Hellenistic influences in its design and sculptural decorations. Originally excavated by Garstang, the 'Royal Bath' has been reinvestigated since 1999 by Simone Wolf and Hans-Ulrich Onasch

from the German Archaeological Institute in cooperation with the Sudan Antiquities Service. New components including a quarter-circular exedra and the complex's enclosure wall have been found. Because of its central water tank and plumbing system, Garstang erroneously thought it was a Roman-style bath, hence its name, but it does not demonstrate features typically associated with this type of structure, so its purpose remains something of an enigma. Wolf and Onasch's work reveals that the waters needed to fill the bath were not dependent on the rising levels of the Nile inundation, and so this structure was probably not a water sanctuary associated with the annual Nile flood, as sometimes suggested. Decorations and sculptures in the 'Royal Bath' honored Dionysus as well the indigenous god, Apedemak. Both gods were associated with rebirth and linked to well-being and fertility, qualities that caused the cult of Dionysus to become popular in contemporary Egypt under the Ptolemies and, it seems, in Meroe, because the elite inhabitants of Meroe appear to have created the 'Royal Baths' to celebrate these aspects of Dionysus and linked him to a Nubian god who shared them, Apedemak.

Like the 'Royal Bath,' the 'Sun Temple,' published by Friedrich Hinkel in 2001, which stands alone on a plain west of the town, relied on its architecture and decoration to express aspects of Meroitic kingship theology. Renovations to its architecture and relief decoration suggest that it may have been understood and/or used differently over time. The first, Napatan Period, structure was on a raised platform. The most significant Meroitic Period rebuilding (late first century AD) created a more elaborate colonnaded platform. Raised on this platform was a sanctuary that stood within a columned court. Battle scenes (whose dates are disputed) carved on the lower platform's outer walls suggest that the temple was at some point in its history intended to commemorate a military victory. The temple may have been renovated to celebrate the military prowess of the Meroitic ruler, which was another important aspect of divine kingship. A Meroitic Period processional way linked the temple to the Royal City, creating another means through which the ruler and his or her subjects could experience a communal confirmation of royal power.

By the mid-first century AD, the character and pace of construction at Meroe changed. A significantly smaller palace (M 950, late first century AD) and an increase in the number of non-royal houses (late first–third centuries AD) suggest a weakening in royal power and the growth of a functionary class. Although building continued through the third century AD, excavations by Grzymski have revealed that there was a decline in the size and maintenance of public buildings as early as AD 250. We know that by the mid-fourth century AD, the central government had collapsed. Some dwellings, rural in plan with animal pens and flimsier construction, suggest that Meroe had ceased to be an urban center. Therefore, the Axumite invasion of Meroe (mid- to late fourth century AD), which has sometimes been considered a significant precipitating factor in Meroe's end, more likely only hastened or completed its decline. While burials in the late, non-royal Central Cemetery suggest ongoing habitation, there are no later remains in excavated domestic areas, indicating that the settlement may have moved to another as yet unexplored part of the site. The circumstances surrounding the final abandonment of Meroe are uncertain.

The Cemeteries

The last pyramids in Africa were built for Meroitic elites and rulers buried in the three royal cemeteries of Meroe: the Western, Southern, and Northern Cemeteries. The Western and Southern Cemeteries, in use from the early Napatan Period (mid-eighth century BC), also contained pit and mastaba burials (for non-elite Nubians). After the Southern Cemetery was fully occupied (late third century BC), Kushite rulers built their pyramids in a new cemetery to the north. Unlike the earlier two cemeteries, it was used exclusively for royal burials and contains the pyramids of all but the first two generations of Kushite rulers. The Western Cemetery continued to be used for elite and non-elite burials until the end of the Meroitic Period (mid-fourth century AD). The Southern and Northern Cemetery burials are on and around a series of narrow hills approximately four kilometers east of Meroe; the Western Cemetery is in a flat plain between the town and the so-called Sun Temple (M 250).

History of Discovery

After Meroe was rediscovered in the late eighteenth century, its pyramids were visited by numerous travelers. Some, like Frédéric Cailliaud (1821), Linant de Bellefonds (1821), and the Prussian Expedition of Lepsius (1844), came in the spirit of scientific inquiry and created valuable records of their early condition. J.H. Breasted's University of Chicago Expedition further recorded and made the first photographs of the pyramids and their decorated chapels in 1906–1907. Unfortunately, many other visitors who came to the pyramids were seeking treasure and damaged them in their quest. The most famous was the Italian doctor, Giuseppe Ferlini, who in 1834 found the golden jewelry in the pyramid of Queen Amanishakheto (Beg. N 6), which is now in the Staatliche Sammlung für Ägyptische Kunst in Munich and the Ägyptisches Museum in Berlin (see "The Treasure of a Nubian Queen"). His claim that he found this treasure hidden inside a small chamber in the upper part of the pyramid has been widely believed. However, as Dunham and later Markowitz and Lacovara have convincingly argued, Ferlini deliberately falsified the find spot in order to misdirect competing treasure seekers. There is no precedent or logical reason for the queen's personal jewelry to have been buried by her successor in the pyramid's masonry. The jewels found by Ferlini were almost certainly buried with the queen in her burial chamber, as were all other Meroitic grave gifts. Ferlini's falsehood was widely accepted, with unfortunate consequences for the pyramids at the hands of treasure seekers, such as the British Museum curator E.A.W. Budge, who early in the twentieth century dismantled the top half of whatever pyramids were still standing in the Northern Cemetery in his search for another treasure-filled chamber. No special chamber was ever found in the top of another pyramid.

George A. Reisner of the Harvard University–Museum of Fine Arts, Boston Expedition (1920–23) conducted the only scientific excavation of these cemeteries. Using the name of a nearby village, Reisner identified the three royal cemeteries as Begarawiya South (Beg. S), Begarawiya North (Beg. N), and Begarawiya West (Beg. W), and numbered their tombs sequentially. This system is still used to identify individual tombs, that is, Beg. S 4, Beg. N 32, Beg. W 6, and so on. Reisner also established a chronological sequence for these burials based on the desirability of their locations within each cemetery, with burials being made from west to east. He assumed that the most desirable locations, such as hilltops (as opposed to gullies), would have been used first and that tombs in these locations would have been earlier in date than those in the less sought-after locations. Reisner's chronological sequencing of tombs, particularly the royal ones, still forms the basis for Meroitic chronology. With the exception of a few articles, including one presenting the first history of the Meroitic Period (1923), Reisner did not publish the excavation's results. These were finally published more than three decades later by his assistant and successor, Dows Dunham, as

part of the series *The Royal Cemeteries of Kush*. From 1976 to 2005, Friedrich W. Hinkel, a German architect trained in the preservation of monuments, directed efforts on behalf of the Sudan Antiquities Service to conserve the royal pyramids. While dismantling endangered pyramids to create a stable foundation on which to rebuild them, he thoroughly documented them. He also discovered and followed the original methods used to build them, including the ingenious use of a *shaduf* to raise the blocks onto the pyramid. The *shaduf*, a type of weighted lever, was and is more typically used in Egypt and Sudan to lift buckets of water from the Nile to irrigation canals. The data resulting from Hinkel's efforts are being prepared for publication as *The Necropolises of Kush* series.

The Tombs

In the Southern and Western Cemeteries, non-elites were buried in simple pit graves without superstructures, while Napatan and Meroitic elite burials had mastabas or pyramids above single rock-cut burial chambers that were reached via a stairway. The mastabas were typically square, stone-faced, rubble-filled solid structures with single rock-cut burial chambers beneath them. The pyramids are far smaller and more steeply angled than the famous pyramids of Giza and were based on the similarly sized (the largest are thirty meters high) and proportioned pyramids built in Nubia during the New Kingdom by Egyptians living there. With the notable exception of the solid stone construction used for Beg. S 7 (and perhaps Beg. S 9 and S 6), the first Kushite pyramids at Meroe were piles of sandstone with an outer mantle consisting of one or two layers of sandstone blocks. Later in the Meroitic Period (ca. AD 130), rubble-filled brick superstructures replaced the stone superstructures. When completed, the exteriors of the pyramids and decorations carved in the chapels were covered with a lime plaster

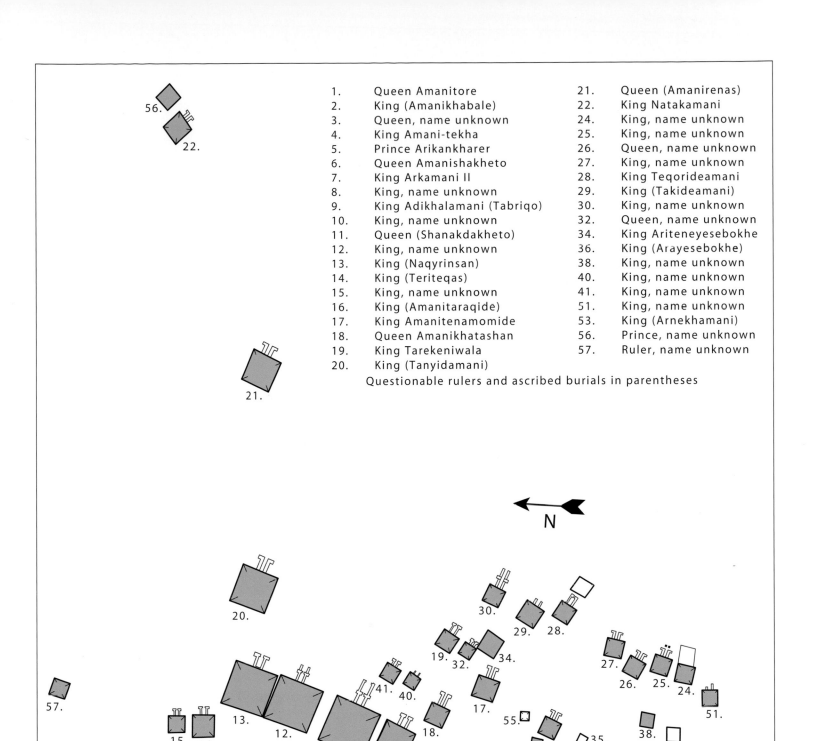

1. Queen Amanitore
2. King (Amanikhabale)
3. Queen, name unknown
4. King Amani-tekha
5. Prince Arikankharer
6. Queen Amanishakheto
7. King Arkamani II
8. King, name unknown
9. King Adikhalamani (Tabriqo)
10. King, name unknown
11. Queen (Shanakdakheto)
12. King, name unknown
13. King (Naqyrinsan)
14. King (Teriteqas)
15. King, name unknown
16. King (Amanitaraqide)
17. King Amanitenamomide
18. Queen Amanikhatashan
19. King Tarekeniwala
20. King (Tanyidamani)

21. Queen (Amanirenas)
22. King Natakamani
24. King, name unknown
25. King, name unknown
26. Queen, name unknown
27. King, name unknown
28. King Teqorideamani
29. King (Takideamani)
30. King, name unknown
32. Queen, name unknown
34. King Ariteneyesebokhe
36. King (Arayesebokhe)
38. King, name unknown
40. King, name unknown
41. King, name unknown
51. King, name unknown
53. King (Arnekhamani)
56. Prince, name unknown
57. Ruler, name unknown

Questionable rulers and ascribed burials in parentheses

Figure 166. The Northern Cemetery at Begarawiya.

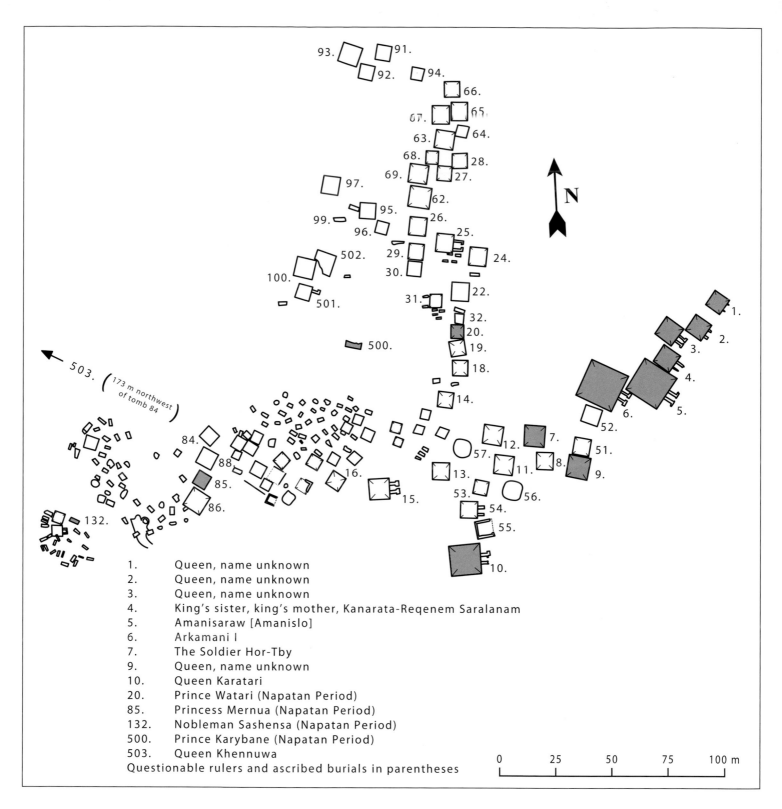

1. Queen, name unknown
2. Queen, name unknown
3. Queen, name unknown
4. King's sister, king's mother, Kanarata-Reqenem Saralanam
5. Amanisaraw [Amanislo]
6. Arkamani I
7. The Soldier Hor-Tby
9. Queen, name unknown
10. Queen Karatari
20. Prince Watari (Napatan Period)
85. Princess Mernua (Napatan Period)
132. Nobleman Sashensa (Napatan Period)
500. Prince Karybane (Napatan Period)
503. Queen Khennuwa
Questionable rulers and ascribed burials in parentheses

0   25   50   75   100 m

Figure 167. The Southern Cemetery at Begarawiya.

that was painted in bright colors. Finally, a finial-like ornament or capstone would have been placed on their truncated summits.

Elite and royal pyramids and mastabas had chapels on their eastern faces that were decorated with scenes of offering and funerary rites. These served as cult and offering places to sustain the tomb owners in the afterlife. A few of the larger Meroitic royal pyramid chapels, such as Beg. N 11 and Beg. N 12, also had forecourts decorated with scenes from the owner's funeral procession. As in Egypt, pyramid chapels and forecourts were entered through a pylon. Roughly oriented to the four points of the compass, the royal pyramids' eastern faces are illuminated each morning by the rising sun, whose life-giving rays play upon the ritual scenes in their offering chapels. These small pyramid chapels were always made of sandstone blocks, and their entrance pylons and interior walls were carved with registers of ritual scenes. Reliefs on the north and south walls show the tomb owner watching and benefiting from a variety of offering rituals, while the west wall had a niche that contained an offering stela, an offering scene, or an Osirian triad (see "Nubian Religion"). The east walls had protective gods and demons facing the entrance into the chapel, while above them baboons stood with arms upraised to salute the rising sun when its light filled the doorway of the chapel.

The subterranean burial chambers had to be constructed and their contents sealed within them before the pyramids could be built on top of them and their staircases. The pyramids were therefore built by the owners' heir(s) after the funerals were completed, and thus the final funeral rites consecrating the chapels would have taken place some months or even a year after the actual burial. The substructures consisted of a stairway typically leading to two (for queens) or three (for kings) small chambers. In the Southern Cemetery, the chamber walls were painted with chapters from the Egyptian *Book of the Dead* (see glossary), while the burial chambers beneath the later Meroitic pyramids of the Northern and Western Cemeteries appear to have been undecorated. In addition to the body, whose coffin was sometimes placed on a stone cut coffin bench, the pyramid and mastaba burial chamber(s) contained vessels filled with food and drink, as well as prized possessions such as the jewelry found by Ferlini in Beg. N 6. Non-elite pit burials were smaller but also contained funerary gifts of food, drink, and

favored objects in addition to the body. All royal and most elite and non-elite burials were robbed well before their excavation in modern times. For the most part, only small objects, such as amulets, or larger objects without much intrinsic value, such as ceramics, occasionally survived tomb robberies. However, several elite tombs in the Western and Southern Cemeteries, which were not thoroughly pillaged, have yielded a variety of valuable objects, including some from Egypt, Greece, and Rome that reflect the wealth controlled by Napatan and Meroitic elites.

The Royal Cemeteries
The Western Cemetery

The Western Cemetery, which is the nearest to the town, had the longest duration of use (mid-eighth century BC to mid- to late fourth century AD), with burials dating from the Early Napatan Period that were perhaps contemporary with the first burials at al-Kurru, to burials dating to the end of the Meroitic Period. It was also the largest of the three cemeteries, with several hundred Early to Late Napatan Period non-elite pit burials and approximately 170 larger burials with mastaba (ninety) or pyramid (eighty) superstructures. The more elaborate tombs belonged to important members of the royal family, including non-ruling queens and princes. Although the tombs were pillaged, numerous grave gifts, including luxury objects that were clearly imported from the Mediterranean world, such as painted Greek vases and Roman bronze objects, were found by Reisner's expedition. In addition, there were the more typical grave gifts consisting mainly of small luxury objects, amulets, and vessels associated with offerings.

It has been suggested that the last Meroitic rulers built their pyramids here. However, the decorations carved on the pyramid chapel walls of these purported royal burials do not show their owners as royal figures.

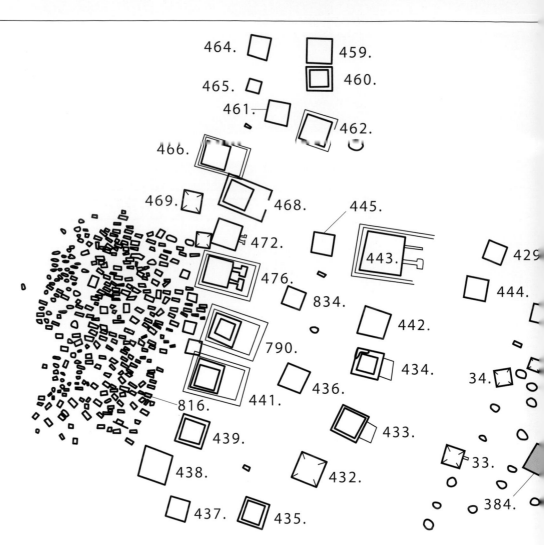

Figure 168. The Western Cemetery at Begarawiya.

1. Queen, name unknown
3. Queen, name unknown, REM 0839 (c. 150-50 BC)
5. Queen, unknown name (late 1st Century BC)
14. Private personage Ñspñasp (c. 116 BC-AD 41)
17. Sa..khadili-mani REM 0841 (170-100 BC)
18. Prince (?) Takatidamani REM 0049 (c. 50 BC)
19. Prince (?) Tedeqene REM 0832 (c. 100 BC)
20. Prince (?)
105(?). Queen (?) Amanipilade REM 0832 (c. AD 250)
113(?). Prince (?) Mashaqadakhel[.] REM 0844 (c. AD 200)
119(?). [...]yali REM 0845 (c. AD 300-350)
129(?). [...]li REM 0846 (c. AD 150-200)
130. Royal personage [...]k[...] (c. AD 300-350)
241. Queen (?)REM 0837 (c. 250-350 BC)
309. Prince (?) Pat.rapeamani REM 0848 (c. AD 250)
342. Royal(?) personage Atedokeya REM 0849 (c. AD 0-100)
816. Great Chief *P3-m3j* (Napatan Period)

Burial place unknown
A. Prince (?) Amanikhe-dolo, (offering table re-used in Beg W 109), REM 0838 (c. AD 200)
B. Royal (?) personage [..]tame (offering table near Beg W 142), REM 0847 (c. AD 100-150)
C. Royal personage [...]nine[...] (offering table near Beg W 384), REM 0850 (c. AD 250)
D. Imenpetiyu, (offering table near Beg W 127)
E. King's son, Iz.i... (inscribed block re-used in Beg W 16)

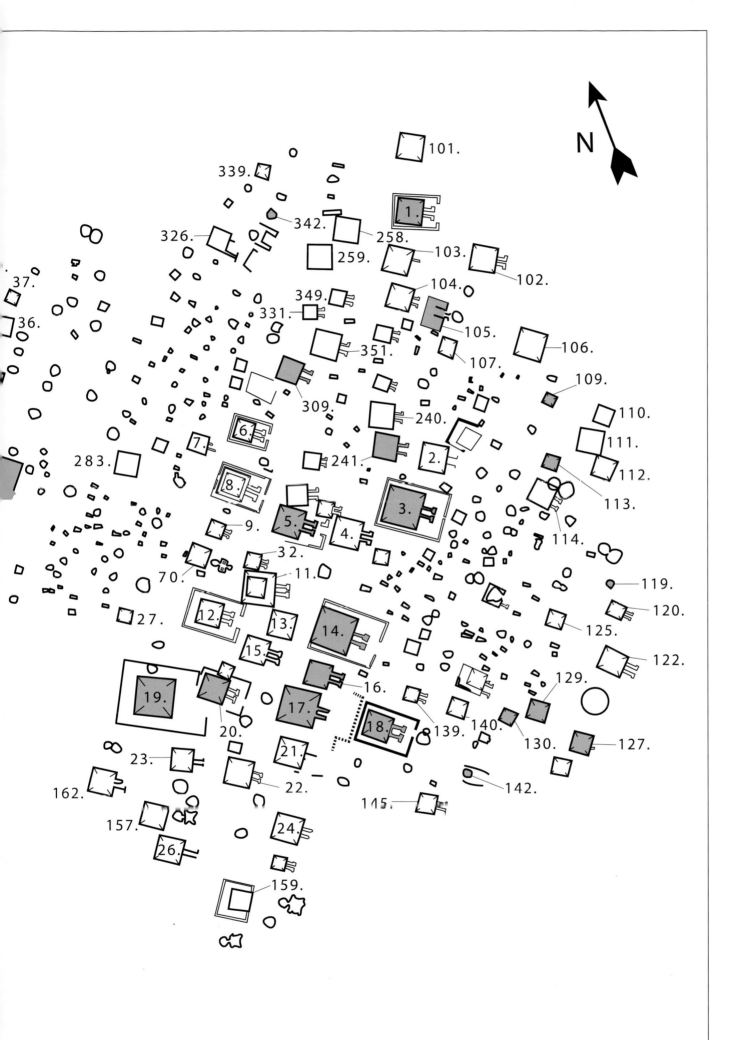

The Southern Cemetery

The Southern Cemetery, located four kilometers from the town on a series of sandstone hills, was in use from approximately the mid-eighth century to the mid-third century BC and contains more than two hundred burials, almost all of which are pit graves dating to the Napatan Period. The first two Meroitic kings and several of their queens were buried beneath pyramids along its easternmost hill-top. All of the other burials, including several other pyramids, belong to ordinary and elite residents of Meroe that predate these royal burials. According to Reisner, some of the earliest elite tombs may be contemporary with Early Napatan burials at al-Kurru. A number of the elite pyramids in this cemetery (among them Beg. S 7, S 8, S 10 and S 503) appear to have been built in the generations immediately preceding the first royal burial at Meroe belonging to King Arkamani I (Beg. S 6, c. 270 BC).

The north and south walls of the decorated chapels of all the pyramids in this cemetery are carved with rows of offering scenes showing the tomb owner watching what may be a depiction of his or her actual funeral. The west wall was surmounted with a scene of the sun god's triumphant emergence from the underworld at dawn, under which was a niche for the owner's funerary stela (see "Nubian Religion"). As will be discussed, the architecture, style, and content of these first royal burials at Meroe are so similar to the late Napatan burials in this cemetery, as well as those in the Napatan royal cemeteries of Nuri, that they should probably be considered as belonging to the Late Napatan Period rather than as inaugurating the new cultural and historical phase known as the Meroitic Period. Both the Northern and Southern Cemeteries were connected to the royal city by a processional way that ended at two wadis leading into them. Two early queens' pyramids (Beg. S 10 and S 503) were atypically built along the wadi's entrance into the Southern Cemetery. As

noted by F.W. Hinkel (cited in Yellin 2009), who spent over four decades working to preserve royal monuments, the two pyramids would have been passed as processions entered into the Southern Cemetery. Perhaps these two early queens were considered significant ancestors of the first Kushite royal dynasty from Meroe and the guardians of their descendants' burials. While the tombs in this cemetery were more pillaged than those from the Western Cemetery, the grave gifts that were found are very similar in type.

The Northern Cemetery

The Northern Cemetery (mid-third century BC– mid-fourth century AD), unlike the Western and Southern Cemeteries, contains only the burials of rulers and three crown princes. Beginning with the third ruler to be buried at Meroe, thirty kings, eight ruling queens, and three crown princes (possibly co-regents) were buried in it. Pyramids were first built along and then below a narrow ridge that lies opposite and to the north of the Southern Cemetery. Unlike the earlier Napatan royal cemeteries at Gebel Barkal and the Southern Cemetery, non-ruling queens were no longer buried in the same cemetery as their husbands after the first or second generation of burials. Instead, their pyramid burials were constructed in the Western Cemetery, along with other important family members. This change in burial customs may have been introduced by a new dynasty with different cultural traditions.

The pyramids in the Northern Cemetery range from those with well-built stone mantles to increasingly smaller and poorly built ones with brick rather than stone mantles encasing their rubble-and-sand cores. In this progression, one can see the decline of the wealth and power of the Meroitic rulers.

During the late third century BC to the early second century AD, the decorations of the pyramid chapels continue to present typical Napatan-

Meroitic funerary offering scenes while also introducing images of New Kingdom Egyptian temple rituals (such as the festival of Sokar) and vignettes from the Egyptian *Book of the Dead* (Beg. N 7, N 11 among others) that were probably derived from texts originating from Egyptian temple archives. In addition, there are occasional images and texts suggesting first-hand knowledge of contemporary Ptolemaic temple rites (Beg. N 1, N 5). The chapels dating to the last centuries of Meroitic rule demonstrate a return to the fundamental beliefs of Kushite funerary religion, and their walls are filled with various types of offering scenes and funerary processions, as discussed by Yellin (1995).

Evidence for Late Napatan and
Early Meroitic History from the
Southern and Northern Cemeteries

Napatan kings were buried near their capital, Napata, beside the holy mountain of Gebel Barkal even after the town of Meroe became an important royal center and perhaps the functional capital of the Napatan state. In the mid-third century BC, the first royal pyramids were constructed in the Southern Cemetery, which is generally considered to mark the inauguration of the Meroitic Period. Yet late Napatan traditions in royal pyramid chapel decoration, as well as in the custom of burying non-ruling queens near their husbands, continued in the Southern Cemetery royal pyramid burials and in the first two generations of royal burials in the Northern Cemetery (Beg. N 4, N 53, N 3). At least one of the late Napatan pyramids at Meroe (Beg. S 7) demonstrates such close structural similarities to contemporary royal pyramids at Napata that workers from the royal capital were apparently sent to Meroe to construct it, demonstrating that important elite burials were being made at Meroe under the auspices of the royal court right before the construction of the first royal ones at Meroe.

The existence of two contemporary Napatan cemeteries (the Western and Southern), which contain similar elite and non-elite burials, suggests that, as found throughout Nubia, clans had their own burial grounds. The inauguration of royal burials in the Southern Cemetery indicates the desire of members of a local branch of the royal family or of a powerful, local Napatan clan to be buried in their family's cemetery; it does not represent the inauguration of a new historical epoch with significant cultural or historical changes known as the Meroitic Period. The Napatan features of earlier elite pyramid burials in the Southern Cemetery (Beg. S 7, S 8, S 9 among others) demonstrate that members of the clan buried in the Southern Cemetery were both powerful and clearly aligned with the royal family at Napata. Members of this clan may well have come into power at the end of the Napatan Period, and following Kushite tradition, these new rulers chose to be buried in their traditional family necropolis at Meroe rather than among less closely related predecessors at Napata.

In fact, the new Kushite, non-Napatan features that mark the Meroitic Period do not appear (Yellin 2009) until a few generations after the first burials in the Northern Cemetery (late third century BC). During the reign of King Arkamani II (Beg. N 7), there is a marked change in the decoration of the royal chapels, as well as the end of the Napatan custom of burying non-ruling queens beside their kings. These changes, along with the contemporaneous appearance of new features in royal titulary and temple decorations at other locales, suggest that a ruling family from the Meroe area with non-Napatan traditions had come into power.

In addition to the three royal cemeteries, there are four non-elite cemeteries near the Western Cemetery, excavated by Garstang early in the twentieth century and containing pillaged tumuli burials dating to the Meroitic and post-Meroitic Periods.

Bibliography

Baud, M. 2010. "Méroé: Visages d'un capital." In M. Baud, A. Sackho-Autissier, and S. Labbé-Toutée, eds., *Méroé: Un empire sur le Nil*, 61–64. Paris: Musée du Louvre Editions.

Breasted, J.H. 1975. The 1905–1907 *Breasted Expeditions to Egypt and the Sudan: A Photographic Study*. Chicago: University of Chicago Press.

Bruce, J. 1790–92. *Voyage aux Sources du Nil, en Nubie et en Abyssynie, pendant les années 1768, 1769, 1770, 1771 & 1772, traduit de l'Anglois par J.H. Castera*. 13 vols. London: n.p.

Budge, E.A.W. 1907. *The Egyptian Sudan*. London: Kegan Paul, Trench, Trübner & Co., Ltd.

Cailliaud, F. 1823. *Voyage à Méroé au fleuve Blanc, au-delà du Fâzoql, à Syouah et dans cinq autres oasis: fait dans les années 1819, 1821, et 1822*. Paris: L'Imprimerie Royale.

Chapman, S., and D. Dunham. 1952. *The Royal Cemeteries of Kush*. Vol. 3: *Decorated Chapels of the Meroitic Pyramids at Meroe and Barkal*. Boston: Museum of Fine Arts.

Dunham, D. 1957. *The Royal Cemeteries of Kush*. Vol. 4: *Royal Tombs at Meroe and Barkal*. Boston: Museum of Fine Arts.

———. 1963. *The Royal Cemeteries of Kush*. Vol. 5: *The West and South Cemeteries at Meroe*. Boston: Museum of Fine Arts.

Edwards, D.N. 1996. *The Archaeology of the Meroitic State: New Perspectives on Its Social and Political Organisation*. Cambridge, U.K.: Tempus Reparatum.

———. 2004. *The Nubian Past: An Archaeology of the Sudan*. London: Routledge.

Garstang, J., and A. Sayce. 1911. *Meroe: The City of the Ethiopians*. Oxford: Clarendon Press.

Grzymski, K.A. 2003. *The Meroe Expedition: Meroe Reports I*. Mississauga, Ont.: Benben Publications.

———. 2004. "Meroe." In D.A. Welsby and J.R. Anderson, eds., *Sudan: Ancient Treasures: An Exhibition of Recent Discoveries from the Sudan National Museum*, 165–67. London: British Museum Press.

———. 2010a. "La fondation de Méroé-ville: Nouvelles données." In M. Baud, A. Sackho-Autissier, and S. Labbé-Toutée, eds., *Méroé: Un empire sur le Nil*, 65–66. Paris: Musée du Louvre Editions.

———. 2010b. "La redécouverte de Méroé." *Dossiers d'Archéologie*. Hors-série 18 (March 2010): 38–43.

Hinkel, F.W. 1986. "Reconstruction Work at the Royal Cemetery at Meroe." In M. Krause, ed., *Nubische Studien: Tagungsakten der 5. Internationalen Konferenz der International Society for Nubian Studies. Heidelberg, 22–25 September 1982*, 99–108. Mainz am Rhein: von Zabern.

———. 1997. "Meroitic Architecture." In D. Wildung, ed., *Sudan: Ancient Kingdoms of the Nile*. Paris and New York: Flammarion.

———. 2001. *Der Tempelkomplex Meroe 250*. Berlin: Verlag Monumenta Sudanica.

Hinkel, F.W., and U. Sievertsen. 2002. *Die Royal City von Meroe und die repräsentative Profanarchitektur in Kusch*. Berlin: Verlag Monumenta Sudanica.

Hinkel, F.W., and J.W. Yellin. Forthcoming. "The Necropolises of Kush I.1, 2. Meroe. The Southern Royal Cemetery." Deutsches Archäologisches Institut.

Lepsius, C.R. 1849–59. *Denkmaeler aus Aegypten und Aethiopien: nach den Zeichnungen der von Seiner Majestät dem Könige von Preussen Friedrich Wilhelm IV. nach diesen Ländern gesendeten und in den Jahren 1842–1845 ausgeführten wissenschaftlichen Expedition auf Befehl Seiner Majestät herausgegeben und erläutert von C.R. Lepsius*. Leipzig: G. Wigand.

Markowitz, Y.J., and P. Lacovara. 1996. "An Amethyst Gaming Piece Transformed." *Cleveland Studies in the History of Art* 1:7–11.

Priese, K.H. 1992. *The Gold of Meroe*. Mainz: Verlag Philipp von Zabern.

Reisner, G.A. 1923. "The Meroitic Kingdom of Ethiopia: A Chronological Outline." *JEA* 9:34–77, 154–60.

Sievertsen, U. 2004. "Meroitic Civic Architecture as a Chronological Reference in Sudan Archaeology." Paper given at Tenth International Conference of Meroitic Studies, Paris.

Torok, L. 1997a. *Meroe City: An Ancient African Capital. John Garstang's Excavations in the Sudan*. 2 vols. London: The Egypt Exploration Society.

———. 1997b. *The Kingdom of Kush: Handbook of the Napatan-Meroitic Civilization*. Leiden: Brill.

Vlach, F. 1984. "Meroitische-hellenistische Plastik aus den sogennannten königlichen Bädern. Ein Arbeitsbericht." *Meroitica* 7:573–77.

Wildung, D. 1996. *Sudan. Antike Königreich am Nil*. Tübingen: Ernst Wasmuth Verlag GmbH.

Wolf, S. 2003. *Meroë Königliche Bäder. Mediterranener Einfluß auf eine afrikanische Hochkultur in griechisch-römischer Zeit*. http://www.deinst.org/index_2963_de.html

Wolf, S., and H.U. Onasch. 2010. "Les 'Bains Royaux' de Méroé. Kouch et le monde méditerranéen au début du notre ère." *Dossiers d'Archéologie*. Hors-série 18 (March 2010): 44–49.

Yellin, J.W. 1995. "Meroitic Funerary Religion." In W. Haase, ed., *Aufsteig und Niedergang der römischen Welt. Part II: Principate*, 18.5, 2869–92. Berlin: Walter de Gruyter.

———. 2009. "La transition entre le Napatéen tardif et l'Epoque méroïtique, d'après les recherches sur la nécropole royale sud de Méroé." *BSFE* 174:8–28.

DANGEIL

Janice W. Yellin

Dangeil is located 350 kilometers northeast of Khartoum, near the Fifth Cataract of the Nile, and has been the focus of excavations by the Berber-Abidiya Archaeological Project under the leadership of Julie Anderson and Saleh al-Din Mohamed Ahmed since 2001. This important Kushite town, which was occupied for nearly the entire Kushite Period (eighth century BC–fourth century AD), was visited in 1822 by Linant de Bellefonds, who wrote about its archaeological remains. Excavations in its central area have led to the discovery of a large Meroitic Period (mid-third century BC–mid-fourth century AD) Amun Temple, dating to the first century AD, and in the South Hall of that temple of four statues belonging to three earlier Kushite kings. The discovery of these statues indicates that the site, previously known to date only to the Meroitic Period, was occupied as early as the seventh century BC. Since the large site is covered by a series of mounds, some as high as four meters, there are almost certainly more interesting discoveries to be made there. In 2007 a small cemetery, Wad Toum Cemetery (WTC), situated northwest of the site on the northern edge of the village, that contained private late Kushite burials was excavated.

Currently only the Meroitic levels of the Amun temple area have been excavated. Carbon-14 dates and cartouches of Queen Amanitore date the Amun temple to the first century AD. Built of red brick and sandstone, the temple was painted and plastered. It was enclosed by a temenos wall and approached through a monumental gateway that opened to a sphinx-lined processional way. A kiosk stood roughly midway between this gateway and the temple's pylon. Like the kiosk in front of the Amun Temple at Naqa, this ten-meter by twelve-meter structure has three engaged columns between screen-walls, broken lintels like those at Philae, and the same harmonic proportions as the Naqa kiosk. Unusually well-preserved plaster and paint reveals that some of its red-brick components were plastered and then painted to imitate the stone with which other unplastered elements, such as its floor, were constructed. Its sandstone capitals and cornices were plastered and painted bright shades of red, yellow, and blue, and there is evidence for painting on its interior walls. The kiosk was used to house the sacred barque that held the temple god's statue during sacred processions from the temple.

In addition to the temple's first pylon, there was a hypostyle hall with columns, and two

274

columned halls in front of a three-part sanctuary. There were also side rooms with altars in the rear part of the temple. As in other Amun temples, a room north of the sanctuary had a freestanding dais at its western end upon which a god's statue might have been placed. These rooms with daises might have served as solar sanctuaries to the sun god Re, Re-Horakhty, or Amun-Re. The temple is not yet completely excavated. The sanctuary had four columns and two altars in it. The inscriptions on the columns were written in Meroitic, and the walls were painted with vivid colors, including images of a fertility god bringing libation fluids. The painted surfaces on the kiosk and within the temple itself demonstrate how colorful a Meroitic temple of this period could be.

In 2008, while excavating a hall on its south side, Anderson and Ahmed's team discovered large fragments of four granite striding statues. A monumental statue belonging to the Nubian ruler Taharqo and two belonging to Senkamanisken had their names inscribed on them. The head from the fourth sculpture has been tentatively identified as Aspelta based on its facial characteristics. The statues offer the first proof that the site was occupied during the Twenty-fifth Dynasty and shortly thereafter. The statue of Taharqo (690–664 BC), who ruled Egypt as a Nubian king of the Twenty-fifth Dynasty, is the only sculpture of an Egyptian ruler to be found this far south in the Nile Valley, indicating that he controlled territory far south of his Kushite capital at Gebel Barkal and the borders of Egypt. Senkamanisken (second half of seventh century BC) and Aspelta (early sixth century BC) ruled Kush during the Napatan Period. The Senkamanisken and Aspelta(?) statues were smaller than Taharqo's, but all are finely carved in the Egyptian/Nubian style that marked representations of Kushite rulers during the Twenty-fifth Dynasty/Early Napatan Period. It is not known why these

statues were deliberately broken centuries later. Two other caches of Napatan statues of these same three rulers were found in 1916 by George Reisner at Gebel Barkal and by Charles Bonnet in 2003 at Doukki Gel-Kerma. The statues in all three locations were ritually broken. Perhaps there was a later dynastic struggle, or the Egyptian army under King Psamtik II, which was known to have led a punitive expedition into Nubia in 593 BC, reached as far south at Dangeil, destroying these statues along with those at Gebel Barkal and Doukki Gel-Kerma. Excavations in this part of the temple revealed that it had been built over one or more earlier structures, and Anderson and Ahmed believe the Dangeil statues once stood in an earlier version of the Amun Temple. The presence of Taharqo's large statue made of granite quarried at the Third Cataract (perhaps near Tombos), so far from Dangeil, indicates both the importance of the site and the power of Taharqo, who commissioned and transported this statue to Dangeil. Traces of paintings on plaster, from the South Hall where these Napatan sculptures were found, indicate that these walls were once covered with images of rulers and gods. The lower half of a sandstone statue of a seated female in late Meroitic style and fragments of a sculptured ram-headed Amun were also found in this room.

The discovery of over 1,200,000 potsherds belonging to broken molds in an area behind the temple is an excellent example of how an archaeological find can lead to new understanding(s). Initially the molds were thought to be used to bake the bread given, as in Egypt, for temple offerings. However, scientific analysis revealed that the molds contained sorghum, which is not made into bread in that type of mold. Rather, these molds were used for sorghum-based porridge or beer, offerings that are not made in Egyptian temples. The offering of sorghum porridge or beer indicates that the Kushites valued offering gifts quite different from those made to Amun in Egyptian temples. Their use further confirms evidence from other Nubian Amun temples that in the first century AD the cult of Amun was becoming distinctly more Kushite in its nature.

Wind erosion to the Amun temple suggests that it and the rest of the site may have been abandoned late in the Meroitic Period. Evidence for a large fire, perhaps caused by disruptions that immediately preceded and followed the collapse of the Meroitic state, may explain its abandonment.

Bibliography

Anderson, J.R., and S.M. Ahmed. 2002. "Recent Fieldwork Conducted by the Berber-Abidiya Archaeological Project." In D.A. Welsby and J.R. Anderson, eds., *Uncovering Ancient Sudan: A Decade of Discovery by the Sudan Archaeological Research Society*, 44–45. London: Sudan Archaeological Research Society.

———. 2005. "Le temple d'Amon à Dangeil (Soudan)." *BSFE* 162:10–27.

———. 2006a. "Bread Moulds and 'Throne Halls': Recent Discoveries in the Amun Temple Precinct at Dangeil." *Sudan & Nubia* 10:95–101.

———. 2006b. "Painted Plaster: A Glimpse into the Decorative Programme Used in the Amun Temple at Dangeil, Sudan." In *Studies in Honor of Nicholas Millet 2. JSSEA* 32:1–15.

———. 2006c. "The 'Throne Room' and Dais in the Amun Temple at Dangeil, Nile State, Sudan." *CRIPEL* 26:1–11.

———. 2008a. "Recent Fieldwork at Dangeil, Nile State in the Amun Temple Complex." *Eleventh International Conference for Meroitic Studies, Vienna, September 1– September 4. 2008*. Vienna: University of Vienna, Department of African Studies.

———. 2008b. "The Kushite Kiosk of Dangeil and Other Recent Discoveries." *Sudan & Nubia* 12:40–46.

———. 2009. "What Are These Doing Here above the Fifth Cataract?!! Napatan Royal Statues at Dangeil." *Sudan & Nubia* 13:78–86.

———. 2010. "Dangeil. A la découverte d'un nouveau temple d'Amon." *Dossiers d'Archéologie*. Hors-série 18 (March 2010): 50–55.

Anderson, J.R., et al. 2007. "Bread Moulds from the Amun Temple at Dangeil, Nile State: An Addendum." *Sudan & Nubia* 11:89–93.

Bellefonds, L.M.A. de. 1958. "Journal d'un voyage a Méroé dans les années 1821 et 1822." In M. Shinnie, ed., *Sudan Antiquities Service Occasional Papers* 4. Khartoum: Sudan Antiquities Service.

Rocheleau, C. 2008. *Amun Temples in Nubia: A Typological Study of New Kingdom, Napatan and Meroitic Temples*. Oxford: Archeopress.

NURI

Susan K. Doll

The cemetery at Nuri preserves the remains of about seventy-three pyramids built for Kushite kings and queens, and the remains of the three mortuary chapels used at their funerals, all dating to the Napatan Period. Nuri's location was chosen by the Twenty-fifth Dynasty Egyptian and Kushite King, Taharqo, sometime after he came to power in 690 BC, and it continued, with breaks, to be used until the reign of Nastasen around 315 BC. The site was occupied in Christian times as well, with the pyramids serving as a source of good stone for later buildings that even included a church, the central aisle of which was actually paved with stelae and offering tables taken from the ancient tombs. Even into the twentieth century, the pyramid field was still regarded as a convenient source of already-cut stone, which could be used for the foundations of buildings and irrigation emplacements. Due to these depredations, most of the smaller Nuri superstructures have been severely damaged or no longer exist, and the larger structures have also suffered much. Additionally, the burial chambers below ground were thoroughly plundered, sometimes shortly after burial, certainly later, and probably often. Now we can only imagine the majestic appearance of the original

necropolis when the pyramids were still standing, painted and decorated, with underground treasure chambers still intact.

Nuri's pyramids are neither the earliest nor the latest tombs of Kushite rulers. They are the resting places for those kings and queens who reigned after the loss of Egypt, and who presided over a transitional period of physical and psychological separation from their lost kingdom to the north, a period which ended in the formation of the Meroitic Empire. In keeping with the strong ties to Egypt still evident at this period, all the traditional essentials for an Egyptian pharaoh's burial were available at Nuri—access by water, reception of the funerary cortege at a mortuary temple, funerary chapels, and pyramids. While earlier and later Kushite cemeteries have pyramids and chapels, Nuri alone had the facilities to provide the full traditional pharaonic burial: it was close enough to the river for a canal to have been built leading from the river to the cemetery, enabling the Napatans to observe the Egyptian custom that a deceased king be borne on water to his final resting place. An early explorer and excavator, George Hoskins, actually saw remains of this canal when he first examined the area. It would have ended somewhere near the three mortuary chapels where the mummies of the Napatan kings were received and where final ceremonies were performed before burial.

We can thus postulate a scenario at Nuri that was reminiscent of those in ancient Egypt upon the deaths of the great pyramid builders. The bodies of the kings proceeded down the river and canal on barges, probably from Gebel Barkal directly to the mortuary temples. There, rites, probably traditionally Egyptian, were enacted before the corpse was taken to the burial chamber and interred. Sadly, we are ignorant of the exact nature of these rites, but since there is evidence of mummification among the Nuri remains, they may have had something to do with the final preparation of the kings' mummies. The remains of reliefs from the central, columned court of Nuri mortuary temple 400 (used in late Napatan times) show processions of gods, offering bearers, and seated kings before laden offering tables. These reliefs may magically recreate some of the scenes that actually took place in this room. Chapel 400 has many additional rooms and structures, including smaller columned spaces and a staircase undoubtedly leading to a second floor, or perhaps even a roof open to the sun, as we find in Ptolemaic temples, and the rites performed here may have been complicated.

These mortuary chapels near the canal were probably shared by many kings (and possibly queens). The major excavator of Nuri, George A. Reisner, believed that this was the case. He thought that the scenes on the temple's walls were conveniently rededicated for each funeral by painting the newly deceased's name into the royal cartouches in the inscriptions. Although the scenes and other inscriptions had been both incised and painted, the cartouches had all been left unincised, with smooth surfaces to receive the painted name of the king (or to be left blank if the deceased had not ruled?). Reisner felt that the chapels were thus 'reusable,' and indeed, the principle of rededication of objects through name change has a long history in the area.

Upon completion of the rites, the royal coffin was borne from the mortuary temple and carried along a processional 'street' leading to the entrance to a ramp or staircase, which headed underground to the burial chambers. When the coffin reached this staircase, the procession gradually disappeared into the earth and arrived at the entrance to the underground complex. Based on the types of inscriptions found in the tomb of Aspelta, for example, there may have been rituals to be performed in the antechambers of the tomb, before the body was actually laid to rest in the main chamber. After the ceremony, there was probably a funerary repast at the foot of the staircase in front of the first chamber. This was celebrated by priests, relatives, and mourners, and the remains of meals, sacrificial animals, and broken pots have sometimes been found in this location. The underground chambers were then sealed off with a door block, and the stairway filled in and covered up to prevent thieves from entering. At some point subsequent to the burial, the pyramid and chapel above the burial chamber were completed. The above-ground chapels, attached to the pyramids, served as sites where priests and families could make offerings to the dead kings. Based on remaining reliefs from this and other pyramid fields, we can assume that important processions and celebrations took place in these chapels, celebrations that involved the deceased/ancestors in the life and society of following generations.

Why King Taharqo chose the site of Nuri to place a new royal cemetery is not entirely clear. Its setting in the larger landscape of the area is a somewhat elevated one, above the flood plain. It is clear from old photographs and new publications that not only was Gebel Barkal visible from Nuri, but Nuri was also visible from Gebel

Barkal, and the choice of Nuri might have been made because the two, when viewed from each other, marked locations along the horizon important for cyclical astronomical events. It also seems that during high inundations, a great expanse of water sometimes covered the many fields between the two sites, perhaps making them reminiscent of the mounds rising up over watery chaos in which creation was believed to have taken place in Egyptian thought. It could be that this effect was created during the very high floods of King Taharqo in year six of his reign. Heavy downpours and a resulting high inundation were commemorated on his Kawa stela, and it is possibly around this time that the appropriateness of Nuri as a future pyramid location attracted Taharqo's attention. If Taharqo did choose Nuri to recall a primeval hill creation scenario with Gebel Barkal as a counterpoint, his pyramid alone enjoyed the efficacy of the symbolism for the first years of the cemetery's existence. His successor Tanwetamani, the last Nubian king to rule Egypt, was apparently not convinced of the suitability of the location for his own tomb, and he returned to al-Kurru to be buried, leaving Taharqo alone in his kingly splendor. Nuri was only used for queens' burials until a successor, King Atlanersa, reopened it.

Taharqo, founder of Nuri, is the best known of the Nubian kings. His fame comes from both his role in the Bible (for example, 2 Kings 19:9 and 2 Chronicles 32:20) and his architectural exploits in Egypt. His pyramid was the largest at Nuri, and also one of the most interesting. It was about one hundred Egyptian ells on each side (that is, 51.75 meters; cf. the 440 ells for each side of the Great Pyramid at Giza) and probably reached a height of just over sixty-seven meters, much smaller than pyramids of the Old Kingdom in Egypt, but nonetheless, a huge structure for its time and place. Because its incline is about 69°, as opposed to the 51° 50' of the Great Pyramid, and because it sat on the highest point of the elevated area comprising Nuri cemetery, its profile against the horizon would have been very impressive. It is probably the remains of Taharqo's pyramid that is visible on the horizon in an Oriental Institute photograph taken from the top of Gebel Barkal during the 1905–1907 Breasted expeditions (O. I. Negative Number 2967). With its height intact, the pyramid would, of course, have appeared much more striking.

Taharqo's monument as we see it today was apparently an enlargement of a smaller pyramid, visible inside the final, larger one in some of the drawings made on the site by early travelers. This enlargement may have been thought appropriate to honor Taharqo's long reign and his initial military successes in the Levant. Perhaps the above-ground monument was even enlarged and finished by his successor, a tradition maintained in later periods, as demonstrated by Friedrich Hinkel. If so, this could mean that Taharqo's pyramid was finished by Tanwetamani, even while the latter was planning his own burial chambers at al-Kurru. However, the excavator, George Reisner, thought that the earlier drawings were in error, as he saw no evidence of a second, earlier structure inside the present pyramid.

Another unusual feature of Taharqo's burial complex is a six-columned burial chamber with arched ceilings under the pyramid, thought to be a copy of the Osireion at Abydos, and intended to provide a burial place for Taharqo as Osiris. It would have been filled with water representing the primeval ocean. Indeed, the structure does have a ground plan reminiscent of the Osireion, and there has long been water in the underground chambers, which could have provided the necessary 'ocean effect' naturally. But was this result of a high water table considered desirable by the builders? The original excavator, Reisner, thought

Following pages:
Figure 170. Pyramids of Nuri.
Photo © Chester Higgins Jr 2012.

not. He reported that the entire floor had been raised and paved over after the initial construction, and not just immediately below the coffin "emplacement" as mentioned in the excavation report, which would have been necessary to provide the visual effect of the coffin resting in the middle of water. The floor had been raised and paved over in the entire room, precisely, he said, in order to avoid the high water table. Reisner also mentioned further measures taken anciently to keep the chamber dry, including an attempt to prevent water from entering the aisles outside of the columns by placing large stone blocks in the aisles. These facts suggest that ground water seeping into the chamber was not one of the original attractions of the site, and that the burial chamber, with its wooden coffin (see below) and many other water-sensitive objects, was probably not intended to contain large amounts of water. Despite the fact that the excavator's notes describe various parts of the underground complex as having inscribed walls, including an inscription along the west wall of the burial chamber, Reisner was not able to read them, and there is no further information available on these texts, which might have helped us put the design of the burial chamber in context.

Whatever the original intention, the chamber could also be conceptually related to another unique underground construction of Taharqo's, namely his building by the lake at Karnak Temple in Egypt. Taharqo seems to have been a king particularly intrigued by the idea of recreating mythic scenarios combining landscapes and architecture, and we may never understand these scenarios completely. As to the design of his burial chamber, even without water it could still have been intended to represent a grave of Osiris, and there are a number of similar designs in royal tombs in Egypt. However, the lack of a stone sarcophagus in Taharqo's tomb still remains a puzzle, since an imperishable container for the remains would have been the central focus of the design for an Osiris tomb. Although other tombs at Nuri yielded stone sarcophagi, or parts of them, the tomb of Taharqo clearly had none. As the excavator stated in his excavation diary, it was "inconceivable that such a [stone] coffin could have been taken away and I am forced to conclude that Taharqo was buried in a wooden coffin (or a series of wooden coffins)."

Accompanying the king were hundreds of *shawabti*s, small statues intended to come to life and do physical labor for him. Given the complexity and mythic significance of the architectural remains, we can only imagine that Taharqo's burial was a splendid one, and that he was laid to rest with gold jewelry, amulets, beautiful vessels, furniture, and containers of a variety of materials. Unfortunately, water damage and the ravages of plunderers over the ages permit only guesses in this respect.

The pyramid and burial chamber of another king at Nuri are much better preserved and perhaps more representative of the 'typical' Nuri royal burial. This is the pyramid of Aspelta, Nuri 8. Aspelta's pyramid was originally about 26.9 meters high, and had a chapel attached at its eastern front, which had probably been entered through a pylon. At the western end of the chapel was a niche, built for a stela that the excavator finally located in the Christian church. The chapel would have been inscribed and decorated. Pyramids and chapels in Kushite architecture were not connected to the burial chambers, as was usual in Egypt, and the entrance to Aspelta's burial chamber was located well in front of his chapel. A long stairway leading underground from this entrance provided access to three stone-lined burial chambers underneath the pyramid. In the third underground room was found a large, well-decorated, lidded granite sarcophagus, which had been sunk into the pavement. Based on remaining fragments of inlay and 'mummy eyes' (stone eyes rimmed in metal, inlaid into coffins), we can assume that Aspelta had been interred within the sarcophagus in at least one gilded anthropoid wooden coffin, inlaid with precious materials. The other funerary objects found in Nuri 8 are unusually numerous. We can thank a roof collapse that buried a floor and the objects lying on it for their preservation. The quality and beauty of these objects suggest the great accumulations of wealth with which at least some of the Napatan kings must have been interred.

Aspelta's reign is also known for the exceptional number and quality of the texts preserved to us from it. Both literary and religious texts are represented, and both categories show masterly control over the Egyptian language and usage. In regard to textual embellishment, the sarcophagus found in the tomb of Aspelta is the most remarkable found in the entire Nile Valley from any period. It was inscribed for his personal reference in the afterlife with a selection of ancient Egyptian religious texts from a variety of periods and traditions. The fact that it had been created in Napata demonstrates the existence of a great library there, with educated personnel able to make use of it. Equally well-designed and inscribed were the burial chambers under Aspelta's pyramid. At the foot of the entrance stairs, incised on the wall in room A, was located the text of *Book of the Dead*, chapter 145, which enabled Aspelta to use his knowledge of word and ritual to pass through the portals of the underworld after death. Room A was a logical location for these texts, as it was the first room through which his coffin would have passed on the way to its final resting place. In the next room, Aspelta declared his innocence of crimes against *maat* (world order) in extracts from the famous Negative Confession (*Book of*

the Dead, chapter 125). These passages describe an afterworld judgment of the worthiness of the deceased, and Aspelta will have been absolved of transgression through the magic contained in this room. In the actual burial chamber, where the king would rest for eternity, interest appropriately shifted to the retention of and control over body parts (*Book of the Dead*, chapter 26), the retention and control over the soul (*Book of the Dead*, chapter 89), control over speech and powers of expression (*Book of the Dead*, chapter 90), and finally, through *Book of the Dead*, chapter 154, an entreaty to Osiris, full of descriptions of mental and physical revulsion, magically preventing the decay of Aspelta's corpse.

As is the case with the texts on Aspelta's sarcophagus, the selections of texts in the chambers are highly appropriate for their locations, and the complexity and erudition behind their choice and use demonstrates that this king's court had a scholarly interest in religion, a good library, probably at Gebel Barkal, and the literate and informed assistants needed to use that library effectively in the creation of his burial complex. Perhaps the scribe Nesmut, responsible for the Gebel Barkal library and named in one of Aspelta's stelae (see "Texts and Writing in Ancient Nubia"), was the creator of this uniquely inscribed and furnished tomb.

A re-creation of Aspelta's burial chamber can be found in the National Center of Afro-American Artists in Boston, Massachusetts. Based on the badly damaged remains of inscriptions and scenes above and below ground in other burial complexes at Nuri, we can assume that other kings and queens were also provided with a similar panoply of texts and pictures, possibly modeled after Aspelta's, in order to ensure their safe passage through the dangers of the underworld to eternal life.

Bibliography

Arnold, D. 2000. *Lexikon der ägyptischen Baukunst*. Dusseldorf: Albatros Verlag.

Baedeker, K. 1929. *Egypt 1929*. Reprint, London: George Allen & Unwin, 1974.

Bianchi, R.S. 2008. "The Ritual of the Royal Ancestors at Nuri." Communication. *Eleventh International Conference for Meroitic Studies, Vienna, September 1–September 4, 2008*. Vienna: University of Vienna, Department of African Studies.

Budge, E.A.W. 1907. *The Egyptian Sudan 1*. London: Kegan Paul, Trench, Trübner & Co. Ltd.

Dunham, D. 1955. *The Royal Cemeteries of Kush*. Vol. 2: *Nuri*. Boston: Museum of Fine Arts.

Hinkel, F. 1997. "Meroitic Architecture." In D. Wildung, ed., *Sudan: Ancient Kingdoms of the Nile*, 391–414. Paris and New York: Flammarion.

Kendall, T. 2006a. "Napatan Temples: A Case Study from Gebel Barkal." http://rmcisadu. let.uniroma1.it/nubia conference/kendall.doc (June 4, 2006).

———. 2006b. "Why Did Taharqa Build His Tomb at Nuri?" In W. Godlewski and A. Łajtar, eds., *Between the Cataracts: Proceedings of the Eleventh International Conference for Nubian Studies, Warsaw University, 27 August–2 September 2006*. Part 1: *Main Papers*, 117–47. PAM Supplement Series 2:1. Warsaw: Warsaw University Press.

National Center of Afro-American Artists, Boston, Massachusetts. Views of Aspelta's burial chamber. http://www.ncaaa.org/exhibitions.html

Oriental Institute. Photographs. http://oi.uchicago.edu/OI/MUS/PA/EGYPT/BEES/IMAGES/GEBEL_BARKAL/I5C5_4 html

Reisner, G. 1917. "Excavation Diary Nuri" (uncut version). In the archives of the Museum of Fine Arts, Boston.

Gebel Barkal

Joyce Haynes and Mimi Santini-Ritt

Gebel Barkal is located twenty-three kilometers downstream from the Fourth Cataract and 1.5 kilometers from the right bank of the Nile. It is an isolated sandstone table mountain rising 104 meters high with a separate eighty-meter-high pinnacle on its southern face. The pinnacle itself resembles a rearing cobra, or uraeus, wearing either the sun disc or White Crown, depending on the angle from which it is viewed.

This unique stone formation was considered sacred. Known from at least the time of Thutmose III as the 'Pure Mountain' *(djew wab)*, Gebel Barkal was interpreted as a representation of the primeval mound, the source of creation. An elaborate temple complex, dedicated to Amun and his associated gods and goddesses, evolved on the south and southeastern sides of the mountain's base. For well over a thousand years, it was the chief cult center of ancient Kush. The main Amun temple was given the same name as Amun's temple in Karnak, Ipet-Sut, as it was considered the residence of a southern form of the Egyptian state god Amun of Karnak. To the west of the mountain was located the site of a royal pyramid cemetery used by the late Napatan and early Meroitic rulers. The town of Napata surrounded the temples

and likely extended to the banks of the Nile. Here an important overland route linking the area of the Sixth Cataract with the region of the Third Cataract crosses the Nile, no doubt contributing to the development of Napata.

European explorers took note of the extensive remains in the 1820s, but it was not until 1916 through 1920 that serious excavation was undertaken by George A. Reisner and the joint Harvard University–Museum of Fine Arts, Boston Expedition. From 1973 until the present, the University of Rome, La Sapienza, has been excavating there, first under Sergio Donadoni and later under Alessandro Roccati from the University of Turin. Timothy Kendall, originally sponsored by the Museum of Fine Arts, Boston, later by Northeastern University, and now by the National Corporation for Antiquities and Museums of the Sudan (NCAM), has worked at the site from 1986 until the present. From 1995 until 1997, a team from Fundacio Clos, of Barcelona, Spain, directed by Francesca Berenguer, excavated in the royal cemetery. The latest survey and magnetic data have identified at least twenty-four temples and palaces. Of these, eleven have been excavated.

There is evidence of very early human presence at Gebel Barkal. Caves in the mountain apparently served as an ancient source of kaolinite. Chipped stone tools and potsherds found both on the mountain and at its base date to the Neolithic, Pre-Kerma, and Kerma periods. Two graves dating to the time prior to the Egyptian presence were found in the area and may suggest an early settlement.

In the Eighteenth Dynasty, Thutmose I conquered Kush southward beyond Gebel Barkal and the Fourth Cataract. Around 1450 BC, Thutmose III established a garrison at Napata to control the region as well as the trade of gold and other luxury goods coming from the south. The site's earliest monument is the Stela of Thutmose III, which refers to this garrison as well as to a local Kushite settlement. On it, he refers to Gebel Barkal as "the throne(s) of the two lands." By the time of Amenhotep II, an Amun temple had been constructed, and this pharaoh's Amada and Elephantine stelae refer to him hanging a Syrian prince from the walls of Napata. This is the first known written mention of the town of Napata.

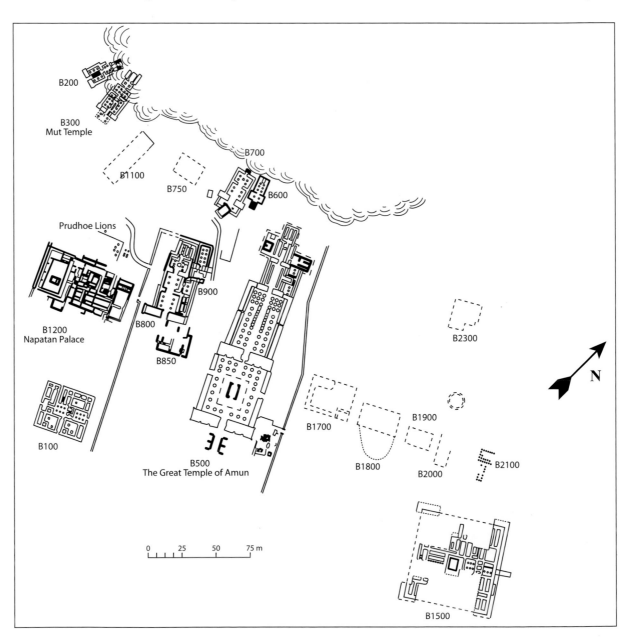

Figure 171. Plan of Gebel Barkal.

Almost every Egyptian pharaoh from Thutmose III through Ramesses II is represented at Gebel Barkal. After Ramesses II, Egyptian building activity appears to have ceased at the site. The latest New Kingdom object found at Gebel Barkal is a fragmentary statue dating to the reign of Ramesses IX. Facing political instability back home during the Twentieth Dynasty, the Egyptians withdrew from Nubia, and the temples fell into disrepair until the rise of the Twenty-fifth Dynasty.

In the eighth century BC, Napata once more became an important religious and political center. A new ruling family emerged in the area, and the powerful kings of this dynasty conquered Egypt and established Egypt's Twenty-fifth Dynasty. Napata became the capital of the Kushite Empire. These pharaohs believed it was the ram-headed Amun of Napata who gave them the right to rule Egypt and Kush. Centered on the pinnacle, an entire temple complex, some of which had New Kingdom foundations, was built and maintained. Piankhi (Piye) and Taharqo, in particular, were responsible for extensive building activity. Napata, as the legitimate center of kingship, was key to the coronation ceremony throughout Kushite history and was one of the cities the king visited as part of his coronation journey. After the Kushites were expelled from Egypt, King Psamtik II sacked Napata in 593 BC as part of a punitive campaign. It was quickly rebuilt, and Napata remained the cult center of Kush even after the court moved to Meroe in the sixth century BC. Napata was destroyed once again around 24 BC by the Roman general Petronius, and once again the religious complex was rebuilt. Meroitic kings and queens, most notably the co-regents Natakamani and Amanitore, restored the temples, built a new palace, and expanded the temple complex to the northeast. After the Meroitic Period, a Christian village gradually occupied the site of Napata, followed by a Muslim village.

The Napatan temples and palaces were often built on top of New Kingdom foundations. The Kushite rulers deliberately restored the religious structures that had been built by the Egyptian pharaohs. The plans of most of the temples roughly follow the Egyptian style, arranged along a central axis with one or more pylons, each followed by a hall or halls, leading back to the sanctuary area. They were oriented according to the Nile, with long axes perpendicular to the river and entryways facing it. In some instances, the sanctuaries were stone-cut chambers carved into the base of the mountain. Construction and reconstruction may have started as early as the reign of Alara, and it continued throughout the Napatan and Meroitic Periods. During this time, building material was typically large blocks of reddish sandstone, as opposed to the small rectangular blocks of yellow sandstone utilized for New Kingdom construction.

Architectural Remains

Palace B100 was erected early in the Meroitic Period. Made of mud brick and roughly square in shape, it had an open central courtyard. Sets of stairs accessed a second floor, which was likely supported by several mud-brick rectangular pillars. Its final phase of restoration was carried out by Natakamani and Amanitore, who are credited with much other restoration work throughout the site.

Taharqo founded B200, a small, partially rock-cut temple with three inner rock-cut sanctuaries. They were dedicated, according to Kendall, to Hathor, Tefnut, and an unknown third goddess.

B300, a temple partly cut directly into the face of the cliff just to the east of B200, was dedicated to Mut of Napata, consort of Amun. It was likely founded as a freestanding tripartite shrine by Thutmose III and rebuilt by Taharqo. In this temple, there are sistrum-headed Hathor capitals, as well as unusual columns carved in the form of Bes. One relief depicts a king making offerings to the ram-headed Amun and Mut. In this scene, the gods are seated inside a structure that is shaped much like Gebel Barkal itself, surmounted by a uraeus crowned with a sun disc.

B350, the imposing pinnacle, was first adorned by King Taharqo. He added an inscription just below its summit (as did later pharaohs such as Nastasen) and had a niche for a statue (probably of himself) hollowed into it. The inscription was covered with sheet gold that would have reflected the sunlight. The great lengths to which he went in order to achieve this embellishment of the all-but-inaccessible peak can be inferred from a series of holes that appear to have been sockets for wooden beams used as scaffolding to access the pinnacle.

The Great Temple of Amun of Napata, B500, was by far the largest and most important of the temples. It measured approximately 150 meters long and was one of the largest temples in Nubia. Several building phases can be identified. The origins date to the New Kingdom, possibly the reign of Thutmose III. According to Kendall, this Thutmoside Amun temple was replaced with an Aten temple by Akhenaten, who also erased the name of Amun throughout the site. *Talatat*-size blocks were found reused in other buildings at Barkal. Kendall contends that Horemheb subsequently rebuilt and rededicated B500 to Amun. Other scholars believe that the first level of construction dates to the late Eighteenth Dynasty, or even as late as the Nineteenth Dynasty, during the time of Sety I. The New Kingdom level of the temple, built right against the base of the mountain, was completed during the reign of Ramesses II. His large hypostyle hall, B502, may have had as many as eighty-four columns arranged in six rows.

Later, Piankhi (Piye) rebuilt the temple in stone on the New Kingdom foundations and enlarged it in several stages. His most notable

work included two pylons, a large hypostyle hall, and a columned courtyard. Little remains of the relief decoration, although some scenes from his *sed* (jubilee) festival and his campaigns against Egypt are visible in B501. Taharqo added a barque stand to B500 and further expanded the temple, which went through many other phases of construction and reconstruction, including the addition of Napatan and Meroitic kiosks. The co-regents Natakamani and Amanitore rebuilt the first pylon and added their own reliefs. Other Meroitic chapels flanking the causeway leading to the entrance have been identified but not excavated, such as B560/570/580. By the beginning of the Christian era, the town encroached on the temple, and the first court was filled with crude-brick dwellings.

B500 Sculpture

The sculpture and fragments that derived from this vast complex are too numerous to include in this brief overview. Throughout the temple, sculpture fragments of various periods were found together. For the most part they were not in their original positions, as the sculptures of earlier kings were revered and reused by later kings who often incorporated them into their new buildings. Some of the more important pieces are mentioned here, many of which are now housed in the Museum of Fine Arts, Boston, with others in museums in Khartoum, Berlin, Toledo, and Richmond.

The earliest is the lower portion of the seated granite sculpture of the nomarch of Asyut in Egypt, Hepdjefa, dating to the Middle Kingdom. It may have been brought from Kerma, where another similar sculpture of him and a statue of his wife, Lady Sennuwy, were found, presumably transported from Egypt. The most notable New Kingdom fragment includes the non-joining head and lower portion of a seated statue of Thutmose

III dressed in the *sed*-festival cloak, from the outer court. An unusual fragmentary granodiorite sculpture of Amenhotep II represents the king as a sphinx, rearing and trampling his Kushite enemies. Numerous joining fragments of a seated sculpture of the viceroy Merymose were found in various rooms of Temple B500 and were also scattered throughout the site. A gray granite ram sphinx of Amenhotep III has been left in situ at the site.

Most scholars credit Piankhi with moving numerous sculptures from the temple of Amenhotep III in Soleb in order to adorn his expanded Great Temple of Amun. These include the rows of granite rams holding images of Amenhotep III that flank the approaches to the first and second pylons of B500. Also from Soleb are the two colossal falcon statues from the inner court, one of Nekhen, and the other of Sopdu. In the outer court, a colossal rearing cobra inscribed for the goddess Selket was found. Several new fragments of this sculpture have recently been found in storage in Boston and permanently joined.

Figure 172. Drawing of Bes columns at Gebel Barkal by Charles Gleyre.

Napatan remains included the sphinx of Senkamanisken, altars of Atlanersa, Piankhi, and Taharqo; a granodiorite statue of Akhratan, and the upper part of a gilded bronze royal statuette holding an image of Maat. Dating to the Meroitic Period is the domed sandstone shrine or 'omphalos.'

A cache of buried statues, destroyed as a result of the raid of Psamtik II, was found by Reisner north of the first pylon in trench B500A. A small seated sculpture of the viceroy Thutmose from the time of Akhenaten was buried with the primarily Napatan sculpture fragments. The Napatan sculptures in B500A were life-size to colossal. These included a statue of Taharqo, two statues of Tanwetamani, three statues of Senkamanisken, one statue of Queen Amanimalol, two statues of Anlamani, and one statue of Aspelta. Another cache of royal statues connected with these was found in temple B800 room 904. Here were sculptures and fragments that joined some of the pieces from B500A, including the colossal head of Taharqo, the body of Senkamanisken, and the top of the feather crown of Anlamani.

A very interesting group of stelae dating from the New Kingdom to the Meroitic Period was also discovered in different areas of B500. These include stelae of Thutmose III (see above) and Sety I; two of Piankhi (one depicts him defeating the Lower Egyptian rulers); several of Aspelta (Adoption Stela, Enthronement Stela; Stela for Prince Khaliut); one each of Tanwetamani (Dream Stela), Queen Sachmach, and Harsiyotef; an Excommunication Stela of an unnamed Napatan king; and a Meroitic stela of King Tanyidamani. These inscribed documents have been invaluable to the reconstruction of Kushite history and religion.

Just east of B700, B600 was a three-room chapel first built by Thutmose IV and restored in the late Napatan/early Meroitic Period after being partially destroyed by a rockfall. It had a staircase that gave access to an elevated portico. Kendall

suggests that it may have been used for coronation or *sed*-festival ceremonies.

Temple B700, another small temple to the north of B800, may have had New Kingdom foundations. Debris east of B701 contained several New Kingdom sculpture fragments. In the sanctuary B704, a statue of Amenhotep III was discovered. The temple was built by Atlanersa, whose faience cartouche was found in the foundation deposit and whose granite barque stand was found in B703. The barque stand was later reinscribed by Senkamanisken, whose granodiorite obelisk fragment was found there, and who likely completed this temple. The temple was enlarged and restored during the Meroitic Period, having succumbed to the same rockfall as B600. An unfinished colossal royal statue of granite was found by the pylon.

Temple B800 stands in front of Gebel Barkal to the west of B500. The original building was made of mud brick with stone columns and was similar in plan to the New Kingdom B500. B800 was founded either by Alara or Kashta and was completed or restored in stone by Piankhi. It is the earliest Kushite temple found at the site. Late in the seventh century BC, B800 was restored again by kings Anlamani and Aspelta and underwent a final rebuilding during the Meroitic Period.

B850 is the area in front of B800; it may have originally been an avenue of sandstone ram statues associated with the earliest level of B800. In early Napatan times, a mud-brick building with painted and plastered interior walls was located here. This was replaced with a large stone building by late Meroitic or early Christian times.

B900 is a small temple overlapping the northeast side of B800. Blocks with reliefs and inscriptions for Piankhi were found in the Meroitic rebuilding of B900. Blocks inscribed for Harsiyotef were also found here. Although originally thought to be two temples, B800 and B900 may be two parts of a single temple, with B800 built first and

B900 added on. In room B904, a second cache of sculpture fragments was found (see above).

Area B1100 is the scant remains of a brick temple in front of the pinnacle (between B300 and B700), built on a north–south axis perpendicular to the pinnacle. There were three building phases: a partially rock-cut New Kingdom (time of Horemheb) temple that was destroyed by a rockfall, the freestanding Twenty-fifth Dynasty (reign of Piankhi or Taharqo?) reconstruction, and a Meroitic building phase dating to the reign of Natakamani and Amanitore. Kendall believes that this was a coronation temple used for ceremonies from the New Kingdom onward and may have been connected to B300 by a corridor.

The large mud-brick Napatan palace B1200 was built by Piankhi, but blocks with cartouches of Ramesses II have been found at the lower levels here, suggesting it may have been constructed on top of an earlier Nineteenth Dynasty building. The palace was completely rebuilt by both Anlamani and Aspelta. This rectangular building had many courtyards and plastered and painted rooms. Some columns were topped with papyrus-bud capitals; in one room inscriptions on the columns indicate that the room was used for New Year ceremonies. Aspelta's palace was apparently destroyed by the army of Psamtik II. Afterward the site was leveled and a new palace constructed, perhaps by Harsiyotef, who claims on his stela to have restored a ruined palace. Some scholars infer a final phase of restoration dating as late as the third century BC on the basis of two colossal red granite lions originally from Soleb, inscribed with

Figure 173. The royal statue cache in situ at Gebel Barkal, February 1916. Photograph © 2012 Museum of Fine Arts, Boston.

the name of Amanislo, discovered on the mountainward side of the palace.

B1300, a small temple with Hathor-headed columns to the southeast of B500, can be dated to the time of Natakamani. Adjacent to it is B1400, another small Meroitic temple.

Natakamani built the vast Great Palace B1500. Roughly square in shape, this 63-square-meter, multi-chambered structure lies far forward and to the east of the mountain and other structures. The building's first floor was erected on a 1.8-meter-high podium, which was accessed by a flight of stairs. There were pillared rooms that opened onto a central colonnaded courtyard. The exterior of the palace had white walls with pilasters, colorful moldings, and glazed roundels.

B1700, east of B500, appears to have been a Napatan temple bakery. Although unexcavated, a large rectangular mud-brick enclosure can be discerned in which countless fragmentary bread molds were found.

A wide scatter of other unexcavated Napatan and Meroitic structures, large and small, lies to the east of B500, including B1800–B2400.

Pyramids

While Gebel Barkal is well known for its vast temple complex, it was also the site of a royal cemetery from the late Napatan to Meroitic Periods. To date, twenty-seven small pyramids have been located in the desert west of the mountain. They are divided into two major groups: Barkal (Bar.) 1–8 constitutes the northern group, and Bar. 9–25 the southern group. In 1995 and 1996, two additional Napatan pyramids were excavated and numbered P. 26 and P. 27, perhaps cenotaphs for Nuri pyramids. Today only twelve pyramids still stand, and they likely indicate a much larger cemetery, still to be excavated.

In the late third century BC a king, perhaps Arnekhamani, selected Barkal as the site for his pyramid and those of his queens. Most of his successors built their tombs at Meroe, but from the first century BC to the first century AD a large number chose to build their pyramids at Barkal. While many of the owners of Barkal pyramids are unknown or unnamed, a few belong to significant historical figures. One such was the independently ruling Meroitic queen Nawidemak (mid-first century BC), whose pyramid is Barkal 6.

The sandstone-faced, steep-sided pyramids with chapels on the east are much like those of Meroe. The burial chamber and associated rooms are directly below the pyramid and are accessed by a long sloping staircase to the east. Barkal Pyramid 3 is one of the best preserved, standing to its full height of 12.9 meters. One interesting feature is that the surfaces of some Barkal pyramids were decorated with faience plaques. For instance, Barkal 3 had three circular faience plaques set one above the other on its upper face. Curiously, the tops of some pyramids, such as Barkal 2 and Barkal 3, were flat, measuring approximately one meter square. Whether there were capstones or features that were set atop the pyramids is uncertain.

Conclusion

The sacred site of Gebel Barkal has been known since prehistoric times. The temple complex was in use for nearly fifteen hundred years, from the early New Kingdom through the late Meroitic Period. However, the original grandeur of this vast and important site is barely discernible by the scant remains visible today. Of the many palaces, temples, and pyramids that have been identified, only a small portion of them have been excavated or published. There is much more to be learned, and it is certain that archaeological work on this site needs to be continued for generations to come in order to bring to life the richness of this most important complex.

Bibliography

Dunham, D. 1970. *The Barkal Temples*. Boston: Museum of Fine Arts.

Dunham, D., and S.E. Chapman. 1952. *Royal Cemeteries of Kush*. Vol. 3: *Decorated Chapels of the Meroitic Pyramids at Meroë and Barkal*. Cambridge, MA: Harvard University Press for the Museum of Fine Arts.

Kendall, T. 1994. "A New Map of the Gebel Barkal Temples." In C. Bonnet, ed., *Études nubiennes: Conférence de Genève. Actes du VIIe Congrès international d'études nubiennes, 3–8 septembre 1990*, vol. 2, 139ff. Geneva: Société d'études nubiennes.

———. 2002. "Napatan Temples: A Case Study from Gebel Barkal. The Mythological Origin of Egyptian Kingship and the Formation of the Napatan State." Presented at the Tenth International Conference of Nubian Studies, University of Rome, Italy, Sept. 9–14, 2002. http://wysinger.homestead.com/ kendall.doc

Kendall, T., and P. Wolf. 2007. "Excavations in the Palace of Aspelta at Gebel Barkal, March 2007." *Sudan & Nubia* 11:82 ff.

Porter, B., and R.L.B. Moss. 1952. *Topographical Bibliography of Ancient Egyptian Hieroglyphic Texts, Reliefs and Paintings*. Vol. 7: *Nubia, the Deserts and Outside Egypt*. Oxford: Griffith Institute.

Reisner, G.A. 1931. "Inscribed Monuments from Gebel Barkal." *ZÄS* 66:76 ff.

Wenig, S. "Gebel Barkal." *LÄ* 2 (1976): 434 ff.

AL-KURRU

Peter Lacovara

The earliest of the cemeteries associated with the Nubian capital at Napata was located at the site of al-Kurru. This was the first and northernmost of all the Napatan royal burial grounds and contained the tombs of the kings of the Twenty-fifth Dynasty, who ruled Egypt and Nubia, and their ancestors. The site was excavated by George A. Reisner for the Harvard University–Museum of Fine Arts, Boston Expedition in 1918 and 1919 and published by Dows Dunham. The unprepossessing ruined tombs of the site, although badly destroyed and plundered

Figure 174. Pyramid 1 of an unknown king at al-Kurru. Photo © Chester Higgins Jr 2012.

for building stone in antiquity, nevertheless yielded a rich array of material overlooked by robbers in the debris of many of the burial chambers.

The cemetery was situated on a low plateau on the west bank of the Nile and cut by two wadis, one on the northern edge of the cemetery and one on the southern end, with several rows of tombs stretched across the site, their demolished superstructures being somewhat difficult to interpret.

Reisner saw the evolution of these tombs as mirroring the development of Egyptian pyramids from a tumulus to a mastaba and then into a true pyramid. However, they seem to have evolved directly from a traditional Nubian tumulus grave with pit and side chamber into a steep-sided pyramid with subterranean burial chamber, following the form of the New Kingdom private pyramid. The 'mastaba' phase of these tombs appears highly questionable, as the superstructures were almost entirely gone and the perimeters of the remains were quite square, suggesting a pyramid base rather than a rectangular tomb.

Access to the grave developed from a simple vertical shaft, as in the ancestral tumuli and earliest pyramids, to a stairway cut into the stone of the plateau leading to a vaulted antechamber and burial chamber. The superstructures were comprised of soft sandstone, quarried locally.

Although the later tombs at al-Kurru indicate a large-scale adoption of Egyptian funerary practice, including the use of canopic jars, *shawabti* figures, and amulets, some Nubian traditions seem to have in part survived, as seen in a modified bed burial with a coffin bench to support an Egyptian-style coffin. Some tombs also had decorated burial chambers. The tombs of Tanwetamani and his mother Qalhata still preserve much of their original paintings on the upper parts of the walls and ceilings.

While even the earliest tumuli contained some imported Egyptian material or Egyptianizing local products, the tombs of the Twenty-fifth Dynasty rulers contained a wealth of exotic objects. Most of the rulers of this dynasty were buried at al-Kurru, including Kashta, Piankhi, Shabaqo, Shebitqo, and Tanwetamani, with Taharqo founding a new cemetery nearby at the site of Nuri.

While there has been some disagreement over the dating of these graves due to the presence of some Egyptian imports found, Lisa Heidorn has clearly shown that the ceramic evidence points to a late date for all these burials, with the ancestral tombs not being much earlier than the ninth century BC. Likewise, most of the imported Egyptian pieces, such as the gilded silver amulets and faience vessels with raised-relief decoration, also date to the later Third Intermediate Period, and the presence of a few stray New Kingdom fragments would not warrant a redating of the site.

Bibliography

Dunham, D. 1950. *The Royal Cemeteries of Kush.* Vol. 1; *El-Kurru.* Boston: Museum of Fine Arts.

Heidorn, L. 1992. "Historical Implications of the Pottery from the Earliest Tombs at El Kurru." *JARCE* 31:115–31.

KAWA

Robert G. Morkot

One of the largest (covering forty hectares) and most significant sites in the Dongola Reach, Kawa lies at the southern end of the Kerma basin some fifty kilometers south of the city of Kerma. Kawa's ancient name was Gem Aten ('the Sun Disc is Found'), suggesting an origin for the cult in the reign of Amenhotep III or Akhenaten.

The principal deity of Gem Aten was a form of Amun. He is depicted as ram-headed with both wavy horns and curled horns, and wearing a large sun disc. He is accompanied by the goddesses Satet and Anukis, indicating a close relationship with the ram-headed god of the First Cataract, Khnum.

The first excavations at Kawa were undertaken by a team from the University of Oxford under the direction of F.Ll. Griffith (1929–31), and completed by M.F.L. Macadam and Laurence Kirwan (1935–36). The excavations concentrated on the central part of the town mound, where a large temple of the reign of the Kushite pharaoh Taharqo (T) was uncovered, along with two smaller temples (A and B), one of which dates to the reign of Tutankhamun. There were numerous important finds, including a series of stelae carrying inscriptions that detail Taharqo's building work and donations to the temple.

Most of the town mounds were left unexcavated, although there was evidence that occupation continued into the later Meroitic Period. New work was begun by the Sudan Archaeological Research Society (SARS) and the British Museum in 1993. They surveyed the site and carried out some targeted stratigraphic excavations in the town and the cemeteries. From this work, it was concluded that the town was most significant, and at its greatest extent, in the earlier Kushite Period, with less evidence from the later first millennium BC and first millennium AD.

At present, the town's origins remain unclear: the earliest standing monument is the temple of Tutankhamun. The principal temple (T) stood at right angles to the river, and temples A and B stand facing the dromos (ceremonial road), which strongly suggests that there was an Eighteenth Dynasty temple on the site of the later Twenty-fifth Dynasty structure. Some evidence for an earlier, but not precisely dateable, building was identified by the Oxford excavations in front of Taharqo's pylon. There is no evidence that Gem Aten was an Egyptian administrative center like Soleb or Amara West, and it is more likely that it served as the seat of an Egyptianized local ruler.

Inscriptional evidence tells of the religious significance of the town to the Kushite King Alara, who dedicated his sister as a priestess to Amun. The inscriptions of Alara's great-nephew, Taharqo, tell us of how, as a prince, summoned to Egypt by Shebitqo, Taharqo saw the temple covered in a sand drift, and how he swore that he would rebuild it. A series of building texts records the foundation and construction work, and details the bronze, silver, and gold furniture and ritual implements. Work continued through the first decade of Taharqo's reign, with masons being sent from Memphis and timber brought from Lebanon for use in the construction and for the flagstaffs in front of the pylon. The temple was dedicated in year 10 of Taharqo's reign (680 BC).

A processional route led from the river to the temple of Taharqo. The route was flanked with rams in pale crystalline gray granite, each protecting an image of the king. These rams are very similar in style to those of Amenhotep III set up along the dromos to the temple at Soleb and later moved to Gebel Barkal, but there are some small stylistic differences, and they are not quite of such fine quality. Archaeologists are therefore uncertain whether these rams were Eighteenth Dynasty and later recut: the figures of Taharqo are certainly altered from larger, perhaps mummiform figures. A number of pits showed that the processional route and one side of the temple were originally surrounded by trees.

The two temples facing the processional route were built in brick with sanctuaries and other elements in stone. The temple of Tutankhamun (A) had a court with six columns, followed by a second court or hall with four columns and a stone sanctuary. Clearly the brickwork had been renewed on one or more occasions, and a stone gateway with scenes and inscriptions of Taharqo was added between the outer and inner courts. The pronaos and sanctuary carried the original relief decoration of the reign of Tutankhamun. In the best-preserved scene in the pronaos, the king was shown with a human-headed form of Amun with the titles "Lord of Thrones of the Two Lands, the Lion who is over the Southland." On the entrance to the sanctuary, Tutankhamun is twice shown presenting offerings to a seated ram-headed lion with a double-plumed crown. Unfortunately, the inscriptions are not fully preserved, but the image certainly represents a form of Amun, and is specified as residing in Gem Aten. In the reign of Taharqo and later, this particular image (the 'crio-sphinx') was revered as the "Amun of Pnubs." In the sanctuary itself, Amun appears in human form, again described as "the Lion who is over the Southland."

Temple B also had a stone sanctuary with brick outer rooms. These outer rooms had columns carrying inscriptions of King Harsiyotef. The sanctuary itself was decorated with extraordinary relief sculpture depicting Amun and other gods, and parallel scenes with images of a king in an elaborate pleated garment making offerings to two groups of four deities. Unfortunately, the top of the wall is missing, with the resultant loss of the cartouches identifying the king, and the names of the deities. Macadam, who published the excavations, argued that the sanctuary belonged to the period around 300 BC and had been inserted into an already-existing brick structure built by Harsiyotef some eighty years before. Macadam's argument was based on a series of presumptions that are no longer valid and were challenged by Robert Morkot, who argued that the temple belonged to the period between the end of the Egyptian New Kingdom and the Twenty-fifth Dynasty. More specifically, Morkot argued that the temple was built by King Ary, whose stela had been discovered in it. This ruler (perhaps the same as the pre-Twenty-fifth Dynasty king Alara) left a long inscription recording events of his reign,

Figure 175. Tutankhamun receiving life from Amun-Re, in the Vestibule of Temple A at Kawa.

has, as its model, a scene in the Fifth Dynasty pyramid temple of Sahure at Abusir. The courtyard was surrounded by a colonnade of ten date-palm columns that were also modeled on those of Sahure's temple. These are examples of the 'archaism' that becomes a feature of the artistic style of the reign of Taharqo: looking back to the past, particularly to the Old Kingdom, and using elements of the earlier style to revitalize art.

The hypostyle hall was supported by sixteen date-palm columns. Between the four columns of the northeast section a small sandstone chamber was constructed, perhaps as a robing room or library (now in the Ashmolean Museum, Oxford). The exterior of this is decorated in high relief with scenes of Taharqo making offerings to a range of gods, notably the ram-headed Amun of Gem Aten, accompanied by the goddesses Anukis, with her conventional tall feather headdress, Satjet, and another form of Anukis whose iconography is that of the goddess Mut. The style of the scenes, as elsewhere in the temple, is typical of the reign of Taharqo, looking back to Old and Middle Kingdom models.

Another room was created later, in the reign of Aspelta, by erecting a wall between the Taharqo shrine, the exterior wall, and the rear wall of the hypostyle. This is also in the Ashmolean Museum, Oxford. The scenes show Aspelta in priestly cheetah skin before the Amun of Gem Aten and the human-headed Amun of Gebel Barkal.

The temple was not preserved to full height, and many of the larger scenes, notably on the external walls, survived only in their lower sections. Of those that were rather better preserved were a series of coronation scenes based on Egyptian models. In the scenes of religious ritual in the hypostyle hall were two groups of musicians: these include harpists, singers, men playing the typically Nubian double-ended drum, and others carrying what are probably trumpets,

which lasted at least twenty-nine years. The dating of Ary and the temple remains controversial.

The temple built by Taharqo was of conventional type with pylon entrance, courtyard, hypostyle hall, and sanctuary rooms. In common with other Twenty-fifth Dynasty temples (for example, Sanam and Tabo), it has a 'coronation hall' with dais to the south of the sanctuary.

The inside of the pylon carried large scenes showing Taharqo as a sphinx trampling on a Libyan chief: the family of the chief is shown and

including what could be elephant-tusk trumpets. Another scene remained, alas, only as a row of feet: it showed a procession of the women relatives of Taharqo and would have been an important historical document. Surviving fragments show that the royal women were ranked, some wearing headdresses with three plumes emerging from small figures of goddesses, whereas younger women had only one plume in a lotus-flower holder.

A number of statues were excavated, including a splendid figure of Taharqo as a lion, his face framed by the lion ruff and mane, rather than the royal headcloth typical of sphinxes. This type of image appears on a colossal scale for Amenemhat III of the Twelfth Dynasty and Hatshepsut in the Eighteenth: another example of Taharqo's artists looking back to the past for inspiration. Many small bronze figures and elements of the temple's furnishings were also recovered, including faience inlay. Notable among these was the large bronze 'aegis' (head with broad collar) of a goddess, originally with inlaid eyes, carrying the name of the Meroitic king Arnekhamani: this probably adorned a processional barque.

The fifth-century BC king Irike-Amanote (Amani-nete-yerike) had four inscriptions carved

Figure 176. The Taharqo temple at Kawa, the south colonnade before complete clearing.

in Taharqo's temple. They were inscribed on the doorjambs and walls of the hypostyle hall, rather than on stelae, and are dated to years 1, 19, and a date higher than 25. The first inscription describes the king's accession in Meroe and the journey to Napata for the coronation (and presumably the burial of his predecessor at Nuri), then the visits to the temples of the Dongola Reach. The prayers to Amun include references to the founding kings of the Kushite state, Alara and Kashta, and the "wonders" that the god had performed for them. The later inscriptions are much more fragmentary, and their main significance is recording a reign that lasted over twenty-five years, and shows several visits to Kawa, or at least a continued interest in the northern part of the kingdom.

Gem Aten was part of the coronation progress of the fourth century BC kings Harsiyotef and Nastasen recorded on stelae from Gebel Barkal. Harisyotef is also recorded at Kawa in the column inscriptions from temple B, and by an added figure and cartouches in the 'coronation hall' adjacent to the sanctuary of temple T. The inscriptions of these later rulers indicate that Gem Aten and the other towns of the Dongola Reach were subject to raids and looting by desert dwellers. Gem Aten is not otherwise clearly recognizable in lists of the Nubian place names of the Ptolemaic and Roman Periods, although some names in those lists have been tentatively identified with it due to their position. The later history of the town therefore awaits archaeological evidence.

In addition to the main temple structures, the Oxford and SARS excavations investigated a range of other buildings that included smaller religious structures, some on processional routes. A number of residential buildings and industrial structures including kilns have also been examined. As an archaeological site, Kawa still has enormous potential for understanding the history and social life of the first millennium BC.

Bibliography
Macadam, M.F.L. 1949. *The Temples of Kawa.* Vol. 1: *The Inscriptions.* London: Oxford University Press.
———. 1955. *The Temples of Kawa.* Vol. 2: *History and Archaeology of the Site.* London: Oxford University Press.
Morkot, R.G. 2000. *The Black Pharaohs: Egypt's Nubian Rulers.* London: Rubicon Press.
Welsby, D. 2002. "Kushite Buildings at Kawa." www.britishmuseum.org/pdf/1d%20Kushite%20buildings.pdf

TABO

Robert G. Morkot

The site of Tabo is located at the southern end of the large (seasonal) island of Argo, south of the Third Cataract of the Nile and at the northern end of the Dongola Reach. Tabo is about forty kilometers north of Kawa and twenty kilometers south of Kerma. Although Argo is an island, it is only during the inundation that the eastern channel is filled and the island created; for the rest of the year, the channel can be crossed on foot and the 'island' is effectively part of the east bank.

The existence of ancient remains has been known since the early nineteenth century, when two broken colossi were drawn by European travelers. These colossi, about seven meters tall, are made of granite and depict the gods Arensnuphis and Sebiumeker. They have parallels from farther south (at Meroe and Musawwarat al-Sufra) and probably date to the first century AD, possibly the reign of Natakamani. The Red Crown on one statue has a fillet of leaves that also appears on diadems worn by Natakamani and his *kandake* (see "Kings and Kingship in Ancient Nubia" and "Women in Ancient Nubia" for discussions of this title) Amanitore, and derives from the laurel wreath of the Roman emperors. These paired statues of Arensnuphis and Sebiumeker flanked entrances to temples, and thus indicated the presence of a major sanctuary at Tabo.

Excavations by the Henry Blackmer Foundation and the University of Geneva were begun in 1965 and exposed the badly ruined temple, probably of the reign of Taharqo. This is similar in size and plan to the other temples of Taharqo's reign at Sanam and Kawa. It is oriented east to west, with its pylon entrance facing east. The temples of Sanam and Kawa were oriented toward the river, and the Tabo temple appears to be facing the seasonal channel, rather than the main course of the river, perhaps indicating some association with the inundation.

A courtyard was surrounded by a colonnade of twenty columns, with a second pylon giving access to a hypostyle hall, also of twenty columns probably with palm-leaf capitals, as at Kawa. The total length of the temple is 75.60 meters and the main part 31 meters broad. The building was constructed in very friable sandstone that eroded easily, and the whole site was later pillaged for building material. Town mounds existed to the south of the temple complex. The only excavated cemetery at the site was of the post-Meroitic Tanqasi culture.

New Kingdom blocks were found reused within the second pylon: these carried the names of a Thutmose (III or IV), of Amenhotep II, Amenhotep III, and Ramesses II, but whether they belonged to a New Kingdom temple on the site, or were brought from elsewhere, is uncertain. The temple was so badly ruined and the stonework in such a poor state of preservation that nothing of significance survived of the relief sculpture or inscriptions. However, on the basis of ancient texts, notably those recording the coronation voyages of the Napatan kings and the 'geographical' lists of the Hellenistic and Roman Periods, the excavators argued that the temple of Tabo should be identified with the ancient city of Pnubs. The ancient sources tell us that Pnubs lay north of Gem Aten (Kawa) and could be reached from there within one day by boat. Pnubs is named as one of the temples where King Anlamani dedicated his sisters as sistrum players to Amun, and it was visited in the coronation voyages of Irike-Amanote, Harsiyotef, and Nastasen. Pnubs is also referred to in the inscriptions recording the invasion of Kush by Psamtik II. That king records that his army reached the land around Pnubs and that there was a battle.

The principal deity of Pnubs was a form of the god Amun, depicted as a ram-headed lion ('crio-sphinx'). This manifestation of Amun is found first in Tutankhamun's small temple at Kawa, although there he is identified as a god of Gem Aten (Kawa) itself and called "the Lion who is over the Southland." In all depictions of the Napatan and Meroitic Periods, this form of the god is associated with Pnubs, a name which itself derives from *pa-nebes* ('the jujube tree'). In many depictions the god is shown seated on a shrine-shaped base with the *nebes*-tree stretching over his back. Some faience inlay ram's heads were excavated at Tabo, but no reliefs or complete inscriptions survived to confirm the dedication.

The archaeological evidence thus seemed to fit that from the ancient texts, and so Tabo was

identified by archaeologists with the ancient Pnubs. However, excavations in a cemetery at Kerma in 1990 recovered a bronze vessel inscribed for a priest of Amun of Pnubs, suggesting that Kerma should actually be identified with the ancient city. This has been confirmed by more recent excavations in the northern part of the Kerma archaeological site, at Doukki Gel, where evidence from the Eighteenth Dynasty identifies the site with Pnubs. The identification of Tabo with a named ancient site now becomes more difficult.

The major artifact discovered at Tabo is a large 'bronze' (copper alloy) statue of a Meroitic king (now in the Sudan National Museum, Khartoum) found in the courtyard. The figure, fifty centimeters tall, is the largest bronze statue discovered in Sudan so far. The king is shown striding in a conventional Egyptian pose, his right arm flexed at the elbow and the left bent with clenched fist, clearly carrying something now lost, probably a bow. On his right hand he wears an archer's thumb ring. The proportions are typical of the earlier Meroitic Period (ca. 300–200 BC), with a smallish rounded head, column-like neck, broad shoulders and chest with powerful upper arms, and very narrow waist. The king wears a cap crown with diadem and double uraeus, ram-head earrings and the cord with ram-head pendants around his neck. He has large bracelets and armlets on the upper arm, an Egyptian-style kilt, and sandals. The figure has a surface covered with a fairly regular pattern of small holes to help a thin layer of plaster adhere. The plaster was then covered in thin gold foil, which survives on the face, neck, and in smaller patches elsewhere. Stylistically, the statue bears a very close resemblance in proportion and facial features to the images of King Arnekhamani on the reliefs of the temple at Musawwarat al-Sufra.

A small group of tumuli of the Tanqasi culture lying south of the temple are the latest ancient

Figure 179. The statue of Sennuwy in situ in Tumulus III at Kerma, April 1914. Photograph © 2012 Museum of Fine Arts, Boston.

extraordinary size of the funerary constructions and the richness of the furniture, uncovered by George A. Reisner during his excavations from 1913 to 1916. The two temples known as K XI and K II, built in the southern sector, which is the latest part of the necropolis, are particularly typical in this respect. Their north–south orientation is highlighted by a northern semicircular bastion. Each building comprised two vaulted rooms with inlaid faience decoration and wall paintings representing either animal processions, with a predominance of the African fauna—giraffes and hippopotami—or navigation and fishing scenes, as well as fighting bovids. K II, also known as the Eastern Deffufa (*deffufa* is an ancient Nubian word for any fortified construction made of mud brick), was connected to the last royal burial installed in the necropolis. Originally, the structure was surmounted by a monolithic stela more than five meters high. The lintel of the entrance door bears a solar disc, displaying increasing Egyptian influence. During restoration works, the vault was replaced by a ceiling supported by columns.

The Western Deffufa was certainly the main temple of the Nubian city of Kerma. If the original building was relatively modest—a mere chapel of wood and mud—it has been continuously modified and enlarged over time, with a religious area comprising chapels and a ceremonial palace, as well as several workshops, including one devoted to bronze work. Even today, the *deffufa*, which rests on a base 52.20 meters long by 26.90 meters wide, reaches a height of nearly eighteen meters. A stairway built through the thick masonries led to a sanctuary consisting of a long blind corridor. In front of it was a large circular base of quartzite used as an altar for the sacrifice of sheep.

Next to the religious complex, the king's residence was the true institution in charge of the traffic of products from Egypt, Central Africa, or the shores of the Red Sea. Seals and very many seal impressions testify to these exchanges. The outer courts were used for the breeding of domesticated animals and for handicrafts, notably those linked with the firing of pottery. A large rounded structure, rebuilt several times on the same spot, could be used as an audience hall, in the manner of those described by the first explorers of Africa: its conical roof supported by three or four rows of wooden columns, its mud-brick wall, and its portico revealed by post holes are all elements of comparison.

This building enables us to grasp the significance of the architecture of this Nubian city, the meeting point between the African world and Egypt. Thus the works carried out at Kerma by the Swiss mission since 1977 have opened a very fascinating field of study. They have allowed for a better definition of the local traditions and know-how, as well as external contributions of the Egyptians and others. Even if the outline of the Western Deffufa can remind us of an Egyptian temple, its internal design remains original, by the narrowness of empty spaces, compared to the thickness of walls, and by its northern bastion.

During the Egyptian occupation of the New Kingdom (ca. 1450 BC), a new city was founded one kilometer away from the Western Deffufa, at a place called Doukki Gel. A circular temple was recently uncovered some forty meters away from the classic Egyptian temples, the external wall of which was strengthened by very closely built rounded buttresses. One must admit that the Nubian divinities could coexist with other gods from the pharaonic pantheon. The religion followed in the *deffufa*s had not vanished and seemed to endure even with the growing Egyptian influence. When the fate of Egypt was eventually in the hands of Nubian rulers, the circular temple was restored again and, many centuries later, the specificities of Kerma are still preserved.

Translated by Pierre Meyrat

Bibliography

Bonnet, C. et al. 2000. *Edifices et rites funéraires à Kerma*. Paris: Errance.

———. 2004. *Le Temple principal de la ville de Kerma et son quartier religieux*. Paris: Errance.

Bonnet, C., and M. Honegger. 2007. "Les fouilles archéologiques de Kerma (Soudan). Rapport préliminaire sur les campagnes de 2005–2006 et 2006–2007." *Genava*, n.s. 55: 183–99.

Bonnet, C., and D. Valbelle. 2007. *The Nubian Pharaohs: Black Kings on the Nile*. Cairo and New York: American University in Cairo Press.

Dunham, D. 1982. *Excavations at Kerma, Part VI: Subsidiary Nubian Graves, excavated by the late George A. Reisner in 1915–1916, not Included in His Excavations at Kerma, I–III and IV–V*. Boston: Museum of Fine Arts.

Kerma et archéologie nubienne: Collection du Musée d'art et d'histoire, Genève. 2006. Geneva: Musée d'art et d'histoire.

Reisner, G.A. 1923. *Excavations at Kerma, Parts I–III and IV–V*. Harvard African Studies 5 and 6. Cambridge, MA: Harvard University Press.

TOMBOS

Janice W. Yellin

Tombos was an important administrative center when Egypt ruled Nubia during the New Kingdom and was perhaps the southernmost point actually inhabited by Egyptians. Only ten kilometers north of Kerma and just south of the Nile's Third Cataract at the entrance into the fertile Dongola area, Tombos was strategically important in the struggle between Egypt and Kerma for control of this region, which was the home territory of the Kerma civilization. Its role in Egypt's conquest of Nubia has long been known, thanks to an inscription carved at Tombos celebrating the conquest of Kerma by Thutmose I. Other inscriptions by Thutmosoid pharaohs are also found in the area.

What is known of the site has been gleaned from James Harrell's investigation of its quarries, which were an important source of granite in pharaonic Egypt, and Stuart Tyson Smith's excavations of its cemetery. Burials in this cemetery have yielded important information about the nature of Egyptian control in this region, the role of Nubians within the Egyptian administration, the nature of Nubian culture after the Egyptians withdrew from Nubia at the end of the New Kingdom, and the origins of the Napatan Dynasty. The largest burial known to date consisted of a brick Eighteenth Dynasty pyramid that belonged to one of Nubia's Egyptian overlords, Siamun, and his wife Weran. The tomb's architecture, size, and decoration with funeral cones testify to the presence of important Egyptian administrators at Tombos; indeed, Siamun's title identified him as the third-highest administrator in Nubia. Mycenaean jars from Greece found in the middle-class area of the cemetery, as well as Mycenaean potsherds from Siamun and Weran's tomb, demonstrate that there was a trade network from the Aegean that reached into central Africa. More modest, middle-class chamber and pit burials in this cemetery have also provided information about Egypt's colonial structure. Of the tombs that have so far been excavated, at least two from the same chronological context contain bodies of males buried according to Egyptian traditions and bodies of females buried according to Nubian practices. These same burials also contained both Egyptian- and Nubian-style objects. An anthropological study published in 2006 by Michele Buzon that discusses four females buried in the flexed posture associated with Nubian traditions confirms that both Nubians and Egyptians were buried alongside each other in the non-elite section of this cemetery. These burials, which also contained objects from both cultures, suggest that the Egyptians married Nubian women who maintained their connection to Nubian religion and culture. Evidence from this group of burials at Tombos also indicates that there were Nubians who acted as administrators of the Egyptian Nubian empire. This is a situation that contradicts the widely held view that the Egyptian colonialists remained separate from, and socially above, the Nubians whom they were ruling. Rather, at Tombos there was a more integrated community of Egyptians and Nubians than previously documented, in which Egyptians and Nubians intermarried and created a culture that preserved both Nubian and Egyptian traditions. This was not a community that existed only within the Egyptian sphere.

This situation would have facilitated the absorption of Egyptian features into the local Nubian culture, which could explain the origins of the Egyptianized Nubian elite who founded the Napatan Dynasty. The unique blend of Egyptian and Nubian features that marks the Napatan Dynasty are similar to those found at Tombos. Smith has excavated tumuli, an indigenous funerary

Figure 180. Tombos quarry with unfinished colossus.

type of burial, that date from the end of the New Kingdom to the Napatan Period. It appears that this Egyptian/Nubian community continued to live at Tombos even after the end of the New Kingdom domination of Nubia, through the ensuing "dark age," and into the Early Napatan Period (Pre- and Early Dynasty Twenty-five) with their Egyptian/Nubian culture intact. For example, in his 2007 article, he describes a tumulus from this "dark age" that contained a bed burial (Nubian feature) upon which there was an extended body (Egyptian feature). Not only are there mud-brick pyramids dating to the early Twenty-fifth Dynasty, but their burials combine Nubian and Egyptian features in a way that is similar to the Pre-Dynasty Twenty-five and Early Napatan burials at al-Kurru. The origins of the Napatan

Dynasty may well have been based on the descendants of an Egyptian /Nubian community such as that found at Tombos, rather than by the influx of new influences from Egypt, and so the rise of this dynasty was most likely the result of an indigenous development rather than contemporary Egyptian influence(s).

Finally, Smith's excavation of a Napatan Period tomb dating to the reigns of Shebitqo or Taharqo (ca. 707–664 BC) may also change our understanding of Nubia's role in the development of the iron industry. Iron spear tips found in the tomb suggest that the iron industry in Nubia, which is among the earliest known, may have developed in that region independent of outside influences and perhaps two hundred years earlier than previously thought.

Bibliography

Buzon, M.R. 2006. "The Relationship between Biological and Ethnic Identity in New Kingdom Nubia: A Case Study from Tombos." *Current Anthropology* 47, no. 3: 683–95.

Harrell, J. 1999. "The Tumbos Quarry at the Third Nile Cataract, Northern Sudan." In D.A. Welsby, ed., *Recent Research in Kushite History and Archaeology:* *Proceedings of the Eighth International Conference for Meroitic Studies*, 239–50. London: British Museum.

Smith, S.T. 2003. *Wretched Kush: Ethnic Identities and Boundaries in Egypt's Nubian Empire.* New York: Routledge.

———. 2007. "Death at Tombos: Pyramids, Iron and the Rise of the Napatan Dynasty." *Sudan & Nubia* 11:2–14.

NAURI

Marjorie M. Fisher

The site of Nauri, located thirty-five kilometers north of the Third Cataract on the east side of the Nile, retains little archaeological material except for a massive rock-cut stela of the famous Abydos decree of Sety I, which dates to his regnal year 4 and is carved on a three-hundred-foot sandstone hill. Next to this hill, on the northern side, another sandstone hill—this one four hundred feet high—represents the remains of a medieval fortress.

Figure 181. The Abydos decree of Sety I at Nauri.

The stela was first reported to J.W. Crowfoot, Director of Education in Sudan, and George Reisner. In 1924, Terence Gray was the first to attempt to take a squeeze, or impression, of the stela, but he was thwarted by its size. After searching for others to document this stela, Frank Addison, the Inspector of Antiquities, eventually engaged people who were able to complete a squeeze; it was sent to F.Ll. Griffith, who translated and published it. This round-topped stela, measuring 1.52 meters wide by 2.79 meters high, discusses the protection of Nubian tribute to the Egyptian temple at Abydos. Little else remains of the site other than two large hills of rocks.

Bibliography

Gardiner, A.H. 1952. "Some Reflections on the Nauri Decree." *JEA* 38:24–33.

Griffith, F.Ll. 1927. "The Abydos Decree of Seti I at Nauri." *JEA* 13:193–208.

Hein, I. 1991. *Die Ramessidische Bautätigkeit in Nubien.* GOF 4, Vol. 22.

Porter, B., and R.L.B. Moss. 1952. *Topographical Bibliography of Ancient Egyptian Hieroglyphic Texts, Reliefs and Paintings.* Vol. 7: *Nubia, the Deserts and Outside Egypt.* Oxford: Griffith Institute.

Sesebi

Robert G. Morkot

Sesebi (Sudla) is the name given to a site in the Abri-Delgo Reach of the Nile. Sesebi lies on the west bank of the river, opposite Delgo, and a little south of the Gebel Sese. The site now lies some two hundred meters from the river, although the river course may have been closer in ancient times. A wadi lies immediately to the north of the site. The excavators found no indications of a quay.

The dominant feature of the site is three standing columns from an ancient temple, and these have attracted visitors and archaeologists since the early nineteenth century. Both Frédéric Cailliaud (in 1823, showing four columns) and Karl Richard Lepsius published views of the ruins. The first major work was that of James H. Breasted, who made a photographic record of the reliefs on the columns. The site was excavated by A.M. Blackman and H.W. Fairman for the Egypt Exploration Society in two seasons, 1936–38. Today the site is being encroached upon by settlement and agriculture. In 2008, a team from the University of Cambridge began a new survey of the site and the surrounding area. This will be followed by some limited excavations to resolve some specific questions about the site's history and development, and will place our understanding of Sesebi more closely in its ancient landscape and environment. One result of the survey near the site suggests that it may have been constructed to exploit local gold reserves.

The site of Sesebi comprises a large rectangular walled enclosure, approximately 270 by 200 meters. The buttressed walls are 4.6 meters thick, with several gateways, lined with stone and with drains. Internally, the town is divided into two sectors by an east–west wall. The northern sector contains the temple and storage areas, and the southern, the settlement. Three cemeteries in the desert to the west of the town belong to the New Kingdom and the Ballana Period: there is no evidence of Napatan or Meroitic occupation. The site is a good example of a New Kingdom 'temple-town' with a short period of occupation. At present, there is no evidence for extramural settlement, as has recently been identified at Amara West.

The ancient name of Sesebi is unknown. In a 1908 report, Breasted identified it with the town 'Gem Aten' ('the Sun Disc is Found,') but the excavations carried out by F.Ll. Griffith and the University of Oxford showed quite clearly that that name was given to the site of Kawa, south of the Third Cataract. At present, the ancient name of Sesebi remains unknown.

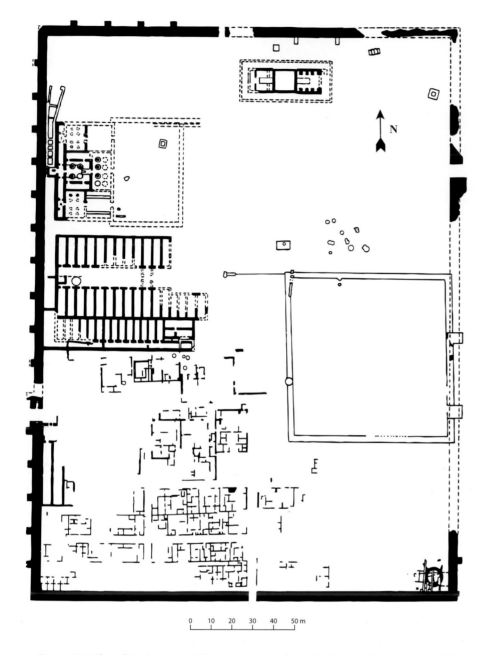

Figure 182. Plan of Sesebi.

father's temple at Soleb, and it is likely that there was a cultic connection between the two sites.

The temple of Sesebi underwent radical alteration during Akhenaten's religious changes. The original dedication is unknown, and there is no evidence that it was, as has sometimes been assumed, dedicated to the Theban triad of Amun, Mut, and Khonsu. The original temple was probably conventional in design, standing on a platform at the western side of an open court, with an entrance in the town wall to the east toward the river. The temple appears to have had a central sanctuary with two flanking chambers preceded by a hall of eight columns. Of the hall, three rather massive date-palm columns remain standing. They are rather squat in proportion to their height, probably for structural rather than aesthetic reasons. The decoration of these reveals something of the complex history of the temple. The columns have two zones of decoration. Above the base is a series of captive figures in raised relief, their bodies emerging from cartouche-shaped rings enclosing the names of captive foreign lands. This band of decoration in shallow raised relief clearly forms part of the original decoration. Above it, the main part of each column has been altered. Fragments of a rather shallow raised relief belong to the redecoration of the columns in the reign of Sety I, but through this can be seen remains of deeply cut sunk relief depicting Akhenaten and Nefertiti worshiping the sun disc, in the style typical of the later part of the king's reign.

From these surviving pieces of decoration, we can reconstruct the phases of alteration of the columns (and presumably the rest of the temple) as:

1. Beginning of the reign of Amenhotep IV: low-relief decoration over all of the column in two zones, with captives around the base and scenes above.

The town was founded at the beginning of the reign of Amenhotep IV, before the king changed his name to Akhenaten. This is clear from the intact foundation deposits excavated beneath the temple and town walls, all of which carry the king's earliest titulary. In 1965 the Schiff Giorgini expedition, working at the temple of Amenhotep III at Soleb, identified remains of a roadway connecting Soleb with Sesebi. The roadway, nine meters wide, was traced for some twenty kilometers. Akhenaten added a columned entrance to his

2. Later in the reign, after the king changed his name to Akhenaten: the earlier scenes removed and new, deeply sunk relief carved with scenes of the king and queen offering to the disc.

3. Reign of Sety I: the Akhenaten reliefs erased and the pillars plastered with new relief carved showing Sety I worshiping the Theban triad.

The temple is unusual for its period in having a crypt. This small chamber was decorated with relief executed in plaster. The whole was poorly preserved, but depicted Akhenaten with various gods, including his father, Amenhotep III, deified as "Nebmaatre-Lord-of-Ta-Sety."

The temple was certainly drastically altered later in Akhenaten's reign to convert it into a more conventional sun temple, but as this structure was later demolished and replaced by the temple of Sety I, its form cannot be reconstructed. The excavations yielded many small fragments of sculpture in the Amarna style, including one with figures of two of Akhenaten's daughters. It might be assumed that the new temple was, like others, constructed using *talatat*, small sandstone blocks typically used in Akhenaten's buildings. It is perhaps possible that the numerous *talatat* reused in the temple at Gebel Barkal, and those recently excavated near Kerma, were from the Sesebi temple.

Much of the stone of the temple has been removed over the centuries, and only fragments of the walls survived. One particularly fine block (now in the Brooklyn Museum) carries a sculpture in low relief depicting a wounded Kushite being helped by a comrade. This motif is found in scenes of Egyptian campaigns in Nubia in the speos of Horemheb at Gebel Silsila, and the temples of Ramesses II at Beit al-Wali and Derr. This piece

possibly belongs to the reign of Sety I. The recent work by the Cambridge team has found numerous small fragments of sculptured sandstone, many from the Sety I phase of the temples.

A platform structure with staircases that stands on the north side of the court preceding the temple has been interpreted as both a solar altar and viewing platform. The original structure appears to have comprised a raised platform with staircase at the west end, suggestive of a solar altar oriented to the rising sun. Later alterations can be dated to the reign of Sety I.

The extensive storage magazines show the importance of Sesebi as both a trading depot and supply center for the local population. A jar reported as containing remains of incense was one of the finds.

A smaller, roughly square enclosure exists within the eastern part of the site. This is defined by a ditch (possibly a foundation trench for a wall), and is generally assumed to represent an earlier occupation of the site. Some pottery dated to the mid-Eighteenth Dynasty has also been discovered. The main temple structure is built on a platform containing unfinished column drums, perhaps also from earlier activity at the site.

The residential area is particularly important, as it is contemporary with the town of Akhetaten (Tell al-Amarna), constructed by Akhenaten as his major residence and religious center in Egypt. Sesebi was a planned settlement, and the houses are of three types: small and slightly larger houses in terraces in the south-west sector, and large houses toward the center of the site. Unlike the larger houses at Akhetaten, those at Sesebi do not stand within their own enclosures and lack the gardens and service and storage areas that are typical of the Amarna 'villas.' There are indications of second stories for many of the houses.

There were numerous small finds from the town and the cemeteries, including scarabs and amulets with close parallels at Amarna. There were also molds for manufacturing amulets, showing that there was at least small-scale production at the site. Significantly, there was a group of sherds of Mycenaean pottery, mainly stirrup jars, again with parallels from Amarna. They are the southernmost significant group of Mycenaean imports known so far. An 'ancestor bust' (a head and shoulders inscribed with names that served as a focus for private religion) was another significant find, these being known mainly from the village of Deir al-Medina (Luxor). A royal head in black granite, depicting a king in the White Crown, has been attributed to the time of Hatshepsut or Thutmose III. The majority of finds were distributed to the Brooklyn Museum, the British Museum, and the Medelhavsmuseet, Stockholm.

Once constructed, Sesebi served as the main administrative center for the Egyptian province of Kush during Akhenaten's reign, but following his death, that function returned to Soleb, slightly to the north. Sesebi was reoccupied as an official center in the early years of the reign of Sety I (or perhaps his predecessor, Horemheb), before the construction of a new town at Amara West. Sety I (or Horemheb) had the solar temple demolished and the first temple restored and rededicated to the Theban triad of Amun, Mut, and Khonsu. The lack of *talatat* from the site suggests that they may

have been taken for building work at Barkal (where many were used in the earliest parts of the Amun temple) and elsewhere.

It is possible that this renewed town was that referred to in Sety I's inscription at Nauri at the Third Cataract. If so, it was called "The House of Millions of Years of King Menmaatre, Heart's-Ease-in-Abydos." The latest evidence from the site belongs to the reign of Ramesses II. It is clear that by the end of the reign of Sety I, the main administrative center was at the newly founded town of Amara West, and that Sesebi was serving as residence for local agricultural workers, and perhaps a few administrators. There is evidence for less formal (more 'organic') development within the settlement.

There is no identifiable material from the late New Kingdom, Napatan, or Meroitic Periods, and we must assume that the town was abandoned sometime in the late Nineteenth or Twentieth Dynasty, except perhaps for a squatter population. Pottery of Napatan date has been identified. The X-Group and Christian cemeteries published by David Edwards suggest that the area had a renewed importance in the later Nubian phases, and in the medieval period, Gebel Sese became a significant center for the Kingdom of Kokka, and has imposing structural remains of medieval and Ottoman date.

Bibliography

Blackman, A.M. 1937. "Preliminary Report on the Excavations at Sesebi, Northern Province, Anglo-Egyptian Sudan, 1936–37." *JEA* 23:145–51.

Breasted, J.H. 1908. "The Monuments of Sudanese Nubia. The Oriental Exploration Fund of the University of Chicago. Second Preliminary Report of the Egyptian Expedition." *AJSL* 25:1–110.

Cailliaud, F. 1826. *Voyage à Méroé au fleuve Blanc, au-delà de Fâzoql dans le midi du royaume de Sennâr, à Syouah et dans cinq autres Oasis; fait dans les années 1819, 1820, 1821, et 1822.* Paris: L'Imprimerie Royale.

Edwards, D.N. 1994. "Post-Meroitic ('X-Group') and Christian Burials at Sesibi, Sudanese Nubia: The Excavations of 1937." *JEA* 80:159–78.

Fairman, H.W. 1938. "Preliminary Report on the Excavations at Sesebi (Sudla) and Amarah West, Anglo-Egyptian Sudan, 1937–38." *JEA* 24:151–56.

Griffith, F.Ll. 1927. "The Abydos Decree of Seti I at Nauri." *JEA* 13:193–208.

Hankey, V. 1980. "The Aegean Interest in el Amarna." *Journal of Mediterranean Anthropology and Archaeology* 1:38–49.

Keith-Bennett, J.L. 1981. "Anthropoid Busts II: Not from Deir el Medina Alone." *BES* 3:43–71.

Lepsius, K.-R. 1849. *Denkmaeler aus Aegypten und Aethiopien nach den Zeichnungen der von Seiner Majestät dem Koenige von Preussen, Friedrich Wilhelm IV., nach diesen Ländern gesendeten, und in den Jahren 1842–1845 ausgeführten wissenschaftlichen Expedition auf Befehl Seiner Majestät.* 13 vols. Berlin: Nicolaische Buchhandlung.

Merrillees, R.S., and J.L. Winter. 1972. "Bronze Age Trade between the Aegean and Egypt: Minoan and Mycenaean Pottery from Egypt in the Brooklyn Museum." *Miscellanea Wilbouriana* 1:101–33.

Morkot, R.G. 1988. "The Excavations at Sesebi (Sudla) 1936–1938." *BSF* 3:159–64.

Peterson, B. 1967. "Archäologische Funde aus Sesebi (Sudla) in Nord-Sudan." *Orientalia Suecana* 16:3–15.

Schiff Giorgini, M. 1967–68. "Soleb-Sedeinga. Résumé des trauvaux de la mission pendant les trois campagnes automne 1965–printemps 1968." *Kush* 15:251–68.

Spence, K., and P. Rose. 2009. "New Fieldwork at Sesebi." *EA* 35:21–24.

Spence, K., P. Rose, R. Bradshaw, P. Collet, A. Hassan, J. MacGinnis, and A. Mason. 2011. "Sesebi 2011." *Sudan & Nubia* 15:34–38.

SOLEB

Marjorie M. Fisher

Soleb Temple was excavated under the direction of Michela Schiff Giorgini from the University of Pisa for six seasons, from 1957 to 1963. She worked with Clément Robichon from the Centre National de la Recherche Scientifique in Paris, Jozef Janssen from the University of Amsterdam, and Jean Leclant, professor at the Sorbonne in Paris and former director of the Institut d'Égyptologie de l'Université de Strasbourg. The primary corpus of information comes from their excavations and documentation of the site. Although they planned a six-volume series to document their work, only four volumes have thus far been produced. Many visitors and scholars have seen Soleb throughout history. Early travelers, such as Lord Prudhoe, Major Orlando Felix, Joseph Bonomi, John Gardner Wilkinson, and George Alexander Hoskins, visited the site between 1813 and 1907. During that time, various scholars who saw the temple of Amenhotep III wrote about the artifacts found in the temple and area, as well as producing paintings and drawings of the site. The Prussian expedition led by Richard Lepsius produced the drawings of Soleb published in his *Denkmäler* in 1844. E.A. Wallis Budge from the British Museum visited Soleb twice in the course of documenting the mon-

uments of Nubia, followed by J. Henry Breasted in 1906–1907. The temple continues to be excavated by the Institut français d'archéologie orientale.

This site, located fifty kilometers south of Amara between the Second and Third Cataracts on the west bank of the Nile, had a long history of use: near the temple are prehistoric graves; a Nubian A-Group, Kerma Culture, and New Kingdom necropolis; and a Meroitic cemetery. The Soleb temple, constructed during the reign of Amenhotep III, was dedicated to Amun, but after Akhenaten assumed power, it was rededicated to Aten. An inscription of the official Ramessu dating to the reign of Ramesses III was also found there, indicating that the temple continued in use over the next several generations.

The fortification walls surrounding the temple reflect the phases of its construction. The sandstone temple of Soleb was built by Amenhotep III and subsequently used by his son Akhenaten. It faces east to the rising sun, as would be expected for a solar temple of this period. It was dedicated to an aspect of Amun-Re of Karnak, and the deified Amenhotep III in his manifestation as Lord of Nubia.

One enters the temple through a pylon doorway and proceeds down a long avenue of ram sphinxes leading to a small courtyard with four pillars, and through a second pylon doorway into a sun court with pillars (peristyle court). There are several religious scenes remaining on the temple as well as *sed*-festival scenes. This sun court leads into a hypostyle court with thirty-six pillars. Continuing along the main axis, one enters the inner hypostyle hall, or vestibule, with twenty-four pillars. Originally this room was not a hypostyle hall/vestibule but contained a ramp leading to the back, where an ancient temple, now missing, had a room with a smaller sanctuary in it, surrounded by pillars. Later this room was converted into the sanctuary, with a room on either side. Uniquely for Nubian temples, there are pillars in each of these rooms, and there is no vestibule (unless the smaller hypostyle hall is considered a vestibule). At least four different varieties of columns are present in this temple, including bound-papyrus pillars in the smaller hypostyle hall and lotus columns with round bases at the entrance.

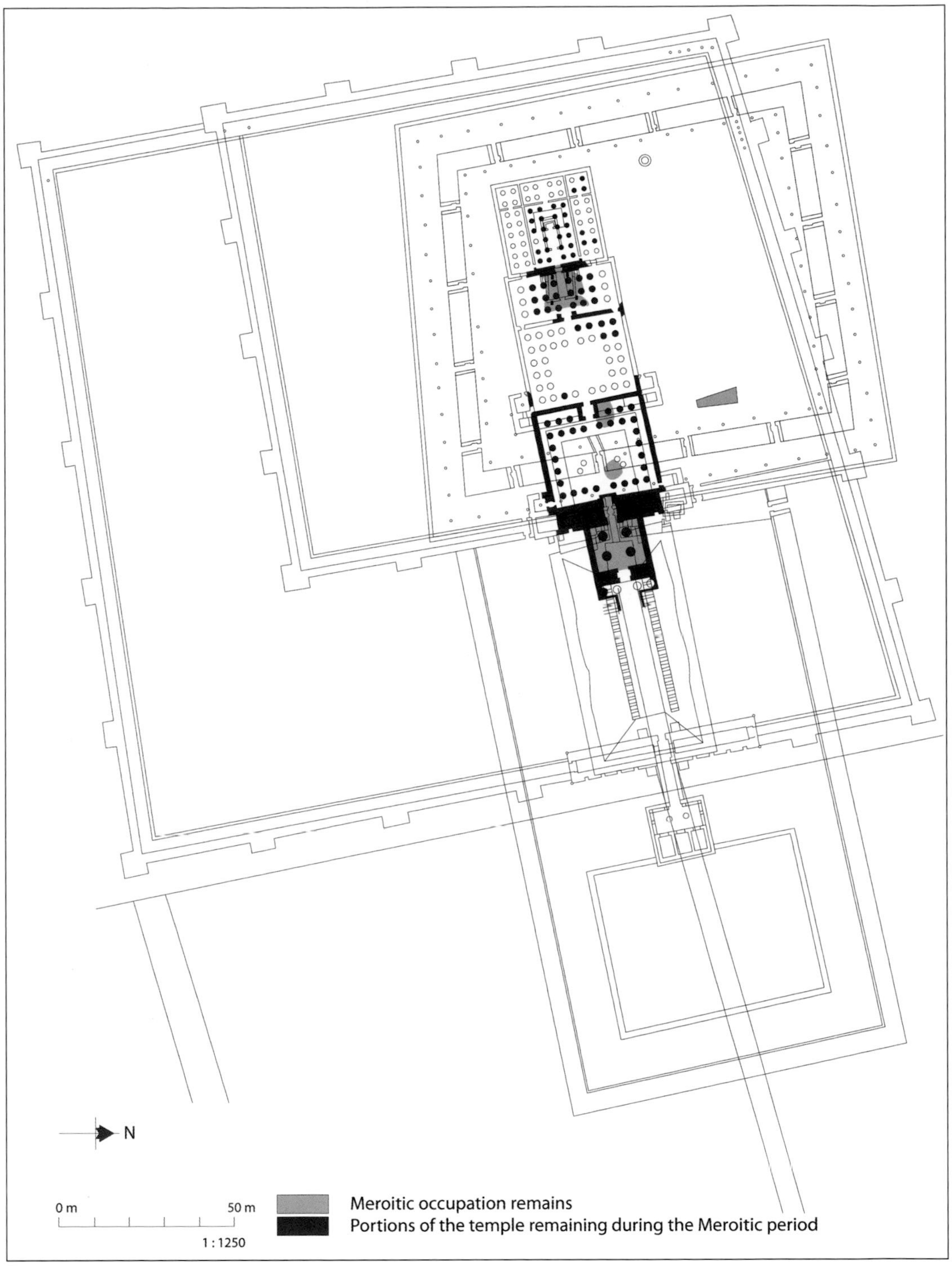

Reliefs in this temple show the identification of the deified Amenhotep III, "Nebmaatre, Lord of Nubia," with Amun, Lord of Nubia. In some scenes, Amenhotep III is depicted worshiping this form of his deified self with ram's horns curled around his ears and the Khonsu headdress of the moon holding the sun

Meroitic occupation remains

Portions of the temple remaining during the Meroitic period

0 m   50 m

1 : 1250

N

on his head. The fragmentary forecourt of the temple preserves doorjambs with figures of Amenhotep IV/Akhenaten worshiping his deified father and Amun, showing the transition from the worship of Amun to the sun god Aten during the reign of Akhenaten.

Figure 183. Plan of the temple of Soleb.

Following pages:
Figure 184. Soleb temple at night. Photo © Chester Higgins Jr 2012.

Bibliography

Fisher, M.M. 2001. *The Sons of Ramesses II*. 2 vols. ÄAT 53.

Gohary, J. 1998. *Guide to the Nubian Monuments on Lake Nasser*. Cairo: American University in Cairo Press.

Hein, I. 1991. *Die Ramessidische Bautätigkeit in Nubien*. GOF 4, vol. 22. Wiesbaden: Harrassowitz.

Kozloff, A., and B.M. Bryan. 1992. *Egypt's Dazzling Sun: Amenhotep III and His World*. Cleveland: Cleveland Museum of Art.

Leclant. J. 1984. "Soleb." In *LÄ* 5:1076–80.

Porter, B., and R.L.B. Moss. 1952. *Topographical Bibliography of Ancient Egyptian Hieroglyphic Texts, Reliefs and Paintings*. Vol. 7: *Nubia, the Deserts and Outside Egypt*. Oxford: Griffith Institute.

Schiff Giorgini, M., in collaboration with C. Robichon and J. Leclant. 1965. *Soleb I: 1813–1963*. Florence: Sansoni.

———. 1971. *Soleb II: Les nécropoles*. Florence: Sansoni.

———. 1998. *Soleb V: Le temple. Bas reliefs et inscriptions*. Cairo: IFAO.

———. 2002. *Soleb III: Le temple. Description*. Cairo: IFAO.

———. 2003. *Soleb IV: Le temple. Plans et photographies*. Cairo: IFAO.

SEDEINGA

Robert G. Morkot

Sedeinga is the name of a significant site in the Abri-Delgo Reach of the Nile, with a New Kingdom temple and town, and evidence for settlement and cemeteries of the Napatan and Meroitic Periods. One of the modern names of the region is Adaya, which is a version of the Meroitic name Atiya (also Twete), itself derived from the Egyptian Hut-Tiye, 'House (Temple) of Tiye.' It might be the Atteva of Pliny's list of places along the Nile.

Although it was visited by European travelers from the early nineteenth century, excavations at Sedeinga began only in 1964, when the expedition led by Michela Schiff Giorgini, Jean Leclant, and Clément Robichon moved there after completion of their work at Soleb, some 14.5 kilometers to the south.

The principal standing monument is the temple constructed in the reign of Amenhotep III and dedicated to his chief wife, Tiye, as a manifestation of the Eye of Re. The temple was little more than one standing column surrounded by a heap of fallen blocks, but the work of the French team is endeavoring to reconstruct the surviving elements. The temple was cultically related to Amenhotep III's own temple at Soleb, which was named after the king himself, using his Horus name Khaemmaat. An inscription from Meroe names the deities of Sedeinga as Isis and Horus, which clearly relates to the divine forms of Tiye and Amenhotep III.

The surviving standing column at Sedeinga is of a nearly fluted type, crowned with the head of Hathor and the naos sistrum. The column was one of eight in a hypostyle hall. At present, the exact plan of the temple remains unclear, but the hypostyle would conventionally have stood between a courtyard and the sanctuary rooms. Such columns were already used in temples associated with the goddess Hathor, such as the chapel in Hatshepsut's temple at Deir al-Bahari (Luxor), in Egypt. Few other elements of the temple sculpture are published so far. The most notable is a large entablature from a doorway with panels containing uraeus cobras and full-faced images of Hathor. It also carries two images of Tiye as a human-head lioness wearing the flat-topped headdress more usually associated with Nefertiti. This certainly identified Tiye with the goddess Tefnut, one of the manifestations of the Eye of Re. Significantly, at the center, the cartouche of Tiye is flanked by two cartouches of Amenhotep III that face inward to hers, a highly unusual instance of the queen taking precedence.

Tiye's cartouche is surmounted by the sun disc, lyre-shaped cow's horns, and two falcon-plumes, and the king's cartouche is surmounted by the double ostrich feathers and sun disc.

One other part of the relief decoration was published by Richard Lepsius. This shows Amenhotep III with the goddess Isis. Lepsius also published an inscription that refers to Tiye as "the Great of Terror in all lands." This too is probably an allusion to the Eye of Re. In Egyptian mythology, the sun god Re sent his burning eye, in the form of the savage lioness, to destroy humankind. The episode is later related to the retreat of the sun into the southland, and the mission of various gods to bring it back to Egypt. The ideology associated with Amenhotep III's celebration of his 'jubilee' festival is very complex, and involves both solar and lunar aspects. The king certainly identified himself with the sun god in a variety of the rites, and Queen Tiye therefore took on the roles of the goddesses associated with Re, most notably Hathor, and her fierce lioness manifestations, Tefnut and Sekhmet.

A number of statue fragments have been attributed to the temple, and these refer to Isis and Weret-hekau, both goddesses closely associated with kingship. A head of Queen Tiye, now in the Boston Museum of Fine Arts, was found much farther south, at Sanam, but probably comes from a statue group that stood in the temple at Sedeinga. It is made of a local Upper Nubian stone, peridotite, and is one of a group of statues of Tiye that show her with an exceptionally large wig decorated with floral garlands, and surmounted by very large cow's horns framing a sun disc. The head was part of a dyad, probably depicting the queen with Amenhotep III: it could be associated with the head of a god with the king's features wearing a double-plumed crown that is now in the Brooklyn Museum.

Of other remains perhaps associated with the temple, there are some reused columns and inscribed hieroglyphic blocks in a Christian church in the nearby village of Nilwa, and the upper part of a broken stela from the temple was excavated in the Meroitic cemetery. It depicts Amenhotep III before the god Amun-Re of Khaemmaat (Soleb) and his own divine form as worshiped in the temple of Soleb, crowned with the lunar disc and crescent and called "Nebmaatre who is in Khaemmaat." This also indicates that the cult of the Sedeinga temple was closely associated with that at Soleb.

The dedication of the temple to the king's Chief Wife was a significant act and without precedent that we know of: it relates very directly to Amenhotep III's development of the royal cult particularly associated with his 'jubilee' festivals. This saw the king reborn, but certainly related him to the moon and Osiris as controllers of the Nile flood. The two temples that Amenhotep III constructed in Upper Nubia, at Soleb and Sedeinga, served as a model for those constructed by Ramesses II at Abu Simbel. The Ramesside temples were much closer together physically, being only a few hundred meters apart, but stood in the same relation, the king's to the south of the queen's. At Abu Simbel, Queen Nefertari was also identified with Isis and Hathor, although she does not achieve quite the pre-eminence that Tiye does at Sedeinga, nor does she appear in lioness form.

A New Kingdom town surrounded the temple. There has been considerable discussion about the nature of the towns in the Abri-Delgo Reach of the Nile. The Egyptian presence in the region in the early Eighteenth Dynasty was on Sai Island, and it has been assumed that the towns of Soleb, Sedeinga, Sesebi, and Amara West represent an Egyptian colonization of the area. This remains unclear. We can be certain that these towns served as major administrative centers for Egyptian rule,

Figure 185. The ruins of
the temple at Sedeinga with
both standing and fallen
Hathor capitals visible.

but they were not best placed to exploit the richest agricultural area of Upper Nubia, which lay south of the Third Cataract. Some writers speculated that Sedeinga was chosen as Tiye's temple town because she came from this region. There is nothing to support this, and all of the evidence suggests that her family was from the region of Akhmim in Upper Egypt, where, indeed there was another temple dedicated to her, at Tahta (Ta-Hut-Tiye).

Sedeinga continued to be an important center in the Napatan and Meroitic Periods, and there are cemeteries surrounding the town. Perhaps significantly, there is no mention of Sedeinga in the inscriptions of the later Napatan Period. The

inscription of Irike-Amanote at Kawa, and the stelae of Kings Harsiyotef and Nastasen from Gebel Barkal, record the journeys made by those kings to the temples as far north as Pnubs (Tabo-Kerma), but not into the Dal-Abri region. It is possible that, following the campaign of Psamtik II, and the Persian conquest of Egypt, Sedeinga and Amara were no longer significant centers with any state building. The Meroitic building work and occupation would thus be analogous with renewed activity in Lower Nubia in the third to second centuries BC. This is speculative but may be answered by the ongoing excavations at both sites.

The first cemetery to be excavated lies five hundred meters west of the temple and contained typical pyramidal tombs with bases measuring from five to nine meters each side, and with heights probably between eight and seventeen meters. Some pyramids had secondary burials and a second pyramid erected over the entrance passage. The finds included Meroitic inscriptions, *ba*-bird statues, and a cavetto cornice with winged sun-disc and Meroitic text. The tomb contents provided evidence for trade with Roman Egypt. One silver ring had a bezel with a silenus head and another a bezel set with a carved agate carrying a profile head of Serapis surrounded by seven stars or planets.

One major find was a group of vessels, some of transparent, some of colored glass. Some were tall flutes on bases and others chalice-shaped with handles. The most impressive were flutes in blue glass, with painted and gilded figures and Greek texts (see illustration in "The Art and Architecture of Meroitic Nubia"). Because of the delicate nature of the glass, it has been suggested that they were local manufactures, but stylistically they relate to other material from the Roman Empire, and it seems far more likely that they were highly prized imports. The nature of the material from the cemeteries shows that the local elites were far from being remote 'provincials' of the Meroitic Empire, and perhaps played an important role in trade

One tomb (W T1) had stone jambs with figures of the Twenty-fifth Dynasty pharaoh Taharqo (690–664 BC). This led to some considerable speculation that following Taharqo's defeat by the Assyrians, he had withdrawn to Kush, and perhaps had been disgraced and deposed and later buried at Sedeinga, rather than in the large pyramid tomb at Nuri. As the Nuri pyramid contained several hundred *shawabti* figures arranged around the burial chamber, along with other funeral equipment, that tomb undoubtedly served as Taharqo's resting place. It is most likely that the Sedeinga jambs are recycled material from a small temple or chapel erected during the king's reign in the town.

A much larger cemetery of the Napatan and Meroitic Periods has been the subject of more recent excavations. Audran Labrousse suggests that some tombs of Napatan date were reused in later Meroitic times. There is evidence for around four hundred tombs with pyramids constructed in mud brick, suggesting that Sedeinga was a major center and may have been the principal administrative town for the Abri-Delgo Reach.

Bibliography

Labrousse, A. 1994. "Sedeinga, état des travaux." In C. Bonnet, ed., *Études Nubiennes: Conférence de Genève, Actes du VIIe Congrès international d'études nubiennes, 3–8 septembre 1990*, vol. 2, 131–33. Geneva: Société d'études nubiennes.

Leclant, J. 1984. "Taharqa à Sedeinga." In *Studien zu Sprache und Religion Ägyptens: zu Ehren von Wolfhart Westendorf*, 1113–19. Göttingen: Herbert.

Lepsius, K.-R. 1849. *Denkmaeler aus Aegypten und Aethiopien nach den Zeichnungen der von Seiner Majestät dem Koenige von Preussen, Friedrich Wilhelm IV., nach diesen Ländern gesendeten, und in den Jahren 1842–1845 ausgeführten wissenschaftlichen Expedition auf Befehl Seiner Majestät*. 13 vols. Berlin: Nicolaische Buchhandlung.

Schiff Giorgini, M. 1965. "Première campagne de fouilles à Sedeinga, 1963–1964." *Kush* 13:112–30.

———. 1967–68. "Soleb-Sedeinga. Résumé des travaux de la mission pendant les trois campagnes automne 1965–printemps 1968." *Kush* 15:251–68.

Sai Island

Janice W. Yellin

Francis Geus, the excavator of Sai Island, called it one of the most beautiful places in Sudan, and the inhabitants of Nubia have concurred for thousands of years. One of the most important and best-preserved sites for understanding both the human and ecological history of Nubia, this island in the middle of the Nile River has been continually occupied from Paleolithic to modern times. Located between the Second and Third Cataracts, south of the barren, rocky area known as the Batn al-Hagar, Sai is among the largest Nile islands, measuring twelve kilometers from north to south and 5.5 kilometers east to west. Visited by the Prussian Royal Expedition of Richard Lepsius in 1842 and formally explored by Anthony Arkell in the 1940s, Sai has been excavated by the French Antiquities Service under the direction of Jean Vercoutter (1954–57, 1969–81), Francis Geus (1993–2004), and now by Didier Devauchelle and Florence Doyen (2006 to the present).

Sai is a rocky, dry island with cultivable lands along the river's edge and basins of fertile soil not far inland. Evidence from very ancient to modern times for the environmental and geological development of the island has been preserved, offering archaeologists and scientists a unique opportunity to understand the relationship between these factors and human habitation. Since 1993 teams of specialists in the sciences and archaeology have formed a working partnership at Sai. There is important evidence for almost all periods of ancient Nubian history in the three known major areas of habitation. In the northeast of the island are Upper Paleolithic, Pre-Kerma, Kerma, Middle Kingdom Egyptian, and New Kingdom settlements. The Northern Necropolis, in use from the second millennium BC to the present, a cathedral, and an Ottoman fort are also in this part of the island. The Northern Necropolis has a large area of Meroitic and X-Group burials. The eastern part of the island's center has Middle Paleolithic, Neolithic, and Kerma sites, as well as a large important Kerma cemetery and two X-Group cemeteries. The other parts of the island are less thoroughly explored. In the western and northwestern areas are cemeteries of the Kerma and X-Group Periods, and to the south another set of Kerma and X-Group cemeteries, as well as some Christian Period dwellings, have been identified.

The long history of human occupation on Sai begins over 300,000 years ago with the Paleolithic sites found by the University of Leuven expedition on a part of the island whose geological structure is such that they are exceptionally well preserved. Other finds belong to the Mesolithic and Neolithic Periods. Pottery and other artifacts belonging to the Pre-Kerma phase, which was contemporary with the Nubian A-Group culture, demonstrate that Sai was settled by the same peoples who founded the great Kingdom of Kerma. Pre-Kerma society on Sai, as at Kerma itself, continued without disruption into a fully developed Kerma culture, one that flourished throughout the entire Kerma period. South of the Batn al-Hagar and thus strategically located at the entry into the Third Cataract territory of the Kerma Kingdom, Sai had an important role as a trading intermediary between Egypt and Nubia throughout the Old Kingdom. During the Middle Kingdom, it served as a bulwark against Egyptian incursions, but was also used by two Twelfth Dynasty rulers, Senwosret I and Senwosret III, as a staging point for attacks on Kerma. Throughout this period, it played an important role in Egyptian-Nubian trade. Its large Kerma population supports the identification of Sai with the political center the Egyptians called Shaât, whose princes are recorded by Egyptians as being among their Nubian adversaries in late Old and early New Kingdom texts. The largest tombs in the Kerma cemetery, which were surmounted by tumuli (up to forty meters) and uniquely constructed with a ring of black stones surrounding a mound of white pebbles, belonged to these local rulers. Indeed Sai's Kerma population was so large and prosperous that the thousands of their graves in the same cemetery provided enough data for Brigitte Gratien, one of the excavators, to define the major phases of the Kerma history, dating from the end of the Old Kingdom to the beginning of the New Kingdom.

The New Kingdom Egyptian rulers, who ultimately triumphed over Kerma, established a walled mud-brick town that was abandoned when they withdrew from Nubia at the end of the New Kingdom (ca. 1077 BC). Thutmose III built a temple to Amun on the remains of an earlier mud brick temple outside the town walls. Two Egyptian cemeteries, one of which had tombs with baked mud-brick pyramids, are south of this town. In the sixteenth century AD, the Ottomans constructed a fort in the same excellent strategic location. A large cemetery west of the fort has Napatan and Meroitic tombs in addition to Christian burials, and at least two others that have ancient burials have been identified. One of the Meroitic Period cemeteries is currently being excavated and documented. Tombs in cemetery 8-B-5.A, as in other Meroitic Nubian elite cemeteries, have small brick pyramids topped with lotus-shaped capstones. Small chapels on their eastern sides were equipped with stone stelae, offering tables, and ba-birds. Gifts from these burials, the inscribed offering table of Waronakel, and funerary stelae published by Claude Rilly, indicate that their owners had sociopolitical connections with inhabitants of Karanog, the seat of the peshto-viceroy. The Sai funerary stelae are particularly telling because they have unusual phrases that are found in the Karanog area rather than at sites closer to Sai.

Sai was an important royal site in the Meroitic Period. During the winter of 2007, Vincent Francigny identified column capitals with the names of Amanitore, Natakamani, and one of their sons and other blocks from a Meroitic temple dating to the first century AD reused in the remains of the Ottoman fort. Column drums from the temple that were decorated with motifs of Nile gods and offerings, which were copied from the Greco-Roman temple at Dakka, well to the north of Sai in Lower Nubia, demonstrate interconnections between religious establishments in these two areas during the first century AD. Along with the numerous Meroitic burials at Sai, the temple further demonstrates its importance within the Meroitic state.

The presence of X-Group burials on the island indicates that the Meroitic culture gave way to the X-Group after the disappearance of the Meroitic central government in the mid-fourth century AD, but little else is yet known about the history of Sai during this time. The remains of a medieval Christian cruciform church, identified as a cathedral, indicate that Sai was the seat of a Nubian bishop, demonstrating that while the reasons for Sai's prominence had changed, its importance in Nubia continued. A familiar role was once again revived when the Ottoman fort was built over part of the walled New Kingdom town.

Bibliography

Edwards, D.N. 2004. *The Nubian Past: An Archaeology of the Sudan.* London: Routledge.

Francigny, V. 2008. "The Meroitic Temple at Saï Island." Communication, Eleventh International Conference for Meroitic Studies, September 1–September 4, 2008. Vienna: University of Vienna, Department of African Studies.

———. 2010. "L'Île de Saï. Méroïtique." *Dossiers d'Archéologie.* Hors-série 18 (March 2010): 62–67.

Geus, F. 2004. "Sai." In D.A. Welsby and J.R. Anderson, eds., *Sudan: Ancient Treasures: An Exhibition of Recent Discoveries from the Sudan National Museum,* 114–17. London: British Museum Press.

Geus, F., et al. 1997. "Tombes napatéennes, méroïtiques et médiévales de la nécropole Nord de l'île de Saï. Rapport préliminaire de la campagne 1994–1995 (archéologie et anthropologie)." *Archéologie du Nil Moyen* 7:99–141.

Gratien, B. 1986. *Saï I: La nécropole Kerma.* Paris: Presses du CNRS.

Rilly, C. 2008. "Les textes méroïtiques de l'île de Saï." *Kush* 19:139–77.

Sackho-Autissier, A. 1998. "Le terme *heqa* et ses applications archéologiques." *Actes de la VIII conférence internationale des Études nubiennes, Lille, du 11 au 17 septembre 1994. CRIPEL* 17, no. 3: 203–18.

Section française de la Direction des Antiquités du Soudan (SFDAS), http://www.diplomatie.gouv.fr/fr/actions-france_830/archeologie_1058/les-carnets-archeologie_5064/afrique-arabie_5068/soudan-nubie-ile-sai_5527/ile-sai_15289.html

Török, L. 1997. *The Kingdom of Kush: Handbook of the Napatan-Meroitic Civilization.* Leiden: Brill.

Zibelius-Chen, K. 1978. *Die ägyptische Expansion nach Nubien: Eine Darlegung der Grundfaktoren.* Wiesbaden: L. Reichert Verlag.

Amara West

Robert G. Morkot

Amara West is a New Kingdom town site in the northern part of the Abri-Delgo reach. The entire ancient site of Amara West is a mound some seven hundred meters long and 230 meters wide with, at its center, a walled enclosure, which is approximately 108 meters square. This enclosure surrounds the temple and planned town. Amara now stands on the west bank of the Nile, although at the time of its construction it was probably on an island. It is part of an extensive series of ancient remains of all periods from prehistoric to medieval, on both sides of the river. These include, on the east bank, the later Meroitic temple of Amara East, and the Napatan cemeteries of Missiminia, published by André Vila.

The site was first the focus of excavations by the Egypt Exploration Society (EES), following their seasons at Sesebi a little farther south. The 1937 to 1939 excavation seasons were directed by Herbert W. Fairman and work was continued by Peter L. Shinnie between 1947 and 1950. These excavations focused on the walled town, with the temple, administrative buildings, and some residential structures being cleared. The EES also made preliminary investigations in the cemeteries. Recently the British Museum has begun a new survey and excavation in the large extramural settlement, which has villa-type compounds, published by R.B. Parkinson and Neal Spencer.

Although some evidence, in the form of scarabs and seal impressions, is of the mid- to late-Eighteenth Dynasty, this may have been brought to the site during its later occupancy, and there is no evidence of any building that can be attributed to the Eighteenth Dynasty. The names that occur most frequently on scarabs, seals, and amulets are Menkheperre (Thutmose III) and Nebmaatre (Amenhotep III). A number of seals with the name of Hatshepsut were also excavated. The name Menkheperre was frequently used as an amulet. There was also building during his reign at Sai, a little to the south of Amara, which was the viceregal administration's major center in his reign. The name of Amenhotep III might have been associated with material brought from Soleb, which Amara replaced as administrative capital in the reign of Ramesses II. The earliest inscription is a stela of the viceroy Usersatjet who served Amenhotep II, but this was probably brought to the site at a later date. Part of a stela dated to year 4 of Sety I, and recording his campaign in Kush, is likely to be associated with the earliest building works at Amara.

The town walls and temple were certainly founded by Sety I, and parallel his Lower Nubian

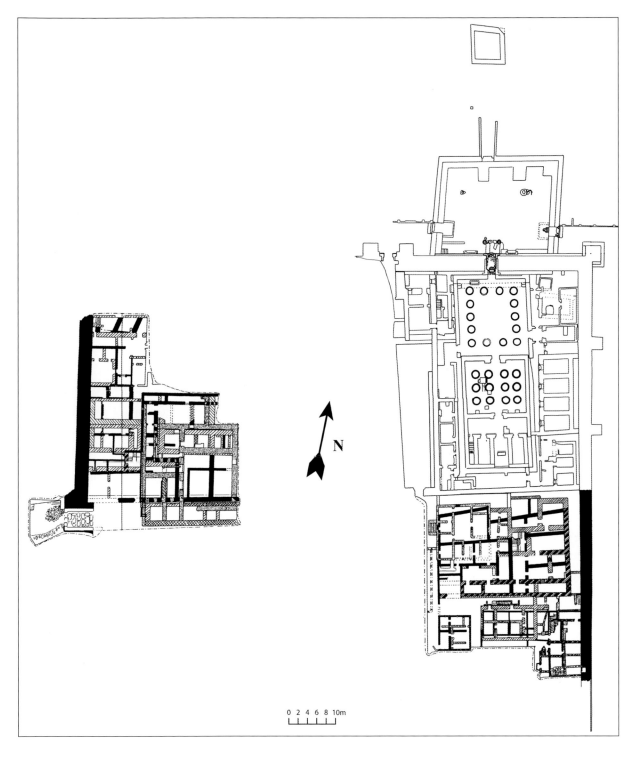

0 2 4 6 8 10m

Figure 186. Plan
of Amara West.

administrative center at Aksha. Like Aksha, the temple and town were unfinished at Sety I's death, and the work was completed, and temple dedicated, early in the reign of Ramesses II. The name of Hekanakht, attested elsewhere as viceroy in year 3 of Ramesses II, has been found on architectural blocks at Amara West, and on others reused at Amara East.

Like Aksha, the religious focus was a temple in which the deified king was dominant. The town was probably founded as "The House of Menmaatre" but was renamed "House of Ramesses, beloved of Amun." The town seems to have been renamed, or given the additional name, "United-with-Waset" ('United with Thebes'), which was also the name given to Ramesses II's mortuary temple at

Thebes (the Ramesseum). This name suggests some sort of cultic association with Thebes.

The temple, constructed of local sandstone, was dedicated to Amun-Re, with a prominent role for the deified Ramesses II. The axis of the temple is north–south, but the internal orientation and layout were altered after construction. The original temple comprised the hypostyle hall, vestibule, and three sanctuary rooms. This structure, built as one unit, measures 25.5 meters north to south and 14.5 meters east to west. Originally the temple was entered from the south, but was reoriented to give it a northern access, with the new main entrance cut through the town wall. This involved the construction of the sanctuary rooms in what had originally been the entrance court, and the addition of a peristyle court between the town wall and the hypostyle hall. Many carved blocks from this first temple were used as building material in the (only slightly) later structure. To protect the entrance in the town wall, a forecourt was added outside the enclosure wall. This outer forecourt had three gates, on the north, east, and west, but the north gate was later blocked up. There was no pylon entrance.

The main north entrance gate is flanked by versions of two well-known texts of Ramesses II: the "Marriage Stela" of year 34 and the "Decree of Ptah" of year 35. These are probably considerably later than the final form of the temple, and both inscriptions were added also at Abu Simbel. An inscription of year 6 of Merenptah is carved in the passage of the main north gate; it is a duplicate of a text at Amada recording rebellion in Nubia, and the defeat of the Libyan invasion of Egypt.

The north gate from the outer forecourt leads into the peristyle court, which is followed by the hypostyle hall, a vestibule, and three sanctuary rooms. The peristyle court, which is 14.7 meters by 15.7 meters, is surrounded by fourteen papyrus-bundle columns. From a door in the east wall, there

is access to a small single-room chapel that was added later in the reign of Ramesses II between the external wall of the temple and the town wall.

The hypostyle hall has twelve papyrus columns originally decorated with small panels of relief sculpture depicting Ramesses II, sometimes accompanied by Queen Nefertari, making offerings to various deities, including his own deified form. These panels were over-carved with much larger reliefs, although the actual content of the scenes remained the same. A considerable amount of color, and in some places gold leaf, survived at the time of the excavations. The walls of the hall are covered with scenes, but most are only partially preserved. Some scenes show large-scale figures of the king, accompanied by the queen and other figures before seated deities; others are of military activities; a frieze of foreign 'name-rings' runs around the lower part of the walls. One scene shows a military campaign (perhaps of year 4) in Lebanon, including the siege of Arqata, and related fragments depict Asiatic captives bringing copper ingots, cattle, and horses.

The most notable addition to the hall is a series of buttresses, one adjoining a column and three others placed against the south wall: these suggest that the roof required some additional support as early as the reign of Ramesses II. The buttresses on the southeast wall were inscribed for the 'usurper' Amenmesse, with later cartouches of Ramesses III. Adjacent to one buttress was a small chapel, also inscribed for Amenmesse. The inscriptions on the buttress were later plastered over and recarved for officials of Ramesses VI and IX.

The vestibule has large-scale scenes of Ramesses II and Queen Nefertari presenting offerings to deities. The central sanctuary has images of the king presenting offerings before the sacred barques.

Following the reorientation and construction of the outer forecourt, there was no significant architectural addition or alteration. Most of the surviving decoration dates to the reign of Ramesses II, and the additional inscriptions of later pharaohs and viceroys were on uncarved areas of walls and columns. The latest dated inscription is of year 6 of Ramesses IX.

The scenes in the temple show a number of gods, but Amun-Re, Mut, and the deified Ramesses II are the most prominent. The deified king appears in a variety of forms, notably as 'Lord of Ta-Sety' (that is, Bow-Land, 'Nubia'). The way that the deified king is described places the decoration, and hence the reorientation, in the earlier part of his reign, either the first or second decade. There are similarities with both Aksha (very early in his reign) and Abu Simbel.

The temple was surrounded by mud-brick storage magazines, and the whole precinct was separated from the rest of the town by a brick wall.

Two sectors of the enclosed town were excavated, one immediately to the south of the temple, and a second adjoining the West Gate of the town. The mud-brick houses and other buildings were attributed to four levels, the earliest (level four) being the original foundation of Sety I continuing into the early part of the reign of Ramesses II. Levels three and two were attributed to the later Nineteenth and Twentieth Dynasties, with level one perhaps being considerably later (that is, during the Napatan Period).

The area of town by the West Gate included a building identified as the "Governor's Palace," as there were stone jambs carrying the names of the *idnw*, the official who headed the administration of Kush (Upper Nubia). This was a substantial building, similar to the houses excavated at Amarna, although not within a compound. The stone sink from the 'bathroom' remained in situ, along with the pottery vessel to catch the drainage water. There were other smaller houses in the vicinity, along with storage rooms.

The West Gate was well preserved, with stone lining the mud brick of the enclosure walls and some roofing slabs in situ. Outside was a paved court and large drainage pipes, both later additions. The original stone facing of the gate was covered with relief decoration showing a military campaign of Ramesses II, which took place about year 20. These reliefs were covered over when the width of the gate was reduced by the erection of brick and stone walls. Doors on both sides of the gate passage gave access to stairs within the walls, leading up to chambers at the top. The enclosure wall had buttresses at regular intervals.

To the east of the town enclosure, a number of garden plots were excavated. These are of a type still made in northern Sudan, with mud walls subdividing the plot into small areas approximately half a meter square, to retain water effectively. Close by was a building of mud brick in which pots containing python skeletons were discovered: these have no absolute parallel from Egypt or Sudan.

Peter Shinnie, director of the later seasons of excavation, was certain that the temple and town had been formally closed down by the Egyptians in response to political changes in Upper Nubia in the late Twentieth Dynasty. The latest dated inscription in the temple belongs to year 6 of Ramesses IX. If the town was closed down, any temple valuables and important administrative material would have been taken, no doubt followed by a period in which usable materials (such as wood) would have been removed. There was a layer of sand about fifty centimeters deep over much of the temple before the evidence of later construction. It is unknown how long the abandonment in this part of the town lasted, although this is a notoriously windy region, and such a layer could build up quite rapidly: the original excavators thought that several centuries separated the levels.

The recent excavations have uncovered 'villas' that had at least two stories, and surrounding service areas: they are thus analogous to those at Amarna and Qantir (Per-Ramesses) in the Delta. One house (E12.10) was in occupation throughout the Twentieth Dynasty. Of particular significance are two hieratic ostraca, one from the 1938 to 1939 season found in the temple magazine area, and one from the recent excavation of E12.10. These both carry sections of a literary text of Middle Kingdom date, *The Teaching of Amenemhat*. This is well known as a scribal training exercise, but the first time that copies have been found outside of Egypt, as Parkinson and Spencer point out.

Some preliminary investigation of the cemeteries was carried out by the EES, and several tombs have been excavated by the British Museum. The material recovered so far belongs largely to the post-Twentieth Dynasty period, with amulets and pottery that parallel material from Missiminia and other Napatan sites. The precise chronology of the material is uncertain, although it is probably to be associated with the latest building levels within the town. The pottery from the EES excavations in the town included New Kingdom and local Nubian wares, and pottery that is of post-Twentieth Dynasty date (Egyptian Third Intermediate Period). Significantly, there were also some fragments of Mycenaean stirrup jars of Late Helladic IIIA and B types.

Although the excavations produced numerous small finds, including votive stelae and some small statues, the excavators noted that there were no larger statues or other material that would be expected. This would be explained if Shinnie's assessment that the town and temple were closed down as part of a systematic withdrawal by the Egyptians sometime following year 6 of Ramesses IX is correct. Some remaining statuary may have been removed and taken to the temples at Gebel Barkal by Piankhi or Taharqo. Piankhi certainly transferred many large sculptures from Soleb, and an inscription of Taharqo refers to the removal of statues from Sai.

Amara is important as a planned Ramesside administrative town in Kush, and the temple parallels those of the reign of Ramesses II in Lower Nubia. It is also important in attempting to understand the archaeology and history of the period between the end of the New Kingdom occupation and the emergence of the independent Kushite kingdom.

Bibliography

Fairman, H.W. 1938. "Preliminary Report on the Excavations at Sesebi (Sudla) and Amarah West, Anglo-Egyptian Sudan, 1937–38." *JEA* 24:151–56.

———. 1939. "Preliminary Report on the Excavations at Amarah West, Anglo-Egyptian Sudan, 1938–39." *JEA* 25:139–44.

———. 1948. "Preliminary Report on the Excavations at Amarah West, Anglo-Egyptian Sudan, 1947–48." *JEA* 34:3–11.

Parkinson, R.B., and N. Spencer. 2008. "The Teaching of Amenemhat at Amara West." *EA* 35:25–27.

Shinnie, P.L. 1951. "Preliminary Report on the Excavations at Amarah West, Anglo-Egyptian Sudan, 1948–49 and 1949–50." *JEA* 37:5–11.

Spencer, P. 1997. *Amara West.* Vol. 1: *The Architectural Report.* London: Egypt Exploration Society.

———. 2002. *Amara West.* Vol. 2: *The Cemetery and the Pottery Corpus.* London: Egypt Exploration Society.

Vila, A. 1977a. *La prospection archéologique de la vallée du Nil au sud de la cataracte de Dal (Nubie Soudanaise).* Fascicle 7: *Le District d'Amara Ouest.* Paris: CNRS.

———. 1977b. *La prospection archéologique de la vallée du Nil au sud de la cataracte de Dal (Nubie Soudanaise).* Fascicle 8: *Le District d'Amara Est.* Paris: CNRS.

———. 1980. *La prospection archéologique de la vallée du Nil au sud de la cataracte de Dal (Nubie Soudanaise).* Fascicle 12: *La nécropole de Missiminia 1.* Paris: CNRS.

GAMMAI

Peter Lacovara

The site of Gammai is located fifteen miles south of Wadi Halfa on the east bank of the Nile, where a spur of the cliffs bordering the river juts out onto the floodplain. Here an expedition under the direction of Oric Bates and Dows Dunham discovered a series of cemeteries dating from the Prehistoric Period to the late Meroitic Period.

The Prehistoric and A-Group graves (Cem. 600) were badly plundered, while a New Kingdom cemetery (Cem. 500) and a large late Meroitic cemetery with large tumuli were better preserved. The burials in the latter contained jewelry similar to that found in the Meroitic south, along with some fairly impressive bronze vessels and containers. In the relatively dry conditions the preservation was excellent, and even the tassels from a Meroitic garment were preserved.

The site was excavated by the Harvard University–Museum of Fine Arts, Boston Expedition under the direction of Oric Bates and Dows Dunham in 1916, and the eventual publication of the expedition fell to Dunham after Bates's death in the 1918 influenza epidemic.

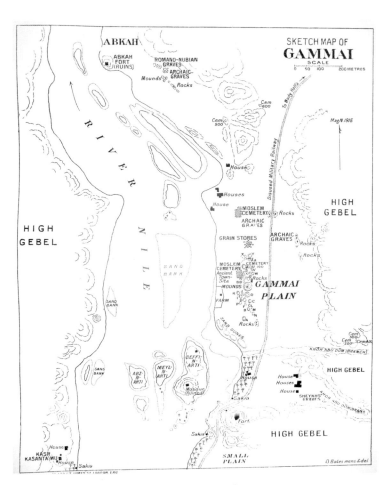

Figure 187. A plan of Gammai made in 1916 by Oric Bates and Dows Dunham.

Bibliography

Bates, O., and D. Dunham. 1927. *Excavations at Gammai.* Harvard African Studies 8, Varia Africana 4, 1–121. Cambridge, MA: Peabody Museum of Harvard University.

GEBEL SHEIKH SULEIMAN

Christian Knoblauch

The corpus of historical documents that attests to the activities of Egyptians in Nubia before the Old Kingdom is slim. By far the most elaborate and widely discussed of these is the major rock carving from Gebel Sheikh Suleiman (see illustration in "The History of Nubia"), a rocky outcrop that straddled the transition from the granite basal complex of the Second Cataract to the sandstone landscape of Lower Nubia. As an indication of the historical significance attributed to this Egyptian monument, the stone bearing the inscription was removed in advance of the flooding of Lower Nubia and now stands in the grounds of the National Museum in Khartoum.

The rock carving, in a combination of raised relief and incised outlines, was located on a sandstone block at the southern end of Gebel Sheikh Suleiman (fig. 11). It is a scene of domination that until very recently was more commonly known to archaeologists from early Egyptian ritual-ceremonial objects, including knife handles, mace heads, and palettes, than from 'rock art': the only parallel is a less carefully executed scene found at Gebel Tjauty in Upper Egypt. To the far left of the scene is a rectangular triple-niched façade of an early Egyptian palace (serekh). In the upper third

of the serekh there are three loosely organized rows of drilled circles that may depict architectural details of the façade. A rightward-facing falcon perches on the top of the serekh. In front of the serekh there is a standing figure. Its arms are pinned behind its back, possibly with the aid of fetters, which are depicted attached to the figure's hands. The suggestion that the fetters are in fact a bow—the hieroglyph sign for 'Ta Sety' ('Nubia')—can be neither proved nor disproved on the available evidence. In the center of the composition are three signs, in order from left to right: a body of water and two circular motifs, one of which is surmounted by a bird, the other by an oblong sign. The circular signs have been interpreted as the city hieroglyph and may be toponyms. To the far right of the scene is a boat. A half-kneeling figure is fastened to its prow by means of a thick rope. The small semicircular object superimposed on the upper edge of the rope has been taken to represent a hut. An arrow pierces the kneeling prisoner's chest. Four dead human figures lie, or perhaps better, float, in unnatural poses around the hull of the boat.

Identifying the theme of the relief is relatively straightforward. The scene contrasts symbols representing the political structure of the Egyptian

Nile Valley—the *serekh* and falcon, the boat—with images of lifeless or subjugated humans. It represents a victory of the representatives of an Egyptian political entity over its enemies. Further interpretation, however, is fraught with uncertainty, as neither the identity of the defeated enemy nor the scale or circumstance of the victory is clearly articulated. The Nubian context at least suggests a Nubian identity for the defeated, but this information by itself is not overly illuminating. Does it refer to a victory over a Nubian political unit (that is, a state, chiefdom, tribe, or village), a geographical unit (all of Nubia or just a part), or an entire Nubian culture (the A-Group or members of the Pre-Kerma Culture beyond the Second Cataract)? Was the armed confrontation and victory the incidental by-product of an armed trading mission; was it a razzia with limited short-term goals, or a large-scale invasion with long-term strategic objectives? Or on the other hand does the carving need to refer to an actual event at all? Could the act of carving in fact be the important event here, magically extending the limits of the Egyptian cosmos by engraving symbols and images in stone? There is no easy answer to these questions, and therefore some hesitancy should be applied when placing the inscription at the beginning of a normative, historical narrative of relations between the Egyptian state and Nubia. The situation is compounded by the elusive identity of the victor: the *serekh*, a symbol related to the Egyptian king, is anonymous, that is, it is not connected with a royal name. The chronological range for the use of anonymous *serekh*s is broad and spans the proto-dynastic Dynasty Zero and the first half of the First Dynasty. The earlier date could suggest the involvement of one of a number of contemporary early proto-states that shared political power in the Nile Valley. The later date suggests action undertaken by representatives of the king of the unified state. It is clear that how we understand the inscription is intrinsically bound up with how we date it.

The earlier date may be supported by a second rock inscription made a few feet away from the major relief. This relief depicts a half-kneeling captive attached by rope to a large scorpion. A figure, possibly holding a weapon, stands next to him. Another figure, holding a bow and arrow, is depicted upside-down nearby. The scene was identified by its discoverer as the record of an expedition by the Egyptian King Scorpion to the Second Cataract. As Scorpion is now assigned to Dynasty Zero, this would place it at the earlier end of the chronological range given to the major relief. The attribution of the inscription to King Scorpion has found some acceptance, although there are a number of reasons not to subscribe to this point of view without circumspection. These include the observation that the scorpion and the human figures appear to have been executed using different engraving techniques, other evidence for later (ancient) additions to the graffiti, and some peculiarities in the depiction of the scorpion. It is unfortunate that the graffiti is now lost and that these details cannot be checked against the original.

Bibliography

Arkell, A.J. 1950. "Varia Sudanica." *JEA* 36:24–40.

Köhler, E.C. 2002. "History or Ideology? New Reflections on the Narmer Palette and the Nature of Foreign Relations in Pre- and Early Dynastic Egypt." In E.C.M. van den Brink and T.E. Levy, eds., *Egypt and the Levant: Interrelations from the 4th through the Early 3rd Millennium BCE*. London and New York: Leicester University Press.

Murnane, W.J. 1987. "Appendix C. The Gebel Sheikh Suleiman Monument: Epigraphic Remarks." In B. Williams and T. Logan, "The Metropolitan Museum Knife Handle and Aspects of Pharaonic Imagery before Narmer." *JNES* 46, no. 3: 245–85.

Needler, W. 1967. "A Rock-drawing on Gebel Sheikh Suleiman (near Wadi-Halfa) Showing a Scorpion and Human Figures." *JARCE* 6:87–91.

Second Cataract Forts

Bruce Williams

Fortresses and their destruction held a place in Egyptian symbolic culture from earliest times, and the Egyptians repeatedly cited their importance to state security in literature and representations. In the late Middle Kingdom, the Egyptians built at their southern frontier the largest complex of fortresses that survived to modern times from the pre-Roman ancient world. Early in the career of Nubian archaeology, they were excavated, and some were re-explored during the great salvage of Nubian antiquities in the 1960s. Only two remain today, Shalfak and Uronarti, which stood on commanding heights.

While the fortresses distributed from Aswan to Buhen by the early and middle Twelfth Dynasty would have served to protect mining and quarrying expeditions, control the local population, and function as bases for patrols, they were not a dense complex. In the reign of Senwosret III, events occurred that triggered the construction of a much-enhanced and truly systematic complex of fortresses at the southern end of Lower Nubia, extending from Serra East and Faras in the north to Semna South. Their size, close proximity to each other, and the relatively small number of inhabitants nearby are strong indications that they were built to confront a

powerful and well-organized enemy. Straddling the difficult rapids of the cataract, they took advantage of the river traffic's vulnerability to serve as something stronger than a tripwire to invading forces. They were both a formidable block and a forward base for campaigns to the south.

The roots of this complex may be seen in three factors. First, the rapid consolidation of a rigorous bureaucratic regime in Egypt produced absconders in abundance who had to be prevented from leaving. Second, Senwosret III felt the need to campaign in Asia personally, with negative results, indicating a new military vulnerability, and third, Kush to the south was rapidly rising to the status of a power. Kush may already have acted against Egypt, although no event is recorded, but such action would go far to explain Senwosret's campaigns and the huge scale of the forts.

In Nubia, the chief enemy was Kush. With its greatest capital just south of the Third Cataract, it already extended its power or influence as far upstream as the Fifth Cataract and downstream almost to the Semna Gate. Senwosret III campaigned against Kush repeatedly, but still had to build his enormous complex. At Semna, which came to be the headquarters of the fortification system as well as the boundary, he erected stelae

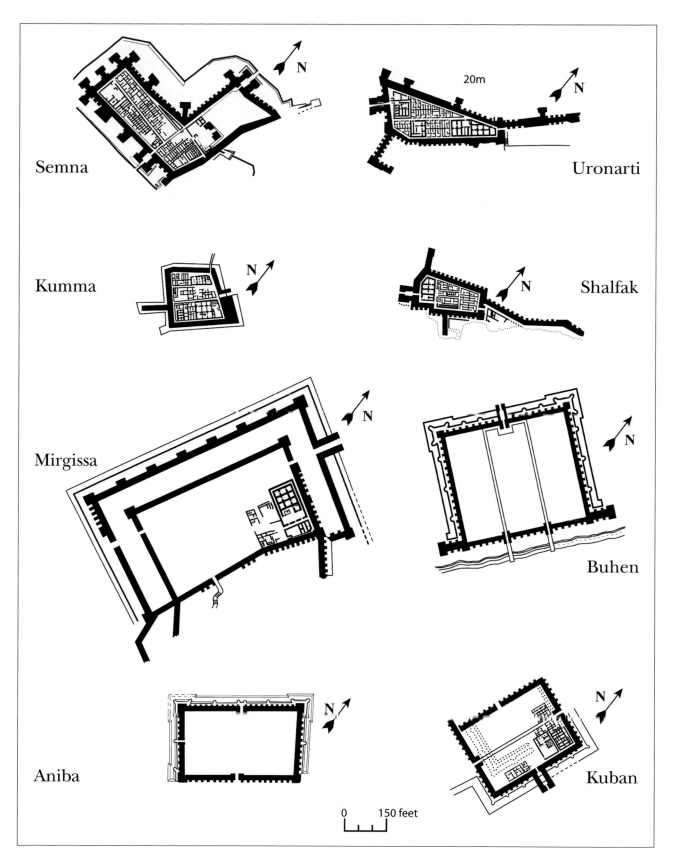

Semna

Uronarti

20m

Kumma

Shalfak

Mirgissa

Buhen

Aniba

Kuban

0   150 feet

Figure 188. Plans of Second Cataract forts.

recording his victories and setting forth his frontier policy that no one from the south could pass by except to trade. The events in Nubia were apparently part of a wider strategy, which unfolded during the Twelfth Dynasty, that saw the suppression of powerful nomarch magnates in Middle Egypt, the erection of a detailed bureaucratic administration, and inconclusive campaigning in Western Asia. Senwosret rebuilt the older forts and established a new fortification complex in the area of the frontier, with its apex at Semna, where the Nile is confined into a narrow chasm. The complex was the most elaborate known before the Romans; only the numerous forts built by the Ottoman government at the Third Cataract were comparable in Nubia. The Second Cataract fortification system was the greatest secular construction that survived from the ancient Nile. It was a remarkable feat of military planning, sophisticated architecture, and engineering. The effort easily surpassed that required to build the pyramid complexes of the day. The fortress system and its ancillary patrols were maintained and regulated with an attention to detail that appears remarkably modern. The older fortresses were enhanced, and those near the frontier, Buhen and the fortified center at Kor, were greatly expanded and incorporated into the new complex.

The most forward area was the region of Heh. The forts there included Kumma (ancient Itnuw-Pdjut) on the east bank, Semna (Sekhem-Khakaure Ma'-kheru, opposite, about six hundred meters away) and Semna South (Dair-Sety) on the west side of the river, as well as the island fortress to the north, Uronarti (Khesef-Iunuw), which had a palace complex nearby. A low wall ran between the two west-bank fortresses that isolated an area that might have been used to beach vessels. Semna and Kumma were sited on the large granite outcrop of the Semna Cataract, over which flowed the Nile.

From Semna to the rapids of the Batn al-Hagar (Belly of Stones) is about forty kilometers, in a direct line. The distance was secured by two fortresses, Shalfak (Wa'f-Khasut) on the west bank, and Askut (Djer-Sety), on an island somewhat to the north. The large fortress of Mirgissa (Iken) was located at the upstream end of the braided channels of the cataract, which were impassable to shipping at low water. The rapids were bypassed by a timber-framed, mud-paved slipway, which ran in a straight line at least two and possibly several kilometers, rejoining the Nile above the prominent *gebel* (see glossary) of Abusir. Nile boats were dragged on it, perhaps on runners, although a much later scene from the tomb of Tutankhamun's viceroy Huy shows only mud against the ship, and the towing. The great, fortified center of Kor (ancient name unknown) lay just beyond, on the west bank. This was greatly expanded, with elaborate fortifications and official complexes. North of Kor was Buhen (ancient Buhen), which was given a great outer enclosure and superbly planned inner fortifications that make it the most famous of Egyptian fortresses. The most northerly were two smaller fortresses, at Faras West (Ink-tawy), and Serra East (Khesef-Medjay), not far from Buhen.

Most of the Second Cataract forts were rectangular, with one wall fronting the Nile at Kumma, Semna South, Mirgissa, Buhen, Faras, and Serra East. Semna, built on the rock of the west bank, was L-shaped, while Uronarti, Askut, and Shalfak were roughly triangular. In size, they ranged from about fifty by fifty meters (Kumma, Semna South) to about two hundred by two hundred meters (Buhen), and the great outer wall at Buhen enclosed some seven hundred by 250–300 meters.

The fortresses were constructed in well-defined phases. The space for the fort was leveled to bedrock, where possible. Masons cut a ditch with sloping sides and a flat bottom into the rock, to surround the fort. If the ditch continued into alluvium, it was lined with stone masonry, or even brick. On this prepared foundation, the work crews constructed the walls and buildings of the fortress.

The first construction was probably the great curtain wall, since that was the most massive part of the structure. This was located some two meters or more from the edge of the ditch. At Serra, the curtain rested on a shallow layer of sand laid on the subsurface, and the crew constructed it in sections, leaving vertical seams between. The main construction consisted of alternating brick headers and stretchers about five meters (or more) thick. Thick mats of local halfa grass were laid at intervals, especially in the lower courses, where the wall was thickest. At Askut, Shalfak, Semna, Kumma, Uronarti, and Serra East, all forts on rocky hills or bluffs, the brick was reinforced, sometimes heavily, with timber, including both longitudinal and transverse beams. Mirgissa, on the other hand, had only transverse logs. Rectangular piers some two meters deep by three meters broad rested against the outer face. Often, the piers had mud plaster, making sloping lower faces; piers were much broader at the corners. In some cases, such as Mirgissa, the walls had flat pier-like bastions. Most of the forts were also equipped with spur-walls or towers connected to the main wall only by a passage on the wall parapet. These were used to occupy commanding ground that could not be effectively enclosed; at Uronarti and Askut, the spur-walls were long and elaborate. The great permanent gates were protected by a pair of barbicans (towers), one on either side. Other gates had smaller spurs, but some small gates were simply breaks in the wall, presumably just stopped up during a siege. Outside the curtain, the surface was paved, and at the edge of the ditch was a low brick wall, which could be simple, as at Serra, or very complex, as at Buhen, where the outer wall

of the citadel had convex bastions, shield-shaped crenellations, and loopholes arranged to let an archer loose arrows in several directions. Buhen also had a simple wall outside the ditch, which may have served to keep animals from falling. The outer works of fortresses without direct access to the river was completed with a covered stair leading to the river.

The interiors of the forts were planned to use space carefully. Buildings were substantial, and had only narrow streets between them, and the walls were lined with even narrower passageways. At Buhen, streets had covered drains, while channels were used at Serra East. Open squares were few and small. Plans were rectilinear, and when the shape of the fort was not rectangular, the buildings were rectilinear facing the streets, but shaped to fit the inside of the wall behind. Where possible, the fortresses were leveled, but when they were on sloping ground, the rock was terraced, and the buildings were sometimes partly rock-cut, while the streets could have rock-cut steps.

Buildings included some kind of headquarters, granaries, and magazines, but some other structures seem to have been residential. Lacking the evidence of second stories, the interior arrangements are partly conjectural.

Also conjectural is much of the activity that took place. We know that in addition to normal military duties, there was some manufacturing, such as shields and spears. Egyptian ordinary pottery was manufactured locally at Mirgissa and Serra East, and in the case of the latter, even inside the fort, although perhaps late in its career.

Most, probably all, forts contained one other structure that remains unexplained. This is a circular basin sloped to a sunken pot or round depression in the center. Draining into the basin are four rectangular slabs, each sloped to a channel.

Small stone-lined rectangular pits existed at a number of forts. Serra East contained a large, roughly rectangular basin, approximately twenty by thirty meters. The walls of irregular stones were sloped very much like an outer ditch and had a smooth, sloping surface of mud brick, which continued over the parapet. The eastern side against the rock was not preserved, and its bottom was below ground water. A stone ramp leads downward along the south and east sides, and it had some simple graffiti. No entry existed on the west side, so it was not a harbor, as once thought, but no other use for this basin is obvious. It was certainly important to the fortress, for it occupies the center; it may have been used to confine captives.

Semna and Semna South were connected by a simple wall, and Mirgissa was located at one end of the slipway, but there were other outbuildings also. North of the fortress was situated a walled town with harbor facilities, apparently the port, Iken, where Nubians who came from the south were allowed to trade. A village of houses constructed of mixed stones and mud had pottery kilns nearby. The island fortresses, Uronarti and Askut, had dwellings, magazines, and even official buildings located close to the walls, and some buildings could be found at a distance. Buhen, on the other hand, had great outer fortifications with ditches, curved bastions, and gate stuctures, but few interior buildings. This would serve as a refuge in times of disturbance. The simpler, non-fortified enclosure walls were probably for staging areas. The smaller and more exposed fortresses, on the other hand, do not appear to have had outbuildings.

In design, appearance, and equipment, the fortresses project a significant military purpose, to stand against a siege by an effective and skilled force. They represented a major commitment of resources, not only large construction crews, but large amounts of scarce timber. The walls alone were small mountains of brick; Serra's alone con-

tained some fifteen thousand cubic meters. The dry ditches would obstruct mining and the piling of combustibles against the walls, and they would keep ladders and siege shelters at a distance. These were used in the earlier Middle Kingdom to protect sappers armed with long, metal-tipped poles that could jab hand- and footholds in the walls for the besieging army to mount an assault. The surviving symbolic documents, essentially stelae, present rules for governing the border, and remaining documents of daily life enhance the picture of the fortresses as securing a frontier of danger, against the infiltration of Medjayu from the desert and assault from the rising power in the south, Kush.

Fragments of dispatches, accounts, and memoranda reveal a detailed administration in the forts, entirely consistent with bodies of documents from contemporary official sites in Egypt. Most revealing are the sealings found in almost all the forts, often in great numbers: sealed documents, chests, bags, and sometimes pots. Especially important are large seals for door bolts. These identify the main offices of the fortress, the fortress itself, the granary, treasury, and sometimes an entity called the Upper Fort, possibly the headquarters. The office seals were shield-shaped stamps impressed on dome-shaped or semi-conical lumps pressed over the bolt and a cord that tied it. The office seal was then counter-stamped with the personal seal, normally a scarab, of the officer on duty. Most of the seals have no names, an audit trail established by conical sample sealings kept on a string for reference. Where named, the officers were of low or moderate rank, mostly *shemsu* (retainer, possibly captain). Where a seal impression of a high-ranking official such as the vizier appears, it is from a document, presumably sent to the fort from one of the capitals; royal document seals are also rare, but were found in several of the fortresses.

On a stela set up at Semna, Senwosret III gave a general order for the southern frontier forts. No Nehesy (valley Nubian) was to pass by on land or on the river, except to trade at Iken (Mirgissa). They might be fed, and every good thing done for them, but they had to return. A rigorous program of patrolling was established to enforce this order, and one of the most vivid records from ancient Egypt describes its details. This papyrus, made in the reign of Amenemhat III or slightly later, was a collection of eight dispatches that were sent to Semna fortress and copied before forwarding to the office of the vizier at Thebes. These 'Semna Dispatches' describe measures taken to enforce the general order, both against the Nehesyu and against the Medjayu. The somewhat fragmentary reports of contacts are presented in a professional style familiar in modern military and police organizations. They include the source of the report (Egyptians are named, with descriptions of the forces), persons encountered, their stated purpose, date and time, and action taken, signed by the reporting officer, with persons who received copies indicated, where appropriate.

Most of the contacts consisted of small parties (up to nine persons) of Nehesy Nubians, including women, who arrived at Semna to trade. After trading their unspecified goods, they returned southward by river the next morning. Three

dispatches reported contacts with the Medjayu. Once, a patrol from Iken (Mirgissa) of seventy(?) Medjay soldiers and two Egyptian officers apprehended three men and three women and questioned them. In the second, the track of thirty-two men and three donkeys was found by a patrol from Khesef-Medjay (Serra East). Finally, a party of Medjayu who volunteered for Egyptian service was intercepted near Elephantine. Although they claimed that the desert was "dying of hunger," they were dismissed to the desert. Apart from the

Figure 189. Drawing of the reconstructed gate at Buhen.

difference in treatment (the Nehesyu were rigorously excluded but carefully handled; the Medjayu were interrogated, but also sometimes employed in the Egyptian forces), the dispatches reveal a policy of complete border control and careful reporting of all contacts, which contrasts with the relatively free access depicted in the tomb-chapels of Middle Egypt less than a century earlier. Despite such events as a visit to Thebes by the Medjay ruler of Webat-Sepet, Lower Nubia and Egypt were to be isolated from dangerous incursion and infiltration by a barrier of mud-brick walls, aggressive patrols, and rigorous administrators.

Tombs and monuments of Egyptian officials and residents become common at some of the forts, especially Buhen, by the later eighteenth century BC. Other forts show signs of rather haphazard internal alterations, which reinforce the impression that the soldiers of the garrisons were becoming settlers, and an Egyptian village was built at Askut. Somewhat later, people from the Eastern Desert left tombs and small cemeteries of Pan Graves in Nubia and Upper Egypt, which show that the frontier no longer held back the Medjayu. Later, probably in the seventeenth century BC, the fortress populations fell under the rule of the rising ruler of Kush. One ruler was recognized as pharaonic overlord by an Egyptian commandant of Buhen. At Wadi al-Sebua on the east bank, Nubians themselves constructed a fort. This fort was a roughly circular fieldstone enclosure whose west side was the edge of the cliff. Equipped with loopholes and three low, narrow gates, one fortified, the entire structure was filled with huts and pens.

Some time after the Middle Kingdom, most of the fortresses were destroyed or damaged by fire. There is little stratigraphy to prove the date, but the smooth social transformation to Kushite rule makes it unlikely that the fires occurred when Lower Nubia came under Kushite rule. Rather, it is more probable that the forts were destroyed by the resurgent New Kingdom rulers, who followed a new policy in Nubia, by conquering at least as far as the Fourth Cataract. Because the New Kingdom expanded so far upstream, the Second Cataract forts became irrelevant militarily. Some became the sites of temples.

During the Napatan, Saite, and Persian Periods (ca. 722–332 BC), the frontier in Lower Nubia was again fortified. Kushite Taharqo built a temple and probably a fort on the rock of Ibrim, and about the same time or later, fortresses on the island of Dorginarti and the rocky hill of Gebel Sahaba were constructed at the Second Cataract. Little remained at Sahaba, which may not have been finished, but it probably closely paralleled Dorginarti's plan. Dorginarti had an elongated plan some one hundred by thirty meters, with an administrative complex or commandant's residence on a low terrace with grain-storage magazines and a village-like complex of small houses against the wall to the south, inside the main gate. Dorginarti was frequently repaired and suffered some water damage, but it continued to be in use during the Persian Period. It is not clear whether the three forts of this period belonged to the rulers of Egypt or Kush; they may have changed hands or even have belonged to semi-independent magnates for a time.

The complexes of fortifications built by Middle Kingdom Egypt in Nubia were unique. No other northern power has since invested so heavily in fortifying a Nubian frontier, and this testifies to the strength of the threat the Egyptians perceived.

Bibliography

Dunham, D. 1967. *Second Cataract Forts.* Vol. 2: *Uronarti Shalfak Mirgissa.* Boston: Museum of Fine Arts.

Dunham, D., and J. Janssen. 1960. *Second Cataract Forts.* Vol. 1: *Semna Kumma.* Boston: Museum of Fine Arts.

Emery, W.B., H.S. Smith, and A. Millard. 1979. *Excavations at Buhen.* Vol. 1: *The Fortress of Buhen: The Archaeological Report.* Egypt Exploration Society Memoir 49. London: Egypt Exploration Society.

Firth, C.M. 1912. *The Archaeological Survey of Nubia: Report for 1908–1909.* Cairo: Government Press.

Knudstad, J. 1966. "Serra East and Dorginarti: A Preliminary Report on the 1963–64 Excavations of the University of Chicago Oriental Institute Sudan Expedition." *Kush* 14:165–86.

Monnier, Frank. 2010. *Les forteresses égyptiennes du Prédynastique au Nouvel Empire.* Connaissance de l'Égypte ancienne, no. 11. Brussels: Éditions Safran.

Smith, H.S. 1976. *Excavations at Buhen.* Vol. 2: *The Fortress of Buhen: The Inscriptions.* Egypt Exploration Society Memoir 48. London: Egypt Exploration Society.

Smith, S.T. 1990. "Administration at the Egyptian Middle Kingdom Frontier: Sealings from Uronarti and Askut." In T.G. Palaima, ed., *Aegean Seals, Sealings and Administration: Proceedings of the NEH-Dickson Conference of the Program in Aegean Scripts and Prehistory of the Department of Classics, University of Texas at Austin, January 11–13, 1989,* 197–216. Aegaeum 5 (Annales d'archéologie égéenne de l'Université de Liège).

———. 1991. "Askut and the Role of the Second Cataract Forts." *JARCE* 28:107–32.

———. 2002. *Askut in Nubia: The Economics and Ideology of Egyptian Imperialism in the Second Millenium B.C.* London: Kegan Paul.

Smither, P.C. 1945. "The Semnah Dispatches." *JEA* 31:3–10.

Steindorff, G. 1937. *Aniba.* Vol. 2. Glückstadt, Hamburg, and New York: J.J. Augustin.

Vercoutter, J. 1970. *Mirgissa I.* With the collaboration of H. Elhai, A. Hesse, C. Karlin, J. Maley, and A. Vila. Mission archéologique française au Soudan sous la direction de Jean Vercoutter 1. Paris: Direction Général des Relations Culturelles, Scientifiques et Techniques, Ministère des Affaires Étrangères, with the Centre National de la Recherche Scientifique.

Vogel, Karola. 2004. *Ägyptische Festungen und Garnisonen bis zum Ende des mittleren Reiches.* Hildesheimer ägyptologische Beiträge 46. Hildesheim: Gerstenberg Verlag.

———. 2010. *The Fortifications of Ancient Egypt.* Oxford: Osprey Publishing.

Williams, B. 1999. "Serra East and the Mission of Middle Kingdom Fortresses in Nubia." In E. Teeter and J. Larson, eds., *Gold of Praise: Studies on Ancient Egypt in Honor of Edward F. Wente,* 435–53. SAOC 58. Chicago: Oriental Institute of the University of Chicago.

Žabkar, L.V., and J.J. Žabkar. 1982. "Semna South: A Preliminary Report on the 1966–68 Excavations of the University of Chicago Oriental Institute Expedition to Sudanese Nubia." *JARCE* 19:7–50.

Zibelius-Chen, K. 1988. *Die ägyptische Expansion nach Nubien: Eine Darlegung der Grundfaktoren.* Beihefte zum Tübinger Atlas des Vorderen Orients, Series B, No. 78. Wiesbaden: L. Reichert Verlag.

THE C-GROUP
IN LOWER NUBIA

Claudia Näser

The prehistoric and early historic cultural groups of the Lower Nubian Nile Valley are peculiar historically as well as in their scientific exploration. Lower Nubia, the region between the First Nile Cataract, traditionally Egypt's southern border, and the rugged area south of the Second Cataract, is today entirely submerged under the waters of Lake Nasser. From 1907 onward, this four-hundred-kilometer stretch was systematically investigated in three extensive archaeological surveys, each of which preceded a new heightening of the Aswan Dam. Together they make Lower Nubia one of the archaeologically most thoroughly explored areas worldwide. At the same time, all research is now confined to the records of these salvage campaigns, with all their biases and limitations. For example, excavation work then focused almost entirely on cemeteries, leaving us with a very poor understanding of associated settlement activities. However, with great ingenuity, the head of the First Archaeological Survey of Lower Nubia, Egyptologist George Andrew Reisner, established already in 1910 a local cultural sequence from late prehistory to late antique times. Using letters to indicate chronological positions, he identified A-, B-, C- and X-Groups.

Around 3000 BC, the A-Group flourished in Lower Nubia. But as the pharaonic state emerged in the north, it fell into decline and around 2800 BC fades from the archaeological record. The B-Group, which according to Reisner filled the succeeding gap, was later revealed by H.S. Smith to be nonexistent: it had been made up from mediocre A- and C-Group material. The actual evidence for this period remains equivocal. While the archaeological record—or rather the absence thereof—suggests that the region was widely depopulated or frequented by a highly mobile population, which left few material traces, textual sources from Egypt report campaigns with large spoils of humans and livestock.

The next problematic point is the emergence of the C-Group. Almost abruptly, its well-defined cultural repertoire appears in Lower Nubia in the later third millennium BC—the exact dating is still debated, due to the lack of C-14 dates and other reliable dating tools. Also, the question of its origin has not yet been resolved. While it has been suggested that the early C-Group people are returnees of the former A-Group from Upper Nubia, others maintain that they represent the latest emigrants from the drying-up Eastern Sahara. A final decision is hampered by the fact that most of the distinct cultural elements of the early C-Group seem to have developed only in Lower Nubia—at least in their supposed regions of origin, few traits of them have been found.

The archaeological definition of the C-Group primarily rests on the funerary record. While about ninety of its cemeteries were investigated in Lower Nubia, not more than ten settlement sites have been excavated. With over 1,100 burials, Cemetery N at Aniba, in southern Lower Nubia, is the largest C-Group burial ground. As is usual with the C-Group, its superstructures are modest sand-filled stone rings, which cover simple grave pits with generally single inhumations. The dead were placed in a flexed position. Grave goods are generally limited to some jewelry, bronze mirrors, and shells containing cosmetics. At the superstructures, ceramic vessels, which may originally have contained nourishment, were deposited. One characteristic of the C-Group is bowls with a specifically rich incised decoration. A further hallmark of the early C-Group is tall sandstone stelae, which were erected without obvious reference to a specific grave. Beyond Aniba, their occurrence is limited to a few other large cemeteries at the exit of Wadi al-Allaqi in central Lower Nubia and the plain of Faras, south of Aniba. Obviously, these three locations were centers of the early C-Group. This assumption accords well with their specific agricultural potential, which attracted and supported larger population groups also in later times—as is witnessed by the concentration and the size of burial grounds from all subsequent periods of Nubian history there.

At the end of the third millennium BC, the pharaonic state conquered Lower Nubia and secured the region with a chain of monumental fortresses. Virtually in their shadow, the C-Group people continued their lives. With no accounts of direct conflicts, a widely peaceful coexistence is assumed, but, interestingly, the number of Egyptian objects in C-Group graves decreases in this period, suggesting a limited exchange between fortresses and plains. Egyptian influences were, however, adopted in other areas, for example, in the grave architecture. But most noteworthy are two introductions into the C-Group burial assemblages, namely small handmade jars with sketchily incised decoration of ornaments, but also cattle, herdsmen, birds, and women, and

Figure 190. Grave superstructures and stelae of the early C-Group.

small pottery figurines of cattle, other domestic animals, and women. With them, not a ready-made object group, but a cultural technique—figured representation—is adopted and adapted to implement native/indigenous funerary concepts. Both object types, decorated jars and figurines, also form a key to the ideational world of the C-Group people. In making cattle a central topic of their culture, they resemble some of the recent East African pastoralist societies, such as the Nuer, Dinka, or Massai. In these societies, cattle are a focus of social communication and religious life, and the central form of material and ideational capital. It has been argued that such a way of social discourse is only possible in small-scale societies with much face-to-face contact and limited status positions. This is corroborated by the archaeological record of the C-Group. Its funerary material for the most part lacks status differentiation, and all known C-Group settlements are very small, without elite architecture or religious or administrative installations. On that basis, the C-Group has been characterized as a small, widely egalitarian society, which lived on animal husbandry and agriculture within the narrow ecological confines of the Lower Nubian river valley.

As for the historical trajectory: when around 1750 BC the central power in Egypt again collapsed, the Egyptian control over Lower Nubia also broke down. The succeeding two hundred years were the heyday of the C-Group. For the first time, status differences appear in the archaeological record. In Cemetery Aniba N, stone-ring superstructures with diameters of up to sixteen meters were constructed, some of them with rectangular cult chapels of mud bricks attached. Also the hilltop settlement of Wadi al-Sebua in central Lower Nubia, which features a fortification wall equipped with loopholes, has been cited as evidence of growing complexity and hierarchization among the C-Group. A closer look, however, shows that it comprised not more than about fifteen units, without any internal differentiation. Still, its fortification hints at political insecurities and a new potential of the C-Group people to confront them.

Another sudden turn came about 1550 BC, when Egypt, after reestablishing the country's

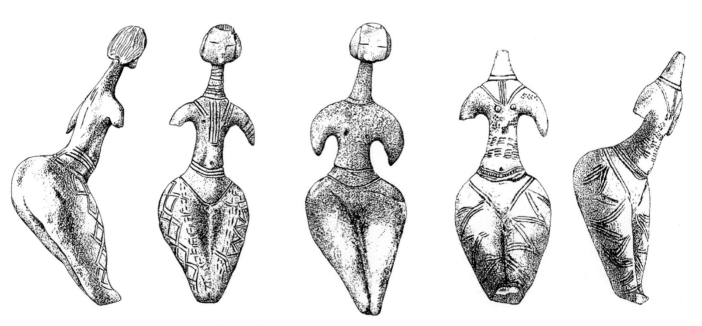

Figure 191. Female statuettes from Aniba Cemetery N.

Figure 192. Monumental stone-ring superstructures and chapels of the late C-Group.

unity, also reconquered Nubia, this time pushing forward much farther south. In the sequel, the C-Group entered a process of acculturation. While its typical cultural elements faded from the archaeological record, population numbers seem to have gone down. When Egyptian control over Lower Nubia once more ceased about 1070 BC, the region seems to have been widely depopulated—a situation very similar to that at the end of the A-Group, more than a thousand years earlier.

All in all, the C-Group is a parade example for the dynamics of early cultures. Favorable conditions triggered its quick social consolidation and the formation of a highly distinct cultural repertoire. Interferences of the Egyptian state strongly affected this trajectory, while the times of crisis of this otherwise overpowering neighbor permitted further internal development and prosperity. The mechanisms and specifics of these dynamics are, however, not nearly satisfactorily explored—as is shown, for example, in the uncertainties surrounding the ascent and the disappearance of the C-Group—leaving much scope for future research.

Bibliography

Adams, W.Y. 1977. *Nubia, Corridor to Africa.* London: Allen Lane, Penguin Books Ltd.

Bietak, M. 1968. *Studien zur Chronologie der nubischen C-Gruppe: Ein Beitrag zur Frühgeschichte Unternubiens zwischen 2200 und 1550 vor Chr.* Berichte des Österreichischen Nationalkomitees der UNESCO-Aktion für die Rettung der Nubischen Altertümer 5. Österreichische Akademie der Wissenschaften, Philosophisch-Historische Klasse, Denkschriften 97, Wien: Hermann Böhlaus Nachfolger.

Glück, B. 2005. "Zur Frage der Datierung der frühen C-Gruppe in Unternubien." *Ägypten und Levante* 15:131–51.

Hafsaas, H. 2006. *Cattle Pastoralists in a Multicultural Setting: The C-Group People in Lower Nubia 2500–1500 BCE.* The Lower Jordan River Basin Programme Publications 10. Bergen: Center for Development Studies, University of Bergen.

Näser, C. In press. "Structures and Realities of Egyptian-Nubian Interactions from the late Old Kingdom to the Early New Kingdom." In S.J. Seidlmayer, D. Raue, and P. Speiser, eds., *The First Cataract: One Region—Various Perspectives: Proceedings of an International Workshop, 3–5 September 2007, Berlin.* Berlin.

Reisner, G.A. 1910. *The Archaeological Survey of Nubia: Report for 1907–1908.* Vol. 1.1. Cairo: National Printing Department.

Sauneron, S. 1965. "Un village nubien fortifié sur la rive orientale de Ouadi es-Sébou." *BIFAO* 63:161–67.

Smith, H.S. 1966. "The Nubian B-Group." *Kush* 14:69–124.

Steindorff, G. 1935. *Aniba.* Vol. 1. Service des Antiquités de l'Égypte. Mission archéologique de Nubie 1929–1934. Glückstadt and Hamburg: J.J. Augustin.

Trigger, B.G. 1965. *History and Settlement in Lower Nubia.* Yale University Publications in Anthropology 69. New Haven, CT: Department of Anthropology, Yale University.

QUSTUL

Peter Lacovara

The site of Qustul is located fifty kilometers north of the Second Cataract, near Abu Simbel, on the eastern bank of the river adjacent to the site of Ballana. Although Shafik Farid and W.B. Emery briefly explored the site, it was not fully explored until the 1960s salvage campaign by an expedition from the Oriental Institute of the University of Chicago, under the direction of Keith C. Seele. In two seasons conducted between 1962 and 1964, a series of cemeteries was excavated ranging in date from the A-Group to the X-Group and given the letter designations: Q (New Kingdom), R (X-Group, Meroitic and New Kingdom), S (New Kingdom),

T (C-Group), U (C-Group), V (A-Group burials and possibly houses, and New Kingdom), W (New Kingdom and A-Group), J (X-Group and C-Group), K (C-Group), and L (A-Group 'royal' cemetery). Although all the cemeteries had been badly plundered in antiquity, they nonetheless provided a wealth of important artifacts.

The X-Group graves uncovered were clearly part of the same cemetery as the large tumuli discovered in the Second Nubian Survey at Ballana, and Seele pointed out that one could see an evolution of that cemetery from earlier Meroitic graves. Also in the same section of the necropolis were burials of the Second Intermediate Period

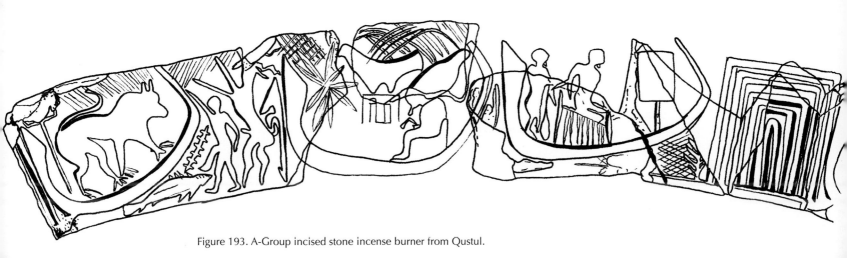

Figure 193. A-Group incised stone incense burner from Qustul.

352

through the New Kingdom, alongside two Classic Kerma tumuli with bed burials along with some Pan-Grave pottery.

The most important material of all unearthed were the large graves in cemetery L belonging to the Nubian A-Group. It has been suggested that the site was the capital of a proto-dynastic state in Lower Nubia. Previously it was thought that the A-Group was a simple, pastoral population of nomadic cattle and sheep and goat herders and hunters living in small villages.

However, the discovery of large, rich graves, some with emblems associated with later Egyptian royalty, suggests that this was the capital of a sophisticated early state with large, royal burial monuments. More importantly, these tombs dated to the Late Predynastic/Naqada III Period, suggesting that the A-Group kingdom was coeval with the emerging proto-states in the Hierakonpolis and Thinite regions in Egypt. Despite being extensively robbed, these tombs contained vast quantities of jewelry, eggshell ware vases, imported Egyptian pottery and stone vessels, and even imported Syro-Palestinian pots.

The results of the excavations were published in an exemplary way by Bruce Williams, and the Oriental Institute was presented with a generous division of the finds.

Bibliography

Farid, S. 1963. *Excavations at Ballana 1958–1959*. Cairo: General Organization for Government Printing Offices.

Seele, K.C. 1974. "University of Chicago Oriental Institute Nubian Expedition: Excavations between Abu Simbel and the Sudan Border, Preliminary Report." *JNES* 33, no. 1: 1–43.

Williams, B.B. 1984. *C-Group, Pan Grave, and Kerma Remains at Adindan: Cemeteries T, K, U, and J.* Excavations between Abu Simbel and the Sudan Frontier, Part 5. *OINE* 5. Chicago: Oriental Institute.

———. 1989. *Neolithic, A-Group, and Post A-Group Remains from Cemeteries W, V, Q, R, S, T and a Cave behind Cemetery K.* Excavations between Abu Simbel and the Sudan Frontier, Parts 2, 3, and 4. *OINE* 4. Chicago: Oriental Institute.

———. 1990. *Twenty-fifth Dynasty and Napatan Remains from Cemeteries W and V at Qustul.* Excavations between Abu Simbel and the Sudan Frontier, Part 7. *OINE* 7. Chicago: Oriental Institute.

———. 1991a. *Meroitic Remains from Qustul Cemetery Q, Ballana Cemetery B, and a Ballana Settlement.* Excavations between Abu Simbel and the Sudan Frontier, Part 8. *OINE* 8. Chicago: Oriental Institute.

———. 1991b. *Noubadian X-Group Remains from Royal Complexes in Cemeteries Q and 219 and from Private Cemeteries Q, R, V, and W, B, J, and M at Qustul and Ballana.* Excavations between Abu Simbel and the Sudan Frontier, Part 9. *OINE* 9. Chicago: Oriental Institute.

———. 1992. *New Kingdom Remains from Cemeteries R, V, S, and W at Qustul and Cemetery K at Adindan.* Excavations between Abu Simbel and the Sudan Frontier, Part 6. *OINE* 6. Chicago: Oriental Institute.

BALLANA

Peter Lacovara and Salima Ikram

Ballana was the site of an important cemetery in Lower Nubia, excavated by Walter Bryan Emery between 1928 and 1931 as part of the second Aswan Dam salvage campaign, and then again in 1958 and 1959 by Shafik Farid under the supervision of Selim Hassan. A total of 148 graves were explored (122 by Emery and 26 by Farid). The tombs' superstructures consisted of vast tumuli that were made of earth, sand, and dolorite pebbles, and the substructures consisted of one or several underground chambers lined with mud brick. Some tombs were found substantially intact, but even the robbed burials still proved to contain many of the original burial goods.

Dating to the time after the collapse of the Meroitic state but before the founding of the Christian Nubian kingdoms, these tombs belong to the post-Meroitic or X-Group culture, which flourished in Lower Nubia around AD 350 to 600.

The objects found in the graves are chiefly of Nubian origin, but there were also many items imported from Byzantine Egypt and the Mediterranean in general. Grave goods included ceramics, stone pestles, bronze lamps, metal vessels, and beads made of different materials. Horses, donkeys, and servants were buried with their masters.

There is very little textual information in the tombs, so the identification of the tomb owners escapes us. It has been suggested that these are the burials of the kings and the court of Nobadia. The kings were buried with all their finery and wore cylindrical crowns inlaid with jewels on their heads. Most remarkable are a set of crowns in silver and inlaid with garnets with the ram of Amun, ostrich plumes, *wedjat* eyes, and uraei that still bear witness to pharaonic traditions long gone in Egypt.

After a tomb was sealed, the passageway leading to the entrance was filled with slaughtered animals: horses, camels, donkeys, and dogs. The larger tombs contained up to seventeen human sacrifices. In some rooms, archaeologists found the remains of a queen and all her servants, who were apparently sacrificed when the king died.

One important tomb discovered here was tomb 118, which consisted of three chambers. It might be described as a classic example of a royal burial at Ballana and contained a main burial chamber and two storage rooms, one of which was filled with food and drink offerings, and the other with the deceased's tools and weapons. The roof of the burial chamber had collapsed and the

Figure 194. X-Group silver crown inlaid with garnets. Photo © Chester Higgins Jr 2012.

tomb, therefore, escaped looting. The body of the person buried here was found on a bier. It was most likely that of a king, as a crown was found upon his head. Under the bier were the remains of a large wooden gaming board, weapons, and a folding chair made of iron. The tomb also contained skeletons of a young male servant and a cow. In the two storerooms, more skeletons of servants, as well as pottery and several bronze lamps, were discovered.

Bibliography

Emery, W.B. 1948. *Nubian Treasure: An Account of the Discoveries at Ballana and Qustul*. London: Methuen and Co.

Farid, S. 1963. *Excavations at Ballana 1958–1959*. Cairo: General Organization for Government Printing Offices.

ABU SIMBEL

Marjorie M. Fisher

The two rock-cut temples of Abu Simbel were originally situated on the west bank of the Nile, 250 kilometers south of Aswan in Lower Nubia. The site was visited by numerous artists and scholars throughout the centuries—for example, Champollion, Belzoni, Roberts, Budge, Breasted, Weigall, Wreszinski, Wilkinson, Hay, Rifaud, and so on—due to its immense size and beauty. It was in 1813 that Johann Ludwig (John Lewis) Burckhardt first wrote about this site in the European historical literature. It has been excavated under the auspices of l'Institut français d'archéologie orientale. During the UNESCO campaign of 1966 to 1968, the two temples were moved to their present location within an artificial hill above the ancient site. Both temples were carved entirely out of the rock face.

Archaeologists have discovered prehistoric finds but no settlements of any period in the area. Artifacts from the A-Group, C-Group, Kerma Culture, and Pan-Grave groups are also prevalent. Votive cliff inscriptions dating to the Middle Kingdom and Eighteenth Dynasty are found nearby as well, and diorite quarries used by kings as early as the Old Kingdom are located northwest of the temples. Also found near the temples are numerous rock-cut votive stelae dating to the reign of Ramesses II and belonging to the viceroys Iuni, Hekanakht, Paser II, and Setau, as well as two sandstone statues of Viceroy Paser II and later material of Amenmesse, Sety II, Siptah, Ramesses IV, and Ramesses IX.

The two temples at Abu Simbel (the Great Temple of Ramesses II and the Small Temple of his wife Nefertari) seem to replicate the style of husband-and-wife temples that Amenhotep III had built for himself and his wife Tiye at Sedeinga. Such paired temples for king and queen were never duplicated later. The front entrance of the Great Temple at Abu Simbel displays sixty-five-foot-tall rock-cut statues of Ramesses II with figures of his children, wife, and mother situated by his legs. The children of Ramesses II are depicted throughout his temples in Nubia and beside his legs on monumental statues, as was also the case at Amenhotep III's Sedeinga temple, from which Ramesses II apparently copied this idea.

The Great Temple of Ramesses II is approached by an ascending terrace leading to the four large statues of Ramesses II, described above. Proceeding between the colossi into the temple, one enters the great hall. Abutting the two groups of four pillars facing each other are

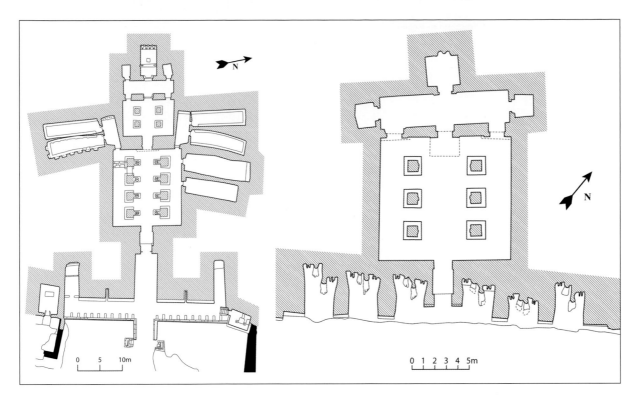

Figure 195. Plans of the Great Temple of Ramesses II and the Small Temple of Nefertari.

statues of Ramesses II in his ceremonial garb. Cultic reliefs cover the columns and other walls of this room. Next to the great hall are eight smaller chambers. Leading from the back of the great hall, a second hall continues into a vestibule connected to a sanctuary. Two minor rooms are also located off the vestibule. Throughout the temple, cultic reliefs portray Re-Horakhty and Amun-Re as well as the deified Ramesses II, all being worshiped by Ramesses II; it is interesting to note that Ramesses II is worshiping himself in the deified form. At the back of the temple, cut into the sanctuary, three gods are represented along with Ramesses II: Amun-Re, Re-Horakhty, and Ptah, creating a group of four figures (similar to those at Derr and Gerf Hussein, while Beit al-Wali had three figures) carved out of the rock face at the back of the sanctuaries). On February 21/22 and October 21/22, the light of the sun enters the temple and illuminates these statues at the back of the temple.

Attached to the terrace of the temple on either side are the north and south chapels. The north chapel, associated with the sun cult, is attached to an enclosure wall with a gate. The south chapel may have been a station for the sun barque, as indicated by reliefs showing the barque of Thoth and that of Re-Horakhty. Another suggests a birth house, but for what reason is unknown.

The Small Temple, dedicated to the goddess Hathor and attributed to the wife of Ramesses II, Nefertari, consists of three rooms: a hall with two sets of three Hathor pillars, a vestibule, and a sanctuary, with smaller rooms situated adjacent to the vestibule. On the façade, four sons of Nefertari are depicted next to the legs of the standing figures of Ramesses II: Amenherkhepeshef, Prehirwenemef, Meryatum, and Meryre. Two daughters of Nefertari are also shown near her legs: Merytamun and Henettawy.

Inside the temple, Nefertari is frequently portrayed with the goddess Hathor and sometimes represented as a 'chantress' carrying a sistrum in her hand, as on a plaque from Deir al-Bahari on the west bank of Thebes in Egypt. At Abu Simbel, she is mentioned with her frequent title, "Beloved of Mut," and associated with Hathor and Isis-Sothis. The goddess Isis appears only once, in association with Hathor. Amun-Re is represented infrequently, mainly on

Figure 196. Aerial view of the Great Temple at Abu Simbel in its original location, 1938.

Opposite: Figure 197. View of two statues of Ramesses II and the south wall in the great hall within the Great Temple of Abu Simbel. Photo © Chester Higgins Jr 2012.

when the battle of Kadesh occurred (see below), while Hein dates it to approximately regnal years 5–10 based upon: first, the early use of the writing of Ramesses II's name in the temple; second, the brevity of the procession of Ramesses' princes carved on the wall in the Great Hall, suggesting the king was too young to have very many sons; third, a stela of the viceroy Iuni, who lived during the early part of Ramesses' reign, carved adjacent to the temple; and fourth, a rock-cut stela of the viceroy Hekanakht, who held this position from approximately year 10 to year 24. Hein and Kitchen maintain that the Small Temple of Nefertari (who died around year 30) must have been dedicated while the queen was alive.

As in other Nubian temples, there are two styles of decoration: military and cultic. The military reliefs in the Great Temple, appearing in the first pillared hall, portray Ramesses II fighting his enemies. A large scene records the Battle of Kadesh in Lebanon/Syria, which was waged against the Hittites, on the north wall, and a fictitious campaign against Dapur, also in Syria, on the south wall. The former military relief takes up most of the wall and is not well preserved. Many parts of the relief are difficult to see clearly, and the paint has not survived. There are no military reliefs in the Small Temple of Nefertari.

The cultic reliefs on the Great Temple of Ramesses II focus on the three gods to whom the temple is dedicated: Amun-Re, Re-Horakhty, and Ptah, a trinity representing all aspects of the sun god. These gods are represented on the façade, in side chapels, and throughout the temple in reliefs. Amun-Re/Amun is seen in every room and on every side of the temple. Re-Horakhty and Re also appear throughout the temple complex. Hathor, the mother goddess, is depicted in the main part of the temple on the north wall, on columns on the south side of the Great Hall, and in two of the northern rooms. Isis, her sister, is

the west side of the temple, and Re-Horakhty and Ptah only on one wall. In the sanctuary is a statue of Hathor in cow form, in front of which is a smaller statue of a standing Ramesses II. This temple, dedicated to Hathor, was the last rock-cut temple built by Ramesses II dedicated to a local god. It was presumably built at the same time as the Great Temple.

Anthony Spalinger dates construction of these temples to before regnal year 5 of Ramesses II,

Figure 198. The Great Temple at Abu Simbel.

portrayed, but Osiris only appears in the main sanctuary and a northern side room. A number of other gods are also represented.

Two very interesting reliefs decorate the first pillared hall. In the first, Amun-Re comes forth from his mountain, and in the second, Ramesses II appears as a god but with ram's horns curled around his ears, a sign both of his deification and also of the syncretism between the Nubian cult of the ram god and that of Amun-Re. All the reliefs use Ramesses II's preferred palette of colors: red, black, and yellow.

Bibliography

El-Achirie, H., and J. Jacquet. 1984. *Le Grand Temple d'Abou-Simbel*. Vol. 1: *Architecture*. Cairo: CEDAE.

Bernard, E., and A. Aly. 1959. *Abou-Simbel: Inscriptions greques, carriennes et sémitiques des statues de la façade*. CEDAE 7.

Burckhardt, J.L. 1819. *Travels in Nubia*. London: Association for Promoting the Discovery of the Interior Parts of Africa.

Černy, J., and E. Edel. 1959. *Abou-Simbel: Décret de Ptah*. CEDAE 4.

Desroches-Noblecourt, C., and C. Kuentz. 1968. *Le petit temple d'Abou Simbel: Nofretari pour qui se leve le Dieu-Soleil*. CEDAE, Mémoires 1–2.

Fisher, M.M. 2001. *The Sons of Ramesses II*. 2 vols. ÄAT 53.

Gaballa, G.A., and M. Maher Taha. 2001. *Le Grand Temple d'Abou Simbel*. Vol. 1. Collection Documentaire 1. Cairo: Ministry of Culture, Supreme Council of Antiquities.

Gohary, J. 1998. *Guide to the Nubian Monuments on Lake Nasser*. Cairo: American University in Cairo Press.

Habachi, L. 1969a. *Features of the Deification of Ramesses II*. Glückstadt: J.J. Augustin.

———. L. 1969b. "Divinities Adored in the Area of Kalabsha, with Special Reference to the Goddess Miket." *MDAIK* 24:169–83.

Hein, I. 1991. *Die Ramessidische Bautätigkeit in Nubien*. GOF 4, Vol. 22.

Kitchen, K.A. 1982. *Pharaoh Triumphant: the Life and Times of Ramesses II*. Warminster, U.K.: Aris and Phillips.

Porter, B., and R.L.B. Moss. 1952. *Topographical Bibliography of Ancient Egyptian Hieroglyphic Texts, Reliefs and Paintings*. Vol. 7: *Nubia, the Deserts and Outside Egypt*, 95–119. Oxford: Griffith Institute.

Spalinger, A. 1980. "Historical Observations on the Military Reliefs of Abu Simbel and Other Ramesside Temples in Nubia." *JEA* 66:83–99.

ARMINNA WEST
AND ARMINNA EAST

Janice W. Yellin

The towns of Arminna West and Arminna East faced each other on the eastern and western banks of the Nile River, some ten miles north of Abu Simbel. The first scientific excavation of the towns, along with the nearby sites of Toshka East and West, was headed by Hermann Junker in 1911–12. This was followed by excavations in the 1930s by Walter B. Emery, L.P. Kirwan, and Ugo Monneret de Villard. The last excavations before the site was flooded by Lake Nasser were made in 1961–63 by the University of Pennsylvania Museum–Yale University Expedition, led by William Kelly Simpson as part of the Nubian Salvage Campaign. Despite all these different expeditions, the sites were never wholly excavated and documented.

The territory surrounding them was essentially arid. Arminna East, which was not too far from fertile lands, was settled by the New Kingdom and continued to be occupied through the Meroitic Period. However, Arminna West lay in a more barren area and was not settled until the Meroitic Period, when a new irrigation device was introduced into the region. Their populations were at their height during the Meroitic reoccupation of Nubia in the late second century AD. Based on a funerary-stela text, André Heyler

(cited in Trigger) has suggested that the Meroitic name of Arminna was Admen. William Y. Adams noted that, like many other Nubian Meroitic towns, residents lived in mud-brick houses so packed together and in no apparent pattern or plan that it is impossible to distinguish individual family units. According to him, the variety of its remains demonstrates that Arminna East had an economically and socially complex population who enjoyed a lively market that supported both local and distant trade.

Much of what is known about Arminna West during the Meroitic Period comes from excavations in Cemetery B, which was, following the Meroitic preference for placing cemeteries on elevated ground, on a nearby desert plateau. Dorian Fuller recognized that these burials demonstrate a pattern seen in other Meroitic Nubian cemeteries like Karanog. In them, the underlying clan structure of Meroitic sociopolitical organization is reflected by the range in the size and complexity of tombs belonging to family members of different status who were buried in family groupings. The most elaborate and high-status burials had rectangular stone superstructures with small chapels. The chapels had stone doorjambs, lintels, stelae, and offering tables that are decorated with mortuary texts as well as images of the deceased and/or gods, such as Anubis, making offerings.

Eleven whole or partial stelae and two offering tables, whose texts yielded information about the social organization and status of the elites, have been published by Bruce Trigger and André Heyler. They indicate that Amun of Luxor and Amun of Napata (Amenap) were worshiped at Arminna, as they were throughout Meroitic Nubia. Two stelae indicate that their owners were priests of the lion god Apedemak, a royal god who originated in the southern Butana region. Any reference to Apedemak is rare north of Meroe, and the presence of his priests at Arminna demonstrates a connection between their families and the royal family at Meroe. Other stelae reveal their owners' family connections to the royal governors who lived in more important Upper Nubian towns like Kara-

nog and Faras. Based on these family connections, Trigger believes that its elites controlled the northern area of Nubia for the central government at Meroe, explaining the establishment of Arminna West in the Meroitic Period and the prosperity of both sites during it. The distinctive and high quality of the offering-table and tomb decorations found with some of the pyramid burials indicates that there was enough wealth at Arminna to support the well-trained priests and artisans responsible for their manufacture.

Arminna West continued to be occupied through the Christian Period, although its population, which shrank over time, lived in a progressively poorer, simpler town. Arminna East, however, was abandoned at the end of the Meroitic Period, perhaps due to increased attacks by nomads like the Blemmyes from the Eastern Desert.

Bibliography

Adams, W.Y. 1977, repr. 1984. *Nubia: Corridor to Africa.* Princeton, NJ: Princeton University Press.

Fuller, D.Q. 1999. "A Parochial Perspective on the End of Meroe: Changes in Cemetery and Settlement at Arminna West." In D.A. Welsby, ed., *Recent Research in Kushite History and Archaeology: Proceedings of the Eighth International Conference for Meroitic Studies,* 203–17. London: British Museum Press.

———. 2003. "Pharaonic or Sudanic? Models for Meroitic Society and Change." In D. O'Connor and A. Reid, eds., *Ancient Egypt in Africa,* 169–84. London: University College London.

Simpson, W.K. 1963. *Heka-nefer and the Dynastic Material from Toshka and Arminna.* New Haven, CT and Philadelphia: Yale University Press.

Török, L. 1997. *The Kingdom of Kush: Handbook of the Napatan-Meroitic Civilization.* Leiden: Brill.

Trigger, B.G. 1965. *History and Settlement in Lower Nubia.* New Haven, CT: Yale University Press.

———. 1967. *The Late Nubian Settlement at Arminna West.* New Haven, CT and Philadelphia: Yale University Press.

———. 1970. *The Meroitic Funerary Inscriptions from Arminna West.* New Haven, CT and Philadelphia: Yale University Press.

———. 1976. *Nubia under the Pharaohs.* Boulder, CO: Westview Press.

———. 1996. "Toshka and Arminna in the New Kingdom." In P. Der Manuelian, ed., *Studies in Honor of William Kelly Simpson* 2, 801–10. Boston: Museum of Fine Arts.

Weeks, K.R. 1967. *The Classic Christian Townsite at Arminna West.* New Haven, CT: Yale Egyptological Seminar.

Zibelius-Chen, K. 1978. *Die ägyptische Expansion nach Nubien: Eine Darlegung der Grundfaktoren.* Wiesbaden: Reichert.

Toshka East and Toshka West

Janice W. Yellin

Like the nearby sites of Arminna East and West, Toshka East and West face each other across the Nile River. Along with Arminna, they were excavated by Hermann Junker in 1911–12 and by Walter B. Emery, Laurence P. Kirwan, and Ugo Monneret de Villard in the 1930s. The last excavations before the site was flooded by Lake Nasser were made in 1961–63 by the University of Pennsylvania Museum–Yale University Expedition led by William Kelly Simpson as part of the Nubian Salvage Campaign.

Although the eastern and western parts of Toshka are on arid land, nearby areas were suitable for agriculture. Prior to the Meroitic Period, as at Arminna East, Nubians at Toshka lived beside the Egyptians who first exploited and then controlled the region. Burials excavated by Emery and Kirwan testify to the presence of Nubian A-Group (Predynastic–Archaic Egypt), C-Group, and Medjayu peoples (Middle Kingdom Egypt). C-Group graves dating from the First Intermediate Period through the Second Intermediate Period, and a few dating to the New Kingdom, were found in several of its cemeteries. Bruce Trigger believed that the settlement of Toshka East owed this longevity to its location on the eastern bank of the Nile, with good access to the fertile areas a bit inland, making it a place where the pastoralists of the Eastern Desert, such as the Medjayu, and riverine settlers, such as the C-Group, interacted. The Nubian population continued to prosper at Toshka East until the end of the Second Intermediate Period, but by the New Kingdom there is no evidence for them, and Trigger proposed that the Nubians were pushed out of the area by Egyptian settlers. However, given the incomplete excavation of Toshka East, it is possible that evidence for a later Nubian presence was missed.

Toshka West may have owed its existence to its use as a debarkation point for Egyptian mining expeditions. Inscriptions found there indicate that in the Fourth and Fifth Dynasties, as well as the Middle and New Kingdoms, Egyptian kings had used the town as their staging point on the Nile for the exploitation of carnelian and diorite quarries in the western desert.

Based on the excavations' findings, Toshka East appears to have been more prosperous than Toshka West. In addition to its role as an access point for Eastern Desert pastoralists and trade, it may have been the birthplace of a powerful Nubian family. Of the three New Kingdom rock-cut tombs found there, the burial place of Hekanefer, the Prince of Miam (the Egyptian name for the area around Toshka and Arminna) is the most notable. Although he lived at Aniba, which was the administrative center of all Lower Nubia, Hekanefer chose to be buried at Toshka East, suggesting that this was his place of birth. He is among the Nubian dignitaries shown bringing tribute in the Theban tomb of Huy, the viceroy of Nubia under Tutankhamun. In his own tomb, Hekanefer depicts himself as an Egyptian, and he may have been among those children of the Nubian elite whom the Egyptians raised in their royal court as a way to assure their loyalty, before sending them back to their birthplaces to rule on Egypt's behalf. A decorated rock-cut shrine at the northern end of Toshka East—which may have been a Medjayu cult place since the Middle Kingdom—has an inscription invoking Horus, Lord of Miam; King Senwosret III (Twelfth Dynasty); and Reshep, a Canaanite god. According to this text, it was ordered by Hu-ma'y, the "Medjay of His Majesty" (=the pharaoh). Like the tomb of Hekanefer, this inscription speaks to the connection between Egyptians and Nubians, particularly the Medjayu, at Toshka East. The Medjayu people, who were buried in pan-shaped graves such as those found at Toshka, appear to have lived in some numbers there. Former foes of Egypt's incursions into Nubia during the Middle Kingdom, the Medjayu were pastoralists who watered their herds at the Nile. Trigger argues that by the end of the Third Intermediate Period, they appear to have aligned their fortunes with the New Kingdom rulers and were allowed to displace C-Group farmers in this area as a reward for helping the early-Eighteenth Dynasty rulers Ahmose and Kamose—whose names occur in an inscription at Toshka East—occupy Lower Nubia. The inscription from the rock shrine in which Hu-ma'y calls himself the "Medjay of His Majesty" is used to support this argument by Trigger, who also raises the possibility that Hekanefer was a Medjay. There is archaeological evidence that Toshka East was inhabited during Meroitic times, but like Arminna East, not after. Both sites, being on the eastern bank of the Nile, were open to attacks from Eastern Desert nomads such as the Blemmyes after the Meroitic state, which had protected them, ended. Toshka West, like Arminna West, continued into the Christian Period in a much reduced state.

Bibliography

Adams, W.Y. 1977, repr. 1984. *Nubia: Corridor to Africa.* Princeton, NJ: Princeton University Press.

Simpson, W.K. 1963. *Heka-nefer and the Dynastic Material from Toshka and Arminna.* New Haven, CT and Philadelphia: Yale University Press.

Trigger, B.G. 1965. *History and Settlement in Lower Nubia.* Yale University Publications in Anthropology 69. New Haven, CT: Department of Anthropology, Yale University.

———. 1967. *The Late Nubian Settlement at Arminna West.* New Haven, CT and Philadelphia: Yale University Press.

———. 1976. *Nubia under the Pharaohs.* Boulder, CO: Westview Press.

———. 1996. "Toshka and Arminna in the New Kingdom." In P. Der Manuelian, ed., *Studies in Honor of William Kelly Simpson* 2, 801–10. Boston: Museum of Fine Arts.

Zibelius-Chen, K. 1988. *Die ägyptische Expansion nach Nubien: Eine Darlegung der Grundfaktoren.* Wiesbaden: Reichert.

Qasr Ibrim

Pamela J. Rose

The fortress of Qasr Ibrim lies about two hundred kilometers south of Aswan on the east bank of the Nile, and was, before the building of the High Dam at Aswan and the creation of Lake Nasser, located on a cliff top some sixty meters above the river. From that position, it was able to control both traffic on the river and routes through the Eastern Desert. Throughout its three-thousand-year history, it served as a fortified stronghold and as a major religious and administrative center in pagan and Christian times. The length of occupation and the excellent preservation of organic materials resulting from the dry Nubian climate have provided a wealth of information about the history of Qasr Ibrim, and unique information on the daily life of the inhabitants of the fortress through time.

At its maximum extent, the fortress covered an area of about 160 by 240 meters. With the flooding of Lake Nasser, Qasr Ibrim became an island, and the lowest-lying parts of the fortress were lost. Qasr Ibrim has been excavated by the Egypt Exploration Society since 1963, and the surrounding cemeteries, now flooded, were excavated first as part of the archaeological campaign preceding the raising of the old Aswan Dam in the late 1920s, and again in 1961–62.

The date of the initial occupation of Qasr Ibrim is still unclear, but a settlement within a defensive wall enclosing part of the hilltop certainly existed by the early Third Intermediate Period. New Kingdom occupation is possible, especially given the presence of a series of small shrines of the period in the cliff face below the fortress and a stela of Sety I on a nearby headland, but there is as yet no unequivocal evidence from the fortress itself. During the Twenty-fifth Dynasty, a small mud-brick temple was built by the pharaoh Taharqo, the sanctuary of which was decorated with paintings of the king standing in front of Amun, and formed part of a wider settlement within the old fortification wall.

Qasr Ibrim entered the world stage when it became caught up in the confrontation between the Sudanese Meroitic state and Roman Egypt in the late first century BC, a conflict that was described by several classical historians, including Strabo. After the Roman victory, Ibrim was occupied and refortified, and a Roman garrison was established there. Military equipment of the period, and particularly stone balls used as ammunition in large catapults, has been found in large quantities.

After the withdrawal of the garrison, Ibrim came under Meroitic rule, and served as a key administrative and religious center in Lower Nubia. There were several temples on the hilltop that attracted pilgrims both from farther south and from Egypt. The pilgrims left mementos of their visits in the form of graffiti in the temples and on the road leading to Ibrim from the Eastern Desert, and offerings of large numbers of coins found embedded in oil on temple floors. Another temple, at the northern end of the fortress, is one of the latest pagan structures known in Egypt. A small number of pyramid burials of the period were found in the cemeteries to the north of Ibrim.

After the collapse of centralized government in the fourth century AD, Qasr Ibrim became the seat of a local ruler, and was often in conflict with other regional tribal groups. However, letters found at Ibrim show that high-level diplomatic contacts took place with Egypt, and suggest that the ruler probably received financial support from

Figure 199. View of Qasr Ibrim from the water.

the Egyptian government in return for maintaining peace on the frontier. At this time there is evidence of a greater density of occupation within the fortress, which is perhaps a reflection of the unstable conditions locally. The coming of Christianity to the area is attested by construction of a church in the Taharqo temple, probably early in the sixth century AD. There are extensive cemeteries of the period around the site.

With the official conversion of the kingdom of Nobadia to Christianity in the late sixth century, a large cathedral was built reusing blocks from one of the temples, and at least three other churches are known to have stood within the walls. On a nearby hilltop, another church and monastic settlement flourished for several hundred years. The cathedral included burial places for the early bishops of Ibrim, and further bishops' burials were found outside, including those of bishops from neighboring cities. One of the last known bishops appointed to Qasr Ibrim, in the mid-fifteenth century, was buried in a makeshift grave in the cathedral with scrolls recording his appointment as bishop. Pilgrims continued to come to Qasr Ibrim, and left graffiti on a nearby hilltop from which travelers could gain their first view of the city when approaching from the Eastern Desert.

Qasr Ibrim continued to function as an administrative center, and was the seat of the eparch (the deputy of the king of Makuria, who was based at Old Dongola) for much of the Christian Period. Large quantities of correspondence found at Ibrim show his role as middleman between the Nubians and Egyptians, acting on matters of diplomacy, frontier policy, and commercial activities. Relations with Egypt were generally peaceful, although Qasr Ibrim was sacked by Shams al-Daula, the brother of the Egyptian ruler Salah al-Din, in AD 1172.

Qasr Ibrim became an Ottoman garrison in the late sixteenth century, and for a short period was the southernmost limit of the Ottoman Empire. This status was lost as the Ottoman frontier moved farther south, and Qasr Ibrim waned in importance. The members of the garrison became settled in the area, and gradually the fortress was abandoned in favor of the valley below. The fortress was seized and briefly occupied by Mamluks fleeing from Egypt. They were driven out by Muhammad Ali Pasha, and the fortress was finally abandoned in 1812.

Bibliography

For the excavations, see *JEA* 49 (1963).

Adams, W.Y. 1996. *Qasr Ibrîm: The Late Medieval Period.* London: Egypt Exploration Society.

Mills, A.J. 1982. *The Cemeteries of Qasr Ibrîm: A Report of the Excavations Conducted by W.B. Emery in 1961.* London: Egypt Exploration Society.

Rose, P.J. 2008. "Early Settlement at Qasr Ibrim." In W. Godlewski and A. Łajtar, eds., *Between the Cataracts: Proceedings of the Eleventh International Conference for Nubian Studies, Warsaw University, 27 August–2 September 2006.* Part 1: *Main Papers*, 195–209. PAM Supplement Series 2:1. Warsaw: Warsaw University Press.

Karanog

Janice W. Yellin

The Town

Although Karanog (about thirty kilometers south of Aswan) is now submerged under Lake Nasser, excavations conducted there in 1907–10 by David Randall-MacIver and Leonard Woolley have provided significant information about the life, religion, and language of its Meroitic inhabitants. Along with the towns of Faras and Qasr Ibrim, Karanog was an important center for the governance of Lower Nubia during the Meroitic Period (mid-third century BC–mid-fourth century AD) and became the region's main center of governance in the second century AD. It continued to be inhabited after the end of the Meroitic kingdom by Blemmyes and other groups until the Christian Period.

Called Nalote by the ancient Meroites, Karanog was a large urban administrative center that covered approximately fifteen to nineteen acres, with a population estimated by various scholars to range between 1000 and 2400 inhabitants. Beginning in the second century AD, the powerful *peshto*-viceroys who governed the province moved to Karanog from Faras along with their administrators, whom László Török estimates were a small but significant percentage of the population (50 to 190 administrators in any given generation). The fertile land surrounding Karanog would have supported its residents, and the many luxury goods found in the tombs of residents would have been brought into the city via the trade routes that connected it with Roman Egypt, and thus to the greater Mediterranean world. Control of these trade routes and the exchange of goods between Roman Egypt and Nubia was an important responsibility borne by the *peshto*-viceroy and his bureaucrats.

In his 1993 re-examination of data from the earlier excavations, David O'Connor describes the excavated area of the town as being composed of two- and three-story mud-brick houses aligned along narrow twisting streets. Other structures made of more temporary materials might have also been crowded among the mud-brick dwellings. As expected, the size of houses varied depending on the status and wealth of their owners, with the southeast side of the town having the larger dwellings and the southwest the smaller, less wealthy ones. O'Connor believes that the houses of the wealthier inhabitants were placed in the northern part of the town so that the prevailing north wind would blow dust and odors away from them.

In addition to these more typical dwellings, there were two large mud-brick buildings that stood on individual hilltops overlooking the town, which were probably the dwellings of the *peshto*-viceroys. The later and larger of the two, called the "castle" by the excavators, was three stories high. Rare examples of multi-purpose Meroitic administrative centers, both buildings are similar in their floor plans, which indicate that one area of their first floors was for public rooms with an audience hall, while other parts of the first and upper floors were used for domestic purposes. For reasons still not understood, Karanog, unlike other important Nubian administrative centers, did not have a protective enclosure wall.

Texts from Karanog indicate that several forms of Amun (Amun of Napata, Amun of Luxor,

Amun) and Isis had cults there, although their temples were never found. In addition to these typically Egyptian/Kushite gods, Mash, an indigenous sun god, was worshiped exclusively in this area, and his priests were buried at Aniba.

The Cemetery

Karanog's cemetery is a surprising distance from the town (about 7.25 kilometers north at modern Aniba), but since no Meroitic town was found near Aniba and no cemetery found at Karanog, Aniba does seem to be the site of the Karanog burials. Randall-MacIver and Woolley excavated 641 burials dating from the first to early fourth centuries AD that represented different social

Figure 200. The west face of the 'castle' at Karanog, taken in 1911.

classes, including elites such as priests and *peshto*s as well as their family members. O'Connor has noted that the segmentary nature of Meroitic society is demonstrated by the general organization of the burials, in which there are clusters of family areas for each of the important clans. The tombs within these family areas reflect the sociopolitical status of their owners. The social structure of these clans can be inferred from these tombs' locations within their family areas and their size and complexity. The greater a tomb's distance from the more important tombs, the lesser their owner's status in the social hierarchy. This is confirmed by their tomb types. The largest, best-equipped pyramid burials belong to the *peshto-viceroys*, while the smaller pyramid burials belong to lesser functionaries or members of their families, including priests and other government officials. The lower-status tombs were simpler and had underground chambers without a superstructure, but the wealthiest and the most complex graves copied royal burials from Meroe with a pyramid, a chapel, and underground burial chambers. The small chapels on their eastern faces had vaulted or flat roofs and contained a funerary stela on which was painted an image of the tomb owner. In front of the chapels was a low brick platform upon which was an offering table, and set on its roof or into the pyramid's east face was a *ba*-bird statue of the owner. The offering tables were sometimes decorated with a scene of Anubis and a goddess pouring a libation with offerings for the tomb owner, which illustrated an actual offering ritual performed at the chapel by a priest and priestess impersonating these gods. Inside the tomb chambers were objects needed in the afterlife, such as clothing, jewelry, personal toilet items (eye make-up, razors, and tweezers), and clay pots for food and drink. Sometimes there were other personal items reflecting the owner's occupation in life or status items imported from Egypt and the Mediterranean. The elevated status of many of these burials can be seen in the high quality of these objects, including examples of finely made and painted Meroitic pots. However, even the poorest tombs contained gifts, typically simple pottery vessels and strings of beads.

Karanog was not abandoned after the collapse of the Meroitic kingdom. New groups moved into the region, including the nomadic Blemmyes who, aside from occasional raids, had been kept at the eastern edge of the Nile Valley by the Meroitic rulers. According to William Y. Adams, evidence from the site shows continuous occupation from the end of the Meroitic Period into the Christian Period, although the population was poorer and the architecture of the site showed deterioration over time.

Bibliography

Adams, W.Y. 1977, repr. 1984. *Nubia: Corridor to Africa.* Princeton, N.J.: Princeton University Press.

O'Connor, D. 1993. *Ancient Nubia: Egypt's Rival in Africa.* Philadelphia: University of Pennsylvania.

Randall-MacIver, D., et al. 1909. *Areika.* Oxford: University Press.

Török, L. 1997. *The Kingdom of Kush: Handbook of the Napatan-Meroitic Civilization.* Leiden: Brill.

Welsby, D.A. 1996. *The Kingdoms of Kush: The Napatan and Meroitic Empires.* London: British Museum Press.

Welsby, D.A., and W.V. Davies, eds. 2002. *Uncovering Ancient Sudan: A Decade of Discovery by the Sudan Archaeological Research Society.* London: Sudan Archaeological Research Society.

Woolley, C.L. 1911. *Karanòg: The Town.* Philadelphia: University of Pennsylvania.

Woolley, C.L., and D. Randall-MacIver. 1910. *Karanòg: The Romano-Nubian Cemetery.* Text and Plates. Philadelphia: University of Pennsylvania.

DERR

Marjorie M. Fisher

The Temple of Derr, dating to regnal years 5–10 of Ramesses II, was originally situated 191 kilometers south of Aswan on the east bank of the Nile; nearby graves date to the same period. The temple was first documented in 1910 by Aylward Blackman of Oxford, England, although various travelers and scholars (Jean-François Champollion, F.C. Gau, John Lewis Burckhardt, Jean-Jacques Rifaud, Hector Horeau, Arthur Weigall, James H. Breasted, Gaston Maspero, Amelia Edwards, and others) had already produced drawings and records of it.

In 1964 UNESCO moved the temple 2.6 kilometers to the west bank near Amada. This rock-cut temple, similar in type to Beit al-Wali, consists of three main rooms: the first pillared hall; the second pillared hall, which has three chambers backing off it; and the central one of these chambers, the sanctuary, which had four statues carved out of the rock face, similar to the Abu Simbel Great Temple and Gerf Hussein sanctuaries (see "Abu Simbel," "Gerf Hussein" [four statues], "Beit al-Wali," and "Wadi al-Sebua" [three statues]). The statues shown at Derr represent Ptah, Amun-Re, deified Ramesses II, and Re-Horakhty.

Figure 201. Plan of the temple of Derr.

371

This temple was unique for four reasons. First, it was the only temple in Nubia situated on the east bank of the Nile, perhaps because of the proximity of ancient settlements or the presence of better-quality cliffs in that area. Second, it was oriented north–south, because at this location the Nile flowed east–west. Third, the pillars adjoining figures of Ramesses II placed in the first pillared hall were traditionally oriented along the main axis, but at Derr they were diagonally placed, as in Theban mortuary temples. And fourth, the name of the temple, "great temple of a million years" (as indicated in one inscription), was a title reserved for New Kingdom Theban mortuary temples, and not those found in Nubia during the Eighteenth or Nineteenth Dynasties.

Due to damage over time, the softness of the stone, and the moving of the structure during flooding following construction of the High Dam at Aswan, little remains of the first pillared hall

and nothing of the original pylon in front of the Temple of Derr. The pillars in the first pillared hall, which are mostly destroyed, depict the figure of Ramesses II garbed in his ceremonial kilt and run perpendicular to the main axis. This is a unique use of Ramesses II's pillars, although I. Hein notes that such an orientation is found in royal mortuary temples in Thebes and in the mummified form of the king in an Osiride statue at Karnak in Thutmose I's temple.

The Temple of Derr was previously thought to be dedicated to Re-Horakhty based upon the fact that his image is prominent in every chamber, including the three in the back of the temple. Hein maintains, however, that the temple is in the domain of Re, even though Re-Horakhty is shown prominently as an object of worship, along with the deified Ramesses II. All the statues and reliefs are crudely cut, possibly due to the quality of the sandstone here, but the painting over the

Figure 202. View of Derr from the water, in its original location.

Figure 203. The interior of the temple at Derr. Photo © Chester Higgins Jr 2012.

reliefs is of higher quality. The primary cultic gods present are Re-Horakhty, Amun-Re, and Ptah, although Ptah is represented less often than the other two. Isis, Hathor, and Mut also appear, but infrequently.

Like other temples of Ramesses II, Derr has military reliefs in the first pillared hall, along with processions of Ramesses II's sons and daughters on opposite sides of the doorway leading into the second pillared hall. The military reliefs are mainly destroyed, and those that remain were recently cleaned by conservators working for the Supreme Council of Antiquities. The rest of the temple is decorated with cultic scenes in which Re-Horakhty figures prominently. The temple is dedicated to the sun god Re, and Amun-Re appears throughout the reliefs. The temple was later reused as a Christian church and its reliefs plastered over.

Two hundred meters north of this temple lay a rock stela of Ramesses II. Next to it is a stela of the viceroy Amenemhab from the time of Siptah.

Bibliography

el-Achirie, H., and J. Jacquet. 1980. *Le Temple de Derr.* Vol. 1: *Architecture.* Cairo: Centre d'étude et de documentation sur l'Ancienne Égypte.

Blackman, A.M. 1913. *The Temple of Derr. Les temples immergés de la Nubie.* Cairo: IFAO.

Fisher, M.M. 2001. *The Sons of Ramesses II.* 2 vols. ÄAT 53.

Gohary, J. 1998. *Guide to the Nubian Monuments on Lake Nasser.* Cairo: American University in Cairo Press.

Habachi, L. 1969. *Features of the Deification of Ramesses II.* Glückstadt: J.J. Augustin.

Hein, I. 1991. *Die Ramessidische Bautätigkeit in Nubien.* GOF 4, Vol. 22.

Porter, B., and R.L.B. Moss. 1952. *Topographical Bibliography of Ancient Egyptian Hieroglyphic Texts, Reliefs and Paintings.* Vol. 7: *Nubia, the Deserts and Outside Egypt.* Oxford: Griffith Institute.

AMADA

Robert G. Morkot

Amada is an elegant small temple (twenty-five meters by ten meters) built during the co-reign of Thutmose III and Amenhotep II, with later additions by Thutmose IV and restorations of the Nineteenth Dynasty. The temple has very fine relief sculpture and a number of important historical inscriptions. The temple was relocated during the UNESCO campaign, and now stands 2.6 kilometers inland and sixty meters higher than its original location. Because of the quality of the decoration and the delicate plasterwork, it was decided to raise the nine-hundred-ton inner part of the temple in one piece onto trolleys and move it on rails. This delicate procedure was possible because of the gentle gradient of the desert here. The outer hall was dismantled conventionally.

The building history of this temple was unraveled by Charles Van Siclen. The original temple, built during the co-regency of Thutmose III and Amenhotep II, consisted of a stone-built suite of rooms with a portico of four proto-Doric columns. This structure stood at the back of a courtyard within an enclosure wall of mud brick, and was entered through a gateway, probably with a pylon of mud brick. By noting the different types of relief decoration used on the square

columns I–III and V–VII, Van Siclen was able to demonstrate that columns I-III had originally stood on the right (north) side of the court, because the king wears the White Crown, which is found on this side in the rooms of the chapel. Also, the use of sunk and raised relief indicates that there was originally a covered colonnade that surrounded an open court. Later the columns were dismantled and re-erected in their present position, so that the raised-relief decoration now lines the central aisle of the hall. New side walls were built with engaged pillars and doors, and the whole structure roofed over, creating a hypostyle hall.

The pylon entrance was made of brick with a stone gateway. This entrance has images of Amenhotep II in the White Crown and Thutmose III in the Red Crown, both being embraced by Re-Horakhty; beneath each scene is a small additional depiction of the viceroy Messuy, holding a fan and adoring the cartouches of Merenptah. There are also inscriptions of Sety I.

The square columns each have a panel showing King Thutmose IV embraced by gods; the three other faces carry cartouches of the king identifying him as "beloved" of various gods. Notable among these are the goddess Hathor of

Ibshek (the region of Abu Simbel); Khakaure (Senwosret III); "the Bull Lord of Nubia who is in Thebes"; and the three Nubian forms of Horus, as "Lord of Miam" (Aniba), "Lord of Baki" (Kuban), and "Lord of Buhen." The scenes on the enclosing walls show various rites associated with the coronation or jubilee festivals of the king. References to the "jubilee," usually celebrated after thirty years of reign, are confusing, as the highest year recorded for Thutmose IV is year 8, and he is generally ascribed ten years by Egyptologists. It is also uncertain when the columns were rearranged to create the columned hall.

The inner part of the temple is notable for its very fine raised-relief sculpture, some with well-preserved color. Thutmose III and Amenhotep II are shown as equal rulers, each dominating one half of the temple, and this dates the construction to their short co-regency. The temple is dedicated to Amun-Re and Re-Horakhty.

In the sanctuary, there is an important inscription of year 3 of Amenhotep II, which records his Asiatic campaign. As with so many of the king's records, it emphasizes his prowess as a warrior. Following the defeat of the Asiatic rulers—killed, we are told, by the king himself with his mace—the bodies of six of them were hung from the walls of Thebes and the body of the seventh was taken to Nubia and hung from the walls of the fortress of Napata at the Fourth Cataract "as a warning to the Kushites."

Structurally, the temple had no further additions or alterations following the reign of Thutmose IV, but there are added inscriptions of viceroys and other officials of the Nineteenth and Twentieth Dynasties. Throughout the temple, the name of Amun was erased during the reign of Akhenaten, and later restored. There are restoration texts of Sety I, and from the reign of Ramesses II, inscriptions of the viceroys Hekanakht and Setau. The most important

inscriptions are from the reign of Merenptah. A large stela of year 4 of that king has a kneeling figure of the viceroy Messuy, and recounts the defeat of a "rebellion" in Wawat. This seems to relate very directly to the invasion of Egypt by

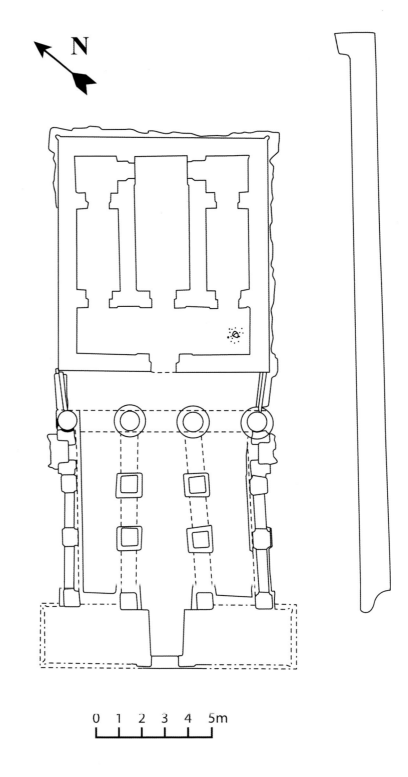

Figure 204. Plan of Amada temple.

0 1 2 3 4 5m

Figure 205. The exterior of the temple at Amada.

the Libyan tribes in that same year, and it has been suggested that the Libyans and Nubians planned a joint attack on Egypt. This failed because the Egyptians learned about it and were able to defeat the Nubians first: the Libyans, however, managed to get close to Memphis before being driven back by the Egyptian army (events recorded on Merenptah's 'Israel Stela' and an inscription at Karnak).

There are other inscriptions of Messuy in the temple. It has been proposed that Messuy was a royal prince, grandson of Merenptah, and eventual usurper of the throne in the reign of Sety II as Amenmesse. In support of this interpretation, some Egyptologists have argued that there are added uraei to the viceroy's forehead in the Amada inscriptions, but this has been challenged by those who think that the 'uraei' are accidental marks on the stone. These royal uraei do not appear on other monuments of the viceroy, and there is no other evidence to support the identification or equation of the two officials.

Two scenes added to the entrance to the inner room are also historically significant. One depicts a kneeling figure of the infamous Chancellor Bay before cartouches of the boy-pharaoh Siptah, and the second depicts the regent, Queen Tawosret, shaking sistra. The text tells us that the two scenes were created by the Overseer of Bowmen of Kush, Piay.

Between the temple and the river, early travelers noted a stone platform with remains of columns, and the name of Sety I: it has been suggested that this was a processional kiosk.

No evidence for a settlement around Amada has been recorded by travelers or archaeologists, but the opposite bank of the river was very fertile, with many palm groves, and so it is possible the settlement may have been there. In the region, there is evidence for C-Group cemeteries, and there are rock inscriptions of many periods, including some of the indigenous rulers probably contemporary with the Eleventh and early Twelfth Dynasties.

Bibliography

Dodson, A. 1997. "Messuy, Amada, and Amenmesse." *JARCE* 34:41–48.

Van Siclen, C.C. 1987. "The Building History of the Tuthmosid Temple at Amada and the Jubilees of Tuthmosis IV." *VA* 3:53–66.

Yurco, F. 1997. "Was Amenmesse the Viceroy of Kush, Messuwy?" *JARCE* 34:49–56.

WADI AL-SEBUA

Marjorie M. Fisher

The site of Wadi al-Sebua, whose ancient name is Per-Amun, has been visited by travelers and scholars throughout the centuries. After Jean-François Champollion, the site was first sketched and documented by Frédéric-Louis Norden in 1737. W.R. Hamilton augmented this documentation in 1801, as did Thomas Legh in 1813–17, J.L. Burckhardt in 1813, Henry Light in 1814, Giovanni Belzoni in 1815, J.J. Rifaud in 1816, Salt and Bankes, Irby and Mangles, and F.C. Gau, who wrote the description that Henri Gauthier eventually used as the basis for his excavations. Other visitors included Frederick Henniker, F. Cailliaud, Anton Prokesch, Ippolito Rosellini, John Taylor, Karl Richard Lepsius, David Roberts, and André Lefèvre, to mention only a few. Because of the visual beauty of the site, it became a destination for most visitors to Nubia.

The site consists of two temples, one of which was built by Amenhotep III and the other by Ramesses II at a late regnal year, 38. The earlier, smaller temple of Amenhotep III is partially rock cut but does not have a niche for statues at the back of the sanctuary, as most rock-cut temples do. The walls were decorated and the temple was intentionally damaged during the Amarna Period as part of Akhenaten's religious transformation, and it was subsequently restored by Ramesses II. The temple was dedicated first to Horus and then, after Ramesses II's restoration, to Amun-Re.

The second temple is one of the most impressive and intact structures in Nubia. It was originally situated 150 kilometers south of Aswan on the west bank of the Nile, but UNESCO moved it four kilometers west of its ancient location in the early 1960s. The temple was transformed into a Coptic church in the early centuries of the Christian era. This structure, known as the temple of Amun-Re and Re-Horakhty (although it seems that it was mainly dedicated to Amun-Re), is partly rock cut and partly freestanding. The temple was surrounded by a mud-brick wall.

One would have entered through a no-longer-extant stone gateway that was set into the mud-brick enclosure wall. This small gateway led to the first court, lined with two sets of three sphinxes wearing double crowns, facing each other. Along the base of these sphinxes the bound enemies of Egypt are depicted: Asiatics appear on the north side and Nubians on the south side. Through another, second pylon made of mud brick is the second court, where four falcon-headed sphinxes represent Horus of Maha, Miam, Baki, and Edfu.

One then ascends a ramp in order to pass through a great stone pylon.

Through this pylon one encounters the next open court/peristyle court, which is filled with reliefs displaying processions of Ramesses II's sons and daughters on both the north and south walls. Two pairs of five pillars in this courtyard adjoin the figure of Ramesses II, who stands with both arms crossed and wearing a sporran kilt. These pillars face the axis running from the front of the temple to the back, as they do in most of the other temples. This part of the temple was

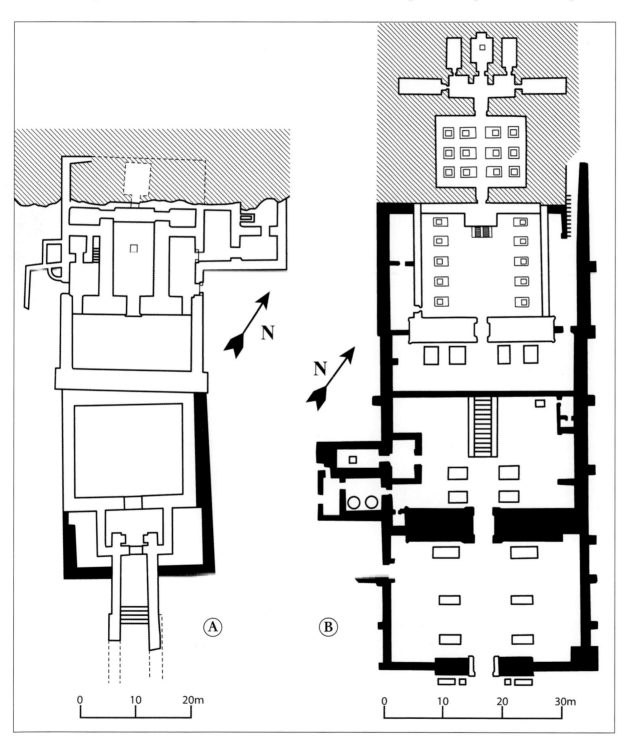

Figure 206. Plans of the temples of (A) Amenhotep III and (B) Ramesses II at Wadi al-Sebua.

freestanding, and visitors had to ascend a small ramp up to a terrace to pass into the next room, the first pillared hall, in order to enter the rock-cut part of the temple, which also featured pillars with Ramesses II (removed when the temple was later reused as a church). This temple and Gerf Hussein appear to be the only ones in which this style of pillars was used in two separate areas. The first pillared hall leads into the vestibule, which has two adjoining rooms on either side. Before it

Figure 207. The approach to the temple of Ramesses II at Wadi al-Sebua. Photo © Chester Higgins Jr 2012.

are three rooms, the center of which is the sanctuary, in which three statues are carved out of the rock face, as at Beit al-Wali (compare this with four statues carved out of the rock face at Abu Simbel, Derr, and Gerf Hussein). Predictably,

only cultic reliefs decorate the inner temple that is part of the rock cliff, for this is where the gods reside. No military reliefs have survived, but the cultic reliefs that do survive are beautiful, prominently portraying Amun-Re, Re-Horakhty, and the deified Ramesses II.

When the temple became a Coptic church, the ancient reliefs at the back were plastered over, which, according to Jocelyn Gohary, had the unintended effect of protecting them. These preserved reliefs show three figures cut out of the rock face: Amun-Re, Re-Horakhty, and the deified Ramesses II. Later, during the reign of Merenptah, an inscription was added on the first pylon doorway, and a grave of a viceroy dating to that reign has been found nearby.

Surrounding these two temples were C-Group and Pan-Grave Nubian settlements. Also nearby are prehistoric cliff paintings, two other Ramesside cemeteries, and three quarries.

Bibliography

Fisher, M.M. 2001. *The Sons of Ramesses II.* 2 vols. ÄAT 53.

Gauthier, H. 1912. *Le Temple de Ouadi es-Sebouâ. Les temples immergés de la Nubie.* 2 vols. Cairo: IFAO.

Gohary, J. 1998. *Guide to the Nubian Monuments on Lake Nasser.* Cairo: American University in Cairo Press.

Haeny, G. 1963. "Rapport préliminaire sur les fouilles à Ouadi es-Sebouâ." *Campagne internationale de l'Unesco pour la sauvegarde des monuments de la Nubie: Fouilles en Nubie (1959–1961),* 53–62. Cairo: Organisme général des imprimeries gouvernementales.

Hein, I. 1991. *Die Ramessidische Bautätigkeit in Nubien.* GOF 4, Vol. 22.

Porter, B., and R.L.B. Moss. 1952. *Topographical Bibliography of Ancient Egyptian Hieroglyphic Texts, Reliefs and Paintings.* Vol. 7: *Nubia, the Deserts and Outside Egypt.* Oxford: Griffith Institute.

MAHARRAQA

Peter Lacovara

The Temple of Maharraqa was begun in the Roman Period and dedicated to Serapis. The modest structure was never finished, and consists only of a small court surrounded on three sides by columns and a sanctuary. Remains of an even smaller temple situated nearer to the river were discovered with decorated blocks invoking Isis, Osiris, Horus, Thoth, and Tefnut.

The temple was originally sited at Hierasykaminos on the border between Meroitic Nubia and Roman Egypt, before it was subsequently relocated to Wadi al-Sebua, along with the Temple of Dakka, as part of the Aswan Dam salvage project.

Bibliography
Gohary, J. 1998. *Guide to the Monuments on Lake Nasser.* Cairo: American University in Cairo Press.
Säve-Söderbergh, T. 1987. *Temples and Tombs of Ancient Nubia: The International Rescue Campaign at Abu Simbel, Philae and Other Sites.* London: Thames and Hudson.

DAKKA

Peter Lacovara

The Temple of Thoth at Dakka was first begun in the third century BC by King Arkamani II, who, in collaboration with Ptolemy IV, dedicated it to the deity. Later, Ptolemy IX enlarged the temple by adding a pronaos with two rows of columns. In the Roman Period, Augustus and Tiberius constructed a second sanctuary, inner and outer enclosure walls, and a massive pylon. Stairways reach to the top of the two towers of the pylon. The pylon was largely undecorated, but is etched with numerous graffiti in Greek and some in Demotic and Meroitic.

The temple is dedicated to the triad of Pselchis (Pnubs): Thoth, Tefnut, and the Nubian god Arensnuphis. Other gods found in the temple decoration include the deified Imhotep and the various local Nubian incarnations of Horus. The complex was surrounded by a fortified enclosure wall in the Roman Period and then converted into a Christian church. The sanctuary of the temple still contains remains of the original granite naos, and a grand processional way stretched from the pylon fifty-five meters to a quay at the river bank.

The temple was originally located about one hundred kilometers south of Aswan, but was disassembled and re-erected by the Egyptian Antiquities Service at Wadi al-Sebua.

Bibliography

Gohary, J. 1998. *Guide to the Monuments on Lake Nasser*. Cairo: American University in Cairo Press.

Säve-Söderbergh, T. 1987. *Temples and Tombs of Ancient Nubia: The International Rescue Campaign at Abu Simbel, Philae and Other Sites*. London: Thames and Hudson.

GERF HUSSEIN

Marjorie M. Fisher

Originally located ninety-nine kilometers south of Aswan, the rock-cut temple of Gerf Hussein, constructed during the reign of Ramesses II, could not be rescued in its entirety by the UNESCO campaign because of its poor condition. Part of the temple was moved near the current site of Beit al-Wali, just south of the Aswan Dam, and one Ramesside pillar, as well as two blocks of the same period, were transferred to the Nubia Museum in Aswan. In its original context, it shared a landscape with New Kingdom Egyptian cemeteries as well as cemeteries of the Nubian A- and C-Groups. To the south of the temple, cliff inscriptions dating to both the Middle and New Kingdoms were discovered, as well as Demotic graffiti. A statue base of Ramesses IV situated outside the temple indicates that some cultic activity continued for some time after the construction of the temple, but it apparently dwindled after the time of Ramesses IV. Some of the pillars abutting the standing forms of Ramesses II in the peristyle court, as well as objects from the site, can currently be found in the Nubia Museum in Aswan.

Under the direction of l'Institut français d'archéologie orientale, the site of Gerf Hussein has been systematically documented and analyzed.

Many early visitors and travelers, such as Rifaud, Legh, Irby and Mangles, Champollion, Weigall, Maspero, Breasted, and Petrie, had written about, documented, painted, and drawn the site; however, it was the French Institute during the UNESCO project of the 1960s that undertook a thorough documentation (published by the Centre d'étude et de documentation sur l'Ancienne Egypte [CEDAE]).

The temple is primarily dedicated to Ptah, but also Ptah-Tatenen and Hathor as well as the deified Ramesses II, and dates to around regnal year 45 of Ramesses II. Its plan is similar to that of the temple of Ramesses II at Wadi al-Sebua. It was constructed under the direction of the viceroy Setau. One of the latest built by Ramesses II, this temple is simpler in form than his others.

When approaching the temple, one proceeds down an avenue flanked by ram sphinxes to the first pylon. The main axis of the temple leads to the forecourt/peristyle court, with two sets of four pillars abutting the forms of Ramesses II. The walls of this forecourt and the first pylon are freestanding but cut from the rock cliff. Also in this court are four bundled papyrus columns. At the farthest end of the forecourt is a ramp leading up to a gateway, which may be another pylon. In front of this gateway, niches on either side held a statue triad of the god. As at Wadi al-Sebua, the deified Ramesses II, Amun-Re, and Ptah are the main cultic gods. The pillars incorporating Ramesses II's statues, although large and crudely cut, are wonderfully painted in black and red. One of them—the best preserved and painted—can be seen in the Nubia Museum in Aswan. Through the gateway, in a hall cut into the rock face, are two sets of three pillars facing each other. On either side of the north and south wall of this hall are four niches displaying additional statue triads cut out of the rock face, similar to those at Beit al-Wali, Derr, and Abu Simbel.

The cultic reliefs in the second pillared hall portray numerous gods: at least ten or eleven on each wall (not including duplicates), unusual for Ramesses' Nubian temples. The temple is dedicated primarily to Ptah, but surprisingly he does not appear frequently on the remaining reliefs.

Continuing along the main access, one enters a vestibule, which has an additional room on either side. At the back of the vestibule are three rooms, the center of which is the sanctuary (again similar to Abu Simbel, Beit al-Wali, and Derr) with four statues cut out of the rock face: Ptah, Ptah-Tatenen, Hathor, and Ramesses II. The figure of Ptah-Tatenen was found to have originally been covered in gold, based on preserved traces, while on Hathor, particles of linen were discovered.

Architecturally, the Great Temple of Abu Simbel, Derr, Wadi al-Sebua, and Gerf Hussein have similar structures. Leaving aside the grand entrances to Abu Simbel and Wadi al-Sebua, each has a peristyle court or hall with pillars abutting figures of Ramesses II through which a pillared hall is entered. The next room, the vestibule, is not as clearly identifiable at Abu Simbel and Derr but is clearly present at Wadi al-Sebua and Gerf Hussein. On either side of the vestibule at Wadi al-Sebua and Gerf Hussein are additional rooms. The vestibule leads to the sanctuary, bracketed by rooms on either side used for rituals.

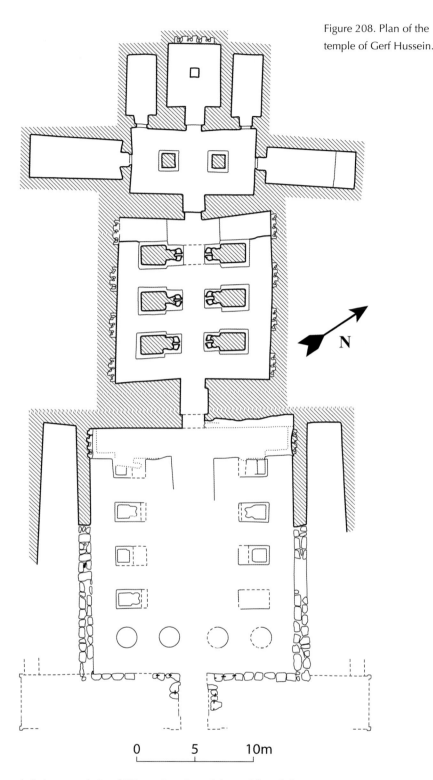

Figure 208. Plan of the temple of Gerf Hussein.

Figure 209. View of the temple of Gerf Hussein in its original location, before it was moved during the UNESCO salvage project.

The surviving decoration of this temple seems to stress the importance of Ptah, Amun-Re, Re, Re-Horakhty, and Horus in his various forms (Baki, Miam, Buhen). In the one surviving military relief on the back wall of the first court (which Hein interprets as being built like a pylon), Ramesses II is smiting the enemies of Egypt before Horus of Buhen and Re-Horakhty. The rest of the surviving documented reliefs are cultic in nature.

Bibliography

Fisher, M.M. 2001. *The Sons of Ramesses II*. 2 vols. ÄAT 53.

Gohary, J. 1998. *Guide to the Nubian Monuments on Lake Nasser*. Cairo: American University in Cairo Press.

Hein, I. 1991. *Die Ramessidische Bautätigkeit in Nubien*. GOF 4, Vol. 22: 9–12.

Jacquet, J., and H. el-Achirie. 1974–78. *Le Temple de Gerf Hussein*. CEDAE 64–67.

Jacquet-Gordon, H. 1981. "Graffiti from the Region of Gerf Hussein." *MDAIK* 37:227–40.

Porter, B., and R.L.B. Moss. 1952. *Topographical Bibliography of Ancient Egyptian Hieroglyphic Texts, Reliefs and Paintings*. Vol. 7: *Nubia, the Deserts and Outside Egypt*. Oxford: Griffith Institute.

DENDUR

Sue D'Auria

The small temple of Dendur was constructed ca. 15 BC, in the reign of Augustus, on the left bank of the Nile near the ancient site of Tuzis, seventy-seven kilometers south of Aswan. The temple was visited by many early travelers, including Robert Hay, ca. 1830, and Amelia Edwards, who executed a watercolor and a romantic description of this "exquisite toy" in 1874. With the building of the first Aswan Dam, Dendur was included in the survey of monuments that were threatened by the rising waters, and the site was investigated in 1901 by Howard Carter

Figure 210. The temple of Dendur before its move during the salvage project.

and in 1906 by Arthur Weigall. The most complete work was done in 1910 by A.M. Blackman, who published two volumes on the site in 1911. After the final raising of the old Aswan Dam in 1933, Dendur was flooded for three-quarters of the year, washing away the red, blue, green, yellow, and black paint used in its decoration. With the construction of the High Dam in the early 1960s, the decision was made to move the temple, and the Centre d'étude et de documentation sur l'Ancienne Égypte spent two seasons recording at Dendur. The temple was dismantled in 1963, and it was offered to the United States in recognition for its support of the UNESCO project to relocate several Nubian temples. It now stands in the Sackler Wing at the Metropolitan Museum of Art in New York.

The temple was built to honor Isis and Osiris, as well as two deified sons, Pedesi and Pihor, of a local Nubian chieftain who was said to have supported Rome in its control over the area. The sons purportedly drowned in the Nile, and their tomb may have been located nearby. The temple was placed behind a thirty-meter-wide cult terrace overlooking the Nile, and consists of a gateway fronting a small court, which leads to the temple proper, comprised of three successive chambers: a pronaos, offering chamber, and sanctuary. The temple is small, only twenty-five meters from the gateway to the rear of the main building, and is constructed of sandstone. The elevation rises eight meters overall.

The gateway, which provided the main access from the river, would have been flanked by a mud-brick pylon, which was never built. The gateway is decorated with four registers of scenes depicting the king, Augustus, presenting offerings to pairs of deities, including many Egyptian gods and goddesses, as well as the Nubian deities Arensnuphis and Mandulis. A variety of offerings are presented: water, milk, beer, and wine; eye paint; crowns, incense, and flowers; and even a water clock. The base of the gateway contains a frieze of lotus and papyrus, a motif that is continued on the temple proper. The gate is surmounted by a cavetto cornice with torus molding and is decorated with a magnificent winged sun disc, representing the god Horus, which also appears at the entrance to the temple.

The pronaos is in the form of a simple, open-fronted entrance porch with two composite columns whose shafts are decorated with lashed bundles of stems, and with papyrus-umbel capitals. These have scenes in sunk relief of men conveying offerings of animals and flowers. On the interior walls, the king, often identified only as "pharaoh," is again represented praying and offering to the gods. The relief here and in other interior areas is raised. The doorway at the rear, along the main axis, has a cavetto cornice with winged sun disc. Two additional doorways, along the north and south walls, lead to the exterior. The thickness of the south doorway contains a Coptic inscription detailing the conversion of the temple into a church in AD 577, at which time the main entrance was changed to this doorway. The ceiling of the pronaos is embellished with vultures, and originally with painted yellow stars on a blue background.

The inner two rooms are undecorated, save for reliefs on the doorframe and the rear wall of the sanctuary, which contains a statue niche where the cult image would have been housed. The relief here portrays offerings made to Isis. Additionally, a crypt was built into the rear wall.

The exterior of the temple is decorated in sunk relief with two horizontal registers of the king again presenting offerings to pairs of deities, who are standing in the lower register and seated in the upper.

The temple was abandoned in the thirteenth century with the conversion of the area to Islam. Much graffiti, dating as early as 10 BC, defaces its surface, and includes inscriptions from many nineteenth-century travelers.

Bibliography

el-Achiri, H., et al. 1972. *Le temple de Dandour*. 2 vols. Cairo: CEDAE.

Aldred, C. 1978. *The Temple of Dendur*. Repr. from Metropolitan Museum of Art Bulletin, Summer 1978: 5–80.

Arnold, D. 1999. *Temples of the Last Pharaohs*. New York: Oxford University Press.

Blackman, A.M. 1911. *The Temple of Dendur*. Cairo: IFAO.

Edwards, A.B. 1891. *A Thousand Miles up the Nile*. London: Routledge.

Metropolitan Museum of Art, New York. The Temple of Dendur. http://www.metmuseum.org/works_of_art/collection_database/egyptian_art/the_temple_of_dendur/objectview.aspx?collID=10&OID=100004628

Monnet-Saleh, J. 1969. "Observations sur le temple de Dendour." *BIFAO* 68:1–13

BEIT AL-WALI

Marjorie M. Fisher

The site of Beit al-Wali was first noticed in the early nineteenth century, when Jean-Jacques Rifaud and Robert Hay mentioned it in their travel journals. They were followed by another explorer, Henry Villiers Stuart, in the later nineteenth century. But it was not until studies by Arthur Weigall in 1907 and Günther Roeder in 1911 that the site truly began to be examined for its historical significance. Even then, no systematic work was undertaken until the building of the Aswan Dam made a thorough examination of the site urgent. Thus in 1960–61, the joint expedition of the Oriental Institute Nubian Expedition and the Swiss Institute (Schweizerisches Institut für ägyptische Bauforschung und Altertumskunde in Kairo) documented the area between Khor Dehmit and Kalabsha. Dr. Herbert Ricke, then director of the Swiss Institute, supervised the excavations, as no archaeologists were associated with the Oriental Institute in Egypt at that time. The Oriental Institute, under Keith Seele, recorded the epigraphy, producing two volumes in collaboration with Labib Habachi and later Louis Žabkar, who aided the study of the Greek inscriptions.

This earliest of the surviving Nubian temples of Ramesses II dates to around 1279 BC—the end of Sety I's reign and regnal year 1 or 2 of Ramesses II's regime. It was not uncommon for a temple to be begun by one king and completed by his successor, since one of the duties of a successor king was to complete the building projects of his father. It is difficult to determine whether these reliefs belong to historical events during the reigns of either Sety I or Ramesses II or whether they serve strictly as propaganda. Later pharaohs (Sety II) and viceroys (Messuy, viceroy of Merenptah) also visited and left their names on this temple. During the Coptic Period, when this temple was used as a church, many of the reliefs in the sanctuary area were covered over and thus destroyed.

The rock-cut temple of Beit al-Wali was originally situated forty kilometers south of Aswan on the west bank of the Nile. With the help of the Polish expedition, the Swiss Institute, and the Oriental Institute, it was relocated to a few kilometers southwest of Aswan by UNESCO in the early 1960s. The layout of this temple is unlike other temples in Nubia, appearing as an elongated tube jutting into the mountainside with perpendicular rooms at its deepest point in the mountain. It, like other rock-cut temples, was carved out of the rock face. The temple consists of three parts: a forecourt, a vestibule with two columns, and a sanctuary. A stone gateway surrounded by a brick wall led into an elongated entrance hall, which was vaulted and made of mud bricks. Through this room was the two-pillared vestibule, in which two niches on the north and south side of the axis each contain three figures carved out of the rock face. The triad Khnum, Ramesses II, and Anukis is represented in the northern niche, while the southern niche contains the triad Horus, Ramesses II, and Isis. Beyond this vestibule is the sanctuary. A niche at the back of the sanctuary probably also had a triad of statues carved out of the rock face. This style of carving figures out of the rock face is similar to that at Gerf Hussein, Derr, and Abu Simbel.

Wall reliefs at Beit al-Wali portray military, presentation, and cultic scenes. In the forecourt/ entrance hall, the south and north walls bear depictions of the king and his princes, as well as Nubians, Syrians, and Libyans. Corresponding to the directions of their homelands, the Nubians appear on the south wall, while the Asiatics and Libyans are depicted on the north walls. The decoration of the temple consists of both sunk and raised reliefs. Interestingly, sunk reliefs appear on the eastern side of the north wall and on the south wall, while raised reliefs appear on the western side of the north wall and throughout the rest of the temple. Very little paint remains on the entrance-hall reliefs because molds for plaster casts (on view in the British Museum) were taken of them in the early nineteenth century, and this process affected the preservation of the paint. Here the king is shown fighting his enemies, accepting their surrender, and receiving tribute from them.

Princes, but no princesses, are shown in the forecourt. Along the south wall, closest to the entrance, a military relief portrays two princes in chariots. To the west of this is a depiction in which the king is seated while his eldest son, Prince Amenherwenemef, presents tribute. Along the north wall, closest to the entrance, the king

is depicted slaying his enemy, while the prince presents captives to him. Farther west are two military scenes representing a prince with the king in battle. Next to this scene the king is shown seated as Amenherwenemef presents him with captives. Amenherwenemef and another prince, Khaemwaset, are the only two sons whose names are listed. One of the unique features of this temple is that these entrance-hall/forecourt reliefs may not reflect actual events. Clearly, the Nubian campaigns portrayed had not yet been conducted during the early years of Ramesses II when this temple may have been decorated. Rather, the

Figure 211. Plan of the Beit al-Wali temple.

Figure 212. Interior of the temple of Beit al-Wali. Photo © Chester Higgins Jr 2012.

Nubian scene may have been meant to indicate symbolically that Ramesses II had control over Nubia. Alternatively, this scene may represent an event that occurred during the reign of Sety I, when the temple was first under construction.

The entrance vestibule recounts the exploits of the king, depicts figures of the gods, and portrays the king in battle. The sanctuary of the temple shows the divine birth of the king and the infant king being suckled by the goddesses Isis and Anukis. This scheme accords with standard Egyptian decorative schemes: as with most Egyptian temples, the earliest decoration and the most sacred scenes occur in the deepest part of the temple; as the temple extends out of the rock, the scenes begin to be more secular. Thus, the vestibule acted as a middle ground between the divine world of the gods, where the king lived, and the mundane world, where his children existed and fought in battle.

During the early Coptic Period, this temple was converted into a church. The long transverse hall became the basilica, with a brick vaulted ceiling supported by three beams. The sanctuary became the altar.

Bibliography

Fisher, M.M. 2001. *The Sons of Ramesses II*. 2 vols. ÄAT 53.

Gohary, J. 1998. *Guide to the Nubian Monuments on Lake Nasser*. Cairo: American University in Cairo Press.

Hein, I. 1991. *Die Ramessidische Bautätigkeit in Nubien*. GOF 4, Vol. 22.

Porter, B., and R.L.B. Moss. 1952. *Topographical Bibliography of Ancient Egyptian Hieroglyphic Texts, Reliefs and Paintings*. Vol. 7: *Nubia, the Deserts and Outside Egypt*. Oxford: Griffith Institute.

Ricke, H., G.R. Hughes, and E.F. Wente. 1967. *The Beit al-Wali Temple of Ramesses II*. OINE 2. Chicago: University of Chicago Press.

Roeder, G. 1938. *Der Felsentempel von Bet el-Wali. Les temples immergés de la Nubie*. Cairo: IFAO.

Spalinger, A. 1980. "Historical Observations on the Military Reliefs of Abu Simbel and Other Ramesside Temples in Nubia." *JEA* 66:83–99.

Stadelman, R. 1981. "Die lange Regierung Ramses' II." *MDAIK* 37:457–63.

KALABSHA

Peter Lacovara

The Temple of Kalabsha is one of the largest sanctuaries constructed in Lower Nubia, measuring seventy-six meters long and twenty-two meters wide. The plan is typical of Ptolemaic temples in Egypt, with a monumental entrance pylon fronting an open court leading to a small hypostyle hall, and a pair of chambers before the sanctuary. The undecorated pylon is set askew from what should have been the perpendicular face of the temple, perhaps to avoid an earlier structure or to reorient the entrance toward the riverbank. It appears that there was a New Kingdom temple on the site, but the construction of the surviving temple appears to date to the early Roman Period, and was dedicated to the local god Merwel or Mandulis. A small, partially rock-cut temple located to the southwest of the temple was dedicated to the Nubian god Dedwen.

The temples were originally situated on the west bank of the Nile, at Bab al-Kalabsha (Gate of Kalabsha), approximately fifty kilometers south of Aswan. The decoration of the temple was never finished but contained brightly painted scenes of Mandulis with Osiris, Isis, and Horus.

A Greek prayer carved into the temple wall reads, "Be benevolent, O Mandulis Son of Zeus. . . . How happy are the people who live in the holy town of Talmis, beloved of Mandulis, the Sun God, and which is under the scepter of Isis, beautiful of hair and many names." Later additions to the temple included an inscription carved by the Roman governor Aurelius Besarion forbidding pigs in the temple, and an inscription of Silko, king of the Nobadia, recording his victory over the Blemmyes, accompanied by a portrait of the king dressed as a Roman soldier on horseback.

Like Philae, Kalabsha had been submerged for a good part of the year by the construction of the First Aswan Dam. During the 1960s salvage campaign, with funding from the West German government, some 16,000 sandstone blocks comprising the temple were dismantled and moved to the site of Khor Ingi overlooking the High Dam. In the course of dismantling the temple, blocks of a monumental gateway of Augustus were discovered reused in the foundations of the temple, and these were awarded in gratitude to Germany and have been reconstructed in Berlin.

Bibliography

Säve-Söderbergh, T. 1987. *Temples and Tombs of Ancient Nubia: The International Rescue Campaign at Abu Simbel, Philae and Other Sites*. London: Thames and Hudson.

Wright, G.R.H. 1972. *Kalabsha: The Preserving of the Temple*. AV 2. Berlin: Mann.

TAFFEH

Elizabeth Cummins

A complete Egyptian temple now stands in the courtyard of the Rijksmuseum van Oudheden (National Museum of Antiquities) in Leiden, the Netherlands. Its journey to the museum from Nubia mirrors the story of many objects and buildings that were saved dur-

ing the massive rescue excavations in the course of the construction of the High Dam in Aswan between 1960 and 1970. The temple of Taffeh was given as a gift to the Netherlands for its participation in, and financial contributions to, the project and is one of four complete Egyptian temples

Figure 213. The temple of Taffeh, as reconstructed in the Rijksmuseum van Oudheden, Leiden.

396

located outside Egypt, along with the temple of Dendur (Metropolitan Museum of Art, New York), the temple of Debod (Madrid), and the temple of Ellesiya (Museo Egizio, Turin).

The Roman town of Taphis was the original site for the temple, which is thought to have been a sanctuary to the goddess Isis, built during the reign of the Roman emperor Augustus (27 BC–AD 14). In its present state, the undecorated temple consists of a small hypostyle hall with six columns. A niche is located on the rear interior wall, with the remains of a Greek inscription located above. The façade of the temple appears to be quite asymmetrical, with a central door, a smaller door on the right side, and a wall panel on the left, but was most likely originally built with a central door flanked by two screen panels. Minor construction and additions were made to the temple over the course of four hundred years, and there is evidence of use during the Christian and Islamic Periods.

After the construction of the first Aswan Dam in 1899, the temple suffered from numerous floods, which allowed a ship to collide with the temple, causing its collapse. In 1960, the building blocks were numbered and prepared for shipment to the Netherlands. However, it was not until 1976 that construction began on the rebuilding of its 657 blocks. Egypt's conditions for the display of the temple included a climate-controlled space and free admission for the public. The temple was inaugurated in April 1979 and is still one of the most popular attractions of Leiden.

Bibliography

Christophe, L.-A. 1960. "Les monuments de (la) Nubie." *La Revue du Caire* 45, no. 243: 362–73 and no. 244: 397–415.

Raven, M.J. 1996. "The Temple of Taffeh: A Study of Details." *OMRO* 76:41–62.

———. 1999. "The Temple of Taffeh, II: The Graffiti." *OMRO* 79:81–102.

Säve-Söderbergh, T. 1987. *Temples and Tombs of Ancient Nubia: The International Rescue Campaign at Abu Simbel, Philae and Other Sites.* London: Thames and Hudson.

Schneider, H.D. 1979. *Taffeh: Rond de wederopbouw van een Nubische tempel.* The Hague: Staatsuitgeverij.

QERTASSI

Peter Lacovara

One of the most picturesque of all the ruins in Lower Nubia is the Kiosk of Qertassi. The structure is composed of a court surrounded by papyrus columns with two Hathor (Bat) columns positioned at the entrance. The construction was never finished but has been suggested to date to the early Roman Period, based on comparison to the Kiosk of Trajan at Philae.

The building may have been associated with a rock-cut shrine of Isis and Osiris located nearby and the local sandstone quarries. During the salvage campaign, the kiosk was disassembled by the Egyptian Antiquities Service and moved to the site of New Kalabsha.

Figure 214. The temple of Qertassi in its original location.

Bibliography

Gohary, J. 1998. *Guide to the Monuments on Lake Nasser.* Cairo: American University in Cairo Press.

Säve-Söderbergh, T. 1987. *Temples and Tombs of Ancient Nubia: The International Rescue Campaign at Abu Simbel, Philae and Other Site*s. London: Thames and Hudson.

DEBOD

Sue D'Auria

There is some indication of early activity in the region of Debod, ten kilometers south of the Aswan Dam on the west bank of the Nile and close to the ancient religious center of Philae. A-Group and C-Group cemeteries have been documented, and a block from a possible chapel of Sety II was also incorporated into the later temple, suggesting a New Kingdom presence at the site.

In the second century BC, the Meroitic king Adikhalamani (Tabriqo) built a chapel dedicated to the god Amun of *t3-ḥwt*, the ancient place name of Debod. It is one of the few places providing documentation of this king. The north and south interior walls of the small structure were decorated with two registers of scenes of the king presenting such offerings as bread, water, milk, wine, incense, amulets and collars, statuettes, and sistra

Figure 215. The temple of Debod, as reconstructed in the Parque de Rosales, Madrid.

to Amun, Mut, and various other deities and pairs of deities, who are standing in the lower register and seated in the upper.

During the Ptolemaic Period, Kings Ptolemy VI, VIII, and XII expanded the temple and rededicated it to Isis, and the Roman rulers Augustus and Tiberius completed its decoration. The additions, on all four sides, included a pronaos with four unfinished composite columns, side chapels at the north and south, a sanctuary at the western end of the building, crypts, a *mammisi* entered from the southern end of the pronaos, and a stairway with access to the rooftop terrace and chapel dedicated to Osiris. The whole was fronted by three freestanding gateways erected during the Roman Period, and a quay adjacent to the Nile. The undecorated sanctuary contained a granite naos placed under the reign of Ptolemy VIII, which was destroyed in the first half of the nineteenth century, and a smaller (nearly two meters high), similar naos decorated with images of kneeling Nile gods binding the *sm3*-sign (representing unity), dating to the time of Ptolemy XII.

The temple ceased to be used in the sixth century AD, when the temples of Isis at nearby Philae were closed. It was visited by many nineteenth-century travelers, who left descriptions and plans. With the construction of the Aswan High Dam and the UNESCO operations to rescue Nubian monuments from the threat of rising waters, Debod temple was dismantled and given to Spain in recognition of its help in saving the temple of Abu Simbel. Debod temple was reassembled in the Parque de Rosales in Madrid, where it has stood since 1972.

Bibliography
Arnold, D. 1999. *Temples of the Last Pharaohs.* New York and Oxford: Oxford University Press.
Porter, B., and R.L.B. Moss. 1952. *Topographical Bibliography of Ancient Egyptian Hieroglyphic Texts, Reliefs and Paintings.* Vol. 7: *Nubia, the Deserts and Outside Egypt.* Oxford: Griffith Institute.
Roeder, G. 1911–12. *Debod bis Bab Kalabsche.* 2 vols. Cairo: IFAO.

PHILAE

Sue D'Auria

The island of Philae, with its magnificent temple dedicated to Isis, the predominant goddess of the Greco-Roman world, was a stronghold of Egyptian religion in the later periods. Indeed, the last known hieroglyphic text in Egypt, dating to August 29, AD 394 and incised by a priest, was found at Philae. A recent study by Jitse Dijkstra, however, challenges the long-held concept of the longevity of the cult into the sixth century AD at Philae, pointing out that no new structure was built in the temple complex after AD 180, that there are indications of the cult's eventual contraction and isolation, and that the last inscription (in Greek) testifying to priestly activity there dates to AD 456–57. Whatever its eventual end, Philae's influence was felt even into modern times, as the Greek and hieroglyphic inscriptions on two obelisks erected here were used by Jean-François Champollion in his quest to decipher the hieroglyphs. Surprisingly for such an important site, however, the earliest inscribed evidence on the island comes quite late in Egyptian history.

Philae is located just south of Aswan, which was the gateway to Nubia during the Pharaonic Period. In Ptolemaic times, however, Philae became increasingly predominant, and it gradually assumed the role previously held by Aswan. Its prominence as a religious site lies partly in its location: the nearby island of Biga, to the west of Philae, was thought to be one of the burial places of the god Osiris, and a cult to this god was located there from earlier times. Philae's temple was dedicated to the wife of Osiris, Isis. One of the most important rituals at Philae was the ferrying of the image of the goddess every ten days across to Biga, to be reunited symbolically with her husband. Because of Philae's position at the confluence of Egypt and Nubia, Nubian deities were also honored there. According to Dijkstra, texts have shown that during the Roman Period there was regular contact between Philae and the Meroitic state, and that Meroe generously supported the priests and cult there. The fall of Meroe seems to have impacted the fortunes of the temple at Philae and contributed to its decline.

With the building of the Aswan High Dam, the monuments on the island were threatened with permanent total immersion, and they were removed to the neighboring island of Agilkia in a UNESCO operation between 1974 and 1980. Upon completion of this work, Gerhard Haeny published a revised architectural history that is invaluable to the understanding of Philae. The

earliest known activity on the island is represented by some sherds of the Middle Kingdom, as
well as New Kingdom inscribed blocks that may
have been brought from elsewhere. The origin of
an altar and some relief blocks dating to the reign
of the Nubian king Taharqo of the Twenty-fifth
Dynasty is also uncertain. These, however, were
dedicated to the god Amun; the first monuments
constructed in honor of Isis were built in the succeeding Twenty-sixth Dynasty. The main Isis
temple and its associated buildings were located
in the central and western areas of the island, near
a granite outcrop that is thought to have represented the primeval mound of creation. Psamtik
II built a small kiosk here, with two rows of four
columns, but its poor foundations and construction suggest that it was a temporary structure,
perhaps connected with Psamtik's visit to the
nearby First Cataract at the beginning of a campaign against Kush, and not necessarily indicative
of a cult of Isis on the island. This was followed by
a three-room shrine built by Amasis that was later
dismantled when a new temple was constructed.
Three hundred decorated blocks from the Amasis
temple were found in the foundations of the
Second Pylon and pronaos of the Isis temple. The
earliest structure that is still standing is a kiosk or
barque station of Nectanebo I of the Thirtieth
Dynasty. Probably used as a processional way
station, as well as a lookout providing good views
to the Nile, it is located at the far southwest of the
island at the entrance to the complex, to which it
had been moved in antiquity from an original
location that is unknown. It had fourteen columns,
with Hathor-headed lotus capitals supporting an
architrave. Stone screens between the columns bear
reliefs of Nectanebo I before the gods. According
to Dieter Arnold, it was Nectanebo I who con-
ceived the overall design of the temple complex,
including a processional way with pylon fronting
the temple, but in his reign only the temple gateway

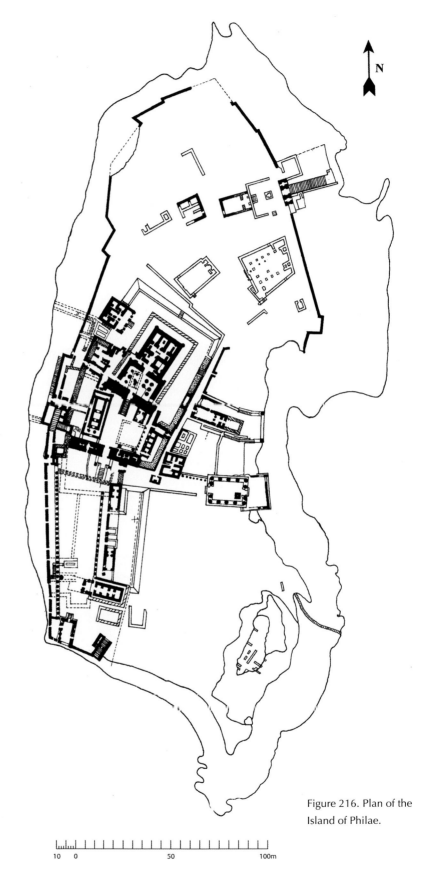

Figure 216. Plan of the
Island of Philae.

10   0   50   100m

was built, which was later incorporated into the First Pylon.

The main temple of Isis was built in the Ptolemaic Period, when the cult of this goddess spread through Egypt and far beyond. Work began under Ptolemy II and was continued by successive rulers, though its decoration was executed over a very long period of time, into the Roman era. In its final form, the temple is entered through the First Pylon, built by Ptolemies V and VI. The towers of the pylon are decorated with images of the king, in this case Ptolemy XII, victorious over his enemies, in the traditional pharaonic fashion of holding them by a hank of hair while smiting them with a club, watched by

Isis, the falcon-headed Horus of Edfu, and Hathor. Above are scenes of the king offering to various gods, and below are reliefs of small figures, representing the Nile, bearing offerings. The pylon leads to a forecourt, on the west side of which is a spectacular birth house (mammisi), one of the most complete and beautiful of these structures, which celebrated the rites relating to the birth of Horus, the son of Isis and Osiris, and his relationship to the reigning king. It originally consisted of two rooms, with the oldest decoration dating to the reign of Ptolemy III, and Ptolemy V recorded actions against a revolt in Upper Egypt on the east side of the porch. Ptolemy VIII enlarged the birth house by adding

Figure 217. The Philae temple of Isis at night. Photo © Chester Higgins Jr 2012.

a new sanctuary at the rear, but the exterior surfaces were decorated from late Ptolemaic into Roman times. To the east, opposite the birth house, a colonnade was built.

The Second Pylon, through which the main temple was accessed, was much smaller, and was completed by Ptolemy VI. At the base of its eastern tower, a section of the granite foundation of the island protrudes, the cult focus, on which was carved an inscription of Ptolemy VI, recording a grant of land made to the goddess, effectively extending the power of the priests at Philae.

According to Haeny, because of the tightly restricted space available to enlarge the temple proper, such usual elements of a Ptolemaic temple as the pronaos (porch or entrance hall) and the peristyle (covered colonnade) of the open court were adapted to the terrain, and reduced in scale. These elements may have also been begun during the reign of Ptolemy VI and decorated later. The sanctuary was dedicated to Isis and her son Harpocrates and still contains a stand for the goddess's barque.

The topography of the island restricted the area upon which the temple could be expanded, and the axis of the structures outside the main temple to the south changes to accommodate the shape of the island.

A number of smaller buildings were constructed during the Ptolemaic Period outside the boundaries of the main temple to the south, along the processional way beginning at the river. These include a temple to Imhotep, the deified sage of the Third Dynasty, and a temple dedicated to the Nubian god Arensnuphis, which was reconstructed as a church in Christian times. A wide, paved terrace, bordered on the east and west by Roman Period colonnades, was created to accommodate the large numbers of pilgrims that must have visited the island. Windows at the back of the western colonnade permitted worshipers to view the tomb of Osiris on the nearby island of Biga. Additional structures, including a temple dedicated to Hathor and a striking though unfinished kiosk overlooking the Nile, attributed to Trajan, were constructed to the east of the main temple, and a monumental gateway with stairs leading to the Nile was built in the Roman Period in the northeast part of the island. Remains of a mud-brick settlement that housed the temple personnel were unfortunately lost with the rising floodwaters.

Bibliography

Arnold, D. 1999. *Temples of the Last Pharaohs.* Oxford: Oxford University Press.

Dijkstra, J.H.F. 2008. *Philae and the End of Ancient Egyptian Religion: A Regional Study of Religious Transformation.* OLA 173.

Haeny, G. 1985. "A Short Architectural History of Philae." *BIFAO* 85:197–233.

MacQuitty, W. 1976. *Island of Isis: Philae, Temple of the Nile.* New York: Scribner's.

Vassilika, Eleni. 1989. *Ptolemaic Philae.* OLA 34.

ELEPHANTINE AND ASWAN

Salima Ikram and Christian Knoblauch

Elephantine Island, located at the northern end of the First Cataract, was a site of major strategic importance throughout the Pharaonic Period, acting as the capital of the first Upper Egyptian nome. This rocky island presumably relied on supplies from the more arable land farther north, as well as from the central administration, particularly during the Fourth and Fifth Dynasties. The main function of the island was to act as a frontier garrison as well as a trading êntrepot for goods from Africa, the mineral wealth of the desert, and the granite from the island and its environs. The current name is presumably derived from the Egyptian *abw*, or Elephant Land. This might be due to the pachyderm-shaped rocks that border the island, the presence of herds of elephants here in antiquity, or the thriving trade in elephant ivory that took place at this location throughout much of its history. Elephantine also played an important role in establishing the height of the inundation, as it was the site of the first Nilometer within Egypt's boundaries. The current Nilometer, located on the eastern face of the island, dates to the Roman Period.

In the late Predynastic Period, the island had a different form, with the southern part, the site of most of the pharaonic and later development, consisting of two large ridges (east and west) that extended well above the waters of the inundation. Declining inundation levels and a series of silt deposits led to the merging of the ridges in the late third millennium BC. The eastern ridge was the first to be settled, and was the site of the island's first temple of many. This very basic temple, dedicated to the goddess Satis, was established in the Naqada III era, and had many subsequent manifestations through the New Kingdom and beyond.

The island has been inhabited almost continuously from the Predynastic Naqada II Period, when an interesting mixture of Egyptian and Nubian features coexisted, until today and has been sporadically excavated from the late nineteenth century onward. Regular excavations were established in 1969 by the Deutsches Archäologisches Institut, joined by the Swiss Institute of Cairo, and these continue today.

Excavations have revealed a series of temples dedicated to Satis as well as to the god Khnum, who replaced Satis in importance during the course of the Dynastic Period, although both deities held sway over the island's populace. The triad of Elephantine was completed by Anukis, and images of all three deities grace the many temples constructed here. In the Greco-Roman

406

era, a cemetery of sacred rams, manifestation of Khnum, was established on the island. The island also housed a sanctuary to Heqaib, the local demigod and erstwhile governor of the island, whose popularity reached its acme during the Middle Kingdom. One of the small pyramids, probably of the Third Dynasty, related to the cult of the king is also located on the island.

The earliest settlement discovered to date was a small collection of dwellings. During the Archaic Period (First and Second Dynasties), Elephantine became the southern border of the newly formed Egyptian state. By the First Dynasty, a small (250 square meters) towered fortress was constructed on the eastern bank, and shortly thereafter the settlement area was surrounded by a defensive brick wall that enclosed the southern part of the eastern ridge, following the contours of the island. This was later enlarged, from the Second Dynasty onward. It has been argued that this was part of a new, more aggressive Egyptian attitude toward the population of Nubia that resulted in the irrecoverable decline of the Lower Nubian A-Group. Setting the evidence for fortification aside, considerable numbers of Nubian ceramics in layers of this date show that Nubian material culture continued to be highly valued by the inhabitants of Elephantine. Whether Nubians lived at Elephantine as they do today, or in surrounding villages, has yet to be determined. The focus of religious life for the local population was the shrine of the local goddess Satis focused on a niche between two boulders north of the fortress wall. It shows little or no evidence of state involvement at this stage of its development.

In the Third Dynasty, the state acted energetically to administratively and ideologically tie the provincial hinterlands to the residence at Memphis. Southern Upper Egypt was no exception, and Elephantine became the site for a royal estate, the administrative components of which were excavated on the western island opposite the Archaic town. A ten- to twelve-meter-high step pyramid was constructed a short distance to the south of here on a granite outcrop and may represent a manifestation of the royal cult in the provincial landscape. Contemporary layers from the East Town show shifting patterns of site use, in particular from food production and storage areas to workshops. Some of these were for stone working, an indication that by the early Old Kingdom, the Aswan region had become an important source for hard stones. Elephantine was also the gateway to the south and was an important stepping stone for expeditions to the copper extraction facility at Buhen, to the granodiorite mines at Gebel al-Asr—the source of the stone used in the famous Khephren statues in the Cairo Museum—as well as for any military expeditions. Seal impressions bearing the names of Fourth and Fifth Dynasty kings, as well as the names and titles of expedition leaders, have been found in the vicinity of the Satis temple and attest to the importance of the site for those charged with missions to the south. During the late Old Kingdom, there is the first evidence for elite burial activity at Qubbet al-Hawa, a distant rocky hill on the west bank of the Nile overlooking Elephantine, which also might have served the tiny town of Syene (Aswan). Some of the tomb owners, including Sabni and Harkhuf, led trading expeditions to Nubia on behalf of the kings of the late Sixth Dynasty. The biographical inscriptions from the façades of their rock-cut tombs are one of the most important textual sources for our understanding of the geopolitical organization of the C-Group and Kerma cultures at that time.

By the end of the Old Kingdom, the area between the two ridges or islands was filled in, creating a larger space for the settlement, which continued to prosper.

Buildings and seal impressions from the Old Kingdom town indicate that it was, at least in the Fourth and Fifth Dynasties, well supplied by the central administration and regarded as being of crucial importance. In the Sixth Dynasty, it gained greater independence from the central authority, which increased during the First Intermediate Period.

The Middle Kingdom saw a resurgence of royal interest in the area, particularly due to the increasing Egyptian control of Nubia, as well as a more lively trading system. During this period, Mentuhotep II constructed a temple to Satis, shortly thereafter replaced by one made by Senwosret I.

This is possibly when the first Khnum Temple was built, and among the administrative and domestic buildings of this new part of town was a shrine where the posthumous cult of Heqaib was celebrated. Heqaib was one of the famed Old Kingdom Elephantine elites buried at Qubbet al-Hawa, and his cult on Elephantine can be traced back to the late Old Kingdom and First Intermediate Period. During the early Middle Kingdom, the scale of the cult reached new heights under the patronage of the powerful chiefs of the local administrative districts (nomarchs) who had statue shrines constructed for themselves in the new temple. Royal involvement in the cult is attested

Figure 218. View of Elephantine Island by David Roberts.

but limited to small statues of late Twelfth and Thirteenth Dynasty date. Rather, from the Eleventh Dynasty onward, royal attention was fixed firmly on the shrine of the goddess Satis. Intef II and III made architectural alterations to the existing shrine, while Mentuhotep II and Senwosret I in turn undertook to fully rebuild the temple and its environs according to an entirely new plan using decorated stone surfaces. In terms of religious practice, of paramount importance was the festival of inundation, which was celebrated in an adjoining courtyard. The unprecedented scale of state incursion into the local temple has contemporary parallels at other Egyptian sites. While on a national level it clearly relates to the consolidation of the power of the new regime, it cannot be divorced from developments at the local level. In particular, Elephantine and its gods gained new religious relevance following the annexation of Lower Nubia during the reign of Senwosret I. A papyrus from the late Middle Kingdom sheds light on another aspect of its existence at this time: although now positioned some 250 kilometers north of the actual border, Elephantine was organized into the string of fortresses that stretched from the Second Cataract into Upper Egypt. These fortresses assisted in the northward movement of mined and traded goods toward the Egyptian heartland and the southward movement of troops and expeditions into Nubia. They also had an important defensive function, and it is significant that a thick mud-brick town wall was constructed on the northwestern side of the island at this time, perhaps an indication for the rising threat posed by Kerma.

The political allegiance of Elephantine during the Second Intermediate Period is unresolved. Lower Nubia came under the political influence of the Kerma kingdom, and Elephantine's status may once again have reverted to that of a border town. Despite the logic of this, there is no uncontested evidence for activity by the Seventeenth Dynasty Theban kings at Elephantine, and one wonders whether it was part of an active zone of engagement between Kerma and Theban territory, where neither power could effectively exercise sovereignty. After the reconquest of Lower Nubia and the conquest of Upper Nubia that began under the pharaohs of the early Eighteenth Dynasty, the religious and economic relevance of Elephantine once again assumed predominance. The town wall of the late Middle Kingdom was destroyed and not replaced, while Hatshepsut and Thutmose III rebuilt the Satis temple and enlarged the Khnum temple. Alterations and additions to the religious setting were undertaken by Thutmose IV, Amenhotep III, and Ramesses II. The temples were part of a much larger precinct that by now covered up to one-third of the town, incorporating important economic and administrative institutions. The prosperity of the local population can be glimpsed in the decorated stone doorways that flanked the entrances to domestic structures. Doubtless, this time of prosperity is when Syene (Aswan) started to gain importance, and it is mentioned in texts and appears in the archaeological record, as is currently being recorded by the Swiss Institute's mission.

The Third Intermediate Period and the loss of Egyptian control over Nubia made Elephantine (and Aswan), once again, an important border post (albeit an area with little in the way of royal monuments of a non-military nature), with an influx of military personnel, including mercenaries from different areas. This changed briefly in the Twenty-sixth Dynasty with a fresh Nilometer being erected, and work resumed on the temples. During the time of the Persian invasion, Elephantine once again played the role of frontier post, and Aramaic-Jewish mercenaries and colonists were stationed on the island and in Syene (Aswan). Their remains include a temple to Yahweh and a significant deposit of papyrus texts pertaining to the daily lives of the local inhabitants, recovered from houses of the period.

From the Thirtieth Dynasty to the Roman era, Elephantine once again was a focus of royal religious activity, with many new components added to the temples, including large terraces that overlooked the riverbank. Nectanebo I and II both built structures in the Khnum precinct. Increasingly, the character of the island came to be almost wholly determined by the nature of its temples, which received particular attention from the Ptolemaic rulers of Egypt. At the same time, the town flourished, and many of the house remains of the period have been excavated. With the advent of Christianity, churches and monasteries replaced the temples, which, in turn, gave way to mosques and more paltry settlements later.

Until the New Kingdom, Elephantine appears to have been the dominant settlement in the far south of Egypt. Thereafter Aswan (Syene) started to rival it in population, and eclipsed it by the late Ptolemaic Period, gradually assuming primacy for administration. In addition to extensive granite quarries, the east bank of the river was the site of harbors, houses, temples, and administrative buildings, and this area continues in use as the main part of the city until today.

Bibliography

Deutsches Archäologisches Institut. Annual Preliminary Reports. http://www.dainst.org/index_54ddb1c8bb1f 14a184920017f0000011_en.html

Dreyer, G. 1986. *Der Tempel der Satet: Die Funde der Frühzeit und des Alten Reiches.* AV 39, Elephantine 8. Mainz: von Zabern.

Franke, D. 1994. *Das Heiligtum des Heqaib auf Elephantine.* SAGA 9. Heidelberg: Heidelberger Orientverlag.

Habachi, L. 1985. *The Sanctuary of Heqaib.* AV 33, Elephantine 4. Mainz: von Zabern.

Jaritz, H. 1980. *Die Terrassen vor den Tempeln des Chnum und der Satet.* AV 32, Elephantine 3. Mainz: von Zabern.

Kaiser, W. 1998a. *Elephantine: Die antike Stadt.* Cairo: Deutsches Archäologisches Institut.

———. 1998b. *Elephantine: The Ancient Town. Official*

Guidebook of the German Institute of Archaeology. Cairo: Deutsches Archäologisches Institut.

Pilgrim, C. von. 1996. *Untersuchungen in der Stadt des Mittleren Reiches und der Zweiten Zwischenzeit.* AV 91, Elephantine 18. Mainz: von Zabern.

Raue, D. 2002. "Nubians on Elephantine Island." *Sudan & Nubia* 6:20–24.

Seidlmayer, S. 1996. "Town and State in the Early Old Kingdom: A View from Elephantine." In J. Spencer, ed., *Aspects of Early Egypt,* 108–27. London: British Museum Press.

Storemyr, P., et al. 2002. "Survey at Chephren's Quarry, Gebel el-Asr, Lower Nubia." *Sudan & Nubia* 6:25–29.

Ziermann, M. 1993. *Befestigungsanlagen und Stadtentwicklung in der Frühzeit und im frühen Alten Reich.* AV 87, Elephantine 16. Mainz: von Zabern.

Notes on Contributors

Charles Bonnet is the former archaeologist of the canton of Geneva. He is a member of the Institute of France (Academy of Inscriptions and Belles-lettres), and former vice president of the Swiss Federal Commission of Historical Monuments. For forty years, he has been the director of the Kerma and Doukki Gel sites. He is professor emeritus at the University of Geneva and former president of the International Society for Nubian Studies. His works in Egypt at Deir al-Medina, Serabit al-Khadim or Pelusium (Sinai) are authoritative.

Elizabeth Cummins is a PhD candidate in the Department of Art History, Emory University. She specializes in New Kingdom Egyptian art and has worked with Egyptian and Nubian collections such as the Boston Museum of Fine Arts and the Michael C. Carlos Museum, Emory University.

Sue D'Auria received her MA in Egyptology from the University of Pennsylvania. She spent nearly twenty years in the Department of Ancient Egyptian, Nubian, and Near Eastern Art of the Museum of Fine Arts, Boston, and is the former associate curator at the Huntington Museum of Art. She has edited several Egyptological publications, most recently *Offerings to the Discerning Eye: An Egyptological Medley in Honor of Jack A. Josephson.*

Susan K. Doll received her PhD in Classical and Oriental Studies from Brandeis University in 1978. She was one of the co-authors of the *Egypt's Golden Age* catalogue and has worked on Napatan use of Egyptian religious texts since completing her thesis on the sarcophagi of Anlamani and Aspelta.

Geoff Emberling is assistant research scientist at the Kelsey Museum, University of Michigan. He co-directed two seasons of salvage work in the Fourth Cataract region in 2007 and 2008 that focused on remains of the Kerma period, including a settlement apparently dedicated to extracting gold.

Marjorie M. Fisher earned her MA from Johns Hopkins University and her PhD from the University of Michigan. She is adjunct assistant professor of Egyptology at the University of Michigan, and associate director for epigraphy of the University of Michigan Abydos Middle Cemetery Project. Her field experience also includes work with Kent Weeks's excavations in the Valley of the Kings, and as Epigrapher with the Epigraphic Survey of Chicago House Luxor. She is the author of *The Sons of Ramses II* and a series of scholarly articles on New Kingdom topics.

World-renowned archaeologist Zahi Hawass is the former minister of state for antiquities in Egypt. He directs important excavations at Giza, Saqqara, and the Valley of the Kings. He has made major discoveries, especially with regard to the royal mummies, and written numerous scientific articles and more than twelve books. He received his PhD from the University of Pennsylvania and has been presented with numerous honors, including five honorary doctorate degrees.

Joyce Haynes has an MA from the University of Toronto and is a doctoral candidate in Egyptian art and archaeology at the University of Toronto. She worked as a research fellow for the Art of the Ancient World at the MFA for twenty years, from 1989 to 2009. She is the author of a number

411

of books on Ancient Nubia and Egypt: *Nubia: Ancient Kingdoms of Africa* and *Egypt in the Age of the Pharaohs and Egyptian Dynasties*. She is also the author of numerous scholarly articles on ancient Egypt and Nubia.

Chester Higgins is the author of the photo collections *Drums of Life, Some Time Ago, Feeling the Spirit: Searching the World for the People of Africa*—a comprehensive look at the African Diaspora—and *Elder Grace: The Nobility of Aging*. His memoir, entitled *Echo of the Spirit: A Photographer's Journey*, was published in 2005. A staff photographer for *The New York Times* since 1975, Higgins's photographs have appeared in *ArtNews, The New York Times Sunday Magazine, Look, Life, Newsweek, Fortune, Geo, The New Yorker*, and *Archaeology*. His work is the topic of two PBS films, *An American Photographer: Chester Higgins, Jr.* and *Brotherman*, and has been featured on CBS *Sunday Morning News*, PBS *The NewsHour*, and ABC *Like It Is* and *Freedom Forum*. www.chesterhiggins.com

Salima Ikram earned her AB from Bryn Mawr College and her MPhil and PhD from Cambridge University. She is a professor at the American University in Cairo, and has excavated in Turkey, Greece, and Sudan, and throughout Egypt, as well as being the co-director of the North Kharga Oasis Survey. She has published extensively on a variety of subjects, including mummies, tombs, and animals, for scholarly and popular audiences, including children.

W. Raymond Johnson has been director of the Epigraphic Survey of the Oriental Institute, University of Chicago, based at Chicago House in Luxor, Egypt, since 1997. He is a research associate (associate professor) of the University of Chicago's Department of Near Eastern Languages and Civ-

ilizations (NELC) and the Oriental Institute and received his PhD in Egyptian archaeology from the University of Chicago in 1992.

Christian Knoblauch is Universitätsassistent (University Assistant) at the University of Vienna. He has a PhD from Macquarie University that explored the unique social lives of Egyptian expatriates living in the Middle Kingdom Nubian fortresses and is currently undertaking research into the production of pottery in Egyptian-controlled Nubia. He has extensive excavation experience in Egypt at Helwan and Abydos.

Peter Lacovara is senior curator of Ancient Egyptian, Nubian, and Near Eastern art at the Michael C. Carlos Museum of Emory University. Before coming to Atlanta, he was assistant curator in the Department of Ancient Egyptian, Nubian, and Near Eastern Art at the Museum of Fine Arts, Boston. He received his PhD in Egyptian archaeology from the Oriental Institute of the University of Chicago.

Yvonne J. Markowitz is the Rita J. Kaplan and Susan B. Kaplan Curator of Jewelry in the Textile and Fashion Arts department at the Museum of Fine Arts, Boston. She was the editor of *Jewelry: Journal of the American Society of Jewelry Historians* and has been an editor of *Adornment Magazine* since 2005. Markowitz is also co-director of the Association for the Study of Jewelry and Related Arts, which organizes an annual conference on jewelry. She has curated several ancient art exhibitions and has published extensively in the area of ancient and contemporary jewelry.

Robert Morkot studied at University College London and the Humboldt University Berlin. He has written many academic papers on Nubia under Egyptian rule during the New Kingdom and on the development of the Napatan Kingdom. Among his books is *The Black Pharaohs: Egypt's Nubian Rulers.*

Claudia Näser is junior professor in the Department of Egyptology and Northeast African Archaeology at Humboldt University, Berlin. Her research and publications have focused on funerary archaeology in Egypt and ancient Nubia, the archaeology of Nubia from prehistory up to the Islamic Period, the history and archaeology of Egypt's expansion into Nubia, the archaeology of nomadism, archaeological theory, and the impact of politics on archaeological practice. She has excavated extensively in Egypt and Sudan, and currently directs two field projects in Sudan. She is co-editor of the series *Meroitica.*

David O'Connor is Lila Acheson Wallace Professor of Ancient Egyptian Art at the Institute of Fine Arts of New York University and co-director of the Yale University–University of Pennsylvania–IFA Excavations at Abydos, Egypt. He has authored many books, including *Ancient Nubia: Egypt's Rival in Africa.*

Pamela Rose is an archaeologist and ceramicist working at the site of Qasr Ibrim in Egyptian Nubia, and Sesebi in Sudan. She is employed by the Austrian Archaeological Institute in Cairo.

Mimi Santini-Ritt has an MA from Brandeis University in Mediterranean Studies. She is currently a senior associate at the Boston Museum of Fine Arts, where she has also been assisting with the cataloguing of ancient Egyptian and Nubian art in the Art of the Ancient World's storage project since 2003.

Bruce Williams earned a PhD in Egyptian and Near Eastern archaeology from the University of Chicago. He has authored eight volumes in the series Oriental Institute Nubian Expedition presenting finds made in the 1960s' salvage of monuments and archaeological remains from the reservoir of the Aswan High Dam. In addition to authoring and co-authoring other works on Nubia and early Egypt, he has done field work in Turkey, Egypt, and Sudan, including co-directing two seasons of the Oriental Institute Nubian Expedition to salvage archaeological remains from the Merowe Dam at the Fourth Cataract in Sudan.

Janice W. Yellin received her PhD from Brandeis University, having completed one of the first theses in ancient Nubian Studies to be written in the United States. The author of articles on Meroitic funerary religion and art, she is currently a professor of art history at Babson College (Wellesley, MA) and has held the Martha Willcomb Lectureship in Ancient Egyptian Civilization at Harvard University. As director of the Royal Pyramids of Kush Project (begun with the late Dr. Friedrich Hinkel, Berlin) she is publishing the pyramids and tombs of Napatan and Meroitic elites at Meroe.

Following pages:
Figure 219. The Temple of Dendur.

Abbreviations

ÄAT   Ägypten und Altes Testament (Wiesbaden)

AJSL   The American Journal of Semitic Languages and Literatures (Chicago)

AV   Archäologische Veröffentlichungen (Berlin)

BES   Bulletin of the Egyptological Seminar (New York)

BIFAO   Bulletin de l'Institut français d'archéologie orientale (Cairo)

BiOr   Bibliotheca Orientalis (Leiden)

BSF   Beiträge zur Sudanforschung (Vienna)

BSFE   Bulletin de la Société française d'égyptologie (Paris)

CA   Current Anthropology (Chicago)

CEDAE   Centre d'étude et de documentation sur l'Ancienne Égypte (Cairo and Paris)

CRIPEL   Cahiers de recherches de l'Institut de papyrologie et d'égyptologie de Lille (Lille)

EA   Egyptian Archaeology: Bulletin of the Egypt Exploration Society (London)

EAZ   Ethnographisch-archaeologische Zeitschrift (Berlin)

FuB   Forschungen und Berichte der Staatlichen Museen zu Berlin (Berlin)

GM   Göttinger Miszellen (Göttingen)

GOF   Göttinger Orientforschungen (Wiesbaden)

IFAO   Institut français d'archéologie orientale (Cairo)

JARCE   Journal of the American Research Center in Egypt (Cairo)

JEA   Journal of Egyptian Archaeology (London)

JNES   Journal of Near Eastern Studies (Chicago)

JSSEA   Journal of the Society for the Study of Egyptian Antiquities (Toronto)

LAA   Liverpool Annals of Archaeology and Anthropology (Liverpool)

LÄ   Lexikon der Ägyptologie, ed. Wolfgang Helck, Eberhard Otto, Wolfhart Westendorf, 7 vols. (Wiesbaden, 1972–92)

MittSAG   Mitteilungen der Sudanarchäologischen Gesellschaft zu Berlin e.V. (Berlin)

MDAIK   Mitteilungen des Deutschen Archäologischen Instituts, Abteilung Kairo (Berlin/Wiesbaden/Mainz)

OINE   University of Chicago, Oriental Institute Nubian Expedition (Chicago)

OLA   Orientalia Lovaniensia Analecta (Leuven)

OMRO   Oudheidkundige Mededelingen uit het Rijksmuseum van Oudheden (Leiden)

PAM   Polish Archaeology in the Mediterranean (Warsaw)

RdE   Revue d'égyptologie (Paris, Louvain)

SAGA   Studien zur Archäologie und Geschichte Altägyptens (Heidelberg)

SAK   Studien zur altägyptischen Kultur (Hamburg)

SAOC   Studies in Ancient Oriental Civilization (Chicago)

SDAIK   Sonderschriften des Deutschen Archäologischen Instituts, Abteilung Kairo (Berlin/Mainz)

SJE   Scandinavian Joint Expedition to Sudanese Nubia (Odense)

VA   Varia aegyptiaca (San Antonio)

ZÄS   Zeitschrift für Ägyptische Sprache und Altertumskunde (Berlin/Leipzig)

Museums with Nubian Collections

Some of the most important collections, as well as museums with significant single pieces, are noted below. Visitors should be careful to check museum hours and gallery openings prior to traveling.

NORTH AMERICA
Canada
Toronto, Ontario
Royal Ontario Museum
100 Queen's Park
Toronto, ON M5S 2C6
(416) 586-5549
www.rom.on.ca

The Royal Ontario Museum has a display collection of Nubian objects from the work of Nicholas Millet at Gebel Adda, additional material from its own excavations, and materials on loan from the Museum of Fine Arts in Boston and elsewhere.

United States
Connecticut
New Haven
Peabody Museum of Natural History, Yale University
170 Whitney Avenue
New Haven, Connecticut 06520
(203) 432-5050
www.peabody.yale.edu

The Peabody Museum has a small collection of material from its participation in the 1960s Salvage Campaign, including a *shawabti* of the Prince of Miam, Hekanefer.

Georgia
Atlanta
Michael C. Carlos Museum of Emory University
571 South Kilgo Circle
Atlanta, Georgia 30322
(404) 727-4282
www.carlos.emory.edu

The Michael C. Carlos Museum has a small collection of Nubian material incorporated into its display of Egyptian art, but plans have been made for a gallery devoted to ancient Nubia.

Illinois
Chicago
The Oriental Institute Museum of the University of Chicago
1155 East 58th Street
Chicago, Illinois 60637
(773) 702-9520
oi.uchicago.edu/museum/

The Oriental Institute Museum has the only gallery devoted to Nubian art currently open in the United States. It showcases material from its participation in the 1960s Salvage Campaign.

Massachusetts
Boston
Museum of Fine Arts
465 Huntington Avenue
Boston, MA 02215
(617) 267-9300
www.mfa.org

The Museum of Fine Arts, Boston probably has the finest collection of Nubian art to be found anywhere in the world. However, currently much of the material is in storage. There are plans to reopen the Nubian gallery. The great sculptures of Aspelta and Anlamani remain on display.

417

Worcester
Worcester Art Museum
55 Salisbury Street
Worcester, MA 01609-3196
(508) 799-4406
www.worcesterart.org
The Worcester Art Museum's small but fine collection boasts the plaque of Prince Arikankharer, one of the finest pieces of Meroitic sculpture known.

New York
Brooklyn
The Brooklyn Museum
200 Eastern Parkway
Brooklyn, NY 11238-6052
(718) 638-5000
www.brooklynmuseum.org
The Brooklyn Museum has an outstanding collection of Egyptian art and a large number of notable pieces from the Twenty-fifth Dynasty.

Manhattan
The Metropolitan Museum of Art
1000 Fifth Avenue at 82nd Street
New York, New York 10028-0198
(212) 536-7710
www.metmuseum.org
The Metropolitan Museum of Art houses the rescued temple of Dendur, awarded to the United States for its participation in the 1960s Nubian Salvage Campaign.

Ohio
Cleveland
Cleveland Museum of Art
11150 East Boulevard
Cleveland, Ohio 44106
(216) 421-7350
www.clevelandart.org
The Cleveland Museum of Art has a number of spectacular reliefs from the tomb of Mentuemhat.

Toledo
Toledo Museum of Art
2445 Monroe St.
Toledo, OH 43620
(419) 255-8000
www.toledomuseum.org
In the collection of the Toledo Museum is an over-life-size statue of King Tanwetamani.

Pennsylvania
Philadelphia
The University of Pennsylvania Museum of
    Archaeology and Anthropology
3260 South Street
Philadelphia, Pennsylvania 19104
(215) 898-4045
www.penn.museum
The University of Pennsylvania Museum's excavations yielded important Nubian material from Buhen and Karanog, though little of this material is currently on display.

Tennessee
Memphis
Art Museum at the University of Memphis
142 CFA Building
University of Memphis
(901) 678-2224
http://www.memphis.edu/amum
The museum at the University of Memphis includes in its collection a number of objects, formerly in the Museum of Fine Arts, Boston, dating from the A-Group through the Meroitic Periods.

EUROPE
Austria
    Vienna
    Kunsthistorisches Museum
    Burgring 5, 1010 Vienna
    01 52524534
    www.khm.at/en/khm

The Kunsthistoriches Museum is a repository for many of the artifacts from Hermann Junker's excavations in Nubia.

Belgium
    Brussels
    Cinquantenaire Museum
    Parc du Cinquantenaire 10, 1000 Brussels
    +32 (0)2 741 72 11
    www.kmkg-mrah.be/cinquantenairemuseum
The collection in Brussels includes objects from the Napatan and Meroitic Periods.

Denmark
    Copenhagen
    Ny Carlsberg Glyptotek
    Dantes Plads 7, 1556 Copenhagen
    +45 33 41 81 41
    http://www.glyptoteket.dk/
Ny Carlsberg Glyptotek has important sculptures from John Garstang's 1910–12 excavations at Meroe and objects from F.Ll. Griffith's excavations in Kawa in 1933.

England
    Bolton
    Bolton Museum
    Le Mans Crescent, Bolton, BL1 1SE
    01204 332211
    www.boltonmuseums.org.uk
Objects from John Garstang's 1909–14 excavations at Meroe, F.Ll. Griffith's excavations at Napata and Sanam Abu Dom in 1912–13, A.M. Blackman's work at Sesebi in the 1930s, and the Egypt Exploration Society excavations at Qasr Ibrim in the 1960s, which includes an important collection of textiles, are in the collection at the Bolton Museum.

Cambridge
The Fitzwilliam Museum
Trumpington St., Cambridge CB2 1RB
01223 332900
www.fitzmuseum.cam.ac.uk/index/html
In the collection of the Fitzwilliam Museum are a lintel from Qasr Ibrim as well as Meroitic pottery and jewelry.

Liverpool
Garstang Museum of Archaeology
School of Archaeology, Classics and Egyptology, Liverpool University
14 Abercromby Square, Liverpool
+44 (0)151 794-2467
http://www.liv.ac.uk/sace/garstang-museum/index.htm
The Garstang Museum contains a significant number of objects from John Garstang's excavations at Meroe, in addition to the original excavation records (including photographic archive). The Garstang Museum also holds (and displays) a small number of objects from Reisner's Kerma excavations.

World Museum
William Brown Street, Liverpool L3 8EN
0151 478 4393
liverpoolmuseums.org.uk/wml/
A large number of objects from John Garstang's work at Meroe went to the World Museum (formerly the Liverpool Museum).

London
The British Museum
Great Russell Street, London WC1B 3DG
44 (0)20 7323 8299
www.britishmuseum.org
The vast British Museum has a gallery devoted exclusively to Nubia, which includes the reliefs from the chapel of Queen Shanakdakheto, the first female ruler at Meroe.

Petrie Museum of Egyptian Archaeology
University College London
Malet Place, London WC1E 6BT
44 (0)20 7679 2884
www.petrie.ucl.ac.uk

The Petrie Museum houses some significant material from the work of John Garstang and Henry Wellcome in Sudan.

Oxford
Ashmolean Museum of Art and Archaeology,
    Oxford University
Beaumont Street, Oxford OX1 2PH
(01865) 278000
www.ashmolean.org

A jewel in the Ashmolean Museum is the small temple of Taharqo from Kawa. A wealth of other Nubian artifacts is grouped around it.

France
Grenoble
Musée de Grenoble
5, place de Lavalette
38000 Grenoble
0476 63 44 44
www.museedegrenoble.fr/accueil.htm

The museum at Grenoble has a *ba*-bird from Gebel Adda in its collection.

Lille
Musée des beaux-arts de Lille
18 Place de la République
59000 Lille 03 20 06 78 00
www.pba-lille.fr

An important collection of Nubian objects excavated by the University of Lille was transferred in 2006 to the Musée des beaux-arts, including material from the excavations of Mirgissa Fort.

Paris
Musée du Louvre
Place des Pyramides
75001 Paris
01 40 20 50 50
www.louvre.fr/llv/commun/home.jsp?bm
    Locale=en

The Louvre has a collection of Nubian objects ranging from Kerma pottery to a Meroitic offering table.

Germany
Berlin
Humboldt Universität
Institut für Archäologie, Lehrbereich Ägyp-
    tologie und Archäologie Nordostafrikas
Mohrenstrasse 40, 10117 Berlin
+49-(0)30-2093-4750
www.archaeologie.hu-berlin.de/aegy_anoa

A collection of archaeological material from the excavations of Humboldt Universität at Musawwarat al-Sufra may be found at the Institute for Archaeology.

Neues Museum
Genthiner Strasse 38, 10785 Berlin
030 26642-4242
www.neues-museum.de

Some of the important sculpture brought back by Karl Richard Lepsius from Gebel Barkal is newly displayed in the renovated Egyptian Galleries of the Neues Museum.

Leipzig
Ägyptisches Museum—Georg Stendorff—
    der Universität Leipzig
Goethestrasse 2, 04109 Leipzig
0341 7 973 7010
www.uni-leipzig.de/~egypt/Museum.htm

The University of Leipzig features material from Georg Steindorff's work at Aniba.

Munich
Staatliche Sammlung Ägyptisches Kunst
Residenzstrasse 1, 80333 Munich
089 298546
http://www.aegyptisches-museum-
muenchen.de/
The Staatliche Sammlung Ägyptische Kunst has
holdings of Meroitic material, including jewelry
of Queen Amanishakheto excavated by Ferlini.

Greece
Athens
National Archeological Museum
44 Patission St., Athens 10682
+30 210 8217724
www.namuseum.gr/wellcome-en.html
The National Archaeological Museum has in its
collection bronze sculptures from Dynasty
Twenty-five, including that of the princess and
wab-priestess Takushit.

The Netherlands
Leiden
Rijksmuseum van Oudheden
Rapenburg 28, 2311 EW Leiden
071 5163163
www.rmo.nl
The temple of Taffeh, given by Egypt in acknowl-
edgment of Dutch participation in the UNESCO
campaign to rescue the monuments, is displayed
in the Rijskmuseum van Oudheden.

Poland
Poznań
Archaeological Museum
ul. Wodna 27, 61-781 Poznań
61-852 51
www.muzarp.poznan.pl/eindex.html
Holdings include objects from Polish work in
Old Dongola and Kadero, and the rescue project
at the Fourth Cataract.

Scotland
Edinburgh
National Museum of Scotland
Chambers St., Edinburgh EH1 1JF
0131 225 7534
www.nms.ac.uk
The National Museum of Scotland features a rich
Second Intermediate Period burial from Thebes
that contained artifacts from the Kerma culture.
There is also a collection of Meroitic material,
including a colossal sculpture of Arensnuphis
from Meroe.

Spain
Madrid
Paseo del Pintor Rosales, 2, 28008 Madrid
913 667 415
The temple of Debod was given to Spain in recog
nition of its support in saving Abu Simbel. It is
displayed in the Parque de Rosales in Madrid.

Switzerland
Geneva
Musée d'Art et d'Histoire
rue Charles-Galland 2
1204 Geneva
022 418 26 00
www.ville-ge.ch/mah
A display in the Musée d'Art et d'Histoire showcases the work of the University of Geneva's mission to Kerma.

AFRICA
Egypt
Aswan
Nubia Museum
al-Fanadek Street (opposite Basma Hotel)
81111 Aswan
(20) 97-319333
www.numibia.net/nubia
The Nubia Museum is a showpiece of the city.

Built by UNESCO to celebrate the work of the Nubian Salvage Campaign, it recounts the history of Nubia in artifacts ranging in date from the Prehistoric Period to the present day in a sleek modern setting. The building itself is a rendering in stone of traditional Nubian mud-brick architecture and is surrounded by a sculpture garden decorated with many more monuments.

Elephantine Island Nubian Museum
The old Nubia Museum on the island of Elephantine, in the picturesque Victorian house that was the home of the architect of the first dam, is awaiting renovation, but beside it is a new museum constructed to illustrate the finds of the German Archaeological Institute's work on the island.

Cairo
Egyptian Museum
Tahrir Square
02 5782448
www.egyptianmuseum.gov.eg
The Egyptian Museum's vast holdings include the Piankhi Victory Stela from Gebel Barkal, the alabaster statue of Amenirdis, and a sample of some of the most significant finds of all three Nubian Salvage Campaigns.

Sudan
Kerma
Kerma Museum
At the site of Kerma
www.kerma.ch/index.php?option=com_content&task=category&sectionid=6&id=31&Itemid=58
A new site museum has opened near the ancient city of Kerma to display some of the treasures unearthed in the Third Cataract area, including a cache of statues from Doukki Gel.

Khartoum
National Museum
Sharia al-Neel, Khartoum
The National Museum in Khartoum houses a vast collection of artifacts from the whole country, including Second Cataract Fort temples of Buhen and Semna and monuments saved from the waters of Lake Nasser.

Glossary

Book of the Dead

What is commonly referred to as the *Egyptian Book of the Dead* is a collection of spells dealing with the passage of the deceased through the underworld, and is more properly named the *Book of Going Forth by Day*. These incantations were inscribed on papyrus, linen, tomb walls, and certain burial goods. Their antecedents lay in the Pyramid Texts carved on the walls of the burial chambers in the royal pyramids in the late Fifth and Sixth Dynasties, and in the subsequent Coffin Texts found inscribed on the interior of wooden coffins of Middle Kingdom elites.

bucranium

A skull or head of a cow or a bull, or an image of one used as a decorative motif.

cataract

A rapid caused by the exposure of underlying rock in a riverbed. There are six cataracts in the Nile River.

deffufa

A local Nubian word for the large constructions made of mud brick found at Kerma. The Upper or Eastern Deffufa was a well-preserved funerary chapel in the cemetery, and the Lower or Western Deffufa was the main temple in the ancient town.

Dongola Reach

The area around the Third Cataract where the Nile returns to its northward flow from the southerly bend ending at the Fourth Cataract. It is named after the modern Sudanese town of Dongola, located on this part of the river.

dromos

A term adapted from ancient Greek referring to the monumental entrance to a building or sacred area.

ell

A term for a unit of measurement, usually a cubit in ancient Egypt. It was traditionally the length of a forearm, but the actual measurement seems to have varied considerably between 45 and 52.5 centimeters.

gebel

The Arabic word for mountain.

hafir

Local Sudanese name for a water reservoir.

kandake/Candace

The title for a female ruler or consort, particularly among the Napatans.

maat/Maat

Cosmic order or balance, rectitude; the name of a goddess personifying the same; she is shown seated and wearing a feather on her head.

mammisi

A building type in temples known as a divine birth house.

Medjay (plural Medjayu)

A semi-nomadic people who played a significant role in the Egyptian police and military (usually equated with the Pan-Grave people).

naos

Holy of holies; a shrine placed in the temple sanctuary.

Nehesy (plural Nehesyu)
Egyptian word for people of Nubia.

peristyle
Covered colonnade surrounding a courtyard or building.

peshto
A Nubian governor during the Meroitic Period who exercised control over both civil and religious institutions.

pronaos
In a Greek or Roman temple, the structure between the shrine and the colonnade.

pyramidion
The capstone of a pyramid.

qore/kor
Title used by a Kushite ruler during the Meroitic Period.

Red Crown
A crown worn by the king representing his rule over Lower Egypt.

sed festival
A 'jubilee' celebrated in Egypt in honor of the first thirty years of the king's rule, after which it was celebrated every three or four years.

serekh
A hieroglyphic symbol containing a royal name, comprising a rectangular triple-niched façade of an early Egyptian palace surmounted by a Horus falcon. It predates the cartouche, the oval ring later used to enclose royal names.

shaduf
A device used to lift water out of the Nile and deposit it in the fields, consisting of a bucket at one end of a pole with a counterpoise attached to it, manipulated by a rope. A person would pull down on the rope to lift the bucket up out of the water, then shift it over the ground and dump the bucket of water onto the earth or into another container.

shawabti
Figurine found in Egyptian and some Nubian tombs representing an individual who does the work for the deceased in the afterlife. In some Egyptian tombs, 365 *shawabti*s have been found, one figure working for each day of the year, and more than a thousand have been found in some Nubian royal tombs of the Twenty-fifth Dynasty.

talatat
Small sandstone blocks characteristically used in the constructions of Akhenaten; they could be carried by one person and were approximately the length of the elbow to the end of the fingers of a hand.

temenos
Taken from an ancient Greek term; a walled-in area or official precinct of a temple.

tumulus
A mound constructed of dirt and/or stones under which a person was buried.

wadi
Valley or water course that remained dry except during torrential rains.

White Crown
A crown worn by the Egyptian king representing his rule over Upper Egypt.

Figure 220. The ram-headed Amun, from the Apedemak temple at Naqa. Photo © Chester Higgins Jr 2012.

Sources of Illustrations

Cover image. Pyramids of Meroe. © Chester Higgins Jr 2012.

Endpaper image. Sandstone relief of lion and elephant, from the Lion Temple at Musawwarat al-Sufra. Photo © Chester Higgins Jr 2012.

1. Soleb temple. © Chester Higgins Jr 2012.
2. Map of Egypt and Nubia. Drawing by Thomas R. James.
3. Map of Lower and Upper Nubia from Aswan to the Third Cataract. Drawing by Thomas R. James.
4. Map of Upper Nubia from the Third Cataract south. Drawing by Thomas R. James.
5. Map of Egypt. Drawing by Thomas R. James.
6. Nubian pyramid at night. © Chester Higgins Jr 2012.
7. The Second Cataract. Etching from *Egypt, Nubia and Ethiopia Illustrated*, published by Dufour Mulat et Boulanger, printed by Gilquin et Dupain (Paris, 1862).
8. Kitchener's Island and dunes. © Chester Higgins Jr 2012.
9. Sand dunes in the Nubian desert. © Chester Higgins Jr 2012.
10. Map of Nubia, 1,000,000 BP–3000 BC, with archaeological sites of the Paleolithic, Mesolithic, and Neolithic Periods. Adapted from D.N. Edwards, *The Nubian Past: An Archaeology of the Sudan* (London: Routledge), and D.A. Welsby and J.R. Anderson, eds., *Sudan: Ancient Treasures* (London: British Museum Press). Drawing by Thomas R. James.
11. Rock inscription at Gebel Sheikh Suleiman. After W.B. Emery, *Lost Land Emerging* (New York: Charles Scribner's Sons, 1967), fig. 13, p. 173. Drawing by Laura Brubaker.
12. Map of Egypt and Nubia, 3000–2000 BC. Adapted from D.B. O'Connor, "Early States along the Nubian Nile," in *Egypt and Africa: Nubia from Prehistory to Islam*, ed. W.V. Davies (London: British Museum Press, 1991), p. 151. Drawing by Thomas R. James.
13. Relief of King Amenemhat I. Lisht North, Pyramid Temple of Amenemhat I. Photograph courtesy of The Egyptian Department, Metropolitan Museum of Art, New York.
14. Map of Egypt and Nubia, 2000–1650 BC. Adapted from D.B. O'Connor, "Early States along the Nubian Nile," in *Egypt and Africa: Nubia from Prehistory to Islam*, ed. W.V. Davies (London: British Museum Press, 1991), p. 154. Drawing by Thomas R. James.
15. Model of Nubian archers, from the tomb of Mesehty, governor of Asyut. Middle Kingdom, Dynasty 11. Photograph courtesy of the Egyptian Museum, Cairo (JE 30969).
16. Map of Egypt and Nubia, 1650–1550 BC. Adapted from D.B. O'Connor, "Early States along the Nubian Nile," in *Egypt and Africa: Nubia from Prehistory to Islam*, ed. W.V. Davies (London: British Museum Press, 1991), p. 155. Drawing by Thomas R. James.
17. Painting in the Eighteenth Dynasty Egyptian tomb of Huy (TT 40) depicting Nubians in procession, carrying offerings to the king. Erich Lessing/Art Resource, New York.
18. Rock-cut inscription at Tombos, late Eighteenth Dynasty. Photograph courtesy of Pamela Rose.
19. The Great Temple of Abu Simbel at sunrise. © Chester Higgins Jr 2012.

20. A fallen statue of Ramesses II at Wadi al-Sebua. Photograph courtesy of Marjorie Fisher.

21. View of Gebel Barkal with a ram statue of Amun in the foreground and the sacred mountain in the background. © Chester Higgins Jr 2012.

22. Map of Egypt and Nubia during Dynasty Twenty-five, ca. 765–655 BC. Adapted from D.B. O'Connor, "Early States along the Nubian Nile," in *Egypt and Africa: Nubia from Prehistory to Islam*, ed. W.V. Davies (London: British Museum Press, 1991), pp. 147 ff. Drawing by Thomas R. James.

23. Palimpsest painting at Wadi al-Sebua of Ramesses II and St. Peter. Photograph courtesy of Martin Davies.

24. Harvard University–Boston Museum of Fine Arts excavations at the Second Cataract: the north end of Dabenarti and the cataract west of Mirgissa, January 1915. Photograph © 2012 Museum of Fine Arts, Boston.

25. Silver and gold objects found by Ferlini at Meroe. From Richard Lepsius, *Denkmaeler aus Aegypten und Aethiopien nach den Zeichnungen der von Seiner Majestät den Koenige von Preussen, Friedrich Wilhelm IV., nach diesen Ländern gesendeten, und in den Jahren 1842–1845 ausgeführten wissenschaftlichen Expedition auf Befehl Seiner Majestät* (Berlin: Nicolaische Buchhandlung, 1849), vol. 5, plate 42.

26. Lotus flower pendant. 2.25 x 2.5 x 0.1 cm. AM 1747, Aegyptisches Museum, Staatliche Museen, Berlin. Photo: Sandra Steiss. Bildarchiv Preussischer Kulturbesitz/Art Resource, New York.

27. Shield ring. H. 5.5 cm. Ant. 2446 b, Staatliche Sammlung Aegyptischer Kunst, Munich. Photo: Margarete Buesing. Bildarchiv Preussischer Kulturbesitz/Art Resource, New York.

28. Signet ring. 2.25 x 2.5 cm. AM 1747, Aegyptisches Museum, Staatliche Museen, Berlin. Photo: Sandra Steiss. Bildarchiv Preussischer Kulturbesitz/Art Resource, New York.

29. Bracelet. 3 x 6.7 x 6.7 cm. AM 1644, Aegyptisches Museum, Staatliche Museen, Berlin. Photo: Sandra Steiss. Bildarchiv Preussischer Kulturbesitz/Art Resource, New York.

30. Nuri camp looking northwest, with *shawabti*s of Taharqo being sorted, March 19, 1917. Harvard University–Boston Museum of Fine Arts Expedition. Photograph © 2012 Museum of Fine Arts, Boston.

31. Golfing in the desert at Meroe Camp. Photograph courtesy of Philippa Dunham Shaplin.

32. Begarawiya North cemetery from the top of Pyramid 7, March 1922. Harvard University–Boston Museum of Fine Arts excavations. Photograph © 2012 Museum of Fine Arts, Boston.

33. Map of sites within Lake Nasser. Adapted from Jocelyn Gohary, *Guide to the Nubian Monuments on Lake Nasser* (Cairo: American University in Cairo Press, 1998). Drawing by Thomas R. James.

34. Blocks from dismantled temples of Dendur, Debod, Ellesiya, and Taffeh on Elephantine Island, 1964. Photograph courtesy of Martin Davies.

35. Heads from the Abu Simbel Great Temple during salvage. SCA Archives.

36. The Great Temple of Abu Simbel during salvage. SCA Archives.

37. Beit al-Wali. Photograph courtesy of Martin Davies.

38. The flooded temple at Wadi al-Sebua. Photograph courtesy of Martin Davies.

59. General plan of a Nineteenth–Twentieth Dynasty rock-cut temple. Drawing by Lorene Sterner.

60. Relief from the tomb of Pennout. © Chester Higgins Jr 2012.

61. The interior of the temple of Beit al-Wali. © Chester Higgins Jr 2012.

62. Relief of the king given life and luck by the god Khnum, from the temple of Beit al-Wali. © Chester Higgins Jr 2012.

63. Ramesses II suckled by goddess Isis in the temple of Beit al-Wali. Photograph courtesy of Marjorie Fisher.

64. Soleb temple at sunset. © Chester Higgins Jr 2012.

65. Relief of Ramesses II worshiping himself in deified form, from the Great Temple at Abu Simbel. From L. Habachi, *Features of the Deification of Ramesses II* (Glückstadt: J.J. Augustin, 1969).

66. The Great and Small Temples at Abu Simbel. © Chester Higgins Jr 2012.

67. The interior of the Great Temple of Abu Simbel, looking down the central axis. © Chester Higgins Jr 2012.

68. Limestone relief from the tomb of Mentuemhat. 15.2 x 12.7 cm. Courtesy of the Michael C. Carlos Museum of Emory University. Photo by Michael McKelvey. 2007.13.1.

69. Bronze statuette of Taharqo. 11.9 x 4.4 cm. Courtesy of the Michael C. Carlos Museum of Emory University. Photo by Michael McKelvey. 2001.16.1.

70. Colossal granite gneiss statue of Aspelta. Nubian, Napatan Period, reign of Aspelta, early sixth century BC. Findspot: Gebel Barkal. H. 332.1 cm (130 ¾ in.). Harvard University–Boston Museum of Fine Arts Expedition (MFA 23.730). Photograph © 2012 Museum of Fine Arts, Boston.

71. Granite gneiss barque stand of King Atlanersa. Nubian, Napatan Period, reign of Atlanersa, second half of seventh century BC. Findspot: Gebel Barkal, Temple B 703. Overall dimensions: 115 x 152.5 x 152.5 cm, 8164.75 kg (45¼ x 60 1/16 x 60 1/16 in., 18,000 lb.). Harvard University–Boston Museum of Fine Arts Expedition (MFA 23.728). Photograph © 2012 Museum of Fine Arts, Boston.

72. Gilded silver and bronze mirror of Shabaqo. Nubian, Napatan Period, reign of Shabaqo, ca. 722–707 BC. Findspot: al-Kurru, Pyramid 15. H. 32.9 cm (13 in.). Harvard University–Boston Museum of Fine Arts Expedition (MFA 21.318). Photograph © 2012 Museum of Fine Arts, Boston.

73. Quartzite statue of Horemakhet. Nubia Museum, Aswan. © Chester Higgins Jr 2012.

74. The pylon of the Lion Temple at Naqa. © Chester Higgins Jr 2012.

75. Meroe at sunset. © Chester Higgins Jr 2012.

76. Bronze hanging lamp. Nubian, Meroitic Period, reign of Takideamani, second century AD. Findspot: Meroe, Pyr. N 29. Overall dimensions: 65.8 x 44 cm (25 7/8 x 17 15/16 in.). Harvard University–Boston Museum of Fine Arts Expedition (MFA 24.966 a-b). Photograph © 2012 Museum of Fine Arts, Boston.

77. The "Venus of Meroe." Sudan National Museum 538. Photograph courtesy of Sudan National Museum and Neil Hewison.

78. Painted and gilded glass chalice from Sedeinga. Courtesy of Collezioni Egittologiche di Ateneo, Pisa.

79. Bronze figure of King Taharqo. Findspot: Gebel Barkal, Great Temple of Amun, B 501. H. 19.9 cm. Harvard University–Boston Museum of Fine Arts Expedition (MFA 21.3096). Photograph © 2012 Museum of Fine Arts, Boston.

80. Carnelian necklace with ram's head pendant. Total length: 49.8 cm. Courtesy of the Michael C. Carlos Museum of Emory University. Photo by Michael McKelvey. 2001.8.2.

81. Objects from the tomb of Aspelta (Nuri Pyramid 8). Harvard University–Boston Museum of Fine Arts Expedition (MFA 20.334, .339, .341, .1070, 21.339, .11739). Photograph © 2012 Museum of Fine Arts, Boston.

82. Scene of the lion god Apedemak. Drawing by Laura Brubaker.

83. Gilded silver figure of Amun. 11.4 x 2.5 cm. Courtesy of the Michael C. Carlos Museum of Emory University. Photo by Bruce M. White, 2006. 2006.36.1.

84. Ram's head. Egyptian, Dynasty Twenty-five, 760–660 BC. Silicified wood. Height x width x length: 12 x 10 x 13 cm (4¾ x 3 15/16 x 5 1/8 in.). Museum of Fine Arts, Boston. Sears Fund with additions. (MFA 03.1557).

85. Relief of Satet, Horus, and Isis from the Lion Temple at Musawwarat al-Sufra. © Chester Higgins Jr 2012.

86. Unfinished granite stela with the figure of Osiris, Sudan National Museum. © Chester Higgins Jr 2012.

87. Sandstone corbel. Sudan National Museum. © Chester Higgins Jr 2012.

88. Apedemak in the form of a snake. © Chester Higgins Jr 2012.

89. Schematic representation of graves of the early and late C-Group. Drawing by Claudia Näser, after M. Bietak, *Studien zur Chronologie der nubischen C-Gruppe: ein Beitrag zur Frühgeschichte Unternubiens zwischen 2200 und 1550 vor Chr.* Berichte des Österreichischen Nationalkomitees der UNESCO-Aktion für die Rettung der Nubischen Altertümer 5. Österreichische Akademie der Wissenschaften, Philosophisch-Historische Klasse, Denkschriften 97. Wien: Hermann Böhlaus Nachf, 1968.

90. Funerary mask from Mirgissa. Musée du Louvre, Département des Antiquités Egyptiennes, E. 25702. H. 22.5 cm, L 20.8 cm. Photograph by Jean-François Gout. Photograph courtesy of Brigitte Gratien.

91. Kerma tumulus. Photograph courtesy of Charles Bonnet.

92. Bed burial at Kerma. Photograph courtesy of Charles Bonnet.

93. Reliefs in the tomb of Pennout. Photograph courtesy of Martin Davies.

94. Painted burial chamber of Queen Qalhata. © Chester Higgins Jr 2012.

95. Stone *shawabti*s of King Taharqo. Nubian, Napatan Period, 690–664 BC. Findspot: Nuri, Pyramid 1. Height range from 10–35 cm (3.9–13.8 in.). Harvard University–Boston Museum of Fine Arts Expedition. Photograph © 2012 Museum of Fine Arts, Boston.

96. Reconstruction of a Meroitic pyramid. Watercolor by F.W. and Marion Hinkel.

97. Reconstruction of a painted stone *ba*-bird statuette from Karanog. From C.L. Woolley and D. Randall-MacIver, *Karanòg: The Romano-Nubian Cemetery*, Plates. University of Pennsylvania Eckley B. Coxe Jr. Expedition to Nubia, vol. 4 (Philadelphia: University Museum, 1910), plate 1.

98. Stela of Nastasen, Berlin 2268. From Richard Lepsius, *Denkmaeler aus Aegypten und Aethiopien nach den Zeichnungen der von Seiner Majestät den Koenige von Preussen, Friedrich Wilhelm IV., nach diesen Ländern gesendeten, und in den Jahren 1842–1845 ausgeführten wissenschaftlichen Expedition auf Befehl Seiner Majestät* (Berlin: Nicolaische Buchhandlung, 1849), vol. 5, plate 16.

99. Sarcophagus of King Aspelta. Nubian, Napatan Period, reign of Aspelta, early sixth century BC. Findspot: Nuri, Pyramid 8. Overall dimensions: 205 x 170 x 310 cm, 14515.1 kg (80 11/16 x 66 15/16 x 122 1/16 in., 32,000 lb.). Harvard University–Boston Museum of Fine Arts Expedition (MFA 23.729). Photograph © 2012 Museum of Fine Arts, Boston.

100. The Coronation Stela of King Aspelta. After E.A. Wallis Budge, *Egyptian Literature*, vol. 2: *Annals of Nubian Kings* (London: Kegan Paul, Trench, Trübner, 1912). Drawing by Gustavo Camps.

101. The Meroitic alphabet. Drawing by Laura Brubaker.

102. Stela with Meroitic text. Sudan National Museum. © Chester Higgins Jr 2012.

103. Stela of King Tanyidamani. Nubian, Meroitic Period, early first century BC. Findspot: Gebel Barkal, Great Temple, Approach (B 551). H. 158 cm (62 3/16 in.). Harvard University–Boston Museum of Fine Arts Expedition (MFA 23.736). Photograph © 2012 Museum of Fine Arts, Boston.

104. Pan-Grave painted cow skull from Mostagedda. Drawing courtesy of Nicholas Thayer.

105. Incised design from a bronze bowl from Karanog, Tomb G 187. Drawing by Laura Brubaker.

106. Wood ration token from the Second Cataract Forts. Drawing courtesy of Barry Kemp.

107. Silver amulet of a goddess suckling Queen Neferukakashta. Findspot: al-Kurru, Pyramid 52. Height x width 5.1 x 1.8 cm (2 x 11/16 in.) Harvard University–Boston Museum of Fine Arts Expedition (MFA 24.928). Photograph © 2012 Museum of Fine Arts, Boston.

108. Relief of the God's Wives of Amun Amenirdis I and Shepenwepet II. Photograph courtesy of Peter Lacovara.

109. Statue of the God's Wife of Amun, Ankhnesneferibre. Nubia Museum, Aswan (CG 42205). © Chester Higgins Jr 2012.

110. Painting of Queen Qalhata. © Chester Higgins Jr 2012.

111. Fragment of stela of King Amanikhabale presenting broad collars to the ram-headed Amun and human-headed Mut. Sudan National Museum 522. © Chester Higgins Jr 2012.

112. Meroitic stela of Lapakhidaye. Sudan National Museum 5261. © Chester Higgins Jr 2012.

113. Queen Amanishakheto smiting enemies. From Richard Lepsius, *Denkmaeler aus Aegypten und Aethiopien nach den Zeichnungen der von Seiner Majestät den Koenige von Preussen, Friedrich Wilhelm IV., nach diesen Landern gesendeten, und in den Jahren 1842–1845 ausgeführten wissenschaftlichen Expedition auf Befehl Seiner Majestät* (Berlin: Nicolaische Buchhandlung, 1849), vol. 5, plate 56.

114. Queen Amanitore and King Natakamani on Naqa temple west wall. From Richard Lepsius, *Denkmaeler aus Aegypten und Aethiopien nach den Zeichnungen der von Seiner Majestät den Koenige von Preussen, Friedrich Wilhelm IV., nach diesen Ländern gesendeten, und in den Jahren 1842–1845 ausgeführten wissenschaftlichen Expedition auf Befehl Seiner Majestät* (Berlin: Nicolaische Buchhandlung, 1849), vol. 5, plate 59.

115. Map of Nubian gold deposits. Drawing by Thomas R. James.

116. Ivory stud earring. Nubian, about 1700–1550 BC. Findspot: Kerma, Tumulus IV, grave 440x. Height x diameter: 2.4 x 2.7 cm (15/16 x 1 1/16 in.). Harvard University–Boston Museum of Fine Arts Expedition (MFA 20.1785). Photograph © 2012 Museum of Fine Arts, Boston.

117. Pair of ivory cuff bracelets. Nubian, 2400–2050 BC. Findspot: Kerma, Tomb KN 35. Height x diameter (.11793): 2.1 x 7.5 cm (13/16 x 2 15/16 in.). Harvard University–Boston Museum of Fine Arts Expedition (MFA 21.11793-4). Photograph © 2012 Museum of Fine Arts, Boston.

118. Ivory cuffs in situ on right wrist, from Kerma, tomb KN 35. From D. Dunham, *Excavations at Kerma, Part VI* (Boston: Museum of Fine Arts, 1982), fig. 151a.

119. Necklaces of carnelian, silver, and blue-glazed quartz. Nubian, about 1700–1550 BC. Findspot: Kerma South Cemetery K 332, K 426, and K 423. L. of carnelian necklace 35 cm (13¾ in.). Harvard University–Boston Museum of Fine Arts Expedition (MFA 20.1727, 20.1668, 20.1717). Photograph © 2012 Museum of Fine Arts, Boston.

120. Necklace of blue faience ball beads and a blue-glazed quartz pendant. Nubian, about 1700–1550 BC. Findspot: Kerma, K XB-61. Length of pendant: 4.6 cm (1 13 /16 in.); diameter of beads: .9 to 1.3 cm; overall length of string 61 cm. Harvard University–Boston Museum of Fine Arts Expedition (MFA 21.1729). Photograph © 2012 Museum of Fine Arts, Boston.

121. Silver, blue-glazed quartz, carnelian, and faience necklace. Nubian, about 1700–1550 BC. Findspot: Kerma, tomb K 1067. Length: 24.5 cm (9 5/8 in.) Harvard University–Boston Museum of Fine Arts Expedition (MFA 13.3969). Photograph © 2012 Museum of Fine Arts, Boston.

122. Fly pendants. Nubian, 1550–1070 BC. Findspot: Semna, tomb S 579. Height x width x depth of a: 7.1 x 3 x 0.5 cm (2 13/16 x 1 3/16 x 3/16 in.). Height x width x depth of b: 6.8 x 3.1 x 0.6 cm (2 11/16 x 1 1/4 x 1/4 in.). Harvard University–Boston Museum of Fine Arts Expedition (MFA 27.878a-b). Photograph © 2012 Museum of Fine Arts, Boston.

123. Mica appliqués. Nubian, 1700–1550 BC. Findspot: Kerma K X, tomb 1039x. Harvard University–Boston Museum of Fine Arts Expedition (MFA 13.4284). Photograph © 2012 Museum of Fine Arts, Boston.

124. Stone weights for weighing gold. Egyptian, 1971–1550 BC. Findspot: Uronarti Island, Halfa Province. Length x width x depth: 4.2 x 3.7 x 1.8 cm. Harvard University–Boston Museum of Fine Arts Expedition (MFA 24.750-52). Photograph © 2012 Museum of Fine Arts, Boston.

125. Gold nugget pendant. Findspot: Meroe, Beg. W 859. L. 3.3 cm (1 5/16 in.) Harvard University–Boston Museum of Fine Arts Expedition (MFA 24.750-52). Photograph © 2012 Museum of Fine Arts, Boston.

126. Reconstructed gold collar. Nubian, 900–760 BC. Findspot: al-Kurru, Tumulus 1. Harvard University–Boston Museum of Fine Arts Expedition (MFA 21.319). Photograph © 2012 Museum of Fine Arts, Boston.

127. Rock crystal and gold Hathor-headed pendant. 743–712 BC. Findspot: al-Kurru, KU 55. Height x diameter: 5.4 x 3.3 cm (2 1/8 x 1 5/16 in.). Harvard University–Boston Museum of Fine Arts Expedition (MFA 21.321). Photograph © 2012 Museum of Fine Arts, Boston.

128. Ram-headed gilt silver and crystal amulet case. 743–712 BC. Findspot: al-Kurru, KU 55. H. 8.9 cm (3½ in.). Harvard University–Boston Museum of Fine Arts Expedition (MFA 24.976). Photograph © 2012 Museum of Fine Arts, Boston.

129. Gold winged-Isis pectoral. 538–519 BC. Findspot: Nuri, pyramid of Amani-nataki-lebte. W. 16.8 cm (6 5/8 in.). Harvard University–Boston Museum of Fine Arts Expedition (MFA 20.276). Photograph © 2012 Museum of Fine Arts, Boston.

130. Faience winged-goddess amulet. 743–712 BC. Findspot: al-Kurru, Pyramid 52. Harvard University–Boston Museum of Fine Arts Expedition (MFA 24.639). Photograph © 2012 Museum of Fine Arts, Boston.

131. Gold and carnelian necklace with human- and ram's-head pendants. 270 BC–AD 320. Findspot: Meroe, Beg. W. 263. L. 33.5 cm (13 3/16 in.). Harvard University–Boston Museum of Fine Arts Expedition (MFA 23.366). Photograph © 2012 Museum of Fine Arts, Boston.

132. Gold and enamel bracelet with an image of Hathor, ca. 100 BC. Findspot: Gebel Barkal, Pyramid 8. Height x length: 1.8 x 12.5 cm (11/16 x 4 15/16 in.). Harvard University–Boston Museum of Fine Arts Expedition (MFA 20.333). Photograph © 2012 Museum of Fine Arts, Boston.

133. Gold Hathor earring, ca. 90 BC–AD 50. Findspot: Meroe, Pyramid 5, no. 6. H. 5.8 cm (2 5/16 in.). Harvard University–Boston Museum of Fine Arts Expedition (MFA 23.340). Photograph © 2012 Museum of Fine Arts, Boston.

134. Gold and enamel ear stud, ca. 270 BC–AD 320. Findspot: Meroe. D. 2.8 cm (1.1 in.). Harvard University–Boston Museum of Fine Arts Expedition (MFA 23.329). Photograph © 2012 Museum of Fine Arts, Boston.

135. Gold signet ring, 185–10 BC. Findspot: Meroe, Beg. W 333. Height x diameter (bezel): 1.2 x 1.3 cm (1/2 x 1/2 in.) height x width (shank): 2.2 x 1.8 cm (7/8 x 11/16 in.). Harvard University–Boston Museum of Fine Arts Expedition (MFA 23.303). Photograph © 2012 Museum of Fine Arts, Boston.

136. Khartoum Mesolithic potsherds. Drawings after A.J. Arkell.

137. Redware bowl with triangle motif. Nubian, A-Group, 3100–3000 BC. Findspot: Dakka, Cemetery 101, Grave 611, number 9. Height x diameter 9.8 x 16 cm (3 7/8 x 6 5/16 in.). Museum of Fine Arts, Boston. Gift of Dr. George A. Reisner. (MFA 19.1546) Photograph © 2012 Museum of Fine Arts, Boston.

138. C-Group incised ware from Aniba N. Egyptian Museum of Leipzig University, inv. nos. 4185, 4207, and 4211. Photograph by Jürgen Liepe.

139. Gilded ware pottery vessel from Mirgissa. Institut de Papyrologie et d'Egyptologie de Lille, no. L135. D: 9.5 cm, H. 15.2 cm. Photograph by Jean-François Gout.

140. Classic Kerma pottery. Nubian, Kerma culture, about 1700–1550 BC. Findspot: Kerma. Height of rilled beaker: 22.5 cm (8 7/8 in.). Harvard University–Boston Museum of Fine Arts Expedition (MFA 13.4080, 13.4076, 20.2006, 20.1714, 13.4102). Photograph © 2012 Museum of Fine Arts, Boston.

141. New Kingdom pot from Buhen. Photograph courtesy of University of Pennsylvania Museum of Archaeology and Anthropology, E 10563.

142. Painted and incised Napatan Period pottery beakers from Gammai. 15.6 x 10.6 cm (black beaker); 15 x 10 cm (red beaker). Michael C. Carlos Museum photo, used by permission of Peabody Museum of Archaeology and Ethnology, Harvard University.

143. Barbotine cup. Nubian, Meroitic Period, first–second century AD. Height: 6.3 cm (2½ in.), diameter (mouth) 7.2 cm (2 13/16 in.), diameter (base) 2.8 cm (1 1/8 in.) Museum of Fine Arts, Boston. Gift in memory of Dows and Marion Dunham (1992.94)

144. Meroitic pottery from Karanog. From C. Leonard Woolley and D. Randall MacIver, *Karanòg: The Romano-Nubian Cemetery*. Eckley B. Coxe, Jr. Expedition to Egypt (Philadelphia: University Museum, 1910), vol. 4, plates, pl. 42.

145. Late Meroitic black-incised pottery beer jar with stamped pattern. Nubian, Meroitic Period, 40 BC–AD 114. Findspot: Meroe, Tomb W 341. Height x diameter 23.5 x 17 cm (9¼ x 6 11/16 in.). Harvard University–Boston Museum of Fine Arts Expedition (24.1804). Photograph © 2012 Museum of Fine Arts, Boston.

146. Meroitic pots from the collection of the University of Pennsylvania Museum of Archaeology and Anthropology, Penn Museum objects E 8232, E8196, E 8486, E 8751, E 8476, E 8488, E 8486, and E 8313, image #150512.

147. C-Group ceramic animals. Leipzig University inv. nos. 4387, 4373, Aegyptisches Museum, Staatliche Museen, Berlin, no. 25545. Bildarchiv Preussischer Kulturbesitz/Art Resource, New York.

148. Cattle skulls in situ. Photograph courtesy of Charles Bonnet.

149. Meroitic painted and gilded glass chalice from Sedeinga, with figure holding ducks and an antelope. Sudan National Museum 20406. © Chester Higgins Jr 2012.

150. Row of rams at Naqa. © Chester Higgins Jr 2012.

151. Petroglyphs at Gerf Hussein showing giraffes. Photograph courtesy of Martin Davies.

152. Petroglyph of elephant near Kalabsha. Photograph courtesy of Marjorie Fisher.

153. Stela of Piankhi, after Mariette.

154. Painted decoration of lions attacking a man, from a Kerma pot. Watercolor by Dows Dunham.

155. Sandstone relief of lion and elephant, from the Lion Temple at Musawwarat al-Sufra. © Chester Higgins Jr 2012.

156. Figure of elephant at Musawwarat al-Sufra. © Chester Higgins Jr 2012.

157. Watercolor of a boy carrying elephants, from Meroe. The Garstang Museum of Archaeology. School of Archaeology, Classics and Egyptology, University of Liverpool, E 8524.

158. Map of Upper and Lower Nubia from the Third Cataract to Aswan. Drawing by Thomas R. James.

159. Map of Upper Nubia from the confluence of the Niles to the Third Cataract. Drawing by Thomas R. James.

160. Meroitic king at Gebel Qeili. Drawing by Laura Brubaker.

161. 'Roman' Kiosk at Naqa in the foreground, and Apedemak temple in the background. © Chester Higgins Jr 2012.

162. Map of the valley of Musawwarat with the known archaeological features. Drawing by Thomas R. James, courtesy of The Archaeological Mission of Humboldt University to Musawwarat es-Sufra.

163. View of the Central Terrace of the Great Enclosure at Musawwarat al-Sufra. Photograph courtesy of Peter Lacovara.

164. Muweis, Palace A, first century AD, view to north. © Michel Baud/Musée du Louvre.

165. Reconstructed pyramids and chapels at Meroe. © Chester Higgins Jr 2012.

166. Northern Cemetery at Begarawiya. Cemetery plan from D. Dunham, *The Royal Cemeteries of Kush*, Vol. 4: *Royal Tombs at Meroe and Barkal* (Boston: Museum of Fine Arts, 1957). List of tomb owner names adapted from *Ancient Egyptian Chronology*, ed. E. Hornung, R. Krauss, and D.A. Warburton (Boston: Brill, 2006): 496–98, and G.A. Reisner, "The Meroitic Kingdom of Ethiopia: A Chronological Outline," *JEA* 9 (1923): 34–77, 154–60. Drawing of cemetery plan by Thomas R. James.

167. Southern Cemetery at Begarawiya. Location of tomb owners adapted from *Ancient Egyptian Chronology*, ed. E. Horning, R. Krauss, and D.A. Warburton (Boston: Brill, 2006): 496–98, with additions for Southern cemetery pyramid/tombs/stela numbers 4 (B.V.1.4), 5 (B.V.1.4), 6 (B.V.1.4; B.V.6), 7 (B.V.1.4), 10 (B.V.1.4), 20 (B.V.3), 85 (B.V.5; B.V.8), 132 (B.V.6), 500 (B.V.4), 503 (B.V.2) by J. Hallof, in J.W. Yellin, in F.W. Hinkel and J.W. Yellin, *Necropolises of Kush I.1. Meroe. The Southern Royal Cemetery* (forthcoming). Tomb 10 (B.IV.7); B.VII.2), 500 (B.IV.4), 503 (B.IV.7; B.VII.2) in J.W. Yellin in Hinkel and Yellin (forthcoming). Cemetery plan from D. Dunham, *The Royal Cemeteries of Kush*, Vol. 5: *The West and South Cemeteries at Meroe* (Boston: Museum of Fine Arts, 1963). Drawing of cemetery plan by Thomas R. James.

168. Western Cemetery at Begarawiya. Cemetery plan from D. Dunham, *The Royal Cemeteries of Kush*, Vol. 5: *The West and South Cemeteries at Meroë* (Museum of Fine Arts, 1963) and The F.W. Hinkel Archive at the German Archaeological Institute, Berlin. Names of tomb owners for Beg. W tombs 1, 3, 5, 14, 20, 241 refer to J.W. Yellin in F.W. Hinkel and J.W. Yellin, *Necropolises of Kush II.1. Meroe. The Western Royal Cemetery* (forthcoming). Tombs 3, 17, 18, 19, 105, 113, 119, 129, 309, 342 refer to C. Rilly, "Palaeographical Evidence for Local Princes in Begrawwiya West," in I. Caneva and A. Roccati, eds., *Acta Nubica: Proceedings of the Tenth International Conference of Nubian Studies, Rome, 9–14 September 2002*, 435–42 (Rome: Istituto Poligrafico e Zecca dello Stato, Libreria dello Stato, 2006). Tombs 3, 17, 18, 19, 105, 113, 119, 129, 130, 309, 342 refer to J. Leclant, A. Heyler, et al., *Répertoire d'Épigraphie Méroïtique: Corpus des inscriptions publiées. REM 0001 à 0387* (Paris: Académie des Inscriptions et Belles-Lettres, 2000) and J. Leclant, A. Heyer, et al., *Répertoire d'Épigraphie Méroïtique: Corpus des inscriptions publiées. REM 0401 à 0851* (Paris: Académie des Inscriptions et Belles-Lettres, 2000). Burial places unknown: A, B, C refer to C. Rilly and to J. Leclant and A. Heyler; D, E refer to J.W. Yellin. Drawing by Thomas R. James.

169. Restored chapel at Meroe. © Chester Higgins Jr 2012.

170. Nuri pyramids. © Chester Higgins Jr 2012.

171. Plan of Gebel Barkal. After D. Dunham, *The Barkal Temples* (Boston: Museum of Fine Arts, 1970) and T. Kendall, "A New Map of the Gebel Barkal Temples," in *Études nubiennes: Conférence de Genève. Actes du VIIe Congrès international d'études nubiennes 3-8 septembre 1990*, edited by C. Bonnet, vol. 2 (Geneva: Société d'études nubiennes, 1994), 139 ff. Drawing by Gustavo Camps.

172. Bes columns at Gebel Barkal. Drawing by Charles Gleyre courtesy of the Lowell Institute.

173. Gebel Barkal trench 500A, royal statue cache, February 1916. Harvard University–Boston Museum of Fine Arts Expedition. Photograph © 2012 Museum of Fine Arts, Boston.

174. Pyramid 1 of an unknown king at al-Kurru. © Chester Higgins Jr 2012.

175. Kawa, Tutankhamun receiving life from Amun-Re. Photograph copyright: Griffith Institute, University of Oxford.

176. Kawa, Taharqo temple. Photograph copyright: Griffith Institute, University of Oxford.

177. Site plan of Kerma. After C. Bonnet, ed., *Kerma, Royaume de Nubie. Catalogue de l'Exposition* (Geneva: Musée de Genève, 1990), p. 20. Drawing by Thomas R. James.

178. Kerma town. © Chester Higgins Jr 2012.

179. Kerma, Tumulus III, statue of Lady Sennuwy (MFA 14.720) in situ, April 1914. Harvard University–Boston Museum of Fine Arts Expedition. Photograph © 2012 Museum of Fine Arts, Boston.

180. Tombos quarry with unfinished colossus. Photograph courtesy of Salima Ikram.

181. The Abydos decree of Sety I at Nauri. Photograph courtesy of Pamela Rose.

182. Plan of Sesebi. After H.W. Fairman, "Preliminary Report on the Excavations at Sesebi (Sudla) and 'Amarah West, Anglo-Egyptian Sudan, 1937–38," *JEA* 24 (1938), pl. 8. Drawing by Gustavo Camps.

183. Plan of Soleb temple. After M. Schiff-Giorgini, *Soleb* IV: *Le Temple. Plans et Photographies* (Florence: Sansoni, 2003), pl. 24. Drawing by Thomas R. James.

184. Soleb temple at night. © Chester Higgins Jr 2012.

185. Ruins of Sedeinga. Photograph courtesy of Salima Ikram.

186. Plan of Amara West. After P. Spencer, *Amara West I: The Architectural Report* (London: Egypt Exploration Society, 1997), pl. 3. Drawing by Gsutavo Camps.

187. Plan of Gammai. From O. Bates and D. Dunham, *Excavations at Gammai*. Harvard African Studies 8, Varia Africana 4 (Cambridge, Mass.: Peabody Museum of Harvard University, 1927).

188. Plans of Second Cataract forts. After W.Y. Adams, *Nubia, Corridor to Africa* (Princeton: Princeton University Press, 1977). Drawing by Gustavo Camps.

189. Drawing of reconstructed gate at Buhen. From W.B. Emery, *Lost Land Emerging* (New York: Charles Scribner's Sons, 1967), fig. 10.

190. C-Group Cemetery N at Aniba. Grave superstructures and stelae of the early C-Group. From G. Steindorff, *Aniba*, vol. 1. Service des Antiquités de l'Égypte. Mission archéologique de Nubie 1929–1934 (Glückstadt, Hamburg: J. J. Augustin, 1935).

191. Female statuettes from Aniba Cemetery N. Egyptian Museum Cairo, inv. nos. JE 65192, 65190 and 65189; drawing after G. Steindorff, *Aniba*, vol. 1. Service des Antiquités de l'Égypte. Mission archéologique de Nubie 1929–1934 (Glückstadt, Hamburg: J.J. Augustin, 1935). Drawing by Isolde Saeuberlich.

192. Superstructures and chapels of the late C-Group. From G. Steindorff, *Aniba*, vol. 1. Service des Antiquités de l'Égypte. Mission archéologique de Nubie 1929–1934 (Glückstadt, Hamburg: J.J. Augustin, 1935).

193. A-Group incised stone incense burner from Qustul. Drawing by Laura Brubaker.

194. X-Group silver crown inlaid with garnets. Nubia Museum, Aswan. © Chester Higgins Jr 2012.

195. Abu Simbel: (A) Plan of the Great Temple of Ramesses II and (B) the Small Temple of Nefertari. Adapted from I. Hein, *Die Ramessidische Bautätigkeit in Nubien*, GOF 4, vol. 22 (Wiesbaden: Otto Harrassowitz, 1991), Pls. 12 and 13. Drawing by Gustavo Camps.

196. Aerial view of the Great Temple at Abu Simbel in its original location, 1938. From the American Geographical Society Library, University of Wisconsin–Milwaukee Libraries.

197. Interior view of the great hall within the Great Temple at Abu Simbel. © Chester Higgins Jr 2012.

198. The Great Temple at Abu Simbel. Photograph courtesy of Marjorie Fisher.

199. View of Qasr Ibrim from the water. Photograph courtesy of Marjorie Fisher.

200. The west face of the 'castle' at Karanog. From C.L. Woolley, *Karanòg: The Town*. Eckley B. Coxe, Jr. Expedition to Nubia (Philadelphia: University Museum, 1911), vol. 5, pl. 3.

201. Plan of Derr temple. Adapted from I. Hein, *Die Ramessidische Bautätigkeit in Nubien*, GOF 4, vol. 22 (Wiesbaden: Otto Harrassowitz, 1991), Pl. 9. Drawing by Gustavo Camps.

202. View of Derr from the water. Photograph courtesy of Martin Davies.

203. The interior of the temple at Derr. © Chester Higgins Jr 2012.

204. Plan of Amada temple. Adapted from I. Hein, *Die Ramessidische Bautätigkeit in Nubien*, GOF 4, vol. 22 (Wiesbaden: Otto Harrassowitz, 1991), Pl. 8. Drawing by Gustavo Camps.

205. The exterior of the temple at Amada. Photograph courtesy of Marjorie Fisher.

206. Plans of the temples of Amenhotep III (A) and Ramesses II (B) at Wadi al-Sebua. Adapted from I. Hein, *Die Ramessidische Bautätigkeit in Nubien*, GOF 4, vol. 22 (Wiesbaden: Otto Harrassowitz, 1991), Pl. 7. Drawing of Amenhotep III temple by Gustavo Camps. Drawing of Ramesses II temple by Thomas R. James.

207. The approach to the temple of Ramesses II at Wadi al-Sebua. © Chester Higgins Jr 2012.

208. Plan of the temple of Gerf Hussein. Adapted from I. Hein, *Die Ramessidische Bautätigkeit in Nubien*, GOF 4, vol. 22 (Wiesbaden: Otto Harrassowitz, 1991), Pl. 2. Drawing by Gustavo Camps.

209. View of the temple of Gerf Hussein in its original location. Photograph by Seba, courtesy of Peter Lacovara.

210. Temple of Dendur before its move. SCA Archives.

211. Plan of the temple at Beit al-Wali. Adapted from I. Hein, *Die Ramessidische Bautätigkeit in Nubien*, GOF 4, vol. 22 (Wiesbaden: Otto Harrassowitz, 1991), Pl. 1. Drawing by Gustavo Camps.

212. Interior of the temple of Beit al-Wali. © Chester Higgins Jr 2012.

213. Temple of Taffeh, as reconstructed in the Rijksmuseum van Oudheden, Leiden. Photograph courtesy Rijksmuseum van Oudheden, Leiden.

214. The temple of Qertassi in its original location. Photograph by Seba, courtesy of Peter Lacovara.

215. The temple of Debod, as reconstructed in the Parque de Rosales, Madrid. Photograph courtesy of Benjamin Beatty.

216. Plan of the Island of Philae. Drawing by Gustavo Camps.

217. The Philae temple of Isis at night. © Chester Higgins Jr 2012.

218. View of Elephantine Island by David Roberts. Courtesy of the Michael C. Carlos Museum.

219. The Temple of Dendur. Egyptian; Nubia, Lower Nubia, Dendur. Roman Period, reign of Augustus Caesar, 15 BC. Aeolian Sandstone. L. from gate to rear of temple 24.6 m (82 ft.). Given to the United States by Egypt in 1965, awarded to the Metropolitan Museum of Art in 1967, and installed in The Sackler Wing in 1978 (68.154). The Metropolitan Museum of Art, New York, New York, U.S.A. Image copyright © The Metropolitan Museum of Art/Art Resource, New York.

220. The ram-headed Amun, from the Apedemak temple at Naqa. © Chester Higgins Jr 2012.

221. The Fourth Cataract in moonlight. © Chester Higgins Jr 2012.

Figure 221. The Fourth Cataract in moonlight. Photo © Chester Higgins Jr 2012.

Index

Page numbers in **bold** refer to maps; page numbers in ***bold italics*** refer to illustrations.

Nabta Playa 201; **xv, 11, 226**
naos 136, 254, 325, 383, 401
Napata 25, 27, 28, 29, 34, 35, 36, 39, 52, 72, 75, 108, 112, 113,
    122, 123, 125, 126, 127, 130, 131, 132, 133, 136,
    139, 140, 141, 142, 143, 152, 153, 156, 158, 163,
    166, 169, 172, 173, 177, 178, 179, 183, 184, 192,
    193, 195, 196, 197, 198, 207, 214, 231, 234, 259,
    264, 267, 270, 272, 275, 277, 278, 283, 285, 286,
    287, 288, 290, 291, 292, 294, 300, 312, 315, 318,
    330, 332, 336, 362, 369, 375; **xvi, 227, 286, 305;** *126*
Napatan kings xix, xx, 36, 115, 121, 127, 130, 142, 162,
    172, 173, 184, 259, 272, 278, 283, 285, 290, 302,
    310, 311, 312
Napatan Period xviii, 10, 33, 34, 36, 52, 54, 72, 75, 76, 84,
    98, 108, 112, 113, 115, 117, 121, 122, 125, 127,
    131, 132, 133, 143, 162, 170, 174, 177, 178, 179,
    184, 185, 207, 238, 242, 262, 263, 267, 270, 272,
    275, 277, 278, 287, 290, 292, 302, 312, 318, 325,
    327, 328, 335, 346; **266, 268;** *74, 205*
Napatan queens 76, 172, 173, 174, 178, 179, 180, 184,
    185, 197
Naqa 38, 48, 88, 116, 132, 133, 136, 137, 141, 163, 184,
    216, 230–37, 244, 245, 253; **xvi, 227;** *215*
    Amun Temple (Temples 100 and 200) 231, 232, 235,
        242, 253, 254, 274
    Lion Temple (Apedemak; Temple 300) 134, 214, 231,
        234, 236; *113, 139, 182, 183, 232, 424*
    'Roman' Kiosk (Temple 361) 231, 235, 274; *232*
Naqada **xvii**
Naqada I Period 14
Naqada II Period 14, 406
Naqada III Period 15, 253, 406
Nasalsa 172, 173, 177
Näser, Claudia 137
Nastasen xix, 34, 163, 173, 214, 277, 288, 300, 302, 327; *155*
Natakamani xx, 133, 184, 231, 232, 234, 238, 244, 251,
    287, 288, 291, 292, 301, 330; **265;** *183*
natural history 223
Nauri 30, 313–14, 318; **xv, 226;** *313*
Nawidemak xx, 182, 185, 292
necklaces 13, 15, 17, 48, 112, 147, 185, 190, 193, 198; *190*
Nefertari 30, 59, 97, 102, 326, 334, 356, 357, 358; *357*
Neferti, prophecies of 21
Nefertiti 316, 325
Neferukakashta 174, 196; *171*
Nehesy/Nehesyu 345, 346
Nekau 36
Nekhen 289; **xvii**
nemes headdress 103
Neolithic Period 12, 141, 203, 210, 214, 219, 330; *10*
Nephthys 132, 146
New Kalabsha 62–66, 67, 398; *see also* Khor Ingi
New Kingdom xviii, 10, 17, 21, 23, 25, 26, 28, 30, 31, 33, 34, 46,
    52, 72, 75, 83, 84, 86, 87, 88, 89, 90, 97, 102, 103, 106,
    108, 109, 110, 121, 125, 126, 127, 128, 129, 131, 132,
    140, 142, 143, 147, 149, 150, 151, 152, 155, 157, 160,
    168, 169, 205, 207, 264, 272, 287, 288, 290, 291, 292,
    295, 297, 301, 302, 308, 310, 312, 315, 318, 320, 325,
    326, 329, 330, 331, 332, 336, 337, 346, 352, 353, 361,
    363, 364, 365, 372, 384, 394, 400, 403, 406, 410; *204*
Nile River 5, 57, 230, 247, 258, 329, 361, 363; **xiv, 11**

Blue Nile 40, 115, 229; **xiv, 11**
White Nile 38, 42, 115; **xiv, 11**
Nile Valley 10, 20, 23, 118, 119, 137, 145, 189, 192, 200,
    201, 202, 230, 238, 239, 242, 244, 275, 283, 304,
    339, 348, 370
Nitokris Adoption Stela 36, 180
Noba 248, 303
Nobadia 39, 40, 41, 354, 367, 394
Nubian Dynasty 34, 192; *see also* Dynasties, Twenty-fifth
Nuer, *see* East African pastoralist societies
Nuri xix, 34, 36, 40, 52, 72, 113, 122, 140, 152, 179, 195,
    198, 207, 270, 277–84, 292, 295, 300, 328; **xvi,
    187, 227;** *53, 121, 130, 194, 279*

O'Connor, David 15, 23, 368, 370
offering tables 108, 137, 140, 143, 166, 179, 184, 277, 278,
    330, 361, 362, 370
Okasha, Tharwat 59, 60, 61, 69
Old Dongola 40, 41, 42, 76, 367; **xvi, 227**
Old Kingdom xviii, 18, 20, 21, 24, 26, 30, 33, 60, 111, 118,
    119, 154, 279, 298, 330, 338, 356, 407, 408
Onasch, Hans-Ulrich 262
Onderka, Pavel 244, 245
Onuris 130, 134
oracles 141
Osiride statue 372
Osiris 62, 63, 65, 90, 99, 116, 129, 130, 132, 136, 137, 141,
    142, 147, 153, 248, 279, 282, 283, 326, 360, 382,
    388, 394, 398, 401, 402, 404, 405; *130*
Osiris-Hekadjet 109
    Chapel, Karnak 174
Osorkon I 34
Osorkon III 177
ostrich 210
    eggs/eggshells 14, 15, 16, 210, 217
    feathers (plumes) 15, 16, 93, 112, 210, 217, 222, 305,
        326, 354
Ottoman Empire 42, 367
Ottomans 330
ovicaprid, *see* goats; sheep
Oxford University 45

Paabtameri 180
Pabatma 180
palace 24, 38, 41, 55, 72, 116, 120, 136, 167, 169, 183, 213,
    222, 230, 239, 244, 245, 250, 251, 252, 258, 259,
    262, 263, 285, 287, 291, 292, 308, 335, 338, 342;
    286; *221, 251*
    Abdin 59
    Spanish Royal 62
Paleolithic Period 10, 12, 72, 200, 213, 329; **10, 11**
Palermo Stone 18
Palestine 15, 162
Panehesy 31
Pan-Grave Culture 46, 79, 145, 147, 186, 205, 222
pan graves 24, 346
papyrus 92, 109, 165, 345, 388, 409, 410
    capitals/columns 291, 321, 334, 384, 388, 398
Papyrus Bulaq 25
Parkinson, R.B. 332, 336
Paser II 356